MOON HANDBOOKS

D0745944

IXTAPA & ZIHUATANEJO

BRUCE WHIPPERMAN

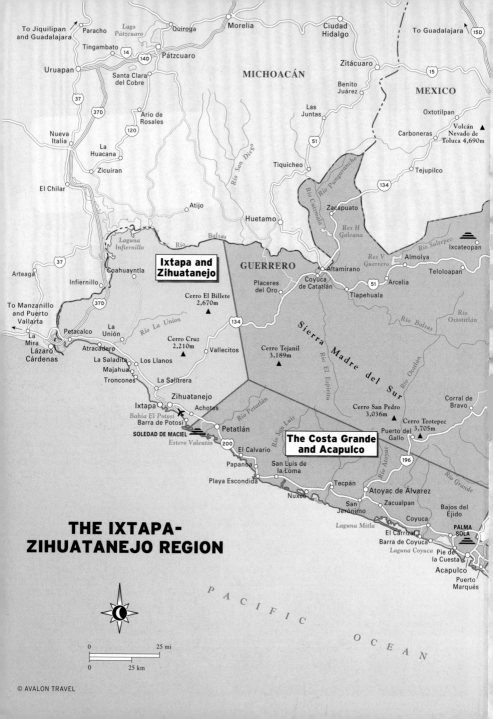

THE IXTAPA-
ZIHUATANEJO REGION

© AVALON TRAVEL

Contents

▶ **Discover Ixtapa
and Zihuatanejo** 6

Planning Your Trip 8
• Where to Go 8
• Ixtapa or Zihuatanejo? 8
• When to Go 10
• Before You Go 11

Explore Ixtapa & Zihuatanejo 13
• The Best of Ixtapa
and Zihuatanejo 13
• Best Beaches 14
• Catch a Wave 16
• The Best of Acapulco
and Guerrero Upcountry 17
• Treasures of Old Mexico 18
• Sportfishing 19

▶ **Ixtapa and Zihuatanejo** **21**

Sights 27
Accommodations 33
Food 48
Entertainment and Events 51
Sports and Recreation 53

Shopping 58
Information and Services 61
Getting There and Away 64
South of Ixtapa and Zihuatanejo ... 66
North of Ixtapa and Zihuatanejo ... 70

▶ **The Costa Grande
and Acapulco** **80**

The Costa Grande 82
Acapulco 104

▶ **Guerrero Upcountry** **138**

Chilpancingo 142
River Country 157
Handicrafts Country 160
Iguala 168
Taxco 179

▶ **The Costa Chica** **202**

The Road to Ometepec 206
Ometepec and Vicinity 211
Pinotepa Nacional and Vicinity 219

▶ **Background**.................. **226**

   The Land 226

   Flora and Fauna................. 229

   History 236

   Government and Economy....... 250

   People and Culture 254

   Festivals and Events 258

   Arts and Crafts 262

▶ **Essentials** **267**

   Getting There 267

   Getting Around 280

   Visas and Officialdom........... 282

   Recreation..................... 285

   Accommodations 290

   Food and Drink 294

   Tips for Travelers 299

   Health and Safety 302

   Information and Services........ 307

▶ **Resources** **312**

   Glossary....................... 312

   Spanish Phrasebook............ 316

   Suggested Reading............. 322

   Internet Resources............. 328

▶ **Index**......................... **331**

▶ **List of Maps** **337**

Discover Ixtapa & Zihuatanejo

The worldwide renown of Mexico's South Seas resort duo is now more deserved than ever. Ixtapa, the younger of the two, remains fashionably modern and brilliant white above creamy golden sands. Neighboring Zihuatanejo still resembles an old-world fishing village slumbering on a diminutive crescent bay. Between them, they offer the best of the old, the new, and the timeless: resort luxury, fine dining, exciting nightlife, brilliant sunsets, hidden beaches, and wild, open ocean.

Along the same sun-drenched coastline, Mexico's original tropical resort, Acapulco, still shines with an emerald-green bay by day, and a gleaming galaxy of city lights by night. Venture beyond the beach resorts, and you'll find much more to explore. Fascinating ancient sites abound, from an ancient rock wall hidden beneath the waters of Zihuatanejo Bay, to the ancient ruined city of Xochipala. Glimpses of the more recent colonial past can be found in nearby Fuerte de San Diego, once proud guardian of the treasures of the fabled Manila galleon, now a world-class historical museum.

The entire state of Guerrero offers diversion and adventure. On the northwest coast, you'll discover getaways at the laid-back beach

resorts of Troncones, Barra de Potosí, and Playa Escondida. On the region's southeastern side, there are the refreshingly downscale beach villages of El Carrizal, Pie de la Cuesta, and Playa Ventura. Farther southeast, follow paths less traveled into the indigenous and African-Mexican heartlands, where a treasury of fetching handicrafts festoon native markets, Spanish is a foreign tongue, and villagers are more likely to speak Mixtec or Amusgo. Finally, all roads seem to lead to Taxco, the celebrated silver-rich colonial gem of the Sierra, set on the slope of a towering mountain. Its narrow winding lanes are decorated with fine silver shops and the baroque monuments of an opulent past.

The many paths to the manifold delights of this region are open and easy to follow, whether you seek glamour and luxury, something offbeat and rustic – or all of the above.

Planning Your Trip

► WHERE TO GO

Ixtapa and Zihuatanejo

Zihuatanejo, with its *lancha*-lined beachfront and pedestrian-friendly downtown, still resembles the original fishing village, while its high-rise cousin Ixtapa, five miles (8 km) to the northwest, appeals to those who prefer something fashionably modern. Country charms blossom beyond both town limits, especially at coral-studded Troncones and beach village and surfing haven La Saladita, both about half an hour north of Ixtapa. On the opposite, southeast side, about 15 miles (24 km) from Zihuatanejo, a growing number of visitors seek heaven on earth in Barra de Potosí and its neighboring wildlife-rich mangrove jungle lagoon.

The Costa Grande and Acapulco

The Costa Grande extends southeast along the 150-mile (242-km) stretch of Highway 200 from Ixtapa-Zihuatanejo to Acapulco. Here you can enjoy tropical Mexico at its purest,

IXTAPA OR ZIHUATANEJO?

Your choice of local lodging sharply determines the tone of your stay. **Zihuatanejo** still resembles the colorful seaside village that visitors have enjoyed for years. Fishing *pangas* (outboard motorboats) decorate its beach side, while *panaderías*, *taquerías*, and *papelerías* line its narrow shady lanes. Many of its hotels – budget to moderate, with spartan but clean fan-only rooms – reflect the tastes of the bargain-conscious travelers who "discovered" Zihuatanejo during the 1960s.

Ixtapa, on the other hand, mirrors the fashionwise preferences of a new generation of Mexican and international vacationers. A broad boulevard fronts your Ixtapa hotel, while on the beach side thatch-shaded chairs on a wide strand, a palmy garden, blue pool, and serene outdoor restaurant are yours to enjoy. Upstairs, your air-conditioned room – typically in plush pastels, with private sea-view balcony, marble bath, room service, and your favorite TV shows by satellite – brings maximum convenience and comfort to a lush tropical setting.

Actually, you needn't be forced to choose. Split your hotel time between Ixtapa and Zihuatanejo and enjoy both worlds.

morning view overlooking Playa Madera, on Zihuatanejo Bay

Acapulco

with groves of swaying palms, wildlife-rich mangrove lagoons, endless beaches, colorful market towns, and a sprinkling of laid-back mini-resorts.

The reward at the end of the Costa Grande road is celebrated Acapulco. A glittering lineup of renowned hotels, restaurants, bars, and dance clubs decorate the east-side new town. The intimate, colonial-era neighborhood nestled around the west-side cove is as picturesque as ever.

Guerrero Upcountry

North from the tropical coast lie the towns of Chilpancingo and Iguala, where a big piece of the rich tapestry of Mexican history was woven. Here, you can also explore the lush valley of the crystalline Río Azul, and take a walk through the wondrous Grutas de Juxtlahuaca limestone caverns. Farther north, craft-rich towns of Chilapa and Olinalá beckon. Past that is picturesque Taxco, renowned for its fine silver jewelry. Other must-sees include the monumental Grutas de Cacahuamilpa limestone caverns and the legendary Xochicalco archaeological site.

The Costa Chica

Highway 200 leaves Acapulco heading due east, traversing the Costa Chica for 150 miles (242 km) before reaching the far southern state of Oaxaca. The town of Ometepec, about

Taxco is known for its fine silver jewelry.

110 miles (177 km) east of Acapulco, is where you'll begin to brush shoulders with indigenous people, many speaking the Amusgo language. Southeast of Ometepec, you'll encounter an entire community of African-Mexican shoppers and sellers in the lively Sunday market town of Cuajinicuilapa. From there, a country road heads south to the laid-back fishing and surfing hamlet of Puerto Maldonado. Another hour east into Oaxaca are the vibrant Amuzgo and Mixtec market towns of Pinotepa Nacional and Jamiltepec.

▶ WHEN TO GO

The Ixtapa-Zihuatanejo region has two sharply defined seasons: wet summer-fall and dry winter-spring.

Some say this region is too hot in the summer. In fact, increased summer cloud cover and showers can actually create average daily temperatures in July, August, and September that are cooler than clear and very warm late-April, May, and early-June temperatures. And near the coast, nights never get warmer than balmy, even during the summer.

If you like lush green landscapes, summer–fall may be your season. This is true everywhere, but especially in the highlands, where myriad multicolored wildflowers decorate the roadsides, and the clouds seem to billow into a 1,000-mile-high blue sky.

During the sunny, more temperate winter, many trees are bare of leaves, grass is brown, and cactuses seem to be the only green. The weather remains sunny during February and March, turning hot in April and May, until the rains arrive and green breaks out again by mid-June.

If you want to pass up the crowds and high prices, avoid the high-season Christmas to New Year's rush (Dec. 20–Jan. 3) and the Semana Santa week up through and including Easter Sunday. However, sunny, temperate January, a low-occupancy mini-season, is a good bet, especially on the beach. The landscape still retains some green and hotels customarily offer discounts.

October through mid-December is also a good time to go. Hotel prices are cheapest, the landscape is lush, beaches are uncrowded, and it's cooler and not as rainy as July, August, and September. Although the first October weeks in Ixtapa-Zihuatanejo may still be a bit too empty for folks who enjoy lots of company, the pace picks up by mid-October and continues through mid-December.

lush summer foliage and a crystal clear waterfall just off the road between Taxco and Ixcateopan

► **BEFORE YOU GO**

Passports, Tourist Cards, and Visas

Your passport is your positive proof of national identity; without it, your status in any foreign country is in doubt. Don't leave home without one. U.S. Immigration rules require that all U.S. citizens must have a valid passport in order to re-enter the United States.

For U.S. and Canadian citizens with a passport, entry by air into Mexico for a few weeks could hardly be easier. Airline officials examine passports at check in, hand out tourist cards *(tarjetas turísticas)* en route; upon arrival, Mexican immigration officers make them official by stamping the tourist cards at the entry gate. Business travel permits for 30 days or fewer are handled by the same simple procedures.

Immunizations and Precautions

A good physician can recommend the proper preventatives for your trip. If you are going to stay pretty much in town, your doctor will probably suggest little more than updating your basic typhoid, diphtheria-tetanus, hepatitis, and polio shots.

For remote tropical areas—below 4,000 feet (1,200 meters)—doctors often recommend a gamma-globulin shot against hepatitis A and a schedule of chloroquine pills against malaria. Use other measures to discourage mosquitoes and other tropical pests. Common precautions include mosquito netting and rubbing on plenty of pure DEET (N,N dimethyl-meta-toluamide) "jungle juice," mixed in equal parts with rubbing alcohol (70 percent isopropyl).

Getting There

Most travelers fly in on regularly scheduled flights from U.S. and Canadian gateways. More options are available with a single plane change in Mexico City. Although few airlines fly directly to the Ixtapa-Zihuatanejo region from the northern United States and Canada, many charters do.

For cost-conscious travelers, express buses provide a safe and sure route to the Ixtapa-Zihuatanejo region. Hundreds of buses head south daily from central bus stations *(camioneras centrales)* in the border towns of Tijuana, Mexicali, Nogales, Ciudad Juárez, Nuevo Laredo, Reynosa, and Matamoros. For

cabañas at Bistro de Roberto at Troncones, north of Zihuatanejo

comfort and speed, go luxury-class ($80–100, 20–30 hours).

Some travelers drive their cars or RVs to the Ixtapa-Zihuatanejo region. Driving time runs 3–5 south-of-the-border days at the wheel, and costs around $80–120 in expressway tolls for passenger cars and light trucks (about triple that for motor homes).

What to Take

"Men wear pants, ladies be beautiful" was once the dress code of one of the Mexican Pacific coast's classiest hotels. Today, men can get by easily without a jacket, women with simple skirts, pants, and blouses. Everyone should bring a hat for sun protection and a light jacket or sweater for the occasional cool evening. Loose-fitting, hand-washable, easy-to-dry clothes make for trouble-free tropical vacationing. If you're going to the highlands (Chilpancingo, Chilapa, Olinalá, Taxco), add a medium-weight jacket. In all cases,

leave showy, expensive clothes and jewelry at home. Stow valuables that you cannot lose in your hotel safe or carry them with you in a sturdy zipped purse or a waist pouch on your front side.

If you're staying at a self-contained resort, you can take the suitcase and one carry-on allowed by airlines. If, on the other hand, you're going to be moving around a lot, you'd do better to condense everything into one easily carried bag with wheels that doubles as luggage and soft backpack.

Campers will have to be careful to accomplish one-bag packing. Fortunately, camping along the tropical coast generally requires no sleeping bag. Simply use a hammock (buy it in Mexico) or a sleeping pad and a sheet for cover. In the winter, you may have to buy a light blanket. A compact tent that you and your companion can share is a must against bugs, as is mosquito repellent. A first-aid kit is absolutely necessary.

Explore Ixtapa & Zihuatanejo

► THE BEST OF IXTAPA AND ZIHUATANEJO

These twin resorts crown the Guerrero Costa Grande, an alluring land of perpetual summer, where the palms always seem to be swaying in the breeze, the frigate birds soaring overhead, and the billows washing the crystalline sand.

Days 1-2

Arrive in Ixtapa or Zihuatanejo. Rest up a few hours, then stroll around downtown Zihuatanejo and along the beachfront Paseo del Pescador. Browse some of the handicrafts shops and enjoy dinner downtown at Tamales y Atoles "Any," Coconuts, or Casa Elvira.

The next morning, after breakfast in Zihuatanejo at the Sirena Gorda (Fat Mermaid), visit the Museo Arqueología de la Costa Grande, then ride a water taxi from the pier to Playa Las Gatas for sunning on the beach, snorkeling, or maybe a scuba lesson. In the afternoon, freshen up at your hotel, then enjoy the sunset and a splurge dinner at Restaurant Il Mare overlooking Zihuatanejo Bay (or, if on a budget, Restaurant La Perla on Playa La Ropa).

Days 3-4

On Day 3, after breakfast at restaurant Mama Norma and Deborah in Ixtapa, browse the handicrafts at the handicrafts and shops, perhaps at the Los Patios shopping complex. Then, either take a taxi, drive, or ride the minibus to Playa Linda to see the crocodiles. Then take the ferry across to Isla Grande for sunning, strolling, swimming, or snorkeling and a seafood lunch at a beachfront *palapa*.

On Day 4 kick back and relax, or follow your own interests. A few options include: unwinding on the beach or by the pool, renting a bike and following the Ixtapa *ciclopista* (bike path), horseback riding at Playa Linda, a fishing trip, or shopping for local

crocodiles at Playa Linda

handicrafts. In the evening, enjoy bar hopping and dancing in Ixtapa: try wacky Señor Frog's and elegant disco Christine across the boulevard. If the night is still young, hop over to Zihuatanejo to check out the band at Restaurant Bandidos, swing and sway at Rumba Caliente, and croon at Splash karaoke bar.

Days 5-6

Get an early start on a two-day getaway in Troncones, an hour's drive northwest. Check in at a comfortable beachfront inn, such as Casa Ki, the Inn at Manzanillo Bay, or Eden Beach Hacienda. After whiling away the afternoon strolling the beach, lazing in a hammock, or swimming beyond

BEST BEACHES

The beach at El Carrizal, on the Costa Grande, is a popular Sunday destination.

MOST PRISTINE

- Playa Coral (Ixtapa and Zihuatanejo, page 32)

- Playa Escondida (Costa Grande, page 90)

BEST SNORKELING

- Playa Las Gatas (Ixtapa and Zihuatanejo, page 29)

- Playa Roqueta (Acapulco, page 115)

BEST SURFING

- Playa Las Gatas and Playa Escolleros (Ixtapa and Zihuatanejo, pages 29, 53)

- Manzanillo Bay (Troncones, page 73)

- Playa Revolcadero (Acapulco, page 130)

- Puerto Maldonado (Costa Chica, page 218)

BEST SURF FISHING

- Playa Las Pozas (Ixtapa and Zihuatanejo, page 66)

- El Carrizal (Costa Grande, page 98)

- Playa Pie de la Cuesta (Acapulco, page 99)

MOST CHILD-FRIENDLY

- Playa Cuachalatate (Ixtapa and Zihuatanejo, page 32)

- Playa Caleta (Acapulco, page 114)

- Playa las Peñitas (Costa Chica, page 209)

BEST SUNSETS

- Playa La Ropa (Ixtapa and Zihuatanejo, page 29)

- Playa El Calvario (Costa Grande, page 88)

the breakers, enjoy dinner at Bistro de Roberto.

Get active for Day 6: Take a surfing lesson or go on a fishing trip from Troncones. Or continue northwest up the coast (drive or get an early start by bus) to check out the beach hamlets of La Saladita and Atracadero. Maybe go all the way to the grand Río Balsas dam, where Highway 200 crosses the border into the state of Michoacán, and Mexico's mightiest river meanders into the Pacific.

Days 7-8

Return southeast past Ixtapa and Zihuatanejo for a day around the village of Barra de Potosí, perhaps combined with a wildlife-

The tranquil waters of Acapulco's Playa Caleta are perfect for child's play.

BEST TENT CAMPING

- Bistro de Roberto (Troncones, page 72)

- Piedra Tlalcoyunque (Costa Grande, page 91)

- Playa Ventura (Costa Chica, page 207)

BEST RV CAMPING

- Ixtapa Trailer Park (Ixtapa and Zihuatanejo, page 47)

- Playa Luces Trailer Park (Pie de la Cuesta, page 102)

- Acapulco Trailer Park (Acapulco, page 102)

MOST BEAUTIFUL

- Playa El Calvario (Costa Grande, page 88)

- Piedra Tlalcoyunque (Costa Grande, page 91)

MOST INTIMATE

- Playa Carey (Ixtapa and Zihuatanejo, page 32)

- Playa Las Palmitas (Acapulco, page 115)

BEST OVERALL

- Playa La Ropa (Ixtapa and Zihuatanejo, page 29)

- Playa Ojo de Agua (Costa Grande, page 90)

- Playa Ventura (Costa Chica, page 207)

CATCH A WAVE

Good surfing spots sprinkle the coastline, including **Playa Las Gatas** on Zihuatanejo Bay and **Playa Escolleros,** right on Ixtapa's main beach.

At the laid-back mini-paradise of Troncones, not far north of Ixtapa-Zihuatanejo, surfing has become a major recreation. The most popular spot is the palm-tufted inlet of **Manzanillo Bay,** location of both the Inn at Manzanillo Bay and Eden Beach Hacienda. A pair of enterprising lovers of the tropics, Michael and Ann Linn of San Luis Obispo, California, operating as **ISA (Instructional Surf Adventures) Mexico,** offer both local day instruction and extended surfing packages during the fall-winter (Nov.-Apr.) season.

Surfing aficionados, hungry for more, often head farther afield, to the idyllic crystalline strands of **La Saladita** (north of Troncones); **Playa Escondida, Playa El Calvario,** and **Piedra Tlalcoyunque** (on the Costa Grande); **Playa Revolcadero** (just south of Acapulco); and **Playa Ventura** and **Punta Maldonado** (on the Costa Chica).

The surf everywhere is highest and best during the July-November hurricane season, when big swells from storms far out at sea attract platoons of surfers to favored beaches.

Consistently dependable waves make Playa El Calvario (on the Costa Grande) a popular surfing destination.

viewing tour, such as with Zoe Kayak Tours, on the grand mangrove Laguna de Potosí. Stay overnight at either of the Barra de Potosí bed-and-breakfasts, Casa Frida or Casa del Encanto, or return to your hotel in Ixtapa or Zihuatanejo.

Spend Day 8 relaxing in either Ixtapa, Zihuatanejo, or Barra de Potosí. If you want more activity, take an excursion south to the Soledad de Maciel archaeological zone and museum, and visit Petatlán's gold

market shops. Enjoy a late lunch or early dinner at Restaurant Mi Pueblito on the plaza.

Days 9-10

Spend your final days letting your body rest and your mind wander. Or consider an excursion south for a picnic at the lovely Playa Ojo de Agua or Piedra Tlalcoyunque. On Day 10, head home, or continue by traveling on to Acapulco and Guerrero Upcountry.

▶ THE BEST OF ACAPULCO AND GUERRERO UPCOUNTRY

Its golden beaches are the stuff of legend, but Acapulco offers much more, both in and around town.

Days 1-2

After arrival in Acapulco, enjoy sunset cocktails at the Hotel Los Flamingos clifftop *mirador* (viewpoint) and dinner in the adjacent restaurant.

The next day, spend the morning around the *zócalo* (old-town plaza), visit the colonial-era Fuerte de San Diego and the nearby Casa de la Máscara (House of Masks). Spend the afternoon relaxing by the pool or on the beach. In the evening, join the crowd viewing the La Quebrada cliff divers.

Days 3-4

In the morning, ride a tour boat from Playa Caleta to offshore Isla Roqueta. Walk the island trail (two hours); then snorkel, swim, and sun at hidden Playa las Palmitas. Enjoy a late lunch or dinner at Restaurant Palao on the island before returning to the mainland.

The next day browse for mementos at Bonita and Linda de Taxco handicrafts stores and Mercado de Parrazal market, all near the old-town plaza. Alternatively, taxi up to Palma Sola Archaeological Site for a stroll and a picnic among the petrolgyphs, or wander the Jardín Botánico (botanical garden). Enjoy a splurge dinner at Restaurant El Olvido or Kookaburra—or if on a budget, at Restaurant Bratwurst, 100 percent Natural, or Restaurant El Zorrito. Spend the evening sampling the nightlife—or really get your adrenaline pumping with a nighttime bungee jump on the Costera Miguel Alemán, just east of the Diana Circle.

Days 5-6

Head into Guerrero Upcountry to explore the valley of the Río Azul. Stop for a swim and maybe kayaking at Balneario Santa Fe, or explore the caves of Juxtlahuaca, near Colotlipa. Continue to Chilpancingo for an overnight stay. Consider an early dinner at Restaurant El Portal or dine a little later at Hotel del Parque.

If Day 6 happens to be a Sunday (or you planned it to be), spend it in Chilapa at the fabulous Sunday handicrafts market, an hour and a half by car or bus east of Chilpancingo. Options in Chilpancingo include the Museo La Avispa and the zoo. Then head north an hour to the intriguing and scenic La Organera Xochipala Archaeological Zone. Continue north by car or bus to Iguala for an overnight stay.

Days 7-8

After breakfast in Iguala at the Hotel María Isabel or Tastee Freeze-La Vaca Negra, stroll the shady Iguala plaza, visit the gold

handicrafts at Chilapa's Sunday market

The Santa Prisca church's baroque front door beckons to visitors.

market a block away, then spend an hour in the Museo y Santuario a la Bandera (Museum and Sanctuary of the Flag). Make the highlight of your Iguala a trip to the colossal Hilltop Memorial Flag south of town.

Continue north to Taxco. Stroll the *zócalo*, browse some silver and handicrafts shops, and enjoy dinner at Del Ángeles or country-style Pozolería Tía Calla.

The next day, after breakfast at Café Dora near the *zócalo*, see the sights, such as Santa Prisca church, Museo Guillermo Spratling, the town market, and maybe ride the cableway to the top of Monte Taxco. Consider dinner with grand sunset views on

the terrace of the Hotel Monte Taxco. Spend the evening enjoying Taxco's nightlife: check out local hangout Bar Berta, loud music at Bar Estación or Concha, or the more soothing piano bar at Mario's.

Days 9-10

On Day 9, visit Grutas de Cacahuamilpa limestone cave national park. If you start early enough (by tour, your own wheels, or taxi), you'll also have time for the legendary Xochicalco UNESCO World Heritage site and museum 25 miles (40 km) beyond Cacahuamilpa. On Day 10, return to Acapulco and head home, or continue southward to the Costa Chica.

▶ TREASURES OF OLD MEXICO

A wealth of Mexican traditions are preserved in this region's museums, handicrafts galleries, cathedrals, pilgrimage shrines, native markets, and archaeological sites.

Ixtapa and Zihuatanejo

First on your list should be the Zihuatanejo regional museum, Museo Arqueología de la Costa Grande, with its treasury of ancient

Costa Grande artifacts. To see an ancient artifact of Zihuatanejo's past, take the water taxi over to Playa Las Gatas for a snorkeling trip to view the underwater remains of the ancient wall, which legend says was built by the Tarascan king around A.D. 1400.

The Costa Grande and Acapulco

Just half an hour south of Zihuatanejo, explore

SPORTFISHING

Ixtapa and Zihuatanjeo have long been world-class sportfishing grounds, known for big-game billfish (marlin, swordfish, and sailfish).

A deep-sea boat charter generally includes the boat and crew for a full or half day, plus equipment and bait for 2-6 people, not including food or drinks. The full-day price depends upon the season. Around Christmas and New Year's and before Easter (when reservations will be mandatory) a big boat can run $450 and up. During low season, however, you might be able to bargain a captain down to as low as $250.

Renting an entire big boat is not the only choice. Winter sportfishing is sometimes so brisk that travel agencies can make reservations for individuals for about $80 per person per day. In season, boats might average one big marlin or sailfish apiece. The best month for **sailfish** (pez vela) is October; for **marlin,** January and February; for **dorado,** March.

But sailfish and marlin are neither the only nor necessarily the most desirable fish in the sea. Competently captained pangas (outboard motor launches) can typically haul in two or three large 15- or 20-pound excellent-eating **dorado** (mahi-mahi, dolphinfish), **huachinango** (snapper), or **atún** (tuna) in two hours just outside Zihuatanejo or Acapulco Bay. Seating 2-6 passengers, pangas are available for as little as $75, depending on the season. Once, six of my friends hired a panga, had a great time, and came back with a boatload of big tuna, jack, and mackerel. A restaurant cooked the fish and served it as a delicious banquet for a dozen of us in exchange for the extra fish.

Sportfishing boats wait for passengers at the dock in Acapulco.

the Soledad de Maciel Archaeological Zone. Start by visiting the new museum, where you can contact a local guide. Continue to the grand reconstructed ball court and the village to view the remarkable life-death motif monolith, the "King of Chole," in front of the church.

Continue south 15 minutes to Petatlán, step inside the pilgrimage church, Parroquia de Padre Jesús, and pay your respects to the town's beloved patron, Padre Jesús. Before you leave town, be sure to see the monumental stone ball-game rings (anillos de piedra), mounted beside the highway through town, a few blocks from the plaza.

In Acapulco's old town, first explore the world-class Fuerte de San Diego and museum. Continue nearby to the Casa de la Máscara, an amazing museum of masks. Back at the *zócalo,* step inside the Our Lady of Solitude cathedral to admire the art deco–style ceiling.

Finally, on a high hillside overlooking the city's west-end old town, enjoy a picnic and a stroll through the leafy Palma Sola Archaeological Site, dotted with a treasury of fascinating petroglyphs.

Guerrero Upcountry

At Chilpancingo, the Guerrero state capital, visit the heroic statue of José María Morelos and the revered Templo de Santa María de la Asunción, where the Congress of Anahuac declared Mexican Independence from Spain in 1813. See it all colorfully illustrated by the grand historical mural in the Museo Regional de Chilpancingo.

statue of José María Morelos in Chilpancingo

On the way north to Iguala, the ancient, partly reconstructed city ruins at La Organera Xochipala Archaeological Zone are worth at least a two-hour stop. At Iguala, an hour farther north, visit the plaza-front Museo y Santuario a la Bandera.

In Taxco, less than an hour north of Iguala, trace the town's colorful history via a self-guided walking tour of the baroque Santa Prisca church, the Museo Guillermo Spratling, and the Casa Humboldt colonial religious art museum.

About 1.5 hours outside of Taxco, visit the legendary Xochicalco archaeological site and museum. History enthusiasts will enjoy a half-day excursion from Taxco to Ixcateopan to visit the museum and shrine honoring the Aztecs' last emperor, Cuauhtémoc, and his (now disputed) remains.

The Costa Chica

The eastern Costa Chica, beginning about a hundred miles east of Acapulco and extending into Oaxaca, is a rich repository of the cultural traditions of both the indigenous people and rural African Mexicans.

The eastern Guerrero market towns north of Highway 200, especially Ometepec (oh-may-tay-PEK) and Xochistlahuaca (soh-chees-tlah-WAH-kah), are the big indigenous centers, where thousands in colorful *traje* (traditional dress) arrive for big Sunday *tianguis* (tee-AHN-geese, native markets).

Nearly all of the African Mexicans live south of Highway 200, around the busy market town of Cuajinicuilapa (kwah-hee-nee-kwee-LAH-pah). Its Museo de las Culturas Afromestizos should be your top priority stop.

Farther east, on the Oaxaca side of the Costa Chica, the market town of Pinotepa Nacional is the hub for the mostly Mixtec-speaking villages. Its native market is biggest on Mondays.

From Pinotepa Nacional, good roads fan north and east to more remote indigenous villages: north to Mixtec-speaking Pinotepa Don Luis (for *pozahuancos* and masks) and Amusgo-speaking San Pedro Amusgos (for lovely hand-embroidered *huipiles*); and east along Highway 200 to Jamiltepec, the Mixtec capital, with a large daily native market.

IXTAPA AND ZIHUATANEJO

The resort pair of Ixtapa and Zihuatanejo present an irresistible opportunity for a season of relaxed vacationing. The choices seem nearly endless. You can sun to your heart's content on luscious beaches, choose from a feast of delicious food, and shop from a trove of fine Mexican handicrafts. Furthermore, outdoor lovers can enjoy their fill of unhurried beach walking and snorkeling, bicycling, horseback riding, kayaking, swimming, surfing, scuba diving, and caving.

Whether you stay in Ixtapa or Zihuatanejo depends on your inclinations. Zihuatanejo still resembles the small fishing village it once was, with many reminders of old Mexico, and has a mix of small to medium-size hotels. Ixtapa, on the other hand, is for modern travelers who prefer the fashionable glitter of a luxuriously comfortable, facility-rich hotel on a crystalline strand. (Though, where you stay may not really matter, because Ixtapa and Zihuatanejo are only five miles (8 km) apart.)

PLANNING YOUR TIME

There's hardly a better place for a balmy winter vacation than the Ixtapa and Zihuatanejo coast, whether it be for simply a four- or five-day-long weekend or a month of Sundays.

If your stay is limited to four or five days, you'll still have time for some sunning and snoozing on the beach or by the pool, sampling some of the excellent Zihuatanejo restaurants, visiting the **Museo Arqueología de la Costa Grande,** browsing Zihuatanejo's irresistible trove of handicrafts, and spending an

© BRUCE WHIPPERMAN

HIGHLIGHTS

◖ Museo Arqueología de la Costa Grande: Zihuatanejo's first stop for history aficionados illustrates the prehistory of the Costa Grande with a treasury of dioramas, paintings, and precious locally discovered and donated artifacts (page 27).

◖ Playa La Ropa: Enjoy this best of all possible resort beaches, tucked along a golden mile of Zihuatanejo Bay's sheltered eastern flank (page 29).

◖ Playa Las Gatas: Only boat accessible, Playa Las Gatas seems like a remote South Seas island, a place where sun, sea, and sand and the rustle of the palms invite relaxation. When you get hungry, a lineup of *palapa* restaurants provide fresh seafood; for exercise, beach stalls rent snorkel gear, which you can use to acquaint yourself with squadrons of tropical fish just a few steps offshore (page 29).

◖ *Teleférico* and Playa del Palmar: In late afternoon, stroll along Ixtapa's creamy resort beach, Playa del Palmar, to the south end where the *teleférico* will whisk you uphill for a panoramic sunset and cocktails and dinner at the El Faro view restaurant (page 30).

◖ Isla Grande: Visitors to this petite, pristine island jewel can enjoy three different beaches, Playa Cuachalatate, Playa Varadero, and Playa Coral, tucked on the island's three sheltered corners. A fourth beach – Playa Carey, for romantics only – is a petite sandy nook accessible by boat only on the island's wild open-ocean shore (page 32).

◖ Barra de Potosí: This rustic palm-shadowed village, with a grand, mangrove-laced,

wildlife-rich lagoon on one side and a luscious beach on the other, seems perfect for a spell of relaxed living (page 68).

◖ Troncones: Once an isolated fishing village on a coral-decorated shoreline, Troncones has become a winter refuge for a loyal cadre of sun-starved Americans and Canadians (page 70).

LOOK FOR ◖ TO FIND RECOMMENDED SIGHTS, ACTIVITIES, DINING, AND LODGING.

afternoon at either secluded **Playa Las Gatas** or **Isla Grande.**

With more time, you can concentrate more on your individual interests. Handicrafts, for example, are a major Zihuatanejo specialty. Start with an hour or two at the tourist market on the west side of town, with many stalls stuffed with tempting treasures from all over Guerrero and Mexico. Then spend the rest of the day browsing the top-pick private handicrafts shops, such as Casa Marina, Artesanías Olinalá, Cerámicas Tonalá, and Galería Maya.

On the other hand, active vacationers will want to get into Ixtapa and Zihuatanejo's great outdoors. You might start off with a day

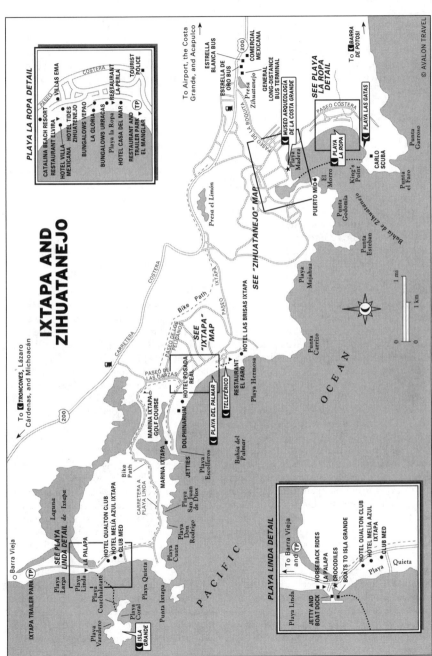

IXTAPA AND ZIHUATANEJO

© AVALON TRAVEL

sunning, hiking, and snorkeling off the beaches of Isla Grande. If you want more, you could try the same at Playa Las Gatas with a scuba-diving lesson thrown in. For still more outdoor adventures, do some bicycling on Ixtapa's new *ciclopista.*

With more days, head out of town south to **Barra de Potosí** on the Laguna de Potosí or north to **Troncones** for a few nights at a comfortable bed-and-breakfast. While in Troncones, adventurers may want to explore the limestone cave, do some deep-sea fishing, or maybe enjoy some surfing lessons. At the village resort of Barra de Potosí, you can easily spend a couple of days sunning and beach-combing; dining on super-fresh seafood at rustic, palm-shaded *palapa* restaurants; and exploring, by boat or kayak, the grand, wildlife-rich Laguna de Potosí.

ORIENTATION

Both Ixtapa and Zihuatanejo are small and easy to get to know. Zihuatanejo's little Plaza de Armas town square overlooks the main beach, Playa Municipal, that fronts the palm-lined pedestrian walkway, Paseo del Pescador. From the plaza looking out toward the bay, you are facing south. On your right is the pier (*muelle,* moo-AY-yay), and on the left the bay curves along the outer beaches of Madera, La Ropa, and finally Las Gatas beneath the far Punta El Faro (Lighthouse Point).

Turning around and facing inland (north), you see a narrow but busy bayfront street, Juan Álvarez, running parallel to the beach past the plaza, crossing the main business streets (actually tranquil shady lanes) Cuauhtémoc and Guerrero. A third street, bustling Benito Juárez, one block to the right of Guerrero, conducts traffic several blocks to and from the shore, passing the market and intersecting a second main street, Avenida Morelos, about 10 blocks inland from the beach. There, a right turn will soon bring you to Highway 200 and, within five miles (8 km), Ixtapa.

Most everything in Ixtapa lies along one three-mile-long (5-km-long) boulevard, Paseo Ixtapa, which parallels the main beach, hotel-lined Playa del Palmar. Heading westerly, arriving from Zihuatanejo, you first pass the Club de Golf Ixtapa, then the big Hotel Barceló on the left, followed by a succession of other high-rise hotels. Soon come the Zona Comercial shopping malls and the Paseo de las Garzas corner on the right. Turn right for both Highway 200 and the outer Playas Cuata, Quieta, Linda, and Larga. At Playa Linda, boats continue to heavenly Isla Grande.

If, instead, you continued straight ahead from the Paseo de las Garzas corner, you would soon reach the Marina Ixtapa condo development and yacht harbor.

GETTING AROUND

In downtown Zihuatanejo, most shops and restaurants are within a few blocks of the plaza. For the beaches, stroll along the beachfront *andador* (walkway) to Playa Madera, hail a taxi ($3) to Playa La Ropa, or enjoy a breezy boat ride from the pier ($5) to Playa Las Gatas.

For Ixtapa or the outer beaches, take a taxi (about $5) or ride one of the very frequent minibuses, labeled by destination, which leave from both Av. Juárez, across from the market, and the northeast downtown corner of Juárez and Morelos, a few blocks farther north from the beach. In Ixtapa, either walk, or ride the minibuses that run along Paseo Ixtapa.

HISTORY
In the Beginning

The Purépecha-speaking people who lived in the area around A.D. 1400 were relative latecomers, preceded by waves of immigrants to Zihuatanejo. The local Archaeolgical Museum of the Costa Grande displays ancient pottery made by Zihuatanejo artisans as many as 5,000 years ago. Later, more sophisticated artists, influenced by the renowned Olmec mother-culture of the Gulf of Mexico coast, left their indisputable mark on local pottery styles.

By the beginning of the Christian era, local people had developed more sophisticated lifestyles. Instead of wandering and hunting and gathering their food, they were living in permanent towns and villages, surrounded by fields where they grew most of what they needed. Besides their staple corn, beans, and squash, these farmers, called Cuitlatecs by the Aztecs, were also cultivating tobacco, cotton for clothes, and cacao for chocolate. Attracted by such a rich bounty of produce, the highland Aztecs, led by their emperor Tizoc, invaded the coast during the late 1400s and extracted a small mountain of tribute yearly from the Cuitlatecs.

Conquest and Colonization

Scarcely months after Hernán Cortés conquered the Aztecs, he sent an expedition to explore the "Southern Sea" and find the long-sought route to China. In November 1522 Captain Juan Álvarez Chico set sail with boats built on the Isthmus of Tehuántepec and reconnoitered the Zihuatanejo coast all the way northeast to at least the Río Balsas, planting crosses on beaches and claiming the land for Spain.

Cortés, encouraged by the samples of pearls and gold that Chico brought back, built more ships and outfitted more expeditions. At a personal cost of 60,000 gold pesos (probably equivalent to several tens of million dollars today) Cortés had three ships built at Zacatula, at the mouth of the Río Balsas. He commissioned Captain Álvaro Saavedra Cerón to command the first expedition to find the route to Asia. Saavedra Cerón set off from Zihuatanejo Bay on October 31, 1527. He commanded a modest force of about 110 men, with 30 cannons, in three small caravels: the flagship *Florida,* the *Espíritu Santo,* and the *Santiago.* The *Florida,* Saavedra Cerón's sole vessel to survive the fierce Pacific typhoons, reached present-day Guam on December 29, 1527, and the Philippines on February 1, 1528. As he did not know any details of the Pacific Ocean and its winds and currents, it's not surprising that Saavedra Cerón failed to return to Mexico. He died at sea in October 1529 in search of a return route to Mexico.

No fewer than seven more attempts were needed (from Acapulco in 1532, 1539, and 1540; from Tehuántepec in 1535; and from Barra de Navidad, two in 1542 and one in 1564) until finally, in 1565, navigator-priest Andrés de Urdaneta coaxed Pacific winds and currents to give up their secret and returned triumphantly to Acapulco from Asia.

The Manila Galleon

Thereafter, the trading ship called the Manila galleon sailed yearly from Acapulco for Asia. For more than 250 years, it returned to Acapulco within a year, laden with a fortune in spices, silks, gold, and porcelain. Although Acapulco's prominence all but shut down all other Mexican Pacific ports, the Manila galleon would from time to time stop off at Zihuatanejo. The same was true for the occasional pirate ship (or fleet) that lurked along the coast, hungry to capture the galleon's riches.

The most famous corsair was Francis Drake, who landed in Zihuatanejo in 1579. Later came the Dutch fleet of Hugo Schapenham in 1624. English Captain William Dampier entered Zihuatanejo Bay in 1704, recording that the shoreline village had about 40 grass huts, inhabited by about 100 unfriendly people who vigorously discouraged his disembarkation. The luckiest of all the corsairs was Captain George Anson, who, in 1715, captured the Manila galleon and returned to England with booty then worth 800,000 pounds sterling—upwards of $50 million today.

On one occasion, no one knows when exactly, a galleon evidently lost some of its precious silk cargo, which washed ashore on one of Zihuatanejo's beaches, now known as Playa La Ropa (Clothes Beach).

Independence

In 1821, Mexico won its independence, stopping the Manila galleon forever. Deprived even of an occasional galleon or pirate ship, Zihuatanejo went to sleep and didn't wake up for more than half a century. The occasion was the arrival of ex-president Lerdo de Tejada, who, during the 1870s, embarked from Zihuatanejo for exile in the United States.

By the 20th century, some of the maritime prosperity of Acapulco, which benefited from

PIRATES OF ZIHUATANEJO

For 10 generations, from the late 1500s to independence in 1821, corsairs menaced the Mexican Pacific coast. They often used Zihuatanejo Bay for repair and resupply.

The earliest was the renowned and feared English privateer Sir Francis Drake. During his circumnavigation of 1577-1580, Drake raided a number of Spanish Pacific ports.

The biggest prize, however, was the Manila galleon, for which he searched the Mexican coast for months. Finally, low on water and food, he dropped anchor and resupplied briefly at Zihuatanejo Bay before continuing northwest.

ENTER THE DUTCH

Dutch corsairs also scoured the seas for the Manila galleon. In October 1624, a Dutch squadron commanded by Captain Hugo Schapenham grouped in a semicircle outside Acapulco Bay to intercept the departing galleon. Port authorities, however, delayed the sailing, and the Dutch began running out of food and water. They tried to trade captives for supplies, but the Spanish refused, offering only inedible gold for the captives. In desperation, Schapenham tried to attack the Acapulco fort directly, but his vessels were damaged and driven off by the fort's effective artillery fire.

The starving Dutch sailors retreated up the coast to Zihuatanejo Bay where, after a few weeks, rested and resupplied, they set sail for Asia on November 29, 1624.

Although most of them arrived in the Moluccas Islands in the East Indies, they disbanded. Most of them, including Schapenham, who was dead by the end of 1625, never returned to Europe.

DAMPIER AND ANSON

A much more persistent and fortunate galleon hunter was English captain William Dampier (1651-1715), who, besides accumulating a fortune in booty, was renowned as a navigator and mapmaker. Lying in wait for the Manila galleon, Dampier anchored in Zihuatanejo Bay in 1704. On December 7, Dampier came upon the Manila galleon *Nuestra Señora del Rosario.*

However, a ferocious Spanish defense forced Dampier's squadron to retreat.

Six years later, commanding another squadron jointly with Captain Woodes Rogers, Dampier captured both the galleon *Encarnación* and the *Nuestra Señora de Begoña* between January 1 and January 5, 1710. Rogers and Dampier returned triumphantly to England in the *Encarnación,* which they had rechristened the *Batchelor.*

Luckiest of all Manila galleon treasure hunters was George Anson (1697-1762), who volunteered for the English navy at the age of 15 and rose rapidly, attaining the rank of captain at the age of 25.

In command of a small fleet of ships and hundreds of sailors, he arrived off Acapulco on March 1, 1742. After waiting three weeks for the galleon to sail, and running low on food and water, Anson sailed northwest, resupplied at Zihuatanejo, and then departed west across the Pacific. On July 1, 1743, off Guam, Anson's forces caught up with and captured the galleon *Nuestra Señora de Covdonga,* with 1.3 million pieces of eight, 35,000 ounces of silver, and a trove of jewels. (A "piece of eight" is an old label for a famous Spanish coin, coveted by pirates the world over.)

Although suffering from the loss of 90 percent of his men, Anson finally returned to England in command of his last remaining ship, carrying booty worth 800,000 pounds sterling, a fortune worth many tens of millions of dollars today.

William Dampier, 1651-1715

George Anson, 1697-1762

the stream of California-bound steamers, spilled over to Zihuatanejo. During the 1920s, nearby resources were exploited, and what is now known as Playa Madera (Wood Beach) earned its label as a loading point for fine hardwood timber exports.

Modern Ixtapa and Zihuatanejo

Recognition of Zihuatanejo's growing importance came on November 30, 1953, when the Guerrero state legislature decreed the formation of the Zihuatanejo *municipio,* whose governmental center was established at the budding town on the bay of the same name.

In the 1960s, a new airport suitable for propeller passenger airplanes, and the paved highway, which arrived from Acapulco around the same time, jolted Zihuatanejo (pop. 1,500) from its final slumber. No longer isolated, Zihuatanejo's headland-rimmed aqua bay began to attract a small colony of people seeking paradise on earth.

Tourism grew steadily. Small hotels and restaurants were built to accommodate visitors. Zihuatanejo had a population of perhaps 5,000 by the late 1970s when Fonatur, the government tourism-development agency, decided to develop Zihuatanejo Bay. Local folks, however, objecting that the proposed lineup of high-rise hotels would block the view of their beautiful bay, squelched the plan.

Fonatur regrouped and alternatively proposed Ixtapa (often translated as White Place, but it more likely means White Top, for the several guano-topped offshore islets), five miles (8 km) north of Zihuatanejo, as a perfect site for a world-class resort. Investors agreed, and the infrastructure—drainage, roads, and utilities—was installed. The jet airport was built, hotels rose, and by 2000, the distinct but inseparable twin resorts of Ixtapa and Zihuatanejo (2010 combined pop. 95,000) were attracting a steady stream of Mexican and foreign vacationers.

Sights

◖ MUSEO ARQUEOLOGÍA DE LA COSTA GRANDE

Zihuatanejo's smallish but fine archaeological museum (Plaza Olaf Palme, Paseo del Pescador, tel. 755/554-7552, 10 A.M.–6 P.M. Tues.–Sun., $3) at the east end of the main town beach authoritatively details the prehistory of the Costa Grande. Professionally prepared maps, paintings, dioramas, and artifacts—many donated by local resident and innkeeper Anita Rellstab—illustrate the development of local cultures, from early hunting and gathering to agriculture and, finally, urbanization by the time of the conquest.

BEACHES AROUND ZIHUATANEJO BAY

Ringed by forested hills, edged by steep cliffs, and laced by rocky shoals, Zihuatanejo Bay would be beautiful even without its beaches. Five of them line the bay.

Playas El Almacén, Municipal, and Madera

Zihuatanejo Bay's west side shelters narrow, tranquil Playa El Almacén (Warehouse Beach), mostly good for fishing from its nearby rocks. Moving east past the pier toward town brings you to the colorful, bustling Playa Municipal. Its sheltered waters are fine for wading, swimming, and boat launching (which anglers, their motors buzzing, regularly do) near the pier end. For maximum sun and serenity, continue walking east away from the pier along Playa Municipal. Cross the pedestrian bridge over the usually dry Agua de Correa creek, which marks the east end of Playa Municipal. Continue along the concrete *andador* (walkway) that winds about 200 yards along the beachfront rocks that run along the west end of Playa Madera. (If you prefer, you can also hire a taxi to take you to Playa Madera, about $3.)

Playa Madera (Wood Beach), once a loading

ZIHUATANEJO

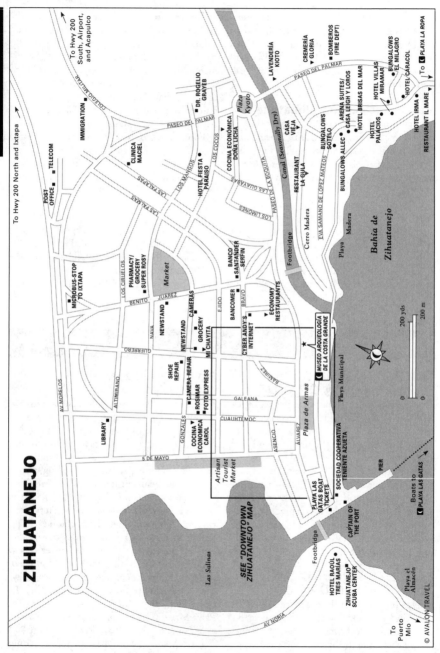

To Hwy 200 North and Ixtapa

To Hwy 200 South, Airport, and Acapulco

COLEGIO MILITAR

IMMIGRATION

TELECOM

POST OFFICE

CLINICA MACIEL

DR. ROGELIO GRAYEB

PASEO DEL PALMAR

LAVENDERIA KIOTO

CREMERIA GLORIA

BOMBEROS (FIRE DEPT)

PASEO DEL PALMAR

Plaza Kyoto

LOS MANGOS

LAS PALMAS

LOS COCOS

HOTEL FIESTA PARAISO

COCINA ECONOMICA DOÑA LICHA

CASA VIEJA

BUNGALOWS EL MILAGRO

HOTEL CARACOL

To PLAYA LA ROPA

ARENA SUITES/ CASA LEIGH Y LOROS

HOTEL VILLAS MIRAMAR

LAS PALMAS

PASEO DE LA BOQUITA

LOS LIMONES

PASEO LAS GUAYABAS

RESTAURANT LA GULA

HOTEL BRISAS DEL MAR

HOTEL PALACIOS

HOTEL IRMA

RESTAURANT IL MARE

MICROBUS-STOP TO IXTAPA

LOS CIRUELOS

PHARMACY/ GROCERY SUPER ROSY

BENITO JUAREZ

Market

BANCO SANTANDER SERFIN

Canal (Seasonally Dry)

BUNGALOWS SOTELO

EVA SAMANO DE LOPEZ MATEOS

BUNGALOWS ALLEC

Cerro Madera

Playa Madera

Bahía de Zihuatanejo

NAVA

NEWSTAND

CAMERAS

E. JIDO

BANCOMER

BRAVO

Footbridge

Playa Madera

GUERRERO

NEWSTAND

GROCERY MI CHAYITA

ECONOMY RESTAURANTS

CYBER ANDY'S INTERNET

AV MORELOS

ALTIMIRANO

SHOE REPAIR

CAMERA REPAIR

ROSIMAR

FOTO EXPRESS

RAMIREZ

MUSEO ARQUEOLOGÍA DE LA COSTA GRANDE

200 yds

200 m

LIBRARY

GALEANA

CUAUHTEMOC

Plaza de Armas

ALVAREZ

Playa Municipal

GONZALES

COCINA ECONOMICA CAROL

ASENCIO

5 DE MAYO

Artisan Tourist Market

SEE "DOWNTOWN ZIHUATANEJO" MAP

SOCIEDAD COOPERATIVA TENIENTE AZUETA

PIER

Boats to PLAYA LAS GATAS

PLAYA LAS GATAS BOAT TICKETS

CAPTAIN OF THE PORT

Las Salinas

Footbridge

HOTEL RAOUL TRES MARIAS

ZIHUATANEJO SCUBA CENTER

Playa el Almacén

To Puerto Mío

AV NOBIA

© AVALON TRAVEL

© BRUCE WHIPPERMAN

It's fun to stroll the *andador* pathway that connects downtown Zihuatanejo with Playa Madera.

point for hardwood lumber, stretches about 300 yards, decorated with rocky nooks and outcroppings and backed by the lush hotel-dotted hill **Cerro Madera.** The beach sand is fine and gray-white. Swells enter the facing bay entrance, usually breaking suddenly in two- or three-foot waves that roll in gently and recede with little undertow. Madera's usually calm billows are good for child's play and easy swimming. Bring your mask and snorkel for glimpses of fish in the clear waters. Beachside restaurant and bars at the Hotel Brisas del Mar and the Hotel Irma, above the far east end, serve drinks and snacks.

Playa La Ropa

Zihuatanejo Bay's favorite resort beach is Playa La Ropa (Clothes Beach), a mile-long crescent of yellow-white sand washed by oft-gentle surf. The beach got its name centuries ago from the apparel that once floated in from an offshore shipwreck. From the summit of the beach's clifftop approach road, **Paseo Costera,** the beach sand, relentlessly scooped

and redeposited by the waves, appears as an endless line of half moons.

Along the 100-foot-wide Playa La Ropa, vacationers bask in the sun, personal watercraft buzz beyond the breakers, rental sailboats ply the waves, and sailboards rest on the sand. The waves, generally too gentle and quick-breaking for surf sports, break close-in and recede with only mild undertow. With its broad horizon and *palapa* restaurants, it's a favorite spot to watch the sun go down. Joggers come out mornings and evenings.

Playa Las Gatas

Secluded Playa Las Gatas, reachable from Playa La Ropa by taxi and a rocky one-mile shoreline hike or much more easily by launch from the town pier, lies sheltered beneath the south-end Punta El Faro headland. Legend has it that the apparent line of rock rubble visible 200 feet off the beach is what remains of a walled-in royal bathing pool that the emperor of the Purépecha people (who still inhabit the highlands of Michoacán) had built to protect his family and friends from the small cat-whiskered nurse sharks that frequent the shoreline. Although the emperor is long gone, the sharks continue to swim off Playa Las Gatas (Cats Beach), named for the sharks' whiskers. (The nurse sharks, however, are harmless; moreover, Las Gatas scuba instructors Thierry and Jean-Claude Duran told me that authoritative archaeological investigators have shown that the rocks are a natural formation.)

Generally calm and quiet, often with super-clear offshore waters, Playa Las Gatas is both a surfing and snorkeling haven and a jumping-off spot for dive trips to prime scuba sites. Beach booths rent gear for beach snorkelers, and a professional dive shop right on the beach, Carlo Scuba, instructs and guides both beginner and experienced scuba divers.

IXTAPA INNER BEACHES

Ixtapa's 10 distinct beaches lie scattered like pearls along a dozen miles of creamy, azure coastline. As you move from the Zihuatanejo end, **Playa Hermosa** comes first. The elevators of the super-luxurious clifftop Hotel Brisas Ixtapa make access to the beach very convenient. At the bottom you'll find a few hundred yards of seasonally-broad white sand, with open-ocean (but often gentle) waves usually good for most water sports except surfing. Good beach-accessible snorkeling is possible off the shoals at either end of the beach. Extensive rentals are available at the beachfront aquatics shop. A poolside restaurant serves food and drinks. Hotel access is only by car or taxi.

◖ *Teleférico* **and Playa del Palmar**

For a sweeping vista of Ixtapa's beaches, bay, and blue waters, ride the *teleférico* (cableway, 7 A.M.–11 P.M. daily) to **El Faro** (tel. 755/555-2510, 8 A.M.–10 P.M. daily in high winter–spring season, shorter hours low season, breakfast $5–10, lunch $8–15, dinner entrées $14–25), a view restaurant at the south end of Ixtapa's main beach, Playa del Palmar.

Long, broad, and yellow-white, Playa del Palmar could be called the billion-dollar beach for the investment money it attracted to Ixtapa. The confidence seems justified. The broad strand stretches for three gently curving miles. Even though it fronts the open ocean, protective offshore rocks, islands, and shoals keep the surf gentle most of the time. Here, most sports are of the high-powered variety—personal watercraft–riding and water-skiing ($50), banana-tubing ($10), and parasailing (despite the considerable risk involved, $25)—although boogie boards can be rented (about $5 an hour) on the beach.

Challenging (usually 3- to 5-foot) surfing breaks roll in consistently off the jetty at **Playa Escolleras,** at Playa del Palmar's far northwest end. Bring your own board.

IXTAPA OUTER BEACHES

Ixtapa's outer beaches spread among the coves and inlets a few miles northwest of the Hotel Zone. Drive, bicycle (rentals, north across the parking lot adjacent to the Supermercado across the street from Hotel Fontan), taxi, or take a minibus marked Playa Linda along the Paseo de las Garzas. Drivers, heading northwest along the Ixtapa hotel row, at the end of the shopping complex, turn right, on Paseo de las Garzas, then fork left at the Hotel Ixtapa Palace after a few hundred yards. After passing the Marina Golf Course (watch out for crocodiles crossing the road, no joke), the road bends west toward the shoreline, winding past a trio of beach gems: Playa San Juan de Dios, Playa Don Rodrigo, and Playa Cuata. Sadly, development has now blocked access to these beaches.

Although Mexican law theoretically allows free public oceanfront access, guards might try to shoo you away from any one of these beaches on the open-ocean side, even if you arrive by boat. If somehow you manage to get there, you will discover cream-yellow strips of sand, nestled between rocky outcroppings, with oft-gentle waves and correspondingly moderate undertow for good swimming, bodysurfing, and boogie boarding. Snorkeling and fishing are equally good around nearby rocks and shoals.

On the peninsula's sheltered northwestern flank, **Playa Quieta** (Quiet Beach) is a place that lives up to its name: a tranquil, sheltered strand of clear water nestled beneath a forested hillside. A ribbon of fine yellow sand arcs around a smooth inlet dotted by a regatta of Club Med kayaks and sailboats plying the water. Get there via the north-end access stairway from the parking lot, signed Playa Quieta Acceso Público. Stop by the beachfront restaurant for refreshments or a fresh seafood lunch.

PLAYA LINDA

Playa Linda, the open-ocean yellow-sand beach at road's end, stretches for miles northwest, where it's known as Playa Larga (Long Beach). Flocks of sandpipers and plovers skitter at the surf's edge and pelicans and cormorants dive offshore while gulls, terns, and boobies skim the wavetops. Driftwood and shells decorate the sand beside a green-tufted palm grove that seems to stretch endlessly to the north.

In addition to the beach, mangrove-fringed **Laguna de Ixtapa,** an arm of which extends south to the bridge before the Playa Linda parking lot, is a must-see. The lagoon's star actors are the huge, toothy crocodiles that sun and snooze below the bridge. Follow the leafy lagoon bank on the beach side of the bridge for rewarding glimpses of other actors, such as a giant, 50–100 pound grandfather freshwater turtle, great white herons, and in season, big nesting flamingo-colored roseate spoonbills and a family of yellow-green iguanas.

Officially, the bicycle path ends at the bridge, but you can continue on foot or by bicycle about 1.5 miles (2.5 km) to sleepy Barrio Viejo village. Take a hat, water, insect repellent, binoculars, and your bird-identification book.

The friendly downscale **La Palapa** beach restaurant, at pavement's end, offers beer, sodas, and seafood, plus showers, toilets, and free parking. Neighboring stable **Rancho Playa Linda** (11 A.M.–6 P.M. daily), managed

© BRUCE WHIPPERMAN

Don't miss the giant turtle that lives below the bridge at Playa Linda, fifteen minutes north of Ixtapa.

by friendly "Spiderman" Margarito, provides horseback rides for about $20 per hour.

The flat, wide Playa Linda has powerful rollers often good for surfing. Boogie boarding and bodysurfing—with caution, don't try it alone—are also possible. Surf fishing yields catches, especially of *lisa* (mullet), which locals have much more success netting than hooking.

(ISLA GRANDE

Every few minutes a boat heads from the Playa Linda embarcadero to mile-long Isla Grande (formerly Isla Ixtapa, 9 A.M.–5 P.M. daily, $5 round-trip). Upon arrival, you soon discover the secret to the preservation of the island's pristine beaches, forests, and natural underwater gardens: "No trash here," the *palapa* proprietors say. "We bag it up and send it back to the mainland." And the effort shows. Great fleshy green orchids and bromeliads hang from forest branches, multicolored fish dart among offshore rocks, and shady native acacias hang lazily over the shell-decorated sands of the island's little beaches.

Boats from Playa Linda arrive at **Playa Cuachalatate** (koo-ah-chah-lah-TAH-tay), the island's most popular beach, named for a local tree whose bark is said to relieve liver ailments. On the island's sheltered inner shore, it's a playground of crystal sand, clear water, and gentle ripples, perfect for families. Many visitors stay all day, splashing, swimming, and eating fresh fish, shrimp, and clams cooked at any one of a dozen beachfront *palapas*. Visitors also enjoy the many sports and equipment on offer: Jet Skis ($50/hr), banana-tube rides ($5), fishing-boat rentals ($60/half-day), aquatic bicycles ($6/hr), snorkel gear ($3/hr), and kayaks ($5/hr).

For a change of scene, follow the short concrete walkway (to the right as you arrive) over the west-side forested knoll to **Playa Varadero** and **Playa Coral,** on opposite flanks of an intimate little isthmus. Varadero's yellow-white sand is narrow and tree-shaded, and its waters are calm and clear.

ZIHUATANEJO, "PLACE OF WOMEN"

An oft-told Costa Grande story says that when Captain Juan Álvarez Chico was exploring at Zihuatanejo in 1522, he looked down on the round tranquil little bay lined with flocks of seabirds and women washing clothes in a freshwater spring. His Aztec guide told him that this place was called Cihuatlán, the "Place of Women." When Chico described the little bay, Cortés tacked *"nejo"* (little) on the name, giving birth to "Zihuatlanejo," which later got shortened to the present Zihuatanejo.

Investigators have offered a pair of intriguing alternative explanations for the "Place of Women" name, a handle that evokes visions of a land of Amazons. They speculate that either Isla Ixtapa (now Isla Grande) or the former royal bathing resort at Playa Las Gatas may have given rise to the name. The bathing resort, founded around 1400 by the Purépecha emperor, was most probably a carefully guarded preserve of the emperor's dozens of wives and female relatives. If not that, Isla Ixtapa may have been used as a refuge for the isolation and protection of women and children against the Aztec invaders who thus attached the label "Place of Women" to the locality.

Behind it lies Playa Coral, a steep coral-sand beach fronting a rocky blue bay. Playa Coral is a magnet for beach lovers, snorkelers, and the scuba divers who often arrive by boat to explore the waters around the offshore coral reef. Women offer massage ($25) to the soothing music of the waves.

Isla Grande's fourth and smallest beach, secluded **Playa Carey,** is named for the sea-turtle species known locally as *carey.* An open-ocean dab of sand nestling between petite, rocky headlands, it's easily accessible by boat from Playa Cuachalatate, but not frequently visited.

Accommodations

The Ixtapa and Zihuatanejo area is one of the Mexican Pacific Coast's loveliest but also most highly seasonal resorts. Hotels and restaurants are most likely to be full during the sunny winter–spring high season, customarily beginning about December 20 and running through Easter week. Low season begins during the oft-hot dry months of May and June. With the beginning of the cooling rains (frequent afternoon thundershowers, drying by evening) in July, vacationers arrive for a medium occupancy season through August. After that, low season begins again, with some restaurants even shutting down during September and October. Nevertheless, for those who crave peace and quiet, bargain hotel prices, just-right balmy weather, and lush verdure, late fall—mid-October through mid-December—is an excellent time to visit. Hotel rates listed here as "low season" are the prices for two that you'll often encounter May–November. Prices listed as "high season" or "holidays" are the steeper tariffs that you will generally encounter during the Christmas–New Year's holidays, often extending through the Easter holiday. Hotels listed here are grouped by location—for Zihuatanejo, Downtown Zihuatanejo, Playa Madera, and Playa La Ropa, and for Ixtapa, Ixtapa and Playa Quieta—and generally listed in ascending order of low-season price.

Zihuatanejo and Ixtapa hotels divide themselves by location (and largely by price) between the budget-to-moderate Zihuatanejo downtown hotels and the more expensive Playa Madera, Playa La Ropa, and Ixtapa hotels. For more information on Zihuatanejo and Ixtapa lodgings, visit the excellent websites www .zihuatanejo.net and www.ixtapa-zihuatanejo .net, or the individual hotel websites listed. Although Zihuatanejo hotels (with the few exceptions noted) provide little or no wheelchair access, all the Ixtapa accommodations described here do.

DOWNTOWN ZIHUATANEJO
Under $50

Right in the middle of the downtown beachfront action is **Casa de Huéspedes Elvira** (Paseo del Pescador 9, tel. 755/554-2061, casa elvira@hotmail.com, $15 s or d in one bed, $20 d in two beds, $25 t low season, add $10 for holidays), founded in 1956 by the late Elvira R. Campos. Every day, Elvira used to look after her little garden of flowering plants, feed rice to her birds—both wild and caged—and pass the time with friends and guests. She would tell of the "way it used to be" when all passengers and supplies arrived from Acapulco by boat, local *almejas* (clams) were as big as cabbages, and you could pluck fish right out of the bay with your hands. Now Elvira's grandmotherly daughter Vicenta carries on her mother's mission. Her petite eight-room lodging divides into an upstairs section, with more light and privacy, and a lower section, with private baths. The leafy, intimate lower patio leads to the airy upper level via a pair of quaint plant-decorated spiral staircases. The rooms themselves are small, authentically rustic, and clean. The four upper rooms share a bathroom and toilet. All rooms come with fans and cable TV. If nighttime noise bothers you, bring earplugs; TV and music from Elvira's adjoining restaurant continues until about 11 P.M. most evenings during the winter high season.

On the west side of downtown, across the lagoon by footbridge from the end of Paseo del Pescador, is the **Hotel Raoul Tres Marias** (Noria 4, Colonia Lázaro Cárdenas, tel. 755/554-2191, $20 s or d in one bed, $25 d, $30 t low season, $30–40 holidays, add $10 for a/c). Its longtime popularity derives from its budget prices and the picturesque lagoonfront boat scene, visible from porches outside some of its 25 rooms. Otherwise, facilities are strictly bare bones with only room-temperature water. Rooms come with TV, fans, and most have private baths.

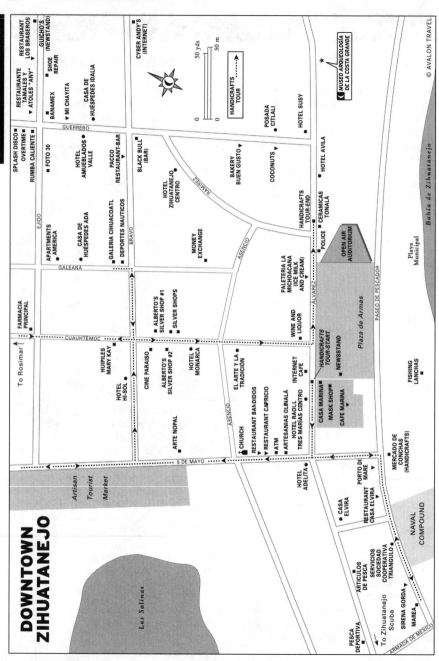

DOWNTOWN ZIHUATANEJO

Las Salinas

Artisan Tourist Market

To Rosimar →

To Zihuatanejo Scuba

Bahía de Zihuatanejo

© AVALON TRAVEL

SPLASH DISCO ■
OVERTIME ■
RUMBA CALIENTE ■

RESTAURANTE TAMALES Y ATOLES "ANY" ▼
GUICHO'S (NEWSTAND) ■
RESTAURANT LOS BRASEROS ■

BANAMEX ■
MI CHAYITA ■
SHOE REPAIR ■
CASA DE HUÉSPEDES IDALIA ■

CYBER ANDY'S (INTERNET) ■

GUERRERO

FOTO 30 ●
HOTEL AMUEBLADOS VALLE ■
PACCO RESTAURANT-BAR ●
BLACK BULL (BAR) ■

POSADA CITLALI ●
HOTEL SUSY ●

EJIDO

APARTMENTS AMERICA ●
CASA DE HUÉSPEDES ADA ●
GALERIA CIHUACOATL ■
DEPORTES NAUTICOS ■

HOTEL ZIHUATANEJO CENTRO ■

BAKERY BUEN GUSTO ▼
COCONUTS ▼

HOTEL AVILA ●

GALEANA

MONEY EXCHANGE ■

HANDICRAFTS TOUR-END ■
POLICE ■
CERAMICAS TONALÁ ●

FARMACIA PRINCIPAL ■

CUAUHTÉMOC

HUIPILES MARY KAY ●
ALBERTO'S SILVER SHOP #1 ●
SILVER SHOPS ●

PALETERIA LA MICHOACANA (ICE MILK AND CREAM) ●

OPEN AIR AUDITORIUM

Plaza de Armas

PASEO DE PESCADOR

Playa Municipal

HOTEL HI-SOL ●
CINE PARAISO ●
ALBERTO'S SILVER SHOP #2 ●
HOTEL MONARCA ●

ARTE NOPAL ■

EL ARTE Y LA TRADICIÓN ■

WINE AND LIQUOR ■

INTERNET CAFE ■

HANDICRAFTS TOUR-START ■
NEWSTAND ■

CHURCH ✝
RESTAURANT BANDIDOS ▼
RESTAURANT CAPRICIO ▼
ATM ■
ARTESANIAS OLINALÁ ■
HOTEL RAOLL TRES MARÍAS CENTRO ■

CASA MARINA MASK SHOP ■
CAFE MARINA ▼

5 DE MAYO

HOTEL ADELITA ●

CASA ELVIRA ●
RESTAURANT CASA ELVIRA ▼

PORTO DI MARE ▼

MERCADO DE CONCHAS (HANDICRAFTS) ■

FISHING LANCHAS ■

NAVAL COMPOUND

PESCA DEPORTIVA ▼
ARTICULOS DE PESCA ▼
SERVICIOS SOCIEDAD COOPERATIVA TRIANGULO ▼
SIRENA GORDA ▼
MAREA ▼

ARMADA DE MEXICO

MUSEO ARQUEOLOGIA DE LA COSTA GRANDE ◀

HANDICRAFTS TOUR ····▶

0   50 yds
0   50 m

A few blocks north and east in the middle of downtown, find unpretentious guesthouse **Casa de Huéspedes Idalia** (Guerrero 9, tel. 755/554-2062, $15 s, $20 d in one bed, $25 d in two beds, add $10 for a/c, $10 for a refrigerator). The elderly owner offers two floors of about a dozen plain but clean rooms, with room-temperature-only shower baths. Don't be put off as you pass through the downstairs entry-level garage; upstairs, Idalia's guests enjoy an airy street-view porch, furnished with hammocks, rocking chairs, and shelves of thick paperback books. Rentals come with TV and fans.

Two blocks behind the market, tucked on a quiet east-side street about five blocks from the beach, budget-conscious travelers will appreciate the attractive **Angela's Hotel and Hostel** (Mangos 25, local cell tel. 044-755/112-2191, from U.S. dial 01152-755/112-2191, angelas hostel@hotmail.com, www.angelashostel .mx; private rooms $25 s or d, $35 t, add $7 for a/c; dorm beds $12). Competently managed by friendly Angela Villalobos and Gregg Thompson, who offer a range of clean, invitingly rustic accommodations, including several private rooms, some with kid-size beds, and dormitories (male, female, and mixed). There is cable TV in the lobby and in-house Internet. Extras include a plant-decorated balcony, with soft couches, cozy for socializing, and a communal-use kitchen.

Back downtown, a block from the beach, long-time favorite **Hotel Susy** (corner of Guerrero and Álvarez, tel./fax 755/554-2339, $30 s or d in one bed, $50 d or t in two beds low season, $40–60 holidays, add $10 for a/c) offers three floors of plain rooms around a shady inner patio. The seven upper-floor bayside rooms have private view balconies (above the busy street, however). Inside corridors unfortunately run past room windows, necessitating closing curtains for privacy, a drawback in these fan-only rooms. Avoid traffic noise by requesting an upper-floor room away from the street. The clean but plain rooms all come with fans and private hot-water baths.

Next door, another solid, moderately-priced choice, if you don't mind a bit of morning noise from the adjacent school, is the popular **Posada Citlali** (Guerrero 3, tel./fax 755/554-2043, no email; $30 s, $35 d, $40 t low season; $40 s, $45 d, $50 t holidays). The hotel (Citlali means star in Náhuatl) rises in a pair of three-story tiers around a shady plant-decorated inner courtyard. Most of the 20 plain, rather small, but clean rooms are thankfully removed from direct street-traffic hubbub. Guests on the upper floors experience less corridor traffic and consequently enjoy more privacy. Reservations are necessary during the high season and strongly recommended at other times. Rentals come with TV, wireless Internet, fans, and hot-water shower baths.

A block west, on a leafy car-free lane, stands Ada Aburto Pineda's modest guesthouse, **Casa de Huéspedes Ada** (Galeana 14, tel. 755/554-2186, nosnos@prodigy.net.mx, www.casade huespedesada.com, rooms $25–75, apartments $400–1,000 per mo.). Her several rentals differ markedly. Downstairs, she offers three plain, dark, and small (barely recommendable) but clean rooms, two with fans, one with air-conditioning (about $20 s, $25 d low season; $30 s, $35 d high season). Her upstairs accommodations are much larger, lighter, and very recommendable. Two are airy, multi-room kitchenette apartments with fans, accommodating up to four or five people ($45 d, $65 t, $65 q low season; $50 d, $70 t, $75 q high season; or $600/mo. in low season, $1,000/mo. high season). They open to a spacious, leafy front porch overlooking the colorful pedestrian-only street scene below. The two remaining upstairs units are in the rear and are smaller but still comfortable and clean, with fans and double beds. The larger of the two has a kitchenette ($40 d low season, $65 d high season; or $400/mo. low season, $700/mo. high season); and the smaller does not have a kitchenette ($35 d low season, $45 d high season). All units come with private hot-water shower baths, TV, in-house Internet, and parking.

If you'd enjoy an airy tropical pool setting, at a reasonable price, check out **Hotel Fiesta Paraíso** (Mangos 5, tel. 755/544-8745, www.hotelfiestaparaiso.com.mx, $35–90 d) on a quiet side street, behind the market, about five blocks from the beach. Lots of pluses here, with two stories of roughly 25 spacious, attractively decorated rooms, with color-coordinated bedspreads and drapes, hot-water shower baths, air-conditioning, cable TV, palm-shaded pool-patio, and parking. It's popular with families, especially on weekends; for peace and quiet, it's best to reserve mid-week.

$50-100

Overlooking the colorful Zihuatanejo downtown action, just two blocks from the beach, rises modest **Hotel Monarca** (Cuauhtémoc 13, tel./fax 755/554-2030 or 744/553-2922, hotelmonarca@live.com, $45 s, $50 d low season, $60 holidays, $1,000/mo.). Choose from six attractive, compact kitchenette (microwave only) studios on three floors. Units are clean, airy, and comfortable; two have private street-view balconies. They accommodate 2–4 people with combinations of double and single beds. Rentals all come with TV, refrigerator, fans, and coffeemaker.

In mid-town, about three blocks from the beach stands **Hotel Amueblados Valle** (Guerrero 33, tel. 755/554-2084, fax 755/554-3220; 1-bedroom unit $50 s or d low season, $60 high season; 2-bedroom unit $75 low season, $100 high season). Inside the front door, find eight furnished apartments on three floors around a leafy-green inner patio. The apartments themselves, all with kitchens and either one or two bedrooms with hot-water shower baths, are clean, spacious, and comfortably appointed. Upper apartments are breezier and lighter. Discounts are possible for monthly rentals. All units come with TV and fans or air-conditioning, but there is no parking and credit cards are not accepted.

Just two blocks from the beach, guests at **Apartments America** (Galeana 16, tel. 755/554-4337, $40–80 d-q, $600–1,000/mo.) enjoy a tranquil, shady street location. The 10 two-bedroom kitchenette apartments, of various sizes, are stacked on two floors around an inner patio-corridor. They are plainly but comfortably furnished with tile floors, bedspreads, curtains, and hot-water shower baths. Apartments can accommodate 4–8 people depending on size and come with fans, air-conditioning, and hot water. There is a modest café-restaurant out front, but no parking. Choose an upstairs apartment for more light and air.

Its location just a block from the beach and two blocks from the town pier draws many fishing enthusiasts to the **Hotel Raúl Tres Marias Centro** (Juan Álvarez 52, at Cinco de Mayo, tel./fax 755/554-6706, toll-free in Mex. tel 800/362-7427, reserve3marias@prodigy.net.mx, www.3marias.net/centro.html, $60 s or d low season, $100 holidays). Some of the 18 clean, comfortable, mostly two-bed rooms have private balconies looking out on the street below. Newcomers might pick up some local fishing pointers after dinner at the hotel's popular restaurant, Los Garrobos. All rooms come with hot-water shower baths, cable TV, and air-conditioning; credit cards are accepted.

Fishing parties are also steady customers at the **Hotel Hi-Sol** (Bravo 120, tel./fax 755/554-0595; $60 s or d, $70 t or q low season; $80 s or d, $90 t, $100 q high season), four blocks from the beach and pier. The hotel offers two floors of about a dozen spacious, clean, and semi-deluxe rooms. All have shiny shower baths and are invitingly decorated with tile and cheery yellow-and-blue-motif bedspreads and curtains. Most rooms open to airy, private, street-view balconies. Rooms come with TV, fans, and telephone.

◖ **Hotel Ávila** (Juan Álvarez 8, tel. 755/554-2010, U.S. tel. 570/688-9466, ixtsptf@verizon.net, www.ixtapasportfishing.com/avila, $45–65 s or d low season, $90–105 high season), downtown Zihuatanejo's only beachfront hostelry, is popular if only for its location. Rooms, although simply decorated, are comfortable. Guests in the hotel's three stories of beachfront rooms enjoy luxurious private-patio bay and beach views. If possible, avoid noise by taking a room on the busy streetfront side. Of the 27 rooms, the cheaper ones face the street and do not have a view, while the more expensive ones come with a beach-view patio. All rooms have fans, cable TV, air-conditioning, hot water, and parking; credit cards are accepted.

Right in the middle of everything is Mexican family favorite **Hotel Zihuatanejo Centro** (Ramírez 2, tel. 755/554-5330 or 755/554-5340, reserve@zihuacentro.com, www.zihua centro.com, $75 s or d low season, $90 high season), Although it's right smack downtown, about two blocks from the beach, guests are nevertheless sheltered from the street noise by rooms that face inward onto an inviting inner pool and courtyard. The 79 rooms, rising in four stories, are clean and simply but comfortably furnished in pastels and vinyl floor tile. Some rooms have two double beds, others have one king- or queen-size bed. For more air and light, ask for a room with a balcony. During the high season, ask for a promotional package to keep the rates down. Rooms come with air-conditioning, fans, cable TV, and hot-water shower baths; there is parking and a restaurant, and credit cards are accepted.

PLAYA MADERA

A sizable fraction of Zihuatanejo's lodgings spreads along and above Playa Madera on the east side of the bay, easily reachable in a few blocks on foot from the town plaza, via the scenic beachfront *andador* (walkway). Many of the lodgings are picturesquely perched along leafy Calle Eva Samano de López Mateos, which runs atop Cerro Madera, the bayfront hill just east of town, while others dot Avenida Adelita at the inland foot of Cerro Madera. Guests in nearly all of the Playa Madera lodgings described here enjoy direct beach access by simply strolling a block or less downhill to luscious Playa Madera.

Note: Because of Zihuatanejo's one-way streets (which fortunately direct most noisy traffic away from downtown), getting to Cerro Madera by car is a bit tricky. The key is Plaza Kioto, the traffic-circle intersection of Paseo de la Boquita and Paseo del Palmar a quarter mile northeast of downtown. As you enter town from Highway 200, keep a sharp eye out and follow the small "Zona Hotelera" signs.

Cerro Madera, the hill rising behind Playa Madera, is home to a sprinkling of comfortable, moderately priced hotels.

At Plaza Kioto, marked by a big Japanese *torii* gate, bear right across the canal bridge and turn right at the first street, Señora de los Remedios. Continue for another block to Avenida Adelita, address of several Playa Madera hotels, which runs along the base of Cerro Madera. From Avenida Adelita, you can either continue along the base of the hill, or turn straight uphill to the lane that runs atop Cerro Madera, Calle Eva Samano de López Mateos, address of several other recommendable lodgings.

$50-100

Playa Madera's only beachfront budget lodging is the 1960s-era **Bungalows Allec** (Calle Eva Samano de López Mateos, Cerro Madera, tel./fax 755/554-2002, reservar@bungalows allec.com, www.bungalowsallec.com, $45–65 d, $80–130 kitchenette apartments), perched on the Cerro Madera hilltop. Clean, comfortable, light, and spacious, the 12 fan-only apartments have breezy bay views from private balconies. Six of the units are very large, with two bedrooms, sleeping at least four, and kitchenettes. The others are smaller studio doubles with refrigerator. There is no pool, but Playa Madera is half a block downhill. Parking is available and credit cards are accepted. Long-term discounts may be available.

Downhill, a couple of blocks inland from the beach find the family-friendly **C Bungalows El Milagro** (Av. Marina Nacional, tel. 755/554-3045, klausbuhrer@hotmail.com, www.ixtapa-zihuatanejo.net/elmilagro/, $55–85 d low season, $105 family-size unit), the life project of Dr. Niklaus Bührer and his wife, Lucina Gomes. Bungalows El Milagro, a hacienda-like walled compound of cottages and apartments, clustered around a shady pool, is winter headquarters for mostly Mexican families and a cordial cadre of long-time German returnees. The welcoming atmosphere and the inviting pool and garden account for El Milagro's success, rather than the 17 plain but clean kitchenette lodgings, which vary in style from rustic Mexican to 1950s Bavarian motel. Look at several before you choose. Add about 25 percent to the rate for high season (Christmas–Easter

and July and August). Discounts of up to 70 percent may be available for long stays. All units come with fully furnished kitchenettes, hot-water shower baths, fans, pool, and parking. No pets are allowed nor credit cards accepted, however.

On Avenida Adelita, right above the Playa Madera, stands the longtime Mexican family–run **Hotel Palacios** (Av. Adelita 15, Col. Playa Madera, tel./fax 755/554-2055, hotelpalacios@ zihuatanejo.net, www.zihuatanejo.net/hotel palacios, $50 s, $55 d low season, $80 holidays), a two-story tier of 28 rooms a short walk downstairs to the beach. Unfortunately, most room windows face corridor walkways, where curtains must be drawn for privacy. Upper units fronting the quiet street avoid this drawback. The rooms themselves are clean, brightly decorated, and comfortable, with fans, air-conditioning, hot-water shower baths, cable TV, and parking. Guests enjoy a small but pleasant blue bayview pool, kiddie pool, and sundeck, perched above the breezy beachfront.

Besides Bungalows Allec, a number of bungalow-style (meaning with kitchen) complexes cluster along the airy Cerro Madera hilltop street. Although their details differ, their basic layouts—which stair-step artfully downhill to private beachfront gardens—are similar. Typical among them is **Bungalows Sotelo** (Calle Eva Samano de López Mateos 13, tel./ fax 755/554-6307, reservar@bungalowssotelo .com, www.bungalowssotelo.com, $65 d low season, $80 d high season; apartments $70–90 low season, $85–180 high season). Guests in a number of the clean and comfortable stucco-and-tile apartments enjoy spacious private or semiprivate terraces with deck lounges and bay views. The smaller units do not have a kitchenette; larger kitchenette suites are available with one or two bedrooms. Rentals vary; look at more than one before deciding. There is no pool and only street parking available, but all units come with air-conditioning, cable TV, and in-house Internet. Make your winter reservations in early.

Also atop Cerro Madera, consider the spiffy **C Arena Suites** (formerly Bungalows Ley)

(Calle Eva Samano de López Mateos s/n, Playa Madera, tel. 755/554-4087, fax 755/554-1365, arenasuites@hotmail.com, $75 d low season, $95 high season). Here, several white-stucco studio apartments stair-step directly downhill to heavenly Playa Madera. Their recent renovations show nicely. Bathrooms shine with flowery Mexican tile, hammocks hang in spacious rustic-chic *palapa*-roofed view patios, and bedrooms glow with wall art, native wood details, and soothing pastel bedspreads. Except for a two-bedroom kitchenette unit at the top, all are kitchenette studios with air-conditioning and telephone. There is no pool, but the beach is straight down the steps from your door. The lovely two-bedroom unit, also with air-conditioning, runs $125 low season for up to four, $140 high season. Long-term low-season discounts (of about 20 percent for 6- to 21-night stays) may be available.

Back downhill, the (**Hotel Villas Miramar** (Av. Adelita, Playa Madera, tel. 755/554-2106 or 755/554-3350, fax 755/554-2149, toll-free Mex. tel. 800/570-6767, reservaciones@hotel villasmiramar.com, www.hotelvillasmiramar .com, garden-view $75 d low season, $150 high season; beach-view $85 d low season, $180 d high season) clusters artfully around gardens of pools, palms, and leafy potted plants. The gorgeous, manicured layout makes maximum use of space, creating both privacy and intimacy in a small setting. The designer rooms have high ceilings, split levels, built-in sofas, and large, comfortable beds. The street divides the hotel into two different, but attractive sections—garden-view and beach-view, but guests may use both—each with its own pool. The restaurant, especially convenient for breakfast, is in the garden-view section but still serves guests who swim, sun, and snooze at the luxurious, beach-view pool-patio on the other side of the street. All rooms come with phones, cable TV, in-house Internet, air-conditioning, and parking; some are wheelchair accessible. Credit cards are accepted. Additional discounts may be available during the May–December 15 low season. Reservations are strongly recommended during the high season.

Zihuatanejo Bay, from the Hotel Irma terrace

© BRUCE WHIPPERMAN

Half a block farther east, overlooking the beach, (**Hotel Irma** (Av. Adelita, Playa Madera, tel. 755/554-8003 or 755/554-8472, fax 755/554-3738, vtasmexhotels@prodigy.net. mx, www.hotelirma.com.mx; no view $65 d low season, $90 high season; with view $75 s or d low season, $125 high season) remains a favorite of longtime lovers of Zihuatanejo, if for no reason other than its view location. Guests enjoy very comfortable, renovated semi-deluxe rooms, a reliable bayview terrace restaurant and bar, and a pair of blue pools perched above the bay. A short walk downhill and you're at creamy Madera beach. Best of all, many of the front-tier rooms have private balconies with just about the loveliest sunset view in Zihuatanejo. The 70 rooms all come with air-conditioning, cable TV, hot-water shower baths, some parking, and wireless Internet connection; credit cards are accepted.

Over $100

Among the plushest Cerro Madera options is the **Hotel Brisas del Mar** (Calle Eva Samano de López Mateos s/n, Cerro Madera, tel./fax 755/554-8332 or 755/554-2142, brisamar@prodigy.net.mx, info@hotelbrisasdelmar.com, www.hotelbrisasdelmar.com; apartments $125 low season, $170 high season; master suites $190 low season, $225 high season; 2-bedroom apartments $380 low season, $470 high season). Owners have completely renovated the original complex and have added a big new wing of a dozen spacious, rustic-chic view suites with native Mexico decor to the original 20 rooms. The brightest spot of this entire complex, besides its sweeping bay views, is the hotel's luxurious beach club, with its shady *palapas,* lounge chairs, and big blue pool. For such amenities, Brisas del Mar asks premium prices. In addition to the original (upgraded) apartments and larger master suites, there are spacious two-bedroom family bungalows that have oceanview patios, kitchens, air-conditioning, wireless Internet, and cable TV.

Also on Playa Madera, perched atop Arena Suites, but completely separate, is upscale **Casa Leigh y Loros** (Calle Eva Samano de López Mateos s/n, Playa Madera, zihua01@gmail.com, www.zihuatanejo-rentals.com, $175 with fans/$205 with a/c low season, $225 with fans/$255 with a/c high season), the lovely life project of friendly California resident Leigh Roth and her pet parrot, Loros. Casa Leigh y Loros, which Leigh rents when she's away, is a multilevel art-decorated white-stucco-and-tile two-bedroom, two-bath villa with roof garden, airy bayview balconies, and up-to-date kitchen appliances. High winter season (except Christmas) runs November 15–April 30 and low season runs May 1–November 14. The villa comes with cable TV and daily maid service; a cook is available at an extra charge. Leigh also manages rentals for many other luxurious villas, apartments, and condominiums. See her website or contact Ignacio, her rental agent, in Zihuatanejo, at local cell tel. 044-755/559-8884.

A few hundred yards farther east along cliffside Paseo Costera toward Playa La Ropa, find ◖ **La Casa Que Canta** (Camino Escénico a Playa La Ropa, tel. 755/555-7030 or 755/555-7000, toll-free Mex. tel. 800/710-9345 or U.S. tel. direct 888/523-5050, fax 755/554-7900, info@lacasaquecanta.com, www.lacasaquecanta.com, $600 d terrace room, $750 d grand suite, $1,000 d master suite), which is as much a work of art as a hotel. The pageant begins at the lobby, a luxurious soaring *palapa* that angles gracefully down the cliffside to an intimate open-air view dining room. Suite clusters of natural adobe sheltered by thick *palapa* roofs cling artfully to the hotel's craggy, wave-washed, precipice, decorated with riots of bougainvillea and gardens of cactus. From petite pool terraces perched above foamy shoals, guests enjoy a radiant aqua bay panorama in the morning and brilliant ridge-silhouetted sunsets in the evening. The 18 art-bedecked, rustic-chic suites, all with private view balconies, come in three grades: super-deluxe "terrace" rooms, more spacious "grand suites," and even more spacious and luxurious "master suites," the latter two options come with their own small pools. All come with air-conditioning, fans, phone, and wireless Internet, but no TV; no kids under 16 are allowed. Make winter reservations very early.

(Furthermore, Casa Que Canta offers the best of all possible upscale worlds within its present grounds: the El Murmullo super-private 10,000-square-foot four-villa inner sanctum compound, built for a maharaja. It includes complete all-exclusive staff, from gardener, chambermaids, butler, waiters, kitchen staff, and gourmet chef, all for only about $4,000 daily.)

PLAYA LA ROPA

Paseo de la Costera, the clifftop access road to Playa La Ropa, skirts Playa Madera and winds southeast downhill to Playa La Ropa, arguably Ixtapa-Zihuatanejo's loveliest resort beach. A mile-long crystal half-moon strand, decorated by lazy coconut palms and washed by gentle surf, set the scene, while an uncluttered collection of low-rise beachfront hotels and bungalows, from downscale-rustic to world-renowned and luxurious, provide the relaxing finale.

The more upscale hostelries spread along the

near (Zihuatanejo) end, while the more moderately-priced hotels, nestle from the middle to the far (southeast) end of the beach.

$50-100

A trio of moderately priced La Ropa lodgings stand out. Check out **◖ Bungalows Urracas** (Playa La Ropa, tel. 755/554-2053 or 755/554-2049 in Spanish only, $65 d low season, $80 high season), made up of about 15 petite brick cottages, like proper rubber planter's bungalows out of Somerset Maugham's *Malaysian Stories,* in a shady jungle of leafy bushes, trees, and vines. Inside, the illusion continues: dark, masculine wood furniture, spacious bedrooms, shiny tiled kitchenettes and baths, and rustic beamed ceilings. From the bungalows, short garden paths lead to the brilliant La Ropa beachfront. About eight additional bungalows occupy beach-view locations out front. Amenities include private, shady front porches (use insect repellent in the evenings), hot-water shower baths, fans, and parking, but no TV or Internet. Ask for a long-term discount. Telephone is the only way to make a reservation. Get your winter reservations in very early (if necessary, ask someone who speaks Spanish to call).

In contrast, find nearby **Bungalows Vepao** (Playa La Ropa, tel. 755/554-3619, fax 755/554-5003, vepao@yahoo.com.mx, www.vepao.com, $80 d low season, $95 d high season). Here you can enjoy a clean, pleasantly tranquil beach lodging, simply but architecturally designed, with floor-to-ceiling drapes, tiled floors, hot-water shower baths, white stucco walls, and pastel bedspreads and shaded lamps. Some units have basic (microwave) kitchenettes as an option. Guests in each of the six side-by side apartments enjoy front patios (upper ones have some views of the bay) that lead right to the hotel's private row of nearby beachfront thatched *palapas.* Rates include parking and fans; long-term discounts are possible. Reserve through owner-manager Verónica Ramírez (in Spanish, 7 A.M.–6 P.M. daily Pacific Time).

Not far from the beach's southeast end, is **Hotel Casa del Mar** (Playa La Ropa, tel./fax

755/554-3873, reserv@zihua-casadelmar.com, www.zihua-casadelmar.com, $75–85 d low season, $90–110 d high season, add $10 for a/c), founded by master scuba diver Juan Barnard Avila and his wife, Margo. In the mid-1990s, they renovated a rickety old hotel, cleaned up the adjacent mangrove lagoon, and nurtured its wildlife (dozens of bird species and a number of crocodiles, take care with pets and toddlers) back to health. Now, new owners carry on Juan and Margo's ecological mission, with a restful hotel and beachfront restaurant where guests may stay and relax for a week or a season, enjoy wholesome food, friendly folks, and sample the good snorkeling, scuba diving, kayaking, turtle hatching, and fishing available right from the beach. Choose a room with an ocean view in front, or a garden view in back. All rooms are immaculate and simply but comfortably furnished with handsomely handcrafted wooden beds, lamps, and cabinets. The garden-view rooms are slightly cheaper than the ocean-view rooms. All rooms come with hot-water shower baths, parking, and small tank pool; credit cards are accepted. Reservations are necessary in winter.

Back near the La Ropa Zihuatanejo end, a block off the beach, **Villas Ema** (Calle Delfines, Playa la Ropa, Zihuatanejo, tel. 755/554-4880, $80 d low season, $105 high season) perches at the top of a flowery hillside garden. Here, the enterprising husband-and-wife owners of downtown Posada Citlali have built 11 apartments, attractively furnished with white tile floors, matching floral drapes and bedspreads, modern-standard shower baths, plenty of windows for light, and sliding doors leading to private view porches for reading and relaxing. Amenities include fans and air-conditioning, hot-water shower baths, beautiful blue pool, and the murmur of the waves on Playa La Ropa nearby. The nine smaller units share a kitchen in common; the three top-level units, although sunnier (and consequently warmer), have the best views and most privacy. Two ground-level larger *villitas,* by the pool, each with its own kitchen and patio and sleeping four, rent for about $110 low season, $120 high season. For reservations, highly recommended in winter, contact either Posada Citlali, tel./fax 755/554-2043, downtown, at Avenida Guerrero 3, Zihuatanejo, Guerr. 40880; or, contact the owner directly, Señora Ema, tel. 755/554-4880, in Spanish, at the Villas Ema on Playa La Ropa. To avoid confusion, be sure to specify your reservation is for Villas Ema.

Over $100

On the central beachfront, adjacent to Bungalows Vepao, also find **C Casa Gloria Maria** (Playa La Ropa, tel. 755/554-3510,

gloriamaria@zihuatanejo.net, www.zihua tanejo.net/casagloriamaria, $100 d low season, $120 high season), a designer white-stucco beachfront house of four apartments. Each of the deluxe units (two upstairs and two down) is attractively decorated with native rustic tile floors, bright floral tile baths, and whimsical hand-painted wall designs at the head of the two double beds. Each unit has its own kitchenette in an outdoor beachview patio. For more breeze and privacy, ask for one of the top-floor units. Rentals come with air-conditioning, hot-water baths, and parking.

OWNING PARADISE

Droves of repeat visitors have fled their northern winters and bought or permanently rented a part of their favorite Mexican Pacific paradises. They happily live all or part of the year in beachside developments that have mushroomed, especially around Ixtapa-Zihuatanejo, Acapulco, Puerto Vallarta, and Guadalajara. Deluxe vacation homes, which foreigners can own through special trusts, run upward from $100,000; condos begin at about half that. Time-shares, a type of rental, start at about $5,000.

TRUSTS

In the past, Mexicans have feared, with some justification, that foreigners were out to buy their country. As a consequence, present laws prohibit foreigners from holding direct title to property within 30 miles (50 km) of a beachfront or within 60 miles (100 km) of a national border.

However, Mexican law does permit *fideicomisos* (trusts), which substitute for outright foreign ownership. Trusts allow you, as the beneficiary, all the usual rights to the property, such as use, sale, improvement, and transfer, in exchange for paying an annual fee to a Mexican bank, the trustee, which holds nominal title to the property. Trust ownership has been compared to owning all the shares of a corporation, which in turn owns a factory. While not owning the factory in name, you have legal control over it.

Although some folks have been bilked into buying south-of-the-border equivalents of the Brooklyn Bridge, Mexican trust ownership is a happy reality for growing numbers of American, Canadian, and European beneficiaries who simply love Mexico. Take note, however, that *the great majority of Mexican real estate sales are cash only.* Real estate mortgage loans in Mexico, while not unheard-of, are definitely the exception.

Mexican *Bienes raíces* (bee-AY-nays rah-EE-says, real estate) business is similar (but with nevertheless significant differences) to the United States and Canada. Agents handle multiple listings, show properties, assist negotiations, track paperwork, and earn commissions for sales completed. If you're interested in buying a Mexican property, work with one of the many honest and hardworking agents in Mexico, preferably a member of the Mexico National Realtors Association (AMPI) who is also recommended through a reliable firm back home or trustworthy, property-savvy friends in Mexico.

During your search, best consider purchase of private, legally-owned property, certified with a genuine deed *(título de propiedad)*. Communal or *ejido* property cannot be legally sold until it is officially changed into private property. Once you have zeroed in on an acceptable property, make sure that you and your agent are negotiating only with the owner

Near the beach's Zihuatanejo end is the **Hotel Villa Mexicana** (Playa La Ropa, tel./fax 755/554-3776 or 755/554-3636, www.villamexicana.com.mx, from $110 d low season, $200 holidays) that seems to be popular for nothing more than its stunning location right in the middle of the sunny beach hubbub. Its 75 rooms, comfortable and air-conditioned, are packed in low-rise stucco clusters around an inviting beachfront pool-patio-restaurant. This seems just perfect for the mostly North American winter package-vacation clientele, who ride personal watercraft, parasail, and boogie board from the beach, snooze around the pool, and socialize beneath the *palapa* of the beachside restaurant. Some rooms have wheelchair access. Parking is available; rooms come with air-conditioning, cable TV, hot-water shower baths, and wireless Internet. Credit cards are accepted.

The 40-odd lodgings of the neighboring hillside **Catalina Beach Resort** (Playa La Ropa, tel. 755/554-2137, toll-free U.S. tel. 877/287-2411 or Can. tel. 866/485-4312, fax 755/554-9327, info@catalinabeachresort.com, www.catalinabeachresort.com, $80 d

---

of record or his or her attorney. With a signed sales agreement in hand, your agent should recommend a *notaria pública* (notary) who, unlike most U.S. notary publics, is an attorney, appointed by the state governor, skilled and licensed in property transactions. You will not need another attorney.

A Mexican notary, a semi-judicial officer, functioning much as a title company does in the United States, is the most important person in completing your transaction. The notary traces the title, ensuring that your bank-trustee legally receives it, and makes sure the agreed-upon amounts of money get transferred between you, the seller, bank, agent, and notary.

You and your agent should meet jointly with the notary early on to discuss the deal and get the notary's computation of the closing costs. For a typical trust-sale, closing costs (covering permit, filing, bank, notary, and registry fees) are considerable, typically 8-10 percent of the sale amount. After that, you will continue to owe property taxes and an approximately 1 percent annual fee to your bank-trustee.

TIME-SHARING

Started in Europe, time-sharing has spread all over the globe. A time-share is a pre-paid rental, usually of a condominium, for a specified time period per year. Agreements usually allow you to temporarily exchange your time-share rental for similar lodgings throughout the world.

Your first contact with time-sharing (*tiempo compartido*) will often be someone on a resort street corner who offers you a half-price tour for "an hour of your time." Soon you'll be attending a hard-sell session offering you tempting inducements in exchange for a check written on the spot. The basic appeal is your investment – say $15,000 cash for a two-week annual stay in a deluxe beach condo-hotel – which will earn you a handsome profit if you decide to sell your rights sometime in the future. What isn't mentioned is that time-shares have become increasingly difficult to sell and the interest or mutual fund growth that you could realize from your $15,000 cash would go far toward renting an equally luxurious vacation condo every year without entailing as much risk.

And risk there is, because you would be handing over your cash for a promise only. Read the fine print. Shop around, and don't give away anything until you inspect the condo you would be getting and talk to others who have invested in the same time-share. It may be a good deal, but don't let anyone rush you into paradise. (For an informative collection of Mexico real-estate-related articles, log on to www.mexconnect.com/articles2597.)

low season, $129 d high season) stair-step picturesquely all the way down to the Zihatanejo end of beach. The Catalina's comfortably appointed, 1960s-era tropical-rustic accommodations maximize privacy, with individual view terraces and hammocks. The spacious lodgings, all clean and deluxe, vary from large to huge; look until you find the one that most suits you. Most have fans only (not necessarily a minus on this airy hillside); some do have air-conditioning, however. At the bottom of the hill, a beach aquatics shop offers sailing, sailboarding, snorkeling, and other rentals; those who want to simply rest enjoy chairs beneath the shady boughs of a beachside grove. The Catalina's food and drink facilities include a view restaurant, perching in the middle of the complex, a snack bar down at the beach, and an airy upper-level terrace bar. Access to all of this requires lots of stair climbing, which fitness aficionados would consider a plus. The Catalina's high-season rates for two run as follows: small casita (large room) $129 fan only; standard casita (suite) $169 fan only; deluxe bungalow (even larger suite) $237 with air-conditioning; deluxe honeymoon suite with air-conditioning $177; all with cable TV and phone. Low-season rates for the same categories run about $80, $112, $153, and $177, respectively.

German entrepreneur Helmut Leins left Munich and came to create paradise on Playa La Ropa in 1978. The result was Playa La Ropa's renowned Villa del Sol, now being operated by new owners as the **Hotel Tides Zihuatanejo** (Playa La Ropa, tel. 755/555-5500, toll-free U.S./Can. tel. 866/905-9560, fax 755/554-2758, reservations@tides zihuatanejo.com, www.tideszihuatanejo.com, $460 s or d low season, $690 and up high season). Here, in an exquisite beachside mini-Eden, a corps of well-to-do North American, European, and Mexican clients return yearly to enjoy tranquility and the elegance of Tides Zihuatanejo's crystal-blue pools, palm-draped patios, and gourmet *palapa*-shaded restaurants. The lodgings vary, from luxuriously spacious at the high end to simply large at the low end; all have handsome rustic floor tile,

handcrafted wall art, and big, luxuriously-soft beds. The plethora of extras includes restaurants, bars, pools, night tennis courts, a newsstand, art gallery boutique, beauty salon, and meeting rooms. There are approximately 70 accommodations. Super-plush room options include more bedrooms and baths, ocean views, and small private whirlpool tubs that go for around $1100 and up. All lodgings come with cable TV, phone, air-conditioning, parking and much more; some have wheelchair access. Credit cards are accepted. Children are permitted in two-bedroom suites only.

IXTAPA

Ixtapa's dozen-odd hotels line up in a luxurious strip between the beach, Playa Palmar, and boulevard Paseo Ixtapa. Guests in all of them enjoy deluxe resort-style facilities and wheelchair access. All are high-end (more than $100/day) accommodations.

Near the northwest end, consider the best-buy **Hotel Krystal Ixtapa** (Paseo Ixtapa s/n, tel. 755/553-0333, fax 755/553-0216, reservacionesixtapa@krystal-hotels.com, www .krystal-hotels.com, $113 d low season, $200 high season). The hotel, which towers over its spacious garden compound, has an innovative wedge design that ensures an ocean view from each room. Relaxation centers on the blue pool, where guests enjoy watching each other slip from the water slide and duck beneath the waterfall all day. Upstairs, all of the 260 tastefully appointed deluxe rooms and suites have private view balconies, cable TV, air-conditioning, and phones. Check for additional discounts through extended-stay or other packages. Extras include tennis courts, racquetball, an exercise gym, wireless Internet, parking, and much more. Credit cards are accepted.

Another good-value choice is the smaller **Hotel Posada Real Ixtapa** (Paseo Ixtapa s/n, tel. 755/553-1625 or 755/553-1745, fax 755/553-1805, toll-free U.S./Can. tel. 800/448-8355, ixtapa@posadareal.com.mx, www .posadareal.com.mx, $150 d low season, $190 high season) at Paseo Ixtapa's northwest end. Get there via the street, beach side, just past the

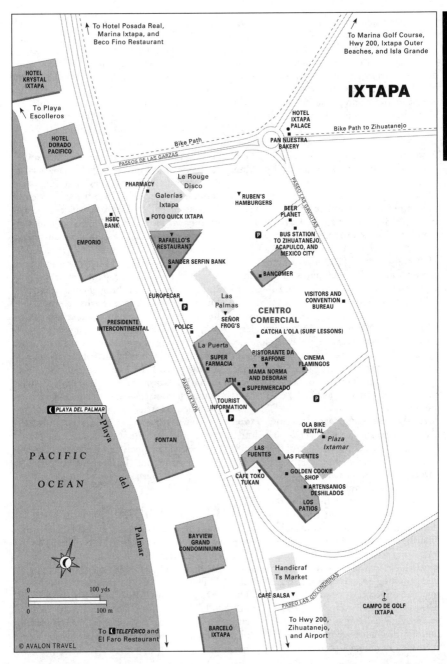

To Hotel Posada Real, Marina Ixtapa, and Beco Fino Restaurant

To Marina Golf Course, Hwy 200, Ixtapa Outer Beaches, and Isla Grande

HOTEL KRYSTAL IXTAPA

IXTAPA

To Playa Escolleros

HOTEL IXTAPA PALACE

Bike Path to Zihuatanejo

HOTEL DORADO PACIFICO

Bike Path

PAN NUESTRA BAKERY

PASEOS DE LAS GARZAS

PHARMACY

Le Rouge Disco

RUBEN'S HAMBURGERS

HSBC BANK

Galerías Ixtapa

BEER PLANET

EMPORIO

FOTO QUICK IXTAPA

PASEO LAS GAVIOTAS

RAFAELLO'S RESTAURANT

BUS STATION TO ZIHUATANEJO, ACAPULCO, AND MEXICO CITY

SANDER SERFIN BANK

BANCOMER

EUROPECAR

Las Palmas

VISITORS AND CONVENTION BUREAU

PRESIDENTE INTERCONTINENTAL

POLICE

SEÑOR FROG'S

CENTRO COMERCIAL

CATCHA L'OLA (SURF LESSONS)

La Puerta

SUPER FARMACIA

RISTORANTE DA BAFFONE

CINEMA FLAMINGOS

PASEO IXTAPA

MAMA NORMA AND DEBORAH

PLAYA DEL PALMAR

ATM

SUPERMERCADO

Playa

TOURIST INFORMATION

PACIFIC

OLA BIKE RENTAL

Plaza Ixtamar

FONTAN

del

OCEAN

LAS FUENTES

LAS FUENTES

GOLDEN COOKIE SHOP

CAFE TOKO TUKAN

ARTENSANIOS DESHILADOS

Palmar

LOS PATIOS

BAYVIEW GRAND CONDOMINIUMS

Handicraf Ts Market

0   100 yds

0   100 m

CAFE SALSA

PASEO LAS GOLONDRINAS

CAMPO DE GOLF IXTAPA

To **TELEFÉRICO** and El Faro Restaurant

BARCELÓ IXTAPA

To Hwy 200, Zihuatanejo, and Airport

© AVALON TRAVEL

big corner restaurant on the left. With a large grassy soccer field instead of tennis courts, the hotel attracts a seasonal following of soccer enthusiasts. Other amenities include a large airy beachfront restaurant and two luscious pools. Although the 110 (rather small) rooms are clean and comfortable, many lack ocean views. Extended-stay or low-season discounts, such as a fourth night free, are seasonally available. Kids under 12 stay for free with parents. Amenities include air-conditioning, satellite TV, phones, wireless Internet, and parking; credit cards are accepted.

Right in the middle of the hotel zone stands the **Hotel Dorado Pacífico** (Paseo Ixtapa s/n, tel. 755/553-2025, fax 755/553-0126, reserv@doradopacifico.com.mx, www.doradopacifico.com.mx, U.S. toll-free tel. 877/936-7236, $110 d low season, $250 high season). Here, three palm-shaded blue pools, water slides, a swim-up bar, tennis courts, and three restaurant-bars continue to satisfy a year-round crowd of vacationers. Upstairs, the rooms, all with sea-view balconies, are pleasingly decorated with sky-blue carpets and earth-tone designer bedspreads. The 285 rooms come with air-conditioning, phones, cable TV, parking, and much more. Low-season and extended-stay discounts may be available; credit cards are accepted.

At the east end, **Hotel Barceló Ixtapa** (Paseo Ixtapa s/n, tel. 755/555-2000, toll-free U.S. tel. 800/227-2356, fax 755/553-2438, reservas@barceloixtapa.com.mx or ixtapa@barcelo.com, www.barceloixtapa.com, all inclusive $340 d low season, $600 high season, kids under six are free, ages 6–12 $60), across from the golf course at the east end of the beach, rises around a soaring lobby/atrium. The Barceló, formerly the Sheraton, offers a long list of resort facilities, including pools, all sports, an exercise gym, several restaurants and bars, cooking and arts lessons, nightly dancing, and a Fiesta Mexicana show-buffet. The 330-odd rooms in standard (which include inland-view balconies only), oceanview, and junior suite grades, are spacious and tastefully furnished in designer pastels and include air-

conditioning, phones, and satellite TV. The Barceló offers only all-inclusive lodging: Rates include all drinks, food, and entertainment.

From its east-end jungly hilltop perch, the queen of Ixtapa hotels, the **◖ Hotel Las Brisas Ixtapa** (Paseo de la Roca, tel. 755/553-2121, toll-free Mex. tel.01-800/227-4727 or U.S./Can. tel. 888/559-4329, fax 755/553-1031, ixtapa@brisas.com.mx, www.brisas.com.mx, $250 d low season, $500 high season, about $1,000 for super-luxury suites) slopes downhill to the shore like a latter-day Aztec pyramid. The monumentally stark hilltop lobby, unadorned except for a clutch of huge stone balls by the front door, contrasts sharply with its surroundings. The hotel's severe lines immediately shift the focus to the adjacent jungle. The fecund forest aroma wafts into the open lobby and the terrace restaurant where, at breakfast during the winter and early spring, guests sit watching iguanas munch hibiscus blossoms in the nearby treetops. The hotel entertains guests with a wealth of luxurious resort facilities, including pools, four tennis courts, a gym, aerobics, an intimate shoal-enfolded beach, restaurants, bars, and nightly piano-bar music. The standard rooms, each with its own spacious view patio, are luxuriously spartan, floored with big designer tiles, furnished in earth tones, and equipped with big TVs, small refrigerators, phones, and air-conditioning. More luxurious options include suites with individual pools and hot tubs. There are 427 rooms in total. In June–October bargain packages can push standard-room prices to as low as $150 d.

PLAYA QUIETA

A trio of all-inclusive luxury resort hotels decorate the luscious, sheltered Playa Quieta beachfront about five miles (8 km) northwest of the main Ixtapa hotel zone.

The original of the three is the **Club Med Ixtapa** (Playa Quieta, toll-free U.S. tel. 800/258-2633, www.clubmed.com, $2300 d per week low season, $4600 d high season), which, as its long-time clients have acquired families, has become kid friendly. Besides deluxe rooms, the usual good Club Med food, and a plethora of included activities, from sailboating and surfing to water aerobics and chess, children can also enjoy a fully supervised program of child-appropriate activities. At Club Med, the usual lodging arrangement is for a minimum of one week, paid in advance for all-inclusive lodging, with all food, drinks, sports, and entertainment included. Kids under 15 go for about half the adult price.

Alternatively, you might consider the Club Med's worthy neighbors, the grand 400-room **Hotel Meliá Azul Ixtapa** (Paseo Punta, Ixtapa, local tel. 755/555-0000, toll-free U.S./Can. tel. 800/336-3542, fax 755/555-0100, www .meliaazulixtapa.com, $300 d per day all-inclusive low season, $600 d high season) and the smaller **Hotel Qualton Club** (Carretera Escenica, Playa Linda, Zihuatanejo, local tel. 755/552-0080, fax 755/552-0070, www.qual ton.com/ixtapa, $200 d per day all-inclusive low season, $300 d high season). Both hotels welcome children and offer deluxe amenities, food, and activities comparable to Club Med, usually at reduced prices.

TRAILER PARKS AND CAMPING

The Ixtapa and Zihuatanejo area has at least three equipped RV-camping parks, two small, on Playa Ropa in Zihuatanejo, and one large government-built site, on Ixtapa's far outer beach, Playa Larga. Other rough, work-in-progress sites offer some RV hookups and camping spaces on Playa La Ropa. Make your winter reservations months in advance.

The new government-run RV park, officially **Ixtapa Trailer Park** (Lote 36, Real Playa Larga, tel. 755/552-0295 or 755/552-0296, trailerparkixtapa@gmail.com, $25/day, $150/ week, $550/month, camping $7 per person) offers basic facilities—including high-power electricity, water, drainage, showers, toilets, and a restaurant. The site, right by breezy, palm-shadowed Playa Larga, fine for all beach pastimes, is promising, but the trailer lot itself, of about 50 unshaded asphalt, RV spaces (big enough for 35-foot rigs) inside a cyclone fence,

is as plain as a supermarket parking lot. Find it about 5 miles (8 km) north from Ixtapa, 10 miles (16 km) from Zihuatanejo. Get there by driving to Playa Linda. Continue north (follow RV park signs), past the Playa Linda bridge and parking lot, continuing about another half-mile to the RV park on the left.

A much smaller and less formal spot to park your RV or put up a tent is at the far end of Playa La Ropa: **El Manglar Restaurant and RV Park** (Playa La Ropa, tel. 755/554-3752, $30 per RV, $10 for tent), on the inland side of the mangrove lagoon adjacent to the beachfront Hotel Casa del Mar. Here, the friendly restaurant owners, who also run the trailer park, offer a parking space, with all hookups, toilets, clean showers, wireless Internet, and resident lagoon crocodiles (watch after your toddlers and pets). Pluses here are a good restaurant, two-minute walk to luscious Playa La Ropa, space for about five large rigs (40-foot) and five small (20-foot), and a locked gate at night. Minuses are lack of shade and evening no-see-ums and mosquitoes. To get to El Manglar, follow the directions to Playa Madera. Because of Zihuatanejo's one-way streets (which fortunately direct most noisy traffic away from downtown), getting there by car is a bit tricky. The key is Plaza Kioto, the traffic-circle intersection of Paseo de la Boquita and Paseo del Palmar a quarter mile northeast of downtown. As you enter town from Highway 200, keep a sharp eye out and follow the small "Zona Hotelera" signs. Past Plaza Kioto and the canal bridge, instead of turning right on Señora de los Remedios street to go to Playa Madera, continue straight ahead two blocks. Pass the Bungalows El Milagro on the right, climb the hill for half a block and bear right for a long block, then turn left where the street forks, and you'll be on your way, with a fine bay view, along Paseo Costera. Continue about a mile, winding toward Playa La Ropa. Downhill, continue straight ahead past a traffic circle and dolphin monument on the right. Continue another mile straight ahead, passing Hotel Real de Palma on the left. Pass under a large arch, then bear right, to the signed El Manglar gate.

If the Manglar park is full, you might find an RV parking space and/or campsite at either of a pair of rustic possibilities on Playa La Ropa. **Playa La Ropa Camping and RV** (near the middle of Playa La Ropa, see Esta Campamento signpost, $15, on the right after the dolphin monument, but before the arch) has several spaces with all hookups. Or continue under the arch straight ahead to **Costa Bella Trailer Park** (tel. 755/554-4967, $20 hookups, $10 campsite), with about 10 unshaded hookups, with drainage, water, and electricity, plus camping spaces at the far south end of the Playa La Ropa road. (For more information and photos of El Manglar and Playa La Ropa Camping and RV trailer parks, visit www.ontheroadin.com/pacificcoast/pacific south/ixtapaandzihuat.htm.)

RENTALS

Zihuatanejo residents sometimes offer their condos and homes for rent or lease through agents. Among the most experienced and highly recommended agents is **Judith Whitehead** (tel./fax 755/554-6226, cell tel. 044-755/557-0078, jude@prodigy.net.mx, www.paradise-properties.com.mx).

Also, owner-agent **Francisco Ibarra** (tel. 755/554-4924 or 755/554-9377, donfranciscoproperties@gmail.com, www.donfrancisco properties.com) rents several moderately priced condos and houses in Zihuatanejo, Ixtapa, and Troncones.

For many more vacation rentals, visit the excellent websites www.zihuatanejo.net and www.zihuatanejo-rentals.com, and www.vrbo .com (Vacation Rentals By Owner).

Food

ZIHUATANEJO
Snacks, Bakeries, and Breakfasts

For something cool, stop by the **La Michoacana** (Álvarez, no phone, 9 A.M.–9 P.M. daily) ice shop across from the police station by the beachfront town plaza. Besides ice cream, popcorn, and wholesome *nieves* (ices), it offers delicious *aguas* (fresh fruit-flavored drinks) that make nourishing, Pepsi-free alternatives.

All roads seem to lead to the excellent downtown Zihuatanejo bakery 【 **Buen Gusto** (Guerrero 11, 8 A.M.–10 P.M. daily, pastries about $0.30–0.80 each), on the west side of the street a few doors up from the restaurant Coconuts. Choose from a simply delicious assortment of fruit and nut tarts and cakes—pineapple, coconut, peach, strawberry, pecan—with good coffee to go with them all.

For hot sandwiches and good pizza on the downtown beach, try the **Cafe Marina** (Paseo del Pescador, tel. 755/554-2462, 8 A.M.–9 P.M. Mon.–Sat., closed approx. June–mid-Sept., $8), just west of the plaza. The friendly, hard-working owner features specials, such as spaghetti and meatballs, or ribs and potato salad,

on some weeknights. The shelves of books for lending or exchange are nearly as popular as the food.

A local stay wouldn't be complete without dropping in for breakfast at the **Sirena Gorda** (Fat Mermaid; Paseo del Pescador, tel. 755/554-2687, 9 A.M.–11 P.M. Thurs.–Tues., $4–9), near the end of Paseo del Pescador across from the naval compound. Here the fishing crowd relaxes, trading stories after a tough night and early morning hauling in the lines. The other unique attractions, besides the well-endowed sea nymphs who decorate the walls, are tempting shrimp-bacon and fish tacos, juicy hamburgers, fish *mole,* and conch and *nopal* (cactus leaves, minus the spines) plates.

Local folks swear by 【 **Cocina Económica Doña Licha** (Calle Cocos, tel. 755/554-3933, 7 A.M.–11 P.M. daily, $3–9) in downtown Zihuatanejo's northeast neighborhood. (From Plaza Kioto, follow Paseo del Palmar west one block, turn left onto Cocos and continue half a block.) The reason is clear: tasty local-style food, served promptly in an airy, spic-and-span setting. Here customers can have it all.

For breakfast try *huevos a la Mexicana* or pancakes; for *lonche*, go for the four-course *comida corrida* set lunch; for *cena* (supper), try one of their super-fresh fish fillets or a seafood brochette (shrimp, oysters, octopus, fish).

Restaurants

Local chefs and restaurateurs, long accustomed to foreign tastes, operate a number of good local restaurants, mostly in Zihuatanejo (where, in contrast to Ixtapa, most of the serious eating occurs *outside* of hotel dining rooms). Note, however, that a number of the best Zihuatanejo restaurants are closed during the low-season months of September and October. If in doubt, be sure to call ahead. The recommendations here move across downtown, generally from east to west.

Zihuatanejo has a pair of good, genuinely Mexican-style restaurants, frequented by a legion of Zihuatanejo longtimers. In the central downtown area, ◖ **Tamales y Atoles "Any"** (corner of Guerrero and Ejido, tel. 755/554-7373, 9 A.M.–11 P.M. daily, $4–8), arguably Zihuatanejo's best, is the spot to find out if your favorite Mexican restaurant back home is serving the real thing. Tacos, tamales, quesadillas, enchiladas, *chiles rellenos,* and such goodies are called *antojitos* in Mexico. At Tamales y Atoles "Any," they're savory enough to please even demanding Mexican palates. Incidentally, Any (AH-nee) is the co-owner, whose perch is behind the cash register, while her friendly husband cooks and tends the tables.

Neighboring **Restaurant Los Braseros** (Ejido 21, tel. 755/554-7522, 4 P.M.–1 A.M. daily, $3–6), half a block farther east along Ejido, midway between between Guerrero and Juárez, is similarly authentic and popular. Waiters are often busy after midnight even during the low season serving seven kinds of tacos and specialties, such as Gringa, Porky, and Azteca, from a menu it would take three months of dinners (followed by a six-month diet) to fully investigate.

Asian-food fanciers have at least one good option, in the tasty offerings of Chinese restaurant **Mi Chayita** (Guerrerro, east side,

three doors south of the Gonzales corner, tel. 755/554-5799, 11 A.M.–9 P.M. Mon.–Sat., $4–8). Here, beneath a cool *palapa*, a California-trained chef satisfies vegetable-hungry appetites, starting with bountifully delicious plates of chow mein and chop suey. On the other hand, meat eaters can choose from a list of many delicious favorites, such as sweet-and-sour pork, breaded shrimp, whole fish, broccoli beef, and much more.

Smack in the middle of town, families fill the tables at petite **Cocina Económica Carol** (Cuauhtémoc, between Ejido and Gonzales, tel. 755/551-1412, 11 A.M.–6 P.M. Mon.–Sat., $2–4). Diners enjoy country-style breakfasts such as *chilaquiles* and *huevos a la Mexicana; comida corrida* (set lunch of soup, rice, meat entrée, and dessert); and supper of tacos, enchiladas, tostadas, and tamales.

Down at the beach, across from the naval compound, longtime **Casa Elvira** (Paseo del Pescador, tel. 755/554-2061, 1–10 P.M. daily, $4–15), founded long ago by the late Elvira Campos, is as popular as ever, still satisfying the palates of a battalion of loyal Zihuatanejo returnees. Elvira's continuing popularity is easy to explain: a palm-studded beachfront, strumming guitars, whirling ceiling fans, and a bounty of fresh salads and soups, hearty fish, meat and chicken entrées, and Mexican specialties, all expertly prepared and professionally served. Reservations are recommended during the high season.

If Elvira's is full, an excellent seafood alternative would be **Porto de Mare** (Paseo del Pescador, tel. 755/554-5902, noon–11 P.M. daily, closed Sept.–Oct., $8–20), half a block east. It's the labor of love of its Italian architect-owner, who designed and crafted its elegant open-air interior himself. As would be expected, his specialties are Italian-style pastas blended with superbly fresh local fish, shrimp, clams, scallops, and oysters.

The owners of up-and-coming **Restaurant Capricio** (Cinco de Mayo, tel. 755/554-3019, 8 A.M.–11 P.M. daily, $8–20), by the church on the southwest corner of downtown, have followed the successful Coconuts restaurant example. Soft background jazz, fairy lights, and a tropical greenery-festooned patio set the scene, while the cuisine of especially good seafood pastas, hamburgers, and steaks provides the main event.

A restaurant that enjoys customers when others don't is (**Casa Viejo** (Josefa Ortiz de Dominguez 7, at the foot of Cerro Madera, tel. 755/554-9770, 2–10 P.M. Mon.–Sat., 9 A.M.–10 P.M. Sun., $13), founded by an American lover of Mexican food. Beneath Casa Viejo's soaring *palapa,* simple guacamole accompanied by *sopa casa viejo* becomes a whole meal, and the barbequed pork ribs are a work of culinary art. On Thursdays the regular menu gives way to the Mexican tradition of *pozole,* with all the trimmings—a treat not to be missed by lovers of true Mexican food.

Splurges

No guide to Zihuatanejo restaurants would be complete without mention of (**Coconuts** (on Guerrero, a block from the beach, tel. 755/554-2518, noon–3:30 P.M. daily for Mexican *comida,* regular menu 6 P.M.–midnight daily in season, closed approx. Sept.–Nov., $12–24). Here, the food—whether it be light (pasta primavera) or hearty (rib-eye steak)—appears to be of importance equal to the airy garden setting and good cheer generated among the droves of Zihuatanejo lovers who return year after year.

For a romantic treat, make a sunset-hour reservation at (**Restaurant Il Mare** (Paseo Costera, on the clifftop, just past Playa Madera a block past Hotel Irma, tel. 755/554-9067, noon–midnight daily high season, 4 P.M.–midnight daily low season, $20). Enter and let the luscious ambience—soothing Italian arias, waves crashing against the rocks far below, the golden setting sun—transport you to somewhere on the Amalfi coast: *O! Sole mio!* The menu extends the impression: Start with *bruschetta alla Romagna;* follow with soup *brodetta di pesce;* salad *pomodoro cipolla rossa con gorgonzola;* and *scampi al vino bianco,* accompanied by a bottle of good Chilean Sendero chardonnay. Finish off with lemon liqueur *Sogna*

di Sorrento. Reservations are strongly recommended on weekends and in the high season.

Enjoy a nouvelle variation by heading east of town to Calle Adelita (foot of Cerro Madera) to sample the "fusion" cuisine of popular **Restaurant La Gula** (Adelita 8, tel. 755/554-8396, 5:30–11 P.M. Mon.–Sat., closed Aug.–Oct., $12–30). Here, chefs practice the craft of small portions and artful presentations of seafood, such as favorites *Eclipses del Sol* (shrimp medallion), *Pesce Solado* (dorado, mahi-mahi,* baked in corn husks), and *Negrito de Zihua* (blackened dorado, in *meuniere* sauce and seasoned with "ten spices"). Reservations are strongly recommended.

IXTAPA
Bakeries, Breakfast, and Snacks

The perfume wafting from freshly baked European-style yummies draws dozens of the faithful to the **Golden Cookie Shop** (Los Patios, upper floor, tel. 755/553-0310, 8 A.M.–2 P.M. Mon.–Sat., closed approx. July–Sept., $4–6), brainchild of local longtimers Helmut and his late wife, Esther Walter. On the inner patio, upper floor of Los Patios shopping complex, Helmut continues their mission of satisfying homesick palates with a continuous supply of scrumptious cinnamon rolls, pies, and hot buns, and hearty American-style breakfasts. In recent years, Helmut has served an authentic German buffet every Friday; call to confirm.

On another day, sample the savory coffee and baked offerings of **Pan Nuestro** (Our Bread; in the Hotel Palacio Ixtapa, tel. 755/553-1585, 9 A.M.–11 P.M. daily for pastries, 1 P.M.–midnight daily for pizza), at the north end of the Ixtapa Centro Comercial shopping complex, one block inland from boulevard Paseo Ixtapa.

Ruben's Hamburgers (tel. 755/553-0027, noon–midnight daily, $3–5) hamburger and taco hall, at the north end of the Ixtapa Centro Comercial shopping complex, behind the corner Galerias Ixtapa center, about a block inland from boulevard Paseo Ixtapa, is by far Ixtapa's most popular eatery, judging from the flocks of Mexican vacationers who occupy its tables. Ruben's is a phenomenon as much as it is a restaurant, outdoing traditional *taquerías* (taco stalls) at their own game, with fresh ingredients and a dozen variations on steaks, hamburgers, and tacos.

Restaurants

Restaurants in Ixtapa have to be exceptional to compete with the hotels. One such restaurant, the **Bella Vista** (Paseo de la Roca, tel. 755/553-2121, 7 A.M.–noon P.M. daily, breakfast buffet $12), *is* in a hotel: It is the Hotel Las Brisas Ixtapa's jungle view–terrace café. Here, you can have the best possible perch for watching the antics of the iguanas in the adjacent treetops. These black, green, and white miniature dinosaurs crawl up and down the trunks, munch flowers, and sunbathe on the branches. The restaurant food and service, incidentally, are exceptional. Lately they've been serving breakfast only in the high season. Call ahead to see if this has changed. Reserve a terrace-edge table; credit cards are accepted.

The Ixtapa restaurant that has customers when most others don't is ◖ **Restaurant Mama Norma and Deborah** (La Puerta shopping center, tel. 755/553-0274, 7:30 A.M.–11 P.M. daily, $12–25). Canadian expatriate proprietor Deborah Thompson manages with aplomb, working from a menu of delicious specialties familiar to North American and European palates. Whatever your choice, be it Greek salad, lobster, steak, or fettuccine Alfredo, Deborah makes sure it pleases. Lately she's been open for breakfast; call to confirm morning hours.

Folks hankering for Italian-style pastas and seafood walk next door to ◖ **Ristorante Da Baffone** (La Puerta shopping center, tel. 755/553-1122, 4 P.M. until about midnight daily, $10–12). The friendly owner, a native of the Italian isle of Sardinia, claims his restaurant is the oldest in Ixtapa. He's most likely right: He served his first meal here in 1978, simultaneous with the opening of Ixtapa's first hotel. While Mediterranean-Mex decor covers the walls, marinara-style shrimp, calamari, clams with linguini, ricotta- and spinach-stuffed cannelloni, and glasses of Chianti and pino grigio load the tables. Call to confirm hours and for reservations.

If Da Baffone is full or closed, or for a splurge, try the highly recommended Italian gourmet restaurant **Becco Fino** (in the Marina Ixtapa, tel. 755/553-1770, noon–midnight daily, $30). Reservations are usually necessary.

Entertainment and Events

In Zihuatanejo, visitors and residents content themselves mostly with quiet pleasures. Afternoons, they stroll the beachfront or the downtown shady lanes and enjoy coffee or drinks with friends at small cafés and bars. As the sun goes down, however, folks head to Ixtapa for its sunset vistas, happy hours, shows, clubs, and dancing.

NIGHTLIFE

Nightlife lovers are blessed with a broad range of enjoyable choices, sprinkled around Ixtapa and Zihuatanejo. In Ixtapa, options vary from the zany Señor Frog's to the relaxed piano bar at El Faro restaurant. Zihuatanejo choices run from raucous Restaurant Bandidos to restful Coconuts lounge bar.

High on the Ixtapa list is the part restaurant, part wacky nightspot **Señor Frog's** (tel. 755/553-2282, restaurant noon–10 P.M., bar until 4 A.M. daily), in the Ixtapa shopping plaza across from the Hotel Presidente InterContinental. Inside, patrons mingle in the cavernous bar, where you needn't risk dancing on your table, since the dance floors are already elevated. The food, while reliable, seems an afterthought.

Christine (in front of the Hotel Krystal, tel. 755/553-0333 or 755/555-0510, 10 P.M.–wee hours Wed.–Sat., cover $10 women, $20 men) is Ixtapa's big-league discotheque. Patrons warm up by listening to relatively low-volume rock, watch videos, and talk while they can still hear each other. That stops around 11:30 P.M. when the fogs descend, the lights begin flashing, and the speakers boom forth their 200-decibel equivalent of a fast freight train roaring at trackside.

For a much calmer diversion, check out upscale restaurant **El Faro** (in Marina Ixtapa, tel. 755/553-2525, 8–11 P.M. Tues.–Sun.), atop the lighthouse, that customarily features live blues-jazz instrumental numbers. Call to verify programs.

Several Ixtapa hotel lobbies bloom with dance music beginning around 7 P.M. during the high winter season. Year-round, however, good medium-volume groups sometimes play for dancing evenings at the **Hotel Presidente InterContinental Ixtapa** (Paseo Ixtapa s/n, tel. 755/553-0018); the **Hotel Barceló Ixtapa** (Paseo Ixtapa s/n, tel. 755/555-2000); and the **Hotel Las Brisas Ixtapa** (Paseo de la Roca, tel. 755/553-2121). Programs change, so call ahead to confirm.

In Zihuatanejo, you'll find nearly all nightlife choices can be best discovered on an evening stroll while looking and listening for what you want. Be sure to check out open-air **Restaurant Bandidos** (Cinco de Mayo, tel. 755/553-8072, noon–2 A.M. nightly in high season), near the church, colorfully decorated in faux 1910 revolution style, with plenty of old Pancho Villa and Emiliano Zapata *bandido* photos. They welcome guests to sing along to the music, both live and recorded. Call to confirm programs.

More Zihuatanejo choices include **Black Bull** (corner of N. Bravo and V. Guerrero, tel. 755/554-2230), a younger-crowd disco; **Rick's** (on Cuauhtémoc downtown, tel. 755/554-2535), live music nightly, from around 6 P.M., sometimes shows, popular with sailboaters; and the upscale **Coconuts** lounge-bar and restaurant (on Guerrero, a block from the beach, tel. 755/554-2518), relaxing garden setting, with hammocks, sofas, and videos.

Additionally, a small nightclub district has bloomed in Zihuatanejo at the corner of Guerrero and Ejido. Towering above it all is gargantuan three-story **Rumba Caliente** (from

9 P.M. Wed.–Sun.) that pounds out its booming Latin offering from the top floor. Next door, trying hard not to be upstaged, **Overtime** booms as long as there are customers. And, next to that, **Splash** (from 7 P.M. Wed.–Sun.) karaoke club patrons belt out vocals.

TOURIST SHOWS

Ixtapa hotels stage **Fiesta Mexicana** extravaganzas, which begin with a sumptuous buffet and go on to a whirling skirt-and-sombrero folkloric ballet. After that, the audience becomes part of the act, with piñatas, games, cockfights, and dancing, while enjoying drinks from an open bar. In the finale, fireworks often boom over the beach, painting the night sky in festoons of reds, blues, and greens.

Entrance runs about $40 per person, with kids under 12 half price. The most reliable and popular shows (sometimes seasonally only, sometimes hotel guests only) are staged on Saturday at the **Hotel Presidente InterContinental Ixtapa** (Paseo Ixtapa s/n, tel. 755/553-0018); Tuesday at the **Hotel Dorado Pacífico** (Paseo Ixtapa s/n, tel. 755/553-2025); and Wednesday at the **Hotel Barceló Ixtapa** (Paseo Ixtapa s/n, tel. 755/555-2000). Call ahead for confirmation and reservations.

SUNSETS

Sunsets are tranquil and often magnificent from the ◖ **Restaurant/Bar El Faro** (tel. 755/553-1027, 5:30–10 P.M. daily low season, longer hours high season), not to be confused with El Faro restaurant in the Marina. It even has a cableway (7 A.M.–7 P.M. daily) that you can ride uphill from the south end of the Ixtapa beach. Many visitors stay to enjoy dinner and the relaxing piano bar. Reservations are recommended during winter and on weekends. Otherwise, drive or taxi via the uphill road toward the Hotel Las Brisas Ixtapa, east of the golf course; at the first fork, head right for El Faro.

For equally brilliant sunsets in a lively but refined setting, try the lobby bar of the ◖ **Hotel Las Brisas Ixtapa** (Paseo de la Roca, tel. 755/553-2121, happy hour 6–7 P.M. daily). The piano bar or seasonal live music for dancing begins around 7:30 P.M. (call to confirm programs). Drive or taxi along the uphill road at the golf course, following the signs to the crest of the hill just south of the Ixtapa beach.

Zihuatanejo Bay's western (sunset-side) headland blocks most Zihuatanejo sunset views, except for spots at the far end of Playa La Ropa. Here, guests congregate at the longtime beachfront favorite **Restaurant La Perla** (Playa La Ropa, tel. 755/554-2700, 10 A.M.–10 P.M. daily).

CRUISES

Those who want to experience a sunset party while at sea ride the big 75-foot catamaran *Picante* (tel. 755/554-2694 or 755/554-8270, picante@picantecruises.com, www.picante cruises.com), which leaves from the Zihuatanejo pier (call to confirm schedule) around 5:00 P.M. daily, returning around 8 P.M. The tariff runs about $50 per person, including open bar.

The *Picante* also heads out daily on a Sunshine Cruise around 10 A.M., returning around 2:30 P.M. Included are open bar, lunch, and snorkeling for about $80 per person. Book tickets (high-season reservations mandatory) for both of these cruises, which customarily include transportation to and from your hotel, through a hotel travel agent or directly through the *Picante* office at Puerto Mío, the small marina about half a mile across the bay from town. Get there from Zihuatanejo on foot or by taxi via the one- mile road that curves around the western, right-hand shore of Zihuatanejo Bay.

MOVIES

Head to the petite **Cine Paraíso** (on Cuauhtémoc, tel. 755/554-2318), three blocks from the beach in downtown Zihuatanejo, to escape into American pop, romantic comedy, and adventure.

Sports and Recreation

SWIMMING AND SURFING

Oft-calm Zihuatanejo Bay is fine for swimming and sometimes good for boogie boarding and bodysurfing at Playa Madera. On Playa La Ropa, although waves generally break too near the shore for either bodysurfing or boogie boarding, swimming beyond the breakers is fine. Surfing is very rewarding at Playa Las Gatas, where swells sweeping around the south-end point give good, rolling left-handed breaks.

Heading northwest to more open coast, waves improve for bodysurfing and boogie boarding along Ixtapa's main beach Playa del Palmar, while usually remaining calm and undertow-free enough for swimming beyond the breakers. As for surfing, good breaks often rise off the **Playa Escolleros** marina jetty at the west end of Playa del Palmar.

Along Ixtapa's outer beaches, swimming is great along calm Playa Quieta. Surfing, bodysurfing, and boogie boarding are correspondingly good but sometimes hazardous in the mountainous open-ocean surf of Playa Linda and Playa Larga farther north.

Surfing lessons have arrived in Zihuatanejo, at **Catcha L' Ola** (Catch a Wave; in Ixtapa in the Centro Comercial Kiosko, behind Restaurant Mama Norma and Deborah, tel. 755/553-1384, catchalola@ixtapasurf.com, www.ixtapasurf.com, surfing lessons $50). Besides surfing lessons and luxury camping trips to the best local surfing beaches, Catcha L' Ola offers surfboard and equipment rentals and repair, and for-sale accessories equipment, information, and cheap beer.

SNORKELING AND SCUBA DIVING

Clear offshore waters (sometimes up to 100-foot visibility during the dry winter–spring season) often draw a steady flow of divers and have nurtured professionally staffed and equipped dive shops. Just offshore, good snorkel and scuba spots, where swarms of multicolored fish graze and glide among the rocks and corals, are accessible from **Playa Las Gatas** in Zihuatanejo Bay and **Playa Carey** on Isla Grande.

Many boat operators take parties for offshore snorkeling excursions. On Playa La Ropa, contact the aquatics shop at the foot of the hill beneath Catalina Resort Hotel. Playa Las Gatas, easily accessible by boat for $4 from the Zihuatanejo pier, also has snorkel and excursion boat rentals. In Ixtapa, similar services are available at beachfront shops at many of the hotels, such as the Posada Real, the Krystal, and the Presidente InterContinental.

Other even more spectacular offshore sites, such as Morros de Potosí, El Yunque, Bajo de Chato, Bajo de Torresillas, Piedra Soletaria, and Sacramento, are accessible with the help of professional guides and instructors.

A trio of local scuba dive shops stand out. Right downtown, licensed long-time instructors Carlos Bustamante and L. Ricardo Gutiérrez carry on Zihuatanejo's professional scuba tradition with **Nautilus Divers** (Juan Álvarez 30, local 4, tel. 755/554-6666, dive@divezihuatanejo.com, www.nautilus-divers.com), across from the Zihuatanejo beachfront basketball court. Beginners start with the resort course: two hours' pool instruction and a guided dive, $80. At the expert end, open-water NAUI certification takes three or four days and runs about $450. For certified divers (bring your certificate) they offer night, shipwreck, deep-water, and marine biology dives at more than a dozen coastal sites.

Also in Zihuatanjeo, long-time scuba instructor and professional marine biologist Juan Barnard Avila offers similar services through his long established **Zihuatanejo Scuba Center** (tel. 755/544-8554, zihdivers@hotmail.com, www.zihuatanejodivecenter.com). Find them at the far west side of downtown, across the lagoon bridge, next to Hotel Raul 3 Marias.

On Playa Las Gatas **Carlo Scuba** (tel. 755/554-6003, carloscuba@yahoo.com, www.carloscuba.com) also provides professional scuba services. PADI-trained instructors offer a resort course, including one beach dive ($60); also a four-day open-water certification course ($450); and a two-tank dive trip for certified participants ($95, one tank $65). They also conduct student referral courses and night dives. Contact the manager-owner, Thierry Duran (son of the renowned diver, late Jean-Claude Duran), at his shop in the middle of Playa Las Gatas.

FISHING

Surf or rock casting with bait or lures, depending on conditions, is generally successful in local waters. Have enough line to allow casting beyond the waves (about 50 feet out on Playa La Ropa, 100 feet on Playa del Palmar and Playa Linda).

The rocky ends of Playas La Ropa, La Madera, del Palmar, and Las Gatas on the mainland, and Playa Coral on Isla Grande, are also good for casting.

For deep-sea fishing, you can launch your own boat or rent one. *Pangas* (launches) are available for hire from individual anglers on the beach, or the boat cooperative at Zihuatanejo pier, or aquatics shops of the Beach Resort Sotavento on Playa La Ropa or the Hotels Las Brisas Ixtapa, Barceló, Krystal, and others on the beach in Ixtapa. Rental for a seaworthy *panga,* including tackle and bait, should run about $80 per half day, depending upon the season and your bargaining skills. An experienced boater can typically help you and your friends hook several big fish in about four hours; local restaurants are often willing to serve them as a small banquet for you in return for your extra fish.

BIG-GAME SPORTFISHING

Zihuatanejo has long been a center for billfish (marlin, swordfish, and sailfish) hunting. Most local captains have organized themselves into cooperatives, which visitors can contact either directly or through town or hotel travel agents. Trips begin around 7 A.M. and return 2–3 P.M. Fishing success depends on seasonal conditions. If you're not sure of your prospects, go down to the Zihuatanejo pier around 2:30 P.M. and see what the boats are bringing in. During good times they often return with one or more big marlin or swordfish per boat (although captains are increasingly asking that billfish be set free after the battle has been won). Fierce fighters, the sinewy billfish ("tigers of the sea") do not make the best eating and are often discarded after the pictures are taken. On average, boats bring in two or three other large fish, such as *dorado* (dolphinfish or mahi-mahi), yellowfin tuna, and roosterfish, all more highly prized for the dinner table.

The biggest local sportfishing outfitter is the blue-and-white fleet of the **Sociedad Cooperativa Teniente Azueta** (tel./fax 755/554-2056, 8 A.M.–5 P.M. daily), named after the naval hero Lieutenant José Azueta. You can see several of its many boats bobbing at anchor adjacent to the Zihuatanejo pier. Arrangements for fishing parties can be made through hotel travel desks or at the cooperative office at the foot of the pier. The larger (28-foot) boats, with three lines, go out for a day's fishing for about $200.

The smaller (18-boat) **Sociedad Cooperativa Triangulo** (tel./fax 755/554-3758, 9 A.M.–7 P.M. daily) is trying harder. Its 38-foot boats for six start around $350; a 25-footer for four, about $180. Contact the office across from the naval compound, near the west end of Paseo del Pescador.

SPORTFISHING TOURNAMENTS

Twice a year, usually in May and January, Zihuatanejo fisherfolk sponsor the **Torneo de Pez Vela** (Sailfish Tournament), with prizes for the biggest catches of sailfish, swordfish, marlin, and other varieties. The entrance fee runs around $800, and the prizes usually include a new pickup truck, outboard motors, and other goodies. For information, contact the local sportfishing cooperative, Sociedad Cooperativa Teniente Azueta (Muelle Municipal, Zihuatanejo, Guerrero 40880, tel./fax 755/554-2056).

SAILING, SAILBOARDING, AND SEA KAYAKING

The tranquil waters of Zihuatanejo Bay, Ixtapa's Playa del Palmar, and the quiet strait off Playa Quieta are good for these low-power aquatic sports. Shops on Playa La Ropa (below Catalina Beach Resort) in Zihuatanejo Bay and at the beachfront at Ixtapa hotels, such as the Krystal, Presidente InterContinental, and Dorado Pacífico, rent small sailboats, sailboards, and kayaks by the hour.

LAGOON KAYAKING AND BIRD-WATCHING

The grand **Laguna de Potosí** and the smaller, more remote **Estero Valentin**, respectively about 10 and 20 miles (16 and 32 km) southeast of Zihuatanejo, have become prime wildlife-viewing sites, due to the enterprise of Ixtapa-based **Zoe Kayak Tours** (contact Brian, tel. 755/553-0496, local cell tel. 044-755/558-8564, from U.S. and Canada dial 011521-755/558-8564, zoe5@aol.com, www.zoekayaktours.com, full-day Potosí $80, Valentin $100). The earnest, wildlife-sensitive operators conduct thoroughly professional excursions, designed to maximize the quality of participants' wildlife-viewing experience and appreciation. Itineraries vary, from full-day outings to extended overnights and more.

For other promising kayaking and bird-watching tour options, check out **Adventours** (tel. 755/553-1069, pablomendizabal@gmail.com, www.ixtapa-adventours.com).

MARINA AND BOAT LAUNCHING

Marina Ixtapa (tel./fax 755/553-2180, 755/553-0222, or 755/553-2365, info@marinaixtapa.com, www.marinaixtapa.com), at the north end of Paseo Ixtapa, offers excellent boat facilities. The slip charge runs about $1 per foot per day for 1–6 days ($0.75 for 7–29 days), subject to a minimum charge per diem. This includes use of the boat ramp, showers, pump-out, trash collection, mailbox, phone, fax, and satellite TV. For reservations and information, contact the marina 9 A.M.–2 P.M. and 4–7 P.M.

© BRUCE WHIPPERMAN

The wildlife-rich mangrove Laguna de Potosí is accessible by either guided tour from Ixtapa-Zihuatanejo or by self-guided kayak adventure.

daily, at the harbormaster's office in the marina-front white building on the right, a block before the big white lighthouse.

The smooth, gradual Marina Ixtapa **boat ramp,** open to the public for a ramp fee (from about $40), is on the right-hand side street, leading to the water, just past the big white lighthouse. Get your ticket beforehand from the harbormaster.

GOLF AND TENNIS

Ixtapa's 18-hole professionally designed **Campo de Golf** (Paseo Ixtapa, across from the Hotel Barceló, tel. 755/553-1062, 7 A.M.–4 P.M. daily, greens fees $75, including cart $110, club rental $25, 18 holes with caddy $25) is open to the public. In addition to its manicured 6,898-yard course, patrons enjoy services of a pro shop, lockers, and tennis courts. Reservations are accepted; morning golfers should get in line early during the high winter season.

The **Marina Golf Course** (tel. 755/553-1410 or 755/553-1424, greens fee $55, cart $35, club rental $35, caddy $25) offers similar facilities and services.

Ixtapa has virtually all of the local tennis courts, all of them private. The **Campo de Golf** (Paseo Ixtapa, across from the Hotel Barceló, tel. 755/553-1062, $7/hour daytime, $10/hour night) has some of the best. Reservations may be seasonally necessary. A pro shop rents and sells equipment. A teaching professional offers lessons for about $25 per hour.

Some hotels welcome outside guests at their tennis courts, for a fee. Call the **Hotel Dorado Pacífico** (tel. 755/553-2025) or the **Hotel Las Brisas Ixtapa** (tel. 755/553-2121) for a reservation.

BICYCLING

Ixtapa's newest popular pastime is bicycling along the 10-mile (16-km) round-trip *ciclopista* bike path to Playa Linda. The rental station **Citi Rental Shop** (south side of the Las Fuentes parking lot, tel. 755/553-0259, 8 A.M.–2 P.M. and 4–8 P.M. daily, bike rentals $5/hour, $25/day) is across the Boulevard from the Hotel Fontan.

The *ciclopista* takes off at the Paseo Las Garzas intersection, at the north-end corner of the Ixtapa shopping-restaurant complex. Officially the *ciclopista* ends 5 miles (8 km) northwest, at the wooden bridge and crocodile-viewing point at the Playa Linda parking lot, but you can go 1.5 miles (2.5 km) farther to Barrio Viejo village at the lagoon's edge. Be sure to take a hat, water, and insect repellent.

If, on your return approach to Ixtapa, you haven't enjoyed your fill of bicycling, you can rack up more mileage along the Zihuatanejo *ciclopista* leg: Heading back to Ixtapa, about 100 yards after the intersection that directs traffic left to Highway 200, bear left where Paseo de los Pelicanos forks left and follow the Zihuatanejo *ciclopista* past the back (northwest) side of the golf course, another eight miles (13 km), two (leisurely) hours to Zihuatanejo and return.

WALKING AND JOGGING

Zihuatanejo Bay is strollable from Playa Madera all the way west to Puerto Mío. A relaxing half-day adventure could begin by taxiing to the Hotel Irma (Av. Adelita, Playa Madera) for breakfast. Don your hats and follow the stairs down to Playa Madera and walk west toward town. At the end of the Playa Madera sand, head left along the *andador* (walkway) that twists along the rocks, around the bend toward town. Continue along the beachfront Paseo del Pescador; at the west end, cross the lagoon bridge, head left along the bayside road to Puerto Mío resort and marina for a drink at the hotel's La Cala restaurant and perhaps a dip in the pool. Allow three hours, including breakfast, for this two-mile (3-km) walk; do the reverse trip during late afternoon for sunset drinks or dinner at the Irma.

Playa del Palmar, Ixtapa's main beach, is good for similar strolls. Start in the morning (during high winter–spring season) with breakfast at the Restaurant/Bar El Faro (tel. 755/555-2510, 7 A.M.–noon daily high season) atop the hill at the south end of the beach. Ride the cableway or walk downhill. With the sun at your back stroll the beach, stopping for refreshments at the hotel pool patios en route. The entire beach stretches about three miles (5 km) to the marina jetty, where you can often watch

surfers challenging the waves and where taxis and buses return along Paseo Ixtapa. Allow about four hours, including breakfast.

The reverse walk would be equally enjoyable during the afternoon. Time yourself to arrive at the El Faro cableway about half an hour before sundown (7:30 P.M. summer, 5:30 P.M. winter) to enjoy the sunset over drinks and/or dinner. Get to El Faro by driving or taxiing via Paseo de la Roca, which heads uphill off the Zihuatanejo road at the golf course. Follow the first right fork to El Faro.

Adventurers who enjoy ducking through underbrush and scrambling over rocks might want to explore the acacia forest and wave-tossed rocky shoreline of the undeveloped far west side of **Isla Grande.** Take water, lunch, and a good pair of walking shoes.

Joggers often practice their art either on the smooth, firm sands of Ixtapa's main beachfront or on Paseo Ixtapa's sidewalks. Avoid crowds and midday heat by jogging in the early mornings or late afternoons. For even better beach jogging, try the flat, firm sands of uncrowded Playa Quieta about three miles (5 km) by car or taxi northwest of Ixtapa. Additionally, mile-long Playa La Ropa can be enjoyed by early-morning and late-afternoon joggers.

SPORTS EQUIPMENT

Sporting goods store **Deportes Náuticos** (corner of N. Bravo and Galeana, downtown Zihuatanejo, tel. 755/554-4411, 10 A.M.–2 P.M. and 4–9 P.M. Mon.–Sat.) sells snorkel equipment, boogie boards, tennis racquets, balls, and other general sporting goods.

A pair of shops on Álvarez, near the pier, sell fishing equipment and supplies. Check out **Pesca Deportiva** (Álvarez 66, corner of Armada de Mexico, tel. 755/554-3651, 9 A.M.–2 P.M. and 4–7 P.M. Mon.–Sat.), which specializes in sportfishing rods, reels, lines, weights, and lures.

Alternatively, another shop a block east and across the street, **Articulos de Pesca** (Álvarez 35, tel. 755/554-6451, 9 A.M.–2 P.M. and 4–8 P.M. Mon.–Sat.), offers a similar selection of heavy-duty fishing goods.

Shopping

ZIHUATANEJO MARKET AND SHOPS

Every day is market day at the Zihuatanejo *mercado* on Avenida Benito Juárez, four blocks from the beach. Behind the piles of leafy greens, round yellow papayas, and huge gaping sea bass, don't miss the sugar and spice stalls. There you will find big cones of raw *panela* (brown sugar); thick, homemade golden honey; mounds of fragrant *jamaica* petals; crimson dried *chiles;* and forest-gathered roots, barks, and grasses sold in the same pungent natural forms as they have been for centuries.

For a huge, handy selection of everything, go to the big Kmart-style **Comercial Mexicana** (Hwy. 200, tel. 755/554-8321 or 755/554-8384, 8 A.M.–11 P.M. daily), behind the bus terminals on Highway 200, about a mile east (Acapulco direction) of downtown. Its shelves are stacked with a plethora of quality goods, from bread and bananas to flashlights and film.

For convenience shopping downtown, try the small grocery **Adriana y Pancho** (plaza-front corner of Álvarez and Cuauhtémoc).

Handicrafts

Although stores in the Ixtapa Centro Comercial shopping center and the adjacent tourist market sell many handicrafts, Zihuatanejo shops offer the best overall selection and prices.

Sometime along your Zihuatanejo tour, be sure to visit the Zihuatanejo **Artisan Tourist Market** stalls (Av. Cinco de Mayo), filled with a flood of attractive handicrafts brought by families who come from all parts of Mexico. Their goods—delicate Michoacán lacquerware, bright Tonalá papier-mâché birds, gleaming Taxco silver, whimsical Guerrero masks, rich Guadalajara leather—spread for blocks along Avenida Cinco de Mayo on the downtown west side. Compare prices; although bargaining here is customary, the glut of merchandise makes it a one-sided buyer's market, with many sellers barely managing to scrape by. If you err in your bargaining, kindly do it on the generous side.

Along the Paseo del Pescador

Private downtown Zihuatanejo shops offer an abundance of fine handicrafts. The best place to start is on the beachfront Paseo del Pescador, at the **Casa Marina** shopping complex (just west of the beachfront town plaza, tel. 755/554-2373, 10 A.M.–2 P.M. and 4–8 P.M. Mon.–Sat., credit cards generally accepted), a family project started by late community leader Helen Krebs Posse. Her adult children and their spouses own and manage stores on the bottom floor of the two-story building.

The original store, **Embarcadero** (Avenida Álvarez side, tel. 755/554-2373), on the lower floor, has an unusually choice collection of woven and embroidered finery, mostly from Oaxaca. In addition to walls and racks of colorful, museum-quality traditional blankets, flower-embroidered dresses, and elaborate crocheted *huipiles,* they also offer wooden folk figurines and a collection of intriguing masks.

Other stores in the Casa Marina that you should visit include **La Zapoteca,** specializing in weavings from Teotitlán del Valle in Oaxaca. Also very worthwhile are **Metzli,** featuring all-Mexico crafts and resort wear selection; **El Jumil,** lacquerware and masks; and **Costa Libre,** one-of-a-kind crafts and hammocks. Furthermore, Zapotec indigenous weavers from Oaxaca demonstrate their craft, often in the Embarcadero and La Zapoteca stores, mornings and afternoons November–April.

A block farther west on the Paseo del Pescador, find the **Mercado de Conchas** (Shell Market). Peruse the several stalls, with many fetching, priced-to-sell offerings including lovely seashells and shell jewelry, paintings, pottery, and much more.

Two blocks farther west, past the Sirena Gorda café, be sure to visit clothing shop **Marea** (Paseo del Pescador, 8 A.M.–10 P.M. daily high season, 8 A.M.–10 P.M. low season), across from the naval compound. It would be easy to pass, because of its mounds of ho-hum T-shirts out front, but if you look inside, you'll find racks stuffed with precious hand-crocheted *huipiles* and blouses from backcountry Guerrero and Oaxaca.

Along Avenida Cinco de Mayo

Return east two blocks along Avenida Álvarez and turn left, inland, at the corner of Cinco de Mayo and find **Artesanías Olinalá** (Cinco de Mayo 2, tel. 755/554-9597, 9 A.M.–9 P.M. daily). Inside, you can enjoy a virtual museum of the venerable Guerrero lacquerware tradition, showcased by their seemingly endless collection of glossy boxes, trays, gourds, plates, and masks, all painstakingly crafted by age-old methods in the remote upcountry town of Olinalá. (After exiting Artesanías Olinalá you could conveniently visit the Artisan Tourist Market stalls on the other side of Cinco de Mayo.)

Continue up Cinco de Mayo, past the church, to **Arte Nopal** (Cinco de Mayo, tel./fax 755/554-7530, 9 A.M.–9 P.M. daily in high season, opens 10:30 A.M. low season), the joy of the owner, who likes things from Oaxaca, especially baskets. He fills his shop with an organized clutter, including unique woven goods and ceramics.

Along Avenida Cuauhtémoc and More

From Arte Nopal on Cinco de Mayo, head right (east) one block along Bravo, to Cuauhtémoc, for a look through several more interesting shops.

At the corner, turn left onto Avenida Cuauhtémoc and continue a block, passing Ejido. A few doors farther, on the right, step into **Rosimar** (Cuauhtémoc, tel. 755/554-2864, 9 A.M.–9 P.M. daily), the creation of Josefina and Manuel Martínez. Inside, they offer a large priced-to-sell collection of Tonalá and Tlaquepaque pottery, papier-mâché, glassware, and more.

Turn around and head back down Cuauhtémoc. A few doors before Bravo, on the right (north) side of the street, admire the collection of lovely native *huipiles* in the **Mary Kay** shop. Then resume, turning left at Bravo, continuing one block and turn left again at Galeana. A few doors from the corner, on the right, step into **Galería Cihuacoatl** (Snake Woman; Galeana 10, tel. 755/544-6697, 9 A.M.–9 P.M. daily) that exhibits the art

© BRUCE WHIPPERMAN

Colorful glassware and ceramic trinkets decorate the shelves at Zihuatanejo's Rosimar store.

of about a dozen local artists. When I visited the gallery, the exhibited works, mostly paintings, some of which were genuinely stunning, tended toward the realistic (even surrealistic), indigenous, and mystical.

Return back to Cuauhtémoc and turn left, to a pair of shops called **Alberto's** (Cuauhtémoc, tel. 755/554-2161, 9 A.M.–9 P.M. daily, credit cards accepted), a few doors below the corner of Bravo, on opposite sides of the street. They offer an extensive silver jewelry collection. As with gold and precious stones, silver prices can be reckoned approximately by weight, at between $1 and $1.25 per gram. The cases and cabinets of shiny earrings, chains, bracelets, rings, and much more are products of a family of artists, taught by master craftsman Alberto, formerly of Puerto Vallarta, now deceased. Many of the designs are one-of-a-kind, and, with bargaining, reasonably priced.

Continue another block downhill on Cuauhtémoc, past the corner of Ascencio, to **El Arte y Tradición** (Cuauhtémoc, tel. 755/554-4625, 10 A.M.–2 P.M. and 4–8 P.M. daily, credit cards accepted), where you can admire a lovely Talavera stoneware collection. This prized ceramic style, the finest of which is made by a few families in Puebla, comes in many shapes, from plates and vases to pitchers and tea cups. Talavera's colorful floral motifs originate from a fusion of traditions, notably Moorish, Italian, Turkish, and Persian, from the Mediterranean basin.

Now that you're again near the beachfront, for a treat head east along Avenida Álvarez, half a block past the plaza to **Cerámicas Tonalá** (Av. Álvarez 12B, beach side, tel. 755/554-6733, 9 A.M.–2 P.M. and 4–8 P.M. Mon.–Sat., credit cards accepted). Here you can view one of the finest Tonalá ceramics collections outside of the renowned source itself. Kindly owner Eduardo López's graceful glazed vases and plates, decorated in traditional plant and animal designs, fill the cabinets, while a menagerie of lovable owls, ducks, fish, armadillos, and frogs, all seemingly poised to spring to life, crowd the shelves.

IXTAPA SHOPS

Ixtapa's **Centro Comercial** complex stretches along the midsection of Paseo Ixtapa across from the hotels. Developers built about 10 sub-complexes within the Centro Comercial, but some of them remain virtually empty. The good news is that the increasing stream of visitors to Ixtapa is adding new life to the Centro Comercial. At this writing, about six sub-complexes, most fronting the boulevard, are welcoming customers.

Los Patios, Las Fuentes, El Kiosco, and Las Palmas

Moving from south to north, first come the Los Patios and Las Fuentes sub-complexes, where designer stores occupy the choice boulevard frontages. Behind them, many small handicrafts stores and ordinary crafts and jewelry shops wait for customers along back lanes and inside patios.

Some stores stand out, however. Especially worth a look is the **La Fuente** (The Source; ground floor, northeast corner of Los Patios complex, tel. 755/553-0812, 9 A.M.–9 P.M. daily). The expertly selected all-Mexico handicrafts collection includes a treasury of picture frames, ranging from polished hardwood to mother-of-pearl; droll Day of the Dead figurines; lots of tinkling glass and ceramic bells; and a trove of women's blouses, dresses, and skirts, both traditional and stylishly up-to-date.

Also in Los Patios, you'll find at least three good Taxco silver shops and a gem of an embroidery store, **Artesanias Deshilados** (Los Patios complex, tel. 755/553-0221, 10 A.M.–2 P.M. and 4–8 P.M. daily), with lovely tablecloths, curtains, *huipiles,* and much more.

At the La Puerta complex 100 yards farther on, a sprinkling of good restaurants is open for business. There's also a *supermercado* (La Puerta complex, tel. 755/553-1514 or 755/553-1508, 8 A.M.–11 P.M. daily) well stocked with veggies, fruit, groceries, and wine. An ATM, pharmacy, telecom money orders, and fax are also available.

Behind the Los Patios, find the up-and-coming El Kiosko sub-complex, with a pair of good restaurants and a surfing shop.

Next comes the boulevard-front police station, and, after that, the Las Palmas sub-complex (Señor Frog's, pharmacy, restaurant, Internet connection) and finally, the busy Las Galerías (corner of Paseo de las Garzas), with mini-super, photo store, and restaurant.

Information and Services

TOURIST INFORMATION

The local **Convention and Visitors Bureau** (Oficina de Convenciones y Visitantes, OCV; Av. Gaviotas, tel. 755/553-1270, fax 755/553-0819, anamoran@visitiz.com, www.travel ixtapazihuatanejo.com, 9 A.M.–2 P.M. and 4–7 P.M. Mon.–Fri.) information office is in Ixtapa near the south end of Avenida Gaviotas, the street that runs behind the entire Ixtapa shopping complex. Call ahead to confirm hours. The generally helpful and knowledgeable staff answers questions, dispenses literature and maps, and can recommend tour agencies and guides.

PUBLICATIONS

The best local English-language book and magazine selection fills the many shelves of the **Hotel Las Brisas Ixtapa** shop (Paseo de la Roca, 9 A.M.–9 P.M. daily). Besides dozens of new paperback novels and scores of popular U.S. magazines, it stocks the *News* from Mexico City, *USA Today,* and a small selection of Mexico coffee table books of cultural and historical interest.

In Zihuatanejo, the **newsstand** (across Juárez from the town market, near the corner of González, tel. 755/554-7943, 9 A.M.–8 P.M. daily) sells the *News.*

If they don't have what you want, go a couple blocks to **Revistas Guicho** (Ejido between Juárez and Guerrero, 9 A.M.–8 P.M. Mon.–Sat., noon–5 P.M. Sun.).

The small Zihuatanejo **Biblioteca** (public library; Cuauhtémoc, 9 A.M.–8 P.M. Mon.–Fri., 9 A.M.–5 P.M. Sat.), five blocks from the beach, also has some shelves of English-language paperbacks.

TRAVEL AGENCIES AND TOUR GUIDES

A number of reliable local agents arrange and/ or guide local excursions. One of the most experienced all-around is **Ixtapa All Inclusive Tours** (at Hotel Brisas del Mar in Zihuatanejo, Cerro Madera, Calle Eva Samano de López Mateos, cell tel. 044-755/102-8664, from U.S. dial 877/234-7469, mexseafish@yahoo.com .mx, www.toursinixtapazihuatanejo). You may choose from Ixtapa-Zihuatanejo Highlight Tour ($45); Countryside ($50); Isla Grande ($37); Horseback Riding ($40); Jungle Canopy ($60); and much more.

Eco-adventuring is the specialty of **Adventours** (tel. 755/553-1069, pablomendiza-bal@gmail.com, www.ixtapa-adventours.com). Highly recommended guide Pablo Mendizabal offers a number of outings, including Isla Grande (bicycling, snorkeling, sea kayaking, bird-watching, $85); Adventure in Potosí (bird- and animal-viewing tower, lagoon kayaking, village exploring, $85); and Ecological Walk (in Aztlán Ecopark: crocodiles, iguanas, great white herons, and much more, $60).

Get way off the beaten track with very professional and wildlife-sensitive **Zoe Kayak Tours** (in Ixtapa, tel. 755/553-0496, cell tel. 044-755/558-8564, zoe5@aol.com, www.zoe kayaktours.com), which specializes in lagoon kayaking and bird-watching.

ECOLOGICAL ASSOCIATION AND HUMANE SOCIETY

The grassroots organization **SOS BAHIA** (Casa Marina, Paseo del Pescador 9, info@sosbahia .org, www.sosbahia.org) leads efforts for local beach and lagoon cleanup and tree planting, saving turtles, political action and much more. Their headquarters shares space and phones with the Animal Protection Society on the upper floor of Casa Marina, just west of the Zihuatanejo beachfront plaza.

The family members of the late Helen Krebs Posse are the guiding lights of the **Sociedad Protectora de Animales** (Animal Protection Society; Casa Marina, Paseo del Pescador 9, tel. 755/554-2373, cell tel. 044-755/112-1648, spaz@zihuatanejo.net, www.zihuatanejo.net/ spaz/), which is working hard to educate people about animal issues. Contact one of the family members at the family's shop complex, in Casa Marina, just west of the Zihuatanejo beachfront plaza.

PHOTOGRAPHY

In Zihuatanejo, **Foto 30** (Ejido between Galeana and Guerrero, tel. 755/554-7610, 9 A.M.–8 P.M. Mon.–Sat., 10 A.M.–2 P.M. Sun.), two blocks from the plaza, offers 30-minute process-and-print service and stocks lots of film and digital accessories, such as many cameras, including SLRs, and filters, tripods, and flashes.

If your camera needs fixing, contact photo genius Joel Guzman at his **camera repair shop** (Calle Gonzales, corner of Cuauhtémoc, tel. 755/544-8021, 8 A.M.–7 P.M. Mon.–Sat.). In Ixtapa, **Foto Quick** (Paseo Ixtapa, tel. 755/553-1956, 9 A.M.–9 P.M. daily), across the boulevard from Hotel Emporio, offers repair services and a modest selection of cameras and supplies.

MONEY EXCHANGE

Several banks, all with ATMs, cluster on the east side of downtown Zihuatanejo. Find **Banamex** (corner of Guerrero and Ejido, tel. 755/554-7293 or 755/554-7294, money exchange 9 A.M.–4 P.M. Mon.–Fri., 10 A.M.–2 P.M. Sat.) two blocks from the beach. If the Banamex lines are too long, use the ATM or walk to **Bancomer** (corner of Bravo and Juárez, tel. 755/554-7492 or 755/554-7493, 8:30 A.M.–4 P.M. Mon.–Fri.).

After bank hours, go to either long-hours HSBC in Ixtapa or to the center of town to **Casa de Cambio Guibal** (at Galeana and Ascencio, tel. 755/554-3522, fax 755/554-2800, 8 A.M.–8 P.M. daily), with long-distance telephone and fax two blocks from the beach, to change U.S., Canadian, French, German, Swiss, and other currencies and travelers checks. For the convenience, it offers you a few percent less for your money than the banks.

In Ixtapa, for long money-changing hours, go to **HSBC** (Paseo Ixtapa, in front of Hotel Emporio, tel. 755/553-0642 or 755/553-0646, 8 A.M.–7 P.M. Mon.–Fri.). Alternatively, go to **Bancomer** (Los Portales complex, tel. 755/553-2112 or 755/553-0525, 8:30 A.M.–4 P.M. Mon.–Fri.) behind the shops across the boulevard from the Hotel Presidente InterContinental Ixtapa.

COMMUNICATIONS

The single **correo** (post office; Centro Federal, tel. 755/554-2192, 8 A.M.–6 P.M. Mon.–Fri., 9 A.M.–1 P.M. Sat.) that serves both Zihuatanejo and Ixtapa is in Zihuatanejo at Centro Federal, in the northeast corner of downtown, five blocks from the beach and about three blocks east of the Ixtapa minibus stop at Juárez and Morelos. Also in the post office is a sub-office of the reliable government **Mexpost** (like U.S. Express Mail—upgraded, secure mail service).

Next door to the **correo** is **Telecomunicaciones** (fax 755/554-2163, 8 A.M.–6:30 P.M. Mon.–Fri., 9 A.M.–noon Sat.), which offers long-distance telephone, public fax, telegrams, and money orders. Another similar telecommunications office serves Ixtapa, in the La Puerta shopping center (rear side), across Paseo Ixtapa from the Hotel Presidente InterContinental.

Money changer Casa de Cambio Guibal is also Zihuatanejo's private telephone and fax office, **larga distancia** (Galeana, corner of Bravo, tel./fax 755/554-3522, 8 A.M.–8 P.M. daily).

In both Ixtapa and Zihuatanejo, many streetside public phone booths provide relatively economical national and international (call the United States for about $1 per three minutes) long-distance service using a Ladatel telephone card. Cards are readily available in grocery, drug, and liquor stores everywhere. First dial 001 for calls to the United States and Canada, and 01 for Mexico long-distance.

Beware of prominent "call home collect," or "use your credit card to call home" phone booths. Such calls customarily run as much as $30 per three minutes (whether or not you use the full three minutes). Best ask the operator for the price before placing your call.

Get on the Internet in Zihuatanejo at one of several downtown spots, such as **Ciber Andy's** (south side of Ejido, between Guerrero and Juárez, tel. 755/544-7984, 9 A.M.–10 P.M. daily), three blocks from the beach.

HEALTH AND EMERGENCIES

For medical consultations in English, contact U.S.-trained **IAMAT associate Dr. Rogelio Grayeb** (Zafiro 12, Zihuatanejo, tel. 755/554-3334 or 755/554-5041, 9 A.M.–2 P.M. and 5–8 P.M. Mon.–Fri., 9 A.M.–3 P.M. Sat.). From northeast-side Plaza Kioto, follow Paseo del Palmar north two blocks to Zafiro, turn right and continue a few doors to Zafiro 12.

Another Zihuatanejo medical option is the very professional **Clínica Maciel** (Palmas 12, tel. 755/554-2380), which has a dentist, pediatrician, gynecologist, and surgeon on 24-hour call, two blocks east and one block north of the market.

Ixtapa and Zihuatanejo have a number of respectable hospitals. In Zihuatanejo, many local folks recommend the state of Guerrero **Hospital General** (Av. Morelos, corner of Mar Egeo, just off Hwy. 200, tel. 755/554-3848 or 755/554-3650) for its generally competent, dedicated, and professional staff.

The most highly recommended hospital in Ixtapa is the **Hospital Naval** (Paseo Ixtapa, tel. 755/553-0599), which, besides military personnel, also services foreign tourists.

For medicines and drugs in Zihuatanejo, go to one of the several downtown pharmacies, such as **Farmacia La Principal** (Cuauhtémoc, two blocks from the beach, tel. 755/554-4217, 9 A.M.–9 P.M. Mon.–Sat.). In Ixtapa, go to **Farmapronto** pharmacy (Las Palmas subcomplex, tel. 755/553-2423, 8 A.M.–9 P.M. daily), located across the parking lot, north, from Señor Frog's. This pharmacy has a delivery service.

For police emergencies in Ixtapa and Zihuatanejo, contact the police headquarters, **cabercera de policía** (Calle Limón, Zihuatanejo, near Hwy. 200, tel. 755/554-2040). Usually more accessible are the police officers at the *caseta de policía* 24-hour police booth at the Zihuatanejo plaza-front, and in Ixtapa on Paseo Ixtapa, across from the Hotel Presidente InterContinental.

IMMIGRATION

If you lose your tourist permit, go to **Migración** (Colegio Militar, tel. 755/554-2795, 9 A.M.–1 P.M. Mon.–Fri.), about five blocks northeast of Plaza Kioto, on the northeast edge of downtown. Bring your passport and some proof of the date you arrived in Mexico, such as your airline ticket, stamped passport, or a copy of your lost tourist permit. Though it's not wise to let such a matter go until the last day, you may be able to accomplish the needed paperwork at the **airport Migración office** (tel. 755/554-8480, 8 A.M.–9 P.M. daily). Call first to confirm.

LAUNDRY

In Zihuatanejo, take your laundry to either **Lavandería Express** (Cuauhtémoc, near corner of González, tel. 755/554-4393, 7 A.M.–7 P.M. daily), five blocks from the beach; or in the Playa Madera district **Lavandería Kioto** (across the canal bridge from Plaza Kioto, 8 A.M.–8 P.M. daily).

Getting There and Away

BY AIR

Several reliable carriers connect Ixtapa-Zihuatanejo directly with U.S. and Mexican destinations year-round. Others operate charter flights, especially during the winter-spring high season.

Many **Aeroméxico** (reservations tel. 755/554-2018, flight information tel. 755/554-2237 or 755/554-2634, www.aeromexico.com) flights (and those of affiliate airline Aeroconnect) connect daily with Mexico City, where connections with U.S. destinations may be made.

Alaska Airlines (direct from Mexico tel. 001-800/426-0333 or 001-800/252-7522, www.alaskaair.com) connects with Los Angeles.

US Airways (direct from Mexico tel. 001-800/235-9292 or 001-800/428-4322, www.usairways.com) connects with Phoenix.

Continental Airlines (tel. 755/554-2549, toll-free Mex. tel. 800/900-5000, www.continentalairlines) connects with Houston daily.

Interjet Airlines (tel. 755/553-7002 or 755/553-7161, toll-free in Mex. tel. 800/011-2345, www.interjet.com.mx) connects with Toluca and Mexico City.

Magnicharter Airlines (tel. 755/553-6290 or 755/553-6291, www.magnichartersmx.com) connects with Mexico City.

Furthermore, a number of seasonal charter flights connect Zihuatanejo with U.S. and Canada destinations: **Frontier Airlines** charter (www.frontier airlines.com) connects with Denver; **Delta Airlines** charter (www.delta.com) connects with Los Angeles and Minneapolis; **Westjet Airlines** (www.westjet.com) connects with Calgary.

Air Arrival and Departure

Ixtapa and Zihuatanejo are quickly accessible, only about 20 minutes (seven miles/11 km) north of the airport via Highway 200. Arrival is generally simple—if you come with a day's worth of pesos (or better, an ATM card) and hotel reservation. Although the terminal does have an ATM for pesos (HSBC, in mid-terminal by the newsstand), a mailbox (*buzón;* outside the front, opposite the check-in counters), restaurant, shops for last-minute purchases, and newsstand with books, magazines, and *USA Today* (for $3.50), it has neither a tourist information booth nor hotel-reservation service. It's best to arrive with a hotel reservation and not to leave the choice up to your taxi driver, who will probably deposit you at a hotel that pays him a commission on your first night's lodging.

Transportation to town is usually by *taxi especial* (private taxi) or *colectivo* van. Tickets are available at booths near the terminal arrival exit. Tariff for a *colectivo* runs about $16 to both Ixtapa and Zihuatanejo, for a *taxi especial,* $28–37 for three or four people. Taxis to Troncones run about $75. Mobile budget travelers can walk the few hundred yards to the highway and flag down one of the frequent daytime Zihuatanejo-bound buses (very few continue to Ixtapa, however). At night, spend the money on a *colectivo* or taxi.

Several major car rental companies staff airport arrival booths. Avoid problems and save money by negotiating your car rental through the agencies' toll-free numbers before departure. Agents at the airport include **Hertz** (tel. 755/112-1683 or 755/554-2592, fax 755/554-3050, lriosabasa.com); **Budget** (tel. 755/554-4837 or 755/553-0397, ixtapa@budgetansa.com); **Alamo** (tel. 755/553-0206 or 755/554-8429, www.alamo-mexico.com.mx); **Thrifty** (tel. 755/553-7020 or 755/553-3019, autzsa@prodigy.net.mx); **Dollar** (tel. 755/553-7050); and **Europcar** (tel./fax 755/553-7158 or 755/553-0869, www.europcar.com.mx).

Departure is quick and easy if you have your passport, tourist permit (which was stamped on arrival), and $19 cash (or the equivalent in pesos) international departure tax if your air ticket doesn't already cover it. Departees who've lost their tourist permits can avoid trouble and a fine by getting a duplicate from Zihuatanejo Immigration at the airport a few hours prior to departure. Simplify this procedure by being prepared with your passport and a copy of the lost permit or at least some proof of your date of arrival, such as an airline ticket.

BY CAR OR RV

Three routes, two easy and one formerly unsafe but now marginally recommended, connect Ixtapa-Zihuatanejo with Playa Azul and Michoacán to the northwest, Acapulco to the southeast, and Ciudad Altamirano and central Guerrero to the northeast.

Traffic sails smoothly along the 76 miles (122 km) of Highway 200, either way, between Zihuatanejo and Lázaro Cárdenas/Playa Azul. Allow about an hour and a half. Several miles before Lázaro Cárdenas the new Highway 37D *cuota* (toll) expressway allows easy access to highland central Michoacán (190 mi/312 km, 4.5 hours to Uruapan, add another half-hour to Pátzcuaro) from Zihuatanejo. The same is true of the 150-mile (242-km, allow four hours) Highway 200 southern extension to Acapulco.

The story is different, however, for the winding, sparsely populated cross-Sierra Highway 134 (intersecting with Hwy. 200 nine mi/15 km north) from Zihuatanejo to Ciudad Altamirano. Rising along spectacular ridges, the paved but sometimes potholed road leads over cool, pine-clad heights and descends to the Ciudad Altamirano high, dry valley of the grand Río Balsas after about 100 miles (160 km). The continuing leg to Iguala on the Acapulco–Mexico City highway is longer, about 112 miles (161 km), equally winding and sometimes busy. Allow about eight hours westbound and nine hours eastbound for the entire trip. Keep filled with gasoline, and be prepared for emergencies, especially along the Altamirano–Zihuatanejo leg, where no hotels and few services exist. *Warning:* This route, unfortunately, was once plagued by robberies and nasty drug-related incidents. Before attempting this trip inquire locally—at your hotel, the tourist information office, or the bus station—to see if authorities deem the road safe.

BY BUS

Zihuatanejo has two major bus terminals. They stand side-by-side on Highway 200 on the Acapulco-bound (east) side of town. The biggest and busiest is the big Estrella Blanca **Central de Autobús** station. Inside its shiny airline-style terminal, travelers have only a few services available: Ladatel card-operated telephones, a left-luggage service, and a small snack bar. If you're going to need supplies for a long bus trip, prepare by stocking up with water and food goodies before you depart.

Estrella Blanca (tel. 755/554-3476), the major carrier, computer-coordinates the service of its subsidiary lines, including first-class Elite, Estrella Blanca, Futura, and luxury-class Turistar Ejecutivo. Tickets can be purchased with cash and some credit cards.

Many departures run along the Highway 200 corridor, connecting with Lázaro Cárdenas/ Playa Azul and northwestern destinations, such as Manzanillo, Puerto Vallarta, and the U.S. at Nogales and Tijuana, and with Acapulco and destinations southeast.

Several luxury- and first-class buses and some second-class buses connect many times daily with Acapulco. A number of them continue north to Mexico City. In the opposite direction, many luxury-, first-, and second-class buses (at least one an hour during the day) connect with Lázaro Cárdenas, Playa Azul junction, and northwest points.

Other departures connect north, via Michoacán. Among them, at least one daily departure connects north with Uruapan and Morelia, via the 37D toll expressway. Another departure connects north by the expressway, via Uruapan, continuing northwest, via Guadalajara and Mazatlán, all the way to the U.S. border at Mexicali and Tijuana.

A number of other reliable carriers operate out of the same terminal. Three of them may be booked through their common reservation number: tel. 755/544-6991. These include major national carrier **Omnibus de Mexico** with northerly departures, via Morelia, via Celaya, Queretaro, Saltillo, Monterrey, all the way to Nuevo Laredo on the U.S. border. Additionally, **Autovias de Mexico** connects both northeast, via Uruapan, Morelia, and Toluca, with Mexico City (Norte and Poniente terminals), and northwest, via Uruapan and Zamora, with Guadalajara. Also Michoacán-based **Parhikuni** connects north, with Morelia, via Nueva Italia, and Uruapan.

Additionally, a few independent carriers provide services, such as **Costa** (tel. 755/554-2912 or 755/554-6327), with connections both southeast along the Costa Grande, with Acapulco, thence north via Chilpancingo with Mexico City (Tasqeña terminal), and northwest, with Lázaro Cárdenas; and finally,

Primera Plus (tel. 75/554-8738) luxury departures connect north, via Morelia, with Irapuato, Leon, Aguascalientes, Celaya, and Queretaro.

Competing major bus carrier **Estrella de Oro** (tel. 755/554-2175) operates out of its separate station on the adjacent, west side of the Estrella Blanca station. It offers some long-distance first-class connections southeast along the coast via Acapulco, thence inland, with Mexico City, via Chilpancingo, Iguala, and Taxco.

South of Ixtapa and Zihuatanejo

Playa Las Pozas, Playa Blanca, and Barra de Potosí, the trio of pocket paradises not far southeast of Zihuatanejo and long known by local people, are now being discovered by a growing cadre of off-the-beaten-track seekers of heaven on earth. Taken together, they offer a feast of quiet south-seas delights: good fishing, beachcombing, camping, wildlife-viewing, and comfortable, reasonably priced lodgings.

Playa Las Pozas, a surf-fishing and seafood haven, is reachable via the Zihuatanejo airport road. Playa Blanca, a mile farther southeast, is a long, lovely golden-sand beach, decorated by a lovely boutique hotel and restaurant. A few miles farther, Barra de Potosí village offers the ingredients of a heavenly one-day or one-week tropical excursion: palm-shaded seafood *palapas,* room for tent or RV camping, stores for supplies, a wildlife-rich mangrove lagoon, and a long beach, ripe for swimming, surfing, fishing, and beachcombing. A trio of petite bed-and-breakfast lodgings and a downscale beachfront hotel offer accommodations.

PLAYA LAS POZAS

Playa Las Pozas rewards visitors with a lagoon, full of bait fish, space for RV or tent camping (be careful of soft sand), a wide beach, and friendly beachside *palapa* restaurants. The beach itself is 100 yards wide, of yellow-white sand, and extends for miles in both directions. It has driftwood but not many shells. Fish thrive in its thunderous, open-ocean waves (and swimmers should take caution). Consequently, casts from the beach can yield 2–5-pound catches by either bait or lures. Local folks catch fish mostly by net, both in the surf and the nearby lagoon. During the June–September rainy season, the lagoon breaks through the bar. Big fish, gobbling prey at the outlet, can themselves be netted or hooked at the same spot.

Camping is popular here on weekends and holidays. Other times you may have the place to yourself. As a courtesy, ask at the friendly family-run *palapa* restaurant (on the west end by the lagoon, which offers some basic hotel rooms) if it's okay to camp beneath their palm grove.

Get to Playa Las Pozas by following the well-marked airport turnoff road from Highway 200, at Km 230. After one mile, turn right before the cyclone wire fence just before entering the terminal complex and follow the bumpy but easily passable straight level road 1.1 miles (1.8 km) to the beach.

PLAYA BLANCA

In 2001, personable, savvy, and hardworking owner-builders from Phoenix, Arizona, decided to create heaven on lazy, lovely Playa Blanca. The result was **Hotel Las Palmas** (cell tel.

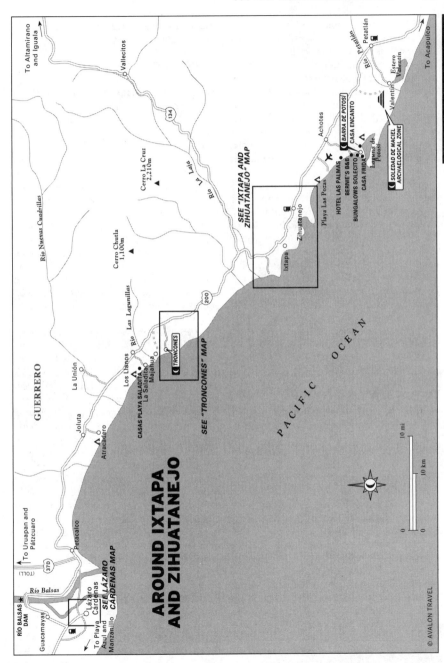

AROUND IXTAPA
AND ZIHUATANEJO

PACIFIC OCEAN

GUERRERO

To Altamirano
and Iguala

To Acapulco

To Uruapan and
Pátzcuaro

To Playa
Azul and
Manzanillo

Vallecitos

134

Cerro La Cruz
2,210m

Cerro Chutla
1,100m

Río Nuevas Cuadrillas

Río Laja

SEE "IXTAPA AND
ZIHUATANEJO" MAP

Achotes

Río Petatlán

Petatlán

Estero
Valentín

Valentín

SOLEDAD DE MACIEL
ARCHAEOLOGICAL ZONE

Laguna de
Potosí

CASA FRIDA

BUNGALOWS SOLECITO

CASA ENCANTO

BERNIE'S B&B

BARRA DE POTOSÍ

HOTEL LAS PALMAS

Playa Las Pozas

Zihuatanejo

Ixtapa

SEE "TRONCONES" MAP

200

TRONCONES

Río Las Lagunillas

Los Llanos

La Unión

La Saladita

CASAS PLAYA SALADITA

Majahua

Joluta

Atracadero

GUERRERO

Petacalco

Lázaro
Cárdenas

Guacamayas

RÍO BALSAS
DAM

Río Balsas

370

(TOLL)

SEE LÁZARO
CÁRDENAS MAP

10 mi

10 km

0

0

© AVALON TRAVEL

044-755/557-0634, from U.S. dial 011-52-1-755/557-0634, reservations@hotellaspalmas.net, info@hotellaspalmas.net, www.hotellaspalmas.net, $290–450 d after Easter–Dec. 20, $329–475 d Jan. 7–Easter, $349–499 d Dec. 21–Jan. 6), replete with precious architecture-as-art, including polished natural tree-trunk–beamed ceilings, elegant tropical hardwood shutters, and massive overhanging thatched *palapa* roofs. A recipe for paradise? Yes, but there's even more: a big blue pool and a good restaurant and bar, all set in cool, green, grassy grounds overlooking a long, creamy, yellow-white strand. Their ten super-comfortable handcrafted rooms, eight with air-conditioning, two with ceiling fans, come with continental breakfast, but without TV or phones; with credit cards not accepted, no kids under 18 allowed, nor any wheelchair access. Get there by continuing about 1.5 miles (2.5 km) along the beach road from Playa Las Pozas to Playa Blanca and Hotel Las Palmas (or alternatively, via the paved road from Hwy. 200 at Achotes). Reservations can be made through the hotel or the owners' Arizona agent, **Gold Coast Travel** (335 W. Virginia Ave., Phoenix, AZ 85003-1020, fax 602/253-3487, goldcoast travel@hotmail.com).

◖ BARRA DE POTOSÍ

At Achotes, on Highway 200, nine miles (15 km) south of Zihuatanejo, a Laguna de Potosí sign points right to Barra de Potosí, an idyllic fishing hamlet at the sheltered south end of the Bahía de Potosí. After a few miles through green, tufted groves, the paved road reaches a fork. Bear left (or right for Hotel Las Palmas) for Barra de Potosí. The road continues, paralleling the beach, a crescent of fine white sand, with a scattering of houses, a few comfortable bed-and-breakfasts, and one modest beach-front hotel.

The waves become even more tranquil at the beach's southeast end, where a sheltering headland rises beyond the adjacent broad Bahía de Potosí. Beneath its swaying palm grove, the hamlet of Barra de Potosí (pop. 500) has all the ingredients for tranquil living. Past the village, at road's end, several hammock-hung *palapa*

restaurants (here called *enramadas*) front the serene Laguna de Potosí.

Sights and Recreation
Home for flocks of birds and waterfowl and shoals of fish, the **Laguna de Potosí** stretches for miles to its far mangrove reaches. Adventure out with your own boat or kayak, or go with Orlando (ask at Restaurant Teresita), who regularly takes parties out for fishing or wildlife-viewing tours. Bring water, a hat, and insect repellent.

If you want to do more but don't have your own kayak, Ixtapa-based **Zoe Kayak Tours** (reserve ahead, tel. 755/553-0496, zoe5@aol.com, www.zoekayaktours.com) leads kayaking trips on Laguna de Potosí's pristine waters.

Bait fish, caught locally with nets, abound in the lagoon. Fishing is fine for bigger catches (jack, snapper, mullet) by boat or casts beyond the waves. Launch your boat easily in the lagoon, then head past the open sandbar like the local fisherfolk.

Lovers of the outdoors must visit **El Refugio de Potosí** (tel. 755/100-0743 or 755/557-2840, laurel@elrefugiodepotosi.org, www.elrefugiode potosi.org) on the way to or from the village. The refuge is a homegrown life project of a dedicated cadre of conservationists who created a local wildlife refuge from scratch, beginning with a complete gigantic sperm whale skeleton (on display) that they rescued from the beach. Gradually, they built up their site, and now it encompasses about 20 acres of tropical forest habitat, with a walking trail, and is home to a community of wild creatures, from woodpeckers and green iguanas, to *zopilotes* and cormorants. While you're there, be sure to take a look inside their butterfly pavilion (with a dozen seasonal species) and climb atop a 50-foot viewing tower to feel the breeze, soak in the bay view, and enjoy a quiet wait for an armadillo or a roseate spoonbill to appear in the forest below. Find it (see the big sign) beside the paved road from Achotes, three miles from Highway 200.

Accommodations and Food
In the village, a pair of bed-and-breakfast–style

hotels offer lodging. First consider the charming flower-bedecked **Casa del Encanto** (House of Enchantment; local cell tel. 044-755/104-6709, from U.S. 011-52-1-755/124-6122, lauragecko2@hotmail.com, www.ninos encantados.com, $65–80 d low season, $70–100 d high season—Oct. 31–May 1), on a village side street. Owner Laura Nolo rents her lovingly decorated rooms, which include fan, private hot-water shower bath, and full breakfast; massages are available at extra cost.

Beneath the grove nearby, guests at **(Casa Frida** (local cell tel. 044-755/558-5839, or tel. 044-755/557-9872, casafridabarra@gmail.com, www.casafrida.net, $45–65 d), life project of a Mexican-French couple, enjoy fondly decorated rooms, built around a charmingly compact pool-patio garden. Room furnishings, based on a Frida Kahlo theme, include handcrafted art and furniture, mosquito curtains over the double beds, and bright Talavera-tiled hot-water bathrooms. Rooms come with fans; breakfast is not included. Only adults are welcome; no pets are allowed.

On the beachfront, about half a mile from the village, settle into the lap of luxury at **(Bungalows Solecito** (local cell tel. 044-755/100-5976, from U.S 011-52-1-755/100-5976, www.bungalows-solecito.com, $120 s or d, Casa Solecito $400). Friendly owner-builder Manuel Romo offers nine airy, rustic-chic South-Seas bungalows all artfully arranged around a flowery, palm-shadowed beachfront garden and pool-patio. Stroll out just a few steps and you're on lovelier-than-life Playa Barra de Potosí. There are four bungalows with full kitchen and king-size beds (one or two adults only); four others, with double beds, but without kitchen (also for one or two adults only); and one large two-bedroom, two-bath suite with kitchen and king-size beds. All units come with fans and hot-water shower baths and many lovely extras. Furthermore, the owner also rents Casa Solecito, an adjacent grand two-bedroom, two-bath beach house, with everything, including gardener and private pool. Get your reservations in early. Sorry, no kids under 18 nor pets are allowed; there is parking and Internet access.

About a mile out of the village, back toward Zihuatanejo, the downscale **Hotel Barra de Potosí** (Petatlán tel. 755/554-8290, Zihuatanejo tel. 755/554-3445, fax 755/554-7060, info@hotel-barradepotosi.com, www .hotel-barradepotosi.com, $35–70 d) perches

© BRUCE WHIPPERMAN

view of the palm-lined beach and bay from the Hotel Barra de Potosí

right on the beach. The surf near the hotel is generally tranquil and safe for swimming and child's play, although the waves, which do not roll but break rather quickly along long fronts, do not appear suited for surfing. The hotel, once neglected, has been renovated: Its pool is brilliant blue, and rooms are reasonably well-maintained at the present writing. The owner says that the restaurant will be open during the high winter season and most weekends, but will close during the low fall season. The beach, however, remains inviting and kid-friendly year-round. The 20-odd rooms, in rising order of price, start with hot and stuffy interior rooms downstairs, improving to exterior rooms with view of the parking lot, then better rooms with private oceanview balcony, and finally kitchenette suites for four, also with oceanview balcony. All rooms come with fans, but there is only room-temperature water and mostly bare-bulb lighting; bring your own lampshade or booklight.

About a mile farther from town on the same luscious beachfront, near the spot where the road from Achotes arrives at the beach, **Bernie's Bed and Breakfast** (local cell tel. 044-755/556-6333, from U.S. 011-52-1-755/556-6333, playacalli@hotmail.com, www.berniesbedandbreakfast.com, $90 s or d year-round) offers three comfortable rooms with "no TV or piped-in-music" (says personable owner Bernie Wittstock) that open onto a lovely palm-shadowed beachfront pool and patio. Rentals come with breakfast. If you give Bernie a day's notice, he says he will cook a light meal for you.

Camping is common by RV or tent along the uncrowded edge of the lagoon. Village stores can provide basic supplies. Prepared food is available at about a dozen permanent lagoon-side *palapa* restaurants. **Restaurant Teresita** is especially recommended.

Getting There and Away

By car, get to Barra de Potosí by following the signed turnoff road from Highway 200 at Km 225, nine miles (14 km) south of Zihuatanejo, just south of the Río Los Achotes bridge. Continue along the good, mostly paved road; pass the Barra de Potosí at Mile 5 (Km 8) and continue to the village at Mile 5.5 (Km 8.9). Alternatively, get to Barra de Potosí by continuing east about three miles (5 km) along the beach road from Hotel Las Palmas at Playa Blanca.

By bus, follow the same route via a Petatlán-bound bus (Omnibus de Mexico, Estrella Blanca) either from one of the Zihuatanejo bus stations, or the local Petatlán bus from the station on Zihuatanejo Avenida Las Palmas, across from Bancrecer. In either case, ask the driver to let you off at the Barra de Potosí turnoff at Achotes and wait for the Barra de Potosí–bound covered pickup truck (comes about every 30 minutes daytime).

North of Ixtapa and Zihuatanejo

Visitors to Troncones and Majahua (mah-HAH-wah) can enjoy a long, pristine, coral-studded beach as well as the natural delights of a small kingdom of forested wildlife-rich hinterland that stretches for miles above and behind the beach. While Troncones has acquired a modicum of modern travel amenities, including a number of restful bed-and-breakfast inns and gourmet restaurants, Majahua remains charmingly rustic.

◖ TRONCONES

Troncones (pop. 500) has a little bit of everything: shady seafood *ramadas,* cozy seaside inns and houses for rent, a sprinkling of good restaurants, and a few places to park your RV or set up a tent by the beach. Most folks get there by bus or taxi from Ixtapa or Zihuatanejo via the side road off of Highway 200 about 20 miles (32 km) north of Ixtapa.

But that's just the beginning. Troncones

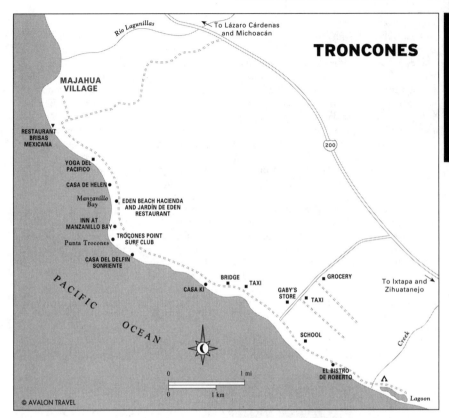

TRONCONES

Rio Lagunillas

To Lázaro Cárdenas and Michoacán

MAJAHUA VILLAGE

200

RESTAURANT BRISAS MEXICANA

YOGA DEL PACIFICO

CASA DE HELEN

Manzanillo Bay

EDEN BEACH HACIENDA AND JARDÍN DE EDEN RESTAURANT

INN AT MANZANILLO BAY

Punta Trocones

TROCONES POINT SURF CLUB

CASA DEL DELFIN SONRIENTE

PACIFIC OCEAN

BRIDGE   TAXI

CASA KI

GROCERY

To Ixtapa and Zihuatanejo

GABY'S STORE   TAXI

SCHOOL

Creek

EL BISTRO DE ROBERTO

Lagoon

0   1 mi
0   1 km

© AVALON TRAVEL

has acquired a growing colony of North Americans, some of who operate accommodations for lovers of peace, quiet, and the outdoors. Besides lazing in hammocks and sunning on the sand, guests at all Troncones lodgings share the same luscious shoreline. You can swim, surf, bodysurf, and boogie board the waves, jog along the sand, explore a limestone cave, and thrill to a treetop cable adventure in the adjacent jungle. Back by the shore, you can beachcomb to your heart's content while enjoying views of the wildlife trove—fish, whales (Dec.–Mar.), dolphins, turtles (Nov.–Jan.), swarms of herons, boobies, egrets, and cormorants—that abounds in the ocean and in nearby lagoons.

Accommodations and Food

Nearly all Troncones accommodations are right on the beach, and rent from about $65 d low season, $90 d high season. As you move northwest (from the entrance road, turn right at the beach) after the bridge, first find **(** **Casa Ki** (P.O. Box 405, Zihuatanejo, Guerrero 40880, tel. 755/553-2815, casaki@yahoo.com, www.casa-ki.com, $65–85 low season, $95–115 high season—Nov. 15–Apr. 30; 2-bedroom house $150 low season, $200 high season), the life project of Ed and Ellen Weston, now managed by daughter Tina Morse. Casa Ki (named for the Japanese word for energy and wholeness) offers four immaculate, charmingly rustic cottages tucked in a lovingly tended seaside garden compound. Each cottage sleeps approximately two adults and two children and comes with shower, toilet, fans, refrigerator, and daily maid service. Guests share a shady outside cooking and dining *palapa*. Breakfast is included in the rates only during the high season. Tina also rents a lovely two-bedroom, two-bath house that sleeps up to six, with full kitchen and daily maid service. Get your winter reservations in early.

Continuing another mile, you'll find one of Troncones' longstanding gems, the **(Inn at Manzanillo Bay** (P.O. Box 5306, Concord, CA 94524, tel. 755/553-2884, fax 755/553-2883, manzanillobay@aol.com, www.manzanillobay .com, *cabañas* $100 d high season, terrace suites $130 d season). Here, owner-chef Michael Bensal has realized his dream of paradise: a haven of a dozen-odd rustic-style *palapa*-roofed *cabañas,* comfortably furnished with deluxe amenities, set around a luscious blue swimming pool and leafy patio. Here you can have it all: a gently curving, wave-washed, surfable shoreline, with the murmur of the billows at night and plenty of hammock time by day. There are oceanfront *cabañas* and larger terrace suites. The rates are discounted by about 20 percent during the low season, June

1–Nov. 14. All units come with fans, hot-water shower baths, and breakfast included. There is a good restaurant and even TV if you want it. Send deposits to P.O. Box in California.

Finally, 100 yards farther along the beach, you arrive at the **Eden Beach Hacienda and Jardín de Eden Restaurant** (P.O Box 128, Zihuatanejo, Guerrero 40880, tel. 755/553-2802, evaandjim@aol.com, www.edenmex .com, $85–115 June–Sept., $105–140 Oct.–May), which shares the same luscious tropical forest oceanfront as all the other lodgings. The amenities include 14 immaculate accommodations—six comfortable rooms with fans in the original house, four spacious beachfront suites with fans, and four beamed-ceiling, air-conditioned suites—all invitingly decorated in stucco and Talavera tile, with king-size beds and private hot-water bathrooms. Rates include breakfast. Make reservations with the hotel directly by phone or email. You may also write or fax them in the United States (41 Riverview Dr., Oak Ridge, TN 37830, fax 801/340-9883). Credit cards are accepted.

At the opposite, southeast end of the Troncones beach, **(Bistro de Roberto** (tel.

Four comfortable sturdy stone *cabañas* accommodate guests at Bistro de Roberto on the Troncones beach.

© BRUCE WHIPPERMAN

755/103-0019, cell tel. 044-755/120-5264, crazytroncones@hotmail.com, www.robertos bistro.com, $45 d low season, $65 d high season), formerly El Burro Borracho (The Drunken Burro), is a beachfront *palapa* restaurant and inn that has become a favorite stopping place for the growing cadre of daytime visitors venturing out from Ixtapa and Zihuatanejo. Here, owner Roberto Rosas Chino attracts a steady stream of visitors with his spicy shrimp tacos, rum-glazed ribs, jumbo shrimp grilled with coconut-curry sauce, and broiled pork chops with mashed potatoes. Besides the shady ocean-view *palapa* restaurant, Roberto's Bistro offers six "elegantly simple" airy rooms, each with a bath, in three stone duplex beachfront cottages. Rooms include a king-size bed, rustic-chic decor, hot water, air-conditioning, and fans. Sports and activities include swimming, surfing, and boogie boarding, plus kayaks, for use by guests. Room rentals include breakfast.

For more choices, consider some of the platoon of guesthouses, bed-and-breakfast inns, hotels, and vacation rental villas that have recently sprouted on the Troncones beachfront. Many choices, mostly upscale, are available. They include bed-and-breakfast **Casa del Delfin Sonriente** (Smiling Dolphin; tel. 755/553-2803, U.S. tel. 831/688-6578, enovey@cruzio.com, www.casadelfinsonriente, rooms $70, deluxe suite $120); **Casa Colorida** (U.S. tel. 303/400-5442, fax 303/680-9685, annmerritt@aol.com, www.casacolorida.com, $200 and up); and luxurious three-bedroom house **Casa de Helen** (tel. 755/553-2800, jenschwab@aol.com, www.tron coneshelen.com, $275 and up). For information on more rentals, visit websites www.troncones .com.mx and www.zihuatanejo.net.

For tenting or RV space, either check with Bistro de Roberto (from the entrance road, at the beach go left a quarter mile) for tenting space or a spot to park your (self-contained) RV; or head to the very welcoming local camping spot, beach *palapa* restaurant La Gaviota, a mile north of Playa Majahua.

Sports and Recreation

Surfing has become a major Troncones recreation. The most popular spot is the palm-tufted inlet, locally known as **Manzanillo Bay** and the location of both the Inn at Manzanillo Bay and Eden Beach Hacienda. Lately, a pair of enterprising lovers of the tropics, Michael and Ann Linn of San Luis Obispo, California, operating as **ISA (Instructional Surf Adventures) Mexico** (cell tel. Nov.–May in Troncones 044-755/558-3821 or 044-755/103-0018, U.S. tel. 541/550-7343, surf@isamexico.com, www .isamexico.com), offer both local day instruction and extended surfing packages during the fall–winter (Nov.–Apr.) season. Classes are small and all equipment and deluxe beachfront lodging is customarily included in packages, which run about $1,000 per person, double occupancy.

Furthermore, the **Inn at Manzanillo Bay** (on the beach, tel. 755/553-2884, fax 755/553-2883, manzanillobay@aol.com, www.man zanillobay.com) operates a shop with surfboards and surfing and snorkeling equipment for rent and sale, and arranges local tours and fishing outings.

Shopping and Services

Eva Robbins, at Eden Beach Hacienda, operates both a gallery offering for-sale art and a shop, **Fruity Keiko** (P.O Box 128, Zihuatanejo, Guerrero 40880, tel. 755/553-2802, evaandjim@aol.com, www.edenmex .com), with a charming collection, mostly of Guerrero country crafts: baskets, toys, silver jewelry, silk scarves, and more.

Folks interested in rentals or buying property in Troncones should contact very knowledgable and locally trusted Troncones pioneer, Dewey McMillin (tel. 755/553-2812).

Some local stores provide drinking water and groceries. For example, on the Zihuatanejo entrance road, on the right as you enter the village, **Gaby's** (tel. 755/553-2891 or 755/553-2892, 8 A.M.–8 P.M. daily) offers some produce, basic groceries, and a long-distance telephone.

A few experienced guides offer local tours. Check out **Blue Morpho Ectotours** (www .williammertz.com/tour.html, $50 half-day and up) of local craftsman and wildlife devotee William Mertz. He and his wife, Belem, lead hiking, kayaking, and wildlife-viewing tours in Troncones lagoon, seashore, and forest locations. You can also explore similar beaten paths with English-speaking Alejandro Rodriguez Pineda's **Costa Nativa Ecotours** (tel. 755/553-2790, cell tel. 044-755/100-7499, info@ tronconesecotours.com, www.tronconeseco tours.com).

Getting There

Follow the signed paved turnoff to Playa Troncones from Highway 200, around Km 30, about 18 miles (29 km) north of Zihuatanejo; or about 42 miles (73 km) south of the Río Balsas dam. Continue 2.2 miles (3.5 km) to the Playa Troncones beachfront *ramadas.* Turn left at Bistro de Roberto bungalows for lodging and possible camping space; turn right for the other described lodgings, beginning with Casa Ki, about a mile farther along the beachfront forest road. From there, the car-negotiable gravel road continues about 1.5 miles (2.5 km) along the beach to Playa Majahua.

MAJAHUA

Here you can enjoy a slice of this beautiful coast as it was before tourism bloomed at Troncones nearby. Instead of cell phones and the Internet, Majahua folks still enjoy plenty of palmy shade, stick-and-wattle houses, and lots of the fresh seafood served in about half a dozen hammock-equipped *ramadas* scattered along the beach. One of the *ramadas* is competently run by a friendly family who calls it **Restaurant de Los Angeles** (sunrise–sunset, $4–8). Another of the best choices is *palapa* **Restaurant Las Brisas,** close by.

The Majahua beach itself curves from a rocky southeast point, past the lagoon of Río Lagunillas, and stretches miles northwest past shoreline palm groves and acacia forest. The sand is soft and dusky yellow, with mounds of driftwood and a seasonal scattering of shells. Waves break far out and roll in gradually, with little undertow. Fine left-breaking surf rises off the southern point. Boats are easily launchable

© BRUCE WHIPPERMAN

Fishing hamlet Majahua, just north of Troncones, remains rustic and tranquil.

(several *pangas* lie along the beach) during normal good weather.

Camping, moreover, is welcomed by local folks. Water is available at local stores, but prepared campers might bring water or purifying tablets and food. The most spacious and welcoming camping spot is at **La Gaviota** beach *palapa* restaurant (cell tel. 044-755/102-8895, http://sites.google.com/site/troncones/camping, tent or RV $7 and up) about a mile north of Majahua village. Here, set up your tent or park your RV on a wide, breezy beach, fine for surfing, surf fishing, beachcombing, fresh fish dining, or simply snoozing in the sun. Get there, traveling from Troncones, north along the beach road, by turning right at the Majahua village center, and shortly turning left at the La Gaviotas sign and continuing another fraction of a mile to the beachfront restaurant.

Get to Playa Majahua, either along the beach road, north via Troncones, or directly, by following the signed turnoff from Highway 200 at Km 33, 20 miles (32 km) northwest of Zihuatanejo (just south of the Río Lagunillas bridge), or 44 miles (70 km) southeast of the Río Balsas dam. Continue 2.9 miles (4.7 km) to the beach.

BEYOND TRONCONES

This northwest corner of the Ixtapa-Zihuatanejo region hides a few small havens for those who yearn for their fill of fresh seafood, uncrowded beach camping, and plenty of swimming, surfing, fishing, and beach-combing. And finally, those who venture to Guerrero's extreme northwest edge can encounter the great Río Balsas, the Mexican Pacific's mightiest river, whose drainage basin extends over five states: Jalisco, Morelos, Michoacán, Guerrero, and Oaxaca.

La Saladita

At La Saladita (The Little Salty Lagoon), the day used to climax when the oyster divers would bring in their afternoon catches. Now, however, the oysters are all fished out. While the oysters recover, divers go for octopus and lobster, which, broiled and served with fixings, sell for about $15 for a one-pounder. You can also do your own fishing via rentable (offer $20/hour) beach *lanchas,* which go out daily and routinely return with three or four 10-pound fish.

The Saladita beach itself is level far out, with rolling waves fine for surfing, swimming, boogie boarding, and bodysurfing. It spreads for at least a mile on both sides of the road's end, with enough driftwood and shells for a season of beachcombing. Permanent beachfront *palapa* restaurants **Paco, Ilianet, Sotelo** and **Enramada Jacqueline** supply fresh fish dinners, as well as shade and camping space ($5 pp). Camping is especially popular during the Christmas and Easter holidays, while at other times you may have the whole place to yourself. You may want to bring your own food and water; the small stores at the highway village may help add to your supplies.

Furthermore, a colony of comfortable lodgings has been built to serve the growing stream of visitors who now frequent this formerly undiscovered mini-paradise. At the low end, you can choose from a number of options: the rustic beachfront *cabañas* ($25 d) offered by most of the *palapa* restaurants; or Sotelo restaurant's modest beachfront hotel ($35 d), with about four plain rooms.

Moving up the economic scale, check out the **House of Waves** (tel. 755/554-4532, elsa_mexico@live.com.mx, elsavale29@hotmailcom, www.houseofwaves.net, $65 mountain view room, $70 sea view room, $140 apartment), a two-story house, with a pair of comfortable two-bedroom seaview veranda apartments upstairs and down. The apartment rooms, each with two double beds for up to four, either have a mountain view or a sea view; both bedrooms together can accommodate up to eight people.

Alternatively, by Ilianet beachfront restaurant, **Casas Playa Saladita** (toll-free U.S. tel. 877/927-6928, info@casasplayasaladita.com, www.casasplayasaladita.com, $80–90 d), offers eight very attractive and comfortable architect-built kitchenette apartments in two stucco buildings. Each apartment has hot-water baths and air-conditioning; the upper level units have better ocean views and breezes.

To get to La Saladita, at Km 40, 25 miles (40 km) northwest of Zihuatanejo and 39 miles (63 km) southeast of the Río Balsas, turn off at the village of Los Llanos. After 0.2 mile, turn right at the church and continue another 3.1 miles (5.1 km) to the beach, where a left fork leads you to Sotelo *palapa* and a right fork leads to the "Embarcadero" sector of the beach and Paco's and Ilianet and the other *palapa* restaurants.

Atracadero

A few miles farther northwest, Playa Atracadero is just being "discovered" and is less frequented than La Saladita. Its two or three beach *palapa* restaurants appear to operate only during weekends, holidays, and the fall–early winter surfing season. Crowds must gather sometimes, however: The main *palapa* has, over time, accumulated a five-foot pile of oyster shells.

The beach sand itself is soft and yellow-gray. The waves, with good, gradual surfing breaks, roll in from far out, arriving gently on the sand. Boat launching would be easy during calm weather. Little undertow menaces casual swimmers, bodysurfers, or boogie boarders. Lots of driftwood and shells—clams, limpets, snails—cover the sand. The beach extends for at least three miles (5 km) past palm groves on the northwest.

To get to Playa Atracadero, turn off at Highway 200 Km 64, near the hamlet of Joluta, 40 miles (64 km) northwest from Zihuatanejo and 24 miles (39 km) southeast from the Río Balsas. Bear left all the way, 2.1 miles (3.3 km) to the beach.

The Río Balsas

It's hard to remain unimpressed as you follow Highway 200 over the Río Balsas dam for the first time. The dam marks the Michoacán–Guerrero state boundary. The hulking rock-fill barrier rises in giant stair-steps to its highway summit, where a grand lake mirrors the Sierra Madre, while on the opposite, downstream side, Mexico's greatest river spurts from the turbine exit gates 500 feet below. The river's power, converted into enough electric energy for a million Mexican families, courses up great looping transmission wires, while the spent river meanders toward the sea. To experience all this, drive directly over the dam, from either the north or south, by following old Highway 200 (bear inland) instead of taking the straight-line, toll expressway direct to or from Lázaro Cárdenas.

LÁZARO CÁRDENAS

The newish industrial port city of Lázaro Cárdenas, named for the Michoacán-born president famous for expropriating American oil companies, is an important transportation and service hub for the northwest Ixtapa-Zihuatanejo region. For travelers it's mainly useful as a stopover for services and bus connections, southeast with Ixtapa-Zihuatanejo, Acapulco, and Mexico City; northwest with the Michoacán coast, Manzanillo, and Puerto Vallarta; and north with the upland Michoacán destinations of Uruapan, Pátzcuaro, and

Morelia. Most of its services, including banks, bus stations, post office, hospital, hotels, and restaurants, are clustered along north–south Avenida Lázaro Cárdenas, the main ingress boulevard, about three miles (5 km) from its Highway 200 intersection.

Accommodations and Food

If you decide to stay overnight, nearby hotels offer reasonably priced lodging. The cheapest and most conveniently located is the **Hotel Delfín** (Av. Lázaro Cárdenas 1633, tel. 753/532-3781 or 753/532-0373, $25 d, $30 d with a/c), across the street from the Galeana bus station. The approximately 20 rooms with baths, in three stories, cluster around an inner pool and patio. Rooms come with fans, hot water, TV, telephone, and wireless Internet.

For more class, go to the high-rise **◖ Hotel Casablanca** (Bravo, tel. 753/537-3480, 753/537-3481, 753/537-3482, 753/537-3483, or 753/537-3484, reservar@hcasablanca.com.mx, www.hcasablanca.com.mx, $55 s, $70 d), a block east from Avenida Lázaro Cárdenas, visible behind and above Bancomer. It offers about six floors of 114 light and comfortable modern-standard deluxe rooms with panoramic private-balcony views. Downstairs, past the lobby, a restaurant overlooks an inviting rear pool and patio. Rooms come with breakfast, air-conditioning, phones, TV, gym, wireless Internet, and parking.

An even fancier hotel option is the executive-class **Krystal Express** (Av. Circuito de las Universidades 60, tel. 753/533-2900 or 753/533-2922, toll-free U.S. tel. 888/726-0528 or Can. tel. 866/299-7096, nhlazaro-cardenas@nh-hotels.com, www.nh-hotels.com, $140 d mid-week, $80 d weekend) on the west side of the ingress boulevard Avenida Lázaro Cárdenas, at the traffic circle, about a quarter mile before the town center. It offers 120 deluxe rooms with air-conditioning, wireless Internet, telephone, cable TV, continental breakfast, restaurant-bar, exercise gym, and whirlpool tub.

Take a break from the sun beneath the shady streetfront awning of the **Restaurant**

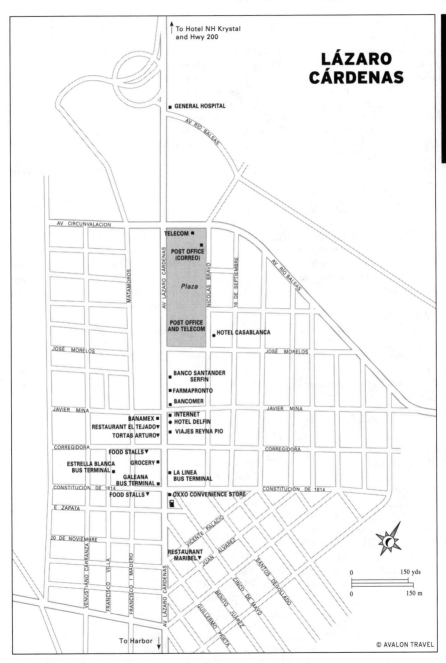

To Hotel NH Krystal and Hwy 200

LÁZARO CÁRDENAS

GENERAL HOSPITAL

AV RÍO BALSAS

AV CIRCUNVALACION

TELECOM

POST OFFICE (CORREO)

MATAMOROS

AV LÁZARO CÁRDENAS

NICOLÁS BRAVO

16 DE SEPTIEMBRE

AV RÍO BALSAS

Plaza

POST OFFICE AND TELECOM

HOTEL CASABLANCA

JOSÉ MORELOS

JOSÉ MORELOS

BANCO SANTANDER SERFIN

FARMAPRONTO

BANCOMER

JAVIER MINA

JAVIER MINA

BANAMEX

RESTAURANT EL TEJADO

TORTAS ARTURO

INTERNET

HOTEL DELFIN

VIAJES REYNA PIO

CORREGIDORA

CORREGIDORA

FOOD STALLS

ESTRELLA BLANCA BUS TERMINAL

GROCERY

GALEANA BUS TERMINAL

LA LINEA BUS TERMINAL

CONSTITUCIÓN DE 1814

CONSTITUCIÓN DE 1814

FOOD STALLS

OXXO CONVENIENCE STORE

E ZAPATA

20 DE NOVIEMBRE

VICENTE PALACIO

JUAN ÁLVAREZ

VENUSTIANO CARRANZA

FRANCISCO VILLA

FRANCISCO I MADERO

AV LÁZARO CÁRDENAS

RESTAURANT MARIBEL

SANTOS DEGOLLADO

CINCO DE MAYO

BENITO JUÁREZ

GUILLERMO PRIETA

0   150 yds

0   150 m

To Harbor

© AVALON TRAVEL

El Tejado (Av. Lázaro Cárdenas, tel. 753/532-0140, 8 A.M.–10 P.M. daily, $4–12), on the main street next to Banamex. (You may need to ask the staff to kindly turn the TV off or at least lower the volume.)

For more economical, but wholesome country cooking, check out the *fondas* (foodstalls) on side street Constitución de 1814, adjacent to the Galeana bus station lot, and on side street Corregidora, the next block north.

Take a break from the street bustle and enjoy supper at the TV-free **Restaurant Maribel** (95 Benito Juárez, tel. 753/532-0642, 7–10 P.M. daily). To get there follow the street that angles diagonally south from Avenida Lázaro Cárdenas, at the Oxxo store, a block from the Galeana bus station. Take a seat and enjoy one of a dozen home-style meals, from *pozole blanco* (savory hominy and pork soup) and *guisado de Puerco* (pork stew) to pineapple tamales, and tostadas.

Travel Agent

A competent and conveniently situated travel agency (and potential information source) is **Viajes Reyna Pío** (Av. Lázaro Cárdenas 9, tel. 753/532-3868 or 753/532-3935, fax 753/532-0723), right across from the Galeana bus station and Banamex.

Money Exchange

Change your money at one of three banks, all with ATMs, clustered nearby: **Banamex** (Av. Lázaro Cárdenas 1646, tel. 753/532-2020, 9 A.M.–4 P.M. Mon.–Sat., 10 A.M.–2 P.M. Sat.); if it's too crowded, try **Bancomer** (Av. Lázaro Cárdenas 1555, tel. 753/532-3888, 8:30 A.M.–4 P.M. Mon.–Fri., 10 A.M.–2 P.M. Sat.), a block north of Banamex and across the street; or **Banco Santander Serfín** (Av. Lázaro Cárdenas 1681, tel. 753/532-0032, 9 A.M.–4 P.M. Mon.–Fri., 10 A.M.–2 P.M. Sat.), on the same side as Bancomer, half a block farther north.

Communications

The *correo* (tel. 755/537-2387, 8 A.M.–4:30 P.M. Mon.–Fri., 8 A.M.–noon Sat.) is at the north end of the big grassy town plaza, with entry facing Av. Nicolas Bravo and the high-rise Casablanca Hotel.

Telecomunicaciones (tel. 753/532-0273, 8 A.M.–7 P.M. Mon.–Sat., 9 A.M.–12:30 P.M. Sun.), with money orders, telephone, and public fax, is behind the post office, facing the center of the plaza.

For telephone, plenty of public street phones accept widely available Ladatel telephone cards.

Connect to the Internet at the small store **Internet Sin Limite** (corner of Av. Lázaro Cárdenas and Javier Mina, tel. 753/532-1480, 8 A.M.–10 P.M. Mon.–Sat., 9 A.M.–9 P.M. Sun.), across the street and south of Bancomer.

Health

The **General Hospital** (tel. 753/532-0900, 753/532-0901, 753/532-0902, 753/532-0903, or 753/532-0904), known locally as "Seguro Social," is on the boulevard into town, left side, corner of H. Escuela Naval, a block before the big right-side traffic circle. Alternatively, visit highly recommended **Dr. Gustavo Cejos Pérez** (Melchor Ocampo 475, tel. 753/532-3902, 8 A.M.–2 P.M. Mon.–Fri.). For routine medicines and drugs, go to conveniently situated **Farmacia Pronto** (tel. 753/537-5002, 7 A.M.–11 P.M. daily), a few doors north of the Galeana bus station.

Getting There and Away

By car or RV, the options to and from Lázaro Cárdenas are virtually the same as those for Ixtapa and Zihuatanejo. Simply add or subtract the 50 miles (80 km) or 1.25-hour travel difference between Ixtapa or Zihuatanejo and Lázaro Cárdenas.

By bus, a trio of long-distance bus terminals serves Lázaro Cárdenas travelers. **Galeana terminal** (Av. Lázaro Cárdenas 1810, tel. 753/532-3006) gets its name from a former, but now non-existent, popular bus line. **Ruta Paraíso** first-class and second-class local-departure buses connect north daily with Apatzingán, Arteaga, Nueva Italia, Uruapan, and Morelia. Very frequent local departures of allied line **Purépechas** also connect northwest along the coast with nearby coastal destinations of La Mira, Playa Azul, and Caleta de Campos. Additionally, several more first- and second-class departures connect northwest with long-distance destination Manzanillo and intermediate points.

In an adjacent booth inside the station, agents (tel. 753/532-3006) sell tickets for **Parhikuni** luxury-class buses (with air-conditioned waiting lounge), connecting north with the Michoacán destinations of Nueva Italia, Uruapan, and Morelia.

Other reliable carriers also operate out of the same station. **Omnibus de Mexico** (tel. 753/537-1119) first-class departures connect north with the U.S. border at Nuevo Laredo, via Uruapan, Morelia, Queretaro, Saltillo, and Monterrey. Additionally, **Autovias de Mexico** (also tel. 753/537-1119) departures connect northeast, with Mexico City (terminal Norte), via Morelia, and Toluca.

Directly across the street, **La Linea** (tel. 753/537-1119) and its associated lines maintain a small streetfront station. It offers a number of options: executive-class "Plus," connecting northwest with Guadalajara via Tecomán and Colima; first- and second-class **Sur** buses, connecting north with Guadalajara via Nueva Italia, Puréapura, and Zamora; first-class Autovias de Mexico buses, connecting north, via Morelia, thence east with Toluca and Mexico City (Poniente and Norte terminals); and second-class stop-anywhere **Autobuses Sur de Jalisco** connecting northwest with Manzanillo and also with Guadalajara, along the coast, via Maruata, Tecomán, Colima, and Ciudad Guzmán.

The big **Estrella Blanca terminal** (Francisco Villa between Constitución de 1814 and Corregidora, tel. 753/532-1111) is two short blocks away, directly behind the Galeana terminal. From there, one or two daily first-class local departures connect north with Michoacán destinations of Uruapan, Morelia, and Mexico City. At least two first-class buses stop, en route both southeast to Zihuatanejo and Acapulco, and northwest to Manzanillo, Puerto Vallarta, Mazatlán, and the U.S. border. In addition, three Futura luxury-class local departures connect daily with Mexico City.

THE COSTA GRANDE AND ACAPULCO

The Costa Grande, the "Big Coast" of the state of Guerrero, stretches 150 miles southeast from Zihuatanejo to Acapulco. Before the highway came during the 1960s, this was a land of corn, coconuts, fish, and fruit. Although it's still that, the road added a new ingredient: a trickle of visitors increasingly enjoying the host of country delights along the way. These include a fascinating archaeological zone, a beloved pilgrimage shrine, historic market towns, and a host of breezy beaches for camping, beachcombing, and surf fishing.

And finally comes the prize at the end of the road: Acapulco, Mexico's original world-class resort, still breezy and beautiful. Here, first-time travelers can discover (while long-timers re-discover) a trove of *tipica* Mexican

diversions, from its shady, vine-hung old-town plaza, bustling market, historic fort and museum, and diadem of crystal-sand beaches, to offshore island and hilltop forest trails.

These Old World delights exist side by side with modern attractions comparable to what you might find in Hollywood or Las Vegas: the new, the brash, and often the very loud. If you're looking for a festive night out, you can sample from dozens of bars, clubs, discotheques, and nightclub extravaganzas— and even a shoreline nighttime bungee jump. Gourmet restaurants add to the allure, attracting the rich and famous with exotic menus as impressive as the views of the city lights reflecting on the water. Today's Acapulco shines as brightly as it ever did.

© BORIS DMITRIENKOV/123RF.COM

HIGHLIGHTS

◖ Soledad de Maciel Archaeological Zone: Visit the grand, reconstructed ball court, the enigmatic King of Chole monolith, and the new museum with its trove of rich artifacts (page 84).

◖ Playa El Calvario: Stop for beachcombing, surfing, boogie boarding, fishing – or at least a drink at one of the clifftop restaurants (page 88).

◖ Piedra Tlalcoyunque: Take a break at this spectacular sheltering sea-rock, where you can surf, wander the wave-tossed tide pools, or visit the turtle-rescue sanctuary (page 91).

◖ Playa Paraíso: Take a breezy afternoon boat ride across the lagoon, or camp and play at picturesque Florentine's Garden Balneario (page 96).

◖ El Carrizal: This mini-Eden offers a pristine open-ocean beach on one side and a rustic, palm-tufted lagoon on the other (page 98).

◖ Laguna Coyuca Boat Tour: Thread through mangrove-laced channels and past islands festooned with nesting herons, cormorants, and pelicans (page 100).

◖ The Acapulco Zócalo: Here, at the charming heart of old Acapulco, stroll in the shade beneath the ancient *higuera* trees, people-watch from park benches, or visit the art deco church (page 110).

◖ Fuerte de San Diego: This grand colonial-era fort protected Acapulco from marauders for more than 300 years (page 112).

◖ La Quebrada: Watch intrepid divers gracefully execute a death-defying 200-foot plunge into a narrow, rockbound, and wave-tossed channel (page 113).

◖ Isla Roqueta: A glass-bottomed boat tour leads to this pristine island, which offers easy trails, a lighthouse, and panoramic clifftop views of the ocean (page 114).

COSTA GRANDE & ACAPULCO

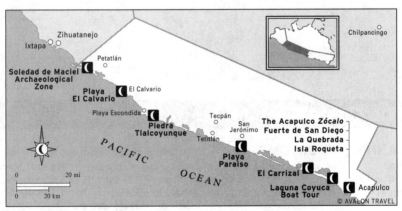

LOOK FOR ◖ TO FIND RECOMMENDED SIGHTS, ACTIVITIES, DINING, AND LODGING.

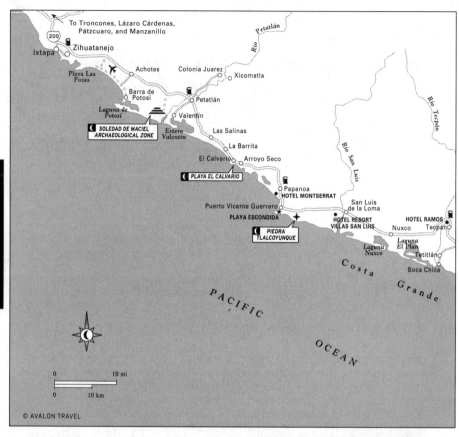

The Costa Grande

PLANNING YOUR TIME

Although the temptation is to drive or bus the entire Costa Grande from Zihuatanejo to Acapulco in one quick half day, that would be a pity. Better, take the scenic route and linger at some of the Costa Grande's paradises en route.

Down the coast, not far from Zihuatanejo, the area around **Petatlán** offers enough for a relaxing day of sightseeing, starting with paying your respects to Petatlán's miraculous patron Padre Jesús, then shopping at Petatlán's gold jewelry market stalls, and relaxing with a walking tour of the nearby **Soledad de Maciel Archaeological Zone.** Continue south for an overnight on intimate **Playa Ojo de Agua** beach at **Hotel Monserrat.**

On the other hand, equipped lovers of the outdoors could be equally content with a few days of camping, surf fishing, beachcombing, and maybe even surfing, or kayaking, off the beach at hidden **Playa Escondida** and/or spectacular and breezy **Piedra Tlalcoyunque.**

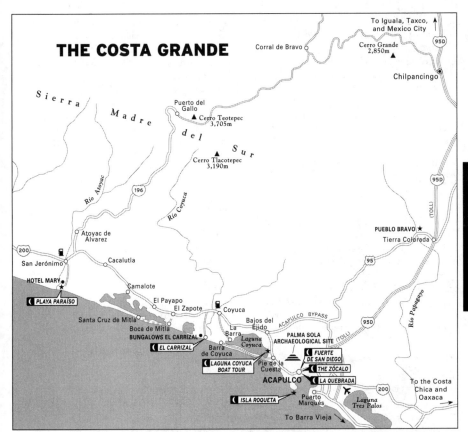

Moreover, if you're into fishing, boating, canoeing, or kayaking you might also consider spending an overnight or more at the lagoon-front informal campgrounds at **Camalote** and **Playa Paraíso.**

Later, spend an overnight in **El Carrizal** at its top-pick Hotel Paraíso Playa Azul, where you can enjoy both the breezy beach on one side and the hotel's lusciously relaxing lagoon-side setting on the other.

HISTORY

Long before Zihuatanejo's latter-day popularity, people had been attracted to the Costa Grande. Their oldest remains, pottery dating from around 3000 B.C., decorates the displays at the Zihuatanejo archaeological museum. Later, around 1000 B.C., the Olmecs (famous for their monumental Gulf coast sculptures) left their unmistakable mark on regional pottery.

After the Olmecs came waves of settlers, including the barbaric Chichimecs (Drinkers of Blood), the agricultural Cuitlatecs, and an early invasion of Aztecs, perhaps wandering in search of their eventual homeland in the Valley of Mexico.

None of those peoples were a match for the armies of Tarascan emperor Hiripan, who during the late 14th century A.D. invaded the Costa Grande from his Michoacán highland capital and established a coastal province, headquartered at the present town of Coyuca de Benítez, less than an hour's drive west of Acapulco.

Three generations later the star of the Aztec emperor Tízoc was rising over Mexico. His armies invaded the Costa Grande and pushed out the Tarascans. By 1500 the Aztecs ruled the coast from their provincial town capital at Cihuatlán, the "Place of Women," not far from present-day Zihuatanejo.

THE ROAD ALONG THE COSTA GRANDE

By bus, go by first- or second-class Acapulco-bound buses (whose drivers, if asked, will let you off most anywhere) from the Zihuatanejo Estrella Blanca terminal.

Drivers, follow Highway 200 southeast, Acapulco direction, out of Zihuatanejo.

◖ SOLEDAD DE MACIEL ARCHAEOLOGICAL ZONE

Find the turnoff from Highway 200 to this important archaeological site 19 miles (31 km)

southeast of Zihuatanejo. At the signed side road at Km 214 turn right and continue five miles (8 km) south of Highway 200 to the new museum, just before Soledad de Maciel village. The site was first explored by INAH (National Institute of Archaeology and History) investigators around 1925. Investigators have identified a classic-era (circa A.D. 300) habitation and ceremonial zone that extends over at least a square mile (2 or 3 square km) around the present Soledad de Maciel village.

The principal artifact uncovered to date is the famous "King of Chole" monolith, visible in front of the town church. Other identified structures include three completely unreconstructed pyramids, ceremonial mounds, and courtyards, a recently reconstructed ball court, and extensive former habitation zones. Many artifacts have been uncovered; examples of these include pottery, on display at the Soledad de Maciel site museum and the Zihuatanejo archaeological museum, and two ball rings beside Highway 200 in town.

At this writing, a sizable **museum** is under

the partially excavated grand ball court at Soledad de Maciel

© BRUCE WHIPPERMAN

construction, and the big **ball court** is being excavated, visible on the road to the village, about a quarter mile, past the museum. All this bodes well, both for visitors and the local community.

King of Chole Monolith and Touring the Archaeological Zone

In Soledad de Maciel village (turn right at first village intersection) find the "King of Chole" monolith, in front of the church. It represents a personage with two faces, looking in opposite right and left directions. One face, representing death, is emaciated, the other, representing life, is plump and vital. (Note: You will probably be able to recognize the life-death faces best from a distance of about 10 feet, rather than close up to the King of Chole.)

Guides at the new museum offer their services for a one- or two-hour tour of the environs. The two-hour tour, which includes the excavated ball court and the museum, should also extend to the 200-foot high, forested **Cerro de las Peñas** (Hill of the Rocks). Ask your guide to point out the plants along the way up. These include the wild plumlike *ciruela;* the *cuachalalope* tree, with buds on the trunk that are boiled for a rejuvenating tonic; the *cacahuanache* tree, whose boiled bark makes a good shampoo; and the *paniko* tree, which makes a sedative tonic.

At the airy summit, the broad hinterland of fields of corn and tobacco (for locally made cigars) and communal coconut groves spread to the ocean, visible on the southern horizon. Also uphill, you will find a giant *órgano* (organ cactus), some petroglyphs (of the Lord of the Hill), and a small cave, complete with bats and more petroglyphs. Bring a flashlight. Among the best qualified of the local guides is Adan Belez Romero (local cell tel. 044-758/100-1953), often available at his house a few doors from the church. Kindly offer $20–30 for a two-hour tour.

PETATLÁN

The town of Petatlán (pop. about 25,000), only 22 miles (35 km) southeast of Zihuatanejo,

besides being Guerrero's most cherished pilgrimage shrine, has a distinguished pre-Columbian heritage that has only recently begun to be appreciated.

Sights

All roads seem to lead to Petatlán's colorful central plaza, *parque municipal,* a few blocks south of Highway 200 at Km 207 (coming from Zihuatanejo, turn right at Calle Bravo). After a stroll around the *parque,* walk two blocks uphill, north, to the **Parroquia de Padre Jesús** (head toward the modern church's pair of white bell towers), hallowed ground for the many thousands of pilgrims who arrive yearly from all over Guerrero and Mexico. Inside the innovative parabolic-arched nave, the faithful pay their respects to the venerated wooden image, above the altar, known affectionately as "Papa Chuy" ("Chooey"), that arrived under miraculous circumstances as the gift of a mysterious but grateful "Christian Pirate" around 1600.

The Petatlán townsfolk fete their beloved Papa Chuy at least twice a year, during the pre-Easter Semana Santa celebration and the August 6–7 Fiesta del Padre Jesús. During both occasions the *parque* is awash with merrymakers watching folkloric dances, eating traditional sweets, and thrilling to the boom and flash of fireworks overhead.

Just out in front of the church, be sure to visit the **Mercado de Oro** (Gold Market) lineup of stalls offering a treasury of bright (some solid but mostly gold-plated) necklaces, amulets, chains, bracelets, and much more.

Accommodations, Food, and Services

Several modest downtown hotels accommodate overnight guests. Ordinarily they're not crowded, but if you're going to stay in Petatlán during the Padre Jesús festival (around Aug. 6 and 7), the week before Easter, or Christmas–New Year's be sure to get reservations far ahead of time.

One of the best hotels is **Hotel Mi Pueblito** (Independencia 108, tel. 758/538-2271, $20 d fan, $30 d a/c, $40 and $50 holidays), next to Telmex. They offer about 10 comfortable, spacious, light, and airy rooms with hot-water shower baths, TV, and parking. Another good choice is plain but clean **Hotel Mary** (on Bravo, three doors west of Independencia, cell tel. 758/103-9437, $14 s, $23 d, $32 t); rooms come with TV and fans.

Petatlán's most highly recommended restaurant is the airy plaza-front *palapa* **Restaurant Mi Pueblito** (tel. 758/538-3104, 8 A.M.–11 P.M. daily, $4–8), on the *parque's*

south side, serving a long menu of Mexican country-style favorites.

While in downtown you can avail yourself of a number of services. These include **Bancomer** (tel. 758/538-2977, 8:30 A.M.–4 P.M. Mon.–Fri.); a *correo* (on Bravo, three doors from Hwy. 200); Ladatel card-operated street telephones; the police (at the *presidencia municipal,* at the plaza, tel. 758/538-4040); and a doctor, **Saul Enríquez Garcia** (Bravo 42, tel. 758/538-2321, 10 A.M.–2 P.M., 4–7 P.M. Mon.–Fri.).

THE LEGEND OF PADRE JESÚS

Sometime during the late 1500s, a priest was assigned to minister to the people of Petatlán. Upon arrival, the priest sympathized with the people's sorry state. For years they had endured both the terrible ravages of smallpox and the greed and cruelty of the Spanish soldiers and colonists. The priest taught them and helped heal them, and after a few years he had gained their confidence.

During the yearly Semana Santa celebration the priest saw that the people had been carrying an old rickety image of San Antonio for the reenactment of the Stations of the Cross. In a church meeting, he convinced his congregation to take up a collection to obtain a true image of Jesus for the upcoming Semana Santa celebration.

Although the collection amounted to only a few small donations, the priest prepared to journey somewhere to get an appropriate new image of Jesus.

Meanwhile, a great storm had been blowing off the coast. Unknown to the priest and the people of Petatlán, a pirate ship, dismasted and waterlogged, was in danger of sinking. On the ship was an image of Jesus, to which the pirate sailors prayed to save their ship. The pirate captain vowed that, if they were saved, he would take the image to the nearest town and donate it to the local people.

The pirates were saved: The storm drove them aground on the Bahía de Potosí's sandy

shoreline. The pirate captain, true to his vow, took the image ashore with two of his crew.

The priest, meanwhile, had been in a quandary; he did not know where he could find a suitable image of Jesus for the few coins that he had collected. Late one night, as he was praying for guidance, the priest was startled by a hard knock on his door. It was the pirate captain, who told the priest that he had the image of Jesus that the priest was looking for. Then, without further explanation, the pirate disappeared into the night.

Barely able to believe the mysterious man who became known as the "Christian Pirate," the priest nevertheless delayed his trek to find a new image.

Easter Sunday came, and the promised image had not appeared. The priest was relating the story of Jesus's death and resurrection to his congregation when a poor woodcutter pushed himself through the assembly and cried out that Jesus with a cross had appeared to him nearby.

The people followed the woodcutter to a clear stream where, under a great tree, was the sculpture of Padre Jesús. The people joyfully carried Padre Jesús back to their church, where he remains in Petatlán to this day.

This is a synopsis of the story of Padre Jesús as researched and written by Petatlán's official historian, Señor Agapito Galeana.

LAS SALINAS AND PLAYA LA BARRITA

These two little roadside spots are interesting for completely different reasons. Playa La Barrita is a lovely beachside mini-paradise, while at Las Salinas people continue to make their living from technology whose origin is lost in time.

Las Salinas

Families of Las Salinas village(pop. 500) harvest salt from the inner flats of the neighboring arm of the ocean, Estero El Cuajo, to make their living. During the dry, low-water winter–spring season, follow the off-highway side road, by the warehouse, around Km 194 to see how they do it. With long-handled wooden trowels, workers fashion diked ponds, about 10 feet (three meters) square, from the mud of the lagoon. They surface the ponds' bottoms with lime, which soon hardens into an impervious basin.

The salt workers channel the seawater into the ponds. The sun evaporates the water and the salt crystallizes on the edges. The workers scoop the salt crystals into small piles outside the ponds, where the salt piles dry in the sun; the salt is then wheeled in carts to the roadside warehouse to be bagged.

Along Highway 200 in the village, around Km 192, you can see the results of all this. Instead of waiting by the roadside for customers, villagers let their salt bags do the waiting, perched on posts, like roadside mailboxes, for someone to stop and leave a dollar (or ten pesos) for a one-kilo sack. They don't mind doing this; the loss of an occasional dollar is small compared to long hours of waiting. And besides, every dollar they earn this way is one they didn't have in the first place.

Las Salinas families maintain roadside stalls around Km 193 to sell both bags of salt and *colorines,* very yummy pastel-colored candied, pure coconut cookies. They're fresh, sweet, delicious, and healthy, to boot.

© BRUCE WHIPPERMAN

harvesting salt at Las Salinas

Playa La Barrita

Of the several small *palapa* restaurants that decorate Playa La Barrita, around Km 188, none enjoys such an attractive setting as **(Restaurant Paraíso Escondido** (Hidden Paradise; tel. 758/538-3381, 8 A.M.–8 P.M. daily, $4–10). Although the food (shrimp, octopus, fish, prawns) is good enough, the site is stunning. The fine yellow-sand beach stretches for about a mile in both directions, and waves wash in from about 100 yards out with little undertow. Surfing, boogie boarding, surf fishing and boat launching appear very doable. For tots, the restaurant even has a blue kiddie pool out front.

Furthermore, grandfatherly owner Isidoro Lombera has built a few small but comfortable beachfront hotel rooms (around $30 d). Rentals, with private hot-water showers and fans, are negotiable. Although at this writing, Isidoro's planned mini-resort is a work in progress, it's certainly worth checking out.

PLAYAS CAYACAL, EL CALVARIO, AND ARROYO SECO

Between Km 183 and Km 178, Highway 200 veers spectacularly close to the ocean. Here, three long beaches, El Calvario, Cayacal, and Arroyo Seco, join in one continuous scenic sweep of sand, sea, and sky. Moving from the Zihuatanejo end, first comes golden Playa Cayacal; then Playa El Calvario, stunningly viewable from any one of a number of clifftop *palapa* restaurants; and finally long, wild, and breezy Playa Arroyo Seco, seemingly stretching forever southeast.

(Playa El Calvario

In contrast to secluded (but not locally recommended for camping) Playa Arroyo Seco at the south end, Playa El Calvario is well frequented, especially by the dozens of daily visitors who stop at one of its several clifftop restaurants perched above the beach. Playa Calvario,

panorama of Playa Calvario, from south-end palapa Restaurant El Mirador

© BRUCE WHIPPERMAN

although especially fine for surfing and nearly everything else (except maybe surf fishing because of the flat shallows), isn't good for camping because it's only about 100 feet wide and vulnerable to flooding at extreme high tide.

Nevertheless, Playa Calvario is an irresistible spot to stop and take in the gorgeous scene. Gulls soar, pelicans dive, waves carry surfers shoreward, and cormorants preen and cackle on the spectacular Piedras Calvarios outcroppings, picturesquely visible from clifftop *palapas* above Playa Calvario.

Along this entire stretch, conditions seem perfect for a day or season of beach diversions. Waves, fine for boogie boarding or surfing, roll in gradually with little undertow. Seasonal storms deposit a few shells and a bit of driftwood. Rock outcroppings provide resting spots for resident gulls, pelicans, boobies, and cormorants, while a sprinkling of visitors strolls the sand and plays in the surf.

Furthermore, at the Playa Calvario clifftop, the sun, at dawn and sunset, graphically demonstrates why the Spanish explorers called the Pacific Ocean the Mar del Sur, the Southern Sea. Here, in late afternoon, you can see the sun (which everywhere in the world rises in the east and sets in the west), shining along a line parallel to the beach line. Thus, the direction south, perpendicular to the east–west beach line, runs straight out to sea.

Enjoy either breakfast or lunch, along with best overall view of this entire breezy strand, at south-end headland **Restaurant El Mirador** (near Km 181, no phone, 7 A.M.–7 P.M. daily, $3–8). The menu includes Mexican-style breakfasts (such as *huevos mexicanos,* omelettes, and *chilaquiles*) until noon, and fresh fish (whole pan fried fillet with garlic or breaded, or in tacos) the rest of the day.

PAPANOA

The small town of Papanoa (pop. 5,000) straddles the highway 47 miles (75 km) southeast of Zihuatanejo and 103 miles (165 km) northwest of Acapulco. Local folks tell the tongue-

in-cheek story of its Hawaiian-sounding name. It seems that there was a flood and the son of the local headman had to talk fast to save his life by escaping in a *canoa* (canoe). Instead of saying "Papa…canoa," the swift-talking boy shortened his plea to "Papa…noa."

At least two recommendable hotels offer accommodations. At the center of town, a block north (left) off the highway, stands the neat, family-run **Hotel La Sirena** (Calle Telecino Moreno, tel. 742/422-2029, $20 d, $35 with a/c, $30 and $40 holidays). Here you'll get a very spacious, clean, and comfortable room with hot-water shower, bath, ceiling fan, and TV. Credit cards are not accepted.

Alternatively, stay at the 1950s-era resort-style **Hotel Club Papanoa** (Hwy. 200, tel. 742/422-0150, $50 s or d, $80 holidays); rooms come with private hot-water shower baths and air-conditioning. Near the beach just off the highway about a mile southeast of Papanoa town, the hotel offers about 30 spacious rooms, a restaurant, and a large, lovely pool, set in airy oceanview garden grounds. Built to be luxurious but is now aging, the hotel is popular during holidays, but nearly empty most other times.

The Hotel Club Papanoa grounds adjoin **Playa Cayaquitos.** The wide, breezy, yellow-gray strand stretches for two miles, washed by powerful open-ocean rollers with good left and right surfing breaks. Additional attractions include surf fishing beyond the breakers and driftwood along the sand. Beach access is via the off-highway driveway just north of the hotel. At the beach, a parking lot borders a seafood restaurant. Farther on, the road narrows (but is still motorhome-accessible) through a defunct beachside home development, past several brush-bordered informal RV parking or tent camping spots.

A clean restaurant, the **Annel** (south side of Hwy. 200, 8 A.M.–9 P.M. daily, $5–8), in the town center, serves passable country-style food.

As for services, Papanoa has friendly **doctor Salvador Zarate** (tel. 742/422-0176), with a small pharmacy; a photo shop, **Universo** (tel. 742/422-0150); a *gasolinera;* first-class bus stops; long-distance telephones both at the gas station and the Hotel Sirena; and Ladatel card-operated public phones.

PLAYA OJO DE AGUA

Nestled in the little nook between a pair of headlands, about half a mile southeast of the Hotel Club Papanoa, is the petite half-moon beach Playa Ojo de Agua, named for its cooling and cleansing freshwater spring. Local families flock here on weekend afternoons to play in the surf, eat fresh seafood at the beachfront *palapas,* and rinse themselves in the community spring (*ojo de agua,* literally eye of water) that trickles from a hillside source, marked by a concrete arch, on the beach. (*Note:* If you use the spring, remember it's usually only a trickle, so kindly conserve water by dipping a bucket, bottle, or can in the collection basin for water to pour over yourself.)

Playa Ojo de Agua is a lovely spot, wide and level, with very surfable waves from about 200 yards out, and a number of shady possible tenting spots (but with little apparent usable space for beachfront RV parking).

Accommodations and Food

Development has arrived at Playa Ojo de Agua in new beachfront **Hotel Monserrat** (cell tel. 044-742/103-0765 or 044/103-3799, $65 d low season, $75 d high season) with about five designer rooms built over an open-air beach-view restaurant and pool-patio. The simply elegant rooms are clean and comfortable, with handsome hardwood highlights, shiny, mod bath fixtures, and king or double beds, plus cable TV; rooms include breakfast, except on holidays.

The restaurant ($6–15), down below, serves from a very recognizable international menu, including breakfast eggs any style, pancakes, and French toast; soups, salads, and sandwiches; and many entrées, which are mostly seafood.

PLAYA ESCONDIDA

Puerto Vicente Guerrero, a small workaday fishing port and naval training center, 52 miles

The hidden spring at Playa Ojo de Agua furnishes cool fresh water, fine for washing off the day's sweat, sand, and salty seawater.

© BR.JCE WHIPPERMAN

(84 km) southeast from Zihuatanejo, 97 miles (156 km) northwest from Acapulco, hides a pearl of a beach, appropriately known as Playa Escondida (Hidden Beach), beyond its southeast headland.

Two miles from the signed highway turnoff continue through the port village, bearing to the left (east), uphill, at the village-center road fork overlooking the harbor. Pass the naval training base at the road's summit, and continue ahead a few blocks downhill to the Hotel Los Arcos at Playa Escondida.

Beyond the few permanent *palapa* restaurants that populate the beachfront spreads a wide yellow-sand beach, sheltered on both sides by rocky headlands. Strong, very surfable waves break and roll in along a nearly level shoreline, receding with only mild undertow.

Playa Escondida (also known locally as Playa Secreta) appears ideal for every kind of beach entertainment, from kiddie play and beachcombing, to surfing and scuba diving. The beach even has ample room for tent camping, especially on the far (east) side.

The most high profile lodging is **Hotel and Restaurant Los Arcos** (tel. 742/427-0252 or 742/424-0556, $35 s, $40 d, $50 t). Its dozen-odd modern, light rooms (somewhat neglected in the past, take a look before moving in) encircle an inviting pool and parking patio. On the beach side, guests also enjoy an open-air (but unkempt at this writing) restaurant with a view of the beach. Room rentals include room-temperature—only private shower baths and air-conditioning.

Folks interested in sportfishing and other ocean diversions might want to book a stay at the **Bahía la Tortuga Fishing Lodge** (U.S. tel. 956/455-6931, www.escapeixtapa.com), which has been receiving guests (by reservation only) at Playa Escondida for several years. Owner-operators John and Angélica Lorenz advertise a number of packages, such as a three-night, four-day package that starts $745 per person for two, including two days of sportfishing, all meals, and airport pickup. They also offer kayaking, snorkeling, scuba diving, surfing lessons, and whale- and turtle-watching, in season. Moreover, John and Angélica accept reservations from non-fishing guests in their comfy lodge. For $75 per person, including three meals, stay for a night or a relaxing week of Sundays on the beach (by advance reservation only, weekly rates negotiable), and get your heart's delight of strolling, beachcombing, headland-hiking, surfing, and snorkeling. Get to the fishing lodge, which is in the middle of the Playa Escondida beach, by turning left at the dirt road after the Naval training base. After about 100 yards turn right and head down to the lodge.

Local homeowners sometimes rent rooms during the winter season. Follow their signs, customarily posted along the ingress street before Hotel Los Arcos.

One pristine and especially recommended local scuba diving site is El Morro, the big rock island visible off the coast northwest, offshore from Papanoa town. Although no dive shop operates locally, certified divers might be able to get there with John Lorenz of the Bahía la Tortuga Fishing Lodge, or **Nautilus Divers** (in Zihuatanejo, tel. 755/554-6666, dive@dive zihuatanejo.com, www.nautilus-divers.com).

◖ PIEDRA TLALCOYUNQUE

At Km 150 (56 mi/90 km from Zihuatanejo, 94 mi/151 km from Acapulco), a signed side road heads seaward to Piedra Tlalcoyunque and the **Carabelas Restaurant** (no phone, open weekends and holidays). Find the restaurant about 1.5 miles (2.5 km) down the mostly paved road (bear right uphill before the beach parking lot). From the restaurant, feast your eyes on a grand panorama, dominated by the monumental sandstone monolith, Piedra Tlalcoyunque, towering above a wave-tossed strand, ripe for beachcombing and surf fishing. Powerful breakers with right-hand surfing breaks roll in and swish up the adjacent beach, while tide poolers poke among the snails and seaweeds in a big sheltered tide pool, under the watchful guard of the squads of pelicans roosting on the surrounding pinnacles.

For fishing, buy some bait from the net fishermen on the beach and try some casts beyond

SAVING TURTLES

Sea turtles were once common on the beaches of the Ixtapa-Zihuatanejo region. Times have changed, however. Now a determined corps of volunteers literally camps out on isolated shorelines, trying to save the turtles from extinction. This is a tricky business because their poacher opponents are invariably poor, determined, and often armed. Since turtle tracks lead right to the eggs, the trick is to get there before the poachers. The turtle-savers dig up the eggs and hatch them themselves, or bury them in secret locations where they hope the eggs will hatch unmolested. The reward – the sight of hundreds of new hatchlings returning to the sea – is worth the pain for this new generation of Mexican eco-activists.

Once featured on dozens of restaurant menus, turtle meat, soup, and eggs are now illegal commodities. Though not extinct, the Mexican Pacific's main sea turtle species –

including the green, olive ridley, hawksbill, and leatherback – have dwindled to a small fraction of their previous numbers.

Turtle activists point out that poaching is only one of the hazards that have driven sea turtles to the edge of extinction. Beach habitat loss; ingestion of floating debris, such as plastic bags and tar balls; disease; and accidental capture by trawler nets continue to take deadly tolls.

The **green turtle** *(Chelonia mydas),* the second-largest sea turtle species, is named for the color of its fat (although in Mexico it's called the *tortuga negra* or *caguama).* Officially endangered, the prolific green turtle nevertheless remains relatively numerous. Female green turtles can return to shore up to eight times during the year, depositing 500 eggs in a single season. When not mating or migrating, the vegetarian greens can be spot-

a hatchling baby turtle

© BRUCE WHIPPERMAN

green turtle

ted often in lagoons and bays, nipping at sea-weed with their beaks. Adults, usually three or four feet long and weighing 200-300 pounds, are easily identified out of water by the four big plates on either side of their shells. Green turtle meat was once prized as the main ingredient of turtle soup.

The **olive ridley** (*Lepidochelys olivacea*, locally *golfina*) turtle population, thanks to persistent government and local volunteer efforts, seems to be stabilizing at several hundred thousand worldwide. Olive ridleys (so-named for their dull green shells) nest in significant numbers at isolated Ixtapa-Zihuatanejo region beaches, notably Playa Piedra Tlalcoyunque, on the Costa Grande, and Playa Larga, east of Acapulco, and Playa Ventura, on the Costa Chica. Among the smaller of sea turtles, olive ridleys (80-100 pounds, with two-foot-long shells at maturity) come ashore to nest, customarily during summer. They lay clutches of around 80-100 eggs, which they bury with their flippers, and quickly return to the sea. They hunt most of the year near shorelines for shellfish, crabs, fish, and squid.

By contrast, the severely endangered **hawksbill** (*Eretmochelys imbricata*) has vanished from many Ixtapa-Zihuatanejo region beaches. Known locally as the *tortuga carey*

(kah-RAY), it was the source of both meat and the lovely translucent tortoiseshell that has been supplanted largely by plastic. Adult *careys*, among the smaller of sea turtles, run 2-3 feet in length and weigh 30-100 pounds. Their usually brown shells are readily identified by shingle-like overlapping scales. During late summer and fall, females come ashore to lay clutches of eggs (around 100) in the sand. *Careys*, although preferring fish, mollusks, and shellfish, will eat almost anything, including seaweed. When attacked, *careys* can be plucky fighters, inflicting bites with their eagle-sharp hawksbills.

You'll be fortunate indeed if you glimpse the rare **leatherback** (*Dermochelys coriacea*), the world's largest turtle. Experts have learned much about the leatherback (*laut* or *tortuga de cuero*) in recent years. About 100,000 female leatherbacks are thought to nest on their favorite egg-laying ground, the Mexican Pacific coast. Tales of the leatherback — of fisherfolk catching seven- or eight-foot individuals weighing nearly a ton — are legend. If you see even a small one you'll recognize it immediately by its back of leathery skin, creased with several lengthwise ridges.

hawksbill

© BRUCE WHIPPERMAN

A jagged garden of granite decorates the beach at Piedra Tlalcoyunque.

the crashing billows on the south side of the Piedra. Later, stroll through the garden of eroded-rock sea stacks on the west side.

The abandoned house on the beach marks the former headquarters of the **Campamento Playa Piedra de Tlalcoyunque,** whose mission remains, to rescue, incubate, and hatch as many turtle eggs as possible. They carry on with aplomb, patrolling, collecting, and burying turtle eggs on the beach during the summer–fall hatching (and egg-poaching) season. Although the volunteers are dedicated to their task, their vigil is a lonely one, and they welcome visitors and contributions of drinks and food.

At the Carabelas Restaurant on the bluff above, you can take in the whole breezy scene while enjoying the restaurant's catch of the day. The name Carabelas (caravels) comes from the owner's admiration of Christopher Columbus. He christened his restaurant's three petite oceanview gazebos after Columbus's three famous caravels: the *Niña,* the *Pinta,* and the *Santa María.*

For an overnight or camping stay, ask at the restaurant if it's okay to set up your tent or

park your (self-contained) RV in the restaurant lot or by the beach below the restaurant. For shower and dishwashing water, ask them if you can drop your bucket down into their well, at the bottom of the rise before the restaurant.

HOTEL RESORT VILLAS SAN LUIS

Little was spared to embellish the pretty hacienda-like corner of a big mango, papaya, and coconut grove that's home to the Hotel Resort Villas San Luis (Carretera Zihuatanejo–Acapulco, Km 142, Buenavista de Juárez, tel./fax 742/427-0282, www.villassanluis.com.mx, $50 s, $60 d, $80 d holidays). It appears as if the owner, tiring of all work and no play, built a park to entertain his friends. Now, his project blooms with lovely swimming and kiddie pools, a big *palapa* restaurant, a smooth *palapa*-housed dance floor, a small zoo, basketball and volleyball courts, and an immaculate hotel.

The hotel is ideal for a lunch/swim break and/or an overnight rest. The 40 rooms are attractively furnished and include air-conditioning, private hot-water shower baths, and parking; credit cards are accepted. If you'll be arriving on a weekend or holiday, be sure to make a reservation. Find it on the right (south) side of the highway, near Km 142, 61 miles (98 km) southeast of Zihuatanejo, 89 miles (143 km) northwest of Acapulco.

SAN LUIS DE LA LOMA

Nearby, two miles past the resort, the picturesque little market town of San Luis de la Loma (pop. 5,000) perches along its hilltop main street, which branches off Highway 200 near Km 140. Besides a number of groceries, fruit stalls, and pharmacies, San Luis has a clean, comfortable guesthouse, **Hotel Hermanos Ruiz** (tel. 742/427-0512 or 742/427-1570, $15 s, $21 d with a/c), and recommendable **Hotel Anita** (tel. 742/427-0288, $18 s, $25 d), on the highway, south side of town. Also, you'll find a post office, a *centro de salud* (health clinic), a *larga distancia,* a dentist, and doctor, general practitioner **Reynaldo Soria** (tel. 742/427-0423). Both first- and second-class buses stop and pick up passengers where the main street intersects the highway.

TECPÁN

The major service center of the central Costa Grande, Tecpán de Galeana (pop. 19,000), commonly shortened to Tecpán, is the birthplace of celebrated independence hero Hermenegildo (air-mah-nay-HEEL-doh) Galeana (1762–1814). Galeana, son of a prominent farming family, successfully operated his family's hacienda until he joined the *insurgente* independence cause in 1811 at the age of 49.

According to scholars, the town's name has two interpretations, both from the Náhuatl (Aztec language): either from *tetl* (stone) and *pan* (atop or on), meaning "atop the stone"; or from *tecutli* (lord) and *pan* (place of), meaning "place of the lord."

Orientation and Sights

Tecpán spreads along the east bank of the broad south-flowing Río Tecpán. A new super-highway bypass conducts Acapulco-bound traffic straight past the town. However, to reach

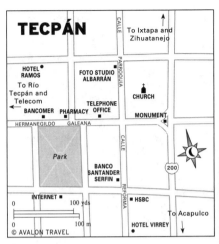

downtown Tecpán, follow the old Highway 200 route: Approaching from Zihuatanejo, before crossing the river, turn off from the bypass and continue north along old Highway 200, which curves right (east), just before crossing the river bridge, then loops to the south, continuing for two miles through the middle of town.

A modern abstract stone monument on the highway's west (right) side marks the center of town. It also marks Tecpán's main east–west street, appropriately named Hermenegildo Galeana. At the monument, turn right (west) onto Galeana; you'll first pass the church on your right, at Calle Parroquia, which crosses Galeana and continues south as Calle Reforma. After another block on Galeana, you arrive at the red-and-pink-adorned town *parque* that harmonizes cheerily with its bougainvillea floral decor.

Accommodations and Food

Tecpán has three or four modest hotels, at least two of which are recommendable. The best is the homey, family-run ◖ **Hotel Ramos** (Ana Acostada de Ramos 3, tel. 742/425-1515, hotel_ramos_tecpan@hotmail.com, $15 d in one bed, $20 d two beds, $25 d a/c). The hotel offers 32 clean, simply but comfortably decorated rooms, built in two stories around a shady parking patio on a quiet side street, one block north of the town plaza. Amenities include private hot-water baths, some rooms with TV, Internet access, and parking.

Also recommendable is the compact **Hotel Virrey** (Reforma 22, tel. 742/425-1342, $30 d fan, $40 d a/c), a block south of the HSBC bank. It offers 19 very clean, sparely but comfortably furnished rooms, all with private hot-water shower bathrooms, TV, and parking. (This hotel is very popular with business travelers; if you're arriving late, call ahead for a reservation.)

Tecpán's best restaurant is the refined Mexican ranch-style family **C Restaurant Fogata** (Campfire Restaurant; tel. 742/425-0033, 7 A.M.–11 P.M. daily, $4–10), fine for breakfast, lunch, or dinner. Find it on the old Hwy. 200 thoroughfare, about four blocks north, Zihuatanejo side, of the town center.

Services

Several service establishments are handily located within a block or two of the plaza. The *telecom* (on Galeana, 9 A.M.–3 P.M. Mon.–Fri., 9 A.M.–noon Sat.) is one block west of the plaza. The *correo* (9 A.M.–3 P.M. Mon.–Fri.) is three blocks south of the plaza. **INNCO Internet** (General Ramos, tel. 742/425-3151, 9 A.M.–10 P.M. daily) is on the south side of the plaza. **Farmacia del Centro** (tel. 742/425-2858, 9 A.M.–8 P.M. daily) is across Galeana from the plaza. To use the ATM at **HSBC bank** (tel. 742/425-2682, 9 A.M.–6 P.M. Mon.–Fri.), walk east from the plaza one block along Galeana, turn right on Reforma and continue south another block. Diagonally across Reforma from HSBC, **Banco Santander Serfín** (9 A.M.–4 P.M. Mon.–Fri.) also has an ATM. Photo supplies and services can be found at **Foto Studio Albarrán** (Calle Parroquia, tel. 742/425-2323, 9 A.M.–8 P.M. daily), across from the church.

For police or medical emergencies, dial 066, or if you're simply sick, see one of the several doctors gynecologist, internist, pediatrician, and traumatologist—available at the **Centro de Especialidades** (old Hwy. 200, tel. 742/425-0258) medical offices, downtown a few blocks

south (Acapulco direction) of the plaza. After medical office hours, go to the town 24-hour **Centro de Salud** (old Hwy. 200, tel. 742/425-0030), two blocks south of the plaza.

SAN JERÓNIMO, PLAYA PARAÍSO, AND CAMALOTE

Visit each of these little places in order to fill entirely different needs: San Jerónimo for a meal, hotel room, supplies, and essential services; Playa Paraíso for a picnic, cooling swim, breezy boat ride, and a petite, but comfortably picturesque hotel; and Camalote for seafood, boating, and tent or RV camping.

San Jerónimo

The small market town of San Jerónimo (pop. 10,000), on Highway 200, 52 miles (84 km) northwest of Acapulco, offers a modicum of services and lodging.

If you're stopping only for a meal, go to the best restaurant in town, **Fonda Santa Rosa** (Hwy. 200), about a mile (Acapulco direction) from town.

Right on the highway, find the bus station. On main ingress street Calle Progreso, a few blocks south from the highway, is the town plaza, with **Telecomunicaciones** (public telephone, money orders, and fax), at the *presidencia municipal* (with police, tel. 781/426-0980). Nearby, find a post office; pharmacy (Farmacia Pronto); a *centro de salud;* **Doctor Felipe Jesus Noguera** (Progreso 17, tel. 781/424-3007); and a pair of modest hotels, the **San Francisco** (Progreso 44, tel. 781/426-0052, guille1978@msn.com, $20 d), with cable TV and private hot-water shower baths, and the nearby **Villa del Mar** (tel. 781/426-0415, $20 d), with restaurant.

C Playa Paraíso

Formerly known as Playa Paraíso Perdido (Lost Paradise Beach), this place has now been found, and for good reason. Local folks love it for its gorgeous swimming-picnicking-camping ground and the breezy boat rides across the Río Atoyac lagoon to good seafood restaurants and a long open-ocean beach.

© BRUCE WHIPPERMAN

a sleepy afternoon at Playa Paraíso

restaurants and long open-ocean beach on the other side. Alternatively, rent a launch for fishing *huachinango* (red snapper), *róbalo* (snook), and *pez gallo* (roosterfish), or launch your own boat or kayak.

If you decide to linger, tent camping space is available at the road's boat landing, on the left beneath the palms, or better, the open-ocean beach across the estuary or Florentine's Garden Balneario.

If you want to stay overnight but lack camping gear, Playa Paraíso has smallish **Hotel Mary** (tel. 742/446-1230, cell tel. 044-781/104-0063 or 044-781/100-5685, $16 d, $20 d with a/c), oddly crowded next to the road, across the lagoon from Florentine's Garden Balneario. (This odd placement, however, allows Hotel Mary's guests to enjoy a spacious, grassy lagoon-front yard with lovely blue pool-patio.) Hotel Mary, originally designed to be a "love" hotel for couples who lack a private place to sleep together, offers two stories of 12 small but clean rooms, some with air-conditioning. Get an upper room for more light and privacy.

Camalote

Reach this lagoon-shore refuge by turning right (Acapulco-bound) 36 miles (58 km) northwest of Acapulco. Follow the signed paved access road about a half mile to the permanent country-style restaurants-campgrounds perched on the airy shoreline of the freshwater Laguna de Mitla.

This pretty spot offers easy boating, fishing, and kayaking on the broad lagoon. Some shady sites beneath lakefront trees also invite tenting and RV parking. However, you may have to start by cleaning a bit of trash from your site.

Never mind the trash: A pair of nearby private campgrounds offer cleaner choices. At the end of the lakefront Camalote road, on the left, find **Restaurant La Bahía,** with space for picnicking, tenting, RV parking, and boat and kayak launching. Even better is the more secluded ◖ **Cabaña Galápagos** (follow the signed dirt road that forks left from the paved road about a quarter-mile from highway), with

Get there via the Highway 200 turnoff signed Hacienda de Cabaña, near the Km 81 highway marker, 50 miles northwest of Acapulco (and 2 miles southeast past San Jerónimo).

Along the Road to Playa Paraíso

After about five miles (8 km) along a good paved road, arrive at family-friendly mini-resort **Florentine's Garden Balneario** (no phone, 8 A.M.–6 P.M. winter, 8 A.M.–8 P.M. summer, admission $5 adults, $2 kids), with pool, kiddie pool, hammocks, restaurant, and more. Cross over on its picturesque hanging bridge and enjoy a swim in the pool, a picnic, or an overnight (bring insect repellent) in the walk-in palm-shaded campground. Like virtually all countryside places, Florentine's Garden Balneario has no telephone and operates only on a drop-in basis.

Continue another 100 yards to the estuary-front boat landing that, on weekends and holidays, buzzes with a swarm of motorboats that whisk families ($1 pp round-trip) to the

all of the above, and the additional plus of much more space to spread out beneath shady lakefront trees. Camping charges run about $10 per day per car during weekends and holidays, free other times when they're empty.

☉ EL CARRIZAL

For something special, follow the paved turnoff, toward the beach, near the Highway 200 Km 37 marker, three miles northwest of (before) Coyuca market town. At the end of the road, you can enjoy all the pleasures of easy country beach living.

If you're on foot, hire a taxi or ride a *colectivo* from the highway. If by car, mark your odometer at the highway just before turning off. At Mile 4.1 (Km 6.6) pass through Epinarillo village, with a sprinkling of stores and a pharmacy and general store.

At Mile 4.6 (Km 7.4), arrive at the beach, a gorgeous miles-long medium-steep, golden-yellow, fine-sand shoreline with powerful, close-in breaks. Flocks of seabirds skitter along the sand, glide over the billows, and dive for fish offshore. Waves seasonally deposit shells and driftwood. The surf, although unsuitable for surfing and generally too rough for swimming, appears excellent for wading and surf fishing. Boat launching, although not impossible, appears only doable with effort in calm weather.

At the beach, you can either go right or left. Go right (west) for a miles-long breezy strand, ripe for solitary tenting or RV camping. Go left (east) for a long lineup of permanent family-friendly *palapa* restaurants and *cabaña* lodgings.

A few of the east-side beachfront establishments stand out. Immediately on your right, find inviting **Restaurant Dunas** (no phone, 8 A.M.–9 P.M. daily, $4–8) and adjacent, away from the beach, **Bungalows El Carrizal** (tel. 781/452-1869, $25 s or d, $35 s or d weekends and holidays). Owned and operated by personable Virginia Díaz, the five small, spartan but clean rooms come with hot-water showers, TV, fans, and shaded parking. Señora Díaz also runs a snack restaurant (separate from neighbor

the view from Resort and Restaurant Nautilus at El Carrizal

© BRUCE WHIPPERMAN

Restaurant Dunas) whose menu features plenty of fruit, vegetables, yogurt, and granola.

Continue east along the beachfront road a few hundred yards, passing a number of *palapas,* to the inviting and popular family-friendly beach **Resort and Restaurant Nautilus** (tel. 781/452-1933, $25 d, $50 d holidays). Managers rent about five plain but clean *cabañas* with private baths next to their large beach-view *palapa* restaurant and blue pool. Although weekdays (except Christmas, Easter, July, and August) are generally quiet here, seekers of peace and quiet on a weekend better stay elsewhere. Nevertheless, tent camping is customary for about $5 per person in the shade on the beach, right in front of the restaurant.

The Nautilus's personable owner, Amado Fajardo Colixto, takes parties of up to eight people on lagoon tours in the adjacent Laguna Coyuca. The fee of $35 per hour covers four people.

Continue east to the palmy, picturesque road's end at Mile 6.3 (Km 10.1), where boats line docks, ready to whisk visitors on lagoon wildlife-viewing and restaurant excursions. Here, lagoon-front **Hotel Paraíso Playa Azul** (tel. 781/452-2051 or 781/452-2052, www.paraisoplayaazul.com.mx, $40 d weekdays, $65 d weekends and holidays) has deluxe accommodations in a cluster of about a dozen attractively decorated rooms around an invitingly grassy pool-patio. Some rooms, however, are unfortunately dark and make little use of the beautiful lagoon-side setting. Nevertheless, they are comfortable, each with a pair of soft double beds, hot-water shower bath, small refrigerator, air-conditioning, and cable TV, A lovely shaded *palapa* sitting area, inviting pool-patio, and restaurant overlook the palm-tufted lagoon. Massages are available at an extra cost. The gorgeous open-ocean beach is only a few steps away across the road. Additional *palapa* restaurants are nearby.

PIE DE LA CUESTA

The translation of the name Pie (pee-YAY) de la Cuesta—Foot of the Hill—aptly describes this downscale resort village. Tucked around the bend a few miles northwest of Acapulco, between a broad open-ocean beach and placid Laguna Coyuca, Pie de la Cuesta appeals to those who want the excitement the big town offers and the peace and quiet that it sometimes doesn't.

Although tranquil, Pie de la Cuesta offers plenty of outdoor fun, such as mangrove-jungle boat tours, horseback riding, beach sunset-watching, hammock snoozing, water-skiing, beachcombing, boat and kayak launching, and swimming and fishing in the adjacent palm-tufted freshwater Laguna Coyuca.

Laguna Coyuca, kept full by the sweet waters of the Río Coyuca, has long been known for its fish and birdlife and tranquil shoreline. During the early 1400s, the Purépecha kings (who ruled from the Michoacán highlands) established a provincial capital near the town of Coyuca. After the Aztecs drove out the Purépecha a century later (and the Aztecs in turn were defeated by the Spanish), Pie de la

Cuesta and its beautiful Laguna Coyuca slumbered in the shadow of Acapulco.

Safety Concerns

As at all resorts, petty thievery is not unknown at Pie de la Cuesta. Keep your eyes peeled and be sure not to leave valuables such as cameras unattended, especially at the beach. It's also unwise to flash too much money in public. Some readers have reported robberies and muggings, so take reasonable precautions.

Sights

Laguna Coyuca is a large, sandy-bottomed lake, lined by palms and laced by mangrove channels. It stretches 10 miles (8 km) along the shoreline west from Pie de la Cuesta, which occupies the southeast (Acapulco) side. The barrier sandbar, wide Playa Pie de la Cuesta, separates the lagoon from the ocean. It extends a dozen miles west to the river outlet, which is open to the sea only during the rainy season. A road runs west along the beach the length of Laguna Coyuca to the tourist hamlet of Barra de Coyuca. There, *palapas* line the beach and serve seafood to busloads of Sunday visitors.

Playa Pie de la Cuesta is a seemingly endless 100-yard-wide (91-meter-wide) stretch of yellow sand. With its powerful close-in breakers, it's a fine spot for surf fishing. It's also good for beachcombing, jogging, and long sunset walks. However, its powerful (mostly March–October) open-ocean waves are unsuited for surfing and hazardous for swimming. They often break thunderously near the sand and recede with strong, turbulent undertow. Fortunately Pie de la Cuesta waves settle down to pleasantly tranquil during invitingly balmy December–February.

On the inland side, the Acapulco (east) end of Laguna Coyuca is an embarkation point for lagoon tours and the center for water-skiing and personal watercraft. Among the best equipped of the shoreline clubs that offer powerboat services is the **Restaurant and Club de Skis Tres Marias** (tel. 744/460-0013). Besides a pleasant lake-view shoreline *palapa* restaurant (9 A.M.–7 P.M. daily), it offers water-skiing

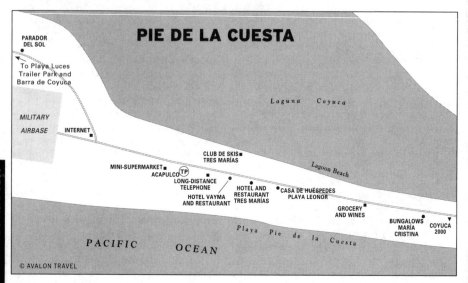

PIE DE LA CUESTA

PARADOR
DEL SOL

To Playa Luces
Trailer Park and
Barra de Coyuca

Laguna   Coyuca

MILITARY
AIRBASE   INTERNET

CLUB DE SKIS
TRES MARÍAS

Lagoon Beach

MINI-SUPERMARKET
ACAPULCO ⓉⓅ
LONG-DISTANCE
TELEPHONE   HOTEL AND   CASA DE HUÉSPEDES
HOTEL VAYMA   RESTAURANT   PLAYA LEONOR
AND RESTAURANT   TRES MARÍAS

GROCERY
AND WINES

BUNGALOWS   COYUCA
MARÍA   2000
CRISTINA

Playa   Pie   de   la   Cuesta

PACIFIC   OCEAN

© AVALON TRAVEL

($35/half-hour, $45/hr) and personal watercraft riding ($70/hr).

If you want to launch your own boat, check with the Skis Tres Marias or Acapulco Trailer park, which both have ramps. The boat traffic, which confines itself mostly to mid-lagoon, does not deter swimming in the lagoon's clear waters. Slip on your bathing suit and jump in anywhere along the sandy shoreline.

◖ Laguna Coyuca Boat Tour

Lagoon tours begin from several landings dotting the Pie de la Cuesta end of the lagoon. Half-day regular excursions (about $8 per person) push off daily around 11 A.M., noon, and 1:30 P.M. They accommodate a maximum of 10 people; make sure they stop at Isla Montosa for an hour or two. Along the way, they pass islands with trees loaded with nesting cormorants, herons, and pelicans. In mid-lake, gulls dip and sway in the breeze behind your boat while a host of storks, ducks, avocets, and a dozen other varieties paddle, preen, and forage in the water nearby. Other times, your boat passes through winding channels hung with vines and lined with curtains of great mangrove roots.

At midpoint, boat tours usually stop for

a bite to eat at **Isla Montosa.** While ashore, be sure to allow time for a stroll to restful **Restaurant Polin,** on the island's palm-shadowed south side, where you'll probably meet some descendants of the pioneer settler known simply as Esteves. As the legend goes, he arrived during the 1930s with six women with whom he founded the present colony, which now numbers about a hundred residents, all related to their illustrious ancestor. For this reason, Isla Montosa is sometimes known as the "La Isla del Hombre Con Seis Mujeres" (The Island of the Man with Six Women).

Barra de Coyuca

On another day, drive your car or ride one of the frequent *colectivo* vans that head from Pie de la Cuesta to Barra de Coyuca village at the west end of the lagoon. Along the way, you will pass some scruffy hamlets and a parade of fenced lots, some still-open meadows where horses graze while others are filled with shady gardens and big houses. Lack of drinkable water, local residents complain, is a continuing problem on this dry sandbar.

At road's end, 10 miles (8 km) west from Pie de la Cuesta, a few tourist stores and a

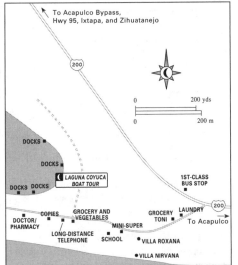

To Acapulco Bypass, Hwy 95, Ixtapa, and Zihuatanejo

200 yds

200 m

DOCKS

DOCKS

LAGUNA COYUCA BOAT TOUR

DOCKS DOCKS

1ST-CLASS BUS STOP

COPIES GROCERY AND VEGETABLES

GROCERY TONI LAUNDRY

DOCTOR/ PHARMACY

MINI-SUPER

To Acapulco

LONG-DISTANCE TELEPHONE SCHOOL

VILLA ROXANA

VILLA NIRVANA

colony of hammock-equipped beach *palapa* restaurants serve holiday crowds. Boats head for tours from the lagoon side, where patrons at the **Restaurant Dos Vistas** enjoy a double view of both beach and lagoon.

(*Note:* Mobile travelers without a lot of luggage can also continue west from here, by cross-lagoon launch to La Barra, thence to Costa Grande points west.)

Accommodations

Approximately 20 bungalows, *casas de huéspedes* (guesthouses), and hotels line Pie de la Cuesta's single beachside road. Competition keeps standards high, management sharp, and prices low. They all cluster along a mile-long strip of road, enjoying highly visible locations right on the beach. Telephone, fax, or email for reservations, especially for the winter season and holidays. Many, but not all of them, have tepid, room-temperature bathwater only and do not accept credit cards; exceptions are noted here. (*Note:* Although all hotels line the single road through Pie de la Cuesta, owners specify the road differently in the addresses they give, mostly either "Playa Pie de la Cuesta" or "Av. Fuerza Aerea.")

UNDER $50

In approximate order of increasing price, first comes **Casa de Huéspedes Playa Leonor** (63 Playa Pie de la Cuesta, tel. 744/460-0348, $45 d year-round), which is very popular with a loyal cadre of Canadian winter returnees. They enjoy camaraderie around the tables of the *palapa* restaurant that occupies the beachside end of a large parking-lot garden. The several breezy, more private, plain but clean units on the upper floor are the most popular. All 10 rooms have two beds, showers, and fans.

Tour boats await customers for a half-day trip around Laguna Coyuca.

© BRUCE WHIPPERMAN

More picturesque are the **Bungalows María Cristina** (P.O. Box 607, Acapulco, Guerrero 39300, tel. 744/460-0262, bungmacris@hot mail.com, www.bungalowsmariacristina.com, $40–120), with eight units (four rooms and four kitchenette-equipped bungalows) set between a street-side parking lot and a palmy beachside restaurant/garden. The clean, fixed-up, and painted rooms come with fans, toilets, and hot-water showers, and can accommodate up to four people. The kitchenette bungalows, most of which face the ocean, can accommodate up to five people.

The enduringly lovely **(Villa Nirvana** (302 Playa Pie de la Cuesta, tel. 744/460-1631, fax 744/460-3573, hotelvillanirvana@prodigy .net.mx, www.lavillanirvana.com, $35–80) attracts a steady stream of repeat guests. A look around and the reason becomes clear: clean, comfortable, semi-deluxe accommodations in an attractive garden beachfront compound, with beachfront pool and patio, restaurant, and parking intelligently screened beyond the tall garden wall in an adjacent lot. The 20 accommodations vary according to season and size. Personable owners Daniel Reams and Pamela Fox offer a wide range, from compact garden-view rooms, some with two beds, to airy, spacious oceanview suites accommodating up to eight people. Discounts for long-term rentals are available; holiday rates may be higher.

The adjacent **Villa Roxana** (302 Playa Pie de la Cuesta, tel. 744/460-3252 or 744/460-5147, $25–40), managed by owner Roxana and her daughter Alexis, also offers attractive choices. They have a dozen-odd, clean, comfortable rooms in two stories around a flowery garden with pool. Although they share the same lot and address with Villa Nirvana (Villa Nirvana in the back by the beach, Villa Roxana out front beside the road), they operate completely separately.

OVER $50

Pie de la Cuesta's class-act lodging is the innovative boutique **(Hotel Vayma** (378 Playa Pie de la Cuesta, tel. 744/460-2882 or 744/460-5260, fax 744/460-0697, vayma@ vayma.com.mx, www.vayma.com.mx; $85 d, $200 suites low season; $155 d, $425 suites high season). Here, guests enjoy the best of all possible rustic chic, including a grandly intimate blue pool, romantically illuminated at night with flickering torches, and 20 individually designed super-deluxe rooms, with names such as Ravel, Berlioz, Debussy, and Pause I and Pause II. Charming Afghan-born owner-manager Parwin Kojani has decorated her rooms with soft, roomy beds, exotic dark-brown hardwood accents, designer lamps, and richly tiled bathrooms. Rentals are often occupied by Parwin's friends—diplomats, entertainers, politicos, and business executives from all over Mexico and the world.

TRAILER PARKS AND CAMPING

RV-equipped Pie de la Cuesta vacationers enjoy a pair of recommendable trailer park choices. The first one to consider is the homey and popular **Acapulco Trailer Park** (P.O. Box 1, Acapulco, Guerrero 39300, tel. 744/460-0010, acatrailerpark@yahoo.com.mx, www.acapulco trailerpark.com.mx; RV $30/day, $425/mo; tent $17 low season, $22 holidays), with about 60 palm-shaded beachfront and choice lagoon-side spaces, with all hookups. A congenial atmosphere, good management, secure fence and gate, and clean restrooms and showers keep the place full most of the winter. Extras include a boat ramp, pool, store, and security guard. Get your winter reservation in early.

Playa Luces Trailer Park (tel. 744/444-4373, playaluces@hotmail.com, www.acapulco trailerpark.com, RV $22–30, tent $20) is about 2.5 miles (4 km) west out of Pie de la Cuesta village, along the Barra de Coyuca road, past the air force base. Formerly a KOA Kampground, the spacious Playa Luces, once the best equipped on the beach, is now somewhat neglected. Although most spaces (many shaded) are not right on the beach, everyone is a stone's throw from the long, silky Playa Pie de la Cuesta, fine for shells, beachcombing, and surf fishing. Facilities include a mini-store, security fence, laundry, playground, and large pool. The spaces all have hookups and are all big enough for motorhomes. They offer a 20 percent discount for monthly rentals.

Food

Most Pie de la Cuesta restaurants are beachfront *palapas* that line the Pie de la Cuesta road. One of the most reliable, especially for breakfast on the lagoon, is the lakeview *palapa* of the ◖ **Restaurant and Club de Skis Tres Marias** (375 Playa Pie de la Cuesta, tel. 744/460-0013, 9 A.M.–7 P.M. daily, $4–12). Here, you can enjoy a brunch omelette, pancakes, or eggs over easy with ham. Later, kick back and pick your favorite from their long list of super-fresh seafood entrées.

If instead you prefer an oceanfront location, you can have it right across the street at **Restaurant Tres Marias** (tel. 744/460-0178, 9 A.M.–8 P.M. daily, $4–12) with similar attentive service, good breakfasts, and seafood and Mexican plates.

Gourmet cuisine has arrived in Pie de la Cuesta at upscale **Restaurant Vayma** (tel. 744/460-5260 or 744/460-2882, 8 A.M.–11 P.M. daily, $5–17), where you can enjoy a great meal while being soothed by the murmur of the waves and the romantic flicker of tiki torches at night. A big menu lays out the finest food. For example, start with Niçoise salad, continue with super-fresh oysters Rockefeller, then either a tasty broccoli-zucchini-tomato-mozzarella pizza or a juicy rib-eye steak. Finish off with tiramisu, accompanied by a savory-smooth Graham's 10 year-old Portuguese port.

On the other hand, a few steps down the economic scale, but also recommended, especially for enjoying the cooling afternoon offshore breeze or watching the sunset, is local favorite **Coyuca 2000** (tel. 744/460-5609, 8 A.M.–10 P.M. daily, $3–6). Here, hearty snack food is the specialty, such as savory chicken *fajitas,* rich guacamole, and a load of tropical margaritas (strawberry, guava, pineapple) to choose from.

Entertainment and Events

Pie de la Cuesta's big fiesta honors the local patron, the **Virgin of Guadalupe,** with masses, processions, fireworks, and dances on December 10, 11, and 12. The fiesta's climax, de rigueur for visitors, is the mass pilgrimage regatta around the lake by boat.

The deluxe all-inclusive resort **Parador del Sol** (tel./fax 744/444-4010 or 744/444-4142, reservaciones@paradordelsol.com.mx, www .paradordelsol.com.mx, day session 9 A.M.–6 P.M.; guest membership per day $40 adult, $20 ages 4–11; overnight $55 pp low season, $130 pp holidays), about a mile west of Pie de la Cuesta village—turn right at the Barra de Coyuca fork—invites visitors to buy day and/or evening guest memberships. Guests enjoy breakfast (9–11 A.M.), lunch (noon–1 P.M.), open bar, and free use of the pools, beach club, kiddie playground, exercise gym, mini-golf course, basketball, volleyball, and tennis courts. If after a day you haven't had your fill, you might want to accept the invitation to stay overnight for all-inclusive double occupancy accommodations.

Services

Although most services are concentrated half an hour away in Acapulco, Pie de la Cuesta nevertheless provides a few essentials. For medical consultations, see either **Doctora Patricia Villalobos** or, her husband, **Doctor Luis Amados Rios** (tel. 744/460-0923) at their pharmacy where the lagoon begins, right in the middle of the village. Between them, they understand both English and French.

Alternatively, telephone **Doctora Paulina Casas Almanza** (tel. 744/444-4076)—watch for her roadside sign, a mile west of Hotel Parador del Sol, next to Playa Luces Trailer Park. Furthermore, she will come to your hotel for consultation.

Among Pie de la Cuesta's scattering of food minimarkets, **Acapulco Trailer Park mini-super** (tel. 744/460-0010, 9 A.M.–8 P.M. daily) is one of the best. Two public long-distance phones are available, one in front of the Acapulco Trailer Park and the other on the highway by the doctors' pharmacy. Internet is available at the small streetfront café on the main Pie de la Cuesta road, east end, about two blocks from the Highway 200 intersection.

For police, fire, or medical emergency, simply dial 066.

GETTING THERE AND AWAY

Pie de la Cuesta is accessible via the fork from Highway 200, near Km 10, six miles (10 km) northwest of the Acapulco old-town *zócalo* by car, taxi ($5), or local bus. The same road fork is also 144 miles (232 km), three hours by road, southeast of Zihuatanejo. Bus drivers, when asked, will customarily drop passengers at the roadside, where they can continue either on foot, by taxi, or in one of the very frequent local *colectivos*.

Acapulco

Acapulco (pop. 1.5 million), the "Queen of Mexican Beach Resorts," is still Mexico's favorite and as sunny and breezy as ever. By day, viewed either from the shore or an airy hilltop, Acapulco's golden strand curves around its picture-perfect half-moon bay. At night, myriad twinkling city lights decorate the same space, bordered below by the bay's ebony darkness and above by the starry firmament.

In Acapulco as in its latter-day metropolitan cousins, Hollywood and Las Vegas, the new, the brash, the loud, and the bright far outshine the quiet, charming side of Acapulco that few visitors know.

But despite the hullabaloo you can easily enjoy Acapulco's hidden feast of old-Mexico diversions: intimate neighborhoods around the *zócalo,* with their upcountry traditional-food restaurants, a fascinating historic fort and museum, and a fetching trove of handicrafts sold all over town.

Of course, modern Acapulco was built for people who like to party, and if you're so inclined you can sample Acapulco's best at a

the "Queen of Mexican Beach Resorts"

© BRUCE WHIPPERMAN

legion of bars, clubs, and discotheques; a shoreline nighttime bungee jump; nightclub extravaganza shows; and with the rich and famous at choice restaurants, where both the cuisine and the view—of a seeming galaxy of twinkling city lights—are equally stunning.

What's more, Acapulco offers manifold outdoor diversions, such as acquainting yourself with tropical fish either through the floor of a glass-bottomed boat or via a snorkeling or scuba diving adventure. On another day, explore the forested corners and hidden beachnooks of offshore Isla Roqueta, and maybe hike through a sylvan mountainside park, decorated by a treasury of ancient petroglyphs, and finally, at day's end, soak up the sunset vista at Hotel Los Flamingos.

PLANNING YOUR TIME

Of course even in a month of Sundays you won't be able to do everything that Acapulco offers, so you might as well save something for your next visit. But spend at least a day around the old-town *zócalo* neighborhood. Start out with breakfast at Café d'Raquel, and sit down and do some people-watching from a bench beneath the shady wild fig trees. Wander south a few blocks to **Fuerte de San Diego** and spend a couple of hours perusing its fascinating displays, climbing to its crenellated battlements to enjoy the airy bay view. On your way back be sure to stop for a half hour at the **Casa de la Máscara.** By late afternoon, it will be time to enjoy the sunset, so taxi over to **Hotel Los Flamingos** for drinks at their sunset gazebo and perhaps supper in their adjacent restaurant. Later continue by taxi on to **La Quebrada** to ooh and aah at the divers' amazingly scary exhibition.

Having hit some of the highlights, you might concentrate on your personal interests. For example, from Playa Caleta, lovers of the outdoors could take a glass-bottomed boat tour, and spend the day hiking the forested paths of **Isla Roqueta** and doing some sunning and snorkeling (bring your own gear) from the island's hidden beaches, and enjoy late lunch at super-scenic Restaurant Palao.

On another day, you might taxi uphill to **Palma Sola Archaeological Site** for a picnic and a shady mountainside stroll among the petroglyphs. On a third day, head to the east side and enjoy the spectacular mountaintop vista from **Capilla de la Paz,** followed up by a stroll around the lush, forested **Jardín Botánico** (botanical garden); or alternatively, take a scuba diving lesson from the Acapulco Scuba Center or go on a fishing trip with Fish-R-Us.

On the other hand, handicrafts shoppers could spend at least half an hour at the (cruise ship-oriented) Bonita handicrafts shop near the *zócalo,* and at least another hour at the nearby Mercado de Parrazal handicrafts market. After lunch (maybe at Sanborn's near the *zócalo*), you could taxi to the Acapulco town market to see the piñatas, then continue east for a couple of hours, browsing the handicrafts arcades and stores in mid-town.

If you want a party you can always find one in Acapulco. A good place to start out would be Restaurant El Olvido for dinner (or if you're on a budget, Restaurant El Zorrito or 100 percent Natural), then continue to the lineup of clubs and the bungee jump just east of the Diana Circle, which will probably occupy you until at least midnight. With time to spare, continue on to more clubs, such as Baby O and Nina's on the Costera, east end. And finally if the night is still young, continue to the super-disco Palladium on the far east-side Las Brisas hillside.

With another day or two you could explore some of Acapulco's country corners. For example, head northwest to Pie de la Cuesta for a boat tour of the wildlife-rich mangrove-laced **Laguna Coyuca** and its delightfully rustic mini-paradise Isla Montosa. You might linger for a day or two more in a comfortable Pie de la Cuesta beachfront hotel, such as Villa Nirvana or upscale Hotel Vayma.

ORIENTATION

In one tremendous sweep, Acapulco curves around its dazzling half-moon bay. Face the open ocean and you are looking due south.

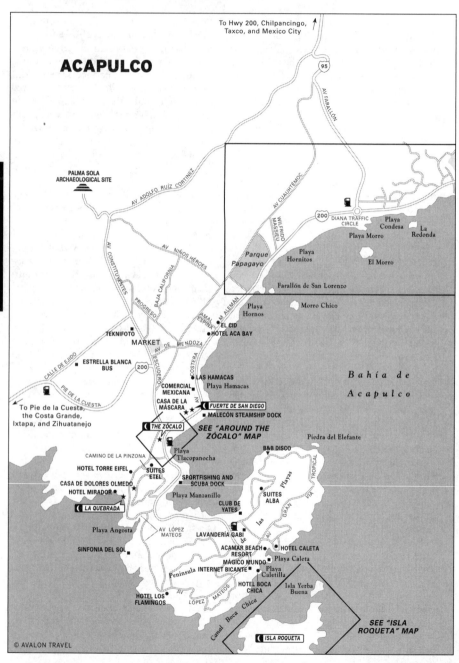

ACAPULCO

To Hwy 200, Chilpancingo, Taxco, and Mexico City

95

AV. FARALLÓN

AV. ADOLFO RUÍZ CORTINEZ

PALMA SOLA ARCHAEOLOGICAL SITE

AV. CUAUHTÉMOC

WILFRIDO MASSIEU

200

DIANA TRAFFIC CIRCLE

Playa Condesa

La Redonda

Playa Morro

AV. NIÑOS HÉROES

AV. CONSTITUYENTES

BAJA CALIFORNIA

PROGRESO

Parque Papagayo

Playa Hornitos

El Morro

Farallón de San Lorenzo

TEKNIFOTO

MARKET

AV. DE MENDOZA

AMAL ESPINA

M. ALEMÁN

Playa Hornos

Morro Chico

CALLE DE EJIDO

ESTRELLA BLANCA BUS

200

AV. ESCUDERO

EL CID

HOTEL ACA BAY

PIE DE LA CUESTA

To Pie de la Cuesta, the Costa Grande, Ixtapa, and Zihuatanejo

COSTERA

LAS HAMACAS

Playa Hamacas

Bahía de Acapulco

COMERCIAL MEXICANA

CASA DE LA MÁSCARA

★ ★ FUERTE DE SAN DIEGO

MALECÓN STEAMSHIP DOCK

THE ZÓCALO

★

SEE "AROUND THE ZÓCALO" MAP

Piedra del Elefante

CAMINO DE LA PINZONA

Playa Tlacopanocha

B&B DISCO

HOTEL TORRE EIFEL

SUITES ETEL

SPORTFISHING AND SCUBA DOCK

las Playas

VIA TROPICAL

CASA DE DOLORES OLMEDO

HOTEL MIRADOR

Playa Manzanillo

CLUB DE YATES

SUITES ALBA

LA QUEBRADA

Playa Angosta

AV. LÓPEZ MATEOS

LAVANDERÍA GABI

AV. GRAN

de las

SINFONIA DEL SOL

ACAMAR BEACH RESORT

MÁGICO MUNDO

HOTEL CALETA

Playa Caleta

Peninsula INTERNET BICANTE

Playa Caletilla

HOTEL BOCA CHICA

Isla Yerba Buena

HOTEL LOS FLAMINGOS

AV. LÓPEZ MATEOS

Canal Boca Chica

ISLA ROQUETA

SEE "ISLA ROQUETA" MAP

© AVALON TRAVEL

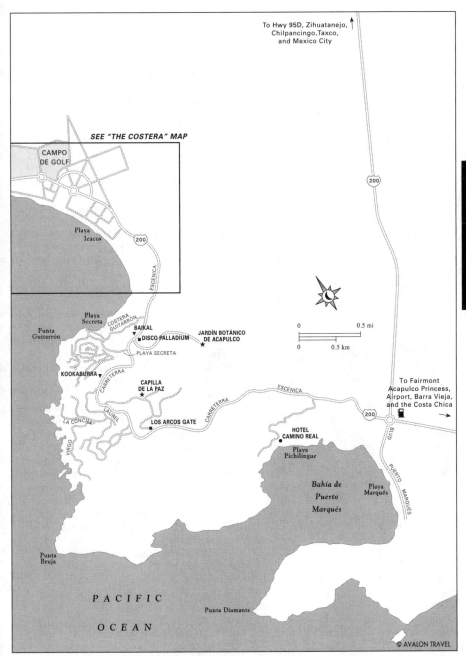

To Hwy 95D, Zihuatanejo,
Chilpancingo, Taxco,
and Mexico City

SEE "THE COSTERA" MAP

CAMPO
DE GOLF

Playa
Icacos

200

ESCENICA

Playa
Secreta

COSTERA GUITARRÓN

Punta
Guitarrón

BAIKAL

DISCO PALLADIUM

JARDÍN BOTÁNICO
DE ACAPULCO

PLAYA SECRETA

KOOKABURRA

CARRETERRA

CAPILLA
DE LA PAZ

LAUREL

LOS ARCOS GATE

CARRETERRA

ESCENICA

200

BLVD

To Fairmont
Acapulco Princess,
Airport, Barra Vieja,
and the Costa Chica

LA CONCHA

VIRGO

HOTEL
CAMINO REAL

Playa
Pichilingue

Bahía de
Puerto
Marqués

Playa
Marqués

PUERTO MARQUÉS

Punta
Bruja

0   0.5 mi

0   0.5 km

Punta Diamante

PACIFIC

OCEAN

© AVALON TRAVEL

West will be on your right hand, east on your left. (Unexpected but true, the Pacific Ocean at Acapulco lies to the south, not the west. Remember that everywhere on earth, the sun sets in the west, and then notice where the sun sets in Acapulco: not out to sea, as in San Francisco or Seattle, but in a direction approximately parallel to the shoreline.)

One continuous beachfront boulevard, appropriately named the Costera Miguel Alemán (the "Costera," for short), unites old (pre-1950) Acapulco, west of the Parque Papagayo amusement zone, with new Acapulco, the lineup of big beach hotels that stretches around the bay to the Las Brisas condo headland. There, a big cross glows at night, marking the hilltop lookout, Mirador La Capilla, above the bay's east end.

On the opposite, old-town side of Parque Papagayo, the Costera curves along the palmy, uncluttered Playas Hornos and Hamacas to the steamship dock. Here the Costera, called the *malecón* as it passes the *zócalo* (town plaza), continues to the mansion-dotted hilly jumble of Península de las Playas.

GETTING AROUND

Buses run nearly continuously along the Costera and the fare averages the equivalent of about $0.40. Bus routes—indicated by such labels as Base (BAH-say, the naval base on the east end), Centro *(zócalo)*, Caleta (the beach, at the far west end), Cine (movie theater near the beach before the *zócalo*), and Hornos (the beach near Parque Papagayo)—run along the Costera.

Taxis, on the other hand, cost $2–6 for any in-town destination. They are not metered, so agree upon the price *before* you get in. If the driver demands too much, hailing another taxi often solves the problem.

HISTORY
In the Beginning

Experts believe that Acapulco Bay, with its bounty of seafood ready for the picking, was home to bands of hunter-gatherers beginning at least 4,000 years ago. They left mute testimony in the rock paintings of their gods at Puerto Marqués, Pie de la Cuesta, and the newly opened site at Palma Sola, uphill from present-day Acapulco town. Moreover, these earliest inhabitants left direct evidence of their daily life at seaside sites: stone metates and pottery utensils that experts have dated to around 2500 B.C.

Acapulco's natural wealth eventually led to more leisure and more sophistication. At Las Sabanas, at the northern edge of the Acapulco suburb, archaeologists unearthed a trove of fetching female statuettes, reminiscent of early Polynesian and Asian artifacts. Such discoveries have added credence to widespread legends of early Chinese influences on the Mexican Pacific coast long before Columbus.

Conquest and Colonization

Enter Hernán Cortés, who in 1519 sailed in command of a small fleet west from Cuba. He didn't find the elusive passage to China, but, hearing of a grand kingdom in the mountains to the west, marched overland and boldly took the Aztec Emperor Moctezuma captive. Nearly immediately, Cortés asked Moctezuma about Mexico's southern coast and dispatched expeditions west and south, founding shipbuilding ports at Huatulco and Tehuántepec on the Oaxaca coast, and at Acapulco and Zacatula, north of Zihuatanejo.

One of the earliest of those expeditions, commanded by Juan Rodríguez de Villafuerte, landed at Acapulco Bay on the feast day of Santa Lucía in 1523. Following Spanish custom, Villafuerte christened his discovery the Bahía de Santa Lucía, a name the bay retained on maps for generations. A safe anchorage, good fresh water, and an abundance of big trees led Villafuerte to establish an outpost and shipbuilding port by the later 1520s. Word got back to the authorities, and by royal decree in 1528 "Acapulco and her land…where the ships of the south will be built…" passed directly into the hands of the Spanish Crown.

Voyages of discovery set sail from Acapulco for Peru, the Gulf of California, and Asia. None returned from across the Pacific, however, until navigator-priest Father Andrés de Urdaneta discovered the northern Pacific trade

THE LEGEND OF ACAPULCO

The *Codex Mendoza* records that, in 1499, en route south from their capital of Tenochtitlán, Aztec commanders and their armies first gazed downward at the blue sweep of Acapulco Bay. Motivated by their need for tropical treasures, such as exotic bird feathers and cacao – so valuable that cacao seeds served as the Aztecs' currency – Aztec forces tried but failed to subdue the fierce Yope tribes that ruled the Acapulco coast.

Nevertheless, the Aztec-origin name, Acapulco, from *acatl*, the Náhuatl (Aztec-language) word for reed, remained. Although translations of Acapulco vary, the meaning "place where the reeds are destroyed" appears most credible. First of all, the traditional Aztec hieroglyph for Acapulco shows a pair of hands, one of which is shown breaking a reed. Moreover,

there is the Yope legend of Acapulco that tells the story of Acatl, the son of the Aztec commander. It seems that Acatl fell hopelessly in love with Quiahuitl (kwee-ahoo-WEE-tl), the comely daughter of the Yope chieftain. When his father forbade him to marry Quiahuitl, Acatl screamed with sorrow. His tears flowed so profusely that they melted him, transforming Acatl into a pond bordered by a reed thicket. Meanwhile, Quiahuitl, vaporized by her all-consuming grief, rose to the heavens as a cloud, condemned to float aimlessly over land and sea. But the lovers nevertheless received fulfillment every year during the summer rains, when Quiahuitl would float over Acapulco and rain upon Acatl's pond, uniting the lovers with so much ardor that the downpour flattened and drowned the reeds lining the pond.

winds, which propelled him and his ship, loaded with Chinese treasure, to Acapulco in October 1565.

The Manila Galleon

From then on, for more than 250 years, a special yearly trading ship, renowned in Mexico and Spain as the Nao de China and in England as the Manila Galleon, set sail exclusively from Acapulco for Asia. Tensely anticipating the Manila galleon's return, Acapulco authorities sent ships to scan the northwestern horizon. Runners and signal fires brought the news to Acapulco and Mexico City, setting in motion a long line of Acapulco-bound traders.

The galleon's arrival sparked an annual trade fair, swelling Acapulco's population with merchants from not only all of Mexico, but from as far as Spain and Peru. Loaded down with gold-filled purses, the traders jostled to bargain for the Manila galleon's shiny trove of silks, satins, damasks, porcelain, gold, ivory, and lacquerware.

Pirates and Forts

Acapulco's yearly treasure soon attracted

marauders. In 1579, Francis Drake, during his celebrated circumnavigation of the globe, and blessed by England's Queen Elizabeth I, threatened the Spanish Pacific coast from Chile to present-day California. One of his most notorious raids was at Huatulco, in Oaxaca, on April 13, 1579, when he even stole the church bell. Drake waited fruitlessly for the Manila galleon as far north as Cape Mendocino, in present-day Northern California, before continuing west across the Pacific.

Later, corsair Thomas Cavendish managed similar mischief, burning Huatulco in 1586. He continued northwest, where, off Cabo San Lucas, Cavendish was the first to capture the Manila galleon, the *Santa Ana*. The cash booty alone, 1.2 million gold pesos, severely depressed the London gold market.

On October 11, 1614, a five-ship Dutch fleet, consisting of the *Sun, Moon, Pechelinga, Jager,* and *Meeuve,* attacked the unfortified village of Acapulco.

Such attacks pushed Viceroy Diego Fernández de Córdoba to build a fort overlooking Acapulco Bay. In 1615, he commissioned, ironically, Dutch architect Adrian Bott, who promptly completed the citadel. Christened three years later as the **Fuerte de San Diego,** it bristled with sturdy crenellated ramparts, arranged in a formidable pentagonal array. The fort limited attacks on Acapulco throughout the 16th and 17th centuries to a few unsuccessful attempts; but old age, termites, and earthquakes took their toll, and in 1776, a terrible earthquake finished the old fort off.

It was resurrected in grand style by military engineers Miguel Costanzo, who drew the plans, and Ramón Panón, who supervised and completed the construction in July 1783. Now serving as a distinguished museum, the Fuerte de San Diego, austere and grand, still proudly stands guard over Acapulco.

Independence
Scarcely a month after Miguel Hidalgo's impassioned *grito* (cry) that inspired revolt against Spain, Hidalgo's *insurgente* compatriot, José María Morelos, led a rebel regiment against the royalist garrison in Acapulco. Attracted by the Manila galleon wealth he assumed was hidden there, Morelos besieged the Fuerte de San Diego. Although he squeezed down on the fort, eventually surrounding it after a several-month siege, the royalist garrison broke out and scattered Morelos's soldiers. Consequently, the Manila galleon was able to land more or less annually until 1820, when rebel forces cut off all support from Mexico City, stopping the Manila galleon forever.

By the mid-1800s, its fine natural harbor began to turn Acapulco's fortunes around. After 1850, Acapulco became a stopover for a flotilla of steamships filled with San Francisco–bound gold-rush adventurers. Subsequently, Acapulco also served as a coaling station for British, American, and French navy steamers that were plying the Pacific in increasing numbers.

Modern Acapulco
On November 11, 1927, the Mexican government blasted through the first Mexico City–Acapulco automobile road, and the first cars began arriving (after a six-day trip, however).

The first luxury hotel, the Mirador, at La Quebrada, went up in 1933; soon airplanes began arriving.

During the late 1940s, Mexican president Miguel Alemán fell in love with Acapulco and thought everyone else should have the same opportunity. He built new boulevards, power plants, and modern Highway 95, which cut the Mexico City driving time to six hours. Investors responded with a lineup of high-rise hotels. Finally, in 1959, U.S. president Dwight Eisenhower and Mexican president Adolfo López Mateos convened their summit conference in a grand Acapulco hostelry.

Movie stars such as Elvis Presley and Lana Turner began coming, staying for weeks, and buying homes. Elizabeth Taylor married movie magnate Michael Todd in the posh Hotel Villa Vera overlooking the new Acapulco. International jet service began in 1964.

However, by the 1980s overdevelopment was beginning to tarnish Acapulco's luster. Hotels had aged; some had become rundown. Untreated sewage was beginning to pollute Acapulco's once pristine bay.

The government responded quickly to reverse Acapulco's decline. By the turn of the new millennium, Acapulco had been largely restored and was attracting new investments. Its sky was again blue, its azure waters were again clean, and it is now a magnet for more than a million foreign and domestic visitors per year.

SIGHTS
Old Acapulco
In old town, traffic slows and people return to traditional ways. Couples promenade along the *malecón* dockfront; fishing boats leave and return. While in the adjacent *zócalo* families stroll past the church, musicians play, and tourists and businesspeople sip coffee in the shade of huge banyan trees.

◖ The *Zócalo*
Start your walk beneath those *zócalo* wild fig trees (*higuera,* a cousin of banyan). Under their pendulous air roots, browse the bookstalls and relax in one of the cafés; at night, watch the

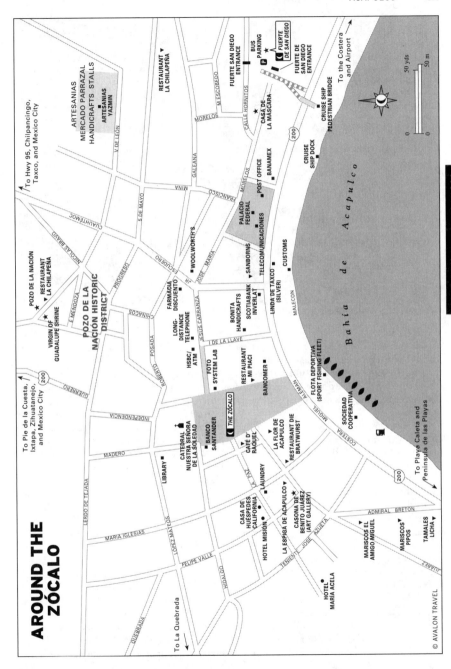

AROUND THE ZÓCALO

© AVALON TRAVEL

Our Lady of Solitude cathedral, near the Acapulco *zócalo*

clowns perform, listen to a band concert, or join in a pitch-penny game. Take a look inside the modern **Our Lady of Solitude cathedral,** constructed in 1930. Admire its angel-filled sky-blue ceiling and visit the Virgin to the right of the altar.

Outside, cross the boulevard to the *malecón* dockside; in mid-afternoon, you may see huge marlin and swordfish being hauled up from the boats.

☙ Fuerte de San Diego

Head out of the *zócalo* and left along the Costera and continue for about three blocks beneath the big pedestrian bridge to the uphill entrance stairway on the left. (Or, alternately, at the big-signalled Costera intersection, at Sanborn's, head inland a block, and turn right at Jesús Carranza, at Woolworth's. Continue uphill about three blocks to the parking lot entrance, on the right.) Continue ahead over the great moat and enter the grand Fuerte de San Diego (tel. 744/482-3828, fuertedesandiego@ prodigy.net.mx, 9 A.M.–6 P.M. Tues.–Sun.,

$5 admission), a pentagonal maze of massive walls, all topped by bristling battlements, completed by engineer Miguel Costanzo in 1783.

Inside, galleries within the original fort storerooms, barracks, chapel, and kitchen illustrate local life during the pre-Columbian era, as well as life after the conquest and colonization. The excellent, unusually graphic displays include much about pirates (such as Francis Drake, Thomas Cavendish, and John Hawkins, known as "admirals" to the English-speaking world); Spanish galleons, their history and construction; and famous visitors. One notable visitor was Japanese ambassador Hasekura Tsunenaga, who in 1613 built a ship and sailed from Sendai, Japan, to Acapulco; he continued overland to Mexico City, by sea to Spain, to the pope in Rome, and back again through Acapulco to Japan. Before you leave, be sure to visit the museum's excellent bookstore on the right after you pass the ticket booth.

Fuerte de San Diego sometimes puts on a seasonal ***espectáculo*** (sound and light show). Ask about it at the museum or at the tourist information office (tel. 744/484-4416 or 744/484-4583, or 744/484-0354, ext. 0354).

Casa de la Máscara

As you exit the Fuerte de San Diego, continue along the lane that begins just west of the museum parking lot. In half a block, you'll arrive at Casa de la Máscara (no phone, call *turismo* tel. 744/484-4416 to verify hours, pedriola240@hotmail.com, 10 A.M.–4 P.M. Tues.–Sun., free). Inside, enjoy six rooms decorated with a trove of fascinating indigenous masks, all handcrafted for the myriad traditional fiestas celebrated in towns and villages all over the state of Guerrero.

Besides the well-known examples, such as the clownish Viejitos (old ones), grinning red devils, scary jaguars, and angelic cherubs, be sure to see the masks that poke fun at the Spanish colonials, with features such as three eyes, double noses, bald heads, and big ears.

◖ La Quebrada

Head back to the *zócalo* and continue west from the front of the cathedral. After three short blocks to Avenida López Mateos, continue uphill to the La Quebrada diver's point ($2 admission), marked by the big parking lot at the hillcrest. There, Acapulco's energy focuses five times a day (at 1 P.M. and hourly 7–10 P.M.) as tense crowds watch the divers plummet more than 100 feet to the waves below. Admission is collected by the divers' cooperative. Performers average less than $100 per dive from the proceeds. The adjacent Hotel Mirador charges about a $10 cover to view the dives from its terrace.

Casa de Dolores Olmedo

Celebrated muralist and painter Diego Rivera (1886–1957), whose renown has received a boost from the latter-day fame of his second wife, Frida Kahlo, spent the last years of his life with his friend Dolores Olmedo, grand dame of Acapulco. Señora Olmedo, who herself passed away in July 2002, was perhaps the world's foremost collector of Rivera works. One of the most visible is a grand rainbow-

hued mosaic that decorates Olmedo's former home compound (Calle Inalambrica 6, best get there by taxi). The mural is visible from its quiet side street in the upscale Península de las Playas neighborhood, not far from La Quebrada. The house itself is private and not typically open to the public, although there are occasional private tours.

Palma Sola Archaeological Site

On a high hillside above Acapulco's west-side neighborhood, a trove of petroglyphs has been excavated for public viewing (approximately 9 A.M.–5 P.M. daily, $2). The site, at an elevation of about 1,200 feet, adjacent to ridgetop El Veladero ecological park, displays a number of big (3–20 feet) geometric-, animal-, and human-form petroglyphs. Created by an ancient people, known generically as "Los Yopes," the stone carvings date from between 200 B.C. and A.D. 600. Get there most easily by taxi, up Avenida Palma Sola to road's end before the hilltop, where a path leads you the last few hundred yards. Take a hat, water, and walking shoes. Local guides will most likely be available on-site.

Jardín Botánico de Acapulco and Capilla de la Paz

Tour, taxi, drive, or bus east along the Costera for a visit to one or both of these very worthwhile sights. Allow at least an hour for each, and at least three hours for the entire excursion.

Arrive in the morning by 9:30 and go first to the botanical garden (Loyola University, Av. Heróico Militar s/n, Cumbres de Llano Largo, tel./fax 744/446-5252, esalinas@acapulco botanico.org, www.acapulcobotanico.org, 9 A.M.–6 P.M. daily, $3). This extensive semi-wild tropical garden nestles in a pair of lush and intimate creek valleys adjacent to the small, new campus of Loyola University. Trails, decorated by exotic palms, cycads, heliconias, gingers, and much more, wind from the parking lot upward to the garden's visitors center, that includes a modest museum gift shop and small café.

Get there by either bus, private car, taxi, or

tour. By bus, take a "Lomas," "Barra Vieja," or "Puerto Marqués" bus heading east on the Costera. Get off the bus at Madieras Restaurant on the right. From there, either hire a taxi ($3) at the restaurant, continue by car, or hike the remaining kilometer uphill from the opposite side of the Costera boulevard (take care in crossing).

For the Capilla de la Paz, continue by bus or car along the Costera uphill. At the first left after the pink Las Brisas resort, bus travelers should hire a taxi; if by car, pass the Los Arcos gate (in view) uphill (tell the guard "Capilla de la Paz") and follow the Capilla de la Paz signs for about another half-mile uphill.

The Capilla de la Paz (Ecumenical Chapel of Peace; 11 A.M.–1:30 P.M. and 4–6 P.M. daily, free) was originally built as a memorial for Milly, the wife of Las Brisas developer Carlos Trouyet. Although the Chapel eventually became the resting place of the Trouyet family (Milly and Carlos's two sons died tragically in an airplane accident in 1967), it wasn't originally intended as such. It was to be a public chapel for meditation and reflection. The monumental 140-foot (42-meter) bronze cross beside the chapel was added in late 1970 as a memorial to his sons by Carlos, who passed away in 1971. The Capilla de la Paz is well worth the visit, if only for its grand panoramic view of Acapulco Bay.

BEACHES
Old Town Beaches

These start not far from the *zócalo*. At the foot of the Fuerte de San Diego, the sand of **Playa Hamacas** (hammocks) begins, changing to **Playa de Los Hornos** (Beach of the Ovens) and curving northeasterly a mile to a rocky shoal-line called Farallón de San Lorenzo. Hornos is the Sunday favorite of Mexican families; boats buzz beyond the very tranquil waves and retirees stroll the wide, yellow sand while vendors work the sunbathing crowd.

Playas Caleta and Caletilla

From anywhere along the Costera, hop onto one of the parade of buses marked Caleta to gemlike Playa Caleta and its twin Playa Caletilla on the far side of the hilly peninsula (named, appropriately, Península de las Playas). The gentle blue ripples at Playa Caleta in particular are fine for the little ones. Caleta and Caletilla are for people who want company. They're often crowded on weekends and holidays (but pleasantly uncrowded mid-week).

The water park **Mágico Mundo** (tel. 744/483-1215, 9 A.M.–5 P.M. daily, $4 adult, $2 child) perches on the little peninsula between the beaches. Although worn, Mágico Mundo still maintains an aquarium, restaurant, water slides, and a swimming pool, plus sea lion, piranha, and turtle shows.

◖ Isla Roqueta

An Isla Roqueta ticket tout will often try to snare you as you get off the Caleta bus. The round-trip, which runs around $3, is usually in a boat with a glass bottom, through which you can peer at the fish as they peer back from their aqua underwater world. On the other side, you can relax on sunny little

Isla Roqueta beckons across the strait from Hotel Boca Chica.

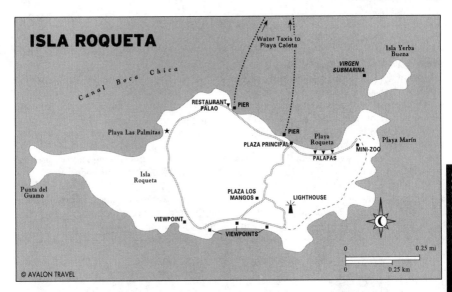

ISLA ROQUETA

Canal Boca Chica

Water Taxis to
Playa Caleta

Isla Yerba
Buena

VIRGEN
SUBMARINA

RESTAURANT
PALAO ■ PIER

Playa Las Palmitas ★

■ PIER

Playa
Roqueta

Playa Marín

PLAZA PRINCIPAL ▼ ▼ ▼
PALAPAS

MINI-ZOO

Isla
Roqueta

Punta del
Guamo

PLAZA LOS
MANGOS ■

LIGHTHOUSE

VIEWPOINT ■

VIEWPOINTS ■

0   0.25 mi
0   0.25 km

© AVALON TRAVEL

Playa Roqueta and have lunch at one of several beachside *palapas*. Sheltered Playa Roqueta is also a great snorkeling spot: Simply pull on your snorkel mask and step into the water to get up close and personal with squadrons of colorful tropical fish.

Other Isla Roqueta options include hiking the mid-island trail uphill from Playa Roqueta, a few hundred yards through the shady tropical deciduous forest, to the *faro* (lighthouse) at the island summit. The few marines who guard the place are lonely and welcome company. Say hello through the gate and they may let you in for a look around.

Afterward, you could cool off with a swimming, snorkeling, and sunning excursion at one of the island's intimate hidden beaches. For example, from the lighthouse continue uphill a few hundred yards, then fork right at the clifftop trail and stroll downhill about a mile, where you can cool off, paddling in the tide pools at **Playa Las Palmitas** at Roqueta's secluded western tip. (Bring your snorkel, mask, and sunscreen.)

A **boat tour** from Playa Caleta (from the Mágico Mundo island) is another way to get to Isla Roqueta. Glass-bottomed boats

leave several times an hour during mid-day for 90-minute tours (about $5 per person, last boat back around 5 P.M.). Trips include viewing underwater life, shoreline vistas, the Virgen Submarina (a holy image of the Virgin of Guadalupe submerged in the Isla Roqueta channel), a stop on the island, and snorkeling.

An especially relaxing spot to linger and kick back after your Isla Roqueta exertions is Polynesian-mode **Restaurant Palao** (noon–6 P.M. daily), perched invitingly above the island's west-side channel-front. If you've got an appetite, satisfy it with their melt-in-your mouth Hawaiian-style pork ribs.

Hotel Los Flamingos

After a spell exploring the delights of Playa Caleta and Isla Roqueta, be sure to stop nearby at gorgeously out-of-date Hotel Los Flamingos (from Playa Caleta, take a taxi west, uphill, along clifftop Av. López Mateos) for a meal, a refreshment in their airy view gazebo *(mirador)*, or just a look around. Former home of Johnny Weismuller, the most famous Tarzan of them all, the Hotel Los Flamingos blooms with delights, from a breathtaking clifftop ocean vista and a lusciously leafy hilltop mango garden-jungle, to a precious blue designer pool.

New Town Costera Beaches

These are the hotel-lined golden shores where affluent Mexicans and foreign visitors stay and play in the sun. They are variations on one continuous curve of sand. Beginning at the west end with **Playa Hornitos** (Little Ovens, also known as Playa Papagayo), it continues, changing names from **Playa Morro** to **Playa Villas Acapulco** (formerly Playa Condesa) and finally **Playa Icacos,** which curves and stretches to its sheltered east end past the naval base. The beaches all feature the same semi-coarse golden silica sand. Playas Hornitos and Morro are

fairly broad—200 feet-wide. The strand narrows sharply to under 100 feet at Playa Villas Acapulco, then broadens again to more than 200 feet along Playa Icacos.

The surf is mostly gentle, breaking in one- or two-foot waves near the beach and receding with moderate undertow. This makes for safe swimming within float-enclosed beachside areas, but waves generally break too near the beach for bodysurfing, boogie boarding, or surfing.

Rocky outcroppings along Playas Hornitos, Morro, and Villas Acapulco add interest and intimacy to an already beautiful shoreline. The rocks are good for tide pooling and fishing by pole-casting (or by net, as locals do) above the waves.

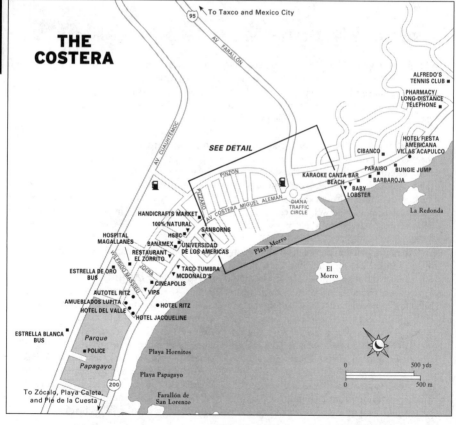

Beaches Southeast of Town

Drive, taxi ($10), or ride a bus marked Puerto Marqués or Lomas along the Costera eastward. Past the naval base entrance on the right, the road climbs the hill, passing a number of panoramic bay viewpoints. After the Las Brisas condo-hotel complex, the road curves eastward around the hill shoulder and heads downward past picture-perfect vistas of **Bahía de Puerto Marqués.**

Continue to the bottom of the hill. If you're driving, mark your odometer at the hill-bottom overpass and intersection and head straight ahead, east, toward the airport. If traveling by bus, continue via one of the Lomas buses, which head east from Acapulco about every half hour. About a mile farther, a turn-off road goes right to the Fairmont Acapulco Princess and the Pierre Marqués hotels and golf course on Playa Revolcadero.

Beach access is by side roads or by walking directly through the upscale hotel lobbies. If you come by bus, hail a taxi from the highway to the Hotel Princess door for the sake of a good entrance.

Playa Revolcadero, a broad, miles-long yellow-white strand, has the rolling open-ocean billows that Acapulco Bay doesn't. The sometimes-rough waves are generally good for boogie boarding, bodysurfing, and inter-mediate-to-advanced surfing, especially near the shoals on the northwest end. Because of

COSTA GRANDE & ACAPULCO

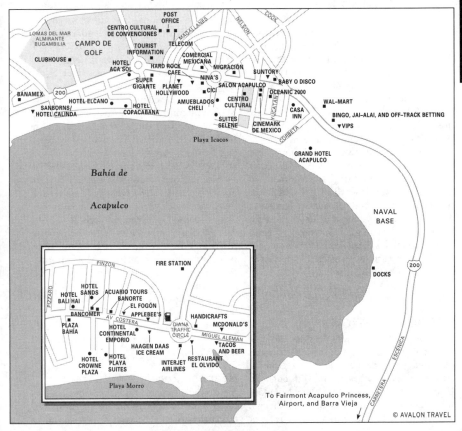

the waves and sometimes hazardous currents, the hotel provides lifeguards. The Playa Revolcadero breeze is also brisk enough for sailing and sailboarding with your own boat or board. Some rentals may be available from the hotel beach concession.

Playa Larga

About seven miles (11 km) from the hill-bottom overpass and intersection, at a monumental sculpture on the right, the road to Playa Larga forks right from the main airport road. By car, follow the fork (as do Lomas-marked buses) and soon you'll be heading east along breezy, wild Playa Larga. The wave-tossed shoreline is rich with seabirds, nesting sea turtles (summer and fall), seasonal shells, and driftwood. If you're in the mood for some exercise, bring a bike (or rent one weekends and holidays) and take advantage of the new *ciclopista* (bike path) that begins at the road fork (Km 11) and parallels the road all the way to Barra Vieja, a sleepy beach village. After that, the road continues over the broad Laguna Tres Palos, past scruffy Las Lomas village, crosses the broad Papagayo River, and finally joins with east-west Highway 200.

For the past several years a hardy group of eco-volunteers has camped and patrolled Playa Larga (Long Beach) during the summer–fall turtle season. At this writing, they were headquarted at Km 32, about 20 miles (32 km) from the fork, at their Campamento Tortuguero Playa Larga. You might stop and say a good word and perhaps donate some food or money to help them sustain their lonely vigil. Even better, set up your own tent nearby and volunteer your help recovering, incubating, and finally releasing the turtle hatchlings.

ACCOMMODATIONS

Location largely determines the price and style of Acapulco hotels. Most of the budget hotels are in old Acapulco, near the *zócalo*. None of them them are on a beach, and with only one deluxe exception (the excellent Hotel Mirador), none have wheelchair access. Nevertheless, their doors lead directly to a nearby feast of old-Mexico sights and sounds, and their prices are certainly right.

Old Acapulco does offer beachfront hotel options, however. A number of good, moderately priced beachfront hotels are available in the Península de las Playas on Playas Caleta and Caletilla. Here, guests enjoy semi-deluxe resort amenities and luscious ocean vistas.

New Acapulco hotels, by contrast, decorate the new town east-side shoreline along the Costera, either right on the beach or within a block or two of it. Guests at the fancier beachfront hostelries enjoy a wealth of resort amenities and luxury view rooms at correspondingly luxurious prices. Most have wheelchair access.

Many Acapulco lodgings, however, defy categorization. Acapulco offers numerous choices to suit individual tastes and pocketbooks. Moreover, *Acapulco occupancy is highly seasonal.* In the new-town luxury hotels, Americans and Canadians crowd in during the winter. In old Acapulco, popular with budget-conscious retirees, vacationers, and middle- and working-class Mexican families, high season is both during holidays and July and August. All hotels are full during the major Christmas–New Year's and Semana Santa (Holy Week) pre-Easter holidays, when prices approximately double. During the low seasons, you can usually save money by requesting a package *(paquete)* and four-night, weekly, or monthly discounts *(descuentos)*. For high-season lodgings, always call, email, fax, or write early for reservations; if writing, use global priority mail and allow two or three weeks for delivery. More information about the hotels listed here is often available at their websites.

Note: Addresses along Acapulco's main boulevard, Avenida Costera Miguel Alemán, do not correspond with location. Instead, numbers seem to have been mostly assigned chronologically.

Near the *Zócalo*

A number of clean, budget-to-moderately-priced hotels cluster in the colorful working-class neighborhood between the *zócalo* and La

Quebrada divers' point. Most of these hotels do not accept credit cards.

UNDER $25

Three blocks west of the *zócalo* on the quiet cul-de-sac end of Avenida La Paz stands the spartan three-story **Hotel María Acela** (Av. La Paz 19, tel. 744/482-0661; $9 s, $15 d low season; $30 s, $40 d holidays). Its family management lends a homey atmosphere more like a guesthouse than a hotel. The 21 austerely furnished fan rooms, although clean enough (but not immaculate), lack hot water. Guests enjoy a small lobby library of paperback books.

Also on quiet side street La Paz stands the good budget buy **Casa de Huéspedes California** (Av. La Paz 12, tel. 744/482-2893, $11 pp low season, $17 pp holidays). Guests enjoy about 20 plainly decorated but clean rooms in two stories surrounding a quiet, tropical inner patio.

Uphill above and south of the La Quebrada parking lot is **❰ Hotel Torre Eifel** (Inalámbrica 110, tel. 744/482-1683, fax 744/483-5727; $15 s, $25 d, $35 d with a/c low season; $35 d, $45 d with a/c holidays). Above a hillside garden overlooking the La Quebrada divers' point tourist mecca, guests enjoy 25 simply but comfortably furnished rooms, with inviting pool and patio, fans, hot water, and parking. Guests in the uppermost rooms enjoy breezy sea views and a sunset horizon. *Note:* The hotel's Inalámbrica address is misleading: You'll find it at the corner of Avenida Pinzona, one block uphill, on the right from the La Quebrada parking lot.

$25-50

Arguably the most charming of the *zócalo*-area hotels is the authentically colonial-era **❰ Hotel Misión** (Felipe Valle 12, tel. 744/482-3643, fax 744/482-2076, hotelmision@hotmail.com; $17 s, $34 d low season; $22 s, $44 d high season) at the corner of La Paz, just two blocks west of the *zócalo*. The owner, María Elena Sayago, relates the history of her hotel-home. It was a school, the Colegio Acapulco, before 1966. Prior to the 1910–1917 revolution, it housed army offices, and before that, it was a bank-like *estango* (depository) for valuables. When she began repairs several years back, her workers uncovered broken antique Chinese porcelain, most likely brought from Asia by the colonial-era Manila galleons. Now, guests enjoy 24 attractive, rustically decorated rooms in two stories around a plant-decorated patio, shaded by a spreading mango tree. Rooms come with fans, hot water, and secure parking in an adjacent fenced lot.

Five blocks west of the *zócalo,* up winding Avenida Pinzona, the **❰ Hotel Etel Suites** (Av. Pinzona 92, tel. 744/482-2240 or 744/482-2241, fax 744/483-8094, etelsuites@terra.com.mx; rooms and suites $35 s, $40 d low season, $70 holidays; kitchen apartments $80 d low season, $130 d holidays) perches on the view hillside above old Acapulco. Well-managed by friendly owner Etel Sutter Álvarez (great-granddaughter of renowned California-Swiss pioneer Johann A. Sutter) and her daughter, the three-building complex stair-steps downhill to a luxurious view garden and pool. Its airy hillside perch lends the Etel Suites a tranquil, luxurious ambience unusual in a moderately priced lodging. Chairs and sofas in a small street-level lobby invite relaxed conversation with fellow guests. The primly but thoughtfully furnished and well-maintained rooms vary from singles to multi-bedroom view apartments. The dozens of rooms and suites come with fans, air-conditioning, hot water, cable TV, some parking, and wireless Internet; credit cards are accepted. For completely furnished view apartments with kitchens discounts are negotiable for monthly rentals. (*Note:* If you arrive in Acapulco on a crowded high-season weekend as I did once, without a reservation, the Etel Suites may be the last decent place in town likely to have a room.)

OVER $100

At the cliff end of Calle Quebrada stands the *zócalo* area's only upscale hostelry, the **Hotel El Mirador Acapulco** (Plazoleta La Quebrada 74, tel. 744/483-1155, toll-free Mex. tel. 800/021-7557, fax 744/483-8800, www.elmiradoracapulco.com; $90 d standard, $160 deluxe low season; $120 d standard, $250 deluxe holidays). Acapulco's first deluxe hotel, El Mirador was built in the early 1930s. El Mirador appropriately uses the La Quebrada diver in its logo. Directly below the hotel restaurant-bar, the divers accomplish their feat to the acclaim of hundreds of spectators five times daily. The hotel has much more to recommend than spectacle, however. Guests choose from a collection of about 50 semi-detached picturesquely perched hillside lodgings. Inside, they are attractively furnished in dark masculine tones, shiny rustic floor tiles, decorator reading lamps, and deluxe bathrooms. Two airy sunset-view restaurants, bars, and three swimming pools complete the attractive picture. All rooms have cable TV, air-conditioning, and parking. Some rooms have wheelchair access.

Península de las Playas Hotels

Many of old Acapulco's mid- to high-end lodgings are spread along one continuous boulevard that winds through the plush Península de las Playas neighborhood. The boulevard starts as the Costera Miguel Alemán as it heads past the *zócalo*. A couple of miles farther southwest, the boulevard curves left as the Gran Via Tropical, rounding the Península de las Playas clockwise. Passing Playas Caleta and Caletilla, the boulevard changes to Avenida López Mateos and continues along the peninsula's sunset (southwest) side past the Hotel Los Flamingos and La Quebrada divers' point before ending back in the *zócalo* neighborhood.

Note: Playas Caleta and Caletilla are customarily crowded with local picnickers and vacationers during all holidays and most weekends, especially Sundays. If crowds pose a problem for you, it is best to stay at the Acamar Beach Resort or the Hotel Boca Chica weekdays only; or, alternatively, stay at the Hotel Los Flamingos, with more spacious grounds and panoramic views, removed from the beachfront hubbub.

$50-100

A trio of very recommendable deluxe hotels decorates the peninsula's luscious south-side oceanfront. Right on the beach stands the ◖ **Acamar Beach Resort** (Av. Costera M. Alemán 26, Fracc. Las Playas, tel. 744/482-0570 or 744/482-0571, or 744/482-0572, toll-free Mex. tel. outside Acapulco 800/719-3684, ventas@acamaracapulco.com, www.acamar acapulco.com; $65 d, $75 t with street view only, $80 d, $90 t with ocean view, kitchenette suite from $80, low season; rates double for holidays), formerly Hotel Playa Caleta. The hotel's popularity among middle-class Mexican vacationers flows from its comfortable amenities and lovely beachfront location, all at moderate prices. Above the 1950s-style but attractively renovated lobby-restaurant-bar rise six floors of 136 rooms, invitingly decorated in white stucco, with shiny marble floors, cheery tropical-bright bedspreads, polished rattan furniture, and modern-standard shower baths. Reserve an upper room (on floors 4, 5, or 6) for more quiet, light, and a gorgeous ocean view. In addition to standard rooms, there are kitchenette suites that sleep up to six people. Rates approximately double during pre-Easter week and during the Christmas–New Year's holidays. Amenities include cable TV, air-conditioning, beachfront pool-patio, restaurant, some rooms with wheelchair access, wireless Internet in lobby, and parking ($3/day); credit cards are accepted.

A mile farther west uphill, a different but equally attractive option is available at the ◖ **Hotel Los Flamingos** (Av. López Mateos s/n, Fracc. Las Playas, tel. 744/482-0690, 744/482-0691, or 744/482-0692, fax 744/483-9806, flamingoo@prodigy.net.mx, www.hotellosflamingos.com; $75 d standard, $85 d superior, $95 d junior suite, low season; respectively $80, $100, $120 in high season). Los Flamingos is the place where oldsters reminisce and youngsters find out who John Wayne, Johnny Weissmuller, and Rory Calhoun were. Personable owner-manager and musician Adolfo Santiago González enjoys playing his guitar and relating his experiences with his famous guests of yesteryear. Vintage Hollywood photos decorate the open-air lobby walls, while pathways lead through a hilltop jungle of palm, hibiscus, and spreading mangoes. The 40-odd rooms, several with private ocean-view balconies, perch on a cliffside that plummets into foaming breakers hundreds of feet below. Soft evening guitar music in an open-air sunset-view restaurant and a luxurious clifftop pool and patio complete the lovely picture. Add about $25 to room rates for an extra person. For about $300, the hotel also offers **Casa Redonda,** a secluded clifftop ocean-view house sleeping six, the former Acapulco home-away-from-home of Johnny Weissmuller (the most famous Tarzan) who died in 1984. All units come with parking, phones, and some air-conditioning; credit cards are accepted.

OVER $100

Back downhill, guests at the **Hotel Boca Chica** (Playa Caletilla s/n, tel. 744/482-7879, fax 744/482-7880, contact@hotel-bocachica.com, www.hotel-bocachica.com, from $120 d low season, $350 d holidays) enjoy an enviable beach vantage and deluxe amenities. Here, views of Playa Caletilla on one hand and the green Isla Roqueta beyond an azure channel on the other are stunning. The hotel perches on a rocky point, not actually on the beach, but invitingly close, as viewed from the hotel's garden paths. The light, beautifully renovated rooms vary; if you have the option, look at two or three before you choose. Early reservations year-round are strongly recommended. The 36 rooms come with phones, air-conditioning, cable TV, wireless Internet, parking, and some wheelchair access; credit cards are accepted.

Costera: West Side

With few exceptions, these hostelries line both beach and inland sides of the busy Costera Miguel Alemán, east of Papagayo amusement park. Hotels are nearly all either right on or just a short walk from the beach.

UNDER $50

Among the more economical is the modest 【 **Hotel del Valle** (G. Gomez Espinosa 8, tel. 744/485-8336 or 744/485-8388, andresvalle@hotmail.com, $30 s or d, with fan only; $45 s or d with a/c, low season; $50 s or d with fan only, $80 s or d with a/c, holidays) on the side street that borders the east end of the Papagayo amusement park. Two motel-style floors of clean, comfortable rooms border a small but inviting pool-patio. On a side street just a block from the beach, away from the noisy boulevard, the del Valle is a tranquil winter headquarters for retirees and youthful budget travelers. The 20 rooms come with hot-water shower baths and street-only parking.

If the Hotel del Valle is full, you might try its similarly budget-priced (but without pools) petite next-door neighbors, **Hotel Jacqueline** (tel./fax 744/485-9338, $50 s or d low season, $70 s or d holidays) and **Amueblados Lupita** (tel. 744/485-9412, $20 pp low season, $35 pp holidays).

$50-100

A trio of moderately priced hotels offer best-buy value about eight blocks (a half mile) down the Costera, east. First comes the relaxing, family-friendly 【 **Hotel Acapulco Park** (Av. Costera M. Alemán 127, tel. 744/485-5992, fax 744/485-5489, toll-free Mex. tel. 800/000-1111, hotel@parkhotel-acapulco.com, www.parkhotel-acapulco.com, $55–65 d low season) with 88 comfortable rooms, some with kitchenettes, around a tranquil palm-shaded pool garden only a short block from the beach. Inside, the rooms are clean, comfortable 1960s-style, with shiny, immaculate bathrooms, ceiling-to-floor drapes, and shiny tile floors, reading lamps, and two or three double beds. This place would be a special plus for tennis players, with its three night-lit tennis courts, tucked on the beach end. Rooms come in three categories by location: standard (looking out on the Costera boulevard, $55 d), garden (by the pool-patio-garden, $60 d) and south side (by the garden or tennis courts, closest to beach, $65 d); prices rise about 20 percent some holiday weekends and just about double during Christmas–New Year and Easter holidays. All rooms come with air-conditioning, cable TV, wireless Internet, and parking; credit cards are accepted. There's a bar but no restaurant.

Directly across the Costera, the **▐ Hotel Bali-Hai** (Av. Costera M. Alemán 186, tel. 744/485-6622 or 744/485-6336, fax 744/485-7972, toll-free Mex. tel. 800/949-6969, balihai@balihai.com.mx, www.balihai.com.mx, $65 d standad, $85 d deluxe low season, rates double for holidays) offers a bit of class at reasonable rates. The superbly maintained hotel offers 108 motel-style rooms in two floors, all enfolding a palmy interior parking-pool-patio, just two blocks from the beach. A pair of designer pools (one of them shallow and kid-friendly) furnished with a collection of chaise lounges set the relaxing tone. Furthermore, the hotel layout, set far back from the boulevard, produces a surprisingly tranquil ambience, shielded from the Costera traffic hubbub. Inside the rooms themselves, spotless marble and tile, handsome Polynesian-mode wood furniture, and modern standard baths complete the inviting picture. The only blot on this lovely portrait is that rooms often must be artificially lit, since they face outward onto the corridor and drapes must be drawn for privacy. Reserve an upper room in the rear for more quiet and privacy. Rooms come in two grades: standard is large and deluxe, sleeping up to four. Superior is larger and more deluxe, sleeping up to six. All room rates just about double during the Christmas–New Year holidays and some national holiday weekends. All rooms come with air-conditioning, cable TV, refrigerator, parking, bar, wireless Internet, and quiet, cool restaurant out front.

On the same, inland side of the Costera, just one block farther east, check out the longtime reliable **Hotel Sands** (Av. Costera M. Alemán 178, tel. 744/484-2260, direct from U.S. toll-free tel. 877/258-1615, toll-free Mex. tel. 800/712-4044, fax 744/484-1053, sands@sands.com.mx, www.sands.com.mx, $45–55 d low season, $70–90 d holidays). In addition to a pool-patio and restaurant next to the main 1960s-modern building, the hotel's spacious grounds encompass a shady green park in the rear that leads to an attractive hidden cluster of garden *cabañas*. Of the main building

rooms, the uppers are best; many have been redecorated with light, comfortable furnishings. Guests in the *cabaña* rooms, on the other hand, enjoy tasteful browns, tile decor, and big windows looking out into a leafy garden. Low-season discounts on weekdays and for longer stays may be available for the asking. All with air-conditioning, cable TV, and phones. Parking and use of squash courts are included; credit cards are accepted.

OVER $100

A mile farther east, the super-popular longtime luxury **▐ Hotel Fiesta Americana Villas Acapulco** (Av. Costera M. Alemán 1220, tel. 744/435-1600, toll-free Mex. tel. 800/696-1313 or U.S./Can. tel. 800/343-7821, fax 744/484-1645, gshfaca@posadas.com, www.fiestamericana.com, $120 d low season, $200 d holidays) presides atop its rocky shoreline perch smack in the middle of the Costera action. Boulevard traffic roars nonstop past the front door and nearby nightclubs rock (on the west side; ask for an east-side room for more peace and quiet). On winter days, ranks of middle-class American and Canadian vacationers sun on the hotel's spacious pool deck and downstairs at its *palapa*-shaded beach club. Resort facilities include multiple restaurants and bars, seasonal live music, shops, auto rental, golf nearby, and all aquatic sports. Rooms, most with private bay-view balconies, are furnished in luscious pastels, rattan, and designer lamps. Rates include cable TV, air-conditioning, phones, wireless Internet, parking, and full wheelchair access; credit cards are accepted. Low-season promotions or discounts may be available.

Costera: East Side

East of the golf course stretches the newest, shiniest part of Acapulco, where seemingly every enterprise, including Wal-Mart, McDonald's, Hooters, and Hyatt Regency, has moved during the recent past. Despite the hubbub, corners of tranquility do exist, especially among many of the high-rise hosteleries and condominiums that occupy the golden beachfront.

$50-100

A few vintage east-side remnants of Acapulco "the way it used to be" live on, seemingly oblivious to the fast-lane world around them. At the CICI water park corner, walk straight toward the beach, along Calle Cristobal Colón. Just before the beach, on the left, you'll find **(Suites Selene** (Called Cristobal Colón 175, tel./fax 744/484-2977 or 744/484-3643, suitesselene@hotmail.com; $45 d low season, $75 d holidays; $75 with kitchenette low season, $85 holidays). Here, just half a block from the beach, by a shady street's-end park, stands a complex of 24 modest apartments. Exterior amenities include a leafy garden, a blue pool and patio, and parking sensitively situated in the rear, away from the garden and apartments. Most of the somewhat worn but clean units have one bedroom, with two double beds, a living-dining room, bathroom, and a kitchenette, with stove, refrigerator, utensils and dishes, and purified water in a five-gallon *garafón* (demijohn) for cooking. The remaining six units have everything but the kitchenette. Discounts are customarily available for weekly or monthly rentals.

For a very worthy moderately priced alternative, return west a few blocks to check out the classy, compact **Hotel Aca Sol** (Av. Costera M. Alemán 53B, tel. 744/484-2700 or 744/484-0255, fax 744/484-0977, ventas@ hotelacasol.com, www.hotelacasol.com, $65 s or d low season, $135 holidays and some long weekends), just two blocks from the beach. Enter the petite but invitingly chic lobby and continue to an airy, palm-decorated rear pool-patio. To one side, an attractive small restaurant, shielded from street noise, serves guests. Upstairs, the 35 rooms in four floors enfold the interior patio. Inside, rooms are white, marbled, and squeaky clean. Guests in most rooms enjoy exterior balconies. Get a room overlooking Calle Almendro, the adjacent quiet side street. Sometimes, if you stay three nights, the fourth night is free; rates include parking, air-conditioning, cable TV, wireless Internet, and telephones. Credit cards are accepted.

OVER $100

Lovers of peace and quiet right on the beach often choose the dignified **(Hotel Elcano** (Av. Costera M. Alemán 75, tel./fax 744/435-1500, ccedeno@elcano-hotel.com, www.hotel elcano.com.mx, $110 d low season, $140 d holidays), two blocks removed—and with room balconies facing the ocean view—from the Costera traffic noise. The hotel was named after Ferdinand Magellan's navigator, Sebastián Elcano (who actually was the one who first circumnavigated the globe 1519–1522; Magellan died en route but got the credit). Hotel Elcano is austerely luxurious, hued in shades of nautical blue, from the breezy, gracefully columned lobby and the spacious turquoise beachside pool to the 180 immaculate, marble-tiled view rooms, with all luxuries included.

On the other hand, those who want a party can have it, also right on the beach, at **Hotel Copacabana** (Tabachines 2, Fracc. Club Deportivo, tel. 744/484-3260 or tel./fax 744/484-6268, toll-free Mex. tel. 800/710-9888 or U.S. tel. 800/562-0197, acapulco@ hotelcopacabana.com, www.hotelcopacabana .com, $120–160 d). Past the inviting, midsize lobby, guests enjoy a live music restaurant-bar, a beachview pool deck, and a squadron of private beachfront *palapas*. Everywhere inside, the marble, brass, and rattan are polished; the guests are mostly 20- and 30-somethings; and the mood is upbeat. Upstairs, the 18 floors of 400-plus rooms are deluxe, comfortable, marble-floored, and cheerily decorated in yellows and whites, with bamboo furniture and bedsteads. Third and fourth guests stay free; holiday rates are much higher, but always include air-conditioning, cable TV, wireless Internet, and parking. Boogie boards, kayaks, water polo, aerobics, and volleyball are available at no extra cost. Other downstairs amenities include shops, a travel agent, and a business center. Credit cards are accepted.

Towering over the Costera's east end is the 20-story high-rise former Hyatt Regency, now **Grand Hotel Acapulco** (Av. Costera M. Alemán 1, tel. 744/469-1234, toll-free Mex. tel. 800/091-2300 or U.S./Can. tel. 866/961-2774, fax 744/484-3087, reservaciones@ghacc.com, www.grandhotelacapulco.com, $100 low season, $200 holidays). Its lavish beachfront facilities include spacious gardens, a blue-lagoon swimming pool, a Tarzan-jungle waterfall, a squadron of personal beach *palapas,* restaurants, bars, seasonal live music in the lobby, shops, all aquatic sports, and tennis and golf nearby. The 690 rooms, all with private view balconies, are large and luxurious, with air-conditioning, cable TV, phones, wireless Internet, parking, and full wheelchair access; credit cards are accepted.

East Side of Town

A number of luxury hostelries spread along the Playa Revolcadero oceanfront, on the beach side of the airport road.

One of the most heavenly choices is the petite **(Villas San Vicente** (tel. 744/462-0149 or fax 744/486-6846, sanvicente_villas@prodigy.net.mx, www.villassanvicente.com.mx, $110–340 d low season), a mini-paradise with plenty of space, sweeping green lawns, and swaying palms, right on a long gorgeous strand. Seekers of peace and quiet can have it all: afternoons in splendid isolation; long walks on the beach; and a view of the sun as it sets. Guests in the five spacious, super-deluxe mini-villas enjoy two bedrooms with king-size beds, two baths, designer living-dining room, completely equipped kitchen, air-conditioning, and individual hot tubs and a small private pool. The two smaller units are more modest but still comfortable studios, with bath, kitchenette, and air-conditioning, set at the upper edge of the property, a bit farther from the beach. All residents share a lusciously inviting main pool and patio, with bar, tennis courts, and parking, all on about 10 palm-shaded beachfront acres. Rates rise by about 40 percent during holidays. Reservations (necessary for the holidays, strongly recommended other times) are available by contacting the Villas' Acapulco office (tel. 744/486-4037, fax 744/485-6846). Get to Villas San Vicente by following the airport road eastbound about seven miles (11 km) past the hill-bottom traffic interchange.

Instead of heading straight ahead to the airport, just before the big monument on the right, fork right, toward Barra Vieja. After a mile or two, you'll reach the Villas San Vicente gate, on the right.

Closer in along the airport road (only about a mile east of the hill-bottom interchange) the showplace **Hotel Fairmont Acapulco Princess** (Playa Revolcadero, tel. 744/469-1000, fax 744/469-1016, toll-free Mex. tel. 800/090-9900 or U.S./Can. tel. 866/540-4401, aca.guestservices@fairmont.com, www.fairmont.com/acapulco; $280 d garden view, $350 ocean view, low season; $320 d garden view, $400 d ocean view, holidays) provides an abundance of resort facilities (including an entire 18-hole golf course), spreading from luscious beachfront garden grounds. Although the hotel centers on a pair of grand neo-pyramids (with a total of 1,019 rooms), the impression from the rooms themselves is of super luxury; from the garden it is of Eden-like jungle tranquility—meandering pools, gurgling cascades, strutting flamingos, swaying palms—that guests seem to soak up with no trouble at all. All rooms are luxurious, with a plethora of up-to-date amenities; guests also enjoy a host of facilities, all sports, and full wheelchair access. Credit cards are accepted.

Rentals and Real Estate

The most useful Internet site for vacation rentals is **Vacation Rentals by Owner** (www.vrbo.com), which links to a broad range of individual Acapulco rentals, from moderate to expensive.

For folks less familiar with the Internet, some good rental sources can also be contacted by telephone and fax. Furthermore, some U.S. and Canadian real estate networks have Acapulco branches. One of the most active is the Century 21 local branch, **Century 21 Realty Mex** (Calle Alonso Martín 43, Fracc. Magellanes, tel. 744/485-9090, toll-free Mex. tel. 800/560-7103, fax 744/486-4187, www.century21acapulco.com.mx/rental.php) in the eastern Costera neighborhood. Although it specializes in high-end villas and condominiums, the staff also may be able to get you a moderately-priced house or villa rental (or suggest someone who can).

Finally, don't forget the two moderately priced apartment complexes: **Hotel Etel Suites** (Av. Pinzona 92, tel. 744/482-2240 or 744/482-2241, fax 744/483-8094, etelsuites@terra.com.mx; rooms and suites $35 s, $40 d low season, $70 holidays; kitchen apartments $80 d low season, $130 d holidays) and **Suites Selene** (Called Cristobal Colón 175, tel./fax 744/484-2977 or 744/484-3643, suitesselene@hotmail.com; $45 d low season, $75 d holidays; $75 with kitchenette low season, $85 holidays).

Trailer Parks and Camping

Although condos and hotels have crowded out virtually all of Acapulco's in-town trailer parks and camping sites, a few good prospects exist nearby. On Acapulco's east side, check out **Diamante Trailer Park** (Playa Diamante, Km 3, tel. 744/466-0200, www.ontheroadin/pacificcoast/pacificsouth/diamante.htm, $15), winter home for a flock of American and Canadian winter sun seekers. Here, you'll find all the basics: 90 large spaces, with all hookups, with 15 or 30 amp electricity, pool, patios, shade pavilion, telephone, pets welcome and tenting allowed, three blocks from Playa Larga (that developers have named Playa Diamante). Find it just off the airport highway, about two miles (3.5 km) east of the hill-bottom intersection. Turn right, about four blocks past the Highway 95 toll expressway junction.

Other good choices are in Pie de la Cuesta. Check out the **Acapulco Trailer Park** (P.O. Box 1, Acapulco, Guerrero 39300, tel. 744/460-0010, acatrailerpark@yahoo.com.mx, www.acapulcotrailerpark.com.mx; RV $30/day, $425/mo; tent $17 low season, $22 holidays) and the **Playa Luces Trailer Park** (tel. 744/444-4373, playaluces@hotmail.com, www.acapulcotrailerpark.com, RV $22–30, tent $20) right on the beach, six miles (9 km) by the coast highway northwest of the Acapulco *zócalo*.

FOOD
Breakfast and Quick Bites
NEAR THE *ZÓCALO*

Start off the day right at **La Flor de Acapulco** (cell tel. 044-744/421-7639, 8 A.M.–10 P.M. daily, $5–12), formerly Restaurant La Parroquia, on the upstairs balcony overlooking the *zócalo*. It's fine for breakfast, snack, or a light lunch as you soak in the scene below.

Another excellent *zócalo* breakfast option is outdoor **C Café d'Raquel** (Calle La Paz, tel. 744/483-8732, 8:30 A.M.–7 P.M. daily, except 7 A.M.–10 P.M. daily on holidays, $4–7).

Alternatively, from the *zócalo*, stroll a block to **Sanborn's** (on the Costera corner of Escudero, tel. 744/482-4095, 7:30 A.M.–11 P.M. daily, $4–16). Here, you can enjoy the cool air-conditioning and a home-style selection, including ham and eggs, hamburgers, roast beef, and apple pie.

On the other hand, **Woolworth's** (tel. 744/480-0072, 9:30 A.M.–8:30 P.M. daily, $3–12), one block from the Costera, behind Sanborn's, also offers air-conditioned ambience and similar fare at cheaper prices.

Finally, for dessert, head back over to the opposite side of the *zócalo* to **La Espiga de Acapulco** (Juárez, tel. 744/482-2699, 7 A.M.–10 P.M. daily, $1), a bakery a block west of the *zócalo* with tasty tarts and cakes.

ON THE COSTERA

Fast food in Acapulco can be found, as it can in most places, at McDonald's, with at least two branches: the original one (corner of Esclavo and Costera M. Alemán), a few blocks east of the landmark Hotel Ritz, and another farther east (on the Costera east of the Diana fountain and traffic circle). For a Mexican alterative, visit **C Taco Tumbra** (tel. 744/485-7261, 6:30 P.M.–2 A.M. Sun.–Thurs., 6:30 P.M.–4 A.M. Fri.–Sat., $2), across the adjacent street from the McDonald's on Alemán. Here, piquant aromas of barbecued chicken, pork, and beef and strains of Latin music fill the air. For a treat, order three of the delectable tacos along with a refreshing *jugo* (fruit juice) or fruit-flavored *agua*.

Diagonally across the street from Taco Tumbra, **Restaurant El Zorrito** (The Little Fox; tel. 744/485-7914 or 744/485-3744, open 24 hours daily, except 6 A.M.–1 P.M. Tues., $6–11) packs in the crowds with just about the tastiest Mexican food in town. If you're in the mood for some serious eating, fill up with a Filete Tampiqueña (beef fillet Tampico style), a *chiles rellenos* plate (enough for two), or *lomo* (roast pork loin).

Three blocks farther east, on the beach side of the boulevard, **Sanborn's** (tel. 744/485-5360, 7 A.M.–1 A.M. daily, $4–12), provides a blessedly cool, refined, and refuge from the street hustle. It's located in a building that was formerly a Denny's, but it's now thoroughly Mexican. Here, almost around the clock, you can sample an international menu of either North American favorites (eggs, pancakes, bacon, and bottomless coffee) or hearty Mexican specialties. Sanborn's also offers a rack of American magazines, such as *Time, Glamour,* and *National Geographic,* and an ATM.

Restaurants

Even though Acapulco has seemingly zillions of restaurants, only a fraction may suit your expectations. Local restaurants come and go like the Acapulco breeze, though a handful of solid longtime eateries continue, depending on a steady flow of repeat customers.

NEAR THE *ZÓCALO* AND PENÍNSULA DE LAS PLAYAS

For plain good eating and homey sidewalk atmosphere morning and night, try outdoor **Café d'Raquel** (Calle La Paz, tel. 744/483-8732, 8:30 A.M.–7 P.M. daily, except 7 A.M.–10 P.M. holidays, $4–7), a few steps off the *zócalo* corner by the churchfront. Shady umbrellas beneath a spreading green tree and many familiar favorites, from tuna salad and chili to waffles, T-bone steak, breaded shrimp, and roast pork with potatoes with gravy, attract a friendly club of Acapulco Canadian and American longtimers during the winter, and mostly local clientele in the summer, when the

menu shifts to Mexican favorites, including a bountiful afternoon *comida corrida.*

Also on the *zócalo*'s west side, two blocks farther west, **Restaurant Bratwurst** (Maria Iglesias 12, corner of Juárez, cell tel. 044-744/127-1523, noon–8 P.M. daily, $5–10) offers home-made German food (cole slaw, bratwurst, sauerbraten, roladen) like your grandma used to make (if your grandma was German). It's one in the restaurant trio, including Café d'Raquel and Tamales Licha, that comprise the budding local gourmet ghetto.

For a very popular variation on local-style cooking go a couple blocks farther west to **Tamales Licha** (Av. Costera M. Alemán 322, corner of Almirante Breton, tel. 744/482-2021, 6–11 P.M. Thurs.–Tues., $2–4). Here, appetizing south-of-the-border specialties—succulent tamales, savory *pozole,* crunchy tostadas, and tangy enchiladas—reign supreme. Portions are generous, the ambience is relaxed, and hygiene standards are impeccable.

Although the very clean, strictly local-style **Restaurant La Chilapeña** (Cinco de Mayo 36, tel. 744/482-0498, 10 A.M.–11 P.M. daily, $2–4) requires a six-block walk from the *zócalo,* it's worth it. Friendly owner Consuela Araiz de Rosario welcomes everyone to sample her Guerrero-style *antojitos,* cooked the way she learned from her mother years ago in upcountry Chilapa. It's best to organize a party so you can sample everything. Besides the tostadas, tacos, enchiladas, and *chalupas,* be sure to order the house specialty, *pozole*— which Señora Consuela claims was invented in Chilapa; see the *Origin of Pozole* wall painting—complete with its bountiful vegetable plate. Get there from the Avenida Escudero corner (at Sanborn's). Walk inland, passing Woolworth's, three blocks north to Cinco de Mayo. Turn right and walk a block and a half to Restaurant La Chilapeña on the right.

Good, reasonably priced seafood restaurants are unexpectedly hard to come by in Acapulco. An important exception is the lineup of local-style seafood eateries along Avenida Teniente Azueta, three blocks west from the *zócalo.* Situated only a block from the fishing dock, they get the freshest morsels first. Local long-timers swear by the excellence of seafood served at **((El Amigo Miguel** (corner of Juárez and Azueta, tel. 744/483-2390, 10 A.M.–9 P.M. daily, $5–15), where continuous patronage assures daily fresh shrimp; prawns; half a dozen kinds of fish, including house specialties *pescado empapelado* and *filete miguel*; and lobster.

If you prefer something a bit fancier, head a block farther from the *zócalo* to tourist favorite **Mariscos Pipos** (Almirante Breton 3, tel. 744/482-2696, noon–8 P.M. daily, $6–18). The freshest of everything is cooked and served to please. Credit cards are accepted.

Many visitors' Acapulco vacations wouldn't be complete without a dinner at the luxuriously scenic clifftop *palapa* restaurant at the **((Hotel Los Flamingos** (Av. López Mateos s/n, tel. 744/482-0690, 8 A.M.–10:30 P.M. daily, $7–15). To get there, take a taxi ($4) about a mile uphill to the west from Playa Caleta. Here all the ingredients for a memorable evening come together: attentive service, tasty seafood, chicken, and meat entrées, soothing instrumental melodies, and an airy sunset view. Credit cards are accepted. A dinner jacket is not necessary (but on breezy winter evenings a windbreaker might feel cozy).

ON THE COSTERA

Moving east to the opposite side of Acapulco Bay, first find **VIPs** (Av. Costera M. Alemán, a block past Papagayo amusement park, tel. 744/486-8574, 8 A.M.–10:30 P.M. daily, $4–12), where you can glimpse the Mexico of the future. Here, Mexican middle-class families flock to a south-of-the-border-style Denny's that beats Denny's at its own game. Inside, the air is cool and the food is tasty (but lately, a bit pricey).

On the other hand, **100% Natural** (tel. 744/485-3982, 24 hours daily, $3–6), in competition five blocks east, across the Costera from Sanborn's, offers appropriately contrasting fare: many veggie and fruit drinks (try the Conga, made of papaya, guava, watermelon, pineapple, lime, and spinach), several egg breakfasts, breads, sandwiches, tacos, and enchiladas.

Enjoy another successful culinary experiment, at the Acapulco branch of the worldwide Japanese restaurant chain **((Suntory** (east end of Av. Costera M. Alemán, tel. 744/484-8088, 2–11 P.M. daily, $8–24), located across from the Oceanic 2000 building. Although a Japanese restaurant in Mexico is as difficult to create as a Mexican restaurant in Japan, Suntory, the giant beer, whiskey, and wine producer, carries it off with aplomb. From the outside, the clean-lined wooden structure appears authentically classic Japanese, seemingly lifted right out of 18th-century Kyoto. The impression continues in the calm, cool interior, where patrons enjoy a picture-perfect tropical Zen garden, complete with lush moss, a stony brook, sago palm, and feathery festoons of bamboo. The food comes from a host of choices—vegetables, rice, fish, and meat—that chefs (who, although Mexican, soon begin to look Japanese) individually prepare for you on the grill built into your table. Credit cards are accepted.

SPLURGE RESTAURANTS

Acapulco visitors and well-to-do residents enjoy a number of fashionable, top-of-the-line restaurants, renowned for their super-scenic locations and fine cuisine. Here's a sampling of the worthy, from west to east.

Although these days it's sometimes overlooked in comparison with the trendy newest restaurants (that appear modeled on its successful example), enduring open-air terrace **((Restaurant El Olvido** (Av. Costera M. Alemán, tel. 744/481-0214 or 744/481-0256, 6 P.M.–2 A.M. daily, $10–304) remains one of Acapulco's best. The Forgotten One, as its name translates, is on the mid-Costera, rear of Plaza Marbella, beach side of the Diana Circle. What's remarkable is that such a tranquil, tropical mini-island could exist so close to the insistent hum of the Costera traffic. By day, guests enjoy a palm-tufted airy bay view and by night an ebony, star-studded sky bordered below by myriad twinkling city lights. The excellent cuisine, nevertheless, provides the main attraction. Choose from a very familiar menu with lots of pasta, meat, and fish, including a number of nouveau international specialties. Reservations, strongly recommended, are necessary on weekends and holidays.

One of Acapulco's classiest spots to be seen is restaurant **Baikal** (Carretera Escénica 22, tel. 744/446-6867, 2 P.M.–midnight Tues.–Sun., $15–40), near the beginning of the Las Brisas uphill bay-view strip, across the boulevard from landmark Palladium disco. Join the well-heeled, mostly Mexico City crowd and soak in the relaxed elegance—massive white columns, draped windows looking out on the gleaming galaxy of the Acapulco night—all to the soothing strains of live jazz. Start off with a fine overview of the entire scene, accompanied by appetizers at the upper bar, then take a main-floor table for your entrée and dessert. After such an introduction, the food may seem like an afterthought, but for an appetizer, try fresh mussels; for salad, arugula with pear; and for the entrée, salmon in honey and balsamic vinaigrette. Reservations are strongly recommended any time.

Another half-mile uphill find █ **Kookaburra** (Las Brisas hillside, tel. 744/446-6020, 6 P.M.–midnight daily, $15–40), where, among the beautiful people, you can gaze out on yet another view of Acapulco. In the cool of the evening, from afar, the heat, fumes, and congestion of the Costera give way to a curtain of twinkling lights, like a galaxy, sliced by the curving ebony line of the bay. The food (for example, start with crab cakes, continue with roast duck with mandarin sauce, finish with almond cake) simply embellishes the effect. Reservations are mandatory.

ENTERTAINMENT AND EVENTS

The old *zócalo* is the best place for strolling and people-watching. Bookstalls, vendors, band concerts, and, on weekend nights especially, pitch-penny games, mimes, and clowns are constant sources of entertainment. When you're tired of walking, take a seat at a sidewalk café, such as La Flor de Acapulco (upstairs balcony, often with evening live music) or Café d'Raquel, and let the scene pass *you* by for a change.

Nightlife

Acapulco's hottest new dance nightclub is Acapulco's "Cathedral of Salsa," the **Salon Q** (Av. Costera M. Alemán 3117, tel. 744/484-3252 or 744/481-0114, 10 P.M.–4 A.M. daily, about $34), on the east end by the Cinemark multiplex. The fun begins quietly at around 10 P.M., then the live music starts, and by midnight a platoon of folks are rocking to salsa. The climax comes with the live show at 12:45 A.M. The cover charge includes open bar.

Turn down the volume and enjoy dancing at some of the Costera hotel lobby bars. As you move east along the Costera, the best possibilities are the **Hotel Crowne Plaza** (Av. Costera M. Alemán, tel. 744/440-5555), formerly Costa Club, with a medium-volume live salsa and rock band nightly except Sunday, and the **Hotel Copacabana** (Tabachines 2, Fracc. Club Deportivo, tel. 744/484-3260), from 8 P.M. nightly. Call ahead to verify programs.

Discotheques usually monitor their entrances carefully and are consequently safe and pleasant places for a night's entertainment (provided you are either immune to the noise or bring earplugs). They open their doors around 10 P.M. and play relatively low-volume music and videos for starters until around 11 P.M., when fog descends, lights flash, and the thumping begins, continuing sometimes till dawn. Admission runs about $10 upwards to $30 or more for the tonier joints.

Acapulco's discos and music hangouts concentrate in three east-side spots. As you move east, a solid lineup of hangouts and discos occupies the Costera's beach side between the Diana Circle and the towering Hotel Fiesta Americana Villas Acapulco. During peak seasons, the dancing crowds spill on to the boulevard. Stroll along and pick out the style and volume that you like.

Of the bunch, **Dora** disco ($5 entrance fee) is the loudest, brashest, and among the most popular. The music and the lights go till dawn. Other neighboring discos, such as Beach, Baby Lobster, Karaoke Canta Bar, Barbaroja, Paraiso (that has customers when no one else does), Crazy Lobster, and Happy Lobster, while sometimes loud, are nevertheless subdued in comparison.

The must-do newcomer is **Mojita,** which is hosting increasingly big crowds, right in the middle of the action.

Rising above everything is the **Bungie Jump** (tel. 744/484-7529), where dozens of spectators get goose bumps watching one soul do his or her death-defying leap (for only $55, half price for seniors), daily until about midnight.

Another mile east, Planet Hollywood and Hard Rock Café, both of which actually serve food, signal the beginning of a second lineup on both sides of the Costera, of about a dozen live-music or disco clubs. The energy they put out trying to outdo each other with brighter lights, louder music, and larger and flashier facades is exceeded only by the frequency at which they seem to go in and out of business. More or less permanently fixed are **Planet Hollywood** (tel. 744/484-0717, noon–1 A.M. daily, bar until 2 A.M. daily, no cover), with recorded music and videos; **Hard Rock Café** (tel. 744/484-0047, live music daily noon–2 A.M., no cover); **Baby O** (tel. 744/484-7474, 10:30 P.M.–4 A.M., cover $20 women, $30 men)—"There's only one Acapulco and only one Baby O"—disco and concert hall; and **Nina's** (tel. 744/484-2400, 10 P.M.–4 A.M., cover about $20 for women, higher for men), "guaranteed fun" concert and *salsa* nightclub, across from the Acapulco Convention Center.

Reigning above all of these lesser centers of discomania is the **Palladium** (tel. 744/446-5490, www.palladium.com.mx, Tues. and Thurs.–Sat. low season, Mon.–Sat. high season, cover $20 women, $35 men), visible everywhere around the bay as the pink neon glow on the east-side Las Brisas hill. Go there, if only to look, though call for a reservation beforehand or they might not let you in. Inside, the impression is of ultramodern fantasy—a giant spaceship window facing outward on a galactic star carpet—while the music explodes, propelling you, the dancing traveler, through inner space. In the Palladium cocktails are around $10, while French champagne runs upward of $300 a bottle.

Tourist Shows

The **Salon Acapulco** (Av. Costera M. Alemán, tel. 744/484-3252 or 744/484-0114, $10 entrance fee, $25 with open bar), Acapulco's nightclub *espectáculo* performance, goes on two, three, or four days a week, in the afternoons until after midnight, depending on the season. Performances generally include a little bit of everything, from folkloric dance and rope twirling, to jugglers and glittering chorus lines. Find it on the Costera's east-end next to the Oceanic 2000 shopping center, across from Baby O disco.

Sunsets

West-side hills block Acapulco Bay's sunset horizon. Sunset connoisseurs remedy the problem by gathering at ocean-view points on the west-side Península de las Playas, such as the Sinfonia del Sol sunset amphitheater, La Quebrada, Playa Angosta, and especially the cliffside restaurant and gazebo/bar of the Hotel Los Flamingos before sunset.

Far east-side beach locations, especially at the Grand Hotel Acapulco beachfront restaurant-bar, and hillside east-end Las Brisas Scenic Highway (Carretera Escénica) bars at super-fashionable restaurants Baikal and Kookaburra also provide unobstructed sunset-viewing horizons.

Bay Cruise Parties

One popular way to enjoy the sunset and a party at the same time is via a cruise aboard the steel excursion boat *Bonanza* (tel. 744/483-1803, $30 pp, kids under 1.4 meters are half price). It leaves from its bayside dock on the Costera half a mile (toward the Península de las Playas) from the *zócalo.* Although cruise schedules vary seasonally, offerings can include mid-day (11 A.M.–2 P.M.), sunset (4:30–7 P.M.), and moonlight (10:30 P.M.–1 A.M.). Tickets are available from hotels, travel agents, or at the dock.

Bullfights

Bloody *corridas de toros* (ticket office tel. 744/483-9561, $30–40 pp) are staged every

Sunday at 5:30 P.M. seasonally, usually December–March, at the arena (here called a *frontón*) near Playa Caletilla. Avoid congestion and parking hassles by taking a taxi. Get tickets through your hotel travel desk, a travel agent, or the ticket office.

SPORTS AND RECREATION
Jai Alai and Bingo
About $10 gains you entrance to Acapulco's big jai alai *frontón* (Av. Costera M. Alemán, tel. 744/484-3195, 9 P.M.–1 A.M. Tues.–Sun.), an indoor stadium—look for the Bingo sign—on the east end of the Costera across from the Grand Hotel (formerly Hyatt Regency). Here, it's hard not to ooh and aah at the skill of players competing in the ancient Basque game of jai alai (Fri. and Sat. beginning at 9 P.M.). With a long, narrow curved basket tied to one arm, players fling a hard rubber ball, at lethal speeds, to the far end of the court, where it rebounds like a pistol shot and must be returned by an opposing player.

Water Park
CICI (short for Centro Internacional de Convivencia Infantil; Av. Costera M. Alemán, tel. 744/484-8210, 10 A.M.–6 P.M. daily, $10 adult, children under 12 free) is the biggest and best-equipped of Acapulco's water parks. An aquatic paradise for families, CICI has acres of liquid games, where you can swish along a slippery toboggan run, plummet down a towering kamikaze slide, or loll in a gentle wave pool. Other pools contain performing whales, dolphins, and sea lions. Sea mammal performances ($1.50 for adults, free for kids) occur at 2 P.M., 4 P.M., and, in season, 5:30 P.M. Patrons also enjoy a restaurant, a beach club, and much more. CICI is on the east end of the Costera between the golf course and the Hyatt Regency.

Swimming and Surfing
Acapulco Bay's oft-tranquil and invitingly clear emerald-green waters usually allow safe swimming from hotel-front beaches. The water is often too calm for surf sports, however. Nevertheless, strong waves off open-ocean **Playa Revolcadero** southeast of the city frequently give good rides. Be aware; the waves can be dangerous. The Fairmont Acapulco Princess on the beach provides lifeguards. Check with them before venturing in. Bring your own equipment; rentals may not be available.

Snorkeling and Scuba Diving
The best local snorkeling is off **Isla Roqueta.** The closest access points are by boat from the docks at Playa Caleta and Playa Tlacopanocha. Such trips usually run about $20 per person for two hours, equipment included. Snorkel trips can also be arranged through beachfront aquatics shops at hotels such as the Ritz, Crowne Plaza, Hotel Fiesta Americana Villas Acapulco, the Grand Hotel Acapulco, and at the scuba shops listed here.

Although local water clarity is often not ideal, especially during the summer–fall rainy season, Acapulco does have a few professional dive shops. A good option is the up-and-coming **Swiss Divers Association** (tel./fax 744/482-1357, info@swissdivers.com, www.swissdivers.com), headquartered at the Hotel Caleta above Playa Caleta. Their services range from beginner beach dives ($35) and two-tank dives for certified divers ($70) up to NAUI and PADI open-water certification courses (four days, $400).

Alternatively, PADI and NAUI instructor José Vasquez and his crew offer similar services and prices at **Acapulco Scuba Center** (Paseo del Pescador, tel. 744/482-9474, reserve@acapulcoscuba.com, www.acapulcoscuba.com. on) on the waterfront near the *Bonanza* tour boat dock, about half a mile west, past the old-town *zócalo*.

Sportfishing
Fishing boats line the *malecón* across the Costera from the *zócalo*. Drop by the dock after 2 P.M. to see what the boats are bringing in. In season, they might average one big marlin or sailfish apiece. At the dockside fishing cooperative office (tel. 744/482-1099, 8 A.M.–4 P.M.

© BRUCE WHIPPERMAN

Boats tied up at the dock attest to Acapulco's sportfishing renown.

daily, big boats $350–400/day, small boats $250/day) you can rent big 40-foot boats, with five or six fishing lines and accommodating eight persons, or smaller boats, with three or four lines and holding five or six passengers.

On the other hand, big-game sailfish and marlin are neither the only nor necessarily the most desirable fish in the sea. Competently captained *pangas* (outboard motor launches) can typically haul in three or four large 15- or 20-pound excellent-eating *róbalo* (snook), *huachinango* (snapper), or *atún* (tuna) in two hours just outside Acapulco Bay. Such lighter boats are rentable (offer $25 per hour) from individual fishermen on Playa Hamacas, the beach just east of the steamship dock. Best ask a Mexican friend to do the negotiating for you.

A number of well-equipped, experienced private captains routinely take fishing parties to Acapulco's rich offshore fishing grounds. Find them along the Costera, half a mile west from the *zócalo* at the dock just past the *Bonzanza* cruise ship landing. A very solid choice is **Fish-R-Us** (tel. 744/482-8282 or 744/487-8787, toll-free Mex. tel. 800/347-4787 or U.S. tel. 877/347-4787, customerservice@fish-r-us.com, www.fish-r-us.com).

Some scuba diving instructors and outfitters also offer fishing trips. One of the most highly recommended is José Vasquez of **Acapulco Scuba Center** (Paseo del Pescador, tel. 744/482-9474, reserve@acapulcoscuba .com, www.acapulcoscuba.com.on).

Marina and Boat Docking

A safe place to dock your boat is the **Club de Yates** (Av. Costera M. Alemán 215, Fracc. Las Playas, tel./fax 744/482-3859, cyates@acabtu .com.mx or gg@clubdeyatesaca.com.mx, www .clubdeyatesaca.com.mx) on the Península de las Playas's sheltered inner shoreline. The slip rate runs around $2.50 per foot per day (for up to 39 feet), and use of the ramp for launching is about $75. The many services include 110/220-volt power, pump-out, toilets, showers, restaurant, repair facilities, access to the swimming pool, and more.

Tennis and Golf

Acapulco's tennis courts are all private and nearly all at the hotels. Try the **Hotel Crowne Plaza** (Av. Costera M. Alemán, tel. 744/440-5555, $10/hr, daytime only) or **Acapulco Park** (Av. Costera M. Alemán, tel. 744/485-5437, $8/hr daytime, $15/hr nighttime), on the Costera, beach side, near the Plaza Bahía shopping center. Lessons by in-house teaching pros customarily run $20–30 an hour. The Acapulco Campo de Golf also rents tennis courts.

The Acapulco **Campo de Golf** (Av. Costera M. Alemán, tel. 744/484-0781 or 744/484-0782, 6:30 A.M.–6 P.M. daily; greens fee $45 9 holes, $65 18 holes, $25 caddy, $10 club rental), right on the mid-Costera, is open to the public on a first-come, first-serve basis.

Much more exclusive are the fairways at the **Club de Golf** (tel. 744/469-1000) of hotels Fairmont Acapulco Princess and Pierre Marqués, about five miles (8 km) past the southeast edge of town. Here, the 18-hole greens fee runs about $135 until noon (then $95 until 4 P.M. and $65 after that), including cart and shared caddy.

Walking and Jogging

The most interesting beach walking in Acapulco is along the two-mile (3-km) stretch of beach between the Hotel Fiesta Americana Villas Acapulco and the rocky point at Parque Papagayo. Avoid the midday heat by starting early for breakfast along the Costera (a good choice is Sanborn's, at Hotel Calinda, tel. 744/481-2426) and walking west along the beach with the sun to your back. You can do the reverse walk just as easily in the afternoon after about 3 P.M. from Playa Hamacas (just east of the steamship dock) after lunch on the *zócalo.*

For a relaxing forest walk, follow the trails either on **Isla Roqueta,** or at **Palma Sola Archaeological Site.**

SHOPPING
Traditional Market

Acapulco, despite its modern glitz, has a very colorful traditional market (corner of Mendoza and Constituyentes, dawn–dusk daily), which is fun for strolling through even without buying anything. Vendors arrive here with grand intentions and mounds of neon-red tomatoes, buckets of *nopales* (cactus leaves), towers of toilet paper, and mountains of soap bars. Don't miss **Piñatas Uva,** one of the market's most colorful shops. The market is a quarter-mile inland from Playa de los Hornos. Ride a Mercado-marked bus or hire a taxi to get there.

Handicrafts

Despite steep competition, asking prices for Acapulco handicrafts are relatively high. Nevertheless, some sources are worth checking out. Near the *zócalo,* try **Bonita** (in the basement of the big old Edificio Oviedo, at I. de la Llave and Costera M. Alemán, tel. 744/482-0590 or 744/482-5240, 9 A.M.–7 P.M. daily), with an eclectic feast of handmade Mexican finery. Here you may see artisans adding to the acre of gleaming silver, gold, copper, brass, fine carving, and lacquerware around you.

For a treat while you're still near the *zócalo,* from Sanborn's walk directly across the Costera to class-act **Linda de Taxco** (adjacent to the cruise ship terminal, tel. 744/483-3347), a silver shop that amounts to a sight all by itself. Their amazingly huge solid-silver pieces, ranging from elephants and hippos to giant crucifixes and noble new-age gods and goddesses, are worth a visit even without buying.

Still another bountiful handicrafts source not far from the *zócalo* is the artisans' market **Mercado de Parrazal.** From Sanborn's, head away from the Costera a few short blocks to Vasquez de León and turn right one block. There, a big shady plaza of semi-permanent stalls offers a galaxy of Mexican handicrafts. Sharp bargaining is necessary, however, to cut the asking prices down to size. The best store in the Parrazal market is **Yazmin** (9 A.M.–6 P.M. daily), in the middle of the complex. Yazmin has an unusual collection of many one-of-a-kind jewelry, ceramics, and woodwork examples.

On the new-town east side a number of handicrafts shopping centers line the Costera.

Check out the pair of handicrafts arcades, **Dalia** and **Pueblito,** across the Costera from the Plaza Bahía shopping mall (just west of the Hotel Crowne Plaza). Stalls along shady interior walkways display a host of moderately priced leather, silver, hand-embroidered dresses, *huipiles,* bedspreads, napkins, ceramics, glass, stoneware, and much more.

For a grand selection of largely inexpensive, but still attractive, native-made handicrafts, go to the large indigenous **mercado de artesanías** warren of stalls, on the mid-Costera, just east of the Diana Circle, inland side.

INFORMATION AND SERVICES
Tourist Information and Travel Agents

An easily accessible local tourist information office is the *modulo* (tel. 744/484-4416, 9 A.M.–10 P.M. daily), in front of the convention center, two blocks east of the golf course. Here, workers staff a small crafts shop and money exchange office.

Although American Express is not among them, Acapulco does have some travel agents. Either start at your hotel travel desk, or contact **Acuario Tours** (Av. Costera M. Alemán 186 #3, tel. 744/469-6100, fax 744/485-7100, www.acuariotours.com, 8 A.M.–9 P.M. Mon.–Sat.) in the mid-Costera, across from the Hotel Crowne Plaza.

Publications

The best new-book sources in town are the three branches of **Sanborn's:** As you move west to east, you'll find the *zócalo* branch (on the Costera across from the steamship dock, tel. 744/482-4093, 7 A.M.–11 P.M. daily); mid-Costera branch (at the Hotel Calinda, tel. 744/482-2426); and east-Costera branch (on the ground floor of the Oceanic 2000 shopping plaza, tel. 744/484-2035).

English-language newspapers, such as the *News* from Mexico City and *USA Today,* are often available in the large hotel bookshops, especially at the Hotel Fiesta Americana Villas Acapulco. In old town, newsstands at the *zócalo*'s inland corner (to the right of the churchfront) regularly sell the *News.*

Money Exchange

In the *zócalo* neighborhood, **HSBC Bank** (Jesús Carranza 8, tel. 744/483-5722, 9 A.M.–5 P.M. Mon.–Fri., 9 A.M.–3 P.M. Sat.), with ATM, is the best option. It is on the one-block side street tucked at the *zócalo*'s northeast corner (right side, facing church). Also, nearby, on the Costera, a block east of the *zócalo,* try **Bancomer** (tel. 744/482-2097 or 744/480-1277, 9 A.M.–4 P.M. Mon.–Fri., 10 A.M.–3 P.M. Sat.), with ATM.

On the new side of town, also change money at **HSBC** (across the Costera from the golf course, tel. 744/485-8727, 9 A.M.–5 P.M. Mon.–Fri., 9 A.M.–3 P.M. Sat.); or at **Bancomer** (a few blocks west of the Diana Circle, tel. 744/484-4065 or 744/484-4848, 8:30 A.M.–4 P.M. Mon.–Fri.).

After normal bank hours, change traveler's checks at **Cibanco** money exchange (tel. 744/484-3108, 9 A.M.–7 P.M. Mon.–Sat.), across the street and a block west from the Hotel Fiesta Americana Villas Acapulco.

Communications

The Acapulco main *correo* (post office; in the Palacio Federal, tel. 744/483-2405, 9 A.M.–6 P.M. Mon.–Fri., 9 A.M.–3:30 P.M. Sat.) is across the Costera from the cruise ship dock, three blocks east from the *zócalo.* In the same building, the main **Telecomunicaciones** (tel. 744/482-2622 or 744/482-0103, 8 A.M.–6 P.M. Mon.–Fri., 9 A.M.–noon Sat.–Sun.) provides money orders, telegrams, and fax services.

There is also a joint **post and telegraph office** (Cuauhtémoc and Massieu, tel. 744/486-7952, 8 A.M.–5 P.M. Mon.–Fri., 9 A.M.–noon Sat.) on the outside upstairs walkway on the west side of the Estrella de Oro bus terminal building.

For the lowest telephone rates, use the widely available Ladatel cards in the many public street telephones. First dial 001 for long distance to the United States and Canada or 01 for Mexico. Otherwise, near the *zócalo,* you can call *larga distancia* (long distance) from the small office next to the HSBC bank (Jesús Carranza at Calle de la Llave, 8 A.M.–9 P.M. daily).

Connect to the Internet at one of the many streetfront stores scattered along the Costera and around the *zócalo*. For example, go to **Foto System Lab** (on the *zócalo*, tel. 744/482-2112, 9 A.M.–10 P.M. daily). Find it at the inland corner of the *zócalo*, on the right side as you face the church.

Health and Emergencies

If you get sick, ask your hotel to call a doctor for you or contact the **Hospital Magellanes** (W. Massieu 2, corner of Colón, tel. 744/469-0270 or 744/485-6544), one of Acapulco's most respected private hospitals, for both office visits and round-the-clock emergencies. Get there from the mid-Costera (at the Hotel Ritz) by going one block directly inland along Massieu. Facilities include a lab, 24-hour pharmacy, and an emergency room with many specialists on call.

A group of American-trained IAMAT (International Association for Medical Assistance to Travelers) physicians offers (24-hour day and night) medical consultations in English. Contact them at the **medical department** (tel. 744/469-1000, ext. 1309) of the Hotel Fairmont Acapulco Princess.

For routine medications near the *zócalo*, go to one of many pharmacies, such as at **Sanborn's** (corner of Escudero and the Costera, tel. 744/482-6167) or the big **Farmacia Discuento** (at Escudero and Jesús Carranza, tel. 744/482-3552, 8 A.M.–10 P.M. daily), across Escudero from Woolworth's.

For police emergencies, contact one of the many tourist police along Costera, or taxi to the **tourist police headquarters** (across Av. Cuauhtémoc from the Estrella Blanca (Papagayo) bus station, tel. 744/485-0490).

Immigration

If you lose your tourist card go to **Migración** (tel. 744/466-9025, 9 A.M.–1 P.M. daily) either at the airport at least three hours prior to your departure or on the Costera (tel. 744/435-

0102, 9 A.M.–1 P.M. Mon.–Fri.), across the side street from Comercial Mexicana. Bring your passport and some proof (such as your stamped passport, airline ticket, or a copy of your lost tourist card) of your arrival date in Mexico.

Consulates

Acapulco has a number of resident consular agents. For Americans, there is the office of Alexander Richards, the **U.S. consular officer** (in the Hotel Continental Emporio, tel. 744/481-1699 or 744/481-0100, fax 744/484-0300, consular@prodigy.net.mx, 9 A.M.–2 P.M. Mon.–Fri.). In genuine emergencies only, contact him at tel. 744/431-0094.

Canadians should contact the **Canadian consul** (at the Centro Comercial Marbella, suite 23, tel. 744/484-1305, fax 744/484-1306 or 744/481-1349, acapulco@canada.org.mx, 9:30 A.M.–12:30 P.M. Mon.–Fri.) for assistance. After hours, in an emergency, call tel. 800/706-2900.

For the **British consul,** check with the Canadian consul. Germans can contact the **German consul** (Antone de Alamino 26, tel. 744/484-1860, fax 744/484-3810).

For additional information and other consulates, see the local telephone directory yellow pages, under "Embajadas y Consulados."

Supermarkets and Department Stores

In the *zócalo* area behind Sanborn's, **Woolworth's** (on Escudero, corner of Morelos, tel. 744/480-0072, 9:30 A.M.–9 P.M. daily) is a good source for a little bit of everything at reasonable prices.

Comercial Mexicana, with at least two Acapulco branches, is a big Mexican Kmart, with everything, plus groceries and a bakery. Find one branch (tel. 744/483-5449, 8 A.M.–11 P.M. daily) on the Costera, across from Playa Hamacas, just east of the Fuerte de San Diego; and on the far east side, the second branch (tel. 744/484-3373, 24 hours daily) is across the Costera from CICI water park.

Alternatively, go to the huge **Walmart** (tel.

744/469-0203, 24 hours daily) at the far east end, across from the Grand Hotel Acapulco.

Photography

The best photo equipment and repair shop in town is **Teknifoto** (Constituyentes 245, tel. 744/483-8316 or 744/482-4741, 10 A.M.–2 P.M. and 4–7 P.M. Mon.–Fri., 10 A.M.–2 P.M. Sat.) near the fire station (bomberos), about half a mile northeast of the zócalo.

For basic camera equipment and services (and Internet access) go to **Foto System Lab** (tel. 744/482-2112, 9 A.M.–10 P.M. daily), on the zócalo's inland corner, the right-hand side as you face the churchfront.

GETTING THERE AND AWAY
By Air

Several airlines connect the **Acapulco airport** (code-designated ACA, officially the Juan N. Álvarez International Airport) with U.S. and Mexican destinations.

Aeroméxico (reservations tel. 744/485-1625 or 744/485-1600, flight information tel. 744/466-9296 or 744/466-9104) and associated Aerolitoral flights connect directly with Mexico City.

Continental Airlines (reservations toll-free Mex. tel. 800/900-5000, flight information tel. 744/466-9063) flights connect with Houston.

Volaris Airlines (tel. 800/122-8000, www.volaris.com.mx) flights connect directly with Tijuana.

Interjet Airlines (tel. 800/322-5050 or 800/011-2345, www.interjet.com.mx) connect directly with Mexico City.

American Airlines (reservations toll-free Mex. tel. 800/904-6000, flight information tel. 744/466-9227) flights connect with Dallas and Chicago during the winter season.

Delta Air Lines (reservations toll-free Mex. tel. 800/902-2100) Aéromexico affiliate charter flights connect with Atlanta during the winter-spring season.

AIR ARRIVAL AND DEPARTURE

After the usually quick immigration and customs checks, Acapulco arrivees can access airport car rentals, efficient transportation for the 15-mile (24-km) trip to town, a magazine and book stand, and ATMs.

Airport car rental booths often open for arriving flights include **Hertz** (tel./fax 744/485-8947 or 744/466-9172); **Avis** (tel. 744/466-9190 or 744/462-0085); **Alamo** (tel. 744/466-9444 or 744/484-3305); and **Budget** (tel. 744/481-2433 or 744/466-9003). You can ensure availability and often save money by bargaining for a reservation with the agencies via their toll-free 800 numbers before you leave home.

Buy tickets for **ground transport** from agents near the exit, by the terminal's far left side. Options include collective GMC Suburban station wagons (about $8 per person) that deposit passengers at individual hotels. There are also compact four-passenger taxis especiales ($20–40, depending on distance). GMC Suburbans can also be hired "especial" ($30–50 for up to seven passengers).

On your departure day, save money by sharing a taxi with fellow departees. Don't get into the taxi until you settle the fare. Having already arrived, you know what the airport ride should cost. If the driver insists on greed, hail another taxi.

If you lost your tourist permit, either go to Migración in town (on the Costera, across the side street from Comercial Mexicana, tel. 744/435-0102, 9 A.M.–1 P.M. Mon.–Fri.) before your departure date, or arrive at the airport three hours early to iron out the problem with Migración officials (tel. 744/466-9025, 9 A.M.–1 P.M. daily). Bring your passport and some proof of your date of arrival—either a stamped passport, airline ticket copy, or a copy of your lost tourist permit.

The Acapulco air terminal building has a number of shops for last-minute handicrafts purchases, a buzón (mailbox), public telephones, and upstairs, good restaurant wings.

By Bus

Major competitors Estrella Blanca and Estrella de Oro operate three separate long-distance *centrales de autobús* (central bus terminals), one Estrella Blanca (the Ejido) station on the west side and two (both Estrella Blanca and Estrella de Oro) stations on the east side of town.

Estrella Blanca (tel. 744/483-2713) coordinates the service of its subsidiary lines Elite, Flecha Roja, Autotransportes Cuauhtémoc, Turistar, and Futura at two separate terminals. Credit cards are accepted. Most first- or luxury-class departures use the immaculate westside **Ejido terminal** (Av. Ejido 47). Facilities include left-luggage lockers, food stands across the street, a hotel booking agency, and Ladatel card-operated public telephones.

Scores of *salidas locales* (local departures) buses connect with destinations in three directions: northern interior, Costa Grande (northwest), and Costa Chica (southeast) coastal destinations. Key northern interior connections include Mexico City (dozens daily, some via Iguala and Taxco), Toluca, Morelia via Chilpancingo and Altamirano (six daily), and Guadalajara (three daily).

Many first-class (about 10 per day) and second-class (hourly daytime) departures connect northwest with Costa Grande destinations of Ixtapa-Zihuatanejo and Lázaro Cárdenas. Southeast Costa Chica connections with Puerto Escondido, some continuing to Huatulco and Salina Cruz, include four first-class daily (one via Ometepec) and several second-class connections per day.

Also from the same Estrella Blanca terminal, one or two daily departures connect with the U.S. border (Mexicali and Tijuana) via the entire Pacific coast route, through Ixtapa-Zihuatanejo, Manzanillo, Puerto Vallarta, and Mazatlán. Other departures connect with the U.S. border at Ciudad Juárez, via San Luis Potosí, Zacatecas, Torreón, and Chihuahua.

Many additional first- and luxury-class buses depart from Estrella Blanca's separate west-side big **Papagayo terminal** (Av. Cuauhtémoc 1605, tel. 744/485-3429). Facilities and services include an air-conditioned waiting room, left-luggage service, a snack bar, and hotel reservations. From the Papagayo terminal, luxury-class and first-class buses connect with northeast Mexico and the U.S. border, via Querétaro, San Luis Potosí, Monterrey, and Nuevo Laredo. Other departures connect northwest, with Guadalajara, León, Celaya, and Irapuato; and north, with Puebla and Mexico City bus stations Norte and Sur; and northwest, with Zihuatanejo.

About five blocks east of the Estrella Blanca Papagayo terminal is the busy, modern **Estrella de Oro terminal** (at Cuauhtémoc and Massieu, tel. 744/485-8758 or 744/485-8705). It provides connections only with the Mexico City corridor (Chilpancingo, Iguala, Taxco, Cuernavaca, Mexico City) and northwest Costa Grande destinations via Zihuatanejo, with Lázaro Cárdenas. Services include left-luggage lockers, but no food except sweets, chips, and drinks. A branch post office (8 A.M.–5 P.M. Mon.–Fri., 9 A.M.–noon Sat.) and *telecomunicaciones* office (8 A.M.–9 P.M. Mon.–Sat.) are on the outside upstairs walkway on the west side of the building.

Estrella de Oro departures include many first- and luxury-class connections with Mexico City and intermediate points. Several connect directly through Taxco. Four departures connect daily with the Costa Grande, three with Zihuatanejo, one only with Lázaro Cárdenas. Estrella de Oro offers no Costa Chica (Puerto Escondido) connections southeast.

By Car or RV

Good highways connect Acapulco north with Mexico City, northwest with the Costa Grande and Michoacán, and southeast with the Costa Chica and Oaxaca.

The Mexico City Highway 95D *cuota* (toll) expressway would make the connection via Chilpancingo easy (73 mi/117 km, about 1.5 hrs) if it weren't for the Acapulco congestion. Avoid congestion by going via the toll tunnel (*tùnel cuota*, $6). The uncluttered extension (another 125 mi/201 km, 2.5 hours) to Cuernavaca is a breeze. For Taxco, stay on the Mexico City–bound expressway north past Chilpancingo a total of about 100 miles (160 km) to a "Taxco *cuota*" (toll) turnoff and follow the signs about another 25 miles (40 km) uphill to Taxco. For Iguala, leave the 95D expressway by following the old Highway 95 turnoff, on the north edge of Chilpancingo. Continue another 62 miles (100 km, two hours) to Iguala.

After reaching Cuernavaca, the over-the-mountain leg to Mexico City (53 mi/85 km) would be simple except for possible Mexico City gridlock, which might lengthen it to two hours. Better allow a minimum of around 5.5 driving hours for the entire 251-mile (404-km) Acapulco–Mexico City trip.

The Costa Grande section of Highway 200 northwest toward Zihuatanejo is generally uncluttered and smooth (except for occasional bumps and potholes). Allow about four hours for the 150-mile (242-km) trip.

The same is true for the Costa Chica stretch of Highway 200 southeast to Ometepec (112 mi/180 km), Pinotepa Nacional (157 mi/253 km), and Puerto Escondido (247 mi/398 km total). Allow about 3 driving hours to Ometepec, 4.5 driving hours to Pinotepa, and 7 hours total to Puerto Escondido.

Avoid congestion by heading east via the coastal **Barra Vieja** bypass, across the new Río Papagayo bridge that connects directly to Highway 200, Costa Chica direction, about 20 miles (32 km) east of Acapulco. Get there, from downtown, by driving east along the Costera as if you were heading to the airport. But, two miles (3 km) before the airport, fork right at the intersection to Barra Vieja, marked by a big monument on the right. Continue another 15 miles (24 km) through Barra Vieja, across the Papagayo bridge to Highway 200 and the Costa Chica.

COSTA GRANDE & ACAPULCO

GUERRERO UPCOUNTRY

A treasury of surprises await travelers who venture out into Acapulco's pine-tufted sierra hinterland. The discoveries begin in Chilpancingo, Mexico's Home of the Brave, which basks in a banana-belt upland valley, ringed by mighty cloud-tipped mountains.

From Chilpancingo as a base, explore upcountry Guerrero River Country, and enjoy both swimming, kayaking, and camping beside the clear, spring-fed Río Azul and exploring stalactite-draped limestone caverns.

Continue deeper into the sierra, to the renowned Handicrafts Country of Chilapa and Olinalá. Select from a treasury of soft palm baskets and sombreros, bright pottery, exotic masks, charmingly rustic furniture, and exquisite lacquerware.

Continue north to Iguala, the tropical fruit, grain, and gold oasis and both a memorial to Mexican Independence and shrine to the flag. Wonder at Iguala's surrealistically large Mexican flag, stroll the shady downtown plazas, and visit the gold market.

And finally, be sure to visit Taxco, the silver-rich colonial jewel of the highlands. After exploring its winding lanes and its museums and baroque monuments, visit Taxco's trio of nearby gems—the monumental limestone Grutas de Cacahuamilpa, the legendary ruined city (and UNESCO World Heritage Site) of Xochicalco, and Ixcateopan, believed to be the final resting place of the heroic "Descending Eagle," Cuauhtémoc, the Aztecs' last emperor.

HIGHLIGHTS

◖ Chilpancingo *Zócalo*: In Chilpancingo's historic center, enjoy exploring the monuments to Mexico's independence and the Templo de Santa María de la Asunción, where much of this history was actually made (page 143).

◖ Headwaters of the Río Azul: It seems a miracle that every minute year-round, and especially on hot, dust-dry May afternoons, thousands of gallons of deliciously pure and cool water, enough to form a whole river, should well up from beneath the ground (page 158).

◖ Chilapa Sunday Handicrafts Market: Every Sunday, indigenous folks from all over central Guerrero bring their finest crafts to Chilapa for a day of bargaining and selling (page 161).

◖ Templo de San Francisco: Olinalá lacquerware artisans have gone all out to decorate the interior of their town church with their art. The result in the finely detailed, traditional, floral and animal designs that embellish the altar, the columns, the walls, the ceiling, and more is attractively unique (page 164).

◖ Hilltop Memorial Flag: Climax your Iguala visit atop the hillside south of town to witness Mexico's largest flag, weighing a quarter ton and requiring a platoon of men to raise it at sunrise and lower it at sunset each day (page 172).

◖ Santa Prisca: Your first stop around the Taxco *zócalo* should be at the celebrated baroque-style church, built with the wealth extracted from Taxco's silver mines (page 182).

◖ Grutas de Cacahuamilpa National Park: Few, if any, cave systems in the world are as grand, lovely, and easily accessible as the Grutas de Cacahuamilpa (page 195).

◖ Xochicalco: Besides the site's world-class museum, be sure to visit the Pyramid of Quetzalcoatl, so named by modern-day archaeologists for its powerful stylized bas-relief design of Quetzalcoatl, Mexico's renowned and feared Plumed Serpent (page 195).

LOOK FOR ◖ TO FIND RECOMMENDED SIGHTS, ACTIVITIES, DINING, AND LODGING.

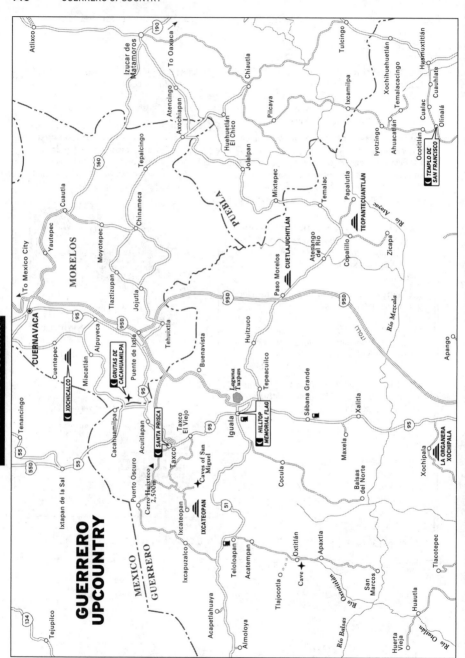

GUERRERO UPCOUNTRY

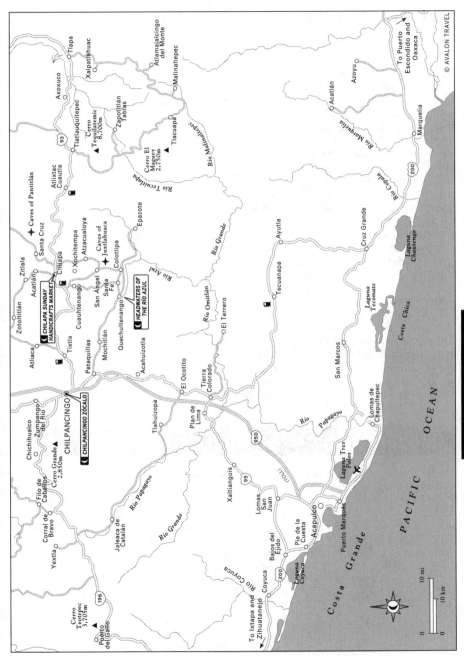

© AVALON TRAVEL

PLANNING YOUR TIME

A minimum of a week would be needed to enjoy the Guerrero Upcountry highlights; visitors with more leisure could easily stretch this out to a month. If, however, you only have three or four days, you should probably enjoy them all in and around Taxco, Mexico's silver capital. Spend a day strolling the winding hillside lanes, visiting the best of the best silver jewelry shops, the Museo Guillermo Spratling, the incomparably baroque **Santa Prisca** church, and the fascinating indigenous market. The next day, ride the stunningly scary *teleférico* (cableway) for a hike, golf, or tennis and lunch or a picnic at mountaintop Hotel Monte Taxco. On a subsequent day or days, make certain to visit the spectacular limestone **Grutas de Cacahuamilpa** (Caves of Cacahuamilpa) and, if you go early enough, continue by tour or car to the storied ruined city and now world-class museum and UNESCO World Heritage Site of **Xochicalco.**

With two or three more days, you could add Guerrero Upcountry's River and Handicrafts Country to your itinerary. On the first day, from Acapulco, head north early to Colotlipa, east of Chilpancingo, for an adventure tour through the exquisite Grutas de Juxtlahuaca limestone cave; in the afternoon, continue to the nearby Río Azul for swimming, inner-tubing, and plenty of general frolicking in the cool, crystal-blue water. Continue to Chilpancingo for an overnight.

Leave early the next day to Chilapa to bargain for treasures at the fascinating **Sunday Handicrafts Market.** (Plan ahead to make sure you visit Chilapa on a Sunday to experience the marketplace.) Continue in the afternoon or the next day to the remote mountain village of Olinalá and spend at least an afternoon visiting home-factory shops filled with the town's renowned glistening lacquerware.

With a day or two more, you could add Iguala, north of Chilpancingo and south of Taxco, to your itinerary. En route from Chilpancingo, you might include a three-hour side trip to an ancient lost city, now La Organera Xochipala Archaeological Zone. In the afternoon, in Iguala, a virtual shrine to the Mexican national flag, be sure to stroll around the three pleasantly shady downtown central plazas and visit the **Museo y Santuario a la Bandera.** An hour before sunset, ride a taxi or *colectivo* to the hillside south of town to witness what must be Mexico's (if not the world's) most awesomely large national flag, powerfully rumbling and snapping, with mini–sonic booms, in the breeze.

Chilpancingo

The formal name of the Guerrero state capital, Chilpancingo de los Bravo (Chilpancingo of the Brave), reflects Mexico's kinship with the United States, "The Home of the Free and Land of the Brave." Historically, in both cases, "the Brave" was more than a mere patriotic turn of phrase. Like the Continental Congress that began meeting in Philadelphia in 1774, the members of the 1813 revolutionary Congress of Anahuac in Chilpancingo did so at the constant risk of their lives.

Chilpancingo, besides being the Guerrero state capital and the cradle of Mexican liberty, is also closely associated with **Vicente Guerrero,** the Mexican hero most comparable to the United States' George Washington. Probably more than any other, Guerrero, Mexico's second president, battled to win Mexico's 1821 independence and continued the struggle to ensure Mexico's 1824 constitution and resulting republican government.

Nevertheless, it's still priest-general **José María Morelos** who holds the hearts of Mexicans, eight generations after his death. It was Morelos who convened Mexico's first revolutionary legislature, the Congress of Anahuac, in Chilpancingo on September 14, 1813.

Morelos had earlier expressed his libertarian

ideas in the celebrated Sentimientos de la Nación, which, with as much force as the ideas of Thomas Jefferson a generation earlier, gave direction to the Congress of Anahuac's work. On November 6, 1813, the Congress declared a manifesto of principles, which notably included the idea that "sovereignty proceeds immediately from the people" and that Mexico should therefore "be free and independent."

It's interesting to note that the Mexican Act of Independence, 37 years after the American Declaration of Independence, took freedom a step farther. Among its principles, the Congress of Anahuac declared that "slavery be prohibited forever," a principle that required 52 more years and a terrible civil war to be established in the United States.

ORIENTATION

Judging from its narrow downtown streets, Chilpancingo (pop. 200,000, elev. 4,000 feet/1,300 meters) is a little town that grew big. Traveling the 62 miles (100 km) by *cuota* (toll) expressway from Acapulco (or 83 mi/133 km by old Highway 95), arrivees must make an effort not to miss the downtown. Both first-class buses and the south–north thruway Avenida Vicente Guerrero bypass the town center completely.

Buses deposit passengers at the Camionera Central (a mile north of the central plaza; taxi or ride a *colectivo* from there).

Drivers, watch carefully for turnoff signs. If you're fortunate, you'll get on to the main south-end ingress Avenida Lázaro Cárdenas, which begins at the Ciudad Universitaria right turnoff. About half a mile (0.8 km) from the turnoff, bear right at a big traffic circle and follow the boulevard, which becomes Bulevar Juan Álvarez and passes, via a one-block tunnel, beneath the Chilpancingo *zócalo*.

SIGHTS
◖ The *Zócalo*

With traffic diverted from it and the surrounding streets, the Chilpancingo *zócalo* (central plaza) makes an enjoyable strolling ground. The best vantage point is the front steps of the

Kick back while you get your shoes polished at the Chilpancingo *zócalo*.

Rebel priest José María Morelos inspired Mexico's Declaration of Independence, signed in Chilpancingo, on Nov. 6, 1813.

GUERRERO UPCOUNTRY

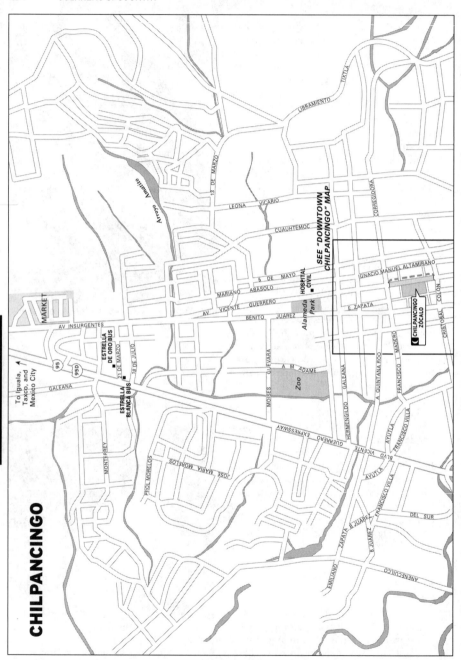

CHILPANCINGO

SEE "DOWNTOWN CHILPANCINGO" MAP

To Iguala, Taxco, and Mexico City

MARKET

AV INSURGENTES

GALEANA

ESTRELLA DE ORO BUS

ESTRELLA BLANCA BUS

Arroyo Amatito

13 DE MARZO

LEONA VICARIO

CUAUHTEMOC

5 DE MAYO

MARIANO ABASOLO

AV. VICENTE GUERRERO

BENITO JUAREZ

HOSPITAL CIVIL

Alameda Park

Zoo

A M ADAME

MOISES GUEVARA

GUERRERO EXPRESSWAY

JOSE MARIA MORELOS

PROL MORELOS

MONTERREY

21 DE MARZO

18 DE JULIO

LIBRAMIENTO

TIXTLA

CORREGIDORA

IGNACIO MANUEL ALTAMIRANO

COLON

CRISTOBAL

E ZAPATA

CHILPANCINGO ZÓCALO

GALEANA

HERMENEGILDO

A QUINTANA ROO

FRANCISCO MADERO

FRANCISCO VILLA

AYUTLA

BLVD VICENTE

AYUTLA

FRANCISCO VILLA

DEL SUR

ZAPATA B JUAREZ

B JUAREZ

EMILIANO

ANENECUILCO

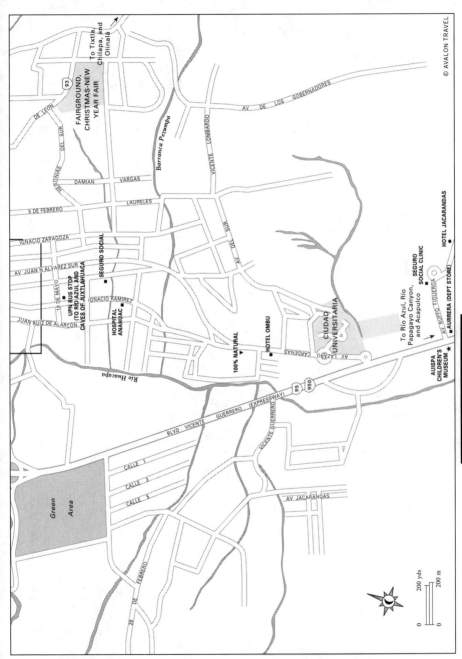

To Tixtla, Chilapa, and Olinalá

FAIRGROUND, CHRISTMAS-NEW YEAR FAIR

93

DE LEÓN

HEROÍNAS DEL SUR

AV DE LOS GOBERNADORES

Barranca Pezunpa

VICENTE LOMBARDO

DAMIAN

VARGAS

LAURELES

5 DE FEBRERO

IGNACIO ZARAGOZA

AV. JUAN N ÁLVAREZ SUR

SEGURO SOCIAL

AV. DEL SUR

18 DE MAYO

UPN BUS STOP (TO RÍO AZUL AND CAVES OF JUXTLAHUACA)

IGNACIO RAMIREZ

JUAN RUIZ DE ALARCÓN

HOSPITAL ANAHUAC

100% NATURAL

HOTEL OMBU

CIUDAD UNIVERSITARIA

AV. LÁZARO CÁRDENAS

Río Huacapa

To Río Azul, Río Papagayo Canyon, and Acapulco

SEGURO SOCIAL CLINIC

AV. RUFFO FIGUEROA

AURRERA (DEPT STORE)

HOTEL JACARANDAS

AUISPA CHILDREN'S MUSEUM

95   950

BLVD VICENTE GUERRERO (EXPRESSWAY)

VICENTE GUERRERO

CALLE 1

CALLE 3

CALLE 5

AV JACARANDAS

Green Area

28 DE FEBRERO

0   200 yds
0   200 m

GUERRERO UPCOUNTRY

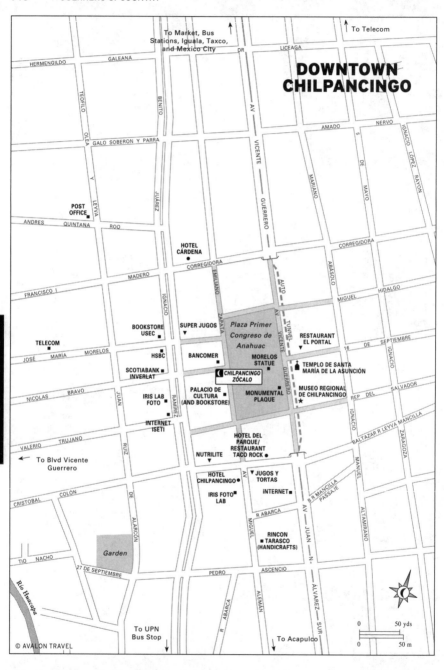

DOWNTOWN CHILPANCINGO

tall Guerrero **Biblioteca Del Estado** (state-house), formerly the Palacio de Gobierno. Face (or imagine you're facing) the plaza, officially the "Plaza of the First Congress of Anahuac," and you're looking east. North is on your left, south on your right. East across the plaza rises the classical facade of the Museo Regional de Chilpancingo, and to the left of that, the twin white bell towers of the Templo de Santa María de la Asunción, where the Act of Independence from Spain was declared on November 6, 1813.

Note the noble gilded **statue of José María Morelos,** at the plaza's northeast corner, below and in front of the church. It memorializes his Sentimientos de la Nación, with the pivotal pronouncement that "No nation has the right to prevent another from the free use of its sovereignty."

On the adjacent, east side of the plaza, below and in front of the museum, see the grand plaque, placed on September 13, 1985, that honors the 175th anniversary of the opening of the Congress of Anahuac. Its inscription, quoting Morelos, commemorates the end of the long period of Spanish dominion from August 12, 1521, until September 14, 1813: "On that day the chains of our servitude to Mexico-Tenochtitlán were broken forever in the brave town of Chilpancingo."

Through art, antiques, artifacts, and displays, the **Museo Regional de Chilpancingo** (east side of the *zócalo,* tel. 747/472-8088, 9 A.M.–6 P.M. Tues.–Sun., $2) illustrates Guerrero geology, flora, fauna, archaeology, history, and folkways. A major attraction is the now-faded but epic historical mural by Roberto Cueva del Río and Luis Arenal that wraps around the entire inner patio. The mural begins at the patio's northeast corner (across the patio, left as you enter) and continues clockwise. The first panel shows the infant future emperor Cuauhtémoc (notice his birth sign, the descending eagle above the infant). Continue to the panel of the encounter of Cuauhtémoc with Cortés, then to the first corner, where another panel depicts the burial of the remains of Cuauhtémoc in Ixcateopan, near Taxco. Farther on, panels represent the independence heroes Morelos, Guerrero, and Hermenegildo Galeana, the Revolution of 1910, and, finally, the latter-day development of Guerrero state.

Step next door to the church, **Templo de Santa María de la Asunción,** the site revered in Mexico, not unlike Independence Hall in Philadelphia, as the place where the Congress of Anahuac formally declared Mexico's independence, on November 6, 1813. Note the polished hand-carved church doors, with reliefs of Mexico's independence heroes: Morelos, first president Nicolás Bravo, Guerrero, and the magnificent eagle-and-serpent national symbol.

Beyond Downtown

Children will most certainly enjoy the modest Chilpancingo **zoo** (near the corner of Moises Guevara and Arturo M. Adame, tel. 747/472-5906, 9 A.M.–5:30 P.M. Tues.–Sun., $2), about half a mile northwest of the *zócalo.* The entrance is on the north side of a large park, with plenty of room to run around and spread a picnic.

Another fun place for kids is the **Museo La Avispa** (a block west of the corner of Bulevar Vicente Guerrero and Av. Rulfo Figueroa, tel. 747/471-2422 or 747/471-3149, info@museolaavispa.org, www.museolaavispa.org, 9 A.M.–6 P.M. Mon.–Fri., 10 A.M.–6 P.M. Sat.–Sun., closed major holidays, $2), south of town. The museum's mission is to introduce technology with a host of hands-on, child-friendly (ages 4–12) activities.

ACCOMMODATIONS

Considering its many visitors on government or commercial business, Chilpancingo has relatively few hotels. Be certain to reserve at least a day (or better a week) in advance. Some, but not all, Chilpancingo hotels accept credit cards. All hotel rates fall in the under-$50 category. Most are compact, business-style hotels, with one exception: the restful, resort-style but moderately priced Hotel Jacarandas, in the southern suburb, convenient for drivers.

By location, starting downtown, the best city-

JOSÉ MARÍA MORELOS: CHAMPION OF MEXICAN INDEPENDENCE

As did his famous predecessor, George Washington, Mexican Independence general José María Morelos y Pavón convened his nation's first constitutional convention. The First Congress of Anahuac, an assemblage of leaders from all over Mexico, convened in Chilpancingo on September 14, 1813. It was virtually three years to the day after martyr-priest Miguel Hidalgo had ignited revolution from the balcony in Dolores, Guanajuato. Later, Morelos remembered: "On that day the chains of our servitude to Mexico-Tenochtitlán (Mexico City) were broken forever."

Those early days of revolution were heady times for a poor priest of such obscure origin. José María Morelos y Pavón was born in Valladolid (now Morelia, named in his honor), Michoacán, on September 30, 1765. Among experts, opinion is divided on Morelos's possible African-Mexican ancestry. Most historians go along with the major evidence: Morelos's swarthy, dark-eyed complexion and the well-known old legal document certifying that one of his grandmothers was a *"mujer libre,"* a standard legal phrase for a free, non-slave woman of African descent.

Young Morelos no doubt was a devout Catholic. Early on, he wanted to study for the priesthood. While waiting to be admitted to seminary, he supported himself by working as a mule driver until he was admitted to the Valladolid Colegio San Nicolas in the mid-1780s.

While a student, Morelos came under the influence of Father Miguel Hidalgo, who was the rector at San Nicolas. Hidalgo was not the usual role model for a budding acolyte. He was ambitious and much more interested in politics than in his priestly duties. Hidalgo's inner circle, which quickly included Morelos, debated the ideas of the French Enlightenment philosophers Jean-Jacques Rousseau (*The Social Contract*) and Count Montesquieu (*The Spirit of the Laws*), who had strongly influenced the founding fathers of the brand-new United States of America.

Hidalgo, always seeking advancement, got an assignment to a rich Guanajuato parish, while Morelos went west and served in a poor isolated corner of Michoacán.

After igniting revolution on September 15, 1810, Hidalgo led his raggedy peasant army, which grew rapidly to about 100,000 at its peak. Inspired, Morelos offered his services to Hidalgo, who told him to go south, raise an army, and capture Acapulco and the riches of the Manila galleon.

Morelos returned to his Michoacán homeland, raised a scruffy platoon of volunteers, and marched toward the coast. Along the way, Morelos recruited droves of volunteers, many of them African Mexican. They passed Zacatula and followed the coast east to Acapulco, arriving as an eager but ill-equipped 3,000-man guerrilla brigade.

In Acapulco, the only point of resistance (albeit stiff resistance) was the old Fuerte

---

center lodging choice is the busy, business-style **{** **Hotel del Parque** (Colón 5, tel. 747/472-3012 or 747/472-1364, fax 747/472-1285, alarcoma@prodigy.net.mx, $40 s, $50 d), a block south of the *zócalo*. Its 28 very clean rooms rise in four floors (but with no elevator) around a small inner lobby-patio. Inside, the rooms are comfortable, modern, semi-deluxe, with hot-water shower baths, TV, phone, fans, wireless Internet, and a good restaurant downstairs, but no pool. Parking nearby costs extra (about $5).

In the same bustling south-of-*zócalo* neighborhood, but more economical, is the skillfully managed **Hotel Chilpancingo** (Miguel Alemán 8, tel./fax 747/472-2446, $18–55). The 40 clean, invitingly decorated, compactly arranged rooms connected by a maze of blue-tiled passageways offer many options. They range from the most basic and dark to spacious, light rooms with 1–3 double beds. The bigger rooms can hold up to six people. All rooms include private hot-water shower baths,

de San Diego, where Morelos, after weeks of besieging the fort, divided his force. He left half surrounding the fort and led the remainder north to Chilpancingo, which he captured with the help of Hermenegildo Galeana and Nícolas Bravo.

Next, Morelos marched west, capturing Chilapa. Then, with a buoyantly robust force of 4,000, he continued north to Cuautla, in the present state of Morelos. Although besieged for 73 days by a superior royalist division, Morelos broke out with most of his men and marched southeast, where he captured Oaxaca, the prize of the south.

At Oaxaca, his radical egalitarian views, the source of his popularity with his troops, surfaced:

> We must eliminate the outdated classifications separating us into black, mulatto, mestizo, and criollo...and call ourselves Americans for our origin as do the English, the French, and that other European country that is oppressing us.

The time was mid-1813, and Morelos was riding his crest of success. At 48, he was at his prime, cutting a dashing figure, topped by a colorful bandanna that wrapped his balding head. Napoleon Bonaparte is said to have paid Morelos the ultimate compliment: "With three such men as José Morelos, I could conquer the world."

Although a priest, Morelos, like his mentor Miguel Hidalgo, rejected sexual abstinence. He fathered several children by his indigenous common-law wife, Brigida Almonte, of Necupétaro, Michoacán.

One of Morelos's sons, Juan Almonte, born in 1803, gained fame, paradoxically, working for the Mexican conservative cause. He served as President Bustamante's Minister of War during the 1830s, under General Santa Anna at the Alamo in Texas, later as ambassador to the United States and Britain, and finally in Emperor Maximilian's cabinet during the 1860s.

Morelos's signal achievement was the Congress of Anahuac, Mexico's first constitutional convention, which Morelos convened in Chilpancingo on September 14, 1813. Although subsequently driven from Chilpancingo by royalist forces, the Congress reconvened in Apatzingan, Michoacán, where it promulgated Mexico's first constitution on October 22, 1814.

Continually pressed by royalist troops, Morelos fought desperately for the remainder of his days protecting the Congress, which amounted to Mexico's first republican government. Finally, royalist troops captured him and spirited him to Mexico City on November 22, 1815. After a month-long trial during which Morelos argued eloquently for the justice of the *insurgente* cause, he was defrocked and taken to the city of San Cristóbal Ecatepec, where he was executed for treason by firing squad on December 27, 1815.

carpet, flowery bedspreads and comfortable mattresses, fans, and wireless Internet; credit cards are not accepted.

Even more downscale is the homey **Hotel Cárdena** (Madero 13, tel. 747/471-6153, $16 s, $22 d, $26 t), a block north of the *zócalo*. Rooms in this converted old family home open onto an interior patio with chairs and shade umbrellas for relaxing. The plain, barebulb rooms come with fans, private hot-water shower baths, cable TV, and café; credit cards

are not accepted. It's not immaculate, but remains a good value for the price.

Outside of the immediate downtown, visitors have a number of decent hotel choices. About a mile south of the *zócalo*, check out the newish **Hotel Ombu** (Av. L. Cárdenas 28, tel. 747/472-5382 or 747/494-7910, fax 747/474-9911, hotelombu@hotmail.com, $35 s, $40–52 d, $57 t). Above the small lobby, three floors of 33 walk-up rooms rise around a spartan-chic inner atrium. Rooms themselves

The Hotel Jacarandas offers comfortable lodging and a restful pool-patio at very reasonable rates.

© BRUCE WHIPPERMAN

are simply but attractively decorated in tile, natural wood, and earth-tone bedspreads and curtains. There are smallish rooms with one double bed and larger rooms with two double beds. All rooms come with good cable TV, phone, portable fan available, wireless Internet, and parking. There is also a hotel restaurant on the premises.

Farther south, about 1.5 miles (2.5 km) south of the town center, is Chilpancingo's best: the government resort-style **C Hotel Jacarandas** (Av. Jacarandas, tel. 747/472-4444, fax 747/472-4987, ventasconujunto@ hotmail.com, www.conjuntojacarandas.tripod .com.html, $40 s, $47 d, $62 t). Guests enjoy a choice of about 50 rooms in a big, curving, white jacaranda-decorated hillside block. Inside, rooms, although a bit worn, are spacious, light, comfortable, and open to airy private balconies overlooking a big blue pool-patio and tropical garden. The rates are reasonable and rooms come with cable TV, fan, phone, private hot-water shower baths, and parking. Credit cards are accepted. There is also a good

hotel restaurant here. Reserve early; this place is often booked completely by conferences.

On the north side of town, bus or car travelers might appreciate the convenience of the newish **Hotel Paradise Inn** (Bulevar Vicente Guerrero, Esquina 21 de Marzo, tel. 474/471-1122 or 474/472-8863, fax 474/471-4691, toll-free Mex. tel. 800/832-4242, admon@ hotelparadise.com, www.paradiseinn.com.mx, from $46 d with one bed, $60 d with two beds) on thruway Bulevar Vicente Guerrero, across from the bus station. Find it about a mile north of the *zócalo,* at the corner of 21 de Marzo. The 100-odd rooms enclose an inner parking-patio. Inside, they're comfortable and immaculate, with all-white semi-deluxe decor and hot-water shower baths. Breakfast is included with the room rate. Rooms come with cable TV, phone, exercise gym, business center, restaurant/bar, air-conditioning, and parking.

FOOD

For snacks, try one of the many very clean streetfront *jugerías* (stalls or small restaurants) and *loncherías* (lunch counters) around the *zócalo*. For example, try **Jugos y Tortas** (on Miguel Alemán, two blocks south of the plaza, corner of Colón). Alternatively, a few blocks north on the *zócalo's* northwest side, an excellent all-around choice is **Super Jugos** (about $2), with plenty of fresh *aguas,* juices, and hot *tortas* and *hamburguesas.*

As for restaurants, downtown's healthiest choice is welcoming **Nutrilite** (Colón 11, tel. 747/494-1932, cell tel. 747/106-9279, 7 A.M.–8 P.M. Mon.–Fri., 8 A.M.–6 P.M. Sat., $2–8), a block south of the *zócalo* and a few doors west of the corner of Miguel Alemán. Here, you can choose from a long list of breakfasts (whole wheat pancakes, eggs any style, fruit plate) or afternoon four-course *comida corrida* (with entrées such as stuffed cactus leaves or meatballs in chipotle sauce), plus a delicious harvest of fruit drinks.

A few more sit-down restaurants provide good food in restful settings near the plaza. High marks go to refined 🄲 **Restaurant El Portal** (just off the *zócalo,* on the north/left side of the church front, tel. 747/472-4668, 7 A.M.–6 P.M. Mon.–Sat., $3–10). In addition to a very recognizable menu of professionally prepared and served breakfasts, salads, soups, pastas, poultry, and meats, it offers a bountiful three-course *comida corrida* (1–5 P.M.).

The **Restaurant Taco Rock** (Colón 5, tel. 747/472-3012, 8 A.M.–midnight daily, $5–10) in the Hotel del Parque, around the block south of the *zócalo,* is a very popular breakfast and lunch stop for business and professional people. At night it becomes a TV bar and nightclub, featuring Latin "taco rock" music. Entrées from a long Mexican-style coffee-shop menu are professionally prepared and presented.

Although it's not strictly vegetarian or macrobiotic, the menu of **100% Natural** (Av. L. Cárdenas 12, tel. 747/472-5457, 9 A.M.–9 P.M. daily, $3–8), half a mile south of downtown, features plenty of healthy and tasty food. Choose from fruits and fruit *licuados,* granola, pancakes, eggs, yogurt, avocado, cheese, soya and meat burgers, french fries, and sandwiches in many styles. Service, by a dedicated squad of twentysomethings in white, beneath an open-air *palapa,* is exemplary.

EVENTS

Chilpancingo people unwind during the big year-end agricultural fair, **Feria de San Mateo, la Navidad, y el Año Nuevo** (Dec. 24–Jan. 8). The festivities kick off with the *teopancolaquio,* a ritual honoring the birth of God on Earth. Offerings include riots of flowers and regional dances, including Los Tlacololeros, Pescados (Fish), Diablos (Devils), and Manueles.

In nearby Tixtla, folks whoop it up for the birthday of their most famous native son, Vicente Guerrero, on August 9, with a feast of cultural events. Three weeks later, the Tixtla plaza is awash with celebrants for the

DANCE OF LOS TLACOLOLEROS

The noise and excitement of the Chilpancingo regional dance Los Tlacololeros remains a favorite of campesinos, who crowd in at fiesta time. The name refers to *tlacoll,* the Aztec word meaning "preparing the fields for planting" by the age-old slash-and-burn method, still widely used in the Sierra Madre backcountry.

The compelling drama centers on the whips, which the hilariously masked cotton-and-sombrero-clothed men snap loudly on each others' padded arms, supposedly to imitate the crackle of the burning brush fire. In one version of the dance a she-dog called *la maravilla* makes a madcap chase after a *tigre* (tiger) that threatens the campesinos.

All of a sudden, without warning, the fire mysteriously goes out while the dumbfounded dancers flail each other with increased desperation, trying frantically to find the culprit for the fire's failure. Soon, however, all is well that ends well as the loud rattling of chains simulates the fire's return, driving the *tigre* from the campesinos' midst.

Fiesta de la Natividad de María (Sept. 1–8). Native Mexican folk flood into town for a parade, carnival, fireworks, *jaripeo* bull roping and riding, and favorite traditional dances Los Manueles, Moros, Diablos, Tigres, and Tlacololeros.

SHOPPING

For supermarket-department stores you have two choices: long-time **Comercial Mexicana** (Calle Baltazar Leyva, tel. 747/472-6355, 8 A.M.–10 P.M. daily), by the tall orange-and-white pelican emblem-sign on the Highway 95 thruway or new south-side, big-box **Aurrera** (tel. 747/116-0290, 8 A.M.–10 P.M. daily), marked by its big green sign, also by the Highway 95 thruway.

The best local source of handicrafts is charming, streetfront store **Rincón Tarasco** (Ramírez 17B, no phone, 9 A.M.–8 P.M. Mon.–Sat.), two blocks south of the *zócalo.* Although grandfatherly Diego Rico hails from the state of Michoacán, he offers an all-Mexico treasury of precious doodads, such as whirling *maltracas* noisemakers, sturdy huaraches, guitars, wriggling snakes, bright lacquerware boxes, and much more.

INFORMATION AND SERVICES
Banks

A number of bank branches, all with ATMs, cluster around the downtown plaza. The best bet is long-hours **HSBC** (Juárez 2, tel. 747/471-3179, 9 A.M.–6 P.M. Mon.–Fri., 9 A.M.–3 P.M. Sat.), a block north and a block west of the plaza's northwest corner. Alternatively, go to **Bancomer** (on the plaza's west side, corner of Bravo, tel. 747/472-2020, 9 A.M.–4 P.M. Mon.–Fri.).

Communications

Find the *correo* (post office; corner of Teofilo Olea y Leyva, tel. 747/472-3562, 8 A.M.–6 P.M. Mon.–Fri.) two blocks west then two blocks north from the *zócalo's* northwest corner.

For phone calls, use one of the many Ladatel card-operated street telephones scattered around the downtown.

Internet connections are commonly available in Chilpancingo. For example, try the small Internet store **Isete** (corner of Ramírez and Trujano, no phone, 8 A.M.–9 P.M. daily), two blocks west of the *zócalo's* center.

Health and Emergencies

Chilpancingo has up-to-date medical facilities. If you get sick, follow your hotel's recommendation. Otherwise, hail a taxi to whisk you to the very highly recommended private **Hospital Anahuac** (Ignacio Ramírez, tel. 747/472-9505), about seven blocks south of the downtown *zócalo.* Alternatively, go to the 24-hour public **Centro de Salud** (Vicente Guerrero 45, tel. 747/471-2640), about four blocks north of the downtown *zócalo,* on the east side of the street. For fire emergencies, call the *bomberos* (tel. 474/472-2280). For police, call the *policia municipal* (emergency number 066).

Photography

For photo supplies and services, go to **Iris Lab** (west side of Ignacio Ramírez between Trujano and Bravo, tel. 747/472-6067, 9 A.M.–3 P.M. and 5–9 P.M. Mon.–Sat.), a block west of the plaza.

Bookstore

The scarcity of printed matter in Chilpancingo makes the collection of the mostly Spanish-language bookstore **Librería de la U.S.E.C.** (corner of Juárez and Morelos, tel. 747/472-8656, 9 A.M.–9 P.M. Mon.–Sat.), one block west of the plaza, all the more precious. Even if you don't buy anything, perusing the piles of many hundreds of volumes, covering myriad subjects from Don Quixote and the history of handicrafts to Faust and French-Spanish dictionaries, can provide a relaxing diversion for book lovers.

GETTING THERE AND AWAY
By Bus

The main long-distance bus station, **Estrella Blanca** (21 de Marzo, between thruway Vicente Guerrero and the municipal market, tel. 474/472-0533) is about 1.5 miles north of downtown.

Out front, a platoon of taxis, local buses, and *colectivos* ferry passengers to dozens of nearby destinations. Ladatel card-operated street telephones are available for calls.

Inside the smallish terminal, agents (tel. 474/472-0533) sell long-distance bus tickets. Both first- and second-class direct departures (including intermediate points) connect with Mexico City, Morelia, Guadalajara, Acapulco, Zihuatanejo, Puerto Vallarta, Iguala, Chilapa, Olinalá, Tlapa de Comonfort, Taxco, and the U.S. border at Nogales and Tijuana.

Outside, a few stands sell snacks, drinks, tacos, and sandwiches. For fresh items, stock up at the market located a block uphill.

Across the street from Estrella Blanca, first-class **Estrella de Oro** (tel. 747/472-2130) buses connect north and south with Acapulco, Iguala, Taxco, and Mexico City.

By Car

Good roads make connections with Chilpancingo easy. To or from Acapulco, follow the *cuota* (toll) expressway a quick 62 miles (100 km; the toll is a steep $20) in about an hour and a quarter. Toll-free Highway 95 (83 mi/133 km) connects with Acapulco in about twice the time, with much more than twice the hazard and wear and tear.

In the opposite direction, the *cuota* (toll) expressway connects Chilpancingo with Mexico City in 148 miles (239 km; auto toll about $30, but worth it) in about 3.5 hours. Make sure you arrive in Mexico City on a permitted day. (Mexico City driving restrictions are as follows: On Monday, no vehicle may be driven with final digits 5 or 6; Tuesday, 7 or 8; Wednesday, 3 or 4; Thursday, 1 or 2; Friday, 9, 0, or a letter. On weekends, all vehicles may be driven.) The old Highway 95 connection, via Iguala and Taxco, with Mexico City, adds about two hours to this drive under the best of conditions.

Connect north with Iguala in 67 miles (108 km, two hours), via old Highway 95 *libre* (that forks west from the toll expressway at the north edge of Chilpancingo). From Iguala, continue to Taxco in another 24 miles (38 km, one hour), for a total of 91 miles (145 km) and three hours.

EXCURSIONS FROM CHILPANCINGO

Roads fan out from Chilpancingo to a number of spots well worth visiting. These include Tixtla de Guerrero, the historic and colorful birthplace of Vicente Guerrero; the fascinatingly exotic La Organera Xochipala Archaeological Zone; the luscious crystal springs of the Rio Azul; and the spectacular Grutas de Juxtlahuaca limestone caverns.

Tixtla de Guerrero

The trip to Tixtla (pop. 20,000) is part of the fun of going there. Although it's only eight miles (12 km), Tixtla is over a high summit, with refreshing breezes and a beautiful view of the mountain-framed green patchwork of fields and orchards of the Tixtla Valley.

The place to arrive is the Tixtla town-center *zócalo*. Bus riders, get off at the adjacent market, at the end of the line. Drivers, turn left on to the main north–south town ingress street, several blocks after entering the town. Let the church's bell tower be your guide to the central *zócalo*.

The *zócalo* focuses around the **Monument to Vicente Guerrero,** a bronze likeness of the great general in a heroic cape.

Next, head across the street, south from the *zócalo,* to the house where Vicente Guerrero lived and directed Mexico's rebellion against Spain. The house is a virtual shrine to Vicente Guerrero, not unlike Mount Vernon is for George Washington. Its main attraction is a mural by Jaime A. Gómez de Payan that dramatically portrays major events and players in Mexican history. Moving clockwise: *insurgente* general Ignacio M. Altamirano (also born in Tixtla) with his hand on a jaguar's head; Benito Juárez surrounded by his contemporaries; José María Morelos passing the flame of liberty to Vicente Guerrero, who completes the struggle for independence; Emperor Cuauhtémoc, tortured for resisting Cortés.

From the *zócalo,* head west (away from the church) to an open ceremonial plaza, fringed by market stalls and with a line of busts of eight of Tixtla's favorite sons and daughters.

VICENTE GUERRERO: FATHER OF THE MEXICAN REPUBLIC

The 1849 proposal for a new Mexican state to be carved from the states of Mexico, Puebla, and Michoacán would seem improbable, except that the proposed state was to be named Guerrero in honor of Mexico's famously popular independence hero and second president, Vicente Ramón Saldana Guerrero.

Vicente Guerrero, Mexico's first African-Mexican president, was born to working-class parents in the village of Tixtla, near Chilpancingo, on August 10, 1782. In 1811, Vicente was working successfully as a gunsmith when, inspired by Father Miguel Hidalgo's *insurgente* cause, he joined with priest-general José María Morelos's ragtag southern rebel forces.

Vicente's valor in battle and natural leadership ability led to his swift promotion. By 1815, however, with most of its original leaders, including Morelos, dead, the *insurgente* cause had lost momentum. Nevertheless, Guerrero grabbed the rebel banner in the south and rallied his men. Guerrero and his *compadre* commanders, Juan Álvarez and Pedro Ascencio, kept royalist brigadier Agustín de Itúrbide's troops in frustrated disarray, chasing the ragtag rebel bands throughout the southern Sierra Madre.

Vicente Guerrero was confronted by a crucial test in 1819. When offered amnesty, the exhausted Guerrero was tempted to give up. Even his father pleaded with him to surrender. But Guerrero remained resolute. In front of his men, Guerrero answered with the now-hallowed words, "Father, to me your voice is sacred...[but] the voice of my country comes first."

In 1821, Mexican royalists, faced with a new unfriendly liberal Spanish government, swallowed hard and joined Guerrero and the rebels. Under the flag (for which Guerrero had personally chosen the colors: red, white, and green) of "Three Guarantees" – independence, Catholicism, equality – Guerrero and Itúrbide rode victoriously into Mexico City.

But quickly, Itúrbide vaulted himself to glory as Emperor Agustín I of Mexico. As could be expected, Guerrero soon revolted, defeating Itúrbide's forces in battle on January 23, 1823, forcing Itúrbide to abdicate on March 19 and later to exile in May.

Mexican republicans took over and put together a national constitution in 1824. An election elevated liberal Guadalupe Victoria to president and conservative Nícolas

---

All of the busts are looking west to the adjacent monument, dedicated jointly to Vicente Guerrero and Ignacio M. Altamirano. A large tablet records the words of Tixtla's most famous son, which translate thus:

Your voice, father, is sacred to me; But the voice of my homeland comes first.

– Vicente Guerrero

From the Guerrero-Altamirano monument, walk left (south) along Calle Federico Encarnación about four blocks. Turn right (west) and continue three blocks to the small park, the **Cuna (Cradle) de Vicente Guerrero.** Guerrero was born in the modest house (which is occupied) at the rear of the park on August 9, 1782.

If you get hungry during your Tixtla visit, a few clean plaza-front *torta* and taco *loncherías* supply wholesome snacks. For a fancier treat, take a seat at the airy upstairs view perch of **Restaurant la Terraza** (Altamirano 3, tel. 754/478-1656, 9 A.M.–11 P.M. daily, $3–10), half a block north from the church, away from the *zócalo.* Enjoy a relaxing lunch (barbequed chicken) or dinner (*albondiagas* meat balls in savory sauce).

From Chilpancingo, get to Tixtla by minibus from the corner of Avenida Insurgentes and 17 de Octubre (near the market) about 10 blocks (0.6 mi/1 km) north of the *zócalo.*

Drivers, get to Tixtla from downtown Chilpancingo's Avenida Juan Álvarez, about eight blocks south of the *zócalo.* Head east, uphill, along Laureles. After two blocks,

Bravo to vice president. Although the restless Bravo revolted in 1827, the breach was temporarily resealed with the election of Vicente Guerrero as Mexico's second president in 1828.

Guerrero, although an able general and enormously popular war hero, was ill at ease among Mexico City's blue bloods. Guerrero left most of the salon politicking to his war minister, Leonardo Zavala (who had organized a popular revolt to get Guerrero elected), and Joel Poinsett, U.S. president Andrew Jackson's savvy ambassador to Mexico.

In the last analysis, although Guerrero's egalitarian views were bad news to Mexico's powerful conservative chosen few, his untutored working-class and mixed-race background was the clincher. He simply didn't fit into Mexico City's upper crust. As it turned out, others were more than willing to take Guerrero's place.

One of those was Antonio López de Santa Anna, who became the darling of Mexican conservatives when his regiment batted down a half-hearted Spanish invasion on the Gulf Coast in July 1829. With Santa Anna's backing, conservative general Anastasio Bustamante mounted a revolt, forcing Guerrero to step down from the presidency in December 1829.

Guerrero again retreated to his southern home territory and drummed up yet another guerrilla revolt against the Mexico City politicos. As usual, Guerrero was master on his own ground. His irregulars outwitted government troops for a year.

Bustamante decided that trickery was the only way to defeat Guerrero. His agents got Guerrero to board the ship *Colombo*, in Acapulco, by bribing the ship's Genoese captain, arch villain Francisco Pichaluga. He took Guerrero, under custody, to Huatulco and handed him over to Bustamante's operatives on January 20, 1831.

Guerrero was next taken to the Valley of Oaxaca; after a bogus trial, he was executed by firing squad at the old Cuilapan basilica on February 14, 1831.

Sadly, the old warrior was gone. But his cause was not lost. Others such as Juan Álvarez, Benito Juárez, Emiliano Zapata, Álvaro Obregón, Lázaro Cárdenas, and many more would carry Guerrero's banner for generations to come.

turn left on Zaragoza; continue three blocks to Heronias del Sur and turn right, uphill. Continue east, going uphill at every intersection, until you arrive at the Tixtla *libramento* highway, where you turn right and follow the traffic.

La Organera Xochipala Archaeological Zone

The half-day (60 mi/100 km) roundtrip to La Organera Xochipala (named for the zone's picturesque gigantic organ cactuses; no phone, 9 A.M.–5 P.M. daily except holidays, admission $5) is well worth the reward at the end of the road: an outstanding example of a trading and ceremonial center identified with the Mezcala culture, which influenced the west and central inland areas of the present state

© BRUCE WHIPPERMAN

a giant organ cactus at La Organera Xochipala Archaeological Zone

LA ORGANERA XOCHIPALA ARCHAEOLOGICAL ZONE

TOMB II

TEMPLE OF THE LIGHTS

NORTH PLAZA

WHITE PALACE

TOMB I

BANQUET ROOM

PALACE OF THE THREE PILARS

NORTH PLAZA

PALACE OF THE WALLS

PALACE OF THE FOUR PILLARS

PATIO OF THE ORGAN CACTUS

PLAZA OF THE CISTERN

PATIO OF THE MEZCAL

PATIO OF THE HIDDEN TOMB

TEMPLE OF SUNSET

SOUTH PATIO

BURNED PALACE

CIRCULAR EDIFICE

ALTAR

0   25 yds

0   25 m

© AVALON TRAVEL

of Guerrero for more than 1,000 years, until about A.D. 1400.

Xochipala, which means "the flower that paints red" in the Aztec language, comprised an urban ceremonial center and defensive refuge for a community that probably lived and farmed in the adjacent river valley, spectacularly visible from the site.

Archaeologists have skillfully restored more than two dozen significant constructions, including colonnaded palaces, false-arched passageways, plazas, patios, temples, rooms, tombs, basements, and a ball court. Its forest of towering organ cactuses adds to La Organera Xochipala's invitingly exotic ambience.

Important clues were uncovered in the trash dumps left by the inhabitants: much pottery, similar to that still used today, stone hatchets,

© BRUCE WHIPPERMAN

La Organera Xochipala Archaeological Zone

metates, tiles, polishing stones, arrow- and spear-heads, leather, copper greenstone beads, and much more. All this, added to the evidence of trade in cotton, fruit, salt, seeds, and medicinal plants recorded at the time of the Spanish conquest, surely indicates a vibrant agricultural and commercial culture, with busy trade ties with both neighboring and distant communities.

Get there from the main Chilpancingo bus station by second-class Tlacotepec-bound bus or *colectivo*. Ask the driver to let you off at the signed Zona Arqueológica side road on the left

before Xochipala. The site is another two miles on foot.

Drivers, head north from Chilpancingo on old Highway 95 about 20 miles (33 km) to the signed Filo de Caballo paved secondary road. Turn left and continue uphill six miles (10 km) to the signed Zona Arqueológica dirt side road on the left. Continue two miles (3 km) to the signed gate on the right. Few facilities, except a small museum and toilet, are available. Bring drinks, food for a picnic, good walking shoes, and a hat.

River Country

Chilpancingo serves as a convenient jumping-off point to enjoy this cluster of uniquely lovely natural attractions, set like gems beneath the pine-tufted Sierra Madre del Sur.

Closest to Chilpancingo is the Río Azul, a popular Sunday picnic route, decorated along the way by a winding, intimate canyon; a lush green farm valley; and colorful, petite market towns, climaxed by an azure ribbon of crystalline springs.

Although all that would be quite enough, a marvelous natural treat hides at the end of the 31-mile road: the Grutas de Juxtlahuaca, a pristine wonderland grotto of varicolored limestone formations, underground rivers, and prehistoric burial remains and wall paintings, all culminating in a wondrous garden of flowery, snow-white aragonite (calcium carbonate) crystals.

THE RÍO AZUL

By bus, this trip could be done from Chilpancingo in one long day. Start out at dawn, via a Colotlipa-bound bus from the Universidad Pedagogical Nacional (UPN, oo-pay-EN-ay) streetfront bus terminal at the corner of Ignacio Ramírez and Niños Héroes, about five blocks south of the Chilpancingo main *zócalo*.

For more leisure, hire a taxi for the day (figure about $50), or stay overnight, camping or staying in a *cabaña* at Balneario Santa Fe or in the Casa de Huéspedes Citlalí in Colotlipa.

Travelers by car could likewise do this 74-mile (119-km) round-trip in a day. Start off around 7 A.M., drive to the Grutas de Juxtlahuaca and explore until around 1 P.M. On the return, stop for a leisurely lunch and swim at the Balneario Santa Fe. In Chilpancingo, fill up with gasoline before you leave; otherwise, gasoline is customarily available en route at the Quechultenango *gasolinera*.

Mochitlán and Quechultenango

Drivers, follow old Highway 95 (not the toll expressway) south from Chilpancingo seven miles (11 km) to the signed Petaquillas–Quechultenango crossroad. Mark your odometer and turn left (east).

Past Petaquillas (pop. 5,000, with stores, local-style restaurants, town plaza, post office), continue east, winding through the narrow, lushly scenic canyon of the upper Río Azul. Although the riverbed may be dry during the winter and spring, don't worry; year-round springs keep the downstream delightfully crystal blue (except perhaps during some muddy summer rainy-season floods).

At Mile 6 (Km 10) arrive at Mochitlán (pop. 4,000, with *centro de salud,* post office, street market, taco shops, and stores), which presides over its verdant, irrigated, river-bottom fields. If you have an extra few minutes, take a look inside the town's venerable barrel-vaulted church. It's the focus of the July 26 **Fiesta de Santa Ana,** when the townsfolk stage a float parade, carnival, fireworks, and enjoy regional dances, including the Tlacololeros, Santiagueros, Diablos, and Huexquitxles.

Continue east to Quechultenango (pop. 10,000), the dominant town of the upper Río Azul Valley, at Mile 17 (Km 27). As if proclaiming the town's importance, the brilliantly decorated church presides over the east side of the plaza. Enter and pass the flowery *retablo* (altarpiece) behind the Virgin of Guadalupe on the left. Overhead, paintings of the Stations of the Cross decorate the ceiling, while up front, behind the altar, Santiago, mounted on a silver horse, brandishes a sword while trampling a hapless band of defeated Moors.

Community celebration focuses yearly at that very altar during the eight-day **Fiesta of Santiago,** combined with the unique indigenous rite of **Ocozuchil,** all of which culminates on the Santiago Feast Day of July 25. People flock in from neighboring communities, among them men decked out in red leather with machetes in hand, to perform the traditional dance Los Santiagueros.

Concurrently during the Santiago fiesta, other folks journey to the sierra to collect *ocozuchil,* an aromatic wild herb. When cut, the herb oozes a strong medicinal odor, thought to be curative. They walk to Quechultenango with the *ocozuchil* branches draped over their bodies and crowd into the church.

◖ Headwaters of the Río Azul

The series of *manantiales* (springs) near Coxcamila, a mile farther east of Quechultenango, at Mile 18, are the marvelous main source of the Río Azul. At the Coxcamila village center, turn right (south) onto the dirt side road to the springs, locally called **El Borbollón.** Follow the dirt side road about a quarter mile to a grove of giant old *tule* trees, from beneath whose gnarled roots cool crystal-clear water wells up, free for everyone to enjoy.

That this is the source is certain. Walk upstream 100 yards and the river is a mere trickle during the dry season. But downstream, many

thousands of gallons a minute of deep, clear aqua-blue water, delightfully cool on a warm day, flow constantly.

Camping in your own tent by the riverbank or self-contained RV in the parking lot is customary at El Borbollón. Police patrols assure nighttime security.

Balnearios

Farther downstream, activity focuses at a pair of *balnearios* (bathing spots) on the Río Azul. These include **Los Manantiales** (Mile 19, Km 31, with several attractive swimming pools and restaurant) and by far the most popular, **Balneario Santa Fe,** reachable by the signed paved side road, right at Mile 19.4 (Km 31.2), about half a mile after Los Manantiales.

For Balneario Santa Fe, continue along the side road two miles (3 km), passing through the small but prosperous Santa Fe town, to the river overlook, then downhill the last quarter mile to the river.

A dozen shady *palapa* restaurants line the clear two-foot-deep flowing stream, a welcome marvel, especially during the dry and oft-hot winter and spring.

Besides food for eating and hammocks for resting, old-fashioned water sports abound. After taking your fill of swimming, inner-tubing, and rafting, cross the river suspension bridge to the other side to the best of all possible swimming holes, complete with rope to swing out and plunge into the cool water.

If you decide to linger, the walk-in **Campamento Santa Fe** (*cabañas* $10 for up to four people, $20 for up to eight; camping spaces $1.50 pp), also across the suspension bridge, offers some options. Choose one of the cramped (but probably fun for kids) *cabañas.* For a more comfortable choice, if you're equipped, set up your tent in one of the roomy camping spaces. Toilets are in shared lavatories. For a bath, jump in the river (or the swimming pool, if it's operating).

RV campers (with medium to small rigs) can park in a large riverside lot that is accessible by turning left from the downhill entrance road a couple hundred yards before the river at the driveway marked by a big tree on the left.

GRUTAS DE JUXTLAHUACA

The lightly touristed but wondrous Grutas de Juxtlahuaca caverns takes their name from the neighboring village, Juxtlahuaca (hooks-tlah-WAH-kah). The small town of Colotlipa, four miles before the Grutas, is the jumping-off point for guides, food, and services.

Get to the Grutas de Juxtlahuaca (10 A.M.–4 P.M. Tues.–Sun., best during Feb.–May dry season) from Colotlipa most conveniently by taxi (about $10). By car, drive to the eastern edge of town, where a Grutas sign directs you left onto a paved secondary road. After three miles, pass a sugar cane–pressing mill on the left, which squeezes out juice for sweet *tepache* (wine fermented from sugarcane juice) or for fermentation into fiery *aguardiente* (cheap liquor made from sugarcane). After four miles, arrive at the cave parking lot. Facilities consist of a toilet and a *palapa* restaurant that is only sometimes open.

Colotlipa

The town of Colotlipa (pop. 4,000) is not far past the Río Azul *balnearios*, 23 miles (37 km) east of old Highway 95. If you arrive during the February 18–26 **Fiesta del Señor de las Misericordias** (Lord of Mercies), the plaza might be filled with the faithful who, by dawn on February 26, climax the festivities by celebrating their *patrón* with jingle bells and *mañanitas* (early morning mass).

Besides local-style restaurants, market fruits and vegetables, grocery stores, *centro de salud,* post office, and street telephones, Colotlipa is the place to hire your guide.

A right-side sign on east–west ingress street Calle Guerrero marks the cave guides' at-home office. Up until the late 1990s, the main guide was Profesor Andrés Ortega Casarrubias, who during the 1950s was first to explore the cave thoroughly. Andrés, known famously as El Chivo (The Goat), passed away in 2004. Now

EXPLORING THE GRUTAS DE JUXTLAHUACA

Although the Juxtlahuaca limestone cave complex, 30 miles (50 km) east of Chilpancingo, is not the world's largest, the treasures that it hides here are exquisite and unique.

The cave complex, used as a burial ground and sacred site, probably by 400 B.C., was explored by latter-day investigators in 1926 and later more thoroughly by Andrés Ortega Covarrubias during the 1950s. Ortega uncovered a then-unknown entrance and eight underground branches, extending a total of about four miles (6 km).

As in all limestone caves, Juxtlahuaca's extensive stalagmites, stalactites, columns, and curtains result from the slight solubility of limestone (calcium carbonate) in water. Thus groundwater, over eons, gradually dissolved the limestone, forming hollow chambers.

The process continues with water droplets falling from the ceiling, leaving a small wet spot above and a similar wet spot below, which dry and deposit some limestone at top and bottom. The dripping continues, gradually building the deposits into long, massive formations that, after many thousands of years, often merge to form grand columns. Water dribbling down the cave walls can deposit limestone similarly, forming magnificent curtains, lovely enough for a maharaja's palace.

Moreover, variations in mineral content, especially iron, causes color variations in the deposits, from pure white to cream, dusty rose, and sienna. Explorers have named many of the formations thus created, such as the Enchanted Fountain, the Cathedral, the Salon of the Ghost, and the Tiger.

Bats and insects make up the bulk of the cave's permanent living inhabitants. Thousands of bats roost on the ceilings not far from the entrance; on the cave floor, cockroaches scurry, feasting on the bats' droppings.

Deep in the cave, humans have left their signs on the cave's walls and floors. Several burial sites, including complete petrified skeletons; much pottery; and *El Chaman, El Serpiente,* and *El Jaguar,* a trio of magnificent cave paintings, attest to the human presence that continues to the present day.

Andrés's son Andrés, his widow, Brenda, and his second son, Enrique, continue his mission as Chivo II, Chivo III, and Chivo IV, respectively.

The Chivo guides have inherited the Grutas de Juxtlahuaca guide franchise (tel. 756/474-7006, 756/474-7034, or 756/474-7047, $20 pp, $10 pp in a group of 4–8), awarded to Andrés by the governor of Guerrero in 1958. They lead individuals and small groups. Although on weekdays you can usually arrange a tour by showing up at the cave entrance, call at least a day in advance to assure yourself a reservation.

Their standard tour (in Spanish), which lasts 2–3 hours and stretches about two underground miles round-trip, is fascinating, but moderately difficult, with some crawling through tight rocky passageways and threading your way carefully down steep limestone inclines. If at all possible, try not to miss the climactic conclusion, which requires wading along a knee-to-waist-deep underground river, then crawling 100 feet along a cramped, damp passageway. You'll get wet, but at the end of the road a marvelous garden of flowery aragonite crystals will reward your effort. Be sure to take along a pair of tennis shoes for wading and a small backpack or camera holster, and seal your camera in a strong watertight bag. For more information and some fine cave photos, visit www.barraganzone.com/ultimopro.html.

For a Colotlipa overnight, stay at **Casa de Huépedes Citlalí** (Calle Neri 21, no phone, $15 per room for up to four people), run by friendly Xochi (SOH-chee) Ortega, two blocks east and half a block south of the Colotlipa *zócalo.* She offers clean rooms with two double beds and shared toilet and hot-water shower. Make reservations through the Chivo guides.

Hearty home-cooked food is available in Colotlipa at restaurant **El Latino** (half a block south of the southeast corner of the town plaza, no phone, 8 A.M.–7 P.M. daily, $3–6). Choose from bountiful breakfasts, an afternoon *comida* (such as *guisado de res,* beef stew), and supper (taco, quesadilla, or tamales) snacks.

Handicrafts Country

The renowned handicrafts of upcountry mountain towns Chilapa and Olinalá draw a steady stream of buyers and visitors. Be sure to arrive in Chilapa (about 1.5 hours east of Chilpancingo) on Saturday night or early Sunday for the Sunday *tianguis* (native market), where craftspeople from all over the Guerrero Sierra Madre bring their best for sale.

Afterward, continue about two hours farther east for an overnight in Olinalá and visit the workshops of the masters of a preconquest lacquerware tradition whose intriguingly mysterious origins are lost in time.

CHILAPA

Presiding over its rich, spring-fed mountain valley, Chilapa de Álvarez (pop. 27,000, elev. 4,300 feet/1,310 meters) was named in honor of the liberal hero general Juan Álvarez (1810–1867). The other part of the town's name comes from Chilapan, a description given by the Aztec—from *chili* (red), *atl* (water), and *pan* (on or above). It translates roughly as "on the red water," or simply, "red river."

In 1522, the Spanish, in the person of Hernán Cortés's lieutenant, conquistador Gonzalo Sandoval, pacified the local people. Soon, Augustinian missionaries arrived and began converting them and building a church and convent, which they dedicated to Saint Augustine on October 5, 1533.

The friars encouraged the local people to expand their long-established weaving tradition. For many centuries before the conquest, their elaborately crafted blankets, *huipiles,* and skirts had been traded all over southern Mexico. Under the Augustinians' guidance, they broadened their skills, eventually crafting the wide variety of baskets, hats, napkins, and pottery that make up the rich Chilapa

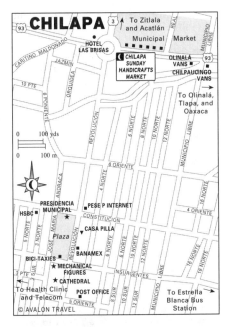

handicrafts tradition that continues to the present day.

Orientation

The prime reference point upon Chilapa arrival is the main highway crossing by the crafts market, marked by the permanent stalls behind the fence just past (east of) the crossing. If you arrive on a Sunday, head straight for the crafts market. Later, from the crossing, you can reach the downtown plaza either on foot (about half a mile south), by *bici-taxi* (bicycle rickshaw, BEE-see), or your own wheels.

☾ Chilapa Sunday Handicrafts Market

Beginning Saturday afternoon, country folks loaded with handmade goods begin arriving for the renowned Sunday handicrafts market. Their wealth of offerings come in a grand array of materials—supple leather bags, handsome belts, handy coin purses, sturdy wallets, comfortable huaraches; glistening shell and horn bracelets,

GUERRERO UPCOUNTRY

Palm-leaf *petates* (mats) are big sellers at the Chilapa Sunday market.

lovely combs, decorative ashtrays, hand-carved desk sets, attractive lampshades; steel machetes, hatchets, gleaming daggers and swords, pocket knives; embroidered *huipiles,* strong *ixtle* (agave fiber) bags, fetching *rebozos* (shawls), napkins, tablecloths, soft palm sombreros, mats, and baskets; and lacquered wooden miniature castles and bulls, scary tiger-masks, colorful paper flowers, pine furniture, select musical instruments, and enticing animal figurines.

Many crafts come from outside Chilapa—for example, shawls from Tenancingo; silver from Taxco; huaraches from Iguala and Tixtla; fireworks from Ayahualulco; lacquerware and tiger masks from Olinalá; papier-mâché from Mezcala; bright earth-red pottery from Atzcualoya; *amate* (painted bark paper) from Amayaltepec; animal figures from Temalacatzingo; and embroidered blouses and skirts from Acatlán.

(Note: Although generally unusual in Guerrero, some pickpockets unfortunately seem to be operating at the Chilapa Sunday *tianguis.* Their technique, which I experienced, was distraction by jostling. Be aware and keep your important items in a secure front waist belt. Moreover, zip your purses and if you normally keep your wallet in a back pocket, keep it in your front pocket with a hand on it.)

Downtown Plaza and Cathedral

For more sights, head south to the downtown plaza and towering neo-Gothic cathedral, dedicated to St. Francis and seat of the local bishop. One of the cathedral's main attractions occurs every Sunday at noon, when the miraculous roses of the Virgin of Guadalupe are revealed to mechanical figures of Don Diego and Archbishop Zumárraga at the door on the right bell tower. Inside the cool nave, spectacularly large stained glass windows, each one donated by a Guerrero locality, add sunny daytime cheer to the cavernous interior.

Back outside the church, a fleet of *bici-taxis,* looking every bit like bicycle rickshaws from the Indian subcontinent, stop and pick up passengers at curbside.

Before leaving the Chilapa plaza, be sure to stop for a drink or snack and admire the marvelous mask collection at the plaza-front Casa Pilla restaurant.

Accommodations and Food

Chilapa visitors enjoy a pair of recommendable hotels. About three blocks north of the plaza is ◖ **Hotel María Hilda** (Av. Revolución 229, tel. 756/475-1840; $15 s, $17 d, one bed; $21 s or d, king-size bed; $21 d, two beds; $24 t, two beds; $29 t, three beds). The hotel's 36 rooms occupy two steep stairway-accessible floors above street level. Rooms are cool, clean, light, and sparsely but comfortably furnished with bedspreads, curtains, and tiled hot-water shower baths. They lack reading lamps, however. Rooms come with cable TV and parking, but no fans or air-conditioning.

"Cleanliness Is Our Rule" is the motto at **Hotel Las Brisas** (Prolongacion Av. Revolución 2, tel. 756/475-0769; $15 s or d, one bed; $28 d, $33 t or q, two beds; $35 for 3–6 people in three beds), at the Chilpancingo highway intersection. Here you get to choose from 36 clean rooms, comfortably furnished with double beds, shiny wood furniture, bright bedspreads, and small but tiled hot-water shower baths. Some rooms have bedside reading lamps. Rooms come with cable TV, parking, fans, and air-conditioning. Reserve the quietest rooms (with the least highway noise): 5, 6, or 7 on the 2nd and 3rd floors.

Some of Chilapa's most wholesome budget food is available at the stalls at the rear of the main Chilapa market (adjacent to the outside crafts stalls). Choicest is *fonda* **Doña Lilia** (7:30 A.M.–7 P.M. daily), which specializes in savory chicken or pork *pozole* and steaming *guisado de res* (beef stew).

Chilapa's best downtown plaza-front eatery is restaurant-bakery **Casa Pilla** (at the northeast downtown plaza corner, tel. 756/475-0263, 8 A.M.–8 P.M. Mon.–Sat., 8 A.M.–7 P.M. Sun., $3–7). If not for the food, Casa Pilla is unforgettable for the spectacular mask collection that adorns its airy dining room.

Equally colorful is the ◖ **Casa Vieja** (474 Calle 6 Norte, two blocks east of the plaza's northeast corner, tel. 756/475-2740,

8 A.M.–8 P.M. Mon.–Sat., 8 A.M.–7 P.M. Sun., $4–10). Within a wall-hung gallery of 1910 Revolution photos and a festoon of ancient *tipica* curios, enjoy a Mexican-style breakfast *(huevos a la Mexicana), comida (chiles rellenos),* or tender ranch *bistec* (steak) for supper.

Events

Chilapa takes time out for a pair of colorful yearly fiestas. First comes the **Fiesta de San Juan** around June 24, when folks crowd the plaza to watch a parade of floats, listen to the oompah of country bands, watch fireworks, and enjoy their favorite regional dances, including the Pescados (Fish) and Moros y Cristianos (Moors and Christians).

Those who didn't get a chance to celebrate earlier get another similar opportunity when townsfolk parade their patron at the August 15 **Fiesta de la Virgen de la Asunción.**

Services

A number of essential services are accessible at (or within walking distance from) the Chilapa plaza. For money, go to **Banamex** (tel. 756/475-0101, 9 A.M.–4 P.M. Mon.–Fri.) on the east side of the plaza.

To get to the *correo* (post office; Calle 12 Sur, between Calles 5 and 7 Oriente, tel. 756/475-0066, 8 A.M.–3 P.M. Mon.–Fri.) from the church-front, walk five blocks east along Insurgentes, to Calle 12 Sur, then turn right and walk south two and a half blocks, passing Calles 3 and 5 Sur, to the post office, before Calle 7 Sur.

For telephone, either buy a Ladatel phone card and use one of the plaza-front street telephones, or go to **Telecom** (Calle 3 Poniente (West), 9 A.M.–3 P.M. Mon.–Fri., 9 A.M.–noon Sat.–Sun.) for public telephone, fax, and money orders. From the southwest (churchfront) plaza corner, walk south a block to Calle 3 Poniente. Turn right and continue three blocks past the Centro de Salud. Internet access is available at **Pese P Internet** (at the northeast plaza corner, tel. 756/475-2400, chelisinc@hotmail.com, 9 A.M.–10 P.M. daily).

For medical attention, let your hotel desk clerk call a doctor for you. Alternatively, go to the **Centro de Salud** (Calle 3 Poniente 703, tel. 756/475-0288), with a doctor on call 24 hours a day, a block east of the Telecom.

Getting There and Away

From Chilpancingo, connect with Chilapa via a first- or second-class bus departure from the Estrella Blanca main bus station. From Acapulco, Chilapa connections (via Chilpancingo) are available from the Estrella Blanca Ejido terminal.

For Chilapa bus departure, go by taxi or *bici-taxi* (bicycle rickshaw) to the local **Estrella Blanca terminal** (Av. Municipio Libre 1804, tel. 756/475-0032). Either walk three blocks east of the plaza to Avenida Municipio Libre, or from the market walk a block east along the highway-front, then right (south) about a mile.

From the terminal, a number of first- and second-class buses connect daily via Tixtla with Chilpancingo, Acapulco, and Mexico City. One (usually late-night) bus per day connects directly east with Olinalá. Alternatively, you can connect with Olinalá via one of the several buses that head to Tlapa de Comonfort. Simply get off en route at the junction to Olinalá and continue north (25 miles, one hour) by *colectivo* or taxi to Olinalá.

More frequent van connections (5 A.M.–7 P.M.) are also available at a pair of terminals across Highway 93 from the Chilapa main market, at the corner of Calle Municipio Libre. **Transportes Guerrerenses** vans connect west several times per day with Chilpancingo and all intermediate points. Across the street, **Ruta Chilapa-Olinalá** vans provide similar connections west with Olinalá and all intermediate points. Neither had phones at this writing.

The good, super-scenic, all-paved but winding Highway 93 connects Chilpancingo with Chilapa in 34 miles (54 km, about 1 hr). In the opposite direction, Highway 93 connects Chilapa with Tlapa de Comonfort over three 7,000-foot ridges in about 75 miles (121 km, about 3 hrs) of smooth, scenic, but winding highway. In all cases, fill up with gasoline at the Chilapa station on the highway.

Reach Olinalá from Chilapa by driving east

toward Tlapa. After about 57 miles (92 km, 2.5 hrs), turn left (north) from Highway 93 at the signed Olinalá junction. Continue north about 25 smooth miles (40 km, 1 hr) to Olinalá, for a total of about 3.5 hours from Chilapa.

OLINALÁ

Reigning over its fertile mountain-rimmed valley on the edge of the sunny basin of the Río Balsas, Olinalá is famous not only for its lacquerware, but also for its masks and furniture. Most Olinalá families are involved in lacquerware, and a number of artisans welcome visitors into their home factory-stores.

Orientation

Olinalá (Place of Earthquakes; pop. 5,000, elev. 4,000 feet/1,300 meters) is basically a large, easy-to-explore village. As in most Mexican towns, Olinalá's streets run north–south and east–west.

Incoming bus travelers from Chilapa-Chilpancingo arrive at the Olinalá street-corner bus terminal, uphill, about five blocks south of (before) town. Continue north on foot or hire a taxi ($1) to the town plaza. Drivers, turn left (west) onto Olinalá main street Ramón Ibarra, a block after the ingress highway bridge. Within about three uphill blocks, you'll arrive at the main town plaza.

Orient yourself by the *presidencia municipal* portals on the plaza's west side and the church on the opposite (east) side. Olinalá's two main streets, Ramón Ibarra and Vicente Guerrero, run east–west along the south and north sides of the plaza, respectively.

Templo de San Francisco

For a revealing preview of the finest of all possible Olinalá lacquerware, head first to the town showplace Templo de San Francisco, one of Mexico's most unique churches, on the plaza's east side.

Inside, a riot of lacquerware, known locally as *linaoe* (lee-nah-OH-ay), dominates the decorations. Although many local artisans have contributed to the decorations, some features stand out. The nave columns, in contrasting cream and maroon, are the work of the acknowledged Olinalá master *artesano* Francisco Coronel.

Also, don't miss the right front side chapel, dedicated to the Virgin of Guadalupe. And before you leave, be sure to look at the mural by the front door, featuring a unique Trinity. Its deity-trio, all of whom resemble Jesus, rain avenging angels down upon devils and sinners in hell.

Handicrafts

Next, go to the source, the workshop-store of *maestro* **Francisco "Don Chico" Coronel** (Juan Aldama 12, tel. 756/473-0084), who welcomes visitors during the day. From the plaza's southwest corner, walk west, uphill, along Ibarra, a few blocks to Aldama, turn right, and continue a few doors to the Coronel's house on the right. Inside, if you're lucky, you'll get to watch him applying the finishing touches to a fine piece of

THE ART OF DON CHICO CORONEL

Olinalá's native son Francisco "Don Chico" Coronel is the nationally acknowledged master of the style of lacquerware that has made Olinalá famous. Born in 1941, young Francisco was apprenticed into the traditional craft of lacquerware as it had been learned by nameless generations of Olinalá youths before him.

Originally, Olinalá craftspeople had made an art of lacquer-decorated gourds. Demand extended the original craft to trinket and jewel boxes, then trays and chests, tables and chairs, and more.

But regardless of size and variety, the method has remained constant. First, the wood is collected, cut, carved to shape, and hand-sanded. A base coat of *chia* seed oil, colored with a locally gathered and ground natural mineral pigment, is applied and left to dry. The piece is then burnished to a shine with a smooth stone, and the whole process is repeated many times over. After the last coat of oil has been applied, the piece is left to dry for a month. Craftspeople next lay out designs that are engraved into the piece, traditionally with a natural agave thorn needle. Vivid colors are painted into the engraving to create a harmonious animal or floral design.

During the 1970s, Don Chico began adding gold to his colors, creating rich and lovely gilded flowers, birds, rabbits, and much more in his designs.

Some Olinalá craftspeople, impatient with the time-consuming traditional materials and processes, are using commercial pigments and oils and faster machine methods. In some cases the quality has suffered.

But that's not true of Don Chico's art. He continues to work by the traditional methods and materials. He's become so famous that presidents have commissioned him to make gifts representative of Mexican craftsmanship. Don Chico responded by making a magnificent tray for Queen Elizabeth II of Great Britain. And when Pope John Paul came to Mexico in July 2002 to canonize the first Latin American indigenous saint, president Vicente Fox presented to John Paul a regal chest made by Francisco "Don Chico" Coronel of Olinalá.

© BRUCE WHIPPERMAN

Acknowledged Olinalá lacquerware maestro Francisco "Don Chico" Coronel finishes a fine lacquerware box.

work. The masterfully crafted and detailed treasury—*bateas* (trays), *cajas* (boxes), *arcas* (chests), *calabazas* (gourds)—that decorates his workshop represents the pinnacle of Olinalá craftsmanship. Collectively, the pieces represent the essence of many centuries of experience and practice. Individually, each piece is the prized product of hours of meticulous work, gathering and processing the natural raw materials, sanding, painting, burnishing, engraving, and finally the fine finish painting that *maestro* Francisco applies. The prices that he asks, typically $40–60 for small-to-medium pieces, are modest indeed.

Several other Olinalá master artisans welcome visitors. (Although they have no formal business hours, keep in mind that these artisans work from their homes. Out of courtesy, one shouldn't arrive too early or too late (no earlier than 9 A.M. and no later than 7 P.M.). Back at the plaza's southeast corner, walk downhill (east) along Ibarra one block. Turn right at Matamoros and continue a few doors to the shop of **Adolfo Escudero Mejía** (Matomoros 5, tel. 756/473-0075). He specializes in beautiful, meticulously designed and adorned boxes, chests, chairs, and trays, many of innovative decoration.

Continue east, downhill, along Ibarra a long block to the corner of Comonfort, where you'll find **Artesanías Olinalá** (corner of Ibarra and Comonfort, tel. 756/473-0022, 8 A.M.–7 P.M. daily), the shop of personable Edilberto Jiménez Barrera. Inside, admire his collection of mostly boxes and chests, but also many unusual-motif gift clocks (representing, for example, lawyers, rancheros, and cockfighters).

Walk a few doors south on Comonfort to find, on the left, **Cajita Linaloe** (Comonfort 3, tel. 756/473-0029, 8 A.M.–7 P.M. daily), the shop of *artesana* Audelia Rendón Franco. Her factory store and workshop, in the rear, are the ongoing result of more than 200 years of family tradition. It abounds with a myriad of lacquerware mirrors, boxes large and small, *calabazas,* picture frames, jaguar masks, and much more.

Accommodations and Food

Olinalá accommodates visitors with at least two acceptable hotels. If you can tolerate roosters

crowing at six in the morning, the best choice is **Hotel Cindy** (Guerrero 46, tel. 756/473-0114; $16 s or d, one bed; $21 d, two beds), two blocks east of the plaza. This loosely run family establishment offers about 15 rooms in three exterior-corridor floors overlooking a parking lot–garden. Rooms (excepting those not rentable) are decently clean with pink bedspreads and tiled baths and come with hot water, fans, TV, and parking. There is an airy upstairs restaurant in the hotel.

The second choice goes to four-story **Hotel Coral** (Ramón Ibarra s/n, no phone; $14 s or d, one double bed; $21 d, two double beds) half a block east of the plaza. A popular stopping place for truck drivers, the Coral offers about 30 plain but clean bare-bulb rooms with colorful tile, fluffy bedspreads, curtains, and hot-water showers. For privacy and a minimum of outside truck noise, take a room on the top floor, away from the street. Rooms come with fans and TV; parking is only available on the street.

As for food, economy meals (soups, stews, tacos, enchiladas, *pozole,* and more) are the specialties of the several **fondas** (food stalls) that set up daily (and nightly) on the north side of the plaza.

For sit-down breakfast, lunch, and supper, the best choice in town is the charming ◖ **Pozolería La Cabaña** (Ramón Ibarra, no phone, 8 A.M.–10 P.M. Mon.–Sat., 8 A.M.–3 P.M. Sun., $2–5), half a block east of the plaza. Savvy owners have turned a rustic, massive-beamed old house into a restaurant that fits its name perfectly. Part of the fun of La Cabaña is the eclectic old-time collection—masks, *cazuelas* (stewing crocks), gourds, wooden spoons, longhorn cattle skulls, and a yellowed portrait of Emiliano Zapata—that decorates the walls.

Alternatively, go to welcoming **Cocina Económica La Guadalupana** (Ramón Ibarra, no phone, 8 A.M.–6 P.M. daily, $2–4), across from the plaza, for breakfast, a hearty *comida* for lunch, or early supper. Friendly, hard-working owner-chef Oralia Garcia specializes in wild game, such as rabbit, opossum, wild pig, and turkey.

Events

If you like old-Mexico color and don't mind

crowds, time your visit to coincide with either of Olinalá's big festivals: the **Fiesta de Pascua** (Passover) during the week before Easter Sunday or the patronal **Fiesta de San Francisco de Asis** (Oct. 2–5).

During the Easter festival, the highlight, besides plenty of food, handicrafts for sale, fireworks, cockfights, and carnival, is the procession of the Stations of the Cross that reenacts the Passion of Jesus.

Later, the San Francisco festival features much of the same, plus a big for-sale handicrafts exposition, *mojigangos* (giant dancing effigies), and favorite traditional dances, including Los Tigres, Los Tecuanes, and the French courtship Danza de los Doce Pares. (Make your hotel reservations early.)

Services

Olinalá provides some essential services close to the plaza.

For ATMs and money exchange, go to **Bancomer** (Ramón Ibarra, tel. 756/473-0332, 8:30 A.M.–4 P.M. Mon.–Fri.), across from the southeast corner of the plaza.

Find the *correo* (8 A.M.–3 P.M. Mon.–Fri.) and **Telecom** (tel. 756/473-0259, 9 A.M.–3 P.M. Mon.–Fri., 9 A.M.–noon Sat.) beneath the *presidencia municipal* portal, west of the plaza. Longer hours for public telephone and fax are available at the Farmacia Discuento.

Internet access is available at **Café@Internet** (Ramón Ibarra 27 Poniente, tel. 756/473-1039, 10 A.M.–10 P.M. daily), a block and a half west of the plaza.

Olinalá provides a number of medical options. For simple medications and advice, try **Farmacia Discuento** (corner of Ramón Ibarra and H. Colegio Militar, tel. 756/473-0346, 8 A.M.–10 P.M. daily), on the north side of Ibarra, a block west of the plaza. For a doctor, drop in to the 24-hour **Centro de Salud** (tel. 756/473-0044, across the street from Farmacia Discuento. Of Olinalá's private physicians, **Dr. Cipriano López Hernandéz** (Guerrero 105) is highly recommended, about four blocks downhill, east of the plaza. Alternatively, visit **Dr. Marizela Jiménez** (Guerrero, half a block east of the plaza).

In an emergency, contact the *policías* (tel. 756/473-0006 or 756/473-0007) in the *presidencia municipal* on the west side of the plaza.

Getting There and Away
BY BUS

Buses and vans arrive and depart from the Olinalá bus station on the ingress highway, uphill five blocks south of town. From Chilpancingo, bus travelers can connect via Estrella Blanca buses via Chilapa, where it's most convenient to continue via Ruta Chilapa-Olinalá van. From eastern locations in Puebla and Oaxaca you can reach Olinalá via Tlapa de Comonfort.

From the same uphill bus station, Sur buses provide two second-class departures per day, connecting with northern and eastern destinations, including Mexico City and the states of Puebla (via Izucar de Matamoros), Morelos (via Cuautla), and Oaxaca (transfer at Tlapa de Comonfort).

Also from the same uphill station, vans provide connections east, with Tlapa de Comonfort, and west, with Chilapa and Chilpancingo, many times per day.

BY CAR

To or from Chilpancingo via Chilapa, drivers can connect with Olinalá, via Highway 93. Westbound, about 57 miles (92 km, 2.5 hrs) after Chilapa, head left (north) from Highway 93 at the signed Olinalá junction. Continue north about 25 smooth miles (40 km, 1 hr) to Olinalá, for a total of about 3.5 hours from Chilapa (or 116 mi/187 km, about 5 hrs, from Chilpancingo).

To or from the north and east (Mexico City and the states of Morelos, Puebla, and Oaxaca), connect via Highway 190 via Izucar de Matamoros, Puebla; or Huajuapan de León, Oaxaca. At the Highway 190 junction with Highway 92, 37 miles (59 km) southeast of Izucar or 57 miles (92 km) northwest of Huajuapan, head south 78 miles (126 km) to the Olinalá junction at Huamuxtitlán. Continue via westbound secondary road another 17 miles (27 km) via Cuauhlote, Cualac, and Xhiacingo to Olinalá. For this trip, figure a total of about four hours from Izucar, five from Huajuapan.

GUERRERO UPCOUNTRY

Iguala

Only a tiny fraction of the vacationers hurrying south to Acapulco bothers to stop in Iguala (pop. 100,000, elev. 2,430 feet/740 meters). Consequently, Iguala is nearly tourist-free. This is remarkable, since the town's official name, Iguala de la Independencia, is much more than a slogan. Iguala is a major patriotic-historic center of Mexico and cradle of Agustín de Itúrbide's Plan de Iguala, which spelled out Mexican independence, and his Bandera de las Trigarantías (Flag of the Three Guarantees)—the red, white, and green tricolor beneath which Itúrbide finally rode triumphantly into Mexico City on September 27, 1821.

Local folks don't seem to mind the lack of tourist hullabaloo, however. They go about their business, living well from both the local mineral riches and the agricultural bounty—fruit, corn, cattle—of their fertile, spring-fed valley.

They also love their pedestrian-friendly downtown, with a number of good restaurants and not one but three shady plazas, sprinkled with juice- and snackstands and cafés.

All this would be easily worth an overnight, but Iguala offers even more: a whole complex

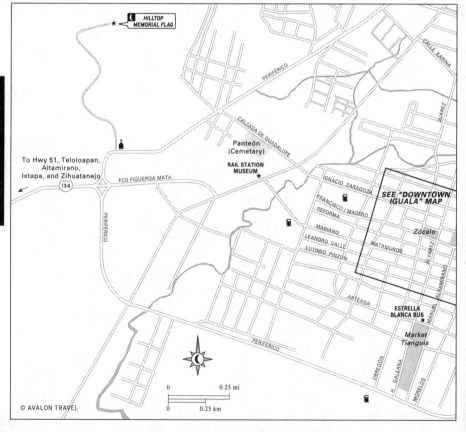

of shops selling gold jewelry, the fascinating Museo y Santuario a la Bandera, and, not to be missed atop a breezy hillside, a spectacularly large Mexican flag billowing gracefully above a monument to the Heroes of the Independence. Furthermore, an easy local excursion leads to Lake Tuxpan for possible boating, camping, and frolicking at the adjacent lovely Quinta Happy bathing resort.

HISTORY

The name Iguala comes from the town's former Aztec-language label, Yohualtépetl, which means, very appropriately, "basin surrounded by mountains." After the conquest, the local Spanish missionaries shifted the name to the more pronounceable Yohuala, and finally, Iguala.

Chontal-speaking people at least as early as A.D. 800 founded the town, which was originally known as Motlacehuatl, an Iguala district still called "old town." During the Aztec expansions of the 1400s, warriors under direction of Emperor Izcoatl conquered Motlacehuatl and erected a temple. Aztec colonists arrived and prospered on the labor of their Chontal-speaking slaves and servants.

The Spanish arrived in 1522 and replaced the Aztec temple, warriors, and settlers with their own church, soldiers, and colonists. They prospered for nearly 300 years until the surrounding region, ignited by Miguel Hidalgo's

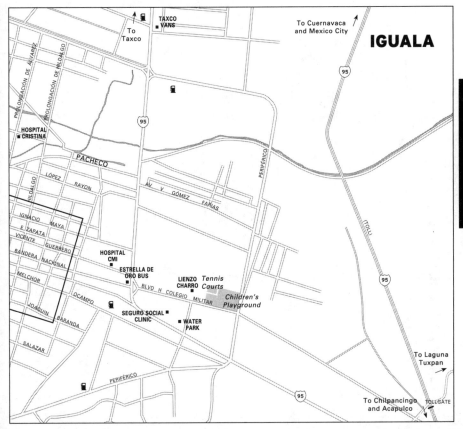

GUERRERO UPCOUNTRY

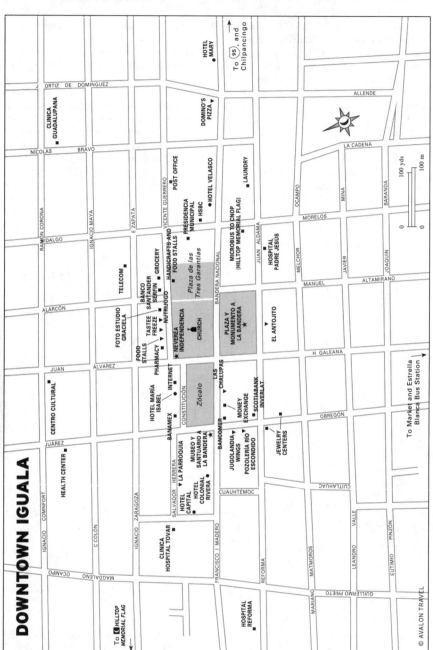

DOWNTOWN IGUALA

To ◀ HILLTOP MEMORIAL FLAG ◀

ORTIZ DE DOMINGUEZ

CLINICA GUADALUPANA ■

ALLENDE

To 95, and Chilpancingo

HOTEL MARY ●

DOMINO'S PIZZA ▼

LA CADENA

100 yds
100 m

NICOLAS BRAVO

POST OFFICE ■

HOTEL VELASCO ●

PRESIDENCIA MUNICIPAL ■

HSBC ■

LAUNDRY ■

OCAMPO

MORELOS

MINA

BARANDA

RAMON CORONA

HIDALGO

IGNACIO MAYA

E ZAPATA

VICENTE GUERRERO

HANDICRAFTS AND FOOD STALLS ■

MICROBUS TO CNOP (HILLTOP MEMORIAL FLAG) ■

JUAN ALDAMA

HOSPITAL PADRE JESÚS ■

JAVIER

MELCHOR

JOAQUIN

ALTAMIRANO

ALARCÓN

TELECOM ■

BANCO SANTANDER SERFIN ■

GROCERY ■

NUTRI-HUGO ■

Plaza de las Tres Garantias

BANDERA NACIONAL

MANUEL

FOTO ESTUDIO GRACIELA ■

TASTEE FREEZE ▼

NEVERÍA INDEPENDENCIA ▼

CHURCH ■

PLAZA Y MONUMENTO A LA BANDERA ★

EL ANTOJITO ■

H GALEANA

JUAN

ALVAREZ

FOOD STALLS ■

PHARMACY ■

★

CENTRO CULTURAL ■

HOTEL MARÍA ISABEL ■

INTERNET ●

BANAMEX ■

Zócalo

CONSTITUCIÓN

LAS CHALUPAS ■

MONEY EXCHANGE ■

SCOTIABANK INVERLAT ■

OBREGÓN

JUÁREZ

HEALTH CENTER ■

BANGOMER ■

MUSEO Y SANTUARIO A LA BANDERA ★

JUGOLANDIA ▼

WINGS ■

POZOLERÍA RÍO ESCONDIDO ●

JEWELRY CENTERS ■

SALVADOR

HERRERA

▼ LA PARROQUIA

HOTEL CAPITAL ■

HOTEL COLONIAL RIVERA ●

CUAUHTÉMOC

CUITLAHUAC

MATAMOROS

VALLE

LEANDRO

PINZÓN

EUTIMIO

To Market and Estrella Blanca Bus Station →

MAGDALENO

OCAMPO

IGNACIO

C COLON

IGNACIO ZARAGOZA

FRANCISCO I. MADERO

CLINICA HOSPITAL TOVAR ■

REFORMA

HOSPITAL REFORMA ■

MARIANO

GUILLERMO PRIETO

To ◀ HILLTOP MEMORIAL FLAG ◀

© AVALON TRAVEL

1810 cry for independence and led by generals José María Morelos and Vicente Guerrero, became the focus of a long, bloody anti-Spanish rebellion. Finally, the struggle climaxed in Iguala on February 24, 1821, when Agustín de Itúrbide, former royalist general turned rebel, joined forces with Guerrero.

Their agreement was based on the *Plan de Iguala,* an Independence strategy that was essentially a moderate compromise that both the conservative European-descendant elite that Itúrbide represented and Guerrero's indigenous and mestizo campesinos could agree upon. It called for an independent Mexico with a parliament presided over by a constitutional Spanish monarchy, much like the 19th-century English monarchs presided over the Dominion of Canada. At the core of the Plan were the Trigarantías (Three Guarantees), three salient principles: Independence from Spain, Catholicism, and equality amongst all Mexicans (men only, however).

On October 27, 1849, Iguala was chosen as the first capital of the new state of Guerrero. Later, the capital shifted to Tixtla, and finally Chilpancingo by the end of the 19th century.

SIGHTS
Arrival and Orientation

Most bus passengers arrive at the Estrella Blanca bus station (corner of Galeana and Salazar), north side of the main market. For the center of town, walk or taxi the seven blocks north along Galeana (to the right as you exit the terminal), or ride a *colectivo* to the zócalo. (If, however, you arrive at the east-side Estrella de Oro bus station on Highway 95, do the same by either taxi or *colectivo* or by walking eight blocks west, away from the highway, along Bandera Nacional to the *zócalo*.)

Drivers arriving via Highway 95 from Taxco heading south, or from Chilpancingo heading north, follow Centro or Zócalo highway signs west after passing the *periférico* (peripheral boulevard)—heading south, turn right; heading north, turn left. Continue about eight blocks west to the *zócalo*.

At the Iguala town center you'll find a trio

of inviting plazas. From east to west, first comes the **Plaza de Trigarantías,** bordered by Avenida Vicente Guerrero on the north and Avenida Bandera Nacional on the south. Move diagonally southwest, across the corner of Bandera Nacional and north–south Calle Altamirano, to find the broad garden **Plaza y Monumento a la Bandera,** bordered on the south by Calle Aldama.

Finally, move diagonally northwest, across the corner of Calle Juan Álvarez and Avenida Bandera Nacional, to the *zócalo,* the very heart of the town. Its bordering streets are one-block Constitución, on its north side; Juárez, on the west side; Reforma, on the south side; and Álvarez, on the east side. Note the landmarks: the Museo y Santuario a la Bandera on the Juárez (west) side and the Hotel María Isabel on its Constitución (north) side.

The *Zócalo*

The downtown *zócalo,* one of the most excitingly pleasant in Guerrero, is a relaxing people-watching sight all in itself. Pause for a refreshment at one of the juice bars and enjoy the shade beneath the 32 leafy tamarind trees, planted in 1832 thanks to general Don Luis Gonzaga Vieyra.

Museo y Santuario a la Bandera

From the *zócalo,* walk west across Juárez to the Museo y Santuario a la Bandera (tel. 733/333-6765, 9 A.M.–6 P.M. Tues.–Sat., 9 A.M.–3 P.M. Sun., $3). The museum has three main *salas* (exhibition halls), all worth a visit.

The **Sala de las Banderas** exhibits a pageant of historic Mexican flags, led off by the celebrated tricolor Bandera de las Trigarantías, with its diagonal white, green, and red stripes. The stripes represent the Plan de Iguala's Three Guarantees: pure white for the Catholic religion, green for independence, and red representing equality for all the races of Mexico.

Also notable is the eagle-and-serpent Aztec "flag," from the Aztec historical document the *crónica* Mexcáyotl, as preserved in the post-conquest record, the Codex Duran.

The 20-odd remaining flags are remarkable partly for their evolutionary linkages to

© BRUCE WHIPPERMAN

the cool and shady main plaza of Iguala

the present Mexican national flag, adopted in 1952, at the end of the hall.

Continue to the **Sala Plan de Iguala,** which exhibits, besides the words of the Mexican national anthem, a copy of the original Plan de Iguala signed by Agustín de Itúrbide on February 24, 1821, and a more readable modern copy. The Plan de Iguala is interesting, partly for its comparison with the revolutionary-period documents of the United States. While the Mexican document effectively declares Catholicism to be the religion of the land and all races to be equal, its U.S. counterparts, such as the Declaration of Independence and the Bill of Rights, say nothing about equality of the races and next to nothing about religion, except the freedom to worship (or not to worship) thereof.

The third hall is the **Santuario a la Bandera,** with a grand illuminated Mexican flag at one end of a hushed and darkened room.

More Downtown Sights

From the museum, head due east to the *zócalo*'s southeast corner. Diagonally southeast, across the corner of Álvarez and Bandera Nacional, spreads the **Plaza y Monumento a la Bandera.** The plaza's grand central memorial, dedicated in 1942 by then president Manuel Ávila Camacho, reflects the Socialist Realism style of the day. It depicts an abnormally husky native couple, the woman with torch in hand, guarding the flag.

The **Centro Joyero de Iguala** (Jewelry Center; corner of Reforma and Obregón, tel. 733/333-3778, 9 A.M.–7 P.M. daily) is both a sight and a shopping ground. Find it just one block south of the *zócalo*'s southeast corner. Inside, a swarm of shops sell seemingly everything possible that can be made of gold.

Outside of the immediate downtown, rail enthusiasts might enjoy a visit to **Museo Ferrocarríl** (Railroad Museum; corner of Calle de la Estación and the railroad track, 9 A.M.–6 P.M. daily), in the former rail station, a mile west of downtown. Currently in the process of restoration, the museum displays a small collection of historic photos and old tools from around 1905 when the rail line reached Iguala.

◖ Hilltop Memorial Flag

Although initially I didn't plan to go to the hilltop west of town for a close-up view of Iguala's big Mexican flag atop its summit, I changed my mind when one day I glanced west across town and noticed the flag for the first time. It was so fantastically huge that it dwarfed every tall building and tree (which were several times closer) in the town foreground.

The hilltop known as C.N.O.P. (pronounced "say-aynay-oh-pay"), where the giant flag was first raised in 1998, is officially the site of the **Monumento a los Héroes de la Independencia** (Monument to the Heroes of the Independence) featuring a shrine inside a summit building (9 A.M.–5 P.M. daily). On a breezy day, the noise alone from the flag's graceful, slow-motion rippling is surprisingly powerful, like the repeated rumble and snap of a chorus of mini sonic booms (which they in fact are). The flagpole, a monumental, twenty-story stack of welded steel about eight feet in diameter at the base, is a wonder in itself.

A small platoon of 25 soldiers is required to carry and fold the 550-pound (250-kg) flag, which is brought down daily before sunset and raised at sunrise. To view the spectacle, arrive before approximately 5:30 A.M. or 5:30 P.M. in summer, 6:00 A.M. or 5:00 P.M. in winter.

Get to the flag by either taxi ($4 roundtrip) from the *zócalo* or by *colectivo* ($0.50 one way) from Calle Morelos (between Guerrero and Bandera Nacional), a block east of the Plaza y Monumento a la Bandera.

By car, head west along *zócalo*-front Calle Ignacio Zaragoza from downtown. Continue for about a mile (across railroad tracks) to the Periferico four-lane thoroughfare. Turn left and continue a half-mile east until you see a chapel on the right, a block before the old Highway 95 underpass. Turn right and pass in front of the chapel, uphill. Continue up the all-paved grade, following the tricolor red, white, and green signs to the top.

ACCOMMODATIONS

Most recommendable Iguala hotels fall in the moderate under-$50 category. During Iguala's very hot and dry spring months of April, May, and June, air-conditioning, if not essential, is certainly a very desirable option if you can afford the extra expense (about $7). The

© BRUCE WHIPPERMAN

Notice the tiny figure at the base of the pole, which is like an ant in comparison to the 200-foot length of Iguala's hilltop memorial flag.

following recommendations start at the *zócalo* and move outward.

Start with Iguala's landmark hotel, the **Hotel María Isabel** (Portal Constitución 5, tel. 733/333-3233 or 733/333-3242, fax 733/333-3240, $45 s, $63 d, $73 t). Once Iguala's pride, now a bit worn but still worthy, the hotel offers about 40 clean (but less than immaculate), conservatively but thoughtfully decorated, dark-wood–paneled rooms with bath. The best and quietest are the upper rear rooms, with small balconies overlooking the tree-shaded pool-patio. Rentals come with air-conditioning, cable TV, and phone. The hotel has an inviting large pool (check to see if it's operating) and patio, parking, and a good plaza-view restaurant upstairs. Credit cards are accepted.

Walk west of the *zócalo* for two more recommendable hostelries. On the short north–south street a block due west of the *zócalo*, find newish **Hotel Capital** (José A. Ocampo 1, tel. 733/334-1399; one double bed: $27 s or d, fan only; $35 s and $40 d with a/c; two beds: $28 d and $30 t fan only; $40 d and $45 t with a/c). Here, guests have the advantage of a quiet side-street location a mere block from the downtown action. Many of the 30-odd smallish rooms in three floors are dark, but invitingly decorated in color-coordinated shades of blue, with hot-water shower baths, tile floors, and attractive wooden furniture. Rentals include cable TV, parking, and a small hotel pool and patio. Credit cards are not accepted.

A block south and a block and a half farther west is the classier old-standby hostelry, **Hotel Colonial Rivera** (Madero 3, tel./fax 733/333-2587, or 733/333-2547; one double bed: $25 s, $29 d fan only; $33 s, $38 d with a/c; two double beds: $30 d or t fan only; $40 d or t with a/c.). The hotel's builders have packed a lot of hotel into a small space. Most of the two floors of 49 rooms line an invitingly leafy but narrow interior patio-garden. Unfortunately, most rooms are dark, with only one window (which must be covered for privacy) facing the exterior corridor. A few lighter, more private rooms face the street but are consequently noisier. The good news is that the rooms are immaculate and have attractive neocolonial decor and some

even have up-to-date noiseless air-conditioning. Rates, furthermore, are very moderate. All rooms come with TV, phone, and security box. There is a restaurant and parking, but no pool. Credit cards are accepted.

On the opposite side of the *zócalo* are a pair of good economy hotel choices, well managed by the same savvy owners. Two blocks east of the *zócalo*, find **Hotel Velasco** (Bandera Nacional 3, tel. 733/332-8120, fax 733/332-5714; one double bed: $18 s, $22 d, fan only; $35 s or d with a/c; two double beds: $25 d, $30 t fan only; $32 d, $40 t with a/c). Clever design has placed the 36 rooms in two floors *above* (rather than beside) the noisy, smoggy, parking patio. Another attractive feature is an airy front upstairs breezeway, with tables beside soft couches for relaxing. All rooms come with fans, hot-water shower baths, phones, cable TV, and parking; credit cards are accepted.

Two blocks farther east, find the **Hotel Mary** (Bandera Nacional 39A, tel. 733/332-5020 or 733/332-5320, fax 733/332-5714; $23 d, with fan; $32 s or d with a/c). The three-floor Mary has modest prices and savvy amenities similar to its brother, the Velasco: breezeways with soft chairs for relaxing and clean, well-maintained rooms.

FOOD
Snacks and Food Stalls

Snacks are plentiful downtown. For example, on one of Iguala's frequent warm afternoons, beat the heat with a *licuado* (ice, fruit, milk, and sugar whipped to a milkshake-like froth but minus the calories) at one of the *jugerías* (juice stalls) that dot the *zócalo* area. If you want more, they usually also serve fresh fruit, hot dogs, *hamburguesas,* and *tortas.*

For a rewarding example, pull up a stool at **Jugolandia Wings** (Juiceland Wings; across Madero from the Museo y Santuario a la Bandera, 6 A.M.–11 P.M. daily), diagonally across from the *zócalo*'s southwest corner. On the *zócalo*'s east side, enjoy about the same tasty options at **Nutrijugo** (Vicente Guerrero), across (north) from the church.

Hearty budget country-style specialties

(tacos, tostadas, *tortas, sincronizadas, pinguinos, quemeyes, alambre*) and more are offered by the platoon of *fondas* (food stalls) in the **Market San Francisco Plaza** (Vicente Guerrero), a block and a half east of the *zócalo*, past the church, across from the Plaza de Trigarantías.

Finally, enjoy an ice cream cone at one of Iguala's quaintest and most venerable institutions, the **(C Nevería Independencia** (on the *zócalo*'s north side, no phone, 10 A.M.–9 P.M. daily), a few doors east of the Hotel María Isabel. Here, the star of the show is an antique ice-cream freezer, complete with a 1920s-era belt-drive compressor, open for everyone to admire. The ice cream, which is excellent (the house specialty is vanilla in a dozen variations), seems an afterthought after witnessing in action the old machine that made it.

Cafés and Restaurants

A sprinkling of downtown restaurants accommodate the Iguala locals who can afford to eat out. One of the town center's classiest is mod **Tastee Freeze-La Vaca Negra** (Vicente Guerrero, tel. 733/332-0177, 8 A.M.–midnight daily, $4–10), half a block east of the *zócalo*, across from the church. Although its name sounds like that of a fast-food joint, it's actually a refined coffee shop trying to appeal to the middle- and upper-class young at heart. It does it quite well with a tasty, professionally prepared and served breakfast, lunch, and dinner menu.

A number of town-center restaurants also serve folks hungering for country fare the way *abuelita hacia* (grandma used to make). The best example is **(C Pozolería Río Escondido** (Obregón, tel. 733/333-3362, 9 A.M.–11 P.M. daily, $2), the place for you to learn even more if you think you already know Mexican food. Start out with appetizer *pata de puerco*, continue with *tacos de longaniza*, then *tostadas de tinga*. If, on the other hand, you hanker for something familiar, go for the house specialty *pozole con todo* (with all the fixin's). Find it half a block south of the southwest *zócalo* corner.

If you want a spell away from old Mexico, go to **Domino's Pizza** (corner of Ortiz de Domínguez and Bandera Nacional, tel. 733/332-4567, 9 A.M.–11 P.M. daily, $5–15), four blocks east of the *zócalo*. Enter the cool white dining room and choose from the lineup of a dozen styles of the usual pizzas, plus half a dozen local favorites you've never heard of.

ENTERTAINMENT AND EVENTS

For child's play, Iguala has both the kid-friendly west-side park and playground

THE FLOWER OF CHRISTMAS

Mexican people tell a story of the lovely red poinsettia flower, which they know as the Flower of Christmas.

Once upon a time, on Nochebuena (Christmas Eve) in a village of southern Mexico, a poor girl named Angelita stood outside the village church sadly watching the faithful carrying rich offerings of fruit, candy, and flowers for the infant Jesus. Angelita was weeping because she had nothing to offer.

At that moment, an angel, shining with a brilliant light, appeared and told Angelita to pick some wild plants beside the road. Angelita did this and returned with a large but humble bunch of weeds. Inside, as she approached the altar, Angelita's weeds miraculously transformed themselves into lovely scarlet flowers.

At the same time, the Virgin above the altar lowered her arm in a gesture of love, and gold stars on her blue cape showered the faithful in the nave. Simultaneously, outside in the black night sky a single star glowed a brilliant white over the little pueblo.

From that time forward, Angelita's brilliant red flowers have blossomed all over southern Mexico just before Christmas. For that reason, people have named that gorgeous bloom the *flor de Nochebuena* and always offer bunches of them to the baby Jesus on December 24.

Parque Infantil del D.I.F. (Integral Family Development; Vicente Guerrero) and its neighboring **CICI Parque Aquatico** water-slide park (Vicente Guerrero, 10 A.M.–6 P.M. daily, $3). Find them on the eastern extension of Vicente Guerrero, on opposite sides of the street a few hundred yards east of old Highway 95, by the *lienzo charro* (rodeo ring).

On Sunday afternoons (around 5 P.M., check with your hotel desk for times) at the *lienzo charro* (rodeo ring) riders practice the art of *jaripeo* (bull riding and roping) and show off their skills of horsemanship. Sometimes daredevil horsewomen in colorful *ropa típica* (traditional dress) compete in *escaramuza charra*. in which they race with abandon around the ring. Get to the *lienzo charro,* on the eastern prolongation of Bandera Nacional, past old Highway 95, about nine blocks east of the *zócalo,* by taxi.

Iguala **Semana Santa** celebrations, in addition to the usual processions, *mañanitas* (mass), stations of the cross, food, and carnival games, also feature a procession of dozens of *penitencias* who may be flaying themselves or crawling on hands and knees to the downtown church altar to ask for forgiveness.

The big patronal **Fiesta de San Francisco** features an October 4 parade of *locos* throwing water and eggs and whatever else in honor of St. Francis of Assisi, who's famous for his sense of humor.

The **Day of the Dead** (celebrated Nov. 1 and 2) is big in Iguala. Families go to the *panteón* (main cemetery; taxi to west-side Calzada de Guadalupe) and tidy up the grave sites of their loved ones. They rebuild the "houses" of the dead and bring the favorite foods of the departed, thus tempting their deceased loved ones to return from the land of the dead and join with the family once again.

SHOPPING

Iguala's prime general shopping ground is the main town market, at the corner of Salazar and Galeana six blocks south of the *zócalo.* Everything—from huaraches and luscious

Iguala high school students create a Day of the Dead shrine.

© BRUCE WHIPPERMAN

mounds of tomatoes, to steaming stews and piquant chiles rellenos—seems to be on sale.

Handicrafts vendors cluster on the Plaza de Trigarantías, two blocks east of the *zócalo,* behind the church. Customarily, several stands offer a large variety, including soft palm-leaf *tenates* (tumpline baskets) and *petates* (mats), wooden bowls and utensils, bright pottery, masks, and much more.

Iguala is famous for its gold market, the **Centro Joyero de Iguala** (corner of Obregón and Reforma, tel. 733/333-3778, 9 A.M.–7 P.M. daily), Mexico's third gold merchandising center after Taxco and Guadalajara. Find its many dozens of shops under one roof a block south of the *zócalo's* southwest corner. Inside is a budget jewelry lover's paradise, where the gold and silver is genuine, but most of the apparent rubies, diamonds, and emeralds are not. (Nevertheless, a few stores, such as Orovel's and Jeisha, do carry genuine low-to-medium-quality gemstones.)

SERVICES
Banks

Banks with ATMs are plentiful near the *zócalo*. You'll find **Banamex** (*zócalo's* northwest corner, tel. 733/333-3049, 9 A.M.–4 P.M. Mon.–Sat.) and **Bancomer** (*zócalo's* southwest corner, tel. 733/333-3401, 8:30 A.M.–4 P.M. Mon.–Fri.). After bank hours, change money at *casa de cambio* **Dimex** (*zócalo's* southwest side, tel. 733/333-6581, 8 A.M.–4 P.M. Mon.–Fri., 9 A.M.–2 P.M. Sat.–Sun.).

Communications

Find the **correo** (south side of Vicente Guerrero, tel. 733/332-0160, 9 A.M.–5 P.M. Mon.–Fri., 9 A.M.–2 P.M. Sat.) two and a half blocks west of the *zócalo*. For telephoning, buy a Ladatel card and use one of the many street telephones. Otherwise, go to **Telecom** (Zapata between Alarcón and Hidalgo, tel. 733/332-1002, 8 A.M.–7 P.M. Mon.–Fri.), northeast of the *zócalo*, for fax and money orders.

Connect to the Internet at **Cyber Vebelde** (Constitución 7, tel. 733/334-0741, 10 A.M.–10 P.M. Mon.–Sat.), two doors east of the Hotel Isabel.

Health and Emergencies

For routine medications and remedies, try one of the many downtown pharmacies, such as **Farmacia Similares** (Bandera Nacional 3A, tel. 732/332-907955, 8 A.M.–midnight daily), near the southeast *zócalo* corner.

If you need a doctor, follow your hotel's recommendation. Otherwise, a handily situated internist, **Dr. Raoul Tovar** (Jose O. Ocampo 8, tel. 733/333-3624, 10 A.M.–4 P.M. and 6–8 P.M. Mon.–Fri.) is available for consultations at Clínica Tovar, his lovely garden-patio hospital-home, a block west of the *zócalo's* northeast corner. His personable English-speaking wife, Ana, runs the reception.

Also, for emergencies a number of reliable hospitals provide round-the-clock services in the downtown area. Hire a taxi to take you to one of the following: **Hospital Reforma** (Reforma 54, tel. 733/333-5892); **Sanatorio**

Padre Jesús (Aldama 24, tel. 733/332-0801); or **Hospital Cristina** (Prolongación Álvarez 153, tel. 733/333-2514 or 733/333-7386).

For other emergencies, call the **police** (tel. 733/332-8005) and in case of fire, contact the *bomberos* (emergency tel. 066).

Laundry

Get your clothes washed at **Lavandería Easy** (tel. 733/332-6189, 10 A.M.–8 P.M. Mon.–Sat.). From the *zócalo's* southeast corner, walk one block south to Aldama, then turn left and walk two and a half blocks west.

GETTING THERE AND AWAY
By Bus

The main bus station, **Central Camionera Estrella Blanca** (at Galeana and Salazar, tel. 733/332-8482), is six blocks south of the *zócalo's* southeast corner.

The terminal has many services, including kept luggage, a long-distance telephone and fax office, air-conditioned first-class waiting room, cafeteria, and money exchange. Buy fresh fruits, vegetables, groceries, and handicrafts at the market across the street.

First- and second-class buses connect with many destinations in all directions, both long-distance and semi-local.

One first-class departure connects daily northwest with the U.S. border at Mexicali and Tijuana, via Cuernavaca, Toluca, Guadalajara, Tepic, and Mazatlán, along the Pacific Coast.

One first-class **Futura** or **Turistar** departure connects daily north with the U.S. border at Nuevo Laredo, via Cuernavaca, Toluca, San Luis Potosí, Saltillo, and Monterrey.

Many first- and second-class buses connect (hourly during the day) north with Mexico City and south with Chilpancingo and Acapulco. Others connect northeast with Puebla via Izucar de Matamoros, where connections southeast with Oaxaca may be made.

Many second-class buses connect east with Altamirano and north with Toluca via Taxco.

A swarm of second-class **Flecha Roja** buses connect with dozens of small regional Guerrero and Morelos destinations, such as Huitzuco, Taxco, Zacapalco, Jojutla, Casahuatlán, and Cuautla.

First-class bus connections, north with Taxco, Cuernavaca, and Mexico City, and south with Chilpancingo and Acapulco, are also available at the alternative **Estrella de Oro bus terminal** (Hwy. 95 north, corner of Bandera Nacional, tel. 733/332-1029), about eight blocks east of the *zócalo*.

By Car

Connect north 22 miles (36 km) with Taxco via old non-toll Highway 95 in about an hour. Alternatively connect north directly with Mexico City via Cuernavaca by *cuota* (toll) expressway Highway 95. (Find the expressway entrance, from old Highway 95, on the southeast, Acapulco, end of town.) Allow about 2.5 hours for this 80-mile (129-km) trip. Make sure you arrive in Mexico City on a permitted driving day.

Connect south with Chilpancingo via old Highway 95, about 64 miles (103 km) in about two hours. Continue to Acapulco via the toll expressway 95D, an additional 62 miles (100 km), in another 1.25 hours.

Connect west with Altamirano from the *periférico's* northwest side, via winding but scenic Highway 51, 114 miles (184 km) in about 3.5 hours.

EXCURSIONS FROM IGUALA
Tuxpan

Nearby Laguna Tuxpan makes an interesting excursion, if not for swimming in the lake, at least for lunch or a picnic by the lake, country views, and the palmy Quinta Happy family resort.

Along the two-mile road to Tuxpan, a major source of Iguala's prosperity becomes immediately apparent. Irrigation has been the key, turning the Iguala valley into an oasis of lush cornfields and a grand orchard of mango trees like the ones you see overhanging the Tuxpan road.

Soon, on the right, pass the refined, *campestre* (country-style) restaurant **Villa Los Ocampo** (no phone, 8 A.M.–9 P.M. daily, $4–8) with plenty of shade and lots of room

doing the laundry in Laguna Tuxpan

for kids to run around. The menu includes shrimp tacos, fish fillets, and brochettes, and also breakfast.

Continue through the Tuxpan village (with small groceries, post office, a pharmacy) to the restaurants on the north Laguna Tuxpan shore. Two of the most inviting are **El Muelle** (no phone, 8 A.M.–8 P.M. daily), with a pier to walk out on; and farther on, **Restaurant El Arbolito** (locally dial tel. 044-733/110-4141, 8 A.M.–8 P.M. daily), shaded by *tabachín* trees (which burst out with lovely red blossoms Dec.–Mar.). Both restaurants offer good bass, shrimp, rib, and beef filet dinners beneath airy lakeview *palapas*.

The lake itself is large, about a mile across, and spring-fed. Despite continual withdrawing of irrigation water, the lake level remains virtually constant year-round. During the dry spring season, the lake becomes an uninviting muddy brown. Sad but true, local folks customarily dirty it up washing clothes on the shoreline.

Nevertheless, the lake is cleaner and more appealing on the far west side, accessible by the lakeshore dirt road after the restaurants. Amenities include some shade trees, plenty of room for RV parking or tent camping (customary and allowed any time), and easy boat- and kayak-launching access.

Much more inviting is the family-friendly **⟨ Balneario Quinta Happy** (tel. 733/332-3562). From the Tuxpan ingress road, follow the fork to the right (signed "Quinta Alegre"). This is a gorgeous spot for at least a picnic and at most a one-week stay. Amenities include five palm-shaded blue swimming pools, three kiddie pools, restaurants, mini-market, basketball, tennis, volleyball and squash courts, and a soccer field, all surrounded by a beautiful orchard of palm, orange, lemon, and mango trees.

The Quinta Happy (*alegre* in Spanish) accommodations ($33 s or d, $44 t or q; add $5 per kid) are no less than you would expect: about 20 clean, semi-deluxe rooms around an inviting pool-patio, separated from the oft-noisy day-use area. Room decor is invitingly rustic, embellished with interior brick and hand-hewn wood furnishings. Rooms come with TV, air-conditioning, and parking. For more peace and quiet, reserve a weekday stay.

Get to Tuxpan by taxi or *colectivo* from the Estrella Blanca bus station, seven blocks south of the Iguala *zócalo*. By car, from the Iguala *zócalo,* go east via Bandera Nacional; after seven blocks turn right (south) at Highway 95. Continue under the *periférico* overpass. Just before a second overpass, bear right onto the lateral road, then turn left under the overpass. Immediately turn right onto the road to Tuxpan. At the signed Quinta Alegre fork either turn right to the *balneario* or continue straight ahead for Tuxpan village and lakeshore after another mile.

GUERRERO UPCOUNTRY

Taxco

As Ixtapa and Acapulco thrive on what's new, Taxco (pop. 100,000) luxuriates in what's old. Nestling beneath forest-crowned mountains and decorated with monuments of its silver-rich past, Taxco now enjoys an equally rich flood of visitors who stop en route to or from Acapulco. They come to enjoy its fiestas and clear pine-scented air and to stroll the cobbled hillside lanes and bargain for world-renowned silver jewelry.

And despite the acclaim, Taxco preserves its diminutive colonial charm *because* of its visitors, who come to enjoy what Taxco offers. They stay in venerable family-owned lodgings, walk to the colorful little *zócalo*, where they admire the famous baroque cathedral, and wander among the awning-festooned market lanes just downhill.

But Taxco offers even more. Travel an hour north to wander within the colossal limestone fairyland of the renowned Grutas de Cacahuamilpa. On the same day, continue

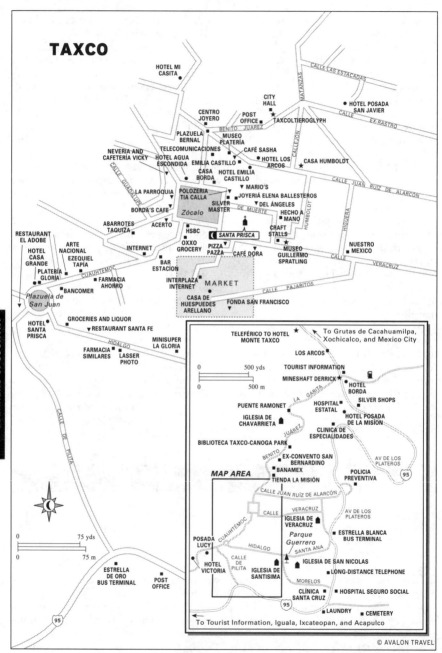

TAXCO

HOTEL MI CASITA

CITY HALL

HOTEL POSADA SAN JAVIER

CENTRO JOYERO

POST OFFICE
TAXCOLTIEROGLYPH

CALLE LAS ESTACADAS

MATANZAS

CALLE EX-RASTRO

BENITO JUAREZ

PLAZUELA BERNAL
MUSEO PLATERÍA
CAFÉ SASHA

TELECOMUNICACIONES
NEVERIA AND CAFETERÍA VICKY
HOTEL AGUA ESCONDIDA
EMILIA CASTILLO
CASA BORDA
HOTEL EMILIA CASTILLO

HOTEL LOS ARCOS
CASA HUMBOLDT

CALLE JUAN RUIZ DE ALARCON

CALLEJON

CALLE GUADALUPE

LA PARROQUIA
POLOZERIA TIA CALLA
MARIO'S
JOYERÍA ELENA BALLESTEROS
DEL ÁNGELES
HECHO A MANO

BORDA'S CAFÉ
Zócalo
SILVER MASTER
DE MUERTE

HUMBOLDT

HIGUERA

ABARROTES TAQUIZA
ACERTO
CRAFT STALLS

NUESTRO MEXICO

RESTAURANT EL ADOBE
HOTEL CASA GRANDE
ARTE NACIONAL EZEQUIEL TAPÍA
INTERNET
HSBC
OXXO GROCERY
SANTA PRISCA
PIZZA PAZZA
CAFÉ DORA
MUSEO GUILLERMO SPRATLING

CALLE VERACRUZ

CALLE

PLATERÍA GLORIA
BANCOMER
FARMACIA AHORRO
CUAUHTEMOC
BAR ESTACIÓN
INTERPLAZA INTERNET

Plazuela de San Juan

MARKET
CALLE PAJARITOS
CASA DE HUESPUEDES ARELLANO
FONDA SAN FRANCISCO

HOTEL SANTA PRISCA
GROCERIES AND LIQUOR
RESTAURANT SANTA FE
MINISUPER LA GLORIA
HIDALGO
FARMACIA SIMILARES
LASSER PHOTO

CALLE DE PILITA

Inset map

TELEFÉRICO TO HOTEL MONTE TAXCO

To Grutas de Cacahuamilpa, Xochicalco, and Mexico City

LOS ARCOS

TOURIST INFORMATION

MINESHAFT DERRICK

HOTEL BORDA

SILVER SHOPS

PUENTE RAMONET
IGLESIA DE CHAVARRIETA

LA GARITA

JUAREZ

HOSPITAL ESTATAL

HOTEL POSADA DE LA MISIÓN

CLÍNICA DE ESPECIALIDADES

BIBLIOTECA TAXCO-CANOGA PARK

BENITO

EX-CONVENTO SAN BERNARDINO
BANAMEX

AV DE LOS PLATEROS

95

MAP AREA

TIENDA LA MISIÓN

POLICIA PREVENTIVA

CALLE JUAN RUÍZ DE ALARCÓN

CALLE
VERACRUZ

AV DE LOS PLATEROS

CUAUHTEMOC
IGLESIA DE VERACRUZ
Parque Guerrero
SANTA ANA

ESTRELLA BLANCA BUS TERMINAL

POSADA LUCY

HIDALGO

IGLESIA DE SAN NICOLAS

HOTEL VICTORIA

CALLE DE PILITA
IGLESIA DE SANTISIMA

LONG-DISTANCE TELEPHONE

MORELOS

CLÍNICA SANTA CRUZ

HOSPITAL SEGURO SOCIAL

95

LAUNDRY
CEMETERY

To Tourist Information, Iguala, Ixcateopan, and Acapulco

HOTEL SANTA PRISCA

ESTRELLA DE ORO BUS TERMINAL

POST OFFICE

95

0   75 yds
0   75 m

0   500 yds
0   500 m

© AVALON TRAVEL

another hour north to marvel at the exquisite untouristed remains of Xochicalco, legendary pre-Columbian capital and internationally acclaimed UNESCO World Heritage site.

On yet another day, travel west an hour to Ixcateopan village and visit the revered resting place of Cuauhtémoc, the last Aztec emperor who, at the eventual cost of his life, rallied his people against the Spanish conquest.

ORIENTATION

Although the present city (elev. 5,850 feet/1,780 meters) spreads much farther, the center of town encompasses the city's original seven hills, wrinkles in the slope of a towering mountain.

For most visitors, the downhill town limit is the *carretera,* the local stretch of old National Highway 95, now named Avenida de los Plateros, after the Taxco *plateros* (silversmiths) who put Taxco on Mexico's tourism map. The highway contours along the hillside from **Los Arcos** (The Arches) on the north (Mexico City) end of town about two miles, passing the Calle

Pilita intersection on the south (Acapulco) edge of town. Along the *carretera,* immediately accessible to a steady stream of tour buses, lie the town's plusher hotels and many silver shops.

The rest of the town is fortunately insulated from the tour bus rush by its narrow winding streets. From the *carretera,* the most important of them climb and converge, like bent spokes of a wheel, to the *zócalo* (main plaza). Beginning with the most northerly, the main streets (and directions they run) are La Garita (uphill), J. R. de Alarcón (downhill), Veracruz (downhill), Santa Ana (downhill), Salubridad (uphill), Morelos (downhill), and Pilita (downhill).

GETTING AROUND

Although walking is by far Taxco's most common mode of transport, taxis go almost anywhere within the city limits ($3 daytime, $4 nighttime). White *combi* collective vans (fare about $0.50) follow designated routes, marked on the windshields. Simply tell your specific destination to the driver. For side trips to nearby towns and villages, a fleet of second-

© BRUCE WHIPPERMAN

Taxco, built on seven hills, affords lovely views in all directions.

class local buses and *colectivo* vans leave frequently from the Estrella Blanca bus terminal on the *carretera* near the corner of Veracruz.

HISTORY

The traditional hieroglyph representing Taxco shows athletes in a court competing in a game of *tlatchtli* (which is still locally played) with a solid natural-rubber *(hule)* ball. "Tlachco," the Náhuatl name representing the place that had become a small Aztec garrison settlement by the eve of the conquest, literally translates as "Place of the Ball Game." The Spanish, more interested in local minerals than in linguistic details, shifted the name to Taxco.

Colonization

In 1524, Hernán Cortés, looking for tin to alloy with copper to make bronze cannon, heard that people around Taxco were using bits of metal for money. Prospectors hurried out, and within a few years they struck rich silver veins in Tetelcingo, now known as Taxco Viejo (Old Taxco), seven miles downhill from present-day Taxco. The Spanish crown appropriated the mines and worked them with generations of native forced labor.

Eighteenth-century enlightenment came to Taxco in the person of José Borda, who, arriving from Spain in 1716, modernized the mine franchise his brother had been operating. José improved working conditions and began paying the miners, thereby increasing productivity and profits. In contrast to past operators, Borda returned the proceeds to Taxco, building the monuments, notably the church of Santa Prisca, that still grace the town.

Independence and Modern Times

The 1810–1821 War of Independence and the subsequent civil strife reduced the mines to but a memory within a generation. They were nearly forgotten when William Spratling, an American artist and architect, moved to Taxco in 1929 and began reviving Taxco's ancient but moribund silversmithing tradition. Working with local artisans, Spratling opened the first cooperative shop, Las Delicias.

Spurred by the trickle of tourists along the new Acapulco highway, more shops opened, increasing the demand for silver, which in turn led to the reopening of the mines. Soon silver demand outpaced the supply. Silver began streaming in from other parts of Mexico to the workbenches of thousands of artisans in hundreds of family- and cooperative-owned shops dotting the still-quaint hillsides of a new, prosperous Taxco.

SIGHTS
🕻 Santa Prisca

All roads in Taxco begin and end on the *zócalo* at Santa Prisca church. French architect D. Diego Durán designed and built the church between 1751 and 1758 with money from the fortune of silver king Don José Borda. The facade, decorated with saints on pedestals, arches, and spiraled columns, follows the baroque churrigueresque style (after Jose Churriguera, 1665–1725, the "Spanish Michelangelo"). Interior furnishings include an elegant pipe organ, brought from Germany by muleback (via boat to Veracruz, thence

Santa Prisca church, the pride of Taxco

© BRUCE WHIPPERMAN

overland) in 1751, and several gilded side altars. The riot of interior elaboration climaxes in the towering gold-leaf main altar, which seems to drip with ornamentation in tribute to Santa Prisca, the Virgin of the Immaculate Conception, the Virgin of the Rosary, and San Sebastian (on the right) who bravely and piously endures his wounds.

Dreamy Bible-story paintings by Miguel Cabrera decorate a chamber behind the main altar, while in a room to the right, portraits of Pope Benedict XIV, who sanctioned all this, José Borda, who paid for it, and his brother, Manuel Borda, Santa Prisca's first priest, hang at the head of a solemn gallery of subsequent padres.

Outside, landmarks around the plaza include the **Casa Borda** (Plaza Borda 1, tel. 762/622-6617, 9 A.M.–9 P.M. daily); it's visible as you face away from the church facade, on the right side of the *zócalo*. This former Borda family town house, built concurrently with the church in typical baroque colonial style, now serves as the Taxco Casa de Cultura, featuring exhibitions by local artists and artisans in the upstairs gallery (10 A.M.–5 P.M. Tues.–Sun.).

Downhill

Heading out and down the Santa Prisca church steps, you can continue downhill in either of two interesting ways. If you walk left immediately downhill from the church, you reach the lane Calle Los Arcos, running alongside and below the church. From there, reach the **market** by heading right before the quaint archway over the street, down the winding staircase-lane, where you'll soon be in a warren of awning-covered stalls.

If, however, you head right from the church steps, another immediate right leads you beside the church along legendary **Calle de Muerte** (Street of Death), so named because of the former cemetery where the workers who died constructing the church were buried. (Note the skeleton on the churchfront corner facing Calle de Muerte.)

Museo Guillermo Spratling

Continuing downhill from Santa Prisca, you'll

A bronze of Don José Borda, Taxco's enlightened 18th-century patron, graces the courtyard of the Museo Guillermo Spratling.

© BRUCE WHIPPERMAN

find Museo Guillermo Spratling (fronting the little plaza behind the church, tel. 762/622-1660, 9 A.M.–5 P.M. Tues.–Sat., 9 A.M.–3 P.M. Sun., hours may vary seasonally, $3). William Spratling was instrumental in helping the community revive its silversmithing tradition in the late 1920s. On the main and upper floors of this history and archaeology museum named in his honor, the National Institute of Archaeology displays intriguing carvings and ceramics (including unusual phallic examples), such as a ball-game ring, animal masks, and a priestly statuette with knife in one hand, human heart in the other. Temporary historical, cultural, and archaeological displays are housed in the basement.

Casa Humboldt

A block away stands the Casa Humboldt (Calle J.R. de Alarcón 12, tel. 762/622-5501, 10 A.M.–6 P.M. Tues.–Sat., 10 A.M.–2 P.M. Sun., $3). To get here, exit the Spratling museum, turn right and walk downhill north, along narrow Calle Humboldt to Calle J.R. de Alarcón and Casa Humboldt. Casa Humboldt is named after the celebrated geographer (Baron Alexander von Humboldt, 1769–1859) who is said to have stayed only one night. Now, the state maintains it as the Museum of Viceregal (colonial) Art. Displays feature a permanent collection of historical artifacts, including the Manila galleon, colonial technology, and colonial religious sculpture and painting.

Walking Tour

A short ride, coupled with a walk circling back to the *zócalo,* provides the basis for an interesting half-day exploration. Taxi or ride a *combi* to the Hotel Posada de la Misión, where the **Cuauhtémoc Mural** glitters on a wall near the pool. Executed by renowned muralist Juan O'Gorman with a riot of pre-Columbian symbols—yellow sun, pearly rabbit-in-the-moon, snarling jaguar, writhing serpents, fluttering eagle—the mural glorifies Cuauhtémoc, the last Aztec emperor. Cuauhtémoc, unlike his uncle Moctezuma, tenaciously resisted the conquest, but was captured and later executed by Cortés in 1525. His remains were discovered in 1949 in Ixcateopan, about 24 miles away by local bus or car.

Continue your walk a few hundred yards along the *carretera* (north, Mexico City direction) from the Hotel Posada de la Misión. There, a driveway leading right (just before the gas station) heads to the Hotel Borda grounds. Turn left on the road just after the gate and you'll come to an **antique brick chimney and cable-hung derrick.** These mark an inactive **mineshaft** descending to the mine-tunnel honeycomb thousands of feet beneath the town. The mines are still being worked from another entrance, but for mostly lead rather than silver. You can see the present-day works from the hilltop of the now-closed Hotel Hacienda del Solar on the south edge of town.

Now, return to the *carretera,* cross over and stroll the main town entry street, **Calle la Garita,** about a mile back to the *zócalo.* Of special interest along the way, besides a number of crafts stores and stalls, are the **Iglesia de Chavarrieta,** the **Ex-Convento San Bernardino,** and the **Biblioteca Taxco-Canoga Park** (library; 9 A.M.–1 P.M. and 3–7 P.M. Mon.–Fri., 9 A.M.–1 P.M. Sat.) with many English-language novels and reference books.

Farther on, a block before the *zócalo,* pause to decipher the stone mosaic of the **Taxco Hieroglyph,** which decorates the pavement in front of the Palacio Municipal (City Hall). Inside, climb the stairs for a balcony-front view of the hieroglyph and the wall mural—a graphic review of Mexican history. See the main actors, from left to right: stolid Benito Juárez ("Respect for the rights of all is peace"); elderly general Porfirio Díaz gives away church and communal land to foreigners; banderilla-laden Emiliano Zapata declares his Plan de Ayala; president Lázaro Cárdenas in overalls expropriates foreign oil companies; and Aldolfo López Mateos declares free school textbooks; while Juárez, John F. Kennedy, Henry Kissinger, Charles de Gaulle, and Jawarlal Nehru look on.

Teleférico

A cableway above the highway (8 A.M.–7 P.M. daily, round-trip tickets about $6, kids half price), on the north side of town where the *carretera* passes beneath Los Arcos, lifts passengers to soaring vistas of the town on one side and ponderous, pine-studded mesas on the other. The ride ends at the Hotel Monte Taxco (tel. 762/622-1300), where you can make a day of it golfing, horseback riding, playing tennis, eating lunch, and sunning on the panoramic-view pool deck. Return by taxi if you miss the last car down.

Cristo del Monte

Above the opposite (west) side of town, about two miles uphill from the *zócalo,* stands the colossal new stone statue of Jesus, where folks enjoy an airy panoramic town view framed by lush, green looming mountains. Get there on foot (if you relish a 1,500-foot climb; wear a hat and carry water) or by taxi (about $2.50), *colectivo* ($0.40, to Casahuates village), or car or on foot, west from the *zócalo,* via Calle Cuauhtémoc, past the Hotel Victoria. After about two more uphill miles (3 km), fork right at the Huixteco sign and continue past Casahuates village about 200 yards, where a dirt driveway leads right to the Cristo del Monte park.

In-Town Vistas

You needn't go as far afield as the Hotel Monte Taxco or the Cristo del Monte to get a good view of the city streets and houses carpeting the mountainside. Vistas depend not only on vantage point but time of day, since the best viewing sunshine (which frees you from squinting) should come generally from *behind*. Consequently, spots along the highway (more or less east of town), such as the patios of the Hotel Posada de la Misión and especially the *mirador* atop the Hotel Borda, provide good morning views, while afternoon views are best from points west of town, along the extension of Cuauhtémoc past the Plazuela de San Juan uphill by (or in the hilltop garden of) the Hotel Victoria.

ACCOMMODATIONS

Taxco's dry, temperate climate relegates air-conditioning, ceiling fans, and central heating to frills offered only in the most expensive hotels. All of the hotel recommendations listed here have hot water and private baths, however. The budget hotels do generally not accept credit cards.

Taxco's lower-end hotels cluster in the colorful *zócalo* neighborhood, while many of the more expensive (over $100) lodgings are scattered mostly along the *carretera*.

Under $50

Soak in your fill of old-fashioned Mexico during a stay at **Casa de Huéspedes Arellano** (Calle de Pajaritos 23, tel. 762/622-0215; $14 s, $24 d, $35 t with shared bath; $18 s, $28 d, $38 t with private hot-water bath), an island of graceful tranquility, yet, surprisingly, smack in the middle of the town market. Past the hotel gate, you enter a flowery patio garden blooming with birdsong and enfolded by tropical verandas. Grandmotherly owner Maria Castillo Arellano offers 14 guest rooms, all opening to airy plant-decorated view portico-patios, ideal for shady relaxation. The rooms themselves, many in need of some paint and polish, are nevertheless clean and simply but comfortably furnished. All rooms come with fans and colorful old-world Taxco just beyond the gate. Get there on foot only, by rolling your luggage a couple of long blocks along Calle Pajaritos (get there by taxi), the lane that begins on (one-way downhill) thoroughfare Calle Veracruz, across from Nuestro Mexico handicrafts shop.

From the *zócalo*'s west side, opposite the church, follow Calle Cuauhtémoc one block to the Plazuela de San Juan and the adjacent **(Hotel Santa Prisca** (Cena Obscura 1, tel. 762/622-0080 or 762/622-0980, fax 762/622-2938, htl_staprisca@yahoo.com, $30 s, $44 d, $50 t, $65 suites). This tranquil, dignified hostelry surrounds an oft-fragrant garden of orange trees; its off-lobby dining room shines with graceful old-world details, such as beveled glass, a fireplace, blue-white stoneware, and ivy-hung portals. Its tile-decorated rooms, in two floors around the inner garden, are clean and comfortable. Rooms come with fans, private hot-water baths, some parking, and wireless Internet. Credit cards are accepted.

$50-100

Picturesquely tucked on an uphill lane, just two blocks uphill, north, from the *zócalo,* find **(Hotel Mi Casita** (Altos de Redondo 1, tel./ fax 762/627-1777, reservations@hotelmicasita .com, www.hotelmicasita.com, $40 s, $50 d, $65 suites low season). A charmingly picturesque retreat for a loyal cadre of longtime lovers of Mexico, the Hotel Mi Casita blooms with a treasury of delightful Mexicana. Its 12 rooms (some small) and suites, most with panoramic balcony views of the surrounding city and cloud-tipped mountains, are individually decorated with fetching designer lamps, hand-painted wall art, and colorful Talavera-tiled bathrooms. Rentals, some quaintly petite, all come with fans, cable TV, parking, and wireless Internet; credit cards are not accepted. Add about 15 percent during Christmas and Easter holidays.

Five short blocks northeast of the *zócalo,*

© BRUCE WHIPPERMAN

the Hotel Posada San Javier's lovely garden and pool

find the inviting ◖ **Hotel Posada San Javier** (Estacas 32, tel. 762/622-3177, tel./fax 762/622-2351, www.posadasanjavier.com, posadasanjavier@hotmail.com, $47 s, $52 d, $60 t, $75 suites). Although it's a steep (but short) climb back to the *zócalo,* this is a very popular hotel, built around a tranquil green garden. It offers about 40 immaculate rooms, an idyllic patio with (unheated but usually swimmable) blue pool, framed in lush verdure and airy verandas for relaxing. All units come with fans, hot water, parking, and an inviting reading room with lots of books; credit cards are not accepted. This hotel customarily fills up by late afternoon, especially on weekends. It's best to arrive very early, or reserve several days in advance.

On J. R. de Alarcón just a block downhill, east, from the *zócalo,* plaudits go to the refined, 16th century ◖ **Hotel Los Arcos** (J. R. de Alarcón 4, tel. 762/622-1836, fax 762/622-7982, reservaciones@hotelosarcostaxco.com, www.hotellosarcos.net, $52 s, $59 d, $65 t).

The 21 rooms rise in three vine-draped tiers around an inner patio, replete with reminders of old Mexico. The rooms, with thoughtfully selected, handmade, polished wooden furniture, tile floors, rustic wall art, and immaculate hand-painted cobalt-on-white tile bathrooms, come with hot water, fans, and Internet available in the patio.

The renovated **Hotel Borda** (Cerro de Pedregal, tel. 762/622-0225, fax 762/622-0617, info@hotelborda.com, www.hotelborda.com, $65 s or d in one bed, $70 d in two beds, $75 and $83 weekends, suites from $120), on a knoll above the *carretera* about a kilometer from the town center, has been restored to approximate the luxury hotel that it once was. This is fortunate, for the hotel's deluxe assets—grand vistas, spacious garden, and luxurious blue pool and patio—remain as attractive as ever. The 110 clean, comfortable, and pleasingly decorated motel-modern rooms come with fans, cable TV, wireless Internet, and parking; credit cards are accepted. The hotel also has a restaurant and bar. Two kids up to age 12 can stay for free.

Taxco's only *zócalo*-front hostelry, the oft-bustling **Hotel Agua Escondida** (Calle Guillermo Spratling 4, tel. 762/622-0726 or 762/622-1166, fax 762/622-1306, reservas@aguaescondida.com, www.hotelaguaescondida.com, $52 s, $72 d, $80 t), stands on the diagonally opposite corner from the *zócalo* church. A multilevel maze of hidden patios, rooftop sundecks, and dazzling city views, the Agua Escondida, popular with families and package tour groups, offers dozens of clean, comfortable rooms. The name, which translates as "Hidden Water," must refer to its big (but unheated) swimming pool, which is tucked away in a far rooftop corner. Rooms vary; if you have the choice, look at several. Try to avoid the oft-noisy street-front rooms. If you don't mind climbing, some of the upper-floor rooms offer airy penthouse-style views. The 76 rooms come with fans, TV, hot water, and wireless Internet; there is limited parking and credit cards are accepted. If prices are steep, ask for a mid-week package.

Over $100

Resort-style ◖ **Hotel Monte Taxco** (Lomas de Taxco, tel. 762/622-1300 or 762/622-1301, fax 762/622-1428, reservaciones@monte taxcohotel.com, www.montetaxcohotel.com; weekdays $110 s, $120 d; weekends $125 s, $140 d) stands atop a towering mesa accessible by either a steep road or cableway (*teleférico;* 8 A.M.–7 P.M. daily, adult round-trip tickets $6, kids half price) from the highway just north of town. On weekends, the hotel is often packed with well-heeled Mexico City families, whose kids play organized games while their parents enjoy the panoramic poolside view or enjoy golf and tennis. The 156 deluxe rooms, most with view balconies, come with air-conditioning, phone, cable TV, and wireless Internet. Guests can take advantage of the hotel's restaurants, shops, piano bar, disco, live music on the weekend, parking, a gym, pool, and steam room; the spa is available at an extra cost. Credit cards are accepted. The adjacent hotel country club offers a nine-hole golf course, tennis courts, and horseback riding. To get here from Highway 95, look for the Hotel Monte Taxco sign about half a mile north of town, and turn steeply uphill to the left, in the direction of Mexico City.

FOOD
Stalls and Snacks

The numerous *fondas* (food stalls) atop the *artesanías* (ar-tay-sah-NEE-ahs) handicrafts section of the Taxco market (downhill from Los Arcos) are Taxco's prime source of wholesome country-style food. The quality of their fare is a matter of honor for the proprietors, since among their local patrons word of a little bad food goes a long way.

Here, you can choose from a potpourri of food that might include steaming bowls of menudo or *pozole,* or plates of pork or chicken smothered in *mole* and much more.

On the *zócalo,* stalls appear late afternoons, offering favorite evening snacks, including tacos, *pozole,* menudo, hot dogs, popcorn, potato chips (deep-fried on the spot), and sweets such as french-fried bananas and churros.

For a sit-down snack or light lunch or supper, go to the **Nevería and Cafetería Vicky** (above the *zócalo*'s northwest corner, tel. 762/622-4085, noon–9:30 P.M. Mon.–Sat., noon–11 P.M. Sun., $2–3), above the street (upper story) fronting the Hotel Agua Escondida. Take a balcony seat and take in the fascinating *zócalo* view, with an espresso *café Americano,* fruit plate, hamburger, and/ or ice cream.

Restaurants

Although its restaurants are not what draws most Taxco's visitors, Taxco nevertheless offers some recommendable dining options.

Judging from its crowd of daily customers, the ◖ **Pozolería Tía Calla** (at the *zócalo*'s northeast corner, downstairs, tel. 762/622-5602, 1–10 P.M. Wed.–Mon., $2–4) seems to be Taxco's most popular restaurant. Locals and families come to feast on the delicious country-style tacos, enchiladas, *pozole* (stew), and even salads (try the good tuna salad, full of crunchy veggies, enough for two).

Another good bet on the *zócalo* is **Pizza Pazza** (half a block to the right, from the cathedral front, upstairs, tel. 762/622-5500, 9 A.M.–11 P.M. daily, $5–12). Take a balcony view table and choose from a little bit of everything Italian and more; there is especially good pizza in about 15 varieties. If the TV is too loud, ask them to lower the *volumen* for you.

For both hearty and economical daytime meals, visit friendly **Café Dora** (Calle Los Arcos 13, tel. 762/622-2850, 8 A.M.–6 P.M. daily, $3–6) on the downstairs lane (before the arch) behind the church. The specialties here are good coffee, breakfasts, and a bountiful afternoon *comida.*

On the other hand, join in a 30-year Taxco tradition at **Mario's** (Plaza Borda 1, south side of the *zócalo,* tel. 762/622-7797, 10 A.M.–midnight daily, $3–12). Favorites here are Sicilian burritos, chili American-style, spaghetti, and pizzas in many varieties. Musician-owner Mario Esquivel (a 1960s-era headliner) continues his long custom, entertaining at his piano bar along with a trio Saturdays and holidays (call to check).

At least recommendable for its refined old-world ambience, the restaurant ◖ **Del Ángeles** (Calle de Muerte—now Celso Muñoz—4, 2nd floor, tel. 762/622-5525, 8 A.M.–10:30 P.M. daily, $5–10) adds an airy view and good food (soups, salads, pasta, Mexican specialties) to the reasons for going there. Inside, rustic old-adobe walls, regal stone columns, and baroque statuary enhance the pleasing effect. Find it, a few steps downhill, left side, from the Santa Prisca churchfront.

A long block from the *zócalo,* at the end of Calle Cuauhtémoc, overlooking Plazuela de San Juan, try old-Mexico motif **Restaurant El Adobe** (Plazuela de San Juan 13, tel. 762/622-1416, 8 A.M.–10:30 P.M. daily, $5–12) for breakfast (juice, eggs, hotcakes), lunch (hamburgers, tacos, enchiladas) or dinner (steak Adobe-style or shrimp brochette).

Of the restaurant options, one of the best for genteel non-tourist ambience is the local favorite **Restaurant Santa Fe** (on the left a few doors downhill from Plazuela de San Juan, tel. 762/622-1170, 7:30 A.M.–10 P.M. daily, $4–8). Tasty country fare (*pozole,* roast chicken, grilled fish, and daily four-course afternoon *comida*) keeps a battalion of faithful customers happy.

At bohemian-style **Café Sasha** (8 A.M.–11 P.M. daily, $4–10) pick from a tasty menu of breakfasts (one cup of coffee included), with home fries; salads (Roquefort and spinach), pizzas, sandwiches, falafel, chow mein, and apple pie. From the *zócalo,* by the Casa Borda, walk a block downhill to Ruiz de Alarcón, then fork right half a block.

ENTERTAINMENT AND EVENTS

Taxco people mostly entertain each other. Such spontaneous diversions are most likely around the *zócalo,* which often seems like an impromptu festival of typical Mexican scenes. Around the outside stand the monuments of the colonial past, while on the sidewalks sit the native people who come in from the hills

© BRUCE WHIPPERMAN

A diverse group of Taxco folks regularly dances to live music at the town *zócalo.*

to sell their onions, tamales, and pottery. Kids run around, their parents and grandparents people-watch, while young men and women flirt, blush, giggle, and jostle one another until late in the evening.

Nightlife

A number of night spots, around or near the *zócalo,* are popular with both local folks and visitors. For example, either join the locals at **Bar Berta** (on the church corner, 11 A.M.–8 P.M. daily, $4–10) or enjoy bouncy music at **Bar Estación** (on Cuauhtémoc, by Bancomer, a block west of the *zócalo,* hours vary depending on customer demand, usually noon–11 P.M. Mon.–Thurs., noon–2 A.M. Fri.–Sun.).

Alternatively, climb the economic scale up the *zócalo*-front stairs to fashionable, restaurant-sports bar **Acerto** (Plaza Borda 12, tel. 762/622-0064, noon–midnight daily, $6–16). Here, either watch the international soccer battles, enjoy a choice people-watching perch, or simply relax over dinner.

For a contrasting but equally entertaining scene, walk to tiny *zócalo*-front **Borda's Café** (Plaza Borda 6A, cell tel. local 044-762/107-9328, 8 A.M.–11 P.M. daily, $5–10), where owner Efrain fills his small space with humor and good cheer. Decor shifts seasonally— Christmas, Independence Day, Day of the Dead—while his permanent display features vintage James Dean, Marlon Brando, Marilyn Monroe, and Elvis Presley photos.

On another day, continue your Taxco party via the jazzy recorded music blaring out of the speakers at restaurant-bar **Concha** (upstairs at Hotel Casa Grande, Plazuela de San Juan, usually noon–11 P.M. Mon.–Thurs., noon–2 A.M. Fri.–Sun.). There is live music on Saturdays. In contrast, at **Mario's** (Plaza Borda 1, south side of the *zócalo,* tel. 762/622-7797, 10 A.M.–midnight daily) a piano accompanies a trio playing oldies but goodies Saturdays from around 9 or 10 P.M.

For more music, in an upscale setting, the **Hotel Monte Taxco** (tel. 762/622-1300 or 762/622-1301, piano bar 8–11 P.M. Fri.–Sat. and on holidays) offers a piano bar in the

restaurant. At the similarly upscale **Hotel Posada de la Misión** (tel. 762/622-0063 or 762/622-0533, roving trio 1–4 P.M., piano bar 8–10 P.M. nightly) patrons enjoy a roving trio for lunch and a cozy piano bar in the evenings. Programs may vary; call to confirm.

Festivals

An abundance of local fiestas provide the excuses for folks to celebrate, starting with the **Festival of Santa Prisca** (Jan. 18–20). On the initial day, kids and adults bring their pet animals for blessing at the church. At dawn the next day, pilgrims arrive at the *zócalo* for *mañanitas* (dawn Mass) in honor of the saint, then head for folk dancing inside the church.

During the year Taxco's many neighborhood churches celebrate their saints' days (such as Chavarrieta, Mar. 4; Veracruz, the four weeks before Easter; San Bernardino, May 20; Santísima Trinidad, June 13; Santa Ana, July 26; Asunción, Aug. 15; San Nicolas, Sept. 10; San Miguel, Sept. 19; San Francisco, Oct. 4; and Guadalupe, Dec. 12) with food, fireworks, music, and dancing.

Taxco's prime religious festival begins with **Carnaval** the few days before Ash Wednesday (usually in Feb.) and climaxes six weeks later during Semana Santa (Easter week). On the Thursday and Good Friday before Easter, cloaked penitents proceed through the city, carrying gilded images and bearing crowns of thorns.

On the Monday after the November 2 Día de los Muertos (Day of the Dead), Taxco people head to pine-shaded Parque Huixteco (PAR-kay weesh-TAY-koh) atop the Cerro Huixteco above the town to celebrate their unique **Fiesta de los Jumiles.** In a ritual whose roots are lost in pre-Columbian legend, people collect and feast on *jumiles* (small crickets)—raw or roasted—along with music and plenty of beer and fixings. Since so many people go, transportation is easy. Drive or ride a *colectivo* (labeled Huixteco on the windshield) along the west-side road (westward extension of Cuauhtémoc from the *zócalo*) uphill about two miles. Fork right at the Huixteco

TLATCHTLI: THE BALL GAME

Basketball fever is probably a mild affliction compared to the enthusiasm pre-Columbian crowds felt for *tlatchtli,* the ball game that was played throughout Mesoamerica and is still played in some places. Contemporary accounts and latter-day scholarship have led to a partial picture of *tlatchtli* as it was played centuries ago. Although details varied locally, the game centered around a hard natural-rubber ball called a *tlatchtli,* which players batted back and forth across a center dividing line with hip, arm, and torso blows.

Play and scoring was vaguely similar to tennis. Opponents, either individuals or in small teams, tried to smash the ball past their opponents into scoring niches at the opposite ends of an I-shaped, sunken court. Players also could garner points by forcing their opponents to make wild shots that bounced beyond the court's retaining walls.

Courts were often equipped with a pair of stone rings fixed above opposite ends of the lateral center dividing line. One scoring variation awarded immediate victory to the team who could manage to bat the *tlatchtli* through the ring.

Like tennis, players became very adept at batting the ball at high speed. Unlike tennis, the ball was solid and perhaps as heavy as two or three baseballs. Although protected by helmets and leather, players were usually bloodied, often injured, and sometimes even killed from opponents' punishing *tlatchtli-*inflicted blows. Matches were sometimes decided like a boxing match, with victory going to the opponent left standing on the court.

As with everything in Mesoamerica, tradition and ritual ruled *tlatchtli.* Master teachers subjected initiates to rigorous training, prescribed ritual, and discipline, not unlike the ascetic lifestyle of a medieval monastic brotherhood.

Potential rewards were enormous, however. Stakes varied in proportion to a contest's ritual significance and the rank of the players and their patrons. Champion players could win fortunes in gold, feathers, or precious stones. Exceptional games could result in riches and honor for the winner and death for the loser, whose heart, ripped from his chest on the centerline stone, became food for the gods.

sign. Continue for several miles to the mountaintop Parque Huixteco.

About three weeks later, the Taxco year-end holiday season kicks off in earnest, with the weeklong **National Silver Fair** (last Sat. in Nov.–first Fri. in Dec.). A month of partying continues with the **Fiesta of the Virgin of Guadalupe** (Dec. 12), climaxing with a week of continuous Christmas and New Year merrymaking, concluding with Day of the Kings gift-giving (Jan. 6).

SPORTS AND RECREATION

Stay in shape as local folks do, by walking Taxco's winding, picturesque side streets and uphill lanes. And, since all roads return to the *zócalo,* getting lost is rarely a problem.

For more formal sports, the **Monte Taxco Country Club** (hotel tel. 762/622-1300, horseback riding $15/hr, tennis $14/hr, golf $50 pp) has horses ready for riding, three good tennis courts, and a nine-hole golf course available for use by non-guests. Contact the country club sports desk, in the little house about 100 yards away from the Hotel Monte Taxco's front entrance, or call the hotel. Rough informal *senderos* (hiking paths) head north, uphill, into the luscious pine- and cedar-forested mesa country. Take sturdy shoes, water, and a hat.

SHOPPING
Market

Taxco's big market day is Sunday, when the town is loaded with people from outlying villages selling produce and live pigs, chickens, and ducks. The market is just downhill from Los Arcos, the lane that runs below the Santa Prisca churchfront's right side. From the lane, head right before the arch and down the staircase. Soon you'll be descending through a warren of market stalls. Don't miss the spice stall, **Yerbería Castillo,** piled with the intriguing wild remedies collected by owner Elvira Castillo and her son Teodoro.

Farther on you'll pass mostly scruffy meat stalls but also some clean juice stands, such as **Licuados Memo** (7 A.M.–6 P.M. daily), where you can rest with a delicious fresh *zanahoria* (carrot), *toronja* (grapefruit), or *sandía* (watermelon) juice.

Before leaving the market, be sure to ask for *jumiles* (hoo-MEE-lays), live crickets that are sold in bags for about a penny apiece, ready for folks to pop into their mouths.

If *jumiles* don't suit your taste, you may want to drop in for lunch at one of the *fondas* (food stalls) upstairs, above the market's *artesanías* section.

Handicrafts

Before visiting the individual private handicrafts shops, you might look around the submarket **Mercado de Artesanías** (watch for the sign above the main Taxco market downhill

souvenir masks for sale

© BRUCE WHIPPERMAN

staircase) that offers an abundance of priced-to-sell mini-treasures such as silver chains, necklaces, earrings, belts, huaraches, and wallets. Furthermore, if you're in town on Saturday, you might also taxi down to the Estrella Blanca bus station on the highway and browse around the **Saturday Silver Market** that spreads along the street out front of the station.

And furthermore, while in town be sure not to miss the common but colorful handicrafts such as the host of charming hand-painted ceramic cats, turtles, doves, fish, and other figurines that local vendors sell very cheaply. If you buy, bargain—but not too hard, for the people are poor and have often traveled far.

Taxco abounds in private handicrafts shops, most of them specializing in silver but a number of others specializing in Guerrero and Oaxaca masks, woodcrafts, pottery, and much more.

I have arranged my list of favorite stores so that, without too much backtracking, you can get a good look at lots of lovely handicrafts in an afternoon's stroll around town.

Start at Calle Cuauhtémoc, across the *zócalo* from the church at the store of master silversmith **Ezequiel Tapia** (15 Cuauhtémoc, tel. 762/622-0416, 9 A.M.–8 P.M. daily), winner of a score of national prizes. His shop, as much a museum as it is a store, displays a choice collection of mostly spectacular pieces, tending toward the large and the avant-garde.

A few doors farther west (away from *zócalo*), check out the longtime (since 1950) silver shop **Arte Nacional** (Cuauhtémoc 9, tel. 762/622-1096, fax 762/622-2202, noon–7 P.M. daily), with a grand selection of virtually everything silver. Specialties range from a museum-quality selection of gleaming table silver (chafing dishes, large platters, tea sets, candelabras) to a treasury of necklaces, bracelets, rings, and much, much more.

Half a block farther, find **Platería Gloria** (Plazuela de San Juan 7, tel. 762/622-2047 or 762/622-0410, fax 762/622-6498, 9 A.M.–8 P.M. Mon.–Sat., 11 A.M.–6 P.M. Sun.), winner of two-dozen-odd national prizes. Besides an exquisite collection of one-of-a-kind earrings, necklaces, and cameos, his shop glows with huge, lovely sculptures in solid silver. For sheer volume and selection of everything lovely, this is the place, with literally thousands of charming silver necklaces, bracelets, rings, place settings, pendants, and candlesticks.

Return east along Cuauhtémoc back to the *zócalo's* east, downhill side. Just past the Santa Prisca churchfront, turn right at former Calle de Muerte (now Calle Celso Muñoz), and nearly immediately on the left find what must be Taxco's most elegantly extravagant silver shop, the **Joyería Elena Ballesteros** (Calle Celso Muñoz 6, tel. 762/622-3767, fax 762/622-3907, info@ebaplata.com, 9 A.M.–7 P.M. Mon.–Sat.). More than just a labor of love, this is a virtual shrine to silver, beginning with the simply exquisite, moving to dining-room tables loaded with enough plates for a maharaja's banquet.

For a contrasting, but equally elegant, selection, continue downhill to **Hecho a Mano** (end of Calle Celso Muñoz, 10 A.M.–5 P.M. Mon.–Sat.) of master silversmith Manuel Porcayo. If originality is what you prefer, he can provide you with a treasury of one-of-a-kind necklaces, bracelets, rings, collars, pendants, and much more.

Return uphill to the *zócalo* corner, then turn right for a look around the bright white grotto-like interior of **Silvermaster** (tel. 762/622-6447, 9 A.M.–8 P.M. daily) in the *zócalo*-front complex Patio de las Artesanías, on the right before the Casa Borda. Inside you'll find showrooms decorated with pendulous plaster stalacites hanging above faux stalagmites, seemingly dripping with fine silver jewelry (all of which, owners say with a smile, was the model for the Grutas de Cacahuamilpa complex).

Continue, passing the Casa Borda. At the corner, just before the Hotel Agua Escondida, head right steeply downhill a block to the petite Plazuela Bernal and to **Hilda** crafts shop (no phone, 9 A.M.–8 P.M. daily), named after the grandmother of the owner. She specializes in masks, devilish to angelic; faux skeletons,

The Silvermaster store in Taxco seemingly drips with fine silver jewelry.

© BRUCE WHIPPERMAN

and miniature dolls and pocket chess sets, all easy to carry home.

Bear right, downhill, onto J. R. de Alarcón, at the fork with Avenida Juárez. Continue downhill a block to one of Taxco's most venerable institutions, the family-owned shop of **Emilia Castillo** (J. R. de Alarcón 7, tel. 762/622-1396, 10 A.M.–7 P.M. Mon.–Sat., 10 A.M.–4 P.M. Sun.), at the Hotel Emilia Castillo on the right side of the street. Run by a branch of the industrious and prolific Castillo clan, the shop offers all in-house work, specializing in porcelain and silver at reasonable prices. Here, unlike at many shops, you can bargain a bit.

Continue east along J. R. de Alarcón, passing Casa Humboldt; after two short blocks, turn right at Calle Higuera, arriving after one block at **Nuestro Mexico** (Veracruz 8, tel. 762/622-0976, nuestromexico@hotmail.com, 10 A.M.–10 P.M. daily except Thurs.) on the left, at the corner of Veracruz. Inside, enjoy a look around at their interesting all-Guerrero clutter of wood and ceramic reproduction masks, soaring angels, ceramic coffee cups, silver, and more.

Finally, return uphill along Veracruz, a short block to Humboldt lane, the small (right-side) plaza in front of the Guillermo Spratling museum. Here, choose your favorites among a trove of priced-to-sell indigenous handicrafts: fetching painted pottery animals, cheerful Father Suns, colorful *amate* (fig-tree-bark) placemats, emerald-hued beads, cool sombreros, polished wooden bowls, and much, much more.

INFORMATION AND SERVICES
Tourist Information

Taxco has a pair of **tourist information offices** (both beside the highway at opposite ends of town, 9 A.M.–7 P.M. daily). The knowledgeable and English-speaking officers readily answer questions and furnish whatever maps and literature they may have. The north office (tel. 762/622-0798) is next to the north-end Pemex gas station; the south office (no phone) is about a quarter mile south of the south-end Pemex station.

Personable veteran Mexico guide **Benito Flores Batalla** (tel./fax 762/622-0542, 3.5 hr city tour $35 without car), who staffs the north-side tourist information office, offers his services as a guide. For starters, he offers a 3.5-hour city tour. Longer trips might include the Grutas de Cachuamilpa, Xochicalco, and Ixcateopan. The same is approximately true for **Enrique Viveros,** who staffs the south-end office. If Benito and Enrique are unavailable, they highly recommend guide **Juan Menatel** (tel. 762/622-0986, $70/day including car).

One of the most reliable travel agents in town is **Turismo Misión** (at the Hotel Posada de la Misión reception desk, tel. 762/622-1125 or 762/622-0063, info@posadamision.com, www.posadamision.com, all-day tour $160, including car for 2–4 people), who provides tours plus all the usual travel agency services.

Groceries and Laundry

Silver shops have driven most groceries from the Taxco town center. However, convenience store **Oxxo** (Cuauhtémoc, west side of the

zócalo, 7 A.M.–midnight daily) brings in the crowd with its decent selection of cheese, milk, yogurt, eggs, lunchmeat, bread, some fruit, wine, beer, chips, cookies, pastries, and more.

Alternatively, go to **Minisuper La Gloria** (Hidalgo, tel. 762/622-3878, 8 A.M.–10 P.M. daily), a long block downhill from Plazuela de San Juan.

For laundry, go to the *Lavanderí* (Av. Los Plateros 346, tel. 762/622-8288, 9 A.M.–7 P.M. Mon.–Sat.), on the *carretera* on the south side, a block south of the big Seguro Social Hospital.

Photography

The photo shop **Foto Hidalgo** (Hidalgo 13, tel. 762/627-6232, 9:30 A.M.–8 P.M. Mon.–Sat.), a block downhill from the Plazuela San Juan, offers a modest stock of merchandise, including batteries, point-and-shoot cameras, popular print film and development, and digital services and accessories.

Publications

English-language books and newspapers are hard to find in Taxco. The most convenient place to find used paperbacks will probably be your hotel.

Nevertheless, you might benefit from the collection at the small local library, **Biblioteca Taxco-Canoga Park** (no phone, 9 A.M.–1 P.M. and 3–7 P.M. Mon.–Fri., 9 A.M.–1 P.M. Sat.). Browse its several shelves of English-language novels, nonfiction, magazines, and reference books. Most of the books were donated by volunteers from Taxco's sister city, Canoga Park, California. The library is a five-minute walk downhill along Juárez (east) from the *zócalo.* About a block past the city hall, turn right at an alley (watch for the Taxco–Canoga Park sign) and continue a few steps downhill to the library.

Money Exchange

Banks near the *zócalo* and their ATMs are Taxco's cheapest source of pesos. Try either **HSBC** (tel. 762/622-7506, 9 A.M.–5 P.M. Mon.–Fri.) to the right, facing the church, or

Bancomer (Cuauhtémoc, tel. 762/622-2393, 8:30 A.M.–4 P.M. Mon.–Fri.), a block from the *zócalo.*

Communications

The town center **correo** (post office; Juárez, tel. 762/627-2503, 8 A.M.–6 P.M. Mon.–Fri., 8 A.M.–3 P.M. Sat.), with after-hours mailbox out front, is in the *presidencia municipal,* downhill (east) from the *zócalo.* The highway branch downhill (tel. 762/622-0501, 8 A.M.–4:30 P.M. Mon.–Fri., 8 A.M.–noon Sat.) is half a block north (Mexico City direction) of the Estrella de Oro bus station.

Telecomunicaciones (off the *zócalo* behind the Casa Borda downhill, tel. 762/622-4885, fax 762/622-0001, 9 A.M.–3 P.M. Mon.–Fri., 9 A.M.–noon Sat.) offers computer, money order, and public fax services.

Public street telephones all over the town center allow inexpensive, easy, long-distance direct dialing with widely available Ladatel telephone cards. Get them at pharmacies and liquor and grocery stores.

For Internet access, go to either the small Internet store on Cuauhtémoc (upstairs, half a block west of the *zócalo,* no phone, 11 A.M.–11 P.M. daily) or computer center **Interplaza** (tel. 762/622-0789, 9:30 A.M.–9 P.M. Mon.–Sat., 10 A.M.–4 P.M. Sun.) in the town market, 200 feet down the steps below the right (west) side of the church.

Health and Emergencies

Taxco has a pair of respected private hospitals, both on the *carretera:* The **Clínica de Especialidades** (33 Av. de los Plateros, tel. 762/622-1111 or 762/622-4500) with 24-hour emergency room, X-rays, a laboratory, a 24-hour pharmacy, and many specialists on call; or the **Clínica Santa Cruz** (Plateros, at the corner of Morelos, tel. 762/622-3012) with similar services, across from the government Seguro Social hospital.

For routine medicines and remedies, go to a good town-center pharmacy, such as **Farmacia de Ahorro** (Cuauhtémoc, half a block west of the *zócalo,* tel. 762/627-3444, 7 A.M.–11 P.M. daily) or **Farmacia Similares** (Hidalgo, one block downhill from Plazuela de San Juan, tel. 762/627-2214, 8 A.M.–9 P.M. daily).

For police emergencies, contact the **policía** (tel. 762/622-0007) or find them on duty on the *zócalo;* at the city hall (Juárez 6, tel. 762/622-0007), two blocks downhill; or at the substation on the side street Calle Fundaciones—walk one block below the *carretera* from the corner of J. R. de Alarcón.

GETTING THERE AND AWAY
By Car or RV

National Highway 95 provides a major direct connection south with Acapulco in a total of about 159 miles (256 km) of driving via Iguala (22 mi/36 km), thence to Chilpancingo (a total of about 86 mi/138 km), and finally Acapulco in another 73 miles (117 km) via the *cuota* (toll) *autopista* (about $20). Allow about 4.5 hours' driving time for the entire trip, either direction.

Alternatively, save about an hour to Acapulco by following toll expressways (about $40) the whole way, by first heading north (Cuernavaca–Mexico City direction) out of town. Follow the Mexico City *cuota* signs all the way about 25 miles (40 km) to the Highway 95D *cuota* expressway, where you fork south (Chilpancingo–Acapulco direction). Allow about 3.5 hours for this longer but quicker 192-mile (310-km) Taxco–Acapulco route.

Non-toll old Highway 95 also connects Taxco north via Cuernavaca with Mexico City, a total of about 106 miles (170 km). The new leg of the Taxco–Mexico City *cuota* (toll) expressway splits off from old Highway 95 about two miles north of town. For those who want to save time, the expressway cuts about half an hour off the driving time. Otherwise, follow the winding old Highway 95 about 20 miles (32 km) to its intersection with Highway 95D *cuota* (toll) superhighway. Congestion around Mexico City may lengthen the driving time to about three hours in either direction.

(*Note:* Authorities limit driving your car in Mexico City according to the last digit of your license plate; make sure you know the restrictions in advance.)

By Bus

Competing lines **Estrella Blanca** (tel. 762/622-0648) and **Estrella de Oro** (tel. 762/622-0131) operate separate stations on the downhill *carretera* several blocks apart. Both offer several luxury- and first-class connections north with Mexico City via Cuernavaca and south with Acapulco via Iguala and Chilpancingo.

Estrella Blanca also offers connections with Puebla, plus the very useful option for northwest-bound travelers of bypassing Mexico City via the superscenic Highway 55 route via Ixtapan del Sal (an interesting spa town) to Toluca. There, you can connect either via Pátzcuaro, Michoacán, or Guadalajara, Jalisco, with the palmy Mexican Pacific beach destinations of Playa Azul, Manzanillo, Puerto Vallarta, San Blas, and Mazatlán.

EXCURSIONS FROM TAXCO

The monumental duo of the Grutas de Cacahuamilpa (caves) and the regal ruins of ancient Xochicalco makes for a fascinating, although long, day trip, by tour or car (two days if by public transportation). If you're going to do them both, head out by 8 or 9 A.M.; the Grutas are 15 miles (25 km) north (Mexico City direction) of town and Xochicalco is 25 miles (40 km) farther.

◖ Grutas de Cacahuamilpa National Park

This trip is well worth the effort. The colossal Grutas de Cacahuamilpa (kah-kah-ooah-MEEL-pah; park office tel. 721/1040-0155 or 721/104-0156, hourly walking tours in Spanish 10 A.M.–4 P.M. daily, $6 admission, $5 for kids) comprise one of the world's most spectacular cavern complexes. Forests of stalagmites and stalactites, in myriad shapes—Pluto the Pup, the Holy Family, a desert caravan, asparagus stalks, cauliflower heads—festoon a series of gigantic limestone chambers. The finale is a grand 30-story hall that meanders for half a mile, like a fairyland in stone. A few gift

shops sell souvenirs; *fondas* (food stalls) supply food.

The hourly walking tours are three miles long and last two hours. They are conducted in Spanish and are included in the general admission cost.

Moreover, experienced guides lead more extensive one or two-day Cacahuamilpa cave tours ($50 or $100 pp) for robust, determined hikers only, during the February–May dry season. Highlights include walking (and sometimes crawling) about five miles (8 km) along sinuous, sometimes steep and slippery subterranean tunnels and paths, and fording waist-deep (and perhaps even shoulder-deep) underground rivers. Make arrangements, at least a week ahead of time, directly with chief guide Lorenzo Amates Muñoz (amates_m@hotmail.com). For more information, call the Cacahuamilpa park office.

GETTING THERE

Combi collective vans ($2 one-way) leave hourly for the caves, beginning at 8:30 A.M., just north of the Estrella Blanca bus station on the *carretera*. Watch for "Grutas" written on the windshields. By car, get there via Highway 95 north from Taxco; 10 miles (16 km) from the north-side Pemex station, fork left onto Highway 55 toward Toluca. Continue five more miles (8 km) and turn right at the signed Grutas de Cacahuamilpa junction. After a few hundred yards, turn right again into the entrance driveway.

◖ Xochicalco

Regal Xochicalco (soh-shee-KAHL-koh), an hour farther north from Cacahuamilpa, although lightly touristed, is a fountainhead of Mesoamerican legend. The archaeological zone (9 A.M.–6 P.M. daily, last visitor entry at 5 P.M.), officially designated as a UNESCO World Heritage site, spreads over a half dozen terraced pyramid hilltops overlooking a natural lake-valley, which at one time sustained a large population. Xochicalco flowered during the late classic period around A.D. 800, partly filling the vacuum left by the decline

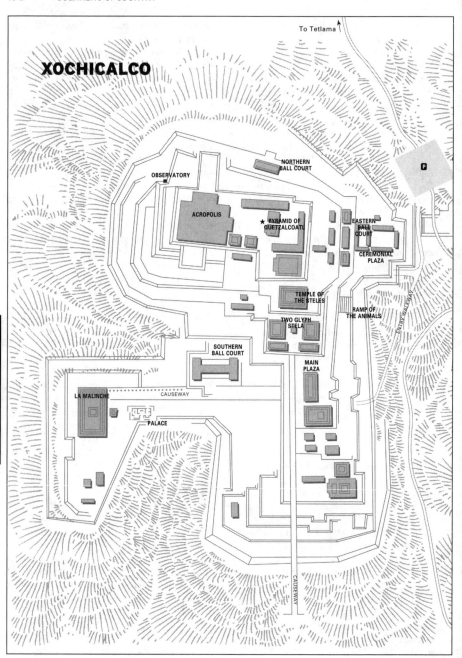

XOCHICALCO

To Tetlama

P

NORTHERN BALL COURT

OBSERVATORY

ACROPOLIS

★ PYRAMID OF QUETZALCOATL

EASTERN BALL COURT

CEREMONIAL PLAZA

TEMPLE OF THE STELES

RAMP OF THE ANIMALS

TWO GLYPH STELA

SOUTHERN BALL COURT

MAIN PLAZA

LA MALINCHE

CAUSEWAY

PALACE

ENTRY WALKWAY

CAUSEWAY

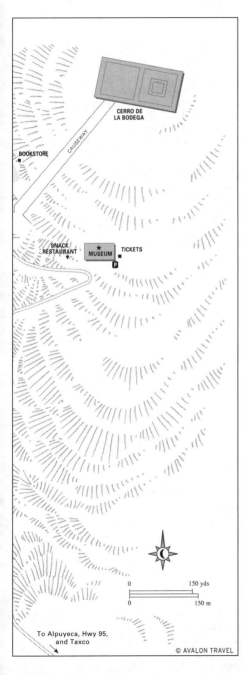

CERRO DE
LA BODEGA

CAUSEWAY

BOOKSTORE

SNACK
RESTAURANT

TICKETS

★ MUSEUM

P

0   150 yds

0   150 m

To Alpuyeca, Hwy 95,
and Taxco

© AVALON TRAVEL

of Teotihuacán, the previously dominant Mesoamerican classic-era city-state. Some archaeologists speculate that Xochicalco at its apex was the great center of learning, known in legend as Tamanchoan, where astronomer-priests derived and maintained calendars and where the Living Quetzalcoatl legend was born.

Your first stop should be the world-class **museum** (tel. 737/374-3090, xochicalco.mor@inah.gob.mx, 9 A.M.–5 P.M. daily, admission $5) via the signed driveway east of the archaeological site; there is a café in the museum. A grand entrance hall leads to six masterfully executed galleries that illustrate the main currents of Xochicalco civilization: Earthly Gifts (flora, fauna, and trade); Warlords and Priests (don't miss the headless Lord-in-Red sun god); Xochicalco, Guardian of the People (centered around a pair of calendar-glyph stelae that undoubtedly records an historic Xochicalco calendric event); Creators and Artists (don't miss the sensitively executed jaguar and coyote pieces); World of the Gods (dramatic illustration of the ball court and ring found on the site); and Daily Spaces (replica of a typical house, family altars and utensils and realistic "Lord of Xochicalco").

EXPLORING THE SITE

Save at least two hours (mandatory visitor exit time 5:45 P.M. daily) to cover the site highlights. After visiting the excellent bookstore (which closes at 5 P.M.), your first stop should be the **Pyramid of Quetzalcoatl** on the site's north side. From the parking lot, head south uphill for about 100 yards, where a wide path forks right, uphill. After approximately another 100 yards, when you reach level ground again, turn right and pass the beautifully reconstructed **eastern ball court** on your right. Continue another 50 yards or so until, on the wall about 200 feet to your left, you see some stairs that you should climb to the next upper level where the platform-like Pyramid of Quetzalcoatl (The Plumed Serpent) rises on the hilltop.

Vermilion paint remnants hint at the

CUAUHTÉMOC: THE LAST AZTEC EMPEROR

Cuauhtémoc (koo-ah-oo-TAY-mok) is more than just a national hero; he's the celebrated Aztec leader who said no to the Spanish conquistadores and, spitting on the spineless example of his uncle Moctezuma before him, did something about it. Faced with the disastrous reality that most of imperial Tenochtitlán's population of 250,000 was either dead or sick with smallpox, Cuauhtémoc rallied his people to hold out for 75 days against Spanish cannons and their 100,000-strong army of native allies.

That the story of Cuauhtémoc was more than a legend became clear when, on September 26, 1949, official investigators announced the discovery of Cuauhtémoc's long-missing remains in the small municipality of Ixcateopan, not far from the famous Acapulco-region silver town of Taxco, Guerrero.

Cuauhtémoc was born into the comfort and privilege of the Mexican imperial family on February 23, 1501. His father, Ahuitzotl, was the son of the eighth Aztec emperor, also Ahuitzotl. His mother, princess Cuayautitalli, was the daughter of the lord of Zompancuahuitl (now Ixcateopan, Guerrero).

His given name, Cuauhtémoc, translates from the Aztec language as "descending eagle." Cuauhtémoc's traditional hieroglyph is thus marked by a stylized diving eagle.

Orphaned by his father when still an infant, Cuauhtémoc was brought up by his mother. At the age of 15 he entered Calmécac, the academy for sons of noble military officers and priests. His formal education initiated him into the secrets of the gods and the sciences of astronomy and the calendar.

After completing his schooling, Cuauhtémoc followed his uncle, Moctezuma II, in his infamous "War of the Flowers" conquests. During this time he proved his valor and skill, gaining the high rank of *tlacetechutli*, the command equivalent of a modern colonel.

Moctezuma II, upon returning home in glory with thousands of captives, presided over the elevation of his nephew, Cuauhtémoc, as governor of the important Tlatelolco and Teotecuhtli districts of the capital Tenochtitlán.

The good times didn't last, however, for soon Hernán Cortés and his small but determined band of armored soldiers and cavalry entered the gates of Tenochtitlán. Cuauhtémoc's uncle, frozen by fear that Cortés might be the returned god Quetzalcoatl, quickly surrendered himself and all of his golden treasure to the wily Cortés. On July 1, 1520, angered by Spanish brutality and their emperor's fearful acquiescence, the Tenochtitlán populace rebelled, killing Moctezuma II and forcing the

---

pyramid's original appearance, which was perhaps as brilliant as a giant birthday cake. In bas-relief around the entire base a serpent writhes, intertwined with personages, probably representing chiefs or great priests. Above these are warriors, identified by their helmets and *atlatl,* or lance-throwers.

Most notable, however, is one of Mesoamerica's most **remarkable bas-reliefs,** on the right flank of the staircase. It shows the 11th week sign, *ozomatli* (monkey), being pulled by a hand (via a rope) to join with the 5th week sign, *calli* (house). Latter-day scholars generally interpret this as describing a calendar correction that resulted from a grand conclave

of chiefs and sages from all over Mesoamerica, probably at this very spot.

About 100 yards south of the Pyramid of Quetzalcoatl rises the **Temple of the Steles,** so named for three large stone tablets found beneath the floor. They narrate the events of the Quetzalcoatl legend, wherein Quetzalcoatl (discoverer of corn and the calendar) was transformed into the morning star (the planet Venus); he continues to rule the heavens as the brightest star and the Lord of Time.

About 100 yards farther south, the **Main Plaza** was accessible to the common people via roads from below. This is in contrast to the sacrosanct **Ceremonial Plaza** by the Eastern

Spanish into their disastrous Noche Triste (Sad Night) retreat, at the end of which an exhausted Cortés sat down and cried for the loss of half of his men.

The Aztecs' triumph was short-lived, however. Although they had rid themselves of the Spanish, smallpox – the Spaniards' deadly legacy – began spreading among the people. When the Spanish, returned to Tenochtitlán in late May 1521 reinforced by a vast corps of native allies, Cuauhtémoc, by contrast, ruled a city decimated by smallpox. Nevertheless, with herculean resolve, he united his people, exhorting those who could to care for the wounded, gather rocks, or help pile bricks for a barricade.

After a bloody siege that lasted for 2.5 months, Cortés resorted to leveling the capital to capture it. On August 13, 1521, Cuauhtémoc, desperate for reinforcements, set out to find them, but he was captured and brought before Cortés and his translator-mistress, Malinche. Cuauhtémoc pointed to the dagger that Cortés held in his belt and said to Malinche, "Malintzin, since I've resisted you in the defense of my city and my people, and come by coercion and in chains before you, take that dagger and kill me with it."

Cortés, however, didn't allow Cuauhtémoc such an honorable death. Perhaps hoping that he could convince him to be his puppet emperor, Cortés kept him in captivity for another four years. He even took Cuauhtémoc and a retinue of Aztec nobles along on his ill-fated expedition to Honduras in 1523-1525. Tortured with foreboding that Cuauhtémoc and his compatriots were plotting against him, Cortés had Cuauhtémoc hanged on February 28, 1525.

Cuauhtémoc's grisly remains were still suspended in the hanging tree when Cuauhtémoc's warrior companion, Tzilactzín, rescued them. Afraid that vandals would desecrate the body, he took down Cuauhtémoc's corpse and wrapped it in aromatic leaves. He and a band of about 30 companions, all deserters of Cortés's expedition, carried the remains for 40 days and nights and buried them secretly at Ixcateopan, the home of Cuauhtémoc's mother. There, 424 years later, Cuauhtémoc's lineal descendant, Salvador Rodrigo Juárez, and historian and professor Eulalia Guzmán announced the discovery of Cuauhtémoc's remains. They are on public display before the altar of Ixcateopan town church, Santa María de la Asunción, in a glass casket above the spot where they were found.

Ball Court nearby. South of the Ceremonial Plaza, the **Ramp of the Animals** (named for the carved animal-motif stones found along its length) slopes upward from east to west.

On the far northwest side of the complex is the **Observatory,** a room hollowed into the hill, stuccoed, and fitted with a viewing shaft for timing the sun and star transits essential for an accurate calendar.

GETTING THERE

Get to Xochicalco by tour guide (contact Benito Flores Batalla or Enrique Viveros, at the Taxco information offices, or Misión Tours, at the Hotel Posada de la Misión, tel. 762/622-1125 or 762/622-0065) or taxi or car. Get there by continuing past the Caves (Grutas) of Cacahuamilpa driveway entrance (mark your odometer). The route is straightforward, continuing by a single main road generally northeast, through Coatlá del Río (12 mi/19 km), Mazatepec (20 mi/33 km), and finally Miacatlán (23 mi/37 km). There you bear right (east) at a fork (watch for Xochicalco signs) and continue past Rodeo hamlet (and lake on the right) to the Xochicalco signed left side road that leads a mile or two uphill to the archaeological site, a total of 29 miles (46 km), about an hour, from Cacahuamilpa, or 48 miles (77 km), two hours, from Taxco.

Ixcateopan

The picturesque little furniture-making town of Ixcateopan (eeks-kah-tay-OH-pan, Land of Cotton) has become famous for the remains of the last Aztec emperor, Cuauhtémoc, which archaeologists discovered there on September 26, 1949.

EXPLORING IXCATEOPAN

The renown has been beneficial. The town streets and plaza are smartly cobbled with the local white marble, and houses and shops are neatly painted and whitewashed. At the center of all of this stands Cuauhtémoc's resting place, the venerable **Iglesia de Santa María de la Asunción** church, beside the town plaza. Inside, volunteers maintain the sanctuary and its small adjoining museum (9 A.M.–3 P.M. and 4–5 P.M. Mon.–Sat., 9 A.M.–3 P.M. Sun.). Cuauhtémoc's relics themselves, which were subjected to thorough investigation when they were unearthed, were believed to be authentic

A gorgeous waterfall on the Taxco-Ixcateopan road invites lingering.

(although some latter-day doubters dispute this claim). The bones lie in a glass case directly over the spot where they were buried beneath the altar stones more than four centuries ago.

The museum next door details the story of Cuauhtémoc's heroic defense of the Aztec capital, Tenochtitlán, and his capture, torture, and subsequent execution by Cortés on February 28, 1525. Copies of pictograms, known as codices, such as the codex Vatican-Ríos (1528), displayed in the museum, represent Cuauhtémoc (literally, "The Descending Eagle") with an inverted, stylized eagle above his head. An excellent booklet ($3) details the fascinating story of the discovery and authentication of his ancestor's remains (in Spanish).

Outside the church, be sure to take a look about three blocks downhill past the church, on main street Calle V. Guerrero, at the town **archaeological site** (Calle V. Guerrero, 10 A.M.–5 P.M. Wed.–Sun.). The main remains, called the "Temple of Cotton," echoing the name Ixcateopan, reveal a ceremonial complex, including a pair of pedestals, royal rooms, and a former spring leading through what appear to have been wash basins (presumably for the cotton the high priests may have ritually processed there).

FESTIVALS

Customarily sleepy Ixcateopan wakes up for three annual fiestas. The fun kicks off in February, when folks celebrate their indigenous roots with a weeklong party of daily flower processions, indigenous dances, and fireworks, all climaxing around the February 23 birthday of Cuauhtémoc.

The customary arrival of the governor of Guerrero, the Acapulco Symphony, and maybe even the president of Mexico, on September 26, the discovery date of Cuautémoc's remains, culminates another week of celebrating.

Finally, townsfolk bring in the New Year in grand style with a combined Christmas–carnival–New Year celebration of their patron Santo Niño de Atocha.

ACCOMMODATIONS AND FOOD

Besides its historic interest, Ixcateopan and its environs—the rustic old church and garden, the tranquil plaza, the surrounding lush oak-forested hills—invite lingering. Moreover, the amiable, frankly curious townsfolk—who are not overwhelmed by tourists—are ready for visitors. They operate some pretty fair plaza-front country eateries, such as Cocinas Económicas Amanec, at the south side of the plaza.

Accommodations are also available, on the main street, at the **Posada de los Reyes** (Calle V. Guerrero 14, tel. 736/366-2368, $20 s, $30 d), a block past the plaza, across the street from the church. The welcoming family owners offer eight clean rooms, around a tranquil inner patio, furnished with attractive locally crafted wood furniture and homespun bedspreads. Rooms come with private hot-water shower baths.

GETTING THERE

Reach the town via Ixcateopan-labeled *colectivo* van ($3 one-way). Catch it in front of the Estrella Blanca bus station in Taxco, or at any point on the *carretera* before the south-side signed turnoff road to Ixcateopan.

Drivers, follow the signed fork, west (turn right if traveling south) from the *carretera*, past the Pemex *gasolinera* about a mile south of town. Mark your odometer. Continue about an hour along the very scenic (including a pair of waterfalls, good for picnicking and splashing, at Mile 4.5/Km 7.2 and Mile 11/Km 17.7), sometimes potholed, paved road for 23 miles (37 km) to the town plaza.

THE COSTA CHICA

In reality the Costa Chica, the "Little Coast," which traditionally includes the coast of Guerrero east of Acapulco and the adjoining coast of Oaxaca, isn't so little after all. Highway 200, heading out of the Acapulco hubbub, requires 150 miles to traverse the scattered groves, forests, fields, and villages to the Mixtec and Amusgo indigenous country between Ometepec, Guerrero, and Pinotepa Nacional, Oaxaca.

To many thousands of Costa Chica indigenous peoples, Spanish is a foreign language. Many of them live in remote foothill villages, subsisting as they always have on corn and beans, with few telephones, sewers, schools, or roads. Those who live near towns often speak the Spanish they have learned by coming to market. In the Costa Chica town markets of Ometepec, Xochistlahuaca, and Pinotepa Nacional you will brush shoulders with them—mostly Mixtecs, Amusgos, and Chatinos—men sometimes in pure-white cottons and women in colorful embroidered *huipiles* over wrapped hand-woven skirts.

Besides the indigenous people, you will often see African Mexicans—*morenos* (brown ones)—also known as *costeños* because their settlements cluster near the coast. Descendants of African slaves imported hundreds of years ago, the *costeños* subsist on the produce from their village gardens and the fish they catch.

Costa Chica *indígenas* and *costeños* have a reputation for being unfriendly and suspicious. If true in the past (it's certainly less so in the present), they have had good reason to be wary of outsiders, who in their view have

HIGHLIGHTS

◖ Playa Las Peñitas: "Precious" is the best word to describe this rocky nook on a breezy strand. The main attraction, besides tasty seafood and a comfortable hotel, is a sacred tide-pool-enfolded sea rock that folks visit en masse on May 3, the Día de la Cruz (page 209).

◖ Parroquia de Santiago: Ometepec folks are so proud of their magnificent parish church that, in the evenings, they illuminate its lovely baby-blue-and-white facade and the rooftop statue of the avenging Santiago for all to see (page 211).

◖ Ometepec Sunday Market: In Ometepec, the handicrafts action centers around the downtown plaza, while across town at the formal market a mountain of old-fashioned goods draws a big crowd of traditionally costumed Amusgo- and Mixtec-speaking country folks (page 211).

◖ Xochistlahuaca: Every Sunday, thousands of Amusgo-speaking indigenous peo-

ple put on their holiday best *traje* (traditional dress) and converge on the awning-festooned center *tianguis* (market) to bargain, gossip, and flirt (page 216).

◖ Museo de las Culturas Afromestizos: Besides the bustling market, make your main Cuajinicuilapa stop at this singularly important museum, which skillfully showcases the history and cultural contributions of the Acapulco region's important African-Mexican community (page 218).

◖ Pinotepa Nacional Market: Pinotepa Nacional, an important market town of the Oaxaca Costa Chica, is a magnet for indigenous coastal Mixtec-speaking people (page 219).

◖ Huaxpáltepec Pre-Easter Fair: You will not be able to avoid this best of all possible indigenous market experiences if your arrival coincides with the local festival of Jesus the Nazarene, four days preceding the fourth Friday before Easter Sunday (page 223).

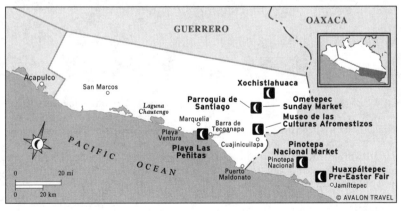

LOOK FOR ◖ TO FIND RECOMMENDED SIGHTS, ACTIVITIES, DINING, AND LODGING.

THE COSTA CHICA

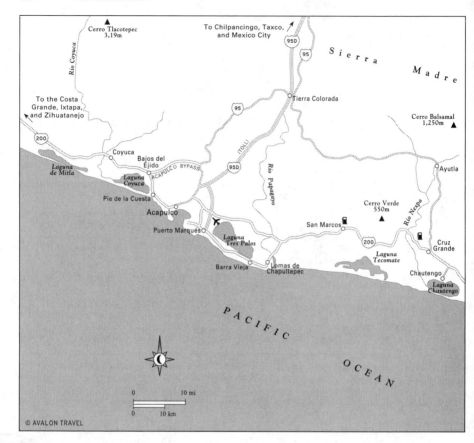

© AVALON TRAVEL

been trying to take away their land, gods, and lives for 400 years.

Communication is nevertheless possible. For the residents of a little mountain or shoreline end-of-road village, your arrival might be the event of the day. People are going to wonder why you came. Smile and say hello. Buy a soda at the store or *palapa*. If kids gather around, don't be shy. Draw a picture in your notebook. If a child offers to do likewise, you've succeeded in making a connection.

PLANNING YOUR TIME

Although you can traverse the Costa Chica in less than a day, try to save some time to linger a few days to soak in the local color of the market towns and enjoy the natural diversions along the way. For example, kayakers and wildlife-viewers might enjoy a whole day exploring the mangrove-laced, wildlife-rich, wetland Laguna Chautengo. If so, you might want to stay even longer for tenting, beach-combing, fishing, and surfing in or near the cross-lagoon breezy barrier-beach village San José de la Barra.

On the other hand, most anyone could easily enjoy an overnight or two at each of the petite south-seas beach resorts of **Playa Ventura** and **Playa Las Peñitas.** At Playa Ventura, you can choose among several beachfront hotels, especially the modest Hotel Caracola or Hotel Tortuguita retreats, whose owners welcome

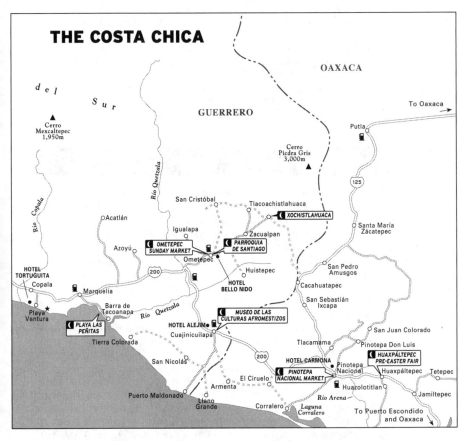

THE COSTA CHICA

del
Sur

OAXACA

GUERRERO

To Oaxaca →

▲ Cerro
Mexcaltepec
1,950m

Cerro
Picdra Gris
3,000m ▲

Putla

Río Quetzala

Río Copala

San Cristóbal

Tlacoachistlahuaca

☾ **XOCHISTLAHUACA**

125

○ Acatlán

Igualapa

Santa María Zácatepec

Azoyú ○

☾ **OMETEPEC SUNDAY MARKET**

○ Zacualpan

☾ **PARROQUIA DE SANTIAGO**

Ometepec

200

Huistepec ○

San Pedro Amusgos

HOTEL BELLO NIDO

Cacahuatepec ○

San Sebastián Ixcapa

HOTEL TORTUGUITA

Copala

Marquélia

Barra de Tecoanapa

Río Quetzala

☾ **MUSEO DE LAS CULTURAS AFROMESTIZOS**

Playa Ventura ★

☾ **PLAYA LAS PEÑITAS**

HOTEL ALEJIM

Cuajinicuilapa

San Juan Colorado ○

Tierra Colorada

Tlacamama ○

Pinotepa Don Luis ○

San Nicolás ○

200

HOTEL CARMONA

☾ **HUAXPÁLTEPEC PRE-EASTER FAIR**

Pinotepa Nacional

Huaxpáltepec ○

Tetepec ○

☾ **PINOTEPA NACIONAL MARKET**

El Ciruelo ○

Puerto Maldonado ○

Armenta ○

Llano Grande

Huazolotitlan ○

Jamiltepec ○

Corralero ○

Laguna Corralero

Río Arena

To Puerto Escondido and Oaxaca

---

guests with rustic but comfortable accommodations and beachfront pools and patios. Tenters and RV campers could linger for a day, a week, or a season enjoying the miles-long wild Playa Ventura strand, ripe for surf fishing, camping, and beachcombing.

In contrast, **Playa Las Peñitas,** a scenically petite golden strand, offers a modest hotel; a unique natural tide-pool bathing pool; a luscious serene lagoon, with crocodiles for viewing; and super-fresh fish, shrimp, and oysters, from a lineup of rustic beachfront *palapa* restaurants.

Farther east, Ometepec, the capital of the indigenous Costa Chica Guerrero hinterland, deserves at least two days, one of which should be a Sunday. That will give you time to visit both the fascinating Xochistlahuaca *tianguis* (market) and the big **Ometepec Sunday Market** back in town on the same Sunday. Stay overnight in the relaxing top-pick Ometepec Hotel Bello Nido.

Moving farther east, just before the Oaxaca border, be sure to stop in Cuajinicuilapa and visit the unique **Museo de las Culturas Afromestizos.** With another day or two you could explore the nearby African-Mexican coastal country hinterland around the breezy beach fishing hamlet of Puerto Maldonado. There, you can overnight by parking your RV or setting up your tent near the beachfront Las Brisas *palapa* restaurant or stay overnight at the modest guesthouse Casa de Huéspedes Valle Encantado nearby.

Continue east into Oaxaca and explore the coastal Amusgo- and Mixtec-speaking country around Pinotepa Nacional. Spend at least one Pinotepa Nacional overnight at the Hotel Carmona; visit the big **Pinotepa Nacional Market;** maybe make a handicrafts side trip to one or two nearby upcountry towns, such as north to Pinotepa Don Luis (for *pozo-huanco* wraparound skirts and masks) or San Pedro Amusgos (for *huipiles*); and maybe visit Huaxpáltepec, which hosts a sprawling, fascinatingly indigenous **Pre-Easter Fair** that virtually blocks Highway 200 10 miles east of Pinotepa.

The Road to Ometepec

If you're going by bus, ride one of the several daily first-class or second-class buses from the Estrella Blanca (Avenida Ejido) terminal in Acapulco. Let the highway kilometer markers (both at roadside and on the asphalt itself) lead you to your chosen destination. Let the driver know a minute ahead of time where to let you off.

If driving from Acapulco, mark your odometer at the traffic circle where Highways 95 and 200 intersect over the hill north from Acapulco. If, on the other hand, you bypass that congested point via the Acapulco airport road, follow straight ahead over the overpass at the hill-bottom Puerto Marques interchange, set your odometer to zero and continue toward the airport. Another couple of miles ahead, pick up the new *cuota autopista* expressway on the left, which will whisk you to the Highway 200 intersection turnoff in less than 10 minutes. Mileages and kilometer markers along the road are sometimes the only locators of side-road turnoffs to hidden villages and beaches.

Fill up the car with gas in Acapulco before starting out. After that, gas is at least available at Cruz Grande (56 mi/91 km), Marquelia (91 mi/146 km), Ometepec (110 mi/177 km), Pinotepa Nacional (157 mi/253 km), Jamiltepec (175 mi/283 km), and Puerto Escondido (247 mi/398 km).

SAN MARCOS

San Marcos (pop. 10,000), 36 miles (58 km) east of Acapulco, is a frequent first stop for essential services along the Costa Chica.

Accommodations and Food

San Marcos's best hotel, **Le Carma** (on the highway, south side, tel. 745/453-0037, $20 d with fan, $30 d with a/c) is recommendable for an overnight. Although the hotel's loose management leaves something to be desired, guests enjoy cooling off in the hotel's inviting blue pool. The approximately 20 clean rooms come with fans, TV, and hot-water shower baths.

For food, try seafood **Restaurant Jaibo** (on the highway, south side, no phone, approx. 9 A.M.–8 P.M. daily, $3–7), about two blocks east of Le Carma hotel. Specialties here include fresh grilled shrimp and tender fish fillets, breaded or grilled with butter and garlic.

Of the local roadside *taquerias* the best is **Dona Chely** (no phone, 9 A.M.–9 P.M. daily, $1–3); you can also get tacos (chicken, *carnitas,* beef), three for a dollar, a block farther east.

Information and Services

San Marcos has a **Banamex** (on the central plaza, tel. 745/453-0036, 9 A.M.–4 P.M. Mon.–Fri.) with a 24-hour ATM. Banamex is accessible from the highway via the entrance arch at Calle Hidalgo; continue about 0.3 mile (0.5 km) to the plaza. San Marcos also has a small government hospital on the highway; a pharmacy, **Farmapronto** (Hidalgo 29, two blocks past the entrance arch, tel. 745/453-1876, 9 A.M.–9 P.M. daily); streetfront Ladatel card-operated telephones; a doctor, Carlo Cortes, at his clinic (on Nicolas Bravo, off the central plaza, near Bancomer); a **correo** and **telecomunicaciones** (on the central plaza, tel. 745/453-0130, 9 A.M.–3 P.M. Mon.–Fri., 9 A.M.–12:30 P.M. Sat.).

LAGUNA CHAUTENGO AND PLAYA VENTURA

These laid-back havens are attractive for different reasons: Playa Ventura is for those who enjoy civilized south-seas delights, while the broad Laguna Chautengo estuary attracts folks hankering for wild things, such as troves of wildlife for viewing and photographing, pristine beaches for camping and beachcombing, and swarms of good-eating *lisa* (mullet), *sierra* (mackerel), and *róbalo* (snook), just for the catching.

Laguna Chautengo

Follow the good turnoff road four miles (about 6 km) east of Cruz Grande (43 mi/69 km east of Acapulco). Continue 3.7 miles (6 km) to the boat landing. Here, the big mangrove lagoon spreads about eight miles in both directions along the coast and four miles across to the barrier sandbar. Most of the year Laguna Chautengo is a freshwater reservoir of the Ríos Nexpa, Jalapa, and Copala. But during the rainy season the lagoon breaks through the sandbar, slicing a channel at the beachfront hamlet of Pico de Monte that beckons far across the lagoon.

Boatmen customarily charge ($10 one-way per person or $20 one-way per boat of up to 10 passengers) for the cross-lagoon round-trip to the village of **San José de la Barra**, which includes waiting for the passengers to enjoy a fish dinner at one of the several beachfront *palapas*. If you're going to camp overnight on the beach, let your boatman know when to return and pick you up.

Although road's-end facilities amount to no more than a dock and a snack restaurant, alternatives exist. Rent a boat and captain (figure $10–20/hr) and mount your own fishing trip. Or do the same with your own boat or kayak. Launching appears easily doable from the calm, gently sloping shoreline.

Playa Ventura

Three miles east of the small town of Copala, 77 miles (123 km) from Acapulco, a roadside sign points toward Playa Ventura. Four miles down a paved road, which a truck-bus from Copala traverses regularly, you arrive at pavement's-end at Playa Ventura village. From there, a miles-long golden beach arcs gently east. Past a lighthouse, the beach leads to a point, topped by a picturesque jumble of weather-rounded granite rocks, known locally as **Casa de Piedra** (House of Stone).

Playa Ventura provides everything for a restful day or season in the sun: a seemingly endless strand of yellow sand, *palapa* restaurants, and friendly folks. It offers surfable rollers and turtles who nest in the summer and fall. Although development is gradually crowding them out, good tent or RV (maneuverable medium rigs, vans, or campers) spots still sprinkle the inviting outcropping-dotted shoreline, on the southeast side, past Casa de Piedra. There, shady *palapas* set up by former campers stand ready for rehabilitation and reuse by new arrivals.

Surf fishing (with net-caught bait fish) is fine from the beach, while *pangas* go out for deep-sea catches. Good surfing breaks angle in from the points, and, during the rainy season, the west-side, behind-the-beach lagoon is good for fishing, shrimping, and wildlife-viewing. (Bring your kayak or inflatable raft.)

The palm-tufted beach stretches southeast for miles. Past the Casa de Piedra outcropping, an intimate *palapa*- and *panga*-lined sandy cove curves invitingly to yet another palmy point, Pico del Monte. Past that lies still another, even more pristine, cove and beach.

Accommodations and Food

Beside supplies from the two or three village stores, food plus space for tenting and RV parking is also available at a number of family-run *loncherías* and beach *palapa* restaurants.

Beginning at village-center landmark Hotel Pérez, move east along the beachfront dirt road immediately past **Las Palmeras,** which offers a shady, spacious grove for informal tenting and

RV parking. Continue next door to beachfront restaurant and campground **Doña Maura,** with space for a few small-to-medium self-contained RVs and tents beneath shady palm-frond *ramadas* (temporary shade roofs). Next comes a trio of inviting restaurants, first **El Faro** ("spaghetti ala Ventura") with a working lighthouse; next, the thatched **Jay** restaurant; and finally **Barbolumba,** with a stunning southeast shoreline view, toward Casa de Piedra.

Virtually all of Playa Ventura's hotel lodgings are on its breezy west-side beachfront. Several are recommendable. Heading west, first find **Hotel Doña Celsa** (local cell tel. 044-741/101-3069; $22 d with fan, $45 d with a/c, low season; $40 d with fan, $60 d with a/c, holidays), with about 20 clean, modern but smallish rooms on two floors around a parking patio. Rentals come with tiled baths and tepid-water showers; there's a hotel pool, restaurant, and small grocery.

Continue west about 100 yards to restaurant and **Hotel Tomy** (local cell tel. 044-741/101-3065; $25 for up to four, $35 with TV, low season; $40 for up to four, $45 with TV, high season), with 22 rooms, some with airy ocean views, encircling a parking-pool-patio. Prices for the clean, sparsely furnished but comfortable tiled rooms are certainly right. All rooms come with fans and private baths.

A hundred yards farther, find **Cabañas la Perla Coyacul** (local cell tel. 044-741/101-3122 or 044-741/101-3022; $30 for up to four, $40 with a/c, low season; $35 for up to four, $45 with a/c, high season; RVs $6 pp) with basic *cabañas* and palm-shaded space for tents and small self-contained RVs. All spaces come with shared toilets and showers. There is a beachfront restaurant, pool, and kiddie pool.

For a more refined hotel choice, continue about another half mile west to **C** **Hotel Caracola** (Costera Antelmo Ventura 68, Playa Ventura, local cell tel. 044-741/101-3047, caracolplayaventura.com, www.playaventura .com, $40 small rooms, $55 *cabañas,* $65 private rooms in thatch house), life project of friendly innkeeper Aura Elena Rodríguez. She offers her vision of paradise, beneath a shady grove of swaying palms, complete with café-restaurant (breakfast and lunch) *palapa* and an inviting beachfront pool-patio. Her several designer-rustic lodgings come in three varieties: a pair of intimate and inviting (but very small) wood-covered teepee-mode rooms for two, with shared bath; two *cabañas* for two, with private baths; and three airy, private rooms, nestled into a three-floor south-seas-in-the-round wood and thatch house, for up to three, with private baths. All lodgings come with fans, mosquito nets, daily maid service, and a kitchen stove and sink for guest use. Sorry, no kids under 15, please.

Finally, about 300 yards farther, comes mini-resort **La Tortuguita** (local cell tel. 044-741/101-3019, julianna5@hotmail.com, www .latortuguitamexico.com; $40 s, $48 d low season, no breakfast; $65 s, $75 d high season, breakfast included; $14 per adult tent and RV), a hotel, restaurant, tenting-RV site, and turtle conservation station. Here, there is no TV or telephone, but instead plenty of fresh sea breeze, the murmur of the waves, and a big, blue pool and palmy patio. Lodging choices include either a big *palapa* to shelter your tent, a grassy palm-shaded yard to park your RV, and five very clean and comfortable sea-view rooms. Rooms come with fans and room-temperature showers. Tenting and RV parking spaces come with shared toilet and shower. Furthermore, friendly European owners Esther (Swiss) and Julio (Lichtenstein) maintain an official turtle conservation station; during the summer-fall hatching season, they encourage guests to help collect, incubate, and finally release turtle hatchlings into the sea.

The increasing popularity of Playa Ventura as a beach destination has led to a growing colony of beachfront homes. A number of the original Playa Ventura families are selling lots, which folks say are going for about $12,000 for a 60-foot-by-60-foot beachfront lot. Before putting your money down, be sure to research the legal details of owning property in Mexico in general and at Playa Ventura in particular. Go through a reputable real estate agent, such as Century 21, and a registered "notario," a

© BRUCE WHIPPERMAN

Horse whisperers feel right at home at La Tortuguita.

lawyer who serves like a title company in the United States, which researches and verifies the property's title.

MARQUELIA

The small market town of Marquelia (pop. 10,000, 91 mi/146 km east of Acapulco) offers a number of services and is a jumping-off point for the charming beachfront haven of Playa Las Peñitas and the country end-of-the-road fishing village of Barra de Tecoanapa. You can't miss Marquelia since its market stalls crowd the highway. Especially worthy is the country-style open-air **Restaurant La Herradura** (north side of the highway, tel. 741/416-9837, 8 A.M.–8 P.M. Tues.–Sun.), at the eastern end of town.

◖ PLAYA LAS PEÑITAS

Just east of Marquelia, turn south (or taxi or catch a truck ride) on the signed Playa Las Peñitas turnoff road. After 3.5 miles (5.7 km) go right at the signed driveway 50 yards to the beach. The main attraction, popular with

local holiday vacationers and Sunday picnicking families, is the long, steep yellow-sand beach, which provides plenty of opportunities for kids to scamper and splash in the gentle waves and sheltered tide pools. It's also lined with seafood *palapas* and Las Peñitas (the Little Rocks), a family of sandstone rocks picturesquely perched on the shoreline. Beside the restaurants is a serene lagoon, current home of a family of crocodiles; ask someone to point them out to you.

At high tide, one of Las Peñitas becomes a small islet, where folks have set a pilgrimage cross around which the faithful congregate for devotions on the May 3 (Día de la Cruz) holiday. It provides a perfect playground for kids scampering and splashing in the waves that curl gently around the islet. Moreover, families frolic in a bathtub-like tide pool on one side of the islet, dunking themselves in the gentle waves that fill its foamy basin.

Just one modest hotel embellishes the lovely Las Peñitas picture. At the beach parking lot, find **Hotel Domi** ($30 d low season, $35 d

THE COSTA CHICA

Tidepooling and fishing are both good at the monumental sacred rock at Playa Las Peñitas.

holidays), run by a friendly, spirited owner-chambermaid. She offers nine plain but new and clean rooms, three of which (numbers 6, 7, and 8) have private ocean-view balconies. Rooms come with fans and hot-water shower baths.

BARRA DE TECOANAPA

Continue past Playa Las Peñitas 1.5 miles by car (or, if without wheels, by truck; offer to pay); cross a river bridge; immediately pass a store; then bear left, passing through Guadalupe village. Continue another 4.5 miles (7.2 km) to the road's end at Barra de Tecoanapa (pop. 1,000).

The village spreads for about a mile along the sandbar of the Río Quetzala, which empties into the sea from its lagoon-estuary about a quarter mile east of town. You can continue (drivers, be careful of soft sand) along the beach track to the embarcadero, decorated with a few dozen fishing *lanchas* pulled up on the lagoon-front. The river channel through the sandbar allows ocean fish *(sierra, róbalo, lisa)* to populate the lagoon.

The village appears to owe its existence to fishing and the holiday and weekend visitors who enjoy fresh seafood at its scattering of humble beachfront *palapa* restaurants. Terns and pelicans diving into onshore waves signal ideal conditions for surf fishing.

Although life on the Barra de Tecoanapa is simple and ruled by the unhurried rhythms of sun and tide, local folks do enjoy a few 21st-century amenities, including a basketball court, two or three small stores, a kindergarten, a primary school, and a potable water system.

All this might spell heaven for experienced visitors equipped to enjoy rustic beachfront living. If you don't mind a few curious townsfolk, plenty of space is available for beachfront tenting and RV parking, especially east of town. Rent a boat or float your own either at the lagoon or right on the beachfront. Waves, which break gradually about 100 yards out, recede with only slight undertow, fine for wading, splashing, and boogie boarding. Although the waves I saw appeared too mild for surfing, stronger swells, a likely seasonal possibility, might produce ideal surfing conditions.

Ometepec and Vicinity

Ometepec (pop. 20,000) is the de facto capital of the Guerrero coastal indigenous heartland. In Ometepec's foothill backcountry, Spanish is a foreign language. About half of the Ometepec *municipio* (pop. 60,000) people are native Amusgo-speaking people. In more remote *municipios* (townships), such as Xochistlahuaca (soh-chees-tlah-WAH-kah), more than three-quarters speak native tongues.

Vibrant markets with piles of fruit and flowers, old-fashioned handmade goods, and crowds of folks in colorful native dress are the reward for visitors who venture uphill to spend time exploring these lively towns.

ORIENTATION

Ometepec is readily accessible via the 10-mile paved road that branches off Highway 200 at a big signed intersection 110 miles (177 km) east of Acapulco. Besides being an important market and service center that draws crowds of native peoples, notably Amusgo and Mixteco speakers, from outlying villages to its big Sunday market, Ometepec (elev. 1,100 feet/330 meters) enjoys a cooler, more temperate climate than the coast. Reflecting its upland location, the town's name, from the Náhuatl (Aztec) language, combines *ome* (two) and *tepec* (hill) to mean "land between two hills."

Ometepec orients itself along a single street, Avenida Cuauhtémoc. Entering town eastbound, via the ingress highway from the coast, you pass under not one, but two entrance arches. The main market is immediately on the right after the second arch.

Avenida Cuauhtémoc continues east past the main (Estrella Blanca) long-distance bus station. After about a quarter mile, the thoroughfare angles right (southeast), through the central business district, passing a parade of shops, taco restaurants, hotels, and banks. Finally, at the petite *zócalo* on the left, Cuauhtémoc bends due south and ends within a block in front of the main church, dedicated to Santiago (St. James).

SIGHTS

◖ Parroquia de Santiago

Ometepec's 1960s-era church, although not old, is both popular and handsome. In the evenings, spotlights keep its lovely blue-and-white facade shining long after dark. During the day, the faithful crowd through its gates and approach the facade, populated with its choir of white-shining saints and angels. Atop all this presides a sculpture of a mounted, sword-brandishing Santiago. Approach even closer and admire the church's grand polished wooden doors, climaxed in the center by yet another Santiago, this time with his horse's hooves trampling the defeated Moors. Inside, swallows swoop beneath the airy nave ceiling and perch and chirp in the chandeliers. Above the altar rises a grand dome whose paintings depict a vista of heaven so pleasing that it seems as luscious as the view must be through the pearly gates themselves.

◖ Ometepec Sunday Market

Ometepec's other famous attraction, the Sunday *tianguis,* operates in two sections: the main one on the west side, just inside the second town entrance arch, and the other around the downtown *zócalo.* At the *zócalo* are most of the handicrafts, including embroidered *huipiles,* huaraches, and sombreros. In the west-side section you'll find a small mountain of everything else: forest-gathered herbs, seeds, and spices, *chiles,* homemade brooms, fruits (mangoes, grapes, and bananas), vegetables (radishes, sweet potatoes, tomatoes), tobacco (in aromatic bunches of big dried leaves), and mounds of dried fish, all in one spreading, semi-organized five-acre area.

ACCOMMODATIONS

Ometepec has a sprinkling of recommendable hotels, all of which accept cash only. They do a brisk business, accommodating the town's many market, business, and festival visitors.

The **Hotel Venus II** (Crucero de Talapa, tel.

THE COSTA CHICA

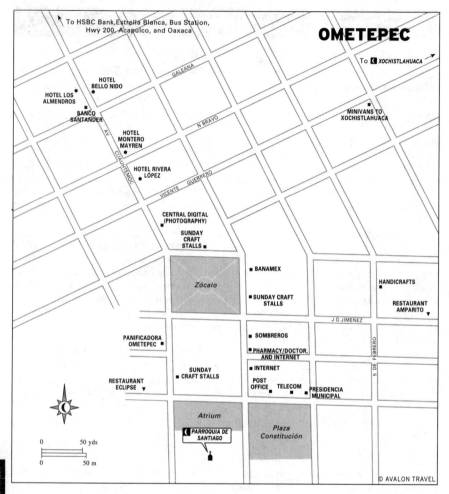

To HSBC Bank, Estrella Blanca, Bus Station, Hwy 200, Acapulco, and Oaxaca

OMETEPEC

To XOCHISTLAHUACA

HOTEL BELLO NIDO

HOTEL LOS ALMENDROS

BANCO SANTANDER

MINIVANS TO XOCHISTLAHUACA

GALEANA

N BRAVO

HOTEL MONTERO MAYREN

AV. CUAUHTÉMOC

HOTEL RIVERA LÓPEZ

VICENTE GUERRERO

CENTRAL DIGITAL (PHOTOGRAPHY)

SUNDAY CRAFT STALLS

Zócalo

BANAMEX

SUNDAY CRAFT STALLS

HANDICRAFTS

RESTAURANT AMPARITO

J G JIMENEZ

PANIFICADORA OMETEPEC

SOMBREROS

PHARMACY/DOCTOR, AND INTERNET

INTERNET

POST OFFICE   TELECOM

PRESIDENCIA MUNICIPAL

SUNDAY CRAFT STALLS

RESTAURANT ECLIPSE

5 DE FEBRERO

Atrium

PARROQUIA DE SANTIAGO

Plaza Constitución

0   50 yds
0   50 m

© AVALON TRAVEL

741/412-2349, hotelrealvenus@hotmail.com; $22 d in one bed, $28 d in two beds, with fan; $32 d in one bed, $40 d in two beds, with a/c) stands prominently on the left, just past the statue of Vicente Guerrero and left of the second arch (about half a mile past the initial ingress highway arch) as you enter Ometepec. The hotel, at the uncongested edge of town and with a secure gated parking lot, is convenient for visitors with cars. Past the reception, the place is modern and clean, with guests in many rooms enjoying balcony vistas (of the parking lot below and hills beyond). The hotel's 20-odd rooms come with private hot-water shower baths, good cable TV, and are a one-block walk to the main town market. (Hotel Venus I, at the downhill Hwy. 200 intersection, tel. 741/415-8026 or 741/415-8027, offers similar lodging services.)

The remainder of Ometepec's hotels is downtown. Moving southwest along main street Avenida Cuauhtémoc, first find relaxing

◖ **Hotel Bello Nido** (Pretty Nest; Cuauhtémoc 50, tel. 741/412-0141 or 741/412-0234; $21 s, $25 d in one bed, with fan; $35 d in two beds, with a/c), about three blocks from the *zócalo*. Past the small but inviting lobby, the hotel rises in three motel-style floors around an appealing pool-patio. Rooms are clean and furnished with dark bedspreads, drapes, and tiled shower baths, but with no bedside reading lamps. All rooms come with TV, fans, and parking. For more tranquility, light, and privacy, reserve a room on an upper floor, in the back above the pool and away from the busy street.

Across the street is worthy newcomer, business-style **Hotel Los Almendros** (Cuauhtémoc 52, tel. 741/412-2691; $15 s, $23 d; $21 s, $26 d with a/c). It offers 18 clean, attractively tiled, tan-motif rooms with shiny modern-standard, hot-water bathrooms. Rentals come with cable TV, fans, wireless Internet, and parking.

THE AMUSGO PEOPLE

If not the most numerous, the Amusgos are the most visible of the Acapulco region's indigenous groups. On Sunday, crowds of Amusgo-speaking people flock to easily accessible market towns in the Costa Chica foothills about 100 miles east of Acapulco.

The Amusgo homeland comprises an approximately 30-by-40-mile territory straddling the Oaxaca-Guerrero border. About one-third of the 30,000 Amusgo speakers live in Oaxaca, around the small centers of Cacahuatepec and San Pedro Amusgos, while the remaining majority live on the Guerrero side, near the centers of Ometepec, Xochistlahuaca, and Tlacoachistlahuaca.

Linguists reckon that the Amusgo language, a member of the Mixtec language subfamily, separated from Mixtec between 2000 and 1000 B.C. Around A.D. 1000, the Amusgos came under the domination of the strong coastal Oaxaca Mixtec kingdom of Tututepec. In A.D. 1457 they were conquered by the Aztecs and, not long after, by the Spanish in the 1520s. Decimation of the Amusgo population by disease during the 16th century led to the importation of African slave labor, whose descendants, known locally as *negros* or *costeños*, live along the Guerrero–Oaxaca coastline.

The Amusgo population eventually recovered; many of the old colonial-era haciendas remained intact until modern times and continued to employ Amusgo people as laborers. Amusgo folks, isolated from the mainstream of modern Mexican life, retain their age-old corn-bean-squash subsistence-farming tradi-

© BRUCE WHIPPERMAN

tion. Moreover, they have received little attention from anthropologists or archaeologists, although several intriguing archaeological mounds exist near Amusgo villages.

Amusgo women are nevertheless famous for their hand-embroidered *huipiles,* whose colorful floral and animal designs fetch willing customers in the Acapulco region and Oaxaca tourist centers. Even better, Amusgo women often wear their *huipiles,* appearing as heavenly visions of spring on dusty small-town side streets.

THE COSTA CHICA

A block farther east, check out **Hotel Rivera López** (Cuauhtémoc 22, tel. 741/412-0028; $16 s, $22 d in one double bed; $22 s, $32 d with a/c; $24 d, $35 d in two double beds with a/c). Choose from 33 sparely furnished, less than immaculate rooms in three floors around an inner parking-patio. Rooms come with TV, fans, parking, and hot-water shower baths.

Finally, half a block from the *zócalo,* lovers of Mexico "the way it used to be" might appreciate the **Hotel Guadalupe** (Cuauhtémoc 20, tel. 741/412-2228, $12 s or d). The approximately 20 plain but clean rooms surround a leafy interior garden patio. They come with room-temperature–water, private shower baths, but no fans.

FOOD

Most eating out in Ometepec occurs in one of two locales. The busiest of these is the westside main market, where *fondas* (food stalls) feature country-style offerings of savory *guisado* (stews of chicken, pork, beef), piles of *antojitos* (chiles rellenos, *pozole,* tamales, tacos), and much more. (Permanent market *fondas* depend on repeat customers and therefore serve wholesome food. If in doubt, remember that cooked food, if it's steaming, will also be safe.)

Most of the other eateries are scattered along Cuauhtémoc near the *zócalo.* From late afternoon until midnight, the best food offerings are the tacos served by the platoon of stalls around the *zócalo,* in a dozen variations, from chicken and pork to barbecued beef, tongue, and brains.

A popular sit-down choice is **Restaurant Eclipse** (on the churchfront street, tel. 741/412-1161, 7:30 A.M.–6 P.M. daily, $2–4); at the end of Cuauhtémoc turn right around the corner. Restaurant Eclipse specializes in breakfasts (eggs any style, pancakes, french toast) and *comida,* a set four-course lunch (noon–6 P.M. daily).

The Ometepec downtown restaurant that everyone seems to recommend is **Amparito** (Juan Garcia Jiménez 11, tel. 741/412-3246, 7:30 A.M.–9 P.M. daily, $4–8), past Banamex, downhill two blocks east of the *zócalo.* Amparito, named after the grandmotherly owner, although specializing in seafood plates (shrimp, octopus, whole fish, fillets), does offer non-seafood specials. These might include *codorniz* (quail) or *guisado de res* (beef stew). For breakfasts, it can serve anything from eggs any style and French toast to pancakes or the good, local *pan dulce* with fresh fruit. If the TV noise bothers you, ask the staff to please lower the volume ("*favor de moderar el volumen*"—fah-VOR day moh-day-RAHR AYL vo-LOO-mayn).

For dessert, sample the fresh baked goods of **Panificadora Ometepec** (Cuauhtémoc 9, no phone, 7 A.M.–9 P.M. daily), a few doors north of the *zócalo.* On the other hand, if you're hankering for something sweet after the bakery closes, listen for someone along the street whistling, it may be the *plátano frito* (fried sweet banana) vendor with his cart.

ENTERTAINMENT AND EVENTS

Ometepec is known for a number of festivals, notably the pre-Easter week **Semana Santa,** which includes, besides the usual religious Masses and processions, cattle, agricultural, and handicrafts expositions, *jaripeo* (bull riding and roping), and a carnival. Festivities climax with regional folk dance performances, including the favorite, Los Chilenos, said to have originated in Ometepec.

If you arrive in town on certain dates, join the festivities—May 3: Fiesta del Día de la Santa Cruz (Holy Cross); July 24–26: Fiesta de Santiago; September 9–11: Fiesta de San Nicolás Tolentino; September 15–16: Fiestas Patrias, including the 11 P.M. reenactment of Father Miguel Hidalgo's Grito de Dolores at the *presidencia municipal,* and the dances of El Mulo y La Tortuga (Mule and the Turtle) and El Macho.

The region's most popular festival is the **Fiesta del Señor del Perdón** (Lord of Pardon) at Igualapa (pop. 3,000), half an hour northwest of Ometepec. You may want to make a special trip for this important indigenous fiesta, which local folks throw yearly on the third

Friday of Lent (16 days after Ash Wednesday, or 29 days before Easter Sunday). The main event is a pilgrimage of thousands, on all fours, on their knees, by foot, or by car or bus to the Santuario del Perdón to ask for favors, or sometimes even miracles, of the Señor. Miracles notwithstanding, merrymaking abounds, especially among the swarm of campesinos—mostly speaking dialects of Amusgo, Mixtec, and Tlapanec languages—decked out in their Sunday-best *traje.* Before departing, make sure to enjoy the whirl and flash of regional dances performed by a number of brightly costumed troupes.

From Ometepec, get to Igualapa either via taxi or *colectivo* from the west-side market or by car. On the west-side exit (toward Hwy. 200) road, about a mile past the western edge of town, turn right at the Igualapa turnoff; continue about 7 miles (11 km) to Igualapa.

SHOPPING

Handicrafts are mostly sold downtown on Sunday at *zócalo*-front stores and stalls. Get huaraches and sombreros at a pair of stores on the *zócalo*'s east side. Women also sell embroidery and embroidered *huipiles* on the *zócalo,* mostly at temporary north-side stalls, on Sunday.

Central Digital (Cuauhtémoc, one-half block northwest of the *zócalo,* local cell tel. 044-741/100-7060, 7 A.M.–7 P.M. daily) offers developing and digital services, popular film varieties, some digital and film supplies, and point-and-shoot cameras.

SERVICES

Several establishments offer essential services near the downtown *zócalo.* (*Note:* At the *zócalo* orient yourself by the church, which is *south* of the *zócalo.*)

Banks, all with ATMs, include **Banamex** (*zócalo*'s northeast corner, tel. 741/412-0880 or 741/412-1354, 9 A.M.–4 P.M. Mon.–Fri.) and longer hours **HSBC** (Cuauhtémoc 52, tel. 741/412-2878 or 741/412-2879, 9 A.M.–6 P.M. Mon.–Fri.), a couple of blocks north of the *zócalo.*

Mail letters at the **correo** (*presidencia municipal,* on Plaza Constitución, 9 A.M.–4 P.M.

© BRUCE WHIPPERMAN

Huipiles for sale

Mon.–Fri., 9 A.M.–1 P.M. Sat.), two short blocks south of the *zócalo*. Money orders and public fax are available at neighboring **Telecom** (*presidencia municipal,* on Plaza Constitución, tel. 741/412-0386, 9 A.M.–2:30 P.M. Mon.–Fri., 9 A.M.–2 P.M. Sat.). For local and long-distance calls, use Ladatel card-operated street-front phones.

A doctor María de los Angeles Miranda (4–9 P.M. Mon.–Fri.), Internet access, and copies are available at **Super Farmacia Mexicana** (southeast *zócalo* corner, tel. 741/412-0657, 8:30 A.M.–9:30 P.M. daily). If you get sick, taxi to the private **Hospital de la Amistad** (tel. 741/412-0985) or **Clínica Seguro Social** (tel. 741/412-0392).

GETTING THERE AND AWAY

Estrella Blanca (tel. 741/412-0035) provides a number of bus connections, most in the morning, with Chilpangingo, Mexico City, Acapulco, and intermediate Costa Chica points. Find the terminal on Cuauhtémoc, just west of its bend toward the *zócalo.*

Although few, if any, long-distance buses from Ometepec connect directly with the very interesting easterly Costa Chica destinations of Cuajinicuilapa and Pinotepa Nacional in Oaxaca, alternatives exist. You can get an early taxi or *colectivo* downhill to the Highway 200 intersection. There, continue by *colectivo,* or wait for an Estrella Blanca (Elite, Gacela, Turistar, Flecha Roja) eastbound bus. (*Note:* Ask the Ometepec Estrella Blanca agent for the bus connection times at the Highway 200 intersection.)

Driving to and from Ometepec is easy. To or from westerly Costa Chica destinations, simply follow Highway 200: one hour to/from Marquelia–Playa Las Peñitas, 33 miles (53 km); 1.5 hours to/from Copala–Playa Ventura, 48 miles (72 km); and 4.5 hours to/from Acapulco, 120 miles (194 km).

Similar good (but winding) road conditions prevail in the easterly direction: three quarters of an hour to/from Cuajinicuilapa, 25 miles (41 km); and two hours to/from Pinotepa Nacional, Oaxaca, 58 miles (93 km).

◼ XOCHISTLAHUACA

Plan your Ometepec visit for a Friday or Saturday arrival (reserve your hotel room a week early) so you can visit the colorful indigenous Sunday markets at both Ometepec and Xochistlahuaca (pop. 3,000), about 17 miles (27 km) northeast. On the other hand, the things you find along the road to Xochi (SOH-chee), as Xochistlahuaca is known locally, may persuade you to linger.

The name Xochistlahuaca (soh-chees-tlah-WAH-kah), which in the Náhuatl (Aztec) language means "plain of flowers," is apt, especially during the summer rains, when wildflowers bloom all over the town's foothill *municipio* (township). Although an interesting destination all on its own, Xochi is a jumping-off point for even more remote Amusgo towns such as Chacalapa, Huistepec, and others with even less pronounceable names, such as Tlacoachistlahuaca.

Although the name Xochistlahuaca is of Aztec origin, the town is virtually all Amusgo speaking, and you can be certain that the Xochi folks have their own name for their town. At the Xochi Sunday market you may have to search around for someone who can translate Spanish into Amusgo well enough to help you bargain for one of the prized embroidered *huipiles* for which Amusgo women are renowned.

Although most Xochi young folks learn Spanish in school, and outside Spanish-speaking vendors descend to sell plastic dishes and transistor radios every Sunday, Xochistlahuaca and its surrounding *municipio* (township) is a domain firmly rooted in Amusgo tradition. Here, *curanderos* (indigenous medicine men or women) still do much of the healing, women often recuperate from childbirth in a *temazcal* (ritual heat bath), and campesinos in their *milpas* (small, family-owned fields) still thank the earth spirits and the Lord of the Mountain for their harvests.

Getting There

Get to Xochi by *colectivo* from the Ometepec downtown corner of Cuauhtémoc and Vicente

Guerrero, a block north of the *zócalo*. If you have only one Sunday to visit, leave early for Xochi (*colectivos* run from at least 7 A.M. and the Xochi market is going strong by 9 A.M.) to allow time upon return to see the Ometepec market by 1 or 2 in the afternoon. Drivers, mark your odometer as you depart along Vicente Guerrero in downtown Ometepec. Along the 17-mile (27-km) route are a number of interesting stops that you may want to visit on a later day.

After about three miles, pass **Balneario Camino Real** (9 A.M.–6 P.M. daily, $3 adults, $2 children under 12), with a big blue swimming pool, kiddie pool, restaurant, and shade for picnicking.

At Mile 3.5 (Km 5.6), arrive at San José village, marked by a gas station and then a road fork. (The right fork, worth exploring on its own, heads down into the lush Río Catarina valley, crosses the river, and continues uphill to indigenous Huistepec village and beyond.)

For Xochi, follow the left fork and continue about nine miles (15 km) from Ometepec, where the road splits. The left fork heads five miles (8 km) to **Tlacoachistlahuaca,** an interesting indigenous market town and *municipio* (township), comparable to Xochi.

For Xochi, bear right at the fork and continue straight ahead. Pass through Zacualpan village at around Mile 11 (Km 17). Continue to the Río San Pedro bridge at about Mile 15 (Km 24). Feast your eyes on the luscious procession of swimming holes decorated by giant, friendly, water-sculptured rocks. (During the June–Sept. rainy season, however, the river may be a yucky muddy brown; but it will clear to an inviting jade-green as the rains abate by October.) Although swimming holes near the bridge are sometimes crowded with noisy local teens, spots upstream, via the strollable (or 4WD-navigable) riverside trail, are probably cleaner, more tranquil, and possible for overnight tenting.

Exploring Xochistlahuaca

Follow the crowd to the Xochi *tianguis* (market) that spreads over the middle of town from the

intersection of Calles Morelos and Reforma. **Museo Comunitario** (along Reforma, a block uphill from the corner, 10 A.M.–5 P.M. Mon.–Fri.) stands on the right. The museum's collection includes donated prehistoric artifacts and historical papers. Plans include adding a handicrafts store in the near future. Although the museum is not ordinarily open on Sunday, someone at the *presidencia municipal* may open it up for you.

As in many backcountry areas, some men and most women wear *traje* unique to their hometowns. Xochi women distinguish themselves with a creamy-white embroidered cotton *huipil* decorated with a pair of crimson over-the-shoulder ribbons, both front and back.

Women dominate both buying and selling. Buyers bustle about, concentrating mostly on staples, perhaps pausing to pick out a bit of ribbon or jewelry as a treat. Sellers wait patiently behind their piles of offerings, which vary from flowers and pork rinds to mameys and machetes.

For a rest and lunch, head to airy **Comedor Velé** (on Morelos, half a block west of Reforma, no phone, 9 A.M.–10 P.M. daily, $2–5), Xochi's best eatery. Take a seat in the shade and choose from a very recognizable list of *tortas, hamburguesas,* enchiladas, tacos, and fresh seafood. Friendly, hardworking owner-chef Aquileo Morales López is *a su servicio* (at your service).

CUAJINICUILAPA

Astride Highway 200, a few miles before the Oaxaca border, Cuajinicuilapa (kwah-hee-nee-kwee-LAH-pah; pop. 12,000) is the major market town and cultural center for the dozen-odd eastern Guerrero *costeño* communities. These include farming villages Los Hoyos, Montecillos, San Nicolas, and the airy, laid-back local fishing port, Puerto Maldonado.

In Cuajinicuilapa, known locally as Cuaji (koo-AH-hee), 125 miles (199 km) east of Acapulco, the market buyers and sellers crowd both the east and west sides of town. The clutter clears, however, at the town center, marked by a big covered basketball court.

◖ Museo de las Culturas Afromestizos

Behind the basketball court stands the Museo de las Culturas Afromestizos (no phone, 10 A.M.–2 P.M. and 4–7 P.M. Tues.–Sun., free admission). The museum shouldn't be missed. It's one of the very few museums dedicated to African-Mexican history and culture. Inside, it offers several fascinatingly graphic and insightful displays, plus a library and dance, theater, guitar, and crafts workshops.

Accommodations and Food

A pair of town-center hotels offer comfortable accommodations. Very recommendable is the 30-room **Hotel Marín** (Calle Principal, tel. 741/414-0021; $16 s, $27 d with fan; $22 s, $36 d with a/c, all with hot-water shower baths), a few doors east of the basketball court. It's built along a shady corridor interspersed with lush green tropical mini-patios. The comfortable, invitingly decorated rooms all have TVs.

First place, however, goes to ◖ **Hotel Alejim** (Calle Rudolfo Rodríguez, tel. 741/414-0310; $18 s, $25 d with fan; $28 s, $34 d with a/c), on the west side of town, a block west of the gas station and half a block off the highway's north side. The hotel, kept cool in the shade of a majestic mango orchard, is an island of tranquility. The 30 spacious, comfortable, and thoughtfully decorated rooms, in two stories, come with hot-water baths, TV, and Internet access.

Cuaji's most popular restaurant is **Restaurant El Ocaso** (Calle Principal, next to Hotel Marin, tel. 741/414-0746, 8 A.M.–8 P.M. daily, $4–6) for breakfast (ham and eggs, hotcakes), afternoon *comida* (baked breast of chicken, fish fillet), and dinner (tacos, hamburgers, or spaghetti bolognese).

Services

Find most services right on the main Highway 200 through street, Calle Porfirio Díaz: **Banamex** with ATM (9 A.M.–4 P.M. Mon.–Fri.), across from the basketball court; **Centro de Salud** (no phone, doctor 24 hours); pharmacy, **Farmapronto** (tel. 741/414-1074, 7 A.M.–10 P.M. daily); *correo* (next to Banamex,

8 A.M.–3 P.M. Mon.–Fri.); Ladatel card-operated street telephones, and *telecomunicaciones* (next to Banamex, tel. 741/414-0337, 9 A.M.–3 P.M. Mon.–Fri., 9 A.M.–noon Sat.–Sun.) for money orders and public fax.

PUERTO MALDONADO

This country coastal fishing village (pop. 1,000), about 20 miles (32 km) south of Cuajinicuilapa, initially got on the map because of its lighthouse. A reassuring beacon, the lighthouse perches atop a point of land called Punta Maldonado, crowning the 100-foot-high bluff that lines this remote coast.

The lighthouse adds a picturesque aspect to the entire scene: a long, breeze-swept beach curving east, while west of the Punta (Point) a few fisherfolks' homes, a couple of stores, a small guesthouse, and a sprinkling of fishing *lanchas* decorate a sheltered strand.

Here, life goes on quietly and easily. You can stroll the beach, picking up a bit of driftwood and a shell or two, joke with the locals, play with the kids, watch the fishermen mend their nets, and rent a boat and mount your own fishing excursion.

Getting There

Get to Puerto Maldonado by minibus from the middle of Cuaji by the basketball court. Drivers, head east from town. After only a mile, turn right (south) onto the signed Puerto Maldonado road near Km 201. Mark your odometer.

After about 10 miles (16 km) pass through Montecillos village (pop. 2,000), a mixed mestizo and African-Mexican community. Farther along, at around 15 miles (24 km), at Tejastruda village, notice the apparently evangelistic church, decorated with both a Christian cross and what appears to be the Star of David. Finally, arrive at Puerto Maldonado just after 19 miles (31 km) from Highway 200.

Sights and Recreation

Get oriented at the rustic **Las Brisas Palapa,** perched on the scenic Punta Maldonado beach-tip. From beneath the *palapa,* drink in the gorgeous panorama as the waves curl around the Punta and swish and disappear into the coral-decorated golden sand of the point's west-side beach.

Use the existing posts in front of the *palapa* for a volleyball game (bring your own ball and net), explore the tide pools, or launch your own boat from the beach. **Surfing** the waves that swell in-shore past the point and break diagonally along the beach line is a regular pastime here.

Practicalities

You can either park your self-contained RV or set up your tent beneath the point's small but sheltering palm grove, or stay at the guesthouse

Hotel El Dorado (tel. 741/411-1992, local cell tel. 044-741/100-1943, $21 s or d) in the beach fishing village about a quarter mile west of the point. The three plain but clean rooms (get the one with the sea view) have air-conditioning and private baths (but room-temperature water only).

A few village stores, such as **Miscelanea Adelita** (next to the hotel), can supply essential groceries and water. For prepared food, visit the beachfront *palapa* **Las Brisas** for breakfast or super-fresh catch of the day for lunch.

If you need medical attention, visit the **Centro de Salud** (tel. 741/596-1245) on the bluff above the beach.

Pinotepa Nacional and Vicinity

On the Oaxaca side of the Guerrero-Oaxaca border, Pinotepa Nacional (pop. 50,000; 157 mi/253 km east of Acapulco; 90 mi/145 km west of Puerto Escondido) and its neighboring communities comprise the hub of an important coastal indigenous region. Mixtec, Amusgo, Chatino, and other peoples stream into town for markets and fiestas in their *traje* (traditional dress), ready to combine business with pleasure. They sell their produce and crafts—pottery, masks, handmade clothes—at the market, then later get tipsy, flirt, and dance.

So many people had asked the meaning of their city's name that the town fathers wrote the explanation on a wall next to Highway 200 on the west side of town. "Pinotepa" comes from the Aztec words *pinolli* (crumbling) and *tepetl* (mountain)—thus "Crumbling Mountain." The second part of the name came about because during colonial times the town was called Pinotepa Real (Royal). This wouldn't do after independence, so the name became Pinotepa Nacional, reflecting the national consciousness that emerged during the 1810–1821 struggle for independence.

The Mixtecs, the dominant regional group, differ with all this, however. To them, Pinotepa has always been Ñií Yo-oko (Little Place). Only

within the town limits do the Mexicans (mestizos), who own most of the town businesses, outnumber the Mixtecs. The farther from town you get, the more likely you are to hear people conversing in the Mixtec language, a complex tongue that uses a number of subtle tones (as do most Chinese dialects) to make meanings clear.

ORIENTATION

On Pinotepa's west side, Highway 200 splits into the town's two major arteries, which rejoin on the east side. The north, westbound branch is called Aguirre Palancares; the south, eastbound branch, the more bustling of the two branches, passes between the town-center *zócalo* and church and is called Avenida Porfirio Díaz on the west side and Avenida Benito Juárez on the east. The main north–south street, Avenida Pérez Gasga, runs past both the churchfront (which faces west) and the *presidencia municipal,* which faces east, toward the *zócalo.*

◖ PINOTEPA NACIONAL MARKET

The main town market, stands a mile west of the *zócalo,* a block south (to the right, eastbound) of

THE COSTA CHICA

Highway 200, by the big fenced-in secondary school. Despite the Pinotepa market's oft-exotic goods—snakes, iguanas, wild mountain fruits, forest herbs, and spices—its people, nearly entirely Mixtec speaking, are its main attraction, especially on the big Monday market days. Men traditionally wear pure-white loose cottons, topped by woven palm-leaf hats. Women wrap themselves in their lovely striped purple, violet, red, and navy blue *pozahuancos* (hand-woven wraparound skirts).

Some women carry atop their heads a polished tan *jicara* (traditional gourd bowl), which, although it's not supposed to, looks like a whimsical hat. Older women (and younger ones with babies at their breasts) go bare-breasted with only their white *huipiles* draped over their chests as a concession to mestizo custom. Others wear an easily removable *mandil,* a light cotton apron-halter above their *pozahuancos.* A few women can ordinarily be found offering colorful *pozahuancos* made with cheaper synthetic thread (that sell for about $30). Traditional handmade *pozahuancos* (hand-spun, hand-sewn, and hand-dyed with naturally gathered pigments) have become difficult to purchase at the Pinotepa market, but are more commonly available in outlying market towns, notably Pinotepa Don Luis.

FESTIVALS

Although the Pinotepa market days are big, they don't compare to the week before Easter (Semana Santa). People get ready for the finale with processions, carrying the dead Christ through town to the church each of the seven Fridays before Easter. The climax comes on Good Friday (Viernes Santa), when a platoon of young Mixtec men paint their bodies white to portray Jews, and while intoning ancient Mixtec chants shoot arrows at Christ on the cross. On Saturday, the people mournfully take the Savior down from the cross and bury him, and on Sunday gleefully celebrate his resurrection with a riot of fireworks, food, and folk dancing.

Although not as spectacular as Semana Santa, there's plenty of merrymaking, food, dancing, and processions around the Pinotepa

---

POZAHUANCOS

To a coastal Mixtec woman, her *poza-huanco* is a lifetime investment symbolizing her maturity and social status, something that she expects to pass on to her daughters. Heirloom *pozahuancos* are wraparound, horizontally-striped skirts of hand-spun thread. Traditionally, women dye the thread by hand, always including a pair of necessary colors: cotton dyed a light purple *(morada)* from secretions of tide-pool-harvested snails, *Purpura patula pansa;* and silk dyed scarlet red with cochineal, a dye extracted from the beetle *Dactylopius coccus,* cultivated in the Valley of Oaxaca. Increasingly, women are weaving *pozahuancos* with synthetic thread, which has a slippery feel compared to the hand-spun cotton. Consider yourself lucky if you can get a traditionally made *pozahuanco* for as little as $200. If someone offers you one for $30, you know it's an imitation.

---

zócalo church on July 25, the day of Pinotepa's patron, Santiago (St. James).

ACCOMMODATIONS

The motel-style **Hotel Carmona** (Av. Porfirio Díaz 127, tel. 954/543-2222, hotel_pepe@hotmail.com; $20 s, $25 d, $30 t with fan; $35 s, $40 d, $45 t with a/c), about three blocks west of the *zócalo,* offers 50 clean, not fancy, but comfortable rooms in three stories; arrive early to enjoy the big backyard garden with pool and sundeck. For festival dates, make advance reservations. Credit cards are not accepted.

If the Carmona is full, check the two high-profile newer hotels, Pepe's and Las Gaviotas, beside the highway on the west side of town. Of the two, **Pepe's** (Carretera Pinotepa Nacional–Acapulco Km 1, tel. 954/543-4347, fax 954/543-3602; $20 s, $25 d with fan; $28 s, $34 d with a/c) is the better choice. It offers 35 spacious semi-deluxe rooms for a reasonable rate, with cable TV, hot-water shower bath, handy passable restaurant, and parking. Rooms at **Hotel Las Gaviotas** (tel. 954/543-2838, $22 d with fan, $30 d with a/c) come with hot-water shower bath, TV, and parking.

Third choice goes to clean **Hotel Marisa** (Av. Juárez 134, tel. 954/543-2101 or 954/543-3190; $18 s or d in one bed, $24 d in two beds, with fan; $33 s or d in one bed, $35 d in two beds with a/c), downtown on the north side of the highway. Rooms come with private baths, TV, and parking.

FOOD

Pinotepa's recommendable eateries sprinkle the town center. Beginning at the *zócalo* and moving west, first, for a light lunch or supper, try the very clean, family-run **Burger Bonny** (southeast corner of the main plaza, no phone, 11 A.M.–10 P.M. daily, $1–4). Besides six varieties of good hamburgers, Burger Bonny offers *tortas,* tacos, french fries, hot dogs, microwave popcorn, fruit juices, and *refrescos.*

A good supper choice is **Tacos Orientales** (Pérez Gasga, half a block north of the church-front, 6–11 P.M. daily, $2.50) with 15 styles of tacos, from fish to *carnitas.*

For a touch of class, take a balcony seat at airy upstairs **Restaurant El Adobe** (on main Hwy. 200 thoroughfare Av. Juárez, across from BanNorte, tel. 954/543-6347 or 954/543-6348, 8 A.M.–10:30 P.M. daily, $3–10). Order from their extensive menu, including breakfast omelets, Caesar salad, spicy *arrachera* steak, and their specialty *plato costeño.*

To enjoy a quick and convenient on-the-road breakfast, lunch, or dinner, stop by the restaurant of high-profile hotel, **Pepe's** (Carretera Pinotepa Nacional–Acapulco Km 1, tel. 954/543-4347, fax 954/543-3602, 8 A.M.–10 P.M. daily, $3–8), west of town.

SHOPPING AND SERVICES

For the freshest fruits and vegetables, visit the town market any day, although it's biggest on Monday. For film and film-processing, step into **Arlette Foto** (tel. 954/543-2766, 8 A.M.–8 P.M. Mon.–Sat., 8 A.M.–3 P.M. Sun.) near the plaza's southwest corner.

Exchange money over the counter or use the

ATMs at all Pinotepa banks. Try **Bancomer** (corner of Díaz and Progreso, tel. 954/543-3022 or 954/543-3190, 8:30 A.M.–4 P.M. Mon.–Fri.), two blocks west of the plaza; or **HSBC** (Av. Progreso, tel. 954/543-3949 or 954/543-3969, 8 A.M.–7 P.M. Mon.–Fri., 8 A.M.–3 P.M. Sat.), also on Avenida Progreso, but across Porfirio Díaz and uphill a block from Bancomer.

Find the *correo* (tel. 954/543-2264, 8 A.M.–7 P.M. Mon.–Fri.) a far half a mile west of downtown, a block past Pepe's hotel and across the street. Find the *telecomunicaciones* office (Av. Pérez Gasga, tel. 954/543-2019, 8 A.M.–7:30 P.M. Mon.–Fri., 9 A.M.–noon Sat.–Sun.) one block north of the plaza church.

For telephone, use Ladatel card-operated street telephones, or go to the long-hours *larga distancia* **Lada Central telephone and fax office** (on the plaza, south side, tel. 954/543-2547). Also nearby on the plaza, answer your email at **Switch Internet** (8 A.M.–9 P.M. daily).

For a doctor, visit **Clínica Rodriguez** (Aguirre 503 Palancares, tel. 954/543-2330), one block north, two blocks west of the central plaza churchfront. Get routine medications at one of several town pharmacies, such as the 24-hour **Super Farmacia** (on Díaz, a block west of the central plaza churchfront, tel. 954/543-4230).

GETTING THERE AND AWAY

From Pinotepa Nacional, by car or RV, Highway 200 connects west from Acapulco (160 mi/258 km) in an easy 4.5 hours at the wheel. The easy 89-mile (143-km) eastward connection with Puerto Escondido takes about 2.5 hours. Additionally, the long, sometimes winding and pot-holed Highway 125–Highway 190 route connects Pinotepa Nacional with Oaxaca city, via Putla de Guerrero and Tlaxiaco (136 mi/219 km) and thence along along Highway 190 via Nochixtlan to Oaxaca City, in a total of 239 miles (385 km).

By bus, from the new **Camionera Central** (Central Bus Station), about half a mile west of downtown, several long-distance bus lines connect Pinotepa Nacional with destinations north, northwest, east, and west. Dominant line **Estrella Blanca** (tel. 954/543-3194), via subsidiaries Turistar, Elite, Futura, Gacela, and Flecha Roja, offers several daily first- and second-class *salidas de paso* (departures passing through): west to Acapulco, Zihuatanejo, and Mexico City; and east to Oaxaca coastal resorts of Puerto Escondido, Pochutla (Puerto Ángel), and Bahías de Huatulco.

First-class competing line **Omnibus Cristóbal Colón** offers broad Oaxaca service, along the Highway 125–Highway 190 corridor, north, via Putla, Tlaxiaco, and Huajuapan de León all the way to Mexico City (Tapo terminal) and northeast, via Highway 190 and Nochixtláan with Oaxaca City.

Some smaller independent lines operate out of the same terminal. **Fletes y Pasajes** (tel. 954/543-6016) offers second-class connections with inland points, via Putla de Guerrero, Tlaxiaco, and Teposcolula along Highway 125, continuing along Highway 190 via Nochixtlán, to Oaxaca City.

First-class **La Nesca** (formerly Estrella del Valle; tel. 954/543-5477) also connects with Oaxaca City, but along the scenic coastal route, via Highway 200 east with Puerto Escondido and Pochutla (Puerto Ángel), thence north along Highway 175, toward Oaxaca City over the high southern sierra.

Finally, for a backcountry adventure, ride on a rickety second-class **Boqueró** bus (with campesino families, bags of carrots, chickens, baby pigs) and connect via the Highway 125–182 route through Putla, thence via Mixteca Baja towns of Juxtlahuaca, and Santiago Tonalá, with Huajuapan de León in one long day.

EXCURSIONS NORTH OF PINOTEPA
Oaxaca Amusgo Country
Cacahuatepec (pop. 5,000; on Hwy. 125 about 25 miles north of Pinotepa Nacional) and its neighboring community San Pedro Amusgos are important centers for the Amusgo-speaking people. Approximately 20,000 Amusgos live in a roughly 30-mile-square region straddling the Guerrero-Oaxaca state border. Their homeland includes, besides Cacahuatepec and San Pedro Amusgos, Ometepec, Xochistlahuaca, Zacoalpán, and Tlacoachistlahuaca on the Guerrero side.

The Amusgo language is linguistically related to Mixtec, although it's unintelligible to Mixtec speakers. Before the conquest, the Amusgos were subject to the numerically superior Mixtec kingdoms until the Amusgos were conquered by the Aztecs in A.D. 1457, and later by the Spanish.

Now, most Amusgos live as subsistence farmers, supplementing their diet with occasional fowl or small game. Amusgos are best known to the outside world for their lovely animal-, plant-, and human-motif *huipiles*, which Amusgo women always seem to be hand-embroidering on their doorsteps.

Although Cacahuatepec enjoys a big market each Sunday, that doesn't diminish the importance of its big Easter-weekend festival, as well as the Día de Todos Santos (All Saints' Day, Nov. 1), and Día de los Muertos (Day of the Dead, Nov. 2), when, at the candle-lit family gravestones, folks welcome their ancestors' return to rejoin the family.

San Pedro Amusgos celebrations are among the most popular regional fiestas. On June 29, the day of San Pedro, people participate in religious processions, and costumed participants dressed as Moors and Christians, bulls, jaguars, and mules dance before crowds of men in traditional whites and women in beautiful heirloom *huipiles*. Later, on the first Sunday of October, folks crowd into town to enjoy the traditional processions, dances, and sweet treats of the fiesta of the Virgen del Rosario (Virgin of the Rosary).

Even if you miss the festivals, San Pedro Amusgos is worth a visit to buy *huipiles* alone. Three or four shops sell them along the main street through town. Look for the sign of **Trajes Regionales Elia** (tel. 954/582-8697), the little store run by sprightly Elia Guzmán when she's not in Oaxaca City. Besides dozens of beautiful embroidered garments, she stocks a few Amusgo books and offers friendly words of advice and local information.

THE MIXTECS

Sometime during the 1980s, southern Mexico's Mixtec-speaking people regained their pre-conquest population of about 500,000. Of that total, around two-fifths speaks only their own language. Their villages and communal fields spread over tens of thousands of square miles of remote mountain valleys north and west of Oaxaca, east and northeast of Acapulco, and south of Puebla.

Their homeland, the Mixteca, spreads over three distinct geo-cultural regions: the Mixteca Alta, Mixteca Baja, and the Mixteca Costera.

The **Mixteca Alta** centers in the high, cool plateau land of Guerrero and Oaxaca (which, on its east side, begins about 100 miles due west from Oaxaca City, and on its west side, about 100 miles due east from Chilpancingo, Guerrero), between the important market centers of Tlapa de Comonfort, Guerrero, and Tlaxiaco, Oaxaca.

Important **Mixteca Baja** communities, some along Highway 190, such as Huajuapan de León in Oaxaca and Izucar de Matamoros in Puebla, dot the dry eastern Guerrero-northwestern Oaxaca mountains and valleys.

In the **Mixteca Costera,** important Mixtec communities exist in or near Ometepec, Guerrero, and Pinotepa Nacional and Jamiltepec, Oaxaca, along Highway 200 in southwestern Oaxaca and southeastern Guerrero.

The Aztec-origin name Mixtecos (People of the Clouds) was translated directly from the Mixtecs' name for their own homeland: Aunyuma (Land of the Clouds). The Mixtecs' name for themselves, however, is Nyu-u Sabi (People of the Rain).

When the Spanish conquistadores arrived in 1519, the Mixtecs were under the thumb of the Aztecs, who, after a long, bitter struggle, had wrested control of most of Oaxaca from combined Mixtec-Zapotec armies in 1486. The Mixtecs naturally resented the Aztecs, whose domination was transferred to the Spanish during the colonial period, and, in turn, to the mestizos during modern times. The Mixtecs still defer to the town Mexicans, but they don't like it. Consequently, many rural Mixtecs, with minimal state or national consciousness, have scant interest in becoming Mexicanized.

In isolated Mixtec communities, traditions still rule. Village elders hold final authority, parents arrange marriages through go-betweens, and land is owned communally. Catholic saints are thinly disguised incarnations of old gods such as Tabayukí, ruler of nature, or the capricious and powerful *tono* spirits that lurk everywhere.

In many communities, Mixtec women exercise considerable personal freedom. At home and in villages, especially in the warm Mixteca Costa, they often still work bare-breasted. And while their men get drunk and carry on during festivals, women dance and often do a bit of their own carousing.

EXCURSIONS EAST OF PINOTEPA

For 30 or 40 miles east of Pinotepa Nacional, where road kilometer markers begin at zero again near the *zócalo,* Highway 200 stretches through the coastal Mixtec heartland, intriguing to explore, especially during festival times.

◖ Huaxpáltepec Pre-Easter Fair

The population of San Andres Huaxpáltepec (oo-wash-PAHL-tay-payk), about 10 miles east of Pinotepa, sometimes swells from about 4,000 to 20,000 or more during the three or four days before the day of Jesus the Nazarene, on the fourth Friday of Lent (or in other words, the fourth Friday after Ash Wednesday). The entire town spreads into a warren of shady stalls, offering everything from TVs to stone metates. The corn-grinding metate, which, including *mano* (stone roller), sells for about $25, is as important to a Mixtec family as a refrigerator is to an American family. A Mixtec husband and wife usually examine several of the concave stones, deliberating the pros and cons of each before deciding.

The Huaxpáltepec Nazarene fair is one of the most colorful of the Mixtec country expositions. Even the highway becomes a lineup of stalls; whole native clans camp under the trees, and mules, cows, and horses wait patiently around the edges of a grassy trading lot as men discuss prices. (The fun begins when a sale is made, and the new owner tries to rope and harness his bargain steed.)

SANTIAGO JAMILTEPEC

About 18 miles (30 km) east of Pinotepa Nacional stands the coastal Mixtec capital of Jamiltepec (hah-meel-teh-PAYK). Two-thirds of its 20,000 are Mixtec-speaking natives, who preserve a still-vibrant indigenous culture. A grieving Mixtec king named the town in memory of his infant son, Jamily, who was carried off by an eagle from this very hilltop.

Around Town

The central plaza, about a mile (1.6 km) from the highway (follow the left-hand signed side road north), stands at the heart of the town. You can't miss it because of the proud town plaza–front clock (and sundials) and the market stalls, always big but even bigger and more colorful on Thursday, the day of the traditional native *tianguis* (market), when a regiment of campesinos crowd in from the Jamiltepec hinterland.

Moreover, several big festivals are instrumental in preserving local folkways. They start off on New Year's Day and resume during the weeks of Cuaresma (Lent), usually during February and March. Favorite dances, such as Los Tejerones (Weavers), Los Chareos, Los Moros (The Moors), and Las Chilenas, act out age-old events, stories, and fables. Los Tejerones, for example, through a cast of animal-costumed characters, pokes fun at ridiculous Spanish colonial rules and customs.

Soon after, Jamiltepec people celebrate their very popular pre-Easter (week of Ramos) festival, featuring neighborhood candlelight processions accompanied by antique 18th-century music. Hundreds of the faithful bear elaborate wreaths and palm decorations to the foot of their church altars on Domingo de Ramos (Palm Sunday).

Later, merrymaking peaks again, between July 23 and 26 during the Fiesta de Santiago Apóstol (Festival of St. James the Apostle) and on September 11 with a festival honoring the Virgen de los Remedios. All this celebrating centers at the town church, the **Templo de Santiago Apóstol,** destroyed by a 1928 earthquake but brilliantly restored from 1992 to 1999, using the same method as the original Dominican padres, who supervised the 16th-century construction of mortar, strengthened with egg yolks. Take a look inside, where the town patron Santiago (St. James, sword in hand) and the Virgen de Los Remedios (Virgin of the Remedies) preside above the altar.

Regardless of the festivals, Jamiltepec at midday is a feast of traditional sights and sounds. For an interesting side excursion, take a stroll to some of the local *ojos de agua* (community springwater sources). From the plaza's northeast side, head east, downhill, along Calle 20 de Noviembre. After about a block, you'll arrive at a covered *pileta* (basin) built into the hillside rocks on the left, where folks fill bottles and jars with drinking water. Continue downhill another couple of blocks to *ojo de agua* **El Aguacate,** where another covered basin, on the left, supplies drinking water, while a cluster of folks wash clothes and bathe in a natural spring beneath an adjacent shady roof.

Shopping

Jamiltepec is well worth a stop if only to visit its market (in two locations, around the town center, and a half-mile north of town in a big building visible from the highway). Especially worthwhile are the handicrafts shops that sell masks, *huipiles,* carvings, hats, and much more. The market action, busiest on the Thursday *tianguis,* peaks around noon, and shuts down by 6 P.M.

Practicalities

Jamiltepec, capital of the vast south coast and mountain Jamiltepec governmental district, has recommendable hotels, restaurants, and services (but not yet a bank) not far from the town plaza. For an overnight option, the best is lovely **℄ Hotel Cádiz** (Calle del Olvido 7, tel. 954/582-8570, $22 s, $26 d) about a quarter mile north of the plaza. The dozen-odd rooms are spacious, with designer tile floors, and thoughtfully furnished with color-coordinated drapes and reading lamps. Views from the windows stretch from the surrounding village to far mountain vistas. All come with private hot-water shower baths, cable TV, fans, and a handy restaurant downstairs.

If the Hotel Cádiz is full, take a look at the clean and comfortable **Hotel Maris** (Calle Josefa Ortíz Dominguez, between de la Cruz and Rayón, tel. 954/582-8042, $15–20). Of the 46 rooms, pick one of the light rooms away from the street; rooms come with private bath, cable TV, and fans, but no restaurant.

For medicines and drugs, go to **Farmacia del Perpetuo Socorro** (Pharmacy of Perpetual Relief; Hidalgo 2, tel. 954/582-9046, 8 A.M.–8 P.M. daily), at the plaza's northeast corner, run by a team of friendly sisters. If you need a doctor, they recommend either **Dr. Manuel Mota** (Hwy. 200, in town barrio Sección 4) or the *seguro social* **hospital** (in town barrio Las Flores) with 24-hour emergency service.

BACKGROUND

The Land

A look at a map of North America reveals that Ixtapa-Zihuatanejo lies very far south, at the 18th parallel of latitude, which, as seen from the north pole, places Ixtapa-Zihuatanjeo four-fifths of the way to the equator. Furthermore, Ixtapa-Zihatuatanejo's longitude, smack on the 102nd parallel, places it both far east and far west, depending on your point of view. From Washington, D.C., Ixtapa-Zihuatanejo is a far 1,500 miles west; from San Francisco, Acapulco is a far 1,300 miles east. And from both, it is a far 1,400 miles south, well into the tropical land of perpetual summer: a paradise where frost never bites.

Ixtapa-Zihuatanejo, the once-hidden, but now famously popular twin resort, presents a charming contrast: Zihuatanejo, the petite fishing village on a half-moon, foothill-rimmed blue bay, and Ixtapa, a luxury mini-metropolis on a palmy, golden strand are a separate, but irresistible pair that continues to draw many thousands of yearly visitors from all over the world.

THE IXTAPA-ZIHUATANEJO REGION

Ixtapa-Zihuatanjo's attractions lie far into its entire region, an ethnically and geographically diverse domain that encompasses, broadly, the entire Mexican state of Guerrero.

The deep-south state of Guerrero (pop. 3,200,000, area 25,000 square mi/65,000 square km) is about the same size as the U.S. state of West Virginia (or the European country of Austria). It stretches about 250 miles (400 km) along Mexico's south Pacific coast

and extends about 150 miles (250 km) inland, over a ruggedly corrugated landscape of coastal plain, foothills, and high sierra, interspersed with a number of upland valleys, many of which drain into the basin of the grand Río Balsas, Mexico's mightiest river.

COSTA CHICA AND COSTA GRANDE

Mountains notwithstanding, Ixtapa-Zihuatanejo's influence extends most strongly along the coast, including a pair of sub-regions that Guerrero folks call the Costa Grande (Big Coast) and Costa Chica (Little Coast). Actually, both coasts are big: From the great Río Balsas, that forms the border with the state of Michoacán, the Costa Grande stretches southeast, past Ixtapa-Zihuatanejo, 150 miles (250 km) to just past Acapulco. From there, the Costa Chica continues southeast 100 miles (160 km) into the neighboring state of Oaxaca.

LAGOONS, BAYS, COVES, AND BEACHES
Lagoons and Barrier Beaches
An example of a landform that defines the entire Ixtapa-Zihuatanejo regional coastline, the blue expanse of mangrove-lined Laguna de Potosí can be viewed by arrivees from their airplane windows a minute before airport touchdown. This is but one of a scenic procession of such mangrove-fringed *lagunas* that decorate the entire Guerrero coastline.

Although all of these placid, blue lagoons are accessible, Laguna de Potosí and Laguna Coyuca (at Pie de la Cuesta), on the Costa Grande, and Laguna Tres Palos (past the Acapulco airport), on the Costa Chica, are the most accessible. All of these coastal *lagunas* result from the opposing forces of surging water: the ocean waves and currents pushing sand shoreward against the flow of the rivers coursing down from the sierra and depositing entire lakes of fresh water at the shoreline.

It's a see-saw struggle that the rivers temporarily win, if only during the summer–fall wet season. Freshwater floods accumulated in the lagoons break though the shoreline sandbars and open channels to the ocean. Pacific waves rush in, carrying with them a bounty of sea creatures and nutrients, and for a spell during the summer the lagoons become slightly salty (brackish).

However, when the river flood abates in the fall, the persistent ocean waves and currents deposit their burden of sand, closing the channels through the *barras* (sandbars). Soon, the lagoons again become fresh, sweet, and clear.

On the ocean side of the lagoons lie the Ixtapa-Zihuatanejo region's hidden barrier beaches, with plenty of fine yellow sand, an abundance of fresh breezes, and seasonal driftwood, seashells, and sometimes even *palapa* restaurants and reusable shady palm-frond *ramadas* (temporary roofs) awaiting new occupants. All are accessible, some easily, such the beach at Barra de Potosí, just south of Zihuatanjeo; Playa Paraíso (by short launch trip), near San Jeronimo; Playa Pie de la Cuesta (by road) a few miles west from Acapulco; and Playa Larga, 20 miles southeast of Acapulco.

Bays and Coves
Gorgeous beaches also decorate many of the Ixtapa-Zihuatanejo region's bays and coves. Besides the famous golden resort strands of Ixtapa-Zihuatanejo and Acapulco, many other breeze-swept sandy coasts and small bays and coves hide lovely beaches. Moving from west to east along the Costa Grande are the gorgeous strands, such as coral-strewn Playa Troncones, Playa Ojo de Agua, Playa Escondida, and Playa Tlalcoyunque. Continuing east along the Costa Chica, especially worth exploring are the untouristed small-resort beaches of Playa Ventura, Playa Las Peñitas, and Punta Maldonado.

COASTAL PLAIN, FOOTHILLS, AND SIERRA
The Ixtapa-Zihuatejo region's coastal plain, source of a major portion of Guerrero's agricultural wealth, concentrates along a relatively narrow strip. It begins at the lagoons' inland edges and, crossed by many south-flowing rivers, extends inland, only about 15 miles in the

west along the Costa Grande, and broadening to about twice that at the eastern, Oaxaca end of the Costa Chica.

North of the coastal strip, the cooler lush, forested foothills, about equal in width to the coastal plain, gradually rise, from an elevation of about 1,000 feet to 3,000 feet (300–900 meters). Several tradition-rich foothill market towns, such as Petatlán and Atoyac on the Costa Grande, and Ayutla, Acatlán, and Ometepec on the Costa Chica, are equally rich centers of lumber, produce (mangoes, papayas, tamarind, coffee, honey), and handicrafts.

The Sierra Madre del Sur

The foothills sharply give way to the Ixtapa-Zihuatanejo region's great mother of ranges, the Sierra Madre del Sur, a succession of gigantic cloud-tipped mountains extending in an unbroken east–west line. Many of their jagged summits top 10,000 feet (3,000 meters). This line of rugged sentinels extends from Cerro Tejamil (10,460 feet/3,190 meters) northeast of Zihuatanejo, all the way east to Cerro San Marcos (10,170 feet/3,100 meters) by the Oaxaca border. In the middle, mightiest of all the Ixtapa-Zihuatanejo region's summits, towers Cerro Teotepec, rising to 11,647 feet (3,550 meters), only 43 miles (70 km) as the crow flies northwest of Acapulco.

The Río Balsas Basin

As precipitously as the sierra rises from the southern shoreline, it drops in the north, into the basin of the Río Balsas, which drains a gigantic realm, including parts of five states—Jalisco, Michoacán, Morelos, Puebla, and Oaxaca—and most of the Ixtapa-Zihuatanejo region.

The people of the Río Balsas basin are both victims and benefactors of the Sierra Madre and the Río Balsas. The mighty sierra forms a great rain shadow, blocking Pacific breeze–borne moisture and turning their homeland into the notorious Tierra Caliente: hot and desert-like most of the year. But the people, by their own ingenuity and with a little government help, benefit from the waters of the river. Aided by dams and irrigation, they have created rich oases of corn, cattle, cotton, mangoes, melons, bananas, and alfalfa by the riverbanks.

CLIMATE

Nature has graced the Ixtapa-Zihuatanejo region with a microclimate tapestry. Although rainfall, offshore breezes, and vegetation introduce refreshing local variations, elevation provides the broad brush. The entire coastal strip (including the mountain slopes and plateaus up to 4,000 or 5,000 feet) luxuriates in the tropics.

The seashore is a land of perpetual summer. Winter days are typically warm and rainless, peaking at 80–85°F (27–30°C) and dropping to 60–70°F (16–21°C) by midnight.

Increasing elevation gradually decreases both temperature and humidity. In Chilpancingo (elev. 4,000 feet) you can expect warm, dry winter days at 75–80°F (24–27°C) and cooler nights around 55–65°F (14–18°C).

Similar but sometimes cooler winter weather prevails in higher 5,800-foot (1,800-meter) Taxco. Days will usually be balmy and spring-like, climbing to around 75°F (24°C) by early afternoon, with nights dropping to a temperate 45–55°F (8–15°C).

Summer days on the beaches are warm, humid, and sometimes rainy. July, August, and September forenoons are typically bright, warming to the high 80s or low 90s (around 33°C). By afternoon, however, clouds often gather and bring short, sometimes heavy, showers. By late afternoon, the clouds part, the sun dries the pavements, and the tropical breeze is just right for enjoying a sparkling sunset.

Chilpancingo and Taxco summers are delightful. Afternoon temperatures rise to the 80s (27–32°C) and cool to the balmy 70s (21–26°C), perfect for strolling during the evenings. In Iguala, however, late-spring and summer temperatures are often hot, typically 85–95°F (30–36°C) during the dry April and May, but cooling a few degrees during the June–September rains.

Flora and Fauna

Abundant sun and summer rains nurture the vegetation of the Ixtapa-Zihuatanejo region. At some roadside spots, crimson bromeliads, pendulous passion fruits, and giant candelabra cactuses luxuriate, beckoning to admirers. Now and then visitors may stop, attracted by something remarkable, such as a riot of flowers blooming from apparently dead branches or what looks like grapefruit sprouting from the trunk of a roadside tree. More often, travelers pass by the long stretches of thickets, jungles, marshes, and dry uplands without stopping; however, a little knowledge of what to expect can blossom into recognition and discovery, transforming the humdrum into the extraordinary.

VEGETATION ZONES

Mexico's diverse landscape and fickle rainfall have sculpted its wide range of plant forms. Botanists recognize at least 14 major Mexican vegetation zones, seven of which occur in the Ixtapa-Zihuatanejo region.

Directly along the coastal highway travelers often pass long sections of three of these zones: savanna, thorn forest, and tropical deciduous forest.

Savanna

Great swaths of pasture-like savanna stretch along Highway 200 between Zihuatanejo and Acapulco. In its natural state, savanna often appears as a palm-dotted sea of grass—green and marshy during the rainy summer, dry and brown by late winter.

Although grass rules the savanna, palms give it character. Most familiar is the **coconut,** the *cocotero (Cocos nucifera)*—the world's most useful tree—used for everything from lumber to candy. Less familiar, but with as much personality, is the Mexican **fan palm,** or *palma real (Sabal mexicana),* festooned with black fruit and spread flat like a señorita's fan.

The savanna's list goes on: the grapefruitlike fruit on the trunk and branches identify the

coconut palm grove on the Costa Chica

gourd tree, or *calabaza (Crescentia alata).* The mature gourds, brown and hard, are famously useful, in a dozen ways, from making music and drinking hot chocolate to carrying water and scooping corn for tortillas.

The waterlogged seaward edge of the savanna nurtures lagoon-front forests of the **red mangrove,** or *mangle colorado (Rhizophora mangle),* short trees that seem to stand in the water on stilts. Their new roots grow downward from above; a time-lapse photo would show them marching, as if on stilts, into the lagoon.

Thorn Forest

Lower rainfall leads to the hardier growth of the thorn forest—domain of the pea family—the legumes marked in late winter and spring by bursts of red, yellow, pink, and white flowers. Look closely at the blossoms and you will see they resemble the familiar wild sweet pea

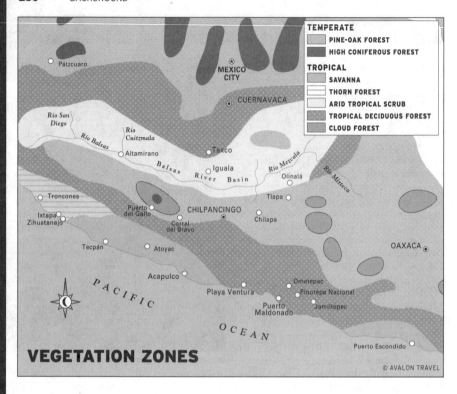

VEGETATION ZONES

TEMPERATE
- PINE-OAK FOREST
- HIGH CONIFEROUS FOREST

TROPICAL
- SAVANNA
- THORN FOREST
- ARID TROPICAL SCRUB
- TROPICAL DECIDUOUS FOREST
- CLOUD FOREST

© AVALON TRAVEL

of North America. Even when the blossoms are gone, you can identify them by seed pods that hang from the branches. Local folks call them by many names. These include the **ta-bachín,** the scarlet Mexican bird of paradise; and its close relative the *flamboyán,* or **royal poinciana,** an import from Africa, where it's called the "flame tree."

Just as abundant (although not so flashy) are the legumes' cousins, the **acacias** and **mimosas.** Long swaths of thorn forest sometimes grow right to the coastal highway and side-road pavements, so that the road appears tunnel-like through a tangle of brushy acacia trees, decorated with riots of tiny yellow flower balls.

If you happen upon a tree with stark gray, leafless branches, apparently lifeless except for a flock of showy white flowers, you've found the **palo del muerto,** "the tree of the dead." It is also called *palo bobo* ("fool tree") in some locales because folks believe if you take a drink from a stream near its foot, you will go crazy.

Tropical Deciduous Forest

In rainier areas, the thorn forest grades into tropical deciduous forest. This is the "friendly" or "short-tree" forest, blanketed by a tangle of summer-green leaves that fall in the dry winter to reveal thickets of branches. Some trees show bright, fall reds and yellows, later blossoming with brilliant flowers—spider lily, cardinal sage, pink trumpet, poppylike yellowsilk *(pomposhuti),* and mouse killer *(mala ratón),* which swirl in the spring wind like blossom blizzards.

The tropical deciduous forest makes up

the lush jungly coat that swathes much of the Ixtapa-Zihuatanejo region's coastal foothills. It is especially lush during the rainy summer, in the uplands along Highway 193, above Atoyac de Álvarez, northwest of Acapulco. Here, vine-strewn thickets overhang the road, like the edges of a lost prehistoric world, where at any moment you expect a dinosaur to rear up.

The biological realities here are nearly as exotic. Beside the road, a spreading, solitary **strangler fig** *(Ficus padifolia)* stands, draped with hairy hanging air roots (which, in time, plant themselves in the ground and support the branches). Its Mexican name, *matapalo* (killer tree), is gruesomely accurate, for strangler figs often entwine themselves in death embraces with less aggressive tree victims.

Well-watered zones of the tropical deciduous forest have become home to a platoon of useful **introduced plants.** These include the common India-native **mango,** "king of fruit" (April–July), and Africa-native **plátano** (banana). Also introduced and common, but not so recognizable, is the **coffee shrub,** or locally *cafeto (Coffea arabica).* Coffee is widely grown in the Ixtapa-Zihuatanejo region, notably in the foothill forests, upcountry from Atoyac de Álvarez. Coffee shrubs, usually trimmed to about five feet in height, grow unobtrusively, often in an apparent wild "jungle" right next to the highway, beneath the shady canopy of taller trees. They're recognizable by their camellia-bush appearance, with shiny dark-green leaves, star-shaped white flowers, and red berries, in season.

Excursions by Jeep or foot along shaded off-highway tracks through the tropical deciduous

POINSETTIA

Although this lovely red flowering plant only became known and appreciated by the wider world during the 1800s, the people of Mexico have enjoyed the poinsettia for millennia. It grows in gorgeous wild profusion in semitropical mountain zones of southwestern Mexico, especially in the Ixtapa-Zihuatanejo region and the neighboring states of Michoacán, Morelos, Oaxaca, and Chiapas.

The Aztecs, who called the poinsettia *cuetlaxochitle*, used its sap to control fevers and its crimson red petals (actually not petals, but colored leaves, called bracts) for dye. The emperor Moctezuma II (1466-1520) especially adored the *cuetlaxochitle*. He ordered caravans of them brought to his capital at Tenochtitlán to honor an Aztec goddess who was said to have died of a broken heart. The *cuetlaxochitle*, a legend recounted, had been born from one drop of the goddess's blood.

Most present-day Mexican folks know the poinsettia as the *flor de Nochebuena* (flower of Christmas Eve). It blooms during the late autumn and early winter, just in time for people to give birthday bouquets to the baby Jesus at churches all over Mexico on December 24.

An eminent German botanist, Karl Lugwig Wilenow, was among the first outsiders to study the poinsettia, from cuttings brought to him from central America. In 1800, recognizing it as a member of the grand Euphorbia family, Wilenow christened it *Euphorbiaceae pulcherrima*, meaning "most beautiful of the Euphoribias."

Although apt, this name has been largely forgotten because of the work of Joel Robert Poinsett, amateur botanist and U.S. ambassador to Mexico during the 1820s. Poinsett, keenly interested in identifying new species wherever he traveled in Mexico, noticed the spectacularly red plant growing beside the road. He brought specimens back to the United States and nurtured them in his South Carolina greenhouse. This led to the plant's spread and ultimate immense popularity all over North and South America, Europe, and most parts of the world.

In 1836, a group of Scottish botanists proposed to honor Poinsett's work by renaming his find *Poinsettia pulcherrima*. The name stuck, and now people everywhere enjoy holiday festoons of the charmingly divine plant known simply as the poinsettia.

forest can reveal delightful jungle scenes; however, unwary travelers must watch out for the poison oak–like *mala mujer,* the "bad woman" tree. The oil on its large five-fingered leaves can cause an itchy rash.

Pine-Oak Forest

Along the upland highways (notably on the higher reaches of north–south Highway 95 and the Chilpancingo–Chilapa–Olinalá Highway 93) the tropical forest gives way to temperate pine-oak forest. Here, many of Mexico's 112 oak and 39 pine species thrive. Oval two-inch cones and foot-long drooping needles (three to a cluster) make the *pino triste,* or sad pine *(Pinus lumholtzii),* appear in severe need of water. Unlike many of Mexico's pines, it produces neither good lumber nor much turpentine, although it *is* prized by guitar makers for its wood.

Much more regal in bearing and commercially important are the tall pines, including the **Mexican white pine** *(Pinus ayacahuite),* known locally as the *pinabete.* It grows to about 100 feet when mature and resembles the white pine of northern regions, with pendulous, scaly 4- to 6-inch often reddish-brown cones that shed winged seeds. Equally recognizable is the **Montezuma pine** *(Pinus montezumae),* or the *ocote macho.* It likewise grows long (but gray) cones and is distinguishable by its interesting drooping needles.

Pines often grow in stands, mixed at lower elevations with **oaks,** which occur in two broad classifications—*encino* (evergreen, small-leafed) and *roble* (deciduous, large-leafed)—both much like the live oaks that dot California hills and valleys. Clustered on their branches and scattered in the shade, *bellota* (acorns) distinctly mark them as oaks.

Arid Tropical Scrub

This desert-like vegetation zone coincides with the semiarid Río Balsas basin, which sprawls for 200 miles (320 km) east–west (reachable both along Highway 51 and north–south Highway 95) between Chilpancingo and Taxco. Although superficially appearing like the temperate deserts of the southwest United States and northern Mexico, the arid tropical scrub zone nurtures a botanic treasury of tropical, frost-sensitive plants, sculpted by extreme heat and drought.

The signature king of all these hardy plants is the spectacular **candelabra cactus** *(Lemaireocereus weberi),* or *candelabro.* Mature specimens, as wide and high as a four-story building, with a dozen or more 10-ribbed vertical columns, resemble a giant dining-table candelabra.

At some spots, great forests of pole-straight *tetetzo* cactuses *(Pachycereus ruficeps)* inhabit the arid tropical scrubland. Up to 50 feet tall, they can collectively resemble a grand army of cactus sentinels, guarding the rocky landscape.

Although not cactuses, many of the 300-odd members of the **agave** family thrive in dryer areas of the Ixtapa-Zihuatanejo region. One such is the charming **cabbage agave** *(Agave perryi),* which grows in families of neat, round, cabbage-like plants, up to three feet in diameter, with broad, bluish-green, spined leaves.

Cloud Forest and High Coniferous Forest

The Ixtapa-Zihuatanejo region's rarest and most exotic vegetation zones are removed from the coastal tourist centers. Adventurers who travel to certain high, dewy mountainsides, beginning around 5,000 feet, can explore the plant and wildlife community of the cloud forest. One such example lies along Highway 196, about 30 miles (50 km) uphill from Atoyac de Álvarez, past the village of El Paraíso. There, abundant cool fog nourishes a Pleistocene remnant forest of dripping tree ferns, liquid amber maples, lichen-draped pines and oaks, above a mossy carpet of orchids, bromeliads, and begonias.

About 20 miles (32 km) farther uphill along the same route, the Ixtapa-Zihuatanejo region's least accessible vegetation zone, the high coniferous forest, swathes the 9,000- to 11,000-foot slopes of Cerro Teotepec. This pristine alpine island, accessible (only with

© BRUCE WHIPPERMAN

The Mexican native maguey *(Agave Americana),* common in dry areas, is prized for its sugary juice.

a guide, inquire locally) on horseback or by foot, nurtures stands of pines, spruce, and fir interspersed with grassy meadows, similar to the Rocky Mountain slopes in the United States and Canada. Here, besides the white and Montezuma pines, you might find hardy stands of **sacred fir** *(Abies religiosa),* or *oyamel;* **Mexican cypress** *(Cupressa lusitanica);* and the high-altitude **alder** *(Alnus firmifolia).*

For a wealth of details, consult books *Meet Flora Mexicana* and *Handbook of Mexican Roadside Flora.*

WILDLIFE

Despite continued habitat destruction—logged forests, filled wetlands, plowed savannas—great swaths of the Ixtapa-Zihuatanejo region still abound with wildlife. Common in the temperate pine-oak forest highlands are mammals seen in the U.S. wilds, such as the mountain lion *(puma, león),* coyote, fox *(zorro),* rabbit *(conejo),* and quail *(codorniz).*

However, the tropical coastal forests and savannas are also home to fascinating species seen only in zoos north of the border. The reality of this dawns on travelers when they glimpse something exotic, such as raucous, screeching swarms of small green parrots rising from the roadside, a giant pea-green iguana lizard, or an armadillo or coati nosing in the sand just a few feet away from them at the forested edge of an isolated beach.

Furthermore, if you're quiet and patient enough, you may be rewarded with a view of the endangered striped cat, the **ocelot** *(ocelotl),* or its smaller cousins, the **margay** *(tigrillo)* and the tan **jaguarundi** *(onza, leoncillo).*

Armadillos, Coatis, and Bats

Armadillos are shy, cat-sized mammals that act and look like opossums but wear reptilian-like shells. If you see one, remain still, and it may walk right up and sniff your foot before it recognizes you and scuttles back into the woods.

A common inhabitant of the tropics is the raccoon-like coati *(tejón, pisote).* In the wild, coatis like shady stream banks, often congregating in large troupes of 15–30 individuals.

They are identified by their short brown or tan fur, small round ears, long nose, and straight, vertically-held tail. They're often kept as pets; the first coati you see may be one offered for sale at a local market.

Mexican bats *(murciélagos)* are widespread, with at least 126 species compared to 37 in the United States. In Mexico, as everywhere, bats are feared and misunderstood. Around sunset, many species come out of their hiding places and flit through the air in search of insects. Most people, sitting outside enjoying the early evening, will mistake their darting silhouettes for those of birds, who, except for owls, do not generally fly so late in the day.

The non-vampire Mexican bats carry their (uncommon) vampire cousins' odious reputation with forbearance. They go about their good works, pollinating flowers, clearing the air of pesky gnats and mosquitoes, ridding cornfields of mice, and dropping seeds, thereby restoring forests. Limestone caves, especially the Grutas de Juxtlahuaca, are the best places to see bats.

The snowy egret is common in coastal lagoons.

BIRDS

The coastal lagoons of the Ixtapa-Zihuatanejo region lie astride the Pacific Flyway, one of the Americas' major north–south paths for migrating waterfowl. Many of the familiar American and Canadian species, including pintail, gadwall, baldpate, shoveler, redhead, and scaup, arrive October–January, when their numbers swell into the millions.

Besides the migrants, swarms of resident species—**herons** and **egrets** *(garzas)*, cormorant-like **anhingas, lily-walkers** *(jacanas)*, and hundreds more—stalk, nest, and preen in the same lagoons.

Few places are better for observing **seabirds** than the beaches of the Ixtapa-Zihuatanejo region. **Brown pelicans** and the soaring black-and-white **frigate birds** are among the prime actors. When a flock of pelicans spot a school of favorite fish, they go about their routine deliberately. Singly or in pairs, they circle and plummet into the waves to come up, more often than not, with a fish in their gullets.

Each bird then bobs and floats over the swells for a minute or two, seeming to wait for its dozen or so fellow pelicans to take their turns. This continues until they've bagged a dinner of 10–15 fish apiece.

Besides the beaches, the blue mangrove lagoons of the Costa Grande and Costa Chica, southeast of Ixtapa-Zihuatanejo, nurture a trove of wildlife, especially birds, ripe for viewing on foot or by boat tour.

For more information, see *Tropical Mexico: The Ecotraveler's Wildlife Guide.*

REPTILES AND AMPHIBIANS
Snakes

Mexico has 460-odd snake species, the vast majority shy and nonpoisonous; they will get out of your way if you give plenty of warning. In the Ixtapa-Zihuatanejo region poisonous snakes have been largely eradicated in city and tourist areas. In the brush or forest, carry a stick or a machete and beat the bushes ahead of you while watching where you put your feet.

When hiking or rock-climbing in the country, don't put your hand in niches you can't see.

You might even see a snake underwater while swimming offshore at an isolated Ixtapa-Zihuatanejo region beach. The **yellow-bellied sea snake,** *Pelamis platurus* (small, grows to about two feet), although rare and shy, can inflict fatal bites. If you see a yellow-and-black snake underwater, get away, pronto.

Some eels, which resemble snakes but have gills like fish and inhabit rocky crevices, can inflict nonpoisonous bites and should also be avoided.

More aggressive and generally more dangerous is the Mexican **rattlesnake** *(cascabel)* and its viper relative, the **fer-de-lance** *(Bothrops atrox).* About the same in size (to six feet) and appearance as the rattlesnake, the fer-de-lance is known by various local names, such as *nauyaca, cuatro narices, palanca,* and *barba amarilla.* It is potentially more hazardous than the rattlesnake because it lacks a warning rattle.

Crocodiles

The crocodile *(cocodrilo, caimán),* once prized for its meat and hide, came close to vanishing in Ixtapa-Zihuatanejo region lagoons until the government took steps to ensure its survival; it's now officially protected. A few isolated breeding populations live on in the wild (such as the very visible crocodile family at Laguna Ixtapa, north of Zihuatanejo), while government and private hatcheries are breeding more for the eventual repopulation of lagoons where crocodiles once were common.

Two crocodile species occur in the Ixtapa-Zihuatanejo region. The true crocodile, *Crocodilus acutus,* has a narrower snout than its local cousin, *Caiman crocodilus fuscus,* a type of alligator *(lagarto).* Although past individuals have been recorded at up to 15 feet long, wild native crocodiles and alligators are usually young and only 3 feet or less in length.

Sea Turtles

The story of Mexican sea turtles is similar: They once swarmed ashore on Ixtapa-Zihuatanejo regional beaches to lay their eggs. Prized for their meat, eggs, hide, and shell, the turtles were severely devastated. Now officially protected, sea turtles are coming ashore in growing numbers at some isolated locations. Of the four locally occurring species, the **olive Ridley turtle** *(tortuga golfina)* and the **green turtle** *(tortuga negra* or *caguama)* are the most common. The green and olive Ridley, although officially endangered, have stabilized because of persistent government and volunteer efforts. The two other, relatively rare, locally occurring sea turtles are the **hawksbill** *(carey)* and the **leatherback** *(tortuga de cuero).*

FISH AND MARINE MAMMALS

Shoals of fish abound in Ixtapa-Zihuatanejo regional waters. Four billfish species (known for their long, pointed beaks, or "bills") are found in deep-sea grounds several miles offshore: **swordfish, sailfish,** and **blue and black marlin.** All are spirited fighters, though the sailfish and marlin are generally the toughest to bring in. The blue marlin is the biggest of the four; in the past, 10-foot specimens weighing more than 1,000 pounds were brought in at Pacific coast marinas. Lately, four feet and 200 pounds for a marlin, and 100 pounds for a sailfish, are more typical. Progressive captains (who now subscribe to the increasingly popular "tag and release") encourage victorious anglers to return these magnificent "tigers of the sea" (especially the sinewy sailfish and blue marlin, which make for poor eating) to the deep after they've won the battle.

Billfish are not the only prizes of the sea, however. Serious fish lovers also seek nonendangered varieties of tuna-like **jack,** such as **yellowtail, Pacific amberjack, pompano, jack crevalle,** and the tenacious **roosterfish,** named for the "comb" atop its head. These, and the **yellowfin tuna, mackerel,** and *dorado,* which Hawaiians call mahimahi, are among the delicacies sought in Ixtapa-Zihuatanejo waters.

Accessible from small boats offshore and by casting from shoreline rocks are varieties of **snapper** *(huachinango, pargo)* and **sea bass** *(cabrilla).* Closer to shore, **croaker, mullet,** and **groupers** can be found foraging along sandy bottoms and in rocky crevices.

Sharks and rays inhabit nearly all depths, with smaller fry venturing into beach shallows and lagoons. Huge **Pacific manta rays** appear to be frolicking, their great wings flapping like birds, not far offshore. Just beyond the waves, local fisherfolk bring in **hammerhead, thresher,** and **leopard sharks.**

Also common is the **stingray,** which can inflict a painful puncture wound with its barbed tail. Experienced swimmers and waders avoid injury by both shuffling (rather than stepping) and watching their feet in shallow waters with sandy bottoms.

Dolphins and Whales

The playful antics of the once numerous **Pacific bottlenosed dolphin** are nevertheless sometimes observable from Ixtapa-Zihuatanejo region-based tour and fishing boats, and sometimes even from beaches. (Sadly, dolphins often get caught and drown in fishing trawlers' nets.)

Larger whale *(ballena)* species, such as the **humpback** and **blue** whale, range the Mexican Pacific tropics and are sometimes visible, both from shore and boat, from the Ixtapa-Zihuatanejo region coastline west to Hawaii and beyond.

History

Once upon a time, maybe as long as 30,000 years ago, the first bands of hunters, probably following great game herds, crossed from Siberia to the American continent. They drifted southward, many of them eventually settling in the lush upland valleys and coastlines of present-day Mexico.

Much later, perhaps around 5000 B.C., these early people began gathering and grinding the seeds of a hardy grass that required only the summer rains to thrive. After generations of selective breeding, this grain, called *teocentli,* the sacred seed (which we call maize or corn), led to prosperity.

EARLY CIVILIZATIONS

With abundant food, villages grew into towns, and towns evolved into small cities. Leisure classes arose—artists, architects, warriors, and ruler-priests—who had the time to think and create. With a calendar, they harnessed the constant wheel of the firmament to life on earth, defining the days to plant, harvest, feast, travel, and trade.

Of Mexico's early urban peoples, the Olmecs were foremost. Around 1500 B.C. they were establishing large ceremonial centers along the Gulf of Mexico Coast. At La Venta, in present-day Tabasco state, archaeologists have uncovered the Olmecs' most spectacular remains: giant stone heads, up to nine feet in height, with football helmet–like caps.

The Olmec influence arrived early in the present-day Ixtapa-Zihuatanejo region. Olmec-style jaguar-motif art has been uncovered at Teopantecuantlán, an upland ceremonial center dating from around 1000 B.C. Moreover, Olmec-style wall paintings decorate caves, notably the Grutas de Juxtlahuaca and Oxtotitlán, in lush highland valleys about 100 miles north of Acapulco.

Monte Albán, Teotihuacán, and Xochicalco

After the decline of the Olmecs, around 500 B.C., other civilizations rose. Monte Albán, in Oaxaca, which was flourishing around the time of Jesus, is thought by many experts to be Mexico's first true city. Later, Teotihuacán, north of present-day Mexico City, grew into one of the world's great metropolises, with a population of about 250,000, by A.D. 500.

Eventually both Monte Albán and Teotihuacán crumbled; they were all but abandoned by A.D. 700, leaving a host of former vassal city-states to tussle among themselves. In the Ixtapa-Zihuatanejo region, first among these was Xochicalco, near Taxco, 150 miles (250 km) north of present-day Acapulco.

The Living Quetzalcoatl

Xochicalco's wise men tutored a young noble who was to become a living legend. In A.D. 947, Topiltzín (literally, Our Prince) was born. Records recite Topiltzín's achievements. He advanced astronomy, agriculture, and architecture and founded the city-state of Tula in A.D. 968, north of old Teotihuacán.

Contrary to the times, Topiltzín opposed human sacrifice. He ruled benignly for two decades, becoming so revered that his people knew him as the living Quetzalcoatl, the plumed serpent god, Quetzocoatl, incarnate.

Bloodthirsty local priests, lusting for human victims, tricked him with alcohol, however; Topiltzín awoke groggily one morning, in bed with his sister. Devastated with shame, Quetzalcoatl banished himself. He headed east from Tula with a band of retainers in A.D. 987, vowing that he would return during the anniversary of his birth year, Ce Acatl. Legends say he sailed across the eastern sea and rose to heaven as the morning star.

The Aztecs

The civilization that Topiltzín founded, known to historians as the Toltec (People of Tula), was eventually eclipsed by others. These included the Aztecs, a collection of seven aggressive immigrant sub-tribes. Migrating around during the 11th century A.D., from a mysterious western land of Aztlán (Place of the Herons) into the lake-filled valley that Mexico City now occupies, the Aztecs survived by being forced to fight for every piece of ground they occupied.

By A.D. 1300 the Aztecs (who called themselves the Máxica) had clawed their way to dominion over the Valley of Mexico. In 1325, They founded their capital, Tenochtitlán, on an island in the middle of the valley-lake. From there, Aztec armies, not unlike Roman legions, marched out and subdued faraway kingdoms and returned with booty of gold, brilliant feathers, precious jewels, and captives, whom they enslaved and sacrificed by the thousands as food for their gods.

Among those gods they feared was Quetzalcoatl, who, legends said, was bearded and fair-skinned. It was a remarkable coincidence, therefore, that the red-bearded, fair-skinned Castilian Hernán Cortés landed on Mexico's eastern coast on April 22, 1519, during the year of Ce Acatl, exactly when Topiltzín, the living Quetzalcoatl, had vowed he would return.

THE CONQUEST

Cortés, a poor Spanish nobleman, then only 34, had promoted an expedition of 11 small ships and 550 men and sailed westward from Cuba in February 1519. Upon landing near present-day Veracruz, he was in trouble. His men, mostly soldiers of fortune, hearing stories of a powerful Aztec empire west beyond the mountains, had realized the impossible odds they faced and became restive.

However, Cortés cut short any thoughts of mutiny by burning his ships. As he led his grumbling but resigned band of adventurers toward the Aztec capital of Tenochtitlán, Cortés played Quetzalcoatl to the hilt, awing local chiefs. Coaxed by Doña Marina, Cortés's native translator-mistress, local chiefs began to add their warrior-armies to Cortés's march against their Aztec overlords.

Moctezuma, Lord of Tenochtitlán

Once inside the walls of Tenochtitlán, the Aztecs' Venice-like island-city, the Spaniards were dazzled by gardens of animals, gold and palaces, and a great pyramid-enclosed square where tens of thousands of people bartered goods gathered from all over the empire.

However, Moctezuma, the lord of that empire, was frozen by fear and foreboding, unsure if these figures truly represented the return of Quetzalcoatl. He quickly found himself hostage to Cortés and then died a few months later during a riot against Spanish greed and brutality. On July 1, 1520, on what came to be called *noche triste* (the sad night), the besieged Cortés and his men broke out, fleeing for their lives along the lake causeway from Tenochtitlán, carrying Moctezuma's treasure.

Aztec Defeat and Spanish Victory

Despite his grievous retreat, Cortés regrouped and reinforced his small army with an armed sailboat fleet and 100,000 Indian warrior-allies and invaded Tenochtitlán a year later. The defenders, greatly weakened by smallpox, led by Cuauhtémoc, Moctezuma's nephew, refused to surrender, forcing Cortés to destroy the city to take it. Tenochtitlán fell on August 13, 1521.

After his triumph, Cortés took former emperor Cuauhtémoc captive. He forced Cuauhtémoc and his retainers to march with him on an ill-fated expedition to Honduras in 1523–1525. Tortured with foreboding that Cuauhtémoc and his compatriots were plotting

against him, Cortés had Cuauhtémoc hanged on February 28, 1525.

But, unknown to Cortés, Cuauhtémoc's followers secretly took his remains hundreds of miles north and may have buried them at Ixcateopan, the home of Cuauhtémoc's mother, near present-day Taxco. There, 424 years later, on September 26, 1949, remains believed by many to be Cuauhtémoc's were discovered and remain enshrined there to this very day.

New Spain

With the Valley of Mexico firmly in his grip, Cortés sent his lieutenants south, north, and west to explore and extend the limits of his domain, which eventually expanded to more than a dozenfold the size of old Spain. In a letter to his king, Charles V, Cortés christened his empire New Spain of the Ocean Sea, a label that remained Mexico's official name for 300 years.

THE SEARCH FOR CHINA

Even during his struggle with the Aztecs, Cortés continued to dream Columbus's old dream. Somewhere west lay China, and he was determined to find it. As early as 1520 Cortés began sending his lieutenants to Mexico's southern Pacific coast to look for safe, timber-rich harbors, where he would build the ships to China.

First on the Pacific shore was Gonzalo de Uribe, who, in 1520, arrived at Zacatula, at the mouth of the Río Balsas, not far northwest of Zihuatanejo. Besides bringing back gold samples, he told Cortés of a good harbor and plenty of timber for building ships.

Discovery of Acapulco Bay

In 1522, conquistador Pedro de Alvarado founded the Ixtapa-Zihuatanejo region's first town, at Acatlán on the Costa Chica. Around the same time, Rodriguez de Villafuerte sailed into Acapulco Bay, which he named Bahía de Santa Lucia, a label that persisted on maps for generations.

After reporting to Cortés of the bay's calm anchorage and abundance of shoreline trees,

MALINCHE AND CORTÉS

If it hadn't been for Doña Marina (received as a gift from a local chief), Hernán Cortés may have become a mere historical footnote. Doña Marina, speaking both Spanish and native tongues, soon became Cortés's interpreter, go-between, and negotiator. She persuaded a number of important chiefs to ally themselves with Cortés against the Aztecs. Clever and opportunistic, Doña Marina was a crucial strategist in Cortés's deadly game of divide and conquer. She eventually bore Cortés a son and lived in honor and riches for many years, profiting greatly from the Spaniards' exploitation of the Mexicans.

Latter-day Mexicans do not honor her by the gentle title of Doña Marina, however. They call her Malinche, after the volcano – an ugly, treacherous scar on the Mexican landscape – and curse her as the female Judas who betrayed her country to the Spanish. *Malinchismo* has become known as the tendency to love things foreign and hate things Mexican.

SIR FRANCIS DRAKE: THE PIRATE EL DRAQUE

The most renowned raider of the Spanish Main was Francis Drake, or the feared "El Draque," as the Spanish called him. The first European corsair to menace Spain's Pacific colonies, Drake left England in 1577 in command of five vessels and 166 men.

Supposedly headed on a trading mission to Africa, Drake's true purpose became clear when he ordered the attack and capture of a Portuguese merchant ship in the eastern Atlantic. By the time he had crossed westward to South America, his disillusioned crew and merchant partners on board mutinied. Executing the leader of the mutineers, Drake abandoned two of his least-seaworthy ships. Next, rallying the remainder of his men, he changed the name of his ship from the stodgy *Pelican* to the proud *Golden Hind*.

In attempting the westward passage through the stormy Strait of Magellan at the extreme southern tip of South America, he lost two of his remaining three ships. Undaunted, Drake sailed his *Golden Hind* up the west coast of South America, raiding and sacking every possible port – Valparaíso, Lima, Arica – and capturing the royal treasure ship the *Cacafuego*.

Contrary to the Spaniards' worst fears, Drake's approach to robbery was very courtly. No one, Spanish or native, was intentionally harmed. Treasure seemed to be Drake's sole objective. During his last attack on the Pacific Coast, at Huatulco on April 13, 1579, he even stole the church bell.

The ultimate prize, however, was the Manila galleon. He lurked offshore at Acapulco for a time, but seeing no treasure ship, Drake skipped northwest and dropped anchor and resupplied at undefended Zihuatanejo. He continued northwest for months, searching doggedly for the Manila galleon.

Finally, Drake stopped to rest at a safe anchorage, probably somewhere on the California coast, at a place that he recorded had cliffs as fair as the white cliffs of Dover (such as at Northern California's Point Reyes peninsula). He records in his log that he stayed for five weeks, traded with the native folks, repaired the *Golden Hind*, and erected his famous "plate of brass," yet to be found. On it he inscribed the claim, in the name of his queen, to the domain of "Nova Albion," now California.

The *Golden Hind* continued west across the Pacific, passing the Spice Islands and India and rounding the south Cape of Africa. Drake arrived in England on September 26, 1580, for a glorious welcome by Queen Elizabeth, having voyaged 35,000 miles and collected a booty of 50,000 pounds of silver.

Villafuerte returned, and by 1530 had built two ships, the *San Miguel* and *San Marcos,* on the shore of Acapulco Bay. For his efforts, Villafuerte was awarded *encomienda* rights (taxes and labor of an indigenous district) over Acapulco and a big slice of the present Ixtapa-Zihuatanejo region. Among the dozen-odd early Pacific expeditions (several of which were personally financed by Cortés), five set out from Acapulco, but none ever returned.

Cortés's Monument

Disheartened by his failure to find China (or, at least, more golden cities), and discouraged with interference by his king's Mexican representatives, Cortés returned to Spain to reassert his authority at court. But mired down by lawsuits, a small war, and his daughter's marital troubles, he fell ill and died in Spain on December 2, 1547. Cortés's remains, according to his will, were eventually laid to rest in a vault at the Hospital de Jesús, which he had founded in Mexico City.

Since latter-day Mexican politics preclude memorials to the Spanish conquest, no monument anywhere in Mexico commemorates Cortés's remarkable achievements. His single monument, historians note, is Mexico itself.

The Manila Galleon

Although a handful of the early Spanish voyages of exploration did actually reach Asia, none had returned to Mexico until priest-navigator Andrés de Urdaneta discovered the north Pacific trade winds that propelled his ship *San Pedro* swiftly east back to America. He (together with the only other shipmate who had enough strength to do it) dropped anchor in Acapulco Bay on October 3, 1565, with a trove of Chinese treasures in his ship's hold.

Thus, more than three generations after Columbus and 40 years of failed trans-Pacific voyages from Mexico that lost dozens of ships and hundreds of lives, the western trade route to Asia was finally a reality.

Not long thereafter, authorities in Spain designated Acapulco as Mexico's sole Pacific trading port. Once a year, at least one silver-laden ship, known to the Spanish as the Nao de China, and to the English as the Manila Galleon, set sail for the Spanish colony of Manila in the Philippines. For more than 250 years thereafter, the Manila Galleon returned with an emperor's dream of rich silks, delicate porcelain, exquisite lacquerware, glittering gold, and rare spices.

Pirate Threats

After a Dutch pirate fleet, greedy for the Manila Galleon's treasure, had attacked Acapulco in 1614, New Spain Viceroy Diego Fernandez de Córdoba decided to build a fort overlooking Acapulco Bay. It successfully deterred hostile attacks, until termites, hurricanes, old age, and finally an earthquake finished the old fort off in 1776. A bigger, stronger fort, the Fuerte de San Diego, replaced it in 1783 and remains to the present day.

COLONIAL MEXICO
The Missionaries

Even while the conquistadores subjugated the Mexicans, missionaries began arriving to teach, heal, and baptize them. A dozen Franciscan brothers impressed natives and conquistadores alike by trekking the entire 300-mile stony path from Veracruz to Mexico City in 1523. Missionary authorities generally enjoyed a sympathetic ear from Charles V and his successors, who earnestly pursued Spain's Christian

mission, especially when it coincided with Spanish political and economic goals.

The King Takes Control

Increasingly after 1525, the crown, through the Council of the Indies, began to wrest power away from Cortés and his conquistador lieutenants, many of whom had been granted rights of *encomienda:* taxes and labor of an indigenous district. From the king's point of view, tribute pesos collected by *encomenderos* from their native serfs reduced the gold that would otherwise flow to the crown. Moreover, many *encomenderos* callously enslaved and sold their native wards for quick profit. Such abuses, coupled with European-introduced diseases, began to reduce the native Mexican population at an alarming rate.

The king and his councilors, realizing that without their local labor force New Spain would vanish, acted decisively, instituting liberal new laws and a powerful viceroy, Don Antonio de Mendoza, to enforce them.

Despite near-rebellion by the colonists, Mendoza and his successors kept the lid on New Spain. Although some *encomenderos* held their privileges into the 18th century, chattel slavery of native Mexicans was abolished and an uneasy peace reigned in Mexico for 10 generations.

The Church

Apart from the missionaries, whose authority flowed directly from the pope in Rome, Mexican parish churches *(parroquias),* most of which remain to the present day, were founded and controlled by local bishops. As did the missionaries, parish churches generally moderated the native Mexicans' toil.

Moreover, the church profited from the status quo. The biblical tithe—one-tenth of everything earned—filled clerical coffers. By 1800, the church owned half of Mexico.

Moreover, both the clergy and the military were doubly privileged. They enjoyed the right of *fuero* (exemption from civil law) and could be prosecuted only by ecclesiastical or military courts.

POPULATION CHANGES IN NEW SPAIN

	Early Colonial (1570)	Late Colonial (1810)
peninsulares	6,600	15,000
criollos	11,000	1,100,000
mestizos	2,400	704,000
indígenas	3,340,000	3,700,000
negros	22,000	630,000

Criollos—The New Mexicans

Nearly three centuries of colonial rule gave rise to a burgeoning population of more than a million *criollos*—Mexican-born, pure European descendants of Spanish colonists, many rich and educated—to whom power to rule was denied.

High government, church, and military office always had been the preserve of a tiny minority of *peninsulares*—whites born in Spain. *Criollos* could only watch in disgust as unlettered, unskilled *peninsulares,* derisively called *gachupines* (wearers of spurs), were boosted to authority over them.

Mestizos, *Indígenas,* and African Mexicans

Upper-class luxury existed by virtue of the sweat of Mexico's mestizo, *indígena* (indigenous), and *negro* laborers and servants. African slaves were imported in large numbers during the 17th century after typhus, smallpox, and measles epidemics had wiped out most of the *indígena* population. Although the African Mexicans, whose communities are still concentrated around Veracruz and the Costa Chica east of Acapulco, contributed significantly (crafts, healing arts, dance, cuisine, music, drums, and marimba), they had arrived last and experienced discrimination from everyone.

INDEPENDENCE

Although the *criollos* stood high above the mestizo, *indígena,* and *negro* underclasses, that seemed little compensation for the false smiles, deep bows, and costly bribes that *gachupines* (wearers of spurs) demanded. Most *criollos,* inspired by the example of the recent American and French revolutions, talked and dreamed of independence. One such group, urged by a firebrand parish priest, acted.

El Grito de Dolores

"¡Viva México! Death to the gachupines!" Father Miguel Hidalgo cried passionately from the church balcony in the Guanajuato town of Dolores on September 16, 1810, igniting action. A mostly *indígena,* machete-wielding army of 20,000 coalesced around Hidalgo and his compatriots. Their ragtag force raged out of control through central Mexico, massacring hated *gachupines* and pillaging their homes.

Hidalgo advanced on Mexico City but, unnerved by stiff royalist resistance, retreated and regrouped around Guadalajara. His rebels, whose numbers had swollen to 80,000, were no match for a disciplined 6,000-strong royalist force. On January 17, 1811, Hidalgo (now "Generalisimo") fled north toward the United States but was soon apprehended, defrocked, and executed.

The 10-Year Struggle

Others carried on, however. Hidalgo's heroic efforts had immediately found crucial support in the Ixtapa-Zihuatanejo region. An African-Mexican former student of Hidalgo, José María Morelos, journeyed south from central Mexico and recruited an entire rebel brigade in the Costa Grande countryside. Drawn by the riches of the Manila galleon deposited at the port, the rebel force laid siege to Acapulco. Morelos, however, took half of his troops north, where he achieved signal victories, capturing Chilpancingo, Tixtla, and Chilapa, in upcountry present-day Guerrero.

Buoyed by success, Morelos focused the independence movement in Chilpancingo, organizing the Congress of Anahuac that declared Mexican independence from Spain on November 6, 1813. Continuously threatened by Spanish counterattacks, Morelos successfully kept the Congress of Anahuac intact by moving the delegates, one step ahead of the Spanish troops, to a number of southern Mexico locations. Tragically, however, Morelos was captured and executed by the Spanish in December, 1815.

After Morelos's death, his compatriot, Vicente Guerrero, also of African-Mexican descent, continued their hit-and-run guerilla campaign for six more years. Finally, with war-weary Mexican conservatives beginning to defect to the cause of Mexican independence, the royalist commander in the south, Brigadier Agustín de Itúrbide, asked for a meeting with Guerrero. Guerrero was impressed by Itúrbide's moderate proposal: that Mexico should become an independent constitutional monarchy, headed by the king of Spain, and based on "Three Guarantees"—the renowned Trigarantías, of independence, Catholicism, and equality—that their army would enforce.

Mexico Wins Independence

On February 24, 1821, in the Acapulco-region town of Iguala, Guerrero and Itúrbide announced their proposal, which became known, famously, as the Plan de Iguala. The plan immediately gained wide support, and on September 21, 1821, Itúrbide rode triumphantly into Mexico City at the head of his Army of Trigarantías. Mexico was independent at last.

The Rise and Fall of Agustín I

After the king of Spain refused titular reign over an independent Mexico, Itúrbide got himself crowned Mexican Emperor Agustín I by the bishop of Guadalajara on July 21, 1822. He soon lost his charisma, however. In a pattern that became sadly predictable for generations of topsy-turvy Mexican politics, an ambitious garrison commander issued a *pronunciamiento,* or declaration of rebellion, against him; old revolutionary heroes endorsed a plan to install a republic. Itúrbide, his braid tattered and brass tarnished, abdicated in February 1823.

The Disastrous Era of Santa Anna

The new Mexican republic, founded in 1824, teetered along, changing hands between conservative and liberal control, for nine chaotic years. By 1833, the government was bankrupt; mobs demanded the ouster of conservative president Anastasio Bustamante, who had executed the rebellious old revolutionary hero, Vicente Guerrero.

Antonio López de Santa Anna, the ambitious military commander whose troops had defeated an abortive Spanish counterrevolution in Veracruz, issued a *pronunciamiento* (declaration of rebellion) against Bustamante; Congress obliged, elevating Santa Anna to "Liberator of the Republic" and naming him president in March 1833.

Santa Anna would pop in and out of the presidency like a jack-in-the-box 10 more times before 1855. First, he foolishly lost Texas to rebellious Anglo settlers in 1836; then he lost his leg (which was buried with full military honors) fighting the emperor of France.

Santa Anna's greatest debacle, however, was to declare war on the United States in 1847, with just 1,839 pesos in the treasury. Within few months, a relatively small 10,000-man American invasion force, led by United States Marines, surged into the "Halls of Montezuma," Chapultepec Castle, where Mexico's six beloved Niños Héroes cadets fell in the losing cause on September 13, 1847.

In the subsequent treaty of Guadalupe Hidalgo, Mexico lost roughly half of its territory—the present states of New Mexico, Arizona, California, Nevada, Utah, and Colorado—to the United States. Eventually, Mexican leaders decided enough was enough, and forced Santa Anna to flee into permanent exile in 1855.

REFORM, CIVIL WAR, AND INTERVENTION

While conservatives searched for a king to replace Santa Anna, liberals, led by Supreme Court Chief Justice Benito Juárez, plunged ahead with three controversial reform laws: the

Ley Juárez, Ley Lerdo, and Ley Iglesias. These *reformas,* augmented by a new Constitution of 1857, directly attacked the privilege and power of Mexico's landlords, clergy, and generals. They abolished *fueros* (the separate military and church courts), reduced huge landed estates, and stripped the church of its excess property and power.

Conservative generals, priests, *hacendados* (landholders), and their mestizo and *indígena* followers revolted. The resulting War of the Reform (not unlike the U.S. Civil War) ravaged the countryside for three long years. The liberal cause was led by Juárez, acting as interim president, and spearheaded by the forces of general Juan Álvarez, whose brigades eventually won out over conservative general Miguel Miramón. Finally, the victorious liberal army paraded triumphantly in Mexico City on New Year's Day, 1861.

Juárez and Maximilian

Benito Juárez, the leading *reformista,* who was officially elected president in March 1861, had won the day. Like his contemporary Abraham Lincoln, Juárez, of pure Zapotec native blood, overcame his humble origins to become a lawyer, a champion of justice, and the savior who held his country together during a terrible civil war. As Lincoln, Juárez had little time to savor his triumph.

Imperial France invaded Mexico in January 1862, initiating the bloody five-year struggle known infamously as the French Intervention. After two costly years, the French pushed Juárez's liberal army into the hills and installed Austrian Archduke Maximilian and his wife, Carlota, the very models of modern Catholic monarchs, as crowned emperor and empress of Mexico in June, 1864.

Juárez, however, refused to yield, stubbornly performing his constitutional duties in a somber black carriage, one jump ahead of the French occupying army. The climax came in May 1867, when liberal forces besieged and defeated Maximilian's army at Querétaro. Juárez, giving no quarter, sternly ordered Maximilian's execution by firing squad on June 19, 1867.

RECONSTRUCTION AND THE PORFIRIATO

Juárez worked day and night at the double task of reconstruction and reform. He won reelection but died, exhausted, at his work-desk, in 1872.

The death of Juárez, the stoic partisan of reform, signaled hope to Mexico's conservatives. They soon got their wish: General Don Porfirio Díaz, the "Coming Man," was elected president in 1876.

Pax Porfiriana

Although Porfirio Díaz's humble Oaxaca mestizo origins were not unlike Juárez's, Díaz was not a democrat: When he was a general, his officers took no captives; when he was president, his country police, the *rurales,* shot prisoners in the act of "trying to escape."

Order and progress, in that sequence, ruled Mexico for 34 years. Foreign investment flowed into the country; new railroads brought the products of shiny factories, mines, and farms to modernized Gulf and Pacific ports.

The human price was high. Don Porfirio allowed more than 100 million acres—one-fifth of Mexico's land area (including most of the arable land)—to fall into the hands of his friends and foreigners. Poor Mexicans suffered the most. By 1910, 90 percent of the *indígenas* had lost their traditional communal land.

REVOLUTION AND STABILIZATION
¡No Reelección!

Porfirio Díaz himself had first campaigned on the slogan *No Reelección,* which expresses the idea that the president should step down after one term. Although Díaz had stepped down once in 1880, he had gotten himself reelected for 26 consecutive years. In 1910, Francisco I. Madero, a short, squeaky-voiced son of rich landowners, opposed Díaz under the same banner.

Although Díaz had jailed him before the election, Madero refused to quit campaigning. From a safe platform in the United States, he called for a revolution to begin on November 20, 1910.

Villa and Zapata

Not much happened, but soon the millions of poor Mexicans who had been going to bed hungry began to stir. In Chihuahua, followers of Francisco (Pancho) Villa, an erstwhile ranch hand, miner, peddler, and cattle rustler, began attacking the *rurales* (federal police force), dynamiting railroads, and raiding towns. Meanwhile, in the south, horse trader, farmer, and minor official Emiliano Zapata and his *indígena* guerrillas were terrorizing rich *hacendados* and forcibly recovering stolen ancestral village lands. Both Villa's and Zapata's movements gained steam and the *federales* (government army troops) began deserting in droves. On May 25, 1911, Díaz submitted his resignation.

As Madero's deputy, general Victoriano Huerta, put Díaz on his ship of exile in Veracruz, Díaz confided, "Madero has unleashed a tiger. Now let's see if he can control it."

The Fighting Continues

Emiliano Zapata, it turned out, was the tiger Madero had unleashed. Meeting with Madero in Mexico City, Zapata fumed over Madero's go-slow approach to the "agrarian problem," as Madero termed it. By November, Zapata had denounced Madero. *"¡Tierra y Libertad!"* ("Land and Liberty!") the Zapatistas cried, as Madero's support faded. The army in Mexico City rebelled; Huerta forced Madero to resign on February 18, 1913, and then murdered him four days later.

But, Huerta was refused U.S. recognition, and pressed on all sides by Zapata in the south, and Villa and newcomer general Venustiano Carranza in the north. Huerta fled into exile in July, 1914.

Fighting sputtered on for three years as authority see-sawed between revolutionary factions. Finally Carranza, whose forces ended up controlling most of the country by 1917, got a convention together in Querétaro to formulate political and social goals. The resulting Constitution of 1917, while restating most ideas of the Reformistas' 1857 constitution, additionally prescribed a single four-year presidential term, labor reform, and subordinated private ownership to public interest. Every village had a right to communal *ejido* land, and subsoil wealth could never be sold away to the highest bidder. In modified form, the Constitution of 1917 has lasted until the present day.

Obregón Stabilizes Mexico

On December 1, 1920, the revolutionary hero, general Álvaro Obregón legally assumed the presidency of a Mexico still bleeding from 10 years of civil war. Although a seasoned revolutionary, Obregón was also a pragmatist who recognized that Mexico needed peace.

Obregon's successful efforts set the stage for Plutarco Elías Calles, his minister of *gobernación* (interior) and handpicked successor, who won the 1924 election. Calles brought the army under civilian control, balanced the budget, and shifted Mexico's social revolution into high gear by redistributing millions of acres to landless campesinos.

But, by single-mindedly enforcing the pro-agrarian, pro-labor, and anti-clerical articles of the 1917 constitution, Calles made many influential enemies. Although he started out brimming with populist zeal, Calles became increasingly dictatorial. Although he bowed out peaceably in favor of Obregón (the constitution had been amended to allow one six-year nonsuccessive term), Obregón was assassinated two weeks after his election in 1928. Calles continued to rule for six more years through three puppet presidents: Emilio Portes Gil (1928–1930), Pascual Ortíz Rubio (1930–1932), and Abelardo Rodríguez (1932–1934). In blessing his minister of war, general Lázaro Cárdenas, for the 1934 presidential election, Calles expected more of the same.

Lázaro Cárdenas, President of the People

The 40-year-old Cárdenas, former governor of Michoacán, immediately set his own agenda, however. He worked tirelessly to fulfill the social prescriptions of the revolution. As morning-coated diplomats fretted, waiting in his outer office, Cárdenas ushered in delegations of campesinos and factory workers and sympathetically listened to their petitions. As a result, he redistributed 49 million acres of farmland, more than any president before or since.

Cárdenas's resolute enforcement of the constitution's Artículo 123 brought him the most renown. Under this pro-labor law, the government turned over a host of private companies to employee ownership and, on March 18, 1938, expropriated all foreign oil corporations.

Although Standard Oil cried foul, U.S. president Franklin Roosevelt did not intervene. Through negotiation and due process, the U.S. companies eventually were compensated with $24 million, plus interest. In the wake of the expropriation, President Cárdenas created Petróleos Mexicanos (Pemex), the national oil corporation that continues to run Mexican oil and gas operations.

Manuel Avila Camacho

Manuel Avila Camacho, elected in 1940, was the last general to be president of Mexico. His administration ushered in a gradual shift of Mexican politics, government, and foreign policy as Mexico allied itself with the U.S. cause during World War II. Foreign tourism, initially promoted by the Cárdenas administration, ballooned.

In both word and deed, moderation and evolution guided President Camacho's policies. *"Soy creente"* ("I am a believer"), he declared to the Catholics of Mexico as he worked earnestly to bridge Mexico's serious church–state schism.

As World War II moved toward its 1945 conclusion, both the United States and Mexico were enjoying the benefits of four years of governmental and military cooperation and mutual trade in the form of a mountain of strategic minerals that had moved north in exchange for a similar mountain of U.S. manufactures that moved south.

CONTEMPORARY MEXICO
The Mature Revolution

During the decades after World War II,

beginning with moderate president Miguel Alemán (1946–1952), Mexican politicians gradually honed their skills of consensus and compromise as their middle-aged revolution bubbled along under liberal presidents and sputtered haltingly under conservatives.

Mexico's revolution hasn't been very revolutionary about women's rights, however. The dominant political party, PRI (Partido Revolucionario Institucional) didn't get around to giving Mexican women, millions of whom fought and died during the revolution, the right to vote until 1953.

Voting for the first time in a national election, women helped keep the PRI in power by electing liberal Adolfo López Mateos in 1958. Resembling Lázaro Cárdenas in social policy, López Mateos redistributed 40 million acres of farmland, forced automakers to use 60 percent domestic components, built thousands of new schools, and distributed hundreds of millions of new textbooks.

In 1964, as several times before, the outgoing president's interior secretary succeeded his former chief. Dour, conservative Gustavo Díaz Ordaz immediately clashed with liberals, labor, and students. The pot boiled over just before the 1968 Mexico City Olympics. Reacting to a student rebellion, the army occupied the National University; shortly afterward, on October 2, government forces opened fire with machine guns on a downtown protest, killing and wounding hundreds of demonstrators. This incident, an open wound on Mexico's body politic, was never investigated until July, 2002, during the presidency of Vicente Fox.

Maquiladoras

Despite its serious internal troubles, Mexico's relations with the United States were cordial. President Lyndon Johnson visited and unveiled a statue of Abraham Lincoln in Mexico City. Later, Díaz Ordaz met with president Richard Nixon in Acapulco.

Meanwhile, bilateral negotiations produced the **Border Industrialization Program.** Within a 12-mile strip south of the U.S.-Mexico border, foreign companies could assemble duty-free parts into finished goods and export them without any duties on either side. Within a dozen years, a swarm of such plants, called maquiladoras, were humming as hundreds of thousands of Mexican workers assembled and exported billions of dollars worth of shiny consumer goods—electronics, clothes, furniture, pharmaceuticals, and toys—worldwide.

Oil Boom, Economic Bust

Discovery, in 1974, of gigantic new oil and gas reserves along Mexico's Gulf coast added fuel to Mexico's already rapid industrial expansion. During the late 1970s and early 1980s billions in foreign investment, lured by Mexico's oil earnings, financed other major developments—factories, hotels, power plants, roads, airports—all over the country.

The negative side to these expensive projects was the huge dollar debt required to finance them. President Luis Echeverría Alvarez (1970–1976), diverted by his interest in international affairs, passed Mexico's burgeoning financial deficit to his successor, José López Portillo. As feared by some experts, a world petroleum glut during the early 1980s burst Mexico's ballooning oil bubble and plunged the country into financial crisis, forcing Mexico's largest holding company to default on it debt payment in 1982, and unleashing inflation and five-fold collapse of the peso.

Although president Miguel de la Madrid (1982–1988) sweated, trying to put Mexico's economic house in order by slicing government, raising taxes, and getting foreign bankers to reschedule Mexico's debt, de la Madrid couldn't stop inflation. Prices skyrocketed as the peso deflated to 2,500 per U.S. dollar, becoming one of the world's most devalued currencies by 1988.

Salinas de Gortari and NAFTA

Public disgust led to significant opposition during the 1988 presidential election. But, despite strong showings by rival conservative PAN (National Action Party) and social-liberal PRD (Partido Revolucionario Democratico),

the PRI's Harvard-educated technocrat Carlos Salinas de Gortari prevailed in a close vote. Salinas climaxed middle-of-the-road presidency by negotiating the North American Free Trade Agreement (NAFTA) with U.S. president George Bush and Canadian prime minister Brian Mulrooney in 1992.

Rebellion, Assassination, and the 1994 Election

But, on the very day in early January 1994 that NAFTA took effect, rebellion broke out in the poor, remote state of Chiapas. A small but well-disciplined campesino force, calling itself Ejército Zapatista Liberación Nacional (Zapatista National Liberation Army or EZLN), or "Zapatistas," captured a number of provincial towns and held the former governor of Chiapas hostage.

To further complicate matters, while Salinas de Gortari's chief negotiator, Manuel Camacho Solís, was attempting to iron out a settlement with the Zapatista rebels, Luis Donaldo Colosio, Salinas's handpicked successor, was gunned down just months before the August balloting. However, instead of disintegrating, the nation united in grief; opposition candidates eulogized their fallen former opponent and later earnestly welcomed his replacement, stolid technocrat Ernesto Zedillo, in Mexico's first presidential election debate.

In a closely watched election relatively unmarred by irregularities, Zedillo piled up a solid plurality against his PAN and PRD opponents. By perpetuating the PRI's 65-year hold on the presidency, the electorate had again opted for the PRI's familiar although imperfect middle-aged revolution.

New Crisis, New Recovery

Zedillo enjoyed little time to savor his victory. The peso, after having been pumped up by Salinas's free and easy monetary policies, crashed, losing half of its value in the few months around Christmas 1994. Mexican financial institutions were in danger of defaulting on their obligations to international investors. To stave off a worldwide financial panic, U.S. President Clinton, in February 1995, secured an unprecedented multibillion-dollar loan package for Mexico.

Furthermore, Mexican democracy got a much-needed boost when notoriously corrupt Guerrero governor Ruben Figueroa was removed from office in disgrace. At the same time, the Zedillo government gained momentum in addressing the Zapatistas' grievances in Chiapas, decreasing federal military presence, building new rural electrification networks, and refurbishing health clinics.

Mexico's economy also began to improve. By mid-1996, inflation had slowed to a 20 percent annual rate, investment dollars were flowing back into Mexico, the peso had stabilized at about 7.5 to the U.S. dollar, and Mexico had paid back half the borrowed U.S. bailout money.

Zedillo's Political Reforms

Although Mexico's justice system left much to be desired, a pair of unprecedented political events signaled an increasingly open political system. In the 1997 congressional elections, voters elected a host of opposition candidates, depriving the PRI of an absolute congressional majority for the first time since 1929. A year later, in early 1998, Mexicans were participating in their country's first primary elections—in which voters, instead of politicians, chose party candidates.

Although President Zedillo had had a rough ride, he entered the twilight of his 1994–2000 term able to take credit for an improved economy, some genuine political reforms, and relative peace in the countryside. The election of 2000 revealed, however, that the Mexican people were not satisfied.

End of an Era: Vicente Fox Unseats the PRI

During 1998 and 1999 the focal point of opposition to the PRI's three-generation rule had been shifting from lackluster left-of-center PRD candidate Cuauhtémoc Cárdenas to relative newcomer Vicente Fox, former president of Coca-Cola Mexico and clean PAN ex-governor of Guanajuato.

Fox, who had announced his candidacy for president two years before the election, seemed an unlikely challenger. After all, the minority PAN had always been the party of wealthy businessmen and the conservative Catholic right. But blunt-talking, six-foot-five Fox, who sometimes campaigned in cowboy boots and a ten-gallon hat, preached populist themes of coalition building and "inclusion." He backed up his talk by carrying his campaign to hard-scrabble city *barrios,* dirt-poor country villages, and traditional outsider groups, such as Jews.

In a closely monitored election on July 2, 2000, Fox decisively defeated the PRI's Francisco Labastida, 42 percent to 38 percent, while Cárdenas received only 17 percent. Fox's win also swept a PAN plurality (223/209/57) into the 500-seat Chamber of Deputies lower house.

In removing the PRI from the all-powerful presidency after 71 consecutive years of domination, Fox had ushered Mexico into a new, hopefully more democratic, era.

Despite stinging criticism from his own ranks, President Zedillo, who historians were already judging as the real hero behind Mexico's new democratic era, made an unprecedented, early appeal, less than a week after the election, for all Mexicans to unite behind Fox.

Vicente Fox, President of Mexico

After his December 1, 2000, inauguration, Fox wasted little time getting started, first heading to Chiapas to negotiate with rebellious indigenous community leaders. Along the way, he shut down Chiapas military bases and removed dozens of military roadblocks. Back in Mexico City, he sent the long-delayed peace plan, including the proposed **indigenous bill of rights,** to Congress. Zapatista rebels responded by journeying en masse from Chiapas to Mexico City, where, in their black masks, they addressed Congress, arguing for more rights for Mexico's native peoples. Although by mid-2001 Congress had passed a modified version of the negotiated settlement, and the majority of states had ratified the required constitutional amendment, indigenous leaders condemned the legislation plan as watered down and unacceptable, while proponents claimed it was the best possible compromise between the Zapatistas' demands and the existing Mexican constitution.

Meanwhile, Fox continued to pry open the Mexican door to democracy. In May 2002, he signed Mexico's first freedom of information act, entitling citizens to timely copies of all public documents from federal agencies. Moreover, Fox's long-promised "Transparency Commission" was taking shape. In July 2002, federal attorneys were taking unprecedented action. They were questioning a list of 74 former government officials, including ex-president Luis Echeverría, about their roles in government transgressions, notably political murders and the University of Mexico massacres during the 1960s and 1970s.

But, Mexico's economy, reflecting the U.S. economic slowdown, began to sour in 2001, losing half a million jobs and cutting annual growth to 2.5 percent.

In the July 7, 2003, congressional elections, voters took their frustrations out on the PAN and gave its plurality in the Chamber of Deputies to the PRI. When the dust settled, the PRI total had risen to 225 seats, while the PAN had slipped to 153. The biggest winner, however, was the PRD, which gained more than 40 seats, to a total of about 100.

In early 2005, reflecting Vicente Fox's victory in 2000, democracy got a big boost in the Ixtapa-Zihuatanejo region as voters broke the PRI's 76-year lock-grip on the Guerrero governorship and state legislature. Furthermore, on February 6, 2005, voters swept the liberal populist PRD Afro-Mexican former mayor of Acapulco, Carlos Zeferino Torreblanca, into a six-year term in the governor's office. In doing so, voters expressed high hopes that the can-do Zeferino would lead Guerrero into a fresh new era of good government.

The Election of 2006

During the first half of 2006, as Vicente Fox was winding down his presidency, Mexicans were occupied by the campaign to elect his successor. Most headlines went to the PRD candidate, the mercurial leftist-populist Andres Manuel López Obrador, former mayor of Mexico City. Trying hard not to be upstaged was the steady, no-nonsense PAN candidate, Harvard-educated centrist-conservative Felipe Calderón, a leading light of President Fox's cabinet.

On Sunday, July 2, 2006, 42 million Mexicans cast their ballots. In an intensely monitored election marred by very few irregularities, unofficial returns indicated that voters had awarded Calderón a paper-thin plurality. Four days later, after all returns were counted, the Federal Electoral Institute announced the official vote tally: only about 22 percent for the PRI candidate, Roberto Madrazo, with the remaining lion's share divided nearly evenly, with 38.7 percent going to Obrador and 39.3 percent for Calderón. This result, the Federal Electoral Institute ruled, was too close to declare a winner without a recount of a doubtful 9 percent of the ballots. Concluded on September 5, 2006, the official recount showed Calderón, with 35.9 percent, the winner over Obrador, with 35.3 percent, and 22.3 percent for Madrazo. The remaining 6.5 percent was distributed among minor candidates (4.4 percent) and nullified (mostly double) votes (2.1 percent).

Besides the razor-thin Calderón-Obrador result, the election results revealed much more. Not only were the 32 electoral entities (31 states and the Federal District) divided equally, with 16 going for Obrador, and 16 for Calderón, the vote reflected a nearly complete north-south political schism, with nearly all of the 16 PAN-majority states forming a solid northern bloc, while the 16 PRD-voting states did the same in the south. Furthermore, the election appeared to signal a collapse of PRI power; with no state (nor the Federal District) giving either a majority or a plurality to Roberto Madrazo.

Election Aftermath

An important result of the 2006 election,

initially overshadowed by the intense struggle over the presidential vote, but potentially crucial, was the federal legislative vote, in which PAN emerged as the biggest winner by far. The final results showed that voters had given PAN candidates strong pluralities of 206/127/106 over the PRD and PRI, respectively, in the 500-seat federal Chamber of Deputies, and 52/29/33 in the 128-seat Senate, with the remainder of seats scattered among minor parties. This result seemed to bode well for Mexican democracy. With some cooperation (most likely from the PRI) Felipe Calderón seemed likely to be able to further the national political and economic reform agenda Vicente Fox had promised six years earlier, but could only partially deliver.

President Calderón Takes Charge

As he prepared for his December 1, 2006, inauguration, Felipe Calderón not only appeared to be both moving ahead with many of his predecessor's original proposals, but he also seemed to be reaching out to the PRI and the PRD with some new proposals. These, although containing much of PAN's pro-business pro-NAFTA ideas, also appeared to borrow considerably from the liberal-populist agenda of Obrador and the PRD and produce much-needed cooperation to push their country closer to the bright but elusive vision of a just and prosperous motherland for all Mexicans.

Calderón got started immediately, tackling Mexico's most immediate problem by declaring war on Mexico's drug lords. Right away he replaced most of the federal police chiefs, many suspected of corruption. He then put the Mexican army in charge of his war on drugs, eventually assigning more than 40,000 Mexican soldiers to seek and destroy criminal drug networks, especially in the drug-infested border states, notably the towns of Tijuana, Ciudad Juárez, and Nuevo Laredo, where criminal drug gangs had been assassinating incorruptible judges and local police officials and officers.

Concurrently, President Calderón skillfully guided the Mexican economy and politics, at both national and international levels. Under his guiding hand, during 2007, the Mexican economy continued to bubble along at a moderate annual growth rate of about 2.5 percent, inflation was kept at a low 4 percent, and the currency steadily held its value, between 10 and 11 pesos to the U.S. dollar.

Unfortunately, during the latter half of Calderón's term, Mexico's economy slumped. Mirroring the U.S. 2008–2009 downturn, Mexico's gross domestic product dropped 6 percent in 2009, but soon recovered, rising to 5 percent in 2010. Although the peso initially dropped a fraction during the same period, it mostly recovered and was holding steady at about 12 to the U.S. dollar during 2010 and 2011.

During the same period, Calderón, by both executive order and in concert with the Mexican federal legislatures, initiated a number of beneficial educational, health, and infrastructure measures. By the end of 2011, Mexico had opened more than 100 new colleges and universities, built at least 1,000 new hospitals and refurbished and enlarged 2,000 more in all corners of the country, providing access to free medical care for a total of 100,000,000 Mexicans (more than 90 percent of the population). Moreover, during the same period, Mexico added more than 10,000 miles (16,000 km) of brand-new interstate expressways to the Mexican highway system.

In the international sphere, behind Calderón, Mexico continued to lead, as a key partner in both the **Puebla-Panama Plan,** fostering democracy and cooperation against organized crime among Mexico's Latin-American neighbor states, and the bilateral **Márida Initiative,** developing security cooperation with the United States.

Also, during the latter three years (2009–2011) of his term, President Calderón increased pressure on Mexico's notorious network of drug cartels, prime traffickers of cocaine, marijuana, amphetamines, and heroin to drug dealers in the United States. Mexican police, soldiers, sailors, and marines killed or jailed approximately 3,000 low-level drug dealers and dozens of their kingpin bosses, thereby ramping up the turf warfare between the drug traffickers, who were desperately killing each other (with a total of 30,000 rival gang shootings) during the same 2009–2011 period.

Security Concerns

Such figures, as reported in sensational news stories must be weighed carefully. First of all, Mexico's "drug war" as President Calderón described it after his 2006 election, is mostly a turf war between the gangsters. Since then, approximately 90 percent of the drug-war casualties (many in deliberately macabre, terrorist-style) have been inflicted by the drug traffickers upon themselves. Only about 10 percent were inflicted on police and the military, and a tiny fraction (a small fraction of 1 percent) were inflicted on innocent Mexican bystanders. Virtually no foreign tourists have suffered any injuries at all.

Furthermore, nearly the entire battle is confined to the border states of Baja California Norte (Tijuana), Sonora (Nogales), Chihuahua (Ciudad Juarez), Coahuila (Saltillo), Nuevo León (Monterrey), and Tamaulipas (Nuevo Laredo). Despite the headlines, in most parts of Mexico (especially in the southern Pacific states of Guerrero, Oaxaca, and Chiapas) local, violent, drug-related incidents are very seldom, if at all.

Government and Economy

THE MEXICAN AND GUERRERO ECONOMIES
Post-Revolutionary Gains

By many measures, Mexico's 20th-century revolution appears to have succeeded. Since 1910, illiteracy has plunged tenfold from 80 to 8 percent; life expectancy has risen from 30 years to more than 70; infant mortality has dropped from a whopping 40 percent to about 2 percent; and, in terms of caloric intake, Mexicans are eating about twice as much as their forebears at the turn of the 20th century.

Decades of steady economic growth account for rising Mexican living standards. The Mexican economy has repeatedly rebounded from recessions by virtue of its plentiful natural resources, notably oil and metals; diversified manufacturing, such as cars, electronics, and petrochemicals; steadily increasing tourism; exports of fruits, vegetables, and cattle; and its large, willing low-wage workforce.

Recent Mexican governments, moreover, have skillfully exploited Mexico's economic strengths. The Border Industrialization Program has led to millions of jobs in thousands of border maquiladora factories, from Tijuana and the mouth of the Río Grande, now spreading to interior centers such as Monterrey, Guadalajara, and Mexico City. The increased manufacturing output has produced manifold economic benefits, including reduced dependency on oil exports and burgeoning job growth and foreign trade as Mexico joined in the General Agreement on Tariffs and Trade (GATT) in 1986 and NAFTA in 1994. Consequently, Mexico has become a net exporter of goods and services to the United States, its largest trading partner.

In 2000, the Fox administration continued Mexico's prudent economic course, which continued under President Calderón, thereby reducing inflation to a healthy level of about 4 percent 2004–2011. This helped stabilize the peso to between 10 and 13 per dollar for most of the 2000–2010 decade. And, despite the double 2001–2003 and 2008–2010 U.S.-Mexico economic slowdowns, Mexico recovered, with a healthy 5 percent growth rate during 2010.

Guerrero Economic Challenges

Many of Mexico's latter 20th-century economic gains have bypassed Mexico's poor southern states of Chiapas, Oaxaca, and Guerrero. Of the three, Guerrero perennially ranks low in many indicators of quality of life, such as income, infant mortality, malnutrition, and illiteracy.

For example, although illiteracy in Guerrero is already high, running at about 20 percent of all adults (compared with only about 9 percent for Mexico as a whole), illiteracy is more than double that (40 percent) among Guerrero's native Mexican adults. This is not surprising, since a large fraction of them have never completed any schooling at all.

As many studies show, poor education is invariably associated with poor health. Infant mortality, as high as 8 percent (1 in 12 babies die) in some indigenous Guerrero communities (with very few, if any, gynecologists), is more than 3 times the (2.8 percent) Mexico average and about 11 times the 0.9 percent (1 baby in 110) U.S. average. This also is not surprising, since the majority of Guerrero's native Mexican people lack regular access to health care.

Although rich in sunshine, mountainous Guerrero lacks arable land and needs more water and capital to irrigate what arable land exists. Under the right conditions, bountiful crops of sesame, corn, tomatoes, citrus, mangoes, peanuts, alfalfa, soy, and *chiles* sprout quickly from bottomland fields.

A potentially valuable crop in Guerrero is coffee, now cultivated by thousands of farmers in the vine-draped lower slopes of the coastal mountains. However, as all over the developing world, growing a crop is the easiest part of trying to make a living from it. Isolation, quality control, and lack of access to markets have kept Guerrero coffee farmers poor. It seems patently unjust that farmers can get only about $1 per pound for the same coffee that, after transport and roasting, sells in U.S. and European grocery stores for $5–10 per pound.

The bright part of the Guerrero economy has been both national and international tourism, which unfortunately has dropped fractionally in recent years, due to stumbling U.S. and Mexican economies and misplaced fears over Mexico's "drug war." Hopefully, as the economic situation improves and travelers learn that the Ixtapa-Zihuatanejo region is as beautiful (and reasonably priced) as ever, tourism

will rebound. This would be a blessing, since, both directly and indirectly, tourism accounts for most of the earnings of half of Ixtapa-Zihuatanejo region families. If it weren't for the resorts of Ixtapa- Zihuatanejo, Acapulco, and Taxco, most Guerrero folks would be even poorer than they are now.

Long-Term Economic Challenges

Despite huge gains, Mexico's Revolution of 1910 is nevertheless incomplete. Improved public health, education, income, and opportunity have barely outdistanced Mexico's population, which has increased more than sevenfold—from 15 million to 113 million—between 1910 and 2012. For example, although the illiteracy rate has decreased, the actual number of Mexican people who can't read, about 10 million, has remained about constant since 1910.

Moreover, the land reform program, once thought to be a Mexican cure-all, has long been a disappointment. The *ejidos* (communal farms) of which Emiliano Zapata dreamed have become mostly symbolic. The fields are typically small and unirrigated. Furthermore, *ejido* land, being communal, is not easily accepted by banks as loan collateral. Capital for irrigation networks, fertilizers, and harvesting machines is consequently lacking. Communal farms are typically inefficient; the average Mexican field produces about *one-quarter* as much corn per acre as a U.S. farm. Guerrero fields average even less. Mexico must accordingly use its precious oil-dollar surplus to import millions of tons of corn—originally indigenous to Mexico—annually.

The triple scourge of overpopulation, lack of arable land, and low farm income has driven millions of campesino families to seek better lives in Mexico's cities and in the United States. Chicago (with many tens of thousands of Guerrero-born residents) is the world's second-largest Guerreran city, ranking only behind Acapulco.

Since 1910, Mexico has evolved from a largely rural country, where 70 percent of the population lived on farms, to an urban nation where 80 percent of the population lives in cities. Fully one-fifth of Mexico's people now live in Mexico City, and one-third of Guerrero's people live in Acapulco.

Staples—wheat for bread, corn for tortillas, milk, and cooking oil—are all heavily imported and consequently expensive for the typical working-class Mexican family, which must spend half or more of its income (typically $500 per month) for food. Recent grain inflation has compounded the problem, particularly for the millions of families at the bottom half of Mexico's economic ladder.

Although average gross domestic product figures for Mexico—about $14,000 per capita (but less than half that for Guerrero) compared to about $47,000 for the United States—place Mexico above nearly all other developing countries, averages, when applied to Mexico (and especially Guerrero), mean little. A primary socioeconomic reality of Mexican history remains: The richest one-fifth of Mexican families earns about 10 times the income of the poorest one-fifth. A relative handful of people own a large hunk of Mexico, and they don't seem inclined to share much of it with the less fortunate. As for the poor, the typical Mexican and Guerrero family in the bottom one-third income bracket often owns neither a car nor a refrigerator, and the children typically do not finish elementary school.

GOVERNMENT AND POLITICS
The Constitution of 1917

Mexico's governmental system is rooted in the Constitution of 1917, which incorporated many of the features of its reformist predecessor of 1857. The 1917 document, with amendments, remains in force, both nationally and in similarly written individual state constitutions. Although drafted at the behest of conservative revolutionary Venustiano Carranza by his handpicked Querétaro "Constitucionalista" congress, it was greatly influenced by liberal Álvaro Obregón and generally ignored by Carranza during his subsequent three-year presidential term.

Although many articles resemble those of its U.S. model, the Constitution of 1917 contains provisions that stem directly from Mexican experience. Article 27 addresses the question of land. Private property rights are qualified by societal need; subsoil rights are public property, and foreigners and corporations are severely restricted in land ownership. Although the 1917 constitution declared *ejido* land inviolate, 1994 amendments allow, under certain circumstances, the sale or use of communal land as loan security.

Article 23 severely restricts church powers. In declaring that "places of worship are the property of the nation," it stripped churches of all title to real estate, without compensation. Article 5 and Article 130 banned religious missionary orders, expelled foreign clergy, and denied priests and ministers all political rights, including voting, holding office, and even criticizing the government.

Article 123 establishes the rights of labor: to organize, bargain collectively, strike, work a maximum eight-hour day, and receive a minimum wage. Women are to receive equal pay for equal work and be given a month's paid leave for childbearing. Article 123 also establishes social security plans for sickness, unemployment, pensions, and death.

On paper, Mexico's constitutional government structures appear much like their U.S. prototypes: a federal presidency, a two-house Congress (single house in Guerrero), and a Supreme Court, with their counterparts in each of the 32 states. Political parties field candidates, and citizens vote by secret ballot.

Mexico's presidents, however, have traditionally enjoyed greater powers than their U.S. counterparts. They need not seek legislative approval for many cabinet appointments, can suspend constitutional rights under a state of siege, can initiate legislation, veto all or parts of bills, refuse to execute laws, and replace state officers (as President Zedillo removed Guerrero governor Ruben Figueroa in 1995). The federal government, moreover, retains nearly all taxing authority, relegating the states to a role of merely administering federal programs.

Although ideally providing for separation of powers, the Constitution of 1917 subordinates both the legislative and judicial branches, with the courts being the weakest of all. The Supreme Court, for example, can only, with repeated deliberation, decide upon the constitutionality of legislation. Five separate individuals must file successful petitions for writs *amparo* (protection) on a single point of law to affect constitutional precedent.

Democratizing Mexican and Guerrero Politics

Reforms in Mexico's stable but top-heavy "Institutional Revolution" came only gradually. Characteristically, street protests were brutally put down at first, with officials only later working to address grievances. Generations of dominance by the PRI, the "Institutional Revolutionary Party," led to widespread cynicism and citizen apathy. Regardless of who gets elected, the typical person on the street may still say that the officeholder is bound to retire with his or her pockets full.

Nevertheless, by 1985, movement toward more justice and pluralism seemed to be in store for Mexico. During the subsequent dozen years, minority parties increasingly elected candidates to state and federal office. Although none captured a majority of any state legislature, the strongest non-PRI parties, such as the conservative pro-Catholic Partido Acción Nacional (PAN, National Action Party) and the liberal-left Partido Revolucionario Democrático (PRD), elected governors.

After his 1994 inaugural address, in which he called loudly and clearly for more reforms, president Ernesto Zedillo quickly began to produce results. He immediately appointed a respected member of the PAN opposition party as attorney general—the first non-PRI cabinet appointment in Mexican history. Other Zedillo firsts were federal Senate confirmation of both Supreme Court nominees and the attorney general, multiparty participation in the Chiapas peace negotiations, and congressional approval of the 1995 financial assistance package received from the United States.

Perhaps most important was Zedillo's campaign and inaugural vow to separate both his government and himself from PRI decision-making. He kept his promise, becoming the first Mexican president, in as long as anyone could remember, who did not choose his successor.

A New Mexican Revolution

Finally, in 2000, like a Mexican Gorbachev, Ernesto Zedillo, the man responsible for many of Mexico's earlier democratic reforms, watched as PAN opposition reformer Vicente Fox swept Zedillo's PRI from the presidency after a 71-year rule. Moreover, despite severe criticism from his own party, Zedillo quickly called for the country to close ranks behind Fox. Millions of Mexicans, still dazed but buoyed by Zedillo's statesmanship and Fox's epoch-making victory, eagerly awaited Fox's inauguration address on December 1, 2000.

But five years later, in early 2006, with his grand vision—reduced poverty, free trade, reformed judiciary, government transparency, indigenous rights—only part fulfilled, no one could fairly say that Vicente Fox didn't try. He remained true to his belief in a democratic presidency: negotiating, haranguing, cajoling, and compromising with a cadre of legislators who stubbornly blocked many of his reform proposals.

Time and again Vicente Fox admitted the messiness and difficulty of the democratic process. But he also remained convinced and committed that there could be no turning from the democratic path for Mexico. In a 2004 interview, he pointed out that, at least, he had ended "Presidencialismo," the decades-old Mexican habit of bowing to a strong, even sometimes ruthless, president.

Upon election in 2006, Felipe Calderón earnestly continued along Vicente Fox's path to Mexican democracy. It is to Calderón's great credit, with the onerously troubling distraction of Mexico's drug cartels, that he's kept Mexico on the democratic path, and even encouraged Mexico's Latin American neighbors to join him.

People and Culture

Let a broad wooden chopping block represent Mexico; imagine hacking it with a sharp cleaver until it is grooved and pocked. That fractured surface resembles Mexico's central highlands, where most Mexicans, divided from each other by high mountains and yawning *barrancas* (ravines), have lived since before history.

The Mexicans' deep divisions, in large measure, led to their downfall at the hands of the Spanish conquistadores. The Aztec empire that Hernán Cortés conquered was a vast but fragmented collection of tribes. Speaking more than 100 mutually alien languages, those original Mexicans viewed each other suspiciously, as barely human barbarians from strange lands beyond the mountains. And even today the lines Mexicans draw between themselves—of caste, class, race, wealth—are the result, to a significant degree, of the realities of their mutual isolation.

POPULATION

The Spanish colonial government and the Roman Catholic religion provided the glue that through 400 years has welded Mexico's fragmented people into a burgeoning nation-state. Mexico's population, around 113 million in 2011, has increased by about 10 percent since 2000, but at a yearly rate diminished to about half that of the previous decade. Increased birth control and emigration largely account for the slowdown.

For similar reasons, Guerrero's population, estimated at about 3.3 million in 2011, is increasing, but at an even slower rate than Mexico in general. Compared to the 18 percent (1.8 percent yearly) increase from 1990 to 2000, Guerrero's population increase has slowed three-fold, to only about a 0.6 percent average yearly increase for the 2000–2011 period. This probably represents Guerrero's large yearly emigration to other places in Mexico and the United States (where, by the beginning of 2011, about a million Guerrero-born folks were living).

Mexico's population has not always been increasing. Historians estimate that European diseases, largely measles and smallpox, wiped out as many as 20 million—perhaps as much as 95 percent—of the *indígena* population within a few generations after Cortés stepped ashore in 1519. The Mexican population dwindled from an estimated 20 million at the eve of the conquest to a mere one million inhabitants by 1600. It wasn't until 1950, four centuries after Cortés, that Mexico's population recovered to its pre-conquest level of about 20 million.

Mestizos, *Indígenas*, *Criollos*, and African Mexicans

Although by 1950 Mexico's population had recovered, it was completely transformed. The mestizo, a Spanish-speaking person of mixed blood, had replaced the pure native Mexican, the *indígena* (een-DEE-hay-nah), as the typical Mexican.

The trend continues. Perhaps three of four Mexicans would identify themselves as mestizo, that class whose part-European blood elevates them, in the Mexican mind, to the level of *gente de razón* (people of "reason" or "right"). And there's the rub. The *indígenas* (or, mistakenly but much more commonly, Indians), by the usual measurements of income, health, or education, squat at the bottom of the Mexican social ladder.

The typical *indígena* family lives in a small adobe house in a remote valley, subsisting on corn, beans, and vegetables from its small, unirrigated *milpa* (family-owned field). They usually have chickens, a few pigs, and sometimes a cow, but no electricity; their few hundred dollars a year in cash income isn't enough to buy even a small gas refrigerator, much less a truck.

The usual mestizo family, on the other hand, enjoys most of the benefits of the 20th century. They typically own a modest concrete house in town. Their furnishings, simple by developed-world standards, will often include an electric refrigerator, washing machine, propane stove, television, and car or truck. The children go to

MEXICAN NAMES

Foreign visitors, confounded by long handles such as Doña Juana María López de Díaz, wonder how Mexican names got so complicated.

The preceding Doña Juana example is especially complicated because it's a typical woman's name, and women's names are generally more complex than typical men's names.

So, let's explain a man's name first. Take the national hero, Vicente Ramón Guerrero Saldaña. Vicente is his first given name; Ramón, his second given name, corresponding to the "middle" name in the United States. The third, Guerrero, is customarily the father's first surname, and the last, Saldaña, his mother's first surname. Only on formal occasions are men referred to with all four of their names. Simply Vicente Guerrero would do most of the time.

Now, back to Doña Juana. I threw a curve at you by introducing "Doña." It's an honorific, used as "Dame," for a distinguished woman. ("Don" is the corresponding honorific for Spanish men.)

So, skipping the honorific, women's names start out like men's: first given name, Juana; second given name, María, and father's first surname, López.

Now, things get more complicated. For unmarried women, the naming is the same as for men. But when a woman gets married, she customarily replaces her second surname with her husband's first surname, preceded by "de," meaning "of." So in the example, Juana is evidently a married woman, who has substituted "de Díaz" (her husband's first surname being Díaz) for her second surname, all adding up to "Juana María López de Díaz."

Thankfully, however, informal names for women also are simplified. Juana, above, would ordinarily shorten her name to her first given name, followed by her husband's first surname: simply Juana Díaz.

All of the above notwithstanding, many Mexican women do not go along with this male-dominated system at all and simply use their maiden names as they were known before they were married.

---

school every day, and the eldest son sometimes looks forward to college.

Sizable *negro* communities, totaling around 150,000 people, descendants of 18th-century African slaves, live along the Guerrero-Oaxaca Pacific coastline. Last to arrive, the *negros* experience discrimination at the hands of everyone else and are integrating very slowly into the mestizo mainstream.

Above the mestizos, a small *criollo* (Euro-Mexican) minority, a few percent of the total population, inherits the privileges—wealth, education, and political power—of its colonial Spanish ancestors.

THE *INDÍGENAS*

Although anthropologists and census takers classify them according to language groups (such as Náhuatl, Mixtec, and Zapotec), *indígenas* generally identify themselves as residents of a particular locality rather than by language or ethnic grouping. And although as a group they are referred to as *indígenas* (native, or aboriginal), individuals are generally uncomfortable being labeled as such.

Recent census figures indicate at least 8 percent of Mexicans are *indígenas*—that is, they speak one of Mexico's 50-odd native languages. The indigenous presence in Guerrero is stronger than in Mexico in general, with four major groups, totaling about 460,000 people, or about 14 percent of the Guerrero population. The largest group, about 200,000, speak **Nahuatl** (the historical Aztec tongue); the others speak **Mixtec** (120,000), **Tlapanec** (100,000), and **Amuzgo** (40,000). Of these, a sizable (about 80 percent) fraction speak no Spanish at all. Moreover, these populations are shifting only gradually. Many *indígenas* prefer the old ways.

While the mestizos are the emergent self-conscious majority class, the *indígenas,* as during colonial times, remain the invisible people of Mexico. They are politically conservative, socially traditional, and tied to the land. On

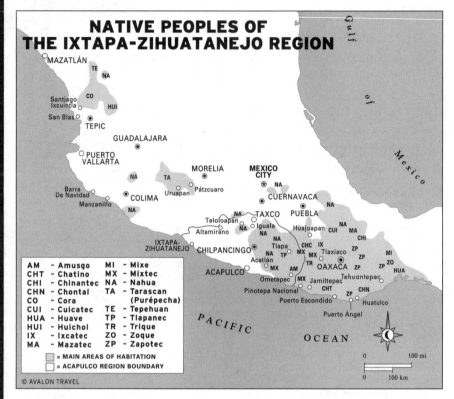

NATIVE PEOPLES OF THE IXTAPA-ZIHUATANEJO REGION

AM	– Amusgo	MI	– Mixe
CHT	– Chatino	MX	– Mixtec
CHI	– Chinantec	NA	– Nahua
CHN	– Chontal	TA	– Tarascan
CO	– Cora		(Purépecha)
CUI	– Cuicatec	TE	– Tepehuan
HUA	– Huave	TP	– Tlapanec
HUI	– Huichol	TR	– Trique
IX	– Ixcatec	ZO	– Zoque
MA	– Mazatec	ZP	– Zapotec

= MAIN AREAS OF HABITATION
= ACAPULCO REGION BOUNDARY

© AVALON TRAVEL

market day, the typical *indígena* family might make the trip into town. They bag tomatoes, squash, or peppers, and tie up a few chickens or a pig. The rickety country bus will often be full and the mestizo driver may wave them away, giving preference to his friends, leaving them to trudge stoically along the road. Indigenous people from all over Mexico, especially the southeast states of Michoacan, Guerrero, and Oaxaca, come to Acapulco, Taxco, and Ixtapa-Zihuatanejo to sell their crafts.

Their lot, nevertheless, has been slowly improving. *Indígena* families now sometimes have access to a local school and a clinic. Improved health has led to an increase in their population. Official census figures, however, are probably low. *Indigenas* are traditionally suspicious of government people, and census takers, however conscientious, seldom speak the local language.

Indígena Language Groups

The Maya speakers of Yucatán and the aggregate of the Náhuatl (Aztec language) speakers of the central plateau are Mexico's most numerous *indígena* groups, totaling three million (one million Maya, two million Nahua).

Official figures of the indigenous population in the Ixtapa-Zihuatanejo region may be misleading. Official counts often do not measure the droves of transient folks—migrants and new arrivals—who sleep in vehicles, shantytowns, behind their crafts stalls, and with friends and relatives. Although they are officially invisible, you will see them in Taxco, Acapulco, and Ixtapa-Zihatanejo, trudging along the beach, for example, laden with their for-sale fruit or handicrafts—men in sombreros and scruffy jeans, women in homemade full-skirted dresses with aprons much like your great-great-grandmother may have worn.

Immigrants in their own country, indigenous people flock to cities and tourist resorts from hardscrabble rural areas. Although of pure native blood, they will not acknowledge it or will even be insulted if you ask them if they are *indígenas.* It would be more polite to ask them where they're from. If from Michoacán, they'll usually speak Tarasco (more courteously, say Purépecha: poo-RAY-pay-chah); if from Oaxaca, they'll probably speak Zapateco, Mixteco, or Chatino; people from Guerrero will typically speak Náhuatl, Tlapaneco, Mixteco, or Amusgo.

As immigrants always have, they come seeking a better life. If you're interested in what they're selling, bargain with humor. And if you err, let it be on the generous side. They are proud, honorable people who prefer to walk away from a sale rather than to lose their dignity.

Dress

Country markets are where you're most likely to see people in traditional dress. There, some elderly men still wear the white cottons that blend Spanish and native styles. Absolutely necessary for men is the Spanish-origin palm-leaf, reed, or straw sombrero (literally, shade-maker) on their heads, loose white cotton shirt and pants, and leather huaraches on their feet.

Women's dress, by contrast, is more colorful. It can include a *huipil* (long, embroidered dress) embroidered in bright floral and animal motifs and a handwoven *enredo* (wraparound skirt that identifies the wearer with a locality; called a *pozahuanco* in the Costa Chica). A *faja* (waist sash) and, in winter, a *quechquémitl* (shoulder cape) complete the ensemble.

RELIGION

"God and Gold" was the two-pronged mission of the conquistadores. Most of them concentrated on gold, while missionaries tried to shift the emphasis to God. They were famously successful; more than 90 percent of Mexicans (about 77 percent of Guerrero people) profess to be Catholics.

Catholicism, spreading its doctrine of equality of all people before God and incorporating native gods into the church rituals, eventually brought the *indígenas* into the fold. Within 100 years, nearly all native Mexicans had accepted the new religion, which raised the universal God of humankind over local tribal deities.

The Virgin of Guadalupe

Conversion of the *indígenas* was sparked by the vision of Juan Diego, a humble farmer. In 1531, on the hill of Tepayac north of Mexico City, Juan Diego saw a brown-skinned version of the Virgin Mary enclosed in a dazzling aura of light. She told him to build a shrine in her memory on that spot, where the Aztecs had long worshipped their "earth mother," Tonantzín. Juan Diego's brown virgin told him to go to the cathedral and relay her instruction to Archbishop Zumárraga.

The archbishop, as expected, turned his nose up at Juan Diego's story. The vision returned, however, and this time Juan Diego's brown virgin realized that a miracle was necessary. She ordered him to pick some roses at the spot where she had first appeared to him (a true miracle, since roses had been previously unknown in the vicinity) and take them to the archbishop. Juan Diego wrapped the roses in his rude fiber cape, returned to the cathedral, and placed the wrapped roses at the archbishop's feet. When he opened the offering, Zumárraga gasped: Imprinted on the cape was an image of the brown virgin herself—proof positive of a genuine miracle.

In the centuries since Juan Diego, the brown virgin—La Virgen Morena, or Nuestra Señora La Virgen de Guadalupe—has blended native and Catholic elements into something uniquely Mexican. In doing so, she has become the virtual patroness of Mexico, the beloved symbol of Mexico for *indígenas,* mestizos, *negros,* and *criollos* alike.

In the summer of 2002, Pope John Paul journeyed to Mexico to perform a historic gesture. Before millions of joyous faithful, on July 31, 2002, the frail aging pontiff elevated Juan Diego to sainthood, thus making him Latin America's first indigenous person to be so honored.

DUENDES: SPIRITS OF MEXICO

Once upon a time, most everyone believed that the world was full of spirits that inhabited every object in creation: trees, rocks, animals, mountains, even the wind and the stars. World mythology is replete with examples, from the leprechauns of Ireland and the fairies of Mount Tirich Mir in Pakistan to the spirits who haunt old Hawaiian *heiaus* (temples) and the *duendes* of Mexico.

Eventually many a campesino will take his children to his mountainside cornfield to introduce them to the *duendes,* the elfin beings that folks sometimes glimpse in the shadowed thickets where they hide from mortals.

At the upper end of his field, the campesino father addresses the *duendes:* "With your permission we clear your brush and use your water because it is necessary to nourish our corn and beans. Please allow us, for otherwise, we would starve."

Modernized city Mexicans, generations removed from country village life, often scoff at such antique beliefs. That is, until the family doctor fails to cure their weakened spouses or sick children. Then they often run to a *curandero* or *curandera* (folk healer).

"*Enduendado*" (affliction by an angry *duende*), the *curandero* sometimes diagnoses. Often the cure is simple and savvy: teas and poultices of forest-gathered herbs; other times it is mystical, such as "purifying" by passing an egg all over the afflicted one's body to draw out the illness, and then breaking the egg into a bowl. The shape the broken yolk takes, maybe of a snake, might determine the treatment, which could be long and intricate: massage with lotions of herbs and oils, followed by a *temazcal* (sweat bath) rubdown with rough maguey fibers, all consummated by intense prayers to the Virgin of Guadalupe to force the *duende* to cease the affliction.

Many times the folk cure fails; other times, however, it succeeds, and with enough frequency to convince millions of Mexicans of the power of the village folk healer to purge a *duende*'s poisonous spell.

With few exceptions, every Ixtapa-Zihuatanejo regional town and village celebrates the cherished memory of its Virgin of Guadalupe on December 12. This celebration, however joyful, is but one of the many fiestas that Mexicans, especially the *indígenas,* live for.

Each village holds its local fiesta in honor of its patron saint, who is often a thinly veiled sit-in for a local preconquest deity. Themes appear Spanish—Christians vs. Moors, devils vs. priests—but the native element is strong, sometimes dominant.

Festivals and Events

Mexicans love a party. Urban families watch the calendar for midweek national holidays that create a *puente* (bridge) to the weekend and allow them to squeeze in a three- to five-day mini-vacation. Visitors should likewise watch the calendar. Such holidays (especially Christmas and Semana Santa, pre-Easter week) mean packed buses, roads, and hotels, especially around the Ixtapa-Zihuatanejo region's beach resorts.

Country people, on the other hand, await their local saint's or holy day. The name of the locality often provides the clue. For example, in San Marcos, on the Costa Chica, 30 miles west of Acapulco, expect a celebration in late April, around April 25, the feast day of St. Mark. People dress up in their traditional best, sell their wares and produce in a street fair, join a procession, get tipsy, and dance in the plaza.

FIESTAS

The following calendar lists national and notable Ixtapa-Zihuatanejo region holidays and festivals. Dates may vary. If you want to attend a specific local fiesta, contact a local travel agent or tourism bureau for information. (But, if you happen to be where one of these is going on, get out of your car or bus and join in!)

January

- Jan. 1: **¡Feliz Año Nuevo!** (New Year's Day); national holiday.
- Jan. 6: **Día de los Reyes** (Day of the Kings); traditional gift exchange.
- Jan. 17–18: **Fiesta de Santa Prisca** in Taxco; families bring their pet animals for blessing at the church. The next day, pilgrims arrive at the *zócalo* for *mañanitas* (mass) in honor of the saint, then head for folk dancing inside the church.
- Jan. 20–21: **Fiesta de San Sebastián;** townsfolk honor the saint martyred in Rome in A.D. 288.
- Jan. 23–Feb. 2: **Fiesta de la Virgen de la Salud;** processions, dancing, food, and fireworks.

February

- Feb. 2: **Día de Candelaria;** plants, seeds, and candles blessed; processions and bullfights.
- February: **Carnaval** (Mardi Gras); during the four days before *Miercoles de Ceniza* (Ash Wednesday, 46 days before Easter Sunday), usually in late February, many towns and villages stage Carnaval extravaganzas; especially in Teloloapan, near Iguala.

March

- March 10–17: **Fiesta de San Patricio** (St. Patrick's Day festival).
- Fifth Friday before Easter Sunday: **Fiesta del Señor del Perdón;** grand pilgrimage festival, in Igualapa, near Ometepec.
- Fourth Friday before Easter Sunday: **Fiesta de Jesús el Nazareno** in Huaxpáltepec; traditional Dance of the Conquest, big native country fair.

- March 19: **Día de San José** (Day of St. Joseph).
- March 21: **Birthday of Benito Juárez,** the "Hero of the Americas"; national holiday.

April

- April 1–7: **Feria de Café** (Coffee Fair) in Atoyac de Álvarez; coffee farmers sell their best; also plenty of horse trading, handicrafts, country food, and bull riding and roping.
- April 1–19: **Fiesta de Ramos** (Palm Sunday); local area crafts fair, food, dancing, mariachis; especially in Jamiltepec.
- April: **Good Friday;** two days before Easter Sunday.
- April: **Semana Santa** (pre-Easter Holy Week culminating in Domingo Gloria, Easter Sunday, a national holiday) especially in Taxco, Pinotepa Nacional, Teloloapan, Petatlán, Ometepec, Iguala, Olinalá, and Jamiltepec.

May

- May 1: **Fiesta del Primer de Mayo** in Atliaca, near Tixtla; age-old indigenous rite; sacrifices, praying for rain, and traditional dances at the sacred site Sótano (Sinkhole) de Oztotempa.
- May 1: **Labor Day;** national holiday.
- May 3: **Fiesta del Día de la Santa Cruz** (Holy Cross); processions to hilltops and sacred sites; many towns, but especially in Ometepec.
- May 3–15: **Fiesta of St. Isador the Farmer;** blessing of seeds, animals, and water; agricultural displays, competitions, and dancing.
- May 5: **Cinco de Mayo;** celebrates the defeat of the French at Puebla in 1862; national holiday.
- May 10: **Mother's Day;** national holiday.

June

- June 24: **Fiesta de San Juan Bautista** (Festival of St. John the Baptist); fairs and religious festivals, playful dunking of people in water, especially in Chilapa.

- June 29: **Día de San Pablo y San Pedro** (Day of St. Peter and St. Paul).

July

- July 20–30: **Fiesta de Santiago Apóstol** (Festival of St. James the Apostle) in many locations, but especially in Pinotepa Nacional, Quechultenango, and Ometepec.

August

- Aug. 6–7: **Fiesta del Padre Jesús;** grand pilgrimage celebration of Petatlán's beloved *patrón,* accompanied by plenty of merry-making, traditional dances, country food, and fireworks.
- Aug. 9: **Fiesta de Vicente Guerrero** in Tixtla; folks celebrate, with cultural events, music, and traditional dances, the birthday of their famous native son, Vicente Guerrero.
- Aug. 14–15: **Fiesta de la Virgen de la Asunción** (Festival of the Virgin of the Assumption); the celebration of the ascension of Mother Mary into heaven, especially in Chilapa.

September

- Sept. 1–8: **Fiesta de la Natividad de María;** indigenous folks flood into Tixtla to sell handicrafts, get tipsy, and watch their favorite traditional dances.
- Sept. 9–11: **Fiesta de San Nicolás Tolentino** in Ometepec.
- Sept. 14: **Charro Day** (Cowboy Day) all over Mexico; rodeos.
- Sept. 15–16: **Dias Patrias** (Patriotic Days); national holiday; mayors everywhere reenact Father Hidalgo's 1810 Grito de Dolores from city hall balconies at 11 P.M. on the night of September 15, especially in Teloloapan and Ometepec.
- Sept. 27–Oct. 2: **Fiesta de San Miguel;** often

with the Danza de los Cristianos y Moros (Dance of the Christians and Moors).

October

- Oct. 4: **Día de San Francisco** (Day of St. Francis of Assisi), especially in Iguala and Olinalá.
- Oct. 12: **Día de la Raza** (Day of the Race); national holiday that commemorates the union of the races.

November

- Nov. 1: **Día de Todos Santos** (All Souls' Day); in honor of the souls of children; the departed descend from heaven to eat sugar skeletons, skulls, and treats on family altars.
- Nov. 2: **Día de los Muertos** (Day of the Dead); in honor of ancestors; families visit cemeteries and decorate graves with flowers and favorite food of the deceased; especially colorful in Iguala and Taxco.
- Monday after the Day of the Dead: **Fiesta de los Jumiles** in Taxco; folks collect and feast on raw or roasted *jumiles* (small crickets) and enjoy music and plenty of fixings.
- Nov. 1–15: **Feria de la Nao de China** in Acapulco; fair celebrating the galleon trade that linked colonial Acapulco with China via the Philippines.
- Nov. 20: **Revolution Day;** anniversary of the Revolution of 1910–1917; national holiday.
- Nov. 28–Dec. 5: **National Silver Fair** in Taxco; Mexico's most skilled silversmiths compete for prizes amid a whirl of concerts, dances, and fireworks.

December

- Dec. 1: **Inauguration Day;** national government changes hands every six years: 2012, 2018, 2024 . . .
- Dec. 8: **Día de la Purísima Concepción** (Day of the Immaculate Conception).
- Dec. 12: **Día de Nuestra Señora de Guadalupe** (Festival of the Virgin of

Guadalupe, patroness of Mexico); processions, music, and dancing nationwide, especially around the Acapulco *zócalo* and the adjacent Pozo de la Nación neighborhood.

- Dec. 16–24: **Christmas Week;** week of *posadas* and piñatas; midnight Mass on Christmas Eve.
- Dec. 24–Jan. 8: **Feria de San Mateo, la Navidad, y el Año Nuevo** in Chilpancingo;

the festivities kick off with the *teopancolaquio,* a ritual honoring the birth of God on Earth. Subsequently folks celebrate with favorite traditional dances, bullfights, carnival, fireworks, cockfights, and plenty of food.

- Dec. 25: **¡Feliz Navidad!** (Christmas Day); Christmas trees and gift exchange; national holiday.
- Dec. 31: **New Year's Eve.**

THE DAY OF THE DEAD

Instead of mourning the dead, Mexicans celebrate the memory of their deceased relatives with a festive holiday, **El Día de los Muertos** (Day of the Dead). The roots of this festival go back for countless generations, long before the Spanish Conquest, to the ancient holiday of Mictecacihuatl, the guardian-goddess of the dead, whom many of the original Mexicans celebrated around the month of August.

The Spanish shifted the date to November 1 and 2 to coincide with the Catholic double holiday of All Saint's Day and All Souls day. Now, Mexicans celebrate November 1 as El Día de los Angelitos (Little Angels), and November 2 as El Día de los Muertos, in remembrance of their deceased children and their deceased adult relatives, respectively. Although universal throughout Mexico, the holiday is most intensely celebrated in the indigenous southern states of Michoacán, Oaxaca, Chiapas, and the entire Ixtapa-Zihuatanejo region.

El Día de los Muertos, named after the second day of the two-day holiday, amounts to a joyous reunion of all family members – both living and dead. At the end of October, people gather in their hometowns and villages to reunite with their loved ones. By noon, on November 1, they arrive at the cemeteries and begin sweeping up the gravesites, polishing the tombstones, scattering flower petals, and lighting candles to mark the path. By early evening, all is ready. The graves are festooned with fruit, flowers, and glowing candles, and decorated with toys and candy for the *angelitos* and dishes loaded with the favorite foods

and drinks of the deceased adults. Most importantly, most everyone has arrived; people drink, eat, and tell favorite family stories. As the evening wears on, people begin to drowse and curl up beneath blankets and spend the night in a happy vigil to welcome their departed loved ones back into the family fold once again.

© BRUCE WHIPPERMAN

Deceased loved ones are honored with flowers and candles on the Day of the Dead.

Arts and Crafts

Mexico is so stuffed with lovely, reasonably priced handicrafts (*artesanías,* ar-tay-sah-NEE-ahs) that many crafts devotees, if given the option, might choose Mexico over heaven. A sizable fraction of Ixtapa-Zihuatanejo region families still depend upon homespun items—clothing, utensils, furniture, native herbal remedies, religious offerings, adornments, toys, musical instruments—which either they or their neighbors craft at home. Many such traditions reach back thousands of years, to the beginnings of Mexican civilization. The accumulated knowledge of manifold generations of artisans has, in many instances, resulted in finery so prized that whole villages devote themselves to the manufacture of a certain class of goods.

Although the resort centers of Ixtapa-Zihuatanejo, Acapulco, and Taxco have plenty of attractive for-sale handicrafts, shoppers who venture away from the coastal resorts to the source towns and villages will most likely benefit from lower prices, wider choices, and, most important, the privilege of encountering the artisans themselves.

The Ixtapa-Zihuatanejo region's three prime handicrafts source towns are **Taxco,** renowned for silver jewelry; **Olinalá,** for fine lacquerware, furniture, and jaguar masks; and **Chilapa,** for the trove of charming handicrafts that folks bring in from outlying villages and sell at the grand Sunday crafts market. Handicrafts lovers should make the extra effort to visit this Sunday market in Chilapa, 2.5 hours by car, 3 hours by direct bus from Acapulco. In Chilapa you will find items made of **horn** (*cuerno):* mescal bottles, combs, pen holders, ash trays, and lampshades; **ironwork** (*hierro):* hachets, daggers, swords, and knives; **maguey fiber** (*ixtle):* hand-painted bags and purses; **embroidery** (*bordado):* napkins, tablecloths, and shawls (*rebozos);* **basketry and woven fiber** (*cestería):* palm sombreros, reed baskets, purses, mats (*petates),* and palm baskets (*tenates);* **wood** (*madera):* masks, lacquerware, miniature human and animal figurines, furniture;

leather (*cuero):* purses, belts, wallets; and **pottery** (*alfarería).*

BARGAINING

Bargaining will stretch your money even further. It comes with the territory in Mexico and needn't be a hassle. On the contrary, if done with humor and moderation, bargaining can be an enjoyable way to meet Mexican people and gain their respect, even friendship.

The local crafts market is where bargaining is most intense. For starters, try offering half the asking price. From there on, it's all psychology: you have to content yourself with not having to have the item. Otherwise, you're sunk; the vendor will probably sense your need and stand fast. After a few minutes of good-humored bantering, ask for *el último precio* (the final price), in which, if it's close, you may have a bargain.

BASKETRY AND WOVEN CRAFTS

Weaving straw, leaves, palm fronds, and reeds is among the oldest of Mexican crafts traditions. Mat and basket-weaving methods and designs 5,000 years old survive to the present day. In the dry sierra and Río Balsas basin of northeastern Guerrero, people weave *petates* (straw mats) upon which vacationers stretch out on the beach and which local folks use for everything, from keeping tortillas warm to shielding babies from the sun. Palm-leaf weaving is a near-universal occupation. The craft spills over to Ixtapa-Zihuatanejo, Acapulco, and the Costa Chica, where you might see a person waiting for a bus or even walking down the street while weaving creamy white palm leaf strands into a coiled basket. (Despite appearances, the product, if made of palm leaf, is not strictly a basket—*canasta* in Spanish—which is made of reeds, but instead a *tenate,* which has no handle like a basket does, but a woven tumpline that folks loop over their foreheads when carrying a load.)

ECOTOURISM

Latter-day jet travel has brought droves of vacationing tourists to developing countries largely unprepared for the consequences. As the visitors' numbers swell, power grids black out, sewers overflow, and roads crack under the strain of accommodating more and larger hotels, restaurants, cars, buses, and airports.

Worse yet, armies of vacationers drive up local prices and begin to change native customs. While visions of tourists as sources of fast money replace traditions of hospitality, television wipes out folk entertainment, Coca Cola and Pepsi substitute for fruit drinks and desserts, and prostitution and drugs flourish.

Some travelers have said enough is enough and are forming organizations to encourage visitors to travel with increased sensitivity to native people and customs. They have developed travelers' codes of ethics and guidelines that encourage visitors to stay at sustainable, local-style accommodations, use local transportation, and seek people- and earth-friendly vacations and tours, such as language-study and cultural programs and people-to-people work projects.

A number of especially active socially responsible travel groups sponsor tours all over the world, including the Ixtapa-Zihuatanejo region. These include organizations such as **Global Exchange, Green Tortoise, Green Globe,** and **Third Eye Travel.** They all have websites that can be accessed via Internet search engines, such as Google and Yahoo, or the super umbrella website www.socially responsible.com.

The related ecotourism movement promotes socially responsible tourism through the strategy of simultaneous enjoyment and enhancement of the natural environment. Neighboring Oaxaca and, to some extent, the Ixtapa-Zihuatanejo region, have become ecotourism centers partly because of the dedication of Oaxaca-based Ron Mader, a moving force behind the superb website www.planeta.com. Log on and you'll find virtually everything you need to know about ecotourism, from nature tour companies and village recycling projects to indigenous handicrafts cooperatives and international conferences.

CLOTHING AND EMBROIDERY

Although *traje* (traditional indigenous dress) has nearly vanished in urban Mexico, significant numbers of Mexican women, especially in country districts of Michoacán, Guerrero, Oaxaca, Chiapas, and Yucatán, make and wear *traje.* Most common is the *huipil,* a full, square-shouldered, short- to midsleeved dress, often hand-embroidered with animal and floral designs. Prized *huipil* designs (Amusgo tribe: white cotton, often embroidered with abstract colored animal and floral motifs) of the Ixtapa-Zihuatanejo region are commonly made in Ometepec, Xochistlahuaca, and neighboring San Pedro de Amusgos in Oaxaca.

Shoppers sometimes can buy other types of *traje,* such as a *quechquémitl* (shoulder cape), often made of wool and worn as an overgarment in winter. The *enredo,* a full-length skirt, wraps around the waist and legs like a Hawaiian sarong. Mixtec-speaking women on the Guerrero-Oaxaca border around Pinotepa Nacional commonly wear the *enredo,* known locally as the *pozahuanco* (poh-sah-oo-AHN-koh), below the waist and, when at home, go bare-breasted. When wearing their *pozahuancos* in public, they usually tie a *mandil,* a wide calico apron, around their front side.

Colonial-era Spanish styles have blended with native *traje,* producing a wider class of dress, known generally as **ropa típica.** Lovely embroidered *blusas* (blouses), *rebozos* (shawls), and *vestidos* (dresses) fill boutique racks and market stalls all over the Ixtapa-Zihuatanejo region.

Fine *bordado* (embroidery) embellishes much traditional Mexican clothing, as well as *manteles* (tablecloths) and *servilletas* (napkins). As everywhere, women define the art of embroidery. Although some still work by hand at home, cheaper machine-made factory lace and needlework is more commonly available in shops.

LEATHER

Ixtapa-Zihuatanejo region shops offer an abundance of leather goods, which, if not manufactured locally, are shipped from the renowned leather centers. These include Guadalajara, Mazatlán, and Oaxaca (sandals and huaraches), and León (shoes, boots, and saddles). For unique and custom-designed articles you'll probably have to confine your shopping to the expensive tourist resort shops. For more usual though still attractive leather items such as purses, wallets, belts, coats, and boots, veteran shoppers go to local city markets.

FURNITURE

Although furniture is usually too bulky to carry back home with your airline luggage, low Mexican prices allow you to ship your purchases home and enjoy beautiful, unusual pieces for a fraction of what you would pay—if you could find them—at home.

A number of classes of furniture (*muebles,* moo-AY-blays) are crafted in villages near the sources of raw materials—either wood, leather, reeds, bamboo, or wrought iron.

Sometimes it seems as if every house in Mexico is furnished with wood **colonial-style furniture.** The basic design of much of it dates at least back to the Middle Ages. Although variations exist, most colonial-style furniture is heavily built. Table and chair legs are massive, often lathe-turned; chair backs are usually straight and vertical. Although usually varnished, colonial-style tables, chairs, and chests sometimes shine with inlaid wood or tile, or animal and flower designs. Family shops turn out good furniture, usually in the highlands, where suitable wood is available. Among the Ixtapa-Zihuatanejo region's best-known places to find these products are Zihuatanejo, Taxco, Ixcateopan (near Taxco), Chilapa (near Chilpancingo), and Olinalá (via Chilapa).

It is intriguing that **lacquered furniture,** in both process and design, has much in common with lacquerware produced half a world away in China. Moreover, Mexican lacquerware tradition both predated the conquest and was originally practiced only on the Pacific, where legends persist of preconquest contact with Chinese traders. Consequently, a number of experts believe that the Mexicans learned the craft of lacquerware from Chinese artists, centuries before Columbus.

Today, artisan families in and around Olinalá in the Ixtapa-Zhuatanejo region carry on the tradition. The process, which at its finest resembles cloisonné manufacture, involves carving and painting intricate floral and animal designs, followed by repeated layerings of lacquer, clay, and sometimes gold and silver to produce satiny jewel-like surfaces. Their creations, ranging from boxes and bowls to chests and chairs, are known commonly as **linaloe** (lee-nah-LOH-ay), after the source tree of the fragrant laquer oil.

GLASS AND STONEWORK

Glass manufacture, unknown in pre-Columbian times, was introduced by the Spanish. Today, factories, especially around Guadalajara, turn out mountains of fetching glass products, notably *burbuja* (boor-BOO-hah) bubbled glass tumblers, goblets, plates, and pitchers, usually in blue, green, or red.

Artisans usually work stone near sources of supply. Puebla, Mexico's main source of onyx (*onix,* OH-neeks), is the manufacturing center for the galaxy of mostly rough-hewn cream-colored items, from animal charms and chess pieces to beads and desk sets, that crowd curio-shop shelves throughout the country.

For a keepsake from a truly ancient Mexican tradition, don't forget the hollowed-out stone metate (may-TAH-tay), a corn-grinding basin, and the three-legged *molcajete* (mohl-kah-HAY-tay), a mortar for grinding *chiles.*

JEWELRY

Gold and silver were once the basis for Mexico's wealth. Her Spanish conquerors plundered a mountain of gold—religious offerings, necklaces, pendants, rings, bracelets—masterfully crafted by a legion of native metalsmiths and jewelers. Unfortunately, much of that indigenous tradition was lost because, for generations, the Spanish denied the Mexicans access to precious metals while they introduced Spanish methods. Nevertheless, a small gold-working tradition survived the dislocations of the 1810–1821 War of Independence and the 1910–1917 revolution. Silver-crafting, moribund during the 1800s, was revived in the Ixtapa-Zihuatanejo region in Taxco, principally through the joint efforts of architect-artist William Spratling and the local community.

Today, spurred by the tourist boom, jewelry-making is thriving in Mexico. Taxco, where a swarm of local families, guilds, and cooperatives produce sparkling silver and gold adornments, is Mexico's acknowledged center.

Additionally, Iguala, not far south of Taxco, and Petatlán, a short ride southeast of Zihuatanejo, are thriving market centers of affordable 14-carat-gold rings, necklaces, chains, bracelets, and pendants.

Buying Silver and Gold

One hundred percent pure silver is rarely sold because it's too soft. Silver (sent from processing mills in the north of Mexico to be worked in Taxco shops) is nearly always alloyed with 7.5 percent copper to increase its durability. Such pieces, identical in composition to sterling silver, should have ".925," together with the initials of the manufacturer, stamped on their back sides. Other, less common grades, such as "800 fine" (80 percent silver), should also be stamped.

If silver is not stamped with the degree of purity, it probably contains no silver at all and is an alloy of copper, zinc, and nickel, known by the generic label "alpaca," or "German" silver. Once, after haggling over the purity and prices of his offerings, a street vendor handed me a shiny handful and said, "Go to a jeweler and have them tested. If they're not real, keep them." Calling his bluff, I took

them to a jeweler, who applied a dab of hydrochloric acid to each piece. Tiny telltale bubbles of hydrogen revealed the cheapness of the merchandise, which I returned the next day to the vendor.

People prize pure gold, partly because, unlike silver, it does not tarnish. Gold, nevertheless, is rarely sold pure (24 karat); for durability, it is alloyed with copper. Typical purities, such as 18 karat (75 percent) or 14 karat (58 percent), should be stamped on the pieces. If not, chances are they contain no gold at all.

METALWORK

Bright copper, brass, and tinware, sturdy ironwork, and razor-sharp knives and machetes are made in a number of regional centers. Copperware, from jugs, cups, and plates to candlesticks—and even the town lampposts and bandstand—all comes from Santa Clara del Cobre, a few miles south of Pátzcuaro, Michoacán.

Especially in Taxco, be sure not to miss the miniature *milagros,* one of Mexico's most charming forms of metalwork. Usually of brass, they are of homely shapes—a horse, dog, or baby, or an arm, head, or foot—and, accompanied by a prayer, are pinned by the faithful to the garment of their favorite saint who they hope will intercede to cure an ailment or fulfill a wish.

POTTERY AND CERAMICS

Although Mexican pottery tradition is as diverse as the country itself, some varieties stand out. Among the most prized is the so-called Talavera (or Majolica), the best of which is made by a few family-run shops in Puebla. The labels Talavera and Majolica derive from Talavera, the Spanish town from which the tradition migrated to Mexico; before that it originated on the Spanish Mediterranean island of Mayorca (thus Majolica), from a combination of still older Arabic, Asian, and African ceramic styles. Shapes include plates, bowls, jugs, and pitchers, hand-painted and hard-fired in intricate bright yellow, orange, blue, and green floral designs. Shops in Zihuatanejo (especially

El Arte y Tradición) and Taxco sell authentic Pueblo Talavera.

So few shops make true Talavera these days that other cheaper look-alike grades, made around Guanajuato, are more common, selling for as little as one-tenth of the price of the genuine article.

More practical and nearly as prized is the stoneware from Tonalá in Guadalajara's eastern suburbs. Made in many shapes, from cuddly dogs, doves and ducks, to complete eight-place dinner settings and embellished with fetching floral designs, Tonala stoneware is hand-painted and high-fired over a reddish clay base. One Zihuatanejo shop, Cerámicas Tonalá, carries a large, lovely selection.

The Ixtapa-Zihuatanejo region itself also sustains a vibrant pottery tradition. In crafts shops and street displays in Ixtapa-Zihuatanejo, Acapulco, and Taxco, you'll find the humble but very attractive unglazed but brightly painted animals—cats, ducks, fish, and many others—that folks bring to resort centers from their village family workshops.

Although most latter-day Mexican potters are aware of the health dangers of lead pigments, some for-sale pottery may still contain lead. The hazard comes from low-fired pottery in which the lead has not been firmly melted into the glaze. Acids in foods such as lemons, vinegar, and tomatoes may therefore dissolve the lead pigments, which, when ingested, might eventually result in lead poisoning. In general, the hardest, shiniest pottery, which has been twice fired—such as the high-quality Tonalá stoneware used for dishes—is the safest.

MASKS

Spanish and native Mexican traditions have blended to produce a multitude of masks—some strange, some lovely, some scary, some endearing, all interesting. The mask tradition flourishes strongly in the Ixtapa-Zihuatanejo region, especially in Chilpancingo, Tixtla, Chilapa, Olinalá, Iguala (in Guerrero Upcountry) and Pinotepa Nacional and Pinotepa Don Luis (in the Costa Chica), where campesinos gear up all year for the masked dances at the village festivals. These especially include Carnaval (Mardi Gras, usually in February), Semana Santa (Easter week), Virgin of Guadalupe (early December), and the festival of the local patron, whether it be San José, San Pedro, San Pablo, Santa María, Santa Barbara, or one of a host of others. Every local such fair has its favored dances, such as the Dance of the Conquest, the Christians and Moors, the Old Men, or the Jaguar, in which masked villagers act out age-old allegories of fidelity, sacrifice, faith, struggle, sin, and redemption.

For singularly fascinating exhibitions of antique Ixtapa-Zihuatanejo region masks, be sure to visit the Casa de la Máscara (House of Masks) in Acapulco and/or the Casa Pilla restaurant in Chilapa.

The popularity of masks has led to an entire made-for-tourist mask industry of mass-produced duplicates, often cleverly antiqued. Many shops in Zihuatanejo, Acapulco, and Taxco, and vendors at the Chilapa Sunday handicrafts market sell attractive reproductions. Examine the goods carefully; if the price is high, don't buy unless you're convinced it's a real antique.

ESSENTIALS

Getting There

BY AIR
From the United States and Canada

The vast majority of travelers reach the Ixtapa-Zihuatanejo region by air. Flights are frequent and reasonably priced. Competition sometimes shaves prices down as low as $400 or less for an Ixtapa-Zihuatanejo or Acapulco low-season round-trip.

Air travelers can save lots of money by shopping around. Don't be bashful about asking for the cheapest price. Make it clear to the airline or travel agent you're interested in a bargain. Ask the right questions: Are there special-incentive, advance-payment, night, midweek, tour package, or charter fares? Check airlines and bargain-oriented travel websites, such as **www.priceline.com, www.orbitz.com, www.expedia.com, www.cheaptickets.com** and **www.travelocity.com.**

Although few airlines fly directly to the Ixtapa-Zihuatanejo region from the northern United States and Canada, many charters do. In locales near Vancouver, Calgary, Ottawa, Toronto, Montreal, Minneapolis, Chicago, Detroit, Cleveland, and New York, consult a travel agent or website for charter flight options. Be aware that charter reservations, which

© BRUCE WHIPPERMAN

often require fixed departure and return dates and provide minimal cancellation refunds, decrease your flexibility. If available charter choices are unsatisfactory, then you might choose to begin your vacation with a connecting flight to one of the Mexico gateways, such as San Francisco, Los Angeles, Phoenix, Dallas, Houston, Chicago, Atlanta, or Miami.

It's wise to reconfirm both departure and return flight reservations, especially during the busy Christmas and Easter seasons. This is a useful strategy, as is prompt arrival at check-in, against getting "bumped" (losing your seat) by the tendency of airlines to overbook the rush of high-season vacationers. For further protection, always try to get your seat assignment and boarding pass included with your ticket.

AIRLINES TO THE IXTAPA-ZIHUATANEJO REGION

A number of airlines offer direct flights to Ixtapa-Zihuatanejo (IX), Acapulco (AC), and/or Mexico City (MX), where quick air or bus connections with Ixtapa-Zihuatanejo and Acapulco may be made. The airlines with the most scheduled flights from the U.S. or Canada, in approximate descending order of activity, are **Aeroméxico, American, Continental, Delta, U.S. Airways, Alaska,** and **Air Canada.** Others offering flights are the reliable Mexican carriers Volaris, Interjet, Magnicharter, and Interjet. Furthermore, Frontier, Delta, Westjet, and others offer seasonal (usually winter-spring) charter flights.

AIRLINE	ORIGIN	DESTINATIONS
Aeroméxico	Los Angeles	MX
tel. 800/237-6639	San Francisco	MX
www.aeromexico.com	Mexico City	IX, AC
	Tijuana	MX
	Phoenix	MX
	San Antonio	MX
	Houston	MX
	New York	MX
	Orlando	MX
	Miami	MX
American	Dallas	AC, MX
tel. 800/433-7300	Chicago	AC
www.aa.com	Miami	MX
Continental	Houston	IX, AC, MX
tel. 800/231-0856	Newark	MX
www.continental.com		
Delta	Los Angeles	MX
tel. 800/221-1212	Dallas	MX
www.delta.com	Atlanta	MX
	New York	MX

Airlines generally try hard to accommodate travelers with dietary or other special needs. When booking your flight, inform your travel agent or carrier of the necessity of a low-sodium, low-cholesterol, vegetarian, or lactose-reduced meal, or other requirements. (My experience has been that such individually prepared meals are tastier than the usual airplane fare.)

From Europe, Latin America, and Australasia

Some airlines fly across the Atlantic directly to Mexico City. These include **British Airways** from London, **Lufthansa,** from Frankfurt, and **Aeroméxico,** from Paris via Madrid.

From Latin America, **Aeroméxico** connects directly with Mexico City, from Sao Paulo, Brazil; Santiago, Chile; and Lima, Peru,

AIRLINE	ORIGIN	DESTINATIONS
U.S. Airways tel. 800/428-4322 www.usairways.com	Phoenix	IX, AC, MX
Alaska tel. 800/426-0333 www.alaskaair.com	Los Angeles	IX
Air Canada tel. 888/247-2262 www.aircanada.com	Toronto	MX
Interjet www.interjet.com.mx	Toluca Mexico City	IX IX, AC
Volaris tel. 866/988-3527 www.volaris.com.mx	Tijuana Oakland	AC, MX MX
Magnicharters www.magnichartersmx.com	Mexico City	IX
SEASONAL CHARTERS		
Delta tel. 800/221-1212 www.delta.com	Los Angeles Minneapolis	IX IX
Frontier tel.800/432-1359 www.frontierairlines.com	Denver	IX
Westjet tel.888/937-8538 www.westjet.com	Calgary	IX

Buenos Aires, Argentina, and San José, Costa Rica. A number of other Latin American flag carriers also fly directly to Mexico City.

A number of carriers cross the Pacific directly to Mexico City, notably, **China Airlines, Thai Airlines, Singapore Airlines,** and **Quantas,** from Hong Kong, Bangkok, Singapore, and Sydney, respectively.

Baggage

The tropical Ixtapa-Zihuatanejo region makes it easy to pack light. Use my packing checklist to double-check (after you've packed) that you're not leaving something important behind. Veteran tropical travelers condense their luggage to carry-ons only. Airlines routinely allow one carry-on (not exceeding 45 inches in combined length, width, and girth), and either a compact book bag or a purse. Thus relieved of heavy burdens, your trip will become much simpler.

Even if you can't avoid checking luggage, loss of it needn't ruin your vacation. *Always carry your irreplaceable items in the cabin with you.* These should include all money, credit cards, travelers checks, keys, tickets, cameras, passport, prescription drugs, and eyeglasses.

Travel Insurance

Travelers packing lots of expensive baggage, or who (because of illness, for example) may have to cancel a nonrefundable flight or tour, might consider buying travel insurance. Travel agents, such as Traveler's Insurance Co. (www.travelers.com) routinely sell packages that cover **lost baggage** beyond your airline's (typically $500), liability limit, **trip cancellation** (if, at the last minute, you can't travel), and **default** (if your tour agency fails to perform) insurance. Carefully weigh your options and the cost (typically $100 for two weeks) against benefits before putting your money down.

BY BUS

As air travel rules in the United States, bus travel rules in Mexico. Hundreds of gleaming luxury- and first-class buses with names such as Elite, Turistar, Futura, Omnibus de Mexico, Primera Plus, Transportes y Autobuses Pacífico, and Estrella Blanca depart the border daily, headed for the Ixtapa-Zihuatanejo region.

Since North American bus lines ordinarily terminate just north of the Mexican border, you must usually disembark and walk to the Mexican *migración* (immigration) office just across the border. After having completed the necessary (passport needed) but very simple paperwork, proceed to the nearby *sitio taxi* (taxi stand) and hire a taxi (agree upon the price before getting in) to take you the few miles to the *camionera central* (central bus station).

First- and luxury-class bus service in Mexico is much cheaper and more frequent than in the United States. Tickets for comparable trips in Mexico cost a fraction of what you'd pay in the United States (around $100 for a 1,000-mile trip, compared to $200 in the United States).

Nevertheless, in Mexico, as on U.S. buses, you often have to take it as you find it. *Asientos reservados* (seat reservations), *boletos* (tickets), and information must generally be obtained in person at the bus station, and credit cards and travelers checks are not often accepted in small-town stations. Neither are reserved bus tickets typically refundable, so don't miss the bus. On the other hand, plenty of buses roll south almost continually.

From California and the West

Cross the border to Tijuana, Mexicali, or Nogales, where you can ride one of several bus lines south along the Mexican Pacific coast route (National Highway 15): Estrella Blanca subsidiaries first-class Elite (which connects the whole way to Ixtapa-Zihuatanejo and Acapulco), luxury-class Turistar, second-class Transportes Norte de Sonora; or first-class independent Transportes y Autobuses del Pacífico (TAP).

At Mazatlán or Tepic, depending on the line, you transfer or continue on the same bus, west via Guadalajara, or south via Puerto Vallarta (the longer but more scenic option). If you choose Guadalajara, you have a pair of options: If your first destination is Ixtapa-Zihuatanejo, transfer there to the Estrella Blanca affiliate bus south via Morelia and Uruapan (in Michocáan) to the coast at Zihuatanejo. If, however, your first destination is Acapulco, take the Estrella Blanca affiliate bus that bypasses Mexico City, via Toluca and Taxco, thence south via expressway 95D to Acapulco.

If however, you choose to go via Puerto Vallarta, from Tepic, continue south through Manzanillo, along the gorgeously scenic Michoacán coast, to Ixtapa-Zihuatanejo. Allow a minimum of two full 24-hour days for either option. Carry liquids and food (which might only be minimally available en route) with you.

Instead of doing the trip in one big bite, you might stop overnight or more for a rest in Guadalajara (go to semi-deluxe tourist Hotel La Serena adjacent to the bus station, tel. 33/3600-0910, fax 33/3600-1774, www.serena.com.mx, $45 d) or, in Puerto Vallarta (Hotel Rosita on the beach, tel. 322/176-1111, tel./fax 322/223-4393, U.S. toll-free tel. 877/813-6712, Canada 888-242/9587, www.hotelrosita.com, $50 d) en route.

From the U.S. Midwest, South, and East

Cross the border from El Paso to Ciudad Juárez and ride one of the Estrella Blanca subsidiaries (luxury-class Turistar or first-class Transportes Chihuahuenses) via Chihuahua and Torreón to either Mexico City Norte (North), or preferably, the Mexico City Sur (South) bus terminal.

From the Sur (sometimes known as Taxqueña) terminal, many buses connect directly with Taxco (Futura, Estrella de Oro) and Acapulco and Zihuatanejo via Chilpancingo (Estrella de Oro, or Estrella Blanca affiliates Turistar, Futura). If you go from the Norte terminal, ride Estrella Blanca affiliates Turistar or Futura, or independent Estrella de Oro to Acapulco and Zihuatanejo. For the entire trip, allow at least two full days to Acapulco, a few hours longer for Ixtapa-Zihuatanejo.

From southern and eastern parts of the United States (and alternatively from the Midwest), cross the border at Laredo, Texas, to Nuevo Laredo and ride one of the Estrella

The 95D Acapulco-Taxco-Mexico City expressway affords spectacular views.

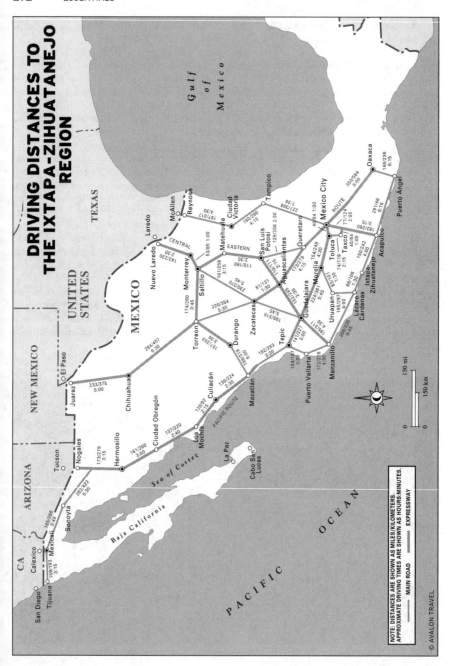

DRIVING DISTANCES TO THE IXTAPA-ZIHUATANEJO REGION

NOTE: DISTANCES ARE SHOWN AS MILES/KILOMETERS.
APPROXIMATE DRIVING TIMES ARE SHOWN AS HOURS:MINUTES.

— MAIN ROAD   — EXPRESSWAY

© AVALON TRAVEL

Blanca deluxe-class subsidiaries (such as Futura for Turistar) to the Mexico City Norte (or possibly Sur) terminal. Continue south, exactly as described above. Allow a minimum of a day and a half (36 hours) for the trip to Acapulco.

BY CAR OR RV

If you're adventurous and like going to out-of-the-way places, but still want to have all the comforts of home, you may enjoy driving your car or RV to the Ixtapa-Zihuatanejo region. On the other hand, consideration of cost, wear and tear on both you and your vehicle, and the congestion hassles in towns may change your mind.

Mexican Car Insurance

Mexico does not recognize foreign insurance. When you drive into Mexico, Mexican auto insurance is at least as important as your passport. At the busier crossings (such as Tijuana, Nogales, El Paso and McAllen), you can purchase insurance at "drive-ins" just north of the border. The many Mexican auto insurance companies are government-regulated; their numbers keep prices and services competitive.

Sanborn's Mexico Insurance (Sanborn's Mexico, P.O. Box 310, McAllen, TX 78502, tel. 956/686-3601, toll-free tel. 800/222-0158, www.sanbornsinsurance.com), one of the most reliable agencies, certainly seems to be trying hardest. With agents all over Mexico and on the border (at San Ysidro, just north of the crossing to Tijuana, Nogales, El Paso, and McAllen, Texas, at the border, just north of the crossing to Reynosa), it offers a range reasonably priced insurance and services. These include handy mile-by-mile travelogs covering "every highway in Mexico," hotel discounts, and much more.

Alternatively, look into "13,000 strong" **Vagabundos del Mar** (tel. 800/474-2252, www.vagabundos.com), an RV-oriented Mexico travel club offering memberships that include a newsletter, caravaning opportunites, discounts, insurance, and much more.

Mexican car insurance runs from a bare-bones rate of about $15 a day for minimal $50,000 (property damage/medical and liability) automobile coverage to a more typical $20 a day for more complete $100,000 coverage. On the same scale, insurance for a $100,000 loaded RV may run more than $30 a day. These daily rates decrease sharply for six-month policies, which run from about $225 for a $50,000 policy ($270 for $100,000) and $400–800 for complete high-end coverage.

If you get broken glass, personal effects, and legal expenses coverage with these rates, you're lucky. Mexican policies don't usually cover them.

You should get something for your money, however. The deductibles should be no more than $500–1,000 and you should be able to get your car fixed in the United States and receive payment in U.S. dollars for losses. If not, shop around.

The Green Angels

The Green Angels have answered many motoring tourists' prayers in Mexico. Bilingual teams of two, trained in auto repair and first aid, help distressed tourists along main highways. They patrol fixed stretches of road at least twice daily by truck. To make sure they stop to help, pull completely off the highway and raise your hood. You may want to hail a passing motorist or trucker with a Mexican cell phone to call the Mexico tourist help line, tel. 800/903-9200, or emergency direct tel. 078, for you.

If, for some reason, you have to leave your vehicle on the roadside, don't leave it unattended. Hire a local teenager or adult to watch it for you. Unattended vehicles on Mexican highways are quickly stricken by a mysterious disease, the symptom of which is rapid loss of vital parts.

Mexican Gasoline

Pemex, short for Petróleos Mexicanos, the government oil monopoly, markets diesel fuel and two grades of unleaded gasoline: 92-octane *premio* (PRAY-mee-oh) and 87-octane Magna (MAHG-nah). Magna (about $0.70/liter, $2.70/gallon) is good gas, yielding performance similar to that of U.S.-style regular unleaded gasoline. (My car, whose manufacturer recommends 91-octane, runs well on Magna.)

Gas Station Thievery

Although the problem has abated considerably in recent years (by the hiring of female attendants), boys who hang around gas stations to wash windows are notoriously light-fingered. When stopping at the *gasolinera,* make sure that everything moveable is out of reach. Also, either insist on pumping the gas yourself or be super-watchful as you pull up to the gas pump to make certain that the pump reads zero before the attendant pumps the gas.

A Healthy Car

Preventive measures spell good health for both you and your car. Get that tune-up (or that long-delayed overhaul) *before,* rather than after, you leave.

Carry a stock of spare parts, which will be more difficult to get and more expensive in Mexico than at home. Carry an extra tire or two, a few quarts of motor oil, gasoline and oil filters, fan belts, spark plugs and fuses. Be prepared with basic tools and supplies, such as screwdrivers, pliers including Vise-Grip, lug wrench, jack, adjustable wrenches, tire pump, steel wire, and duct tape. For breakdowns and emergencies, carry a folding shovel, a husky rope or chain, a gasoline can, and red highway warning markers.

Car Repairs in Mexico

The American big three—General Motors, Ford, and Chrysler—as well as Nissan, Volkswagen and to a lesser extent, Toyota and Honda, are also represented by dealer networks. Getting your car or truck serviced at such big-name agencies is straightforward. While parts will probably be higher in price, shop rates run about one-third to one-half U.S. prices, so repairs will generally come out significantly cheaper than back home.

The same may not be true for repairing all makes, however. Mexico has few other car or truck dealers; consequently, officially certified mechanics for some Japanese, British, and European makes are hard to find.

ROAD SAFETY

Hundreds of thousands of visitors enjoy safe Mexican auto vacations every year. Their success is due in large part to their frame of mind: Drive defensively, anticipate and adjust to danger before it happens, and watch everything – side roads, shoulders, the car in front, and cars far down the road. The following tips will help ensure a safe and enjoyable trip.

- **Don't drive at night.** Range animals, unmarked sand piles, pedestrians, one-lane bridges, cars without lights, and drunken drivers are doubly hazardous at night.

- **Don't exceed the speed limit.** Although speed limits are not often enforced, it's still smart to follow them. Mexican country roads are often narrow and shoulderless. Poor markings and macho drivers who pass on curves are best faced at a speed of 40 mph (64 kph) rather than 75 mph (120 kph).

- **Don't drive on sand.** Even with four-wheel-drive, you'll eventually get stuck if you drive often or casually on beaches. When the tide comes in, who'll pull your car out?

- **Slow down** at the (usually, but sometimes not signed) *topes* (speed bumps) at the edges of towns and for *vados* (dips), which can be dangerously bumpy and full of water.

- **Extend courtesy of the road.** This goes hand-in-hand with safe driving. Both courtesy and machismo are more infectious in Mexico; on the highway, it's much safer to spread the former than the latter.

- **Use *cuota autopistas*** when convenient for your destination; these toll expressways allow for maximum speed and safety.

- **Call the Green Angels.** If you do have car trouble, the Green Angels can help. Call (or ask a passing motorist to call) them at emergency tel. 078, during daytime hours.

The safe and speedy travel possible via Mexican toll expressways *(cuota autopistas)* usually outweighs the cost of the toll.

Nevertheless, many ingenious Mexican independent mechanics can fix any car that comes their way. Their humble *talleres mecánicos* (tah-YER-ays may-KAH-nee-kohs) dot town and village roadsides everywhere.

Although the great majority of Mexican mechanics are honest, beware of unscrupulous operators who try to collect double or triple their original estimate. If you don't speak Spanish, find someone who can assist you in negotiations. *Always* get a cost estimate, including needed parts and labor, in writing, even if you have to write it yourself. Make sure the mechanic understands, then ask him to sign it before he starts work. Although this may be a hassle, it might save you a much nastier hassle later. Shop labor at small, independent repair shops should run $10–20 per hour. For much more information, plus entertaining anecdotes of car and RV travel in Mexico, check out Carl Franz's *The People's Guide to Mexico.*

Bribes (Mordidas)

The usual meeting ground of the visitor and Mexican police is in the visitor's car on a highway or downtown street. To the tourists, such an encounter may seem like mild harassment, accompanied by vague threats of going to the police station or impounding the car for such-and-such a violation. The tourist often goes on to say, "It was all right, though…we gave him $20 and he went away.… Mexican cops sure are crooked, aren't they?"

And, I suppose, if people want to go bribing their way through Mexico, that's their business. But labeling all Mexican cops crooked isn't fair. Police, like most everyone else in Mexico, have to scratch for a living, and they have found that many tourists are willing to slip them a $20 bill (which roughly equals a typical police officer's daily wage) for nothing. Rather than crooked, I would call them hungry and opportunistic.

Instead of paying a bribe, do what I've done a dozen times: Remain cool, and if you're really guilty of an infraction, calmly say, "Ticket, please" *("Boleto, por favor").* After a minute or two of stalling, and no cash appearing, the officer most likely will not bother with a ticket, but will wave you on with only a warning. If, on the other hand, the officer does write you a ticket, he will probably keep your driver's license (which I've always been able to retrieve at the *presidencia municipal* the next day in exchange for paying my fine).

Crossing the Border

Squeezing through the border-traffic bottlenecks during peak holidays and rush hours can easily take two or three hours. Avoid crossing 7–9 A.M. and 4:30–6:30 P.M. Moreover, with latter-day increased U.S. homeland security precautions, the northbound return border crossing, under the best of conditions, generally takes at least an hour of waiting in your car, along with a hundred or more other frustrated drivers. (Note: Do not cross the border *into* Mexico without a **valid passport** for everyone in your party. U.S. border authorities will not let you return without it.)

Highway Routes from the United States

If you decide to drive to the Ixtapa-Zihuatanejo region, you have your choice of three general routes. Maximize comfort and safety by following the broad *cuota* (toll) expressways that often parallel the old narrow *libre* (toll-free) routes. Despite the increased cost (about $150 total to Ixtapa-Zihuatanejo for a car, double or triple that for a motor home) the *cuota* expressways will save you at least two days (including the extra food and hotel tariffs) and wear and tear on both your vehicle and your nerves. Most folks in passenger cars should allow at least four (more likely five or six, depending on the route) full south-of-the-border driving days to Ixtapa-Zihuatanejo and Acapulco. Larger RVs and motor homes should allow at least a day or two more.

PACIFIC ROUTE

From the U.S. Pacific Coast and West, follow National Highway 15 (called 15D as the toll expressway) from the border at Nogales, Sonora, an easy hour's drive south via I-19 from Tucson, Arizona. **California drivers,** unless you have some special reason for doing so, do not cross the border farther west at Tijuana or Mexicali; access by U.S. Interstate Highways 8 and/or 10 to Nogales via Tucson is half a

day quicker than the corresponding two-lane south-of-the-border route.

From Nogales, Highway 15D continues southward smoothly, leading you through cactus-studded mountains and valleys that turn into lush farmland and tropical coastal plain and forest by the time you arrive at Mazatlán. Watch for the **peripheral bypasses** *(periféricos)* and truck routes that guide you past the congested downtowns of Hermosillo, Guaymas, Ciudad Obregón, Los Mochis, and Culiacán. Between these centers, you speed along, via the *cuota* (toll) expressway, all the way to Mazatlán. If you prefer not to pay the high tolls (about $60 Nogales–Mazatlán for a car, much more for motorhome), stick to the old *libre* (toll-free) highway. Hazards, bumps, and slow going might cause you to reconsider, however.

From Mazatlán, continue along Highway 200 to Tepic. There, you can either continue southeast along Highway 15D to Guadalajara, or fork right (south) along Highway 200 to Puerto Vallarta.

If you opt for the Guadalajara route, continue east past Tepic along the easy *cuota autopista* 15D to Guadalajara. There, you link eastward, via crosstown expressway (watch for signs) Avenida Lázaro Cárdenas to Mexico City–bound expressway 15D on the east side of town. Continue east on 15D past Morelia to Toluca, where you *do not continue ahead for Mexico City*. Instead connect, winding through the southeast side of town, with Highway 55 (Boulevard José M. Pino Suárez to Metepec) that, after continuing several miles southeast, connects directly with southbound *cuota autopista* 55D to spa resort Ixtapan del Sal. Continue south on Highway 55 and connect directly with either old Highway 95 to Taxco and Iguala, or expressway 95D south, via Chilpancingo, to Acapulco (total about 1,700 mi/2,730 km, minimum 36 hours at the wheel to Acapulco; 40 hours, 1850 mi/2980 km, to Ixtapa-Zihuatanejo).

Although slower, the Puerto Vallarta route to the Ixtapa-Zihuatanejo region is more scenic and easier to follow. From Tepic, simply continue south, via two-lane Highway 200, through the palmy coastal resorts of Puerto

Vallarta, Manzanillo, and the spectacularly scenic Michoacán coast, to Ixtapa, Zihuatanejo, and Acapulco (total about 1,600 mi/2,580 km, minimum 40 hours at the wheel to Acapulco, 36 hours to Zihuatanejo).

Although choosing between the Puerto Vallarta and Guadalajara options appears to be a toss-up, the Guadalajara route, via expressway nearly all the way, allows for safer driving more hours per day. In effect, this might amount to as little as four days of south-of-the border traveling, in comparison to about five or six days via Puerto Vallarta. However, the extra day or two required by the Puerto Vallarta option might be well worth the scenery and the opportunity to stop in beautiful oceanfront spots along the way. But never mind, you can have it both ways: go one way coming and the other way going.

CENTRAL-EASTERN ROUTE

From the U.S. Midwest, South, and East, a number of routes are possible. Probably fastest and most direct is the route via the southern Texas Laredo–Nuevo Laredo border crossing. Continue south via *cuota autopistas* 85D, 40D, and 57D to Mexico City, thence to Acapulco via *cuota autopista* 95D. Along the way, keep an eye out for the "Mexico" (meaning Mexico City) signs that mark suburban bypasses (commonly labeled *libramiento* or *periférico*): before

Monterrey (*periférico* Highway 40 or 40D); before Saltillo (*libramiento* Highway 57 or 57D); before San Luis Potosí (Highway 57 or 57D); and before Querétaro (Highway 57D).

At the Mexico City northern outskirt, bypass the congested Mexico City downtown the same way by following the right fork Cuernavaca- or Acapulco-direction *periférico*; after several miles also fork right along Boulevard Avila Camacho *periférico*, until finally you see the sign for *cuota* Cuernavaca/Acapulco Highway 95D. From there, you can breeze all the way direct to Acapulco the toll expressway 95D, or the scenic two-lane much improved Highway 95 via Taxco and Iguala.

Also, make sure that you're not in Mexico City on your forbidden day, determined by the last digit of your car's license plate.

BY TOUR AND CRUISE

For travelers on a tight time budget, prearranged tour packages can provide a hassle-free route for sampling the attractions of Ixtapa-Zihuatanejo regional coastal resorts and up-country towns and cities. If, however, you prefer a self-paced vacation, or desire adventure and thrift over comfort and convenience, you should probably defer tour arrangements until after arrival.

By Cruise

Travel agents and websites advertise many cruises that include Acapulco and/or Ixtapa-Zihuatanejo on their itineraries. Vacationers who enjoy being pampered with lots of food and ready-made entertainment (and who don't mind paying for it) can have great fun on cruises. Accommodations on a typical 10-day winter tour or cruise (which would include several days in Ixtapa and Zihuatanejo and/or Acapulco) can run as little as $100 per day per person, double occupancy, to as much as $1,000 or more.

If, however, you want to get to know Mexico and the local people, a cruise is not for you. Included lodging, food, and entertainment are the main events of a cruise; guided shore sightseeing excursions, which generally cost plenty extra, are a sideshow.

MEXICO CITY DRIVING RESTRICTIONS

To reduce smog and traffic gridlock, authorities have limited which cars can drive on which days in Mexico City, depending upon the last digit of their license plates. If you violate these rules, you risk getting an expensive ticket. On Monday, no vehicle may be driven with final digits 5 or 6; Tuesday, 7 or 8; Wednesday, 3 or 4; Thursday, 1 or 2; Friday, 9, 0, or a letter. Weekends, all vehicles may be driven.

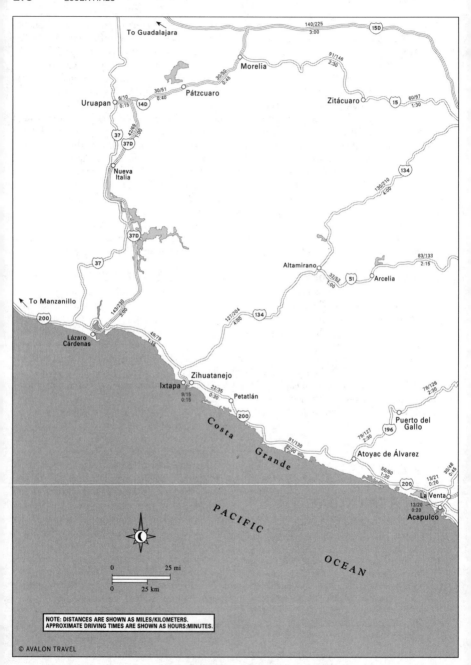

To Guadalajara

Morelia

Uruapan   Pátzcuaro   Zitácuaro

Nueva
Italia

Altamirano   Arcelia

To Manzanillo

Lázaro
Cárdenas

Zihuatanejo
Ixtapa   Petatlán

Puerto del
Gallo

Atoyac de Álvarez

La Venta

Acapulco

Costa   Grande

PACIFIC

OCEAN

0   25 mi

0   25 km

NOTE: DISTANCES ARE SHOWN AS MILES/KILOMETERS.
APPROXIMATE DRIVING TIMES ARE SHOWN AS HOURS:MINUTES.

© AVALON TRAVEL

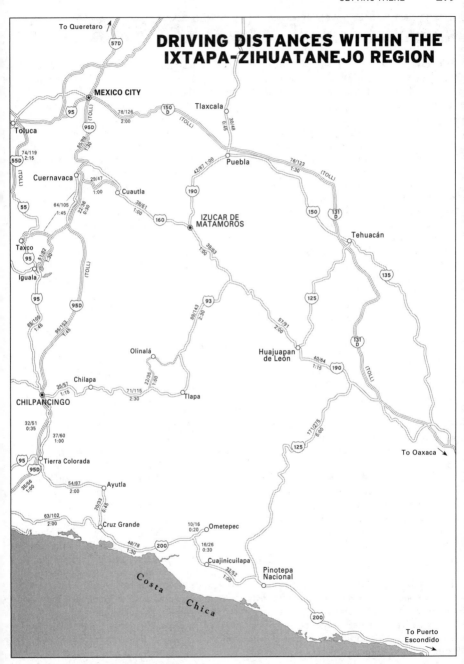

DRIVING DISTANCES WITHIN THE IXTAPA-ZIHUATANEJO REGION

To Queretaro

57D

MEXICO CITY

95

95D (TOLL)

Toluca

55D (TOLL)
74/119
2:15

55 (TOLL)

Cuernavaca

85/68
1:30

78/126 (TOLL)
2:00

150 D (TOLL)

Tlaxcala

30/48
0:45

Puebla

42/67 1:00

78/123 (TOLL)
1:30

131 D

29/47
1:00

Cuautla

38/61
1:00

160

190

150

Tehuacán

64/105
1:45

22/36
0:30

IZUCAR DE MATAMOROS

135

Taxco

51/82
1:30

95

39/63
1:00

125

Iguala

95

95D (TOLL)

93

89/143
2:30

57/91
2:00

131 D

Olinalá

Huajuapan de León

40/84
1:15

190 (TOLL)

85/109
1:45

95/153
1:45

22/35
1:00

Chilapa

35/57
1:15

71/115
2:30

Tlapa

CHILPANCINGO

32/51
0:35

37/60
1:00

125

To Oaxaca

95
95D

Tierra Colorada

54/87
2:00

Ayutla

35/56
1:00

20/33
0:45

171/275
6:00

63/102
2:00

Cruz Grande

10/16
0:20

Ometepec

48/78
1:30

200

16/26
0:30

Cuajinicuilapa

32/52
1:00

Pinotepa Nacional

Costa Chica

200

To Puerto Escondido

Getting Around

BY BUS

The bus is the king of the Mexican road. Dozens of lines connect virtually every town in the Ixtapa-Zihuatanejo region. Three distinct levels of service—deluxe, first-class, and second-class—are generally available. **Luxury-class** (such as Turistar, Futura, Diamante, and Primera Plus, depending upon the line) express coaches speed between major towns, seldom stopping en route. In exchange for relatively high fares (about $50 Acapulco–Zihuatanejo or $70 Acapulco–Taxco, for example), passengers often enjoy rapid passage and airline-style amenities: plush reclining seats, air-conditioning, an on-board toilet, video, and aisle attendant.

Although less luxurious, for about two-thirds the price **first-class** service is frequent and always includes reserved seating. Additionally, passengers enjoy soft reclining seats and air-conditioning (if it is working). Besides their regular stops at or near most towns and villages en route, first-class bus drivers, if requested, will usually stop and let you off anywhere along the road.

Second-class bus seating is unreserved. Second-class buses are not the right choice for travelers with weak knees or stomachs. Often, you will initially have to stand, cramped in the aisle, in a crowd of campesinos. They are warm-hearted but poor people, so don't tempt them with open, dangling purses or wallets bulging in back pockets. Stow your money safely away. After a while, you will be able to sit down. Such privilege, however, comes with obligation, such as holding an old woman's bulging bag of carrots or a toddler on your lap. But if you accept your burden with humor and equanimity, who knows what favors and blessings may flow to you in return.

Tickets, Seating, and Baggage

Mexican bus lines do not usually publish schedules or fares. You have to ask someone who knows (such as your hotel desk clerk), or call the bus station. Only a sprinkling of travel agents bother with handling bus tickets. If you don't want to spend the time to get a reserved ticket yourself, hire someone trustworthy to do it for you. Another option is to get to the bus station early enough on your traveling day to ensure that you'll get a bus to your destination.

Although most luxury and first-class lines accept credit cards and issue computer-printed tickets at their major stations, a sizable fraction of reserved bus tickets are sold for cash and are handwritten, including an assigned *número de asiento* (seat number). If you miss the bus, you lose your money. Furthermore, airlines-style automated reservations systems have not yet arrived at minor Mexican bus stations. Consequently, you can generally buy reserved tickets only at the *salida local* (local departure) station. (An agent in Iguala, for example, may not be able to reserve you a ticket on a bus that originates in Acapulco, 100 miles to the south.)

Request a reserved seat, if possible, with numbers 1–25 in the *delante* (front) to *medio* (middle) of the bus. The rear seats are often occupied by smokers, drunks, and rowdies. At night, you will sleep better on the *lado derecho* (right side), away from the glare of oncoming traffic lights.

Baggage is generally secure on Mexican buses. Label it securely, however. Overhead racks are generally too cramped to accommodate airline-size carry-ons. Carry a small bag with your money and irreplaceables on your person; pack clothes and less-essentials in your checked luggage. For peace of mind, watch the handler put your checked baggage on the bus and watch to make sure it is not mistakenly taken off the bus at intermediate stops.

If your baggage gets misplaced, remain calm. Bus employees are generally competent and conscientious. If you are patient, recovering your luggage will become a matter of honor for many of them. Baggage handlers are at the bottom of the pay scale; a tip for their mostly thankless job is very much appreciated.

On long trips, carry food, beverages, and toilet paper. Station food may be dubious, and the sanitary facilities may be ill-maintained.

If you are waiting for a first-class bus at an intermediate *salida de paso* (passing departure), you have to trust to luck that there will be an empty seat. If not, your best option may be to ride a more frequent second-class bus.

BY CAR OR RV
Rental Car

Car and Jeep rentals are an increasingly popular transportation option for Ixtapa-Zhuatanejo region travelers. A rental offers mobility and independence for local sightseeing and beach excursions. In the resorts, most of the gang's there: Hertz, Avis, Alamo, and Budget, plus a few local outfits. They always require drivers to have a valid driver's license, passport, a major credit card, and may require a minimum age of 25. Some local companies do not accept credit cards, but offer lower rates in return.

Base prices of international agencies such as Hertz and Avis are not cheap. With a 17 percent value-added tax and mandatory insurance, rentals run more than in the United States. The cheapest possible rental car, usually a used, stick-shift VW Beetle, or better, Nissan Tsuru, runs $35–60 per day or $220–400 per week, depending on location and season. Prices are highest and availability lowest during Christmas and pre-Easter weeks. Before departure, use the international agencies' toll-free numbers and websites for availability, prices, and reservations. During nonpeak seasons, you may save lots of pesos by waiting until arrival and renting a car through a local agency. Shop around, starting with the agent in your hotel lobby or with the local Yellow Pages (under *"Automoviles, renta de"*).

Car insurance that covers property damage, public liability, and medical payments is a legal requirement with your rental car. If you get into an accident without insurance, you will be in deep trouble, and may have to spend an overnight in jail. Narrow, rough roads and animals grazing at roadside make driving in Mexico more hazardous than back home.

BY TAXI AND LOCAL TOUR
Taxis

The high prices of rental cars make taxis a viable option for local excursions. Cars are luxuries, not necessities, for most Mexican families. Travelers might profit from the Mexican money-saving practice of piling everyone in a taxi for a Sunday outing. You may find that an all-day taxi and driver, who, besides relieving you of driving, will become your impromptu guide, will cost no more than a rental car.

The magic word for saving money by taxi is *colectivo:* a taxi you share with other travelers. The first place you'll practice getting a taxi will be at either the Ixtapa-Zihuatanejo or Acapulco airport, where *colectivo* tickets are routinely sold from booths near the terminal exit door.

If, however, can pay for your own private taxi (or you need space for more than four people), ask for a *taxi especial,* which will run about three or four times the per-person tariff for a *colectivo.*

Your airport experience will prepare you for in-town taxis, which I've never seen with a meter anywhere in the Ixtapa-Zihuatanejo region. You must establish the price before getting in. Bargaining comes with the territory in Mexico, so don't shrink from it, even though it seems a hassle. If you get into a taxi without an agreed-upon price, you are letting yourself in for a potentially nasty hassle later. If your driver's price is too high, he'll probably come to his senses as soon as you hail another taxi.

After a few days, getting taxis around town will be a cinch. You'll find that you don't have to take the more expensive taxis lined up in your hotel driveway. If the hotel taxi price isn't right, walk toward the street and hail a regular taxi.

In town, if you can't find a taxi, it may be because taxis are waiting for riders at the local stand, called a taxi *sitio.* Ask someone to direct you to it: *"Disculpe. ¿Dónde está el sitio taxi, por favor?"* ("Excuse me. Where is the taxi stand, please?").

Local Tours and Guides

For many Ixtapa-Zihuatanejo region travelers, locally arranged tours offer a hassle-free alternative to sightseeing by rental car or taxi. Hotels and travel agencies, many of whom maintain front-lobby travel and tour desks, offer a bounty of sightseeing, water sports, bay cruise, fishing, and wildlife-viewing tour opportunities.

Visas and Officialdom

PASSPORTS AND TOURIST CARDS

Your passport is your positive proof of national identity; without it, your status in any foreign country is in doubt. Don't leave home without one. In fact, Mexican border inspection officials require that everyone (except babes in arms) must have a valid passport to enter Mexico; U.S. Immigration rules require that everyone, including **U.S. Citizens must have a valid passport in order to re-enter the U.S.** United States citizens may obtain passports (allow 4–6 weeks) at local post offices. For-fee private passport agencies can speed this process and get you a passport within a week, maybe less.

For U.S. and Canadian citizens, entry by air into Mexico for a few weeks could hardly be easier. At the airline check-in desk agents immediately inspect your passport. During the flight, attendants hand out blank tourist cards *(tarjetas turísticas)* and immigration officers make them official by glancing at passports and stamping the cards at the immigration entrance gate. Business travel permits for 30

MEXICO TOURISM BOARD OFFICES

More than a dozen Mexico Tourism Board (Consejo de Promoción Turístico de Mexico, CPTM) offices and scores of Mexican government consulates operate in the United States, Canada, Europe, South America, and Asia. Consulates generally handle questions of Mexican nationals abroad, while Mexico Tourism Boards serve travelers heading for Mexico.

For straightforward dedtination questions and Mexico regional information brochures, contact the Tourism Board (U.S./Can. tel. 800/44-MEXICO or 800/446-3942, www.visitmexico.com). If you need more details and read a bit of Spanish, you might find visiting www.cptm.com.mx helpful also. Otherwise, contact one of the North American, European, South American, or Asian Mexico Tourism Boards directly for guidance.

IN NORTH AMERICA

From Alaska, Arizona, California, Colorado, Hawaii, Idaho, Montana, Nevada, Utah, Washington and Wyoming, contact the **Los Angeles** office (2401 W. Sixth St., Fourth Floor, Los Angeles, CA 90057, tel. 213/739-6336, fax 213/739-6340, losangeles@visitmexico.com).

From Alberta, British Columbia, Alberta, Saskatchewan, and the Yukon and Northwest Territories, contact the **Vancouver** office (999 W. Hastings St., Suite 1110, Vancouver, BC, V6C 2W2, tel. 604/669-2845, fax 604/669-3498, mgarcia@visitmexico.com).

From Arkansas, Colorado, Louisiana, New Mexico, Oklahoma, and Texas, contact the **Houston** office (4507 San Jacinto, Suite 308, Houston TX 77004, tel. 713/772-2581, fax 713/772-6058, houston@visitmexico.com).

From Alabama, Florida, Georgia, Mississippi, Tennessee, North Carolina, Puerto Rico, and South Carolina, contact the **Miami** office (5975 Sunset Drive #305, Miami, FL 33143, tel. 786/621-2909, fax 786/621-2907, miami@visitmexico.com).

From Illinois, Indiana, Iowa, Kansas, Kentucky, Michigan, Minnesota, Missouri, Nebraska, North Dakota, Ohio, South Dakota, and Wisconsin, contact the **Chicago** office (225 North Michigan Ave., 18th Floor, Suite 1800, Chicago, IL 60601, tel. 312/228-0517, fax 312/228-0515, chicago@visitmexico.com).

From Connecticut, Delaware, Kentucky, Maine, Maryland, Massachusetts, New Hampshire, New Jersey, New York, Pennsylvania, Rhode Island, Vermont, Virginia, Washington D.C., and West Virginia, contact the **New York** office (400 Madison Avenue, Suite 11C, New York, NY 10017, tel. 212/308-2110, fax 212/308-9060, mmora@visitmexico.com).

From Ontario, Manitoba, and the Nunavut

days or fewer are handled by the same simple procedures.

Canadian residents must similarly show a valid passport upon entry into Mexico. Nationals of other countries may be subject to different or additional regulations. For advice, consult your regional Mexico Tourism Board Office or local Mexican consulate. (For a detailed list of Mexican consulates in the U.S., see www.mexonline.com/consulate.htm.)

For more complicated cases, get your tourist card early enough to allow you to consider the options. Tourist cards can be issued for multiple entries and a maximum validity of 180 days; photos are often required. If you don't

request multiple entry or the maximum time, your card will probably be stamped single entry, valid for some shorter period, such as 90 days. If you're not sire how long you'll stay in Mexico, request the maximum (180 days is the absolute maximum for a tourist card; long-term foreign residents of Mexico routinely make semiannual "border runs" for new tourist cards).

Don't Lose Your Tourist Card! If you do, be prepared with a copy of the original, which you should present to the nearest federal Migración (Immigration) office (on duty at the Ixtapa-Zihuatanejo and Acapulco airports) and ask for a duplicate tourist permit. Savvy travelers carry copies of their tourist cards while leaving

---

Territory, contact the **Toronto** office (2 Bloor St. West, Suite 1502, Toronto, Ontario M4W 3E2, tel. 416/925-0704, fax 416/925-6061, toronto@visitmexico.com).

From New Brunswick, Newfoundland, Nova Scotia, Prince Edward Island, and Quebec, contact the **Montreal** office (1 Place Ville Marie, Suite 1931, Montreal, Quebec H3B2C3, tel. 514/871-1052 or 514/871-1103, fax 514/871-3825, montreal@visitmexico.com).

IN EUROPE

In Europe, from England, Wales, Scotland, Ireland, Sweden, Estonia, Lithuania, and Latvia, contact the **London** office (Wakefield House, 41 Trinity Square, London EC3N 4DJ, England, UK, tel. 207/488-9392, fax 207/265-0704, uk@visitmexico.com).

From Hungary, Poland, Slovenia, Slovakia, Germany, Austria, German Switzerland, and the Czech Republic, contact the **Frankfurt** office (Taunusanlage 21, D-60325 Frankfurt-am-Main, Deutschland, tel. 697/103-3383, fax 697/103-3755, germany@visitmexico.com).

From France, Belgium, Luxembourg, Monaco, Russia, and French Switzerland, contact the **Paris** office (4 Rue Notre-Dame des Victoires, 75002 Paris, France, tel. 1/428-69612, 1/428-69613, fax 1/428-60580, france@visitmexico.com).

From Spain and Portugal contact the **Madrid** office (Carrera San Jeronimo 46, 28014 Madrid, España, tel. 91/561-3520, 91/561-1827, fax 91/411-0759, spain@visitmexico.com).

From Italy, Turkey, Israel, Cyprus, and Malta, contact the **Rome** office (Via Barbarini 3-piso 7, 00187 Roma, Italia, tel. 06/487-4698, fax 06/487-3630, fax 06/420-4293, italy@visitmexico.com).

IN SOUTH AMERICA

From Brazil, contact the **Sao Paulo** office (Alameda Administrativo, Rocha Azevedo 882, Conjunto 31, Tercer Andador, Sao Paulo, Brazil, 01410-002, tel. 3088-2129, or 3082-3981, fax 3083-5005, brasil@visitmexico.com).

From Argentina, contact the **Buenos Aires** office (Avenida Reconquista 1056, piso 11, 1003 Barrio Retiro CABA, Buenos Aires, Argentina, tel. 1/4139-6670, fax 1/4139-6771, argentina@visitmexico.com).

IN ASIA

From Japan, Korea, India, Indonesia, Malaysia, Singapore, Thailand, Taiwan, and Vietnam, contact the **Tokyo** office (2-15-1-3F, Nagata-Cho, 2-chome, Chiyoda-ku, Tokyo, Japan 100-0014, tel. 335/030-290, fax 335/030-643, japan@visitmexico.com, and pnajar@visitmexico.com).

the original safe in their hotel rooms. Lacking a copy of the original, you might present some alternate proof of your date of arrival in Mexico, such as a stamped passport or airline ticket.

STUDENT AND BUSINESS VISAS

A visa is a notation stamped and signed on your passport showing the number of days and entries allowable for your trip. If you need to stay in Mexico more than 180 days, you may apply (sometimes by enduring considerable red tape) at the consulate nearest your home. However, an ordinary 180-day tourist card may be the easiest student or business visa option, if you can manage it.

ENTRY FOR CHILDREN AND PETS

Mexican rules for traveling children are very specific: Children under 18 traveling in Mexico, must have their own tourist cards and be accompanied either by their parents, or by adults carrying an affidavit that gives permission (including relevant dates and locations), notarized by the children's parents. Parents can smooth the entry process by getting a passport and filling out a Mexican tourist card for each of their children.

Ixtapa-Zihuatanejo travelers should hurdle all such possible delays far ahead of time in the cool calm of their local Mexican consulate rather than the hot, hurried atmosphere of a border or airport immigration station.

A pile of red tape may delay the entry of dogs, cats, and other pets into Mexico. Be prepared with veterinary-stamped health and rabies certificates for each animal. For more information, contact your regional Mexico Tourism Board or your local Mexican consulate.

CAR PERMITS

If you drive to Mexico, you will need a permit for your car. Upon entry into Mexico, be ready with originals and copies of your proof-of-ownership or registration papers (state title certificate, registration, or notarized bill of sale), current license plates, and current driver's license. The auto permit fee runs about $30, payable only by non-Mexican bank MasterCard, Visa, or American Express credit cards. (The credit-card-only requirement discourages those who sell or abandon U.S.-registered cars in Mexico without paying customs duties.) Credit cards must bear the same name as the vehicle proof-of-ownership papers.

The resulting car permit becomes part of the owner's tourist card and receives the same length of validity. Vehicles registered in the name of an organization or person other than the driver must be accompanied by a notarized affidavit authorizing the driver to use the car in Mexico for a specific time.

Border officials generally allow you to carry or tow additional motorized vehicles (motorcycle, another car, large boat) into Mexico but will probably require separate documentation and fee for each vehicle. If a Mexican official desires to inspect your trailer or motor home, go through it with him.

Accessories, such as a small trailer, boat shorter than six feet, CB radio, or outboard motor, may be noted on the car permit and must leave Mexico with the car.

For more details on motor vehicle entry and what you may bring in your baggage to Mexico, you might also consult the AAA (American Automobile Association) *Mexico TravelBook.*

Since Mexico does not recognize foreign automobile insurance, you must buy Mexican automobile insurance.

CROSSING THE BORDER AND RETURNING HOME

Squeezing through border bottlenecks during peak holidays and rush hours can be time-consuming. Avoid crossing 7–9 A.M. and 4:30–6:30 P.M.

Just before returning across the border with your car, park and have a customs *(aduana)* official **remove and cancel the holographic identity sticker that you received on entry.** If possible, get a receipt *(recibo)* or other written verification that it's been canceled *(cancelado).* Travelers have received stiff fines for inadvertently carrying uncanceled car entry stickers on their windshields.

At the same time, return all other Mexican permits, such as tourist cards and hunting and fishing licenses. Also, be prepared for Mexico exit inspection, especially for cultural artifacts and works of art, which may require exit permits. Certain religious and pre-Columbian artifacts, legally the property of the Mexican government, cannot be taken from the country.

If you entered Mexico with your car, you cannot legally leave without it except by permission from local customs authorities, usually the local *aduana* (Customs House) or the Oficina Federal de Hacienda (Federal Treasury Office).

All returnees are subject to U.S. immigration and customs inspection. These inspections have become generally more time-consuming since September 11, 2001. The worst bottlenecks are at busy border crossings, especially Tijuana and, to a lesser extent, Mexicali, Nogales, Ciudad Juárez, Nuevo Laredo, and Matamoros, all of which should be avoided during peak hours.

United States law allows a fixed value ($800 at present) of duty-free goods per returnee. This may include no more than one liter of alcoholic spirits, 200 cigarettes, and 100 cigars. Up to 10 percent duty will be applied to the first $1,000 (fair retail value, save your receipts) in excess of your $800 exemption. You may, however, mail packages (up to $100 value each) of gifts duty-free to friends and relatives in the United States. Make sure to clearly write "unsolicited gift" and a list of the value and contents on the outside of the package. Perfumes (over $5), alcoholic beverages, and tobacco may not be included in such packages.

Improve the security of such mailed packages by sending them by Mexpost class, similar to U.S. Express Mail service. Even better (but much more expensive), send them by Federal Express, DHL or Estafeta international couriers, which maintain offices in Zihuatanejo, Acapulco, Chilpancingo, Iguala, and other larger Ixtapa-Zihuatanejo region towns.

U.S. GOVERNMENT CUSTOMS AND WILDLIFE INFORMATION

For more information on U.S. customs regulations important to travelers abroad, read or download the useful pamphlet *Know Before You Go,* by visiting the U.S. Customs and Border Patrol website (www.cpb.gov). Click on "Travel" at the top of the home page, then scroll down to *Know Before You Go.*

For more information on the importation of endangered wildlife products, contact the Fish and Wildlife Service (1849 C. St. NW, Washington, DC 20240, toll-free tel. 800/344-WILD, www.fws.gov).

Recreation

BEACHES

Their soft sand, gentle waves, and South Seas ambience have made the golden shores of Ixtapa, Zihuatanejo and Acapulco magnets for a generation of seekers of paradise. And while those brilliant strands are justly renowned, travelers are increasingly discovering the many small beach hideaways, such as Pie de la Cuesta, Troncones, Barra de Potosí, Playa Escondida, El Carrizal, Playa Ventura, and Playa Las Peñitas, which beckon beyond the famous resorts.

Other travelers take adventure a step further and set up camp to enjoy the solitude and the rich wildlife of even more pristine shorelines. They explore beaches that vary from pristine driftwood-strewn barrier dunes and wildlife-rich jungle lagoons to foamy tide pools and sand of seemingly innumerable colors and consistencies.

Sand makes the beach—and the Ixtapa-Zihuatanejo region has plenty—from warm golden quartz to cool, velvety white coral. Some beaches drop steeply to turbulent, close-in surf, fine for fishing. Others are level, with gentle, rolling breakers, made for surfing and swimming.

Beaches are fascinating for the surprises they yield. The Ixtapa-Zihuatanejo region's beaches, especially the hidden strands near resorts and the dozens of miles of wilderness beaches and tide pools, yield troves of shells and treasures of flotsam and jetsam for those who enjoy looking for them. Beachcombing is more rewarding during the summer–fall storm season, when big waves deposit acres of fresh shells—among them conch, scallop, clams, combs of Venus, whelks, limpets, olives, cowries, starfish, and sand dollars.

During the summer rainy season, beaches near river mouths are often fantastic outdoor galleries of wind- and water-sculpted snags and giant logs deposited by the downstream flood.

Snorkeling and Scuba Diving

A number of exciting clear-water sites, especially around Ixtapa and Zihuatanejo, and offshore Isla Roqueta in Acapulco, await both beginner and expert scuba divers. Veteran divers usually arrive during the dry winter and early spring when river outflows are mere trickles, leaving offshore waters clear. In Ixtapa, Zihuatanejo, and Acapulco, professional dive shops rent equipment, provide lessons and guides, and transport divers to choice sites.

While convenient, rented equipment is often less than satisfactory. To be sure, serious divers bring their own gear. This should probably include wetsuits in the winter, when many swimmers begin to feel cold after an unprotected half-hour in the water.

Surfing, Sailing, Sailboarding, and Kayaking

The Ixtapa-Zihuatanejo shoreline is blessed by a sprinkling of fruitful surfing spots, notably at Playa Las Gatas in Zihuatanejo Bay and Playa Escolleros and Playa Linda in Ixtapa. Moreover, in Acapulco, surfing enthusiasts challenge the powerful open-ocean waves at Playa Revolcadero not far east of Acapulco Bay. Farther afield, a number of crystalline strands, such as Troncones, Piedra Tlalcoyunque, Playa Escondida, Playa Cayaquitos, Playa El Calvario, Playa Ventura, and Punta Maldonado, also offer good seasonal surfing breaks.

The surf everywhere is highest and best during the July–November hurricane season, when big swells from storms far out at sea attract platoons of surfers to favored beaches.

Sailboarders, sailboaters, and kayakers—who, by contrast, require a bit more tranquil waters—do best in the Ixtapa-Zihuatanejo region's winter or spring. Aquatics shops rent sailboarding outfits, sailboats, and kayaks at a number of resort hotel beaches on both Zihuatanejo Bay and Ixtapa's main beach and Acapulco Bay.

The Ixtapa-Zihuatanejo region's many coastal lagoons offer fine sailboating and kayaking opportunities. To name just a few, check out either Laguna Barra de Potosí, just southeast of Zihuatanejo, or Laguna Coyuca at Pie de la Cuesta, just northwest of Acapulco (both of which may have rentals available).

While beginners can have fun with the equipment available from rental shops, serious surfers, sailboarders, sailboaters, and kayakers should pack their own gear.

POWER SPORTS

Ixtapa, and to a greater extent, Acapulco, have long been a center for motorboating, water-skiing, parasailing, and personal watercraft riding. Crowded conditions on Acapulco Bay have fortunately pushed most water-skiing to spacious Laguna Coyuca (at Playa Pie de la Cuesta) east of town. There, a few well-equipped providers offer equipment and lessons for about $50 per half hour.

In parasailing, a motorboat pulls while a parachute lifts you, like a soaring gull, high over the ocean. After 5 or 10 minutes the driver deposits you—usually gently—back on the sand.

Personal watercraft (such as WaveRunners) are like snowmobiles except that they operate on water, where, with a little practice, beginners can quickly learn to whiz over the waves.

Although Acapulco and Ixtapa resort hotels' aquatic shops generally provide experienced power-sports crews and equipment, crowded conditions increase the hazard to both participants and swimmers. You, as the patron, are paying plenty for the privilege; you have a right to expect that your providers and crew are well-equipped, sober, and cautious.

Beach Buggies and ATVs

Some visitors enjoy racing along the beach and rolling over dunes in beach buggies and ATVs (all-terrain vehicles—*motos* in Mexico), balloon-tired, three-wheeled motor scooters. While certain resort rental agencies cater to the growing use of such vehicles, limits are in order. Of all the proliferating high-horsepower beach pastimes, these are the most intrusive. Noise, exhaust, and gasoline pollution, injuries to operators and bystanders, scattering of wildlife and destruction of their habitats have led (and I hope will continue to lead) to the restriction of dune buggies and ATVs on Ixtapa-Zihuatanejo regional beaches.

FISHING

Experts agree: The Ixtapa-Zihuatanejo region is a world-class deep-sea and surf fishing ground. Sportspeople routinely bring in dozens of species from among the hundreds that have been hooked in Ixtapa-Zihuatanejo regional waters.

Surf Fishing

Most good fishing beaches away from the immediate resort areas will typically have only a few locals (mostly with nets) and fewer visitors. Mexicans typically do little sportfishing. Most either make their living from fishing, or they do none at all. Consequently, a few shops (in Zihuatanejo and Acapulco) sell fishing equipment; plan to bring your own surf-fishing tackle, including net, poles, hooks, lures, line, and weights.

Your best general information source before you leave home is a good local bait-and-tackle shop. Tell the folks there where you're going, and they'll often know the best lures and bait to use and what fish you can expect to catch with them.

In any case, the cleaner the water, the more interesting your catch. On a good day, your reward might be good-eating *cabrillas,* porgies, *sierras* or snook, pulled from the Ixtapa-Zihuatanejo region surf.

You can't have everything, however. Foreigners cannot legally take Mexican abalone, coral, lobster, clams, rock bass, sea fans, shrimp, turtles, or seashells. Neither are they supposed to buy them directly from fishermen.

Deep-Sea Fishing

A deep-sea boat rental generally includes the boat and crew for a full or half day, plus equipment and bait for two to six people, not including food or drinks. The full-day price depends upon the season. Around Christmas and New Year's and before Easter (when reservations will be mandatory) a big boat can run $450 and up at Acapulco and Zihuatanejo. During low season, however, you might be able to bargain a captain down to as low as $250.

Renting an entire big boat is not the only choice. Winter sportfishing is sometimes so brisk at Ixtapa-Zihuatanejo and Acapulco and that travel agencies can make reservations for individuals for about $80 per person per day.

Pangas (outboard launches), seating 2–6 passengers, are available for as little as $75, depending on the season.

Bringing Your Own Boat

If you're going to do lots of fishing, your own boat may be your most flexible and economical option. One big advantage is that you can go to the many excellent fishing grounds the charter boats do not frequent. Keep your equipment simple, scout around the dock, and keep your eyes peeled and ears open for local regulations and customs, plus tide, wind, and fish-edibility information.

FISH

A bounty of fish dart, swarm, jump, and wriggle in the Ixtapa-Zihuatanejo region's surf, reefs, lagoons, and offshore depths. While many make delicious dinners (albacore, dorado, pez gallo, and many more), others are tough (sailfish), bony (bonefish), and even poisonous (puffers). Some grow to half-ton giants (marlin, Goliath fish, sunfish), while others are diminutive poor-eating reef-grazers (parrot fish, damselfish, angelfish), whose bright colors delight snorkelers and divers. Here's a sampling of what you might find underwater or on your dinner plate.

- **albacore** (albacora, atún): 2-4 feet in size; blue; found in deep waters; excellent taste

- **angelfish** (angel): one foot; yellow, orange, blue; reef fish

- **barracuda** (barracuda, picuda): two feet; brown; deep waters; good taste

- **black marlin** (marlin negro): six feet; blue-black; deep waters; good taste

- **blue marlin** (marlin azul): eight feet; blue; deep waters; poor taste

- **bobo** (barbudo): one foot; blue, yellow; found in surf; fair taste

- **bonefish** (macabi): one foot; blue or silver; found inshore; poor taste

- **bonito** (bonito): two feet; black; deep waters; good taste

- **butterfly fish** (muñeca): six inches; black, yellow; reef fish

- **chub** (chopa): one foot; gray; reef fish; good taste

- **croaker** (corvina): two feet; brownish; found along inshore bottoms; rare and protected

- **damselfish** (castañeta): four inches; brown, blue, orange; reef fish

- **dolphinfish, mahimahi** (dorado): three feet; green, gold; deep waters; excellent taste

- **grouper** (garropa): three feet; brown, rust; found offshore and in reefs; good taste

- **grunt** (burro): eight inches; black, gray; found in rocks, reefs

- **jack** (toro): 1-2 feet; bluish-gray; offshore; good taste

- **mackerel** (sierra): two feet; gray with gold spots; offshore; good taste

- **mullet** (lisa): two feet; gray; found in sandy bays; good taste

- **needlefish** (agujón): three feet; blue-black; deep waters; good taste

- **Pacific porgy** (pez de pluma): 1-2 feet; tan; found along sandy shores; good taste

- **parrot fish** (perico, pez loro): one foot; green, pink, blue, orange; reef fish

- **puffer** (botete): eight inches; brown; inshore; poisonous

- **red snapper** (huachinango, pargo): 1-2 feet; reddish pink; deep waters; excellent taste

- **roosterfish** (pez gallo): three feet; black, blue; deep waters; excellent taste

- **sailfish** (pez vela): five feet; blue-black; deep waters; tough, poor taste

- **sardine** (sardina): eight inches; blue-black; offshore; good taste

- **sea bass** (cabrilla): 1-2 feet; brown, ruddy; reef and rock crevices; good taste

- **shark** (tiburón): 2-10 feet; black to blue; in- and offshore; good taste

- **snook** (robalo): 2-3 feet; black-brown; found in brackish lagoons; excellent taste

- **spadefish** (chambo): one foot; black-silver; found along sandy bottoms; reef fish

- **swordfish** (pez espada): five feet; black to blue; deep waters; good taste

- **triggerfish** (pez puerco): 1-2 feet; blue, rust, brown, black; reef fish; excellent taste

- **wahoo** (peto, guahu): 2-5 feet; green to blue; deep waters; excellent taste

- **yellowfin tuna** (atún amarilla): 2-5 feet; blue, yellow; deep waters; excellent taste

- **yellowtail** (jurel): 2-4 feet; blue, yellow; offshore; excellent taste

Fishing Licenses and Boat Permits

Anyone, regardless of age, who is either fishing or riding in a fishing boat in Mexico is required to have a fishing license. Although Mexican fishing licenses are obtainable from certain bait-and-tackle stores and car insurance agents or at government fishing offices everywhere along the coast, save yourself time and trouble by getting both your fishing licenses and boat permits by mail ahead of time from the Mexican Department of Fisheries. Call at least a month before departure (U.S. tel. 619/233-4324, fax 619/233-0344, no website) and ask for (preferably faxed) applications and the fees (which are reasonably priced, but depend upon the period of validity and the fluctuating exchange rate). On the application, fill in the names (exactly as they appear on passports) of the people requesting licenses. Include a cashier's check or a money order for the exact amount, along with a stamped, self-addressed envelope. Address the application to the Mexican Department of Fisheries (Oficina de Pesca, 2550 5th Ave., Suite 15, San Diego, CA 92103-6622).

TENNIS AND GOLF

Most Mexicans are working too hard to be playing much tennis and golf. Consequently, nearly all courses and courts are private. In Ixtapa, one public and one private course serve golfers. Acapulco golfers enjoy one public *campo de golf* (golf course) and at least two plush private ones.

As for tennis, plenty of private courts are available in both Ixtapa and Acapulco. If you are planning on a lot of golf and tennis, check into (or inquire about court rental at) one of the many hotels with these facilities. Use of hotel tennis courts is often, but not always, included in your hotel tariff. If not, fees will run about $10 per hour. Golf greens fees, which begin at about $60 for 18 holes, are always extra.

BULLFIGHTING

It is said there are two occasions for which Mexicans arrive on time: funerals and bullfights.

Bullfighting is a recreation, not a sport. The bull is outnumbered seven to one and the outcome is never in doubt. Even if the matador (literally, killer) fails in his duty, his assistants will entice the bull away and slaughter it in private beneath the stands.

Moreover, Mexicans don't call it a "bullfight"; it's the *corrida de toros,* during which six bulls are customarily slaughtered, beginning at around 5 P.M. After the beginning parade, featuring the matador and his helpers, the picadores and the banderilleros, the first bull rushes into the ring in a cloud of dust. Clockwork *tercios* (thirds) define the ritual: the first, the *puyazos* (stabs), requires that two picadores on horseback thrust lances into the bull's shoulders, weakening it. During the second *tercio,* the banderilleros dodge the bull's horns to stick three long, streamered darts into its shoulders.

Trumpets announce the third *tercio* and the appearance of the matador. The bull—weak, confused, and angry—is ready for the finish. The matador struts, holding the red cape, daring the bull to charge. Form now becomes everything. The expert matador takes complete control of the bull, which rushes at the cape, past its ramrod-erect opponent. For charge after charge, the matador works the bull to exactly the right spot in the ring—in front of the judges, a lovely señorita, or perhaps the governor—where the matador mercifully delivers the precision *estocada* (killing sword thrust) deep into the drooping neck of the defeated bull.

Most sizable Ixtapa-Zihuatanejo region towns, including Zihuatanejo, Taxco, Chilpancingo, Iguala, and Ometepec, stage *corridos de toros.*

In Acapulco, *corridas de toros* are staged late Sunday afternoons seasonally, usually January–March, at the arena (here called a *frontón*) near west-side Playa Caletilla.

Accommodations

The Ixtapa-Zihuatanejo region has many hundreds of lodgings to suit every style and pocketbook: world-class resorts, small beachside hotels, homey *casas de huéspedes* (guesthouses), palm-shaded trailer parks, and many dozens of miles of pristine beaches, ripe for camping.

High seasons depend on whether the visitors are international or domestic: international visitors, mostly from the United States, Canada, and Europe, begin arriving in droves around December 20 and customarily remain in significant numbers through Easter. Mexican vacationers, on the other hand, concentrate in the resorts during holidays, especially Christmas–New Year's, Semana Santa (pre-Easter week), and weekends, especially during *puentes* (long weekends) around national holidays, and July and August.

As for resort preferences, Ixtapa and Zihuatanejo are mostly popular with international visitors in the winter, and Mexicans during Christmas, New Year and Easter holidays, and July and August. The new-town district of Acapulco is most popular with international visitors; both the old town and the new town with Mexicans. Taxco, on the other hand, is mostly popular with Mexico City Mexicans, especially during holidays and weekends.

Do make sure you arrive with reservations everywhere during the Christmas, New Year, and Easter holidays and certain popular weekends, especially around September 15 (Independence Day) and November 20 (Constitution Day).

Hotel Rates

The rates listed in the destination chapters are U.S. dollar equivalents of peso prices, 15 percent IVA (value-added taxes) included, as quoted by the hotel management at the time of writing. Where many hotels are available—Ixtapa-Zihuatanejo, Acapulco, and Taxco—hotels are listed in ascending order of high-season double-occupancy rates. Both low- and high-season rates are quoted whenever possible and are intended as a general guide only. Since rates fluctuate sharply according to local demand, quoted figures will probably only approximate the asking rate when you arrive. (Some readers, unfortunately, try to bargain by telling desk clerks that, for example, the rate should be $35 because they read it in this book. This is unwise, it makes hotel managers and clerks reluctant to quote rates for fear readers might hold their hotels responsible for such quotes years later.)

In the Ixtapa-Zihuatanejo region, hotel rates depend strongly upon season. To cancel the effect of relatively steep Mexican inflation, rates are reported in U.S. dollars. However, when settling your hotel bill, *you should always pay in pesos.*

Saving Money

The hotel prices quoted in this book are rack rates: the maximum tariff, exclusive of packages and promotions, that you would pay if you walked in and rented an unreserved room for a night. Savvy travelers seldom pay the maximum. Always inquire if there are any discounts or packages (*descuentos o paquetes,* des-koo-AYN-tohs OH pah-KAY-tays). At most times other than the super-high Christmas–New Year's and Easter weeks, you can usually get at least one or two free days for a one-week stay. Promotional packages available during slack seasons may include free extras such as breakfast, a car rental, a boat tour, or a sports rental. A travel agent or travel website can be of great help in shopping around for such bargains.

You nearly always save additional money if you deal in pesos only. Insist on both booking your lodging for an agreed price in pesos and paying the resulting hotel bill in the same pesos, rather than dollars. The reason is that dollar rates quoted by hotels are sometimes based on the hotel desk exchange rate, which is customarily about 5 percent, or even as much as 15 percent, less than bank rates. For example, if the clerk tells you your hotel bill is $1,000, instead of handing over the dollars, or having him mark $1,000 on your credit card slip, ask him how much it is in pesos. Using the desk conversion rate, he might say something like 10,000 pesos (considerably less than the 11,000 pesos that the bank might give for your $1,000). Pay the 10,000 pesos in cash or make sure the clerk marks 10,000 pesos on your credit card slip, and save yourself $100.

For stays of more than two weeks, you'll most likely save money and add comfort with an apartment or condominium rental. Monthly rates range $500–1,500 (less than half the comparable hotel per diem rate) for comfortable one-bedroom furnished kitchenette units, often including resort amenities such as pool and sundeck, beach club, and private view balcony.

GUESTHOUSES AND LOCAL HOTELS

As did most of the celebrated Mexican Pacific coast resorts, both Zihuatanejo and Acapulco began with an old town, which expanded to a new *zona hotelera* (hotel strip) where big hostelries rise along a golden strand. In the old town, near the piquant smells, sights, and sounds of traditional Mexico, are the *casas de huéspedes* (guesthouses) and smaller local hotels where rooms are often arranged around a plant-decorated patio.

Such lodgings vary from scruffy to spic-and-span, and humble to semideluxe. At minimum, you can expect a plain but clean room, a shared toilet and hot-water shower, and plenty of atmosphere for your money. High-season rates, depending on the resort and amenities, are typically between $30 and $50 for two. Discounts are often available for long-term stays. *Casas de huéspedes* will rarely be near the beach, unlike many of the medium-to-high-end local hotels.

Medium-to-High-End Local Hotels

Locally owned and operated hotels make up most of the recommendations of this book. Veteran travelers find it hard to understand why people come to Mexico and spend $200–400 a day for a hotel room when good alternatives

run $60–120, high season, depending upon the resort.

Many locally run hostelries are right on the beach, sharing the same velvety sand and golden sunsets as their much more expensive international-class neighbors. Local hotels, which depend as much on Mexican tourists as foreigners, generally have clean, spacious rooms, often with private view balconies, ceiling fans, and toilet and hot-water bath or shower. What they often lack are the plush extras—air-conditioning, cable TV, phones, tennis courts, exercise gyms, and golf courses—of the luxury resort hotels.

Booking these hotels is straightforward. All can be dialed direct: From the United States, dial 011-52, then the local area code/local number (for example, tel. 755/554-4321 for Zihuatanejo) for information and reservations. Like the big resorts, many local hotels have websites and email addresses, and some even have U.S. and Canada toll-free phone numbers. Always ask about money-saving packages *(paquetes)* and promotions *(promociones)* when reserving.

INTERNATIONAL-CLASS RESORTS

The Ixtapa-Zihuatanejo region has many beautiful, well-managed international-class resort hotels. They spread along the pearly strands of Ixtapa, Zihuatanejo, and Acapulco. Their super-deluxe amenities, moreover, need not be overly expensive. During the right time of year you can vacation at many of the big-name spots, such as Fairmont, Copacabana, Melia, Club Med, Las Brisas, Fiesta Americana, Krystal, Best Western—for surprisingly little. While high-season room tariffs ordinarily run $150–350, low-season (May–Nov., and to a lesser degree, Jan.–Feb.) packages and promotions can cut these prices to as low as $100.

APARTMENTS, BUNGALOWS, CONDOMINIUMS, AND VILLAS

For longer stays, many visitors prefer the convenience and economy of an apartment or condominium or the luxurious comfort of a villa vacation rental. Choices vary, from spartan studios to deluxe beachfront suites and rambling view homes big enough for entire extended families. Prices depend strongly upon season and amenities, from $500 per month for the cheapest to at least 10 times that for the most luxurious.

A Mexican variation on the apartment style of accommodation is called a bungalow, although, in contrast to English-language usage, it does not usually imply a detached dwelling. Common in Zihuatanejo, a bungalow accommodation generally means a kitchenette-suite with less service, but with more space and beds. For families or for long stays by the beach, where you want to save money by cooking your own meals, such an accommodation might be ideal.

At the low end, you can expect a clean, furnished apartment within a block or two of the beach, with kitchen and regular maid service. More luxurious condos, very common in Acapulco and Ixtapa and which usually rent for $500 per week and up, are typically high-rise oceanview suites with hotel-style desk services and resort amenities, such as a pool, whirlpool tub, sundeck, and beach-level restaurant.

Higher up the scale, villas and houses vary from moderately luxurious homes to sky's-the-limit beach-view mansions, blooming with built-in designer luxuries, private pools and beaches, tennis courts, and gardeners, cooks, and maids.

Shopping Around

You'll generally find the most economical apartment, condo, and house rental deals through on-the-spot local contacts, such as local newspaper want-ad sections, neighborhood For Rent ("Renta") signs, or local listing agents.

Be smart and let your fingers do the walking with the very useful website for finding affordable long-term vacation rentals, **Vacation Rentals by Owner** (www.vrbo.com), with dozens of leads in Acapulco, Zihuatanejo, Ixtapa, and Troncones.

If you prefer, you can often write, fax, email, or telephone rental managers—many of whom speak English—directly, using the numbers given in the destination chapters of this book.

Rentals are also available through agents who will make long-distance rental agreements. Local real estate agents such as Century 21, which specializes in nationwide and foreign contacts, sometimes list (or know someone who does list) Ixtapa-Zihuatanejo region vacation rentals. Such rentals are becoming increasingly available through the Internet.

Home Exchange and Renting Out Your Own House

You may also want to consider using the services of a home exchange agency/website whereby you swap homes with someone in the Ixtapa-Zihuatanejo region for an agreed-upon time. For a list of agencies, simply enter "home exchange" into an Internet search engine.

On the other hand, it may be easier to rent or lease your own house and use the income to rent a house or apartment in the Ixtapa-Zihuatanejo region. (Although some people—including myself—have found this strategy successful, talk to someone who's done it to find out if it's your cup of tea.)

CAMPING AND TRAILER PARKS
Beach Camping

Informal beach camping is popular among middle-class Mexican families, especially during the Christmas–New Year's week and during Semana Santa. The crowds even overflow onto the resort beaches of Acapulco, Zihuatanejo Bay, and Ixtapa, where folks set up tents or simply sleep under the stars.

On nearly all other Acapulco-region beaches plenty of camping space is always available. The choice spots, such as Playa Ventura, Playa Las Peñitas, and Playa Puerto Maldonado on the Costa Chica; and Playa El Carrizal, Playa Paraíso, the Laguna de Mitla beach, Playa Escondida, and Playa Ojo de Agua on the Costa Grande, typically have a shady palm grove for camping and at least one *palapa* restaurant that serves drinks and fresh seafood.

© BRUCE WHIPPERMAN

camping on the beach in Troncones

(Heads up for falling coconuts, especially when it's windy.) Cost for parking and tenting is often minimal, typically only the price of food at the restaurant.

Days are often perfect for swimming, strolling, and fishing, and nights are balmy—too warm for a sleeping bag, but fine for a hammock (which allows the air circulation that a tent does not). However, good tents keep out mosquitoes and other pesties, which may be further discouraged by a good bug repellent. Tents can get hot, requiring only a sheet or very light blanket for sleeping cover.

As for the safety of camping on isolated beaches, opinions vary from dire warnings of *bandidos* (bandits) to bland assurances that all is peaceful along the coast. The truth is somewhere in between. Trouble is most likely to occur in the vicinity of resort towns, where a few local thugs sometimes harass isolated campers.

When scouting out an isolated beach for camping, a good rule is to arrive early enough in the day to get a feel for the place. Buy a soda

at the *palapa* or store and take a stroll along the beach. Say *"Buenos días"* to the people along the way; ask if the fishing is good *("¿Pesca buena?").* Above all, use your common sense and intuition. If the people seem friendly, ask if it's *seguro* (safe). If so, ask permission: *"¿Es bueno acampar acá?"* ("Is it okay to camp around here?"). You'll rarely be refused.

Camping Upcountry

Scenic river canyons provide some of the most inviting informal tenting opportunities in the Ixtapa-Zihuatanejo region's vast upcountry hinterland. Two of the best are at Campamento Santa Fe and El Borbollón on the spring-fed Río Azul (Blue River) about 20 miles east of Chilpancingo. Another promising spot is on the Río Papagayo at Pueblo Bravo (below the old Highway 95 bridge crossing, about 30 miles south of Chilpancingo).

You can enjoy one of the most informative and entertaining discussions of camping in Mexico in *The People's Guide to Mexico,* by Carl Franz.

Trailer Parks

Campers who prefer company to isolation usually stay in trailer parks. Unfortunately, development has squeezed out many Ixtapa-Zihuatejo–region trailer parks. Nevertheless, a decent well-equipped beachfront trailer park, the Ixtapa Trailer Park, is newly open, a few miles north of Ixtapa. Also, the bare-bones but popular Trailer Park and Restaurant El Manglar, with all hookups, is operating on Playa La Ropa in Zihuatanejo. Near Acapulco, you'll find three good trailer parks, two on Playa Pie de la Cuesta and a big one on breezy Playa Diamante, by the airport, southeast of town.

Food and Drink

Some travel to the Ixtapa-Zihuatanejo region for the food. True Mexican food is old-fashioned, home-style fare requiring many hours of loving preparation. Such food is short on meat and long on corn tortillas, beans, rice, tomatoes, onions, eggs, and cheese.

Mexican food is the unique product of thousands of years of native tradition. It is based on corn—*teocentli,* the Aztec "holy food"—called *maíz* (mah-EES) by present-day Mexicans. In the past, a Mexican woman spent much of her time grinding and preparing corn: soaking the grain in lime water, which swells the kernels and removes the

---

MEXICAN FOOD

On most Mexican-style menus, diners will find variations on a number of basic themes:

Carnes (meats): *Carne asada* is grilled beef, usually chewy and well-done. Something similar you might see on a menu is *cecina* (say-SEE-nah), dried salted beef grilled to a shoe-leather-like consistency. Much more appetizing is *birria,* a Guadalajara specialty. Traditional *birrias* are of lamb or goat, often wrapped and pit-roasted in maguey leaves. In addition to *asada,* meat cooking styles are manifold, including *guisado* (stewed), *al pastor* (spit barbecue), and *barbacoa* (grill barbecued). Cuts include *lomo* (loin), *chuleta* (chop), *milanesa* (cutlet), and *albóndigas* (meatballs).

Chiles rellenos: Fresh roasted green *chiles,* usually stuffed with cheese but sometimes with fish or meat, coated with batter, and fried. They provide a piquant, tantalizing contrast to tortillas.

Enchiladas and *tostadas:* variations on the filled-tortilla theme. Enchiladas are stuffed with meat, cheese, olives, or beans and covered with sauce and baked, while tostadas consist of toppings served on crisp, open-faced corn tortillas.

Guacamole: This luscious avocado, onion, tomato, lime, and salsa mixture remains the delight it must have seemed to its indigenous inventors centuries ago. In non-tourist Mexico, it's served sparingly as a garnish, rather than in appetizer bowls as is common in the U.S. Southwest (and Mexican resorts catering to North Americans). (Similarly, in non-tourist Mexico, burritos and fajitas, both stateside inventions, seldom if ever appear on menus.)

Moles (MOH-lays): uniquely Mexican specialties. *Mole poblano,* a spicy-sweet mixture of chocolate, *chiles,* and a dozen other ingredients, is cooked to a smooth sauce, then baked with chicken (or turkey, a combination called *mole de pavo*). So *típica* it's widely regarded as the national dish.

Quesadillas: made from soft flour tortillas, rather than corn, quesadillas resemble tostadas and always contain melted cheese.

Sopas: Soups consist of vegetables in a savory chicken broth, and are an important part of both *comida* (afternoon) and *cena* (evening) Mexican meals. *Pozole,* a rich steaming stew of hominy, vegetables, and pork or chicken, often constitutes the prime evening offering

tough seed-coat, and grinding the bloated seeds into meal on a stone metate. Finally, she patted the meal into tortillas and cooked them on a hot baked-mud griddle.

Fewer women these days make tortillas by hand. The gentle pat-pat-pat has been replaced by the whir and rattle of the automatic tortilla-making machine in myriad *tortillerías,* where women and girls line up for their family's daily kilo-stack of tortillas.

Tortillas are to the Mexicans as rice is to the Chinese and bread to the French. Mexican food is invariably some mixture of sauce, meat, beans, cheese, and vegetables wrapped in a tortilla, which becomes the culinary be-all: the food, the dish, and the utensil wrapped into one.

If a Mexican has nothing to wrap in his lunchtime tortilla, he will content himself by rolling a thin filling of salsa (*chile* sauce) in it.

HOT OR NOT?

Much food served in Mexico is not "Mexican." Eating habits, as most other customs, depend upon social class. Upwardly mobile Mexicans typically shun the corn-based *indígena* fare in favor of the European-style food of the Spanish colonial elite: chops, steaks, cutlets, fish, clams, omelets, soups, pasta, rice, and potatoes.

Such fare is often as bland as Des Moines on a summer Sunday afternoon. *No picante*—not spicy—is how the Mexicans describe bland food. *Caliente,* the Spanish adjective for "hot" (as in hot water), does not, in contrast to English usage, imply spicy, or *picante.*

---

of small side-street shops. *Sopa de taco,* an ever-popular country favorite, is a medium-spicy cheese-topped thick *chile* broth served with crisp corn tortillas.

Tacos or **taquitos:** corn tortillas served open or wrapped around any ingredient.

Tamales: as Mexican as apple pie is American. This savory mixture of meat and sauce imbedded in a shell of corn dough and baked in a wrapping of corn husks is rarely known by the singular, however. They're so yummy that one *tamal* invariably leads to more *tamales.*

Tortas: the Mexican sandwich, usually broiled beef, pork, or chicken, topped with fresh tomato and avocado, and stuffed between two halves of a crisp *bolillo* (boh-LEE-yoh) or Mexican bun.

Tortillas y frijoles refritos: cooked brown or black beans, mashed and fried in pork fat, and rolled into tortillas with a dash of vitamin C-rich salsa to form a near-complete combination of carbohydrate, fat, and balanced protein.

BEYOND THE BASICS

Mexican food combinations seem endless. Mexican corn itself has more than 500 recog-nized culinary variations, nearly all from indigenous tradition. This has led to a myriad of permutations on the taco, such as *sopes* (with small and thick tortillas), *garnacho* (flat taco), *chilaquile* (breakfast specialty: shredded tortilla, smothered in sauce and baked with grated cheese and onion), *chalupa* (like a tostada), and *gorditas* (thick corn tortillas).

Taking a lesson from California nouveau cuisine, avant-garde Mexican chefs are returning to traditional ingredients. They're beginning to use more and more *chiles* – habanero, poblano, jalapeño, serrano – prepared in many variations, such as chipotle, ancho, *piquín,* and *mulato. Flor de calabaza* (squash flowers) and *nopal* (cactus) leaves are increasingly finding their way into soups and salads.

More often chefs are serving the wild game – *venado* (venison), *conejo* (rabbit), *guajalote* (turkey), *codorniz* (quail), *armadillo,* and *iguana* – that country Mexicans have always depended upon. As part of the same trend, *cuitlacoche* (corn mushroom fungus), *chapulines* (small french-fried grasshoppers), and *gusanos de maguey* (maguey worms) are being increasingly added as ingredients in fancy restaurants.

CATCH OF THE DAY

- **Ceviche** (say-VEE-chay): A chopped raw-fish appetizer as popular in Zihuatanejo beaches as sushi is on Tokyo side streets. Although it can contain anything from conch to octopus, aficionados say the best ceviche consists of diced *tiburón* (young shark) or *sierra* (mackerel) fillet and plenty of fresh tomatoes, onions, garlic, and *chiles*, all doused with lime juice (the acid of which "cooks" the fish).

- **Filete de pescado:** A fish fillet, sautéed *al mojo* (ahl MOH-hoh) – with butter and garlic, or breaded *(en gabardinas)*.

- **Pescado frito:** Fish, pan-fried whole; if you don't specify that it be cooked *a medio* (lightly), the fish may arrive well done, like a big, crunchy french fry.

- **Pescado veracruzana:** A favorite everywhere. Best with *huachinango* (red snapper), smothered in a savory tomato, onion, *chile*, and garlic sauce. *Pargo* (snapper), *mero* (grouper), and *cabrilla* (sea bass) are also popularly used in this and other specialties.

- **Shellfish:** These are abundant and include *ostiones* (oysters) and *almejas* (clams) by the dozen; *langosta* (lobster) and *langostina* (crayfish) *asado* (broiled), *al vapor* (steamed), or fried. Pots of fresh-boiled *camarones* (shrimp) are sold on the street by the kilo; cafés will make them into *cóctel*, or prepare them *en gabardinas* (breaded) at your request.

© BRUCE WHIPPERMAN

Freshly caught steamed whole lobsters are a frequent treat for Mexican *comida* (afternoon meal).

VEGETARIAN FOOD

Although the availability of healthy food is increasing, strictly vegetarian and vegan cooking is the exception in Mexico, as are macrobiotic restaurants, health-food stores, and organic produce. Meat is such a delicacy for most Mexicans that they can't understand why people would give it up voluntarily. If, as a vegetable-lover, you can manage with corn, beans, cheese, eggs, *legumbres* (vegetables), and fruit, Mexican cooking will suit you fine.

Furthermore, wholesome **Chinese food** is a good source of veggies at several Ixtapa-Zihuatanejo and Acapulco locations, plus at least one each in Chilpancingo, Iguala, and Taxco.

SEAFOOD

Early chroniclers wrote that Aztec Emperor Moctezuma employed a platoon of runners to bring fresh fish 300 miles every day from the sea to his court. In the Ixtapa-Zihuatanejo region, fresh seafood is fortunately much more available from many dozens of shoreline establishments, varying from thatched beach *palapas* to five-star hotel restaurants.

Despite the plenty, Ixtapa-Zihuatanejo region seafood prices reflect high worldwide demand, even at the humblest seaside *palapa*. The freshness and variety, however, make even the typical dishes seem bargains at any price.

FRUITS AND JUICES

Squeezed vegetable and fruit juices (*jugos,* HOO-gohs) are among the widely available delights of the Ixtapa-Zihuatanejo region. Among the many establishments—restaurants, cafés, and *loncherías*—willing to supply you with your favorite *jugo,* the *jugerías* (juice bars) are often the most fun. Colorful fruit piles usually mark *jugerías.* If you don't immediately spot your favorite fruit, ask anyway; it might be hidden in the refrigerator.

Besides your choice of pure juices, a *jugería* will often serve *licuados.* Into the juice, they whip powdered milk, your favorite fruit, and sugar to taste for a creamy afternoon pick-me-up or evening dessert. One big favorite is a cool banana-chocolate *licuado,* which comes out tasting like a milkshake minus the calories.

ALCOHOLIC DRINKS

The Aztecs sacrificed anyone caught drinking fermented beverages without permission. The later, more lenient, Spanish attitude toward getting *borracho* (soused) has led to a thriving Mexican renaissance of native alcoholic beverages: tequila, mescal, Kahlúa, pulque, and *aguardiente.* Tequila and mescal, distilled from the fermented juice of the maguey, originated in Oaxaca, where the best are still made. Quality tequila (named after the Guadalajara-area distillery town) and mescal come 76 proof (38 percent alcohol) and up. A small white worm, endemic to the maguey, is customarily added to each bottle of factory mescal for authenticity.

Pulque, although also made from the sap of the maguey, is locally brewed to a modest alcohol content between that of beer and wine. The brewing houses are sacrosanct preserves, circumscribed by traditions that exclude women and outsiders. The brew, said to be rich in nutrients, is sold to local *pulquerías* and drunk immediately. If you are ever invited into a *pulquería,* it is an honor you cannot refuse.

Aguardiente, by contrast, is the notorious fiery Mexican "white lightning," a locally distilled, dirt-cheap ticket to oblivion for poor Mexican men.

While pulque comes from age-old indigenous tradition, beer (introduced by 19th-century German brewers) is the beverage of modern mestizo Mexico. More full-bodied than "light" U.S. counterparts, Mexican beer enjoys an enviable reputation.

Those visitors who indulge usually know their favorite among the many brands, from light to dark: Superior, Corona, Pacífico,

Tecate, Carta Blanca, Modelo, Dos Equis, Bohemia, Tres Equis, and Negro Modelo. Nochebuena, a hearty dark brew, becomes available only around Christmas.

Mexicans have yet to develop much of a taste for *vino tinto* or *vino blanco* (red or white table wine), although some domestic wines (such as the Baja California labels Cetto and Domecq and the boutique Monte Xanic) and newcomer Chilean (Concha y Toro and more) are at least very drinkable and at best excellent.

BREAD AND PASTRIES
Wonderful, locally-baked bread is a delightful surprise to many first-time visitors to the Ixtapa-Zihuatanejo region. Small bakeries everywhere put out trays of hot, crispy-crusted *bolillos* (rolls) and *panes dulces* (sweet pastries).

A TROVE OF FRUITS AND NUTS

Besides carrying the usual temperate fruits, *jugerías* and especially markets are seasonal sources of a number of exotic (followed by an *) varieties.

- **avocado** (*aguacate* – ah-wah-KAH-tay): Aztec aphrodisiac

- **banana** (*plátano*): many kinds – big and small, red and yellow

- **chirimoya***: green scales, white pulp, sometimes called an *anona*

- **ciruela***: looks like (but tastes better than) a small yellow-to-red plum

- **coconut** (*coco*): coconut "milk," called *agua coco*, is a wonderful and healthy thirst quencher

- **grapes** (*uvas*): August-November season

- **guanabana***: looks, but doesn't taste, like a green mango

- **guava** (*guava*): delicious juice, widely available as all-natural Jumex yummy canned juice

- **lemon** (*lima real* – LEE-mah ray-AHL): uncommon and expensive; use lime instead

- **lime** (*limón* – lee-MOHN): abundant and cheap; douse salads with it

- **mamey*** (mah-MAY): yellow, juicy fruit; excellent for jellies and preserves

- **mango:** king of fruit, in 100 varieties April-September

- **orange** (*naranja* – nah-RAHN-ha): greenish skin but sweet and juicy

- **papaya:** said to aid digestion and healing

- **peach** (*durazno* – doo-RAHS-noh): delicious and widely available as Jumex all-natural canned juice

- **peanut** (*cacahuate* – kah-kah-WAH-tay): home roasted and cheap

- **pear** (*pera*): fall season

- **pecan** (*nuez*): for a treat, try freshly ground pecan butter

- **piña anona***: looks like a thin ear of corn without the husk; tastes like pineapple

- **pineapple** (*piña*): huge, luscious, and cheap

- **strawberry** (*fresa* – FRAY-sah): local favorite

- **tangerine** (*mandarina*): common around Christmas

- **watermelon** (*sandía* – sahn-DEE-ah): perfect on a hot day

- **yaca*** (YAH-kah): a relative of the Asian jackfruit, with pebbly green skin, round and sometimes as large as a football; yummy mild taste

- **zapote*** (sah-POH-tay): yellow, fleshy fruit, said to induce sleep

- **zapote colorado***: brown skin, red, puckery fruit, like persimmon; commonly, but incorrectly, called *mamey*

Pastries are a pleasant Mexican culinary surprise.

The sweets vary from simple cakes, muffins, cookies, and doughnuts to fancy fruit-filled turnovers and puffs. Half the fun occurs before the eating: grab a tray and tongs, peruse the goodies, and pick out the most scrumptious. With your favorite dozen or so finally selected, you take your tray to the cashier, who deftly bags everything up and collects a few pesos (two or three dollars) for your entire mouth-watering selection.

Tips for Travelers

ACCESS FOR TRAVELERS WITH DISABILITIES

Mexican airlines and hotels (especially the large ones) have become sensitive to the needs of travelers with disabilities. Open, street-level lobbies and large, wheelchair-accessible elevators and rooms are available in nearly all Ixtapa-Zihuatanejo region luxury (and some smaller, especially boutique) hotels. Furthermore, a growing number of street-corner curbs accommodate wheelchairs.

Both Mexico and United States law forbids travel discrimination against otherwise qualified people with disabilities. As long as your disability is stable and not liable to deteriorate during passage, you can expect to be treated like any passenger with special needs.

Make reservations far ahead of departure and ask your agent to inform your airline of your needs, such as boarding wheelchair or in-flight oxygen. Be early at the gate to take advantage of the preboarding call.

For many helpful details to smooth your trip, get a copy of *Survival Strategies for Going Abroad* by Laura Hershey, published in 2005 by **Mobility International USA** (132 E. Broadway, Suite 343, Eugene, Oregon 97401, www.miusa.org, tel. 541/343-1284 voice/TTY, fax 541/343-6812). Mobility International is a valuable resource for many disabled lovers of Mexico, for it encourages disabled travelers with a goldmine of information and literature and can provide them with valuable Mexico connections. They publish a regular newsletter and provide information and referrals for international exchanges and homestays.

Similarly, **Partners of the Americas** (1424 K St. NW, Suite 700, Washington, D.C. 20005, tel. 202/628-3300 or 800/322-7844, fax 202/628-3306, info@partners.net, www .partners.net), with chapters in 45 U.S. states, works to improve understanding of disabilities and facilities in Mexico and Latin America. It maintains communications with local organizations and individuals whom disabled travelers may contact at their destinations.

TRAVELING WITH CHILDREN

Children are treasured like gifts from heaven in Mexico. Traveling with kids will ensure your welcome most everywhere. On the beach, take extra precautions to make sure they are protected from the sun.

A sick child is no fun for anyone. Fortunately, clinics and good doctors are available even in most small towns. When in need, ask a storekeeper or a pharmacist, *"¿Dónde hay un doctor, por favor?"* ("¿DOHN-day eye oon doc-TOHR por fah-VOHR?"). In most cases, within five minutes you will be in the waiting room of the local physician or clinic.

Children who do not favor typical Mexican fare can easily be fed with always available eggs, cheese, *hamburguesas,* milk, oatmeal, corn flakes, tomatoes, avocados, bananas, cakes, and cookies.

Your children will generally have more fun if they have a little previous knowledge of Mexico and a stake in the trip. For example, help them select some library picture books and magazines so they'll know where they're going and what to expect, or give them responsibility for packing and carrying their own small travel bag.

© BRUCE WHIPPERMAN

Most Mexicans welcome children as gifts from heaven.

Be sure to mention your children's ages when making air reservations; child discounts of 50 percent or more are sometimes available. Also, if you can arrange to go on an uncrowded flight, you can stretch out and rest on the empty seats.

For more details on traveling with children, check out *Adventuring with Children* by Nan Jeffries.

SENIOR TRAVELERS

Age, according to Mark Twain, is a question of mind over matter: If you don't mind, it doesn't matter. Mexico is a country where whole extended families, from babies to great-grandparents, live together. Elderly travelers will benefit from the respect and understanding Mexicans accord to older people. Besides these encouragements, consider the number of retirees already in havens in Puerto Vallarta, Guadalajara, Manzanillo, Ixtapa-Zihuatanejo, Acapulco, Oaxaca, and other regional centers.

Certain organizations support and sponsor senior travel. Leading the field is **Road Scholar** (formerly Elderhostel, 11 Ave. de Lafayette, Boston, MA 02111-1746, toll-free tel. 800/454-5768, www.roadscholar.org). Check out their list of Mexico programs, which regularly includes a 10-day Spanish-language and culture program.

Some books also feature senior travel opportunities. One of the pithiest is *Unbelievably Good Deals and Great Adventures You Can't Have Unless You're Over 50,* by Joan Rattner Heilman, published by McGraw Hill (2008). Its 200 pages are packed with details of how to get bargains on cruises, tours, car rentals, lodgings, and much, much more.

For seniors with online access (as close as your neighborhood library these days) the **Internet** is a gold mine of senior-oriented travel information. For example, on the Google search engine (www.google.com) home page, I typed in "Senior Travel" and netted more than 80 million responses. Near the top of the list was the **Transitions Abroad** site (www.transitionsabroad.com), which offers a gold mine of a sub-site (www.transitionsabroad.com/listings/travel/senior) with a load of useful resources, centering around senior traveling and living abroad.

GAY AND LESBIAN TRAVELERS

The great majority of visitors find Ixtapa-Zihuatanejo region people both gracious and tolerant. This extends from racial color-blindness to being broad-minded about sexual preference. As long as gay and lesbian visitors don't flaunt their own preference, they will find acceptance most anywhere in the state of Guerrero.

As a result, both Ixtapa-Zihuatanejo and Acapulco, have acquired a growing company of gay- and lesbian-friendly hotels, bars, and entertainments. For example, for Oaxaca City hotel, restaurant, and nightlife details, visit the gay-oriented travel website www.go-oaxaca.com; for a list of gay-friendly bars, nightclubs, and businesses, log on to the subsite www.go-oaxaca.com/lifestyles.html.

Some gay- and lesbian-oriented Internet and print publishers also offer excellent travel guidebooks. One of the most experienced is **Damron Company** (tel. 415/255-0404 or 800/462-6654, www.damron.com), which publishes, both in print and by Internet subscription, the *Damron Women's Travel Guide* and *Damron Men's Travel Guide* guidebooks, containing a wealth of gay and lesbian travel information, including several hotel and restaurant listings in Ixtapa-Zihuatanejo and Acapulco.

If you're interested in more gay and lesbian travel information, advice, and services, check out the San Francisco **Purple Roofs** Internet agency (wheretostay@purpleroofs.com, www.purpleroofs.com). They offer lesbian and gay-friendly Oaxaca hotel and travel agent listings, plus a multitude of services, from tours and air tickets, to travel insurance and hotel reservations.

Health and Safety

STAYING HEALTHY

In the Ixtapa-Zihuatanejo region as everywhere, prevention is the best remedy for illness. For those visitors who confine their travel to the beaten path, a few basic common-sense precautions will ensure vacation enjoyment.

Resist the temptation to dive headlong into Mexico. It's no wonder that people get sick—broiling in the sun, gobbling peppery food, guzzling beer and margaritas, then discoing half the night—all in their first 24 hours. An alternative is to give your body time to adjust. Travelers often arrive tired and dehydrated from travel and heat. During the first few days, drink plenty of bottled water and juice, and take siestas.

Immunizations and Precautions

A good physician can recommend the proper preventatives for your Ixtapa-Zihuatanejo region trip. If you are going to stay pretty much in town, your doctor will probably suggest little more than updating your basic typhoid, diphtheria-tetanus, hepatitis, and polio shots.

For camping or trekking in remote tropical areas—below 4,000 feet (1,200 meters)—doctors often recommend a gamma-globulin shot against hepatitis A and a schedule of chloroquine pills against malaria. While in backcountry areas, use other measures to discourage mosquitoes—and fleas, flies, ticks, no-see-ums, "kissing bugs," and other tropical pesties—from biting you. Common precautions include sleeping under mosquito netting, burning *espirales mosquito* (mosquito coils), and rubbing on plenty of pure DEET (n,n dimethyl-meta-toluamide) "jungle juice," mixed in equal parts with rubbing alcohol (70 percent isopropyl). Although super-effective, 100 percent DEET dries and irritates the skin.

Safe Water and Food

Although municipalities have made great strides in sanitation, food and water are still potential sources of germs in some parts of the Ixtapa-Zihuatanejo region. Although water sources are clean most everywhere, except in a few upcountry localities, it's still safest to drink bottled water only. Hotels, whose success depends vitally on their customers' health, generally provide *agua purificada* (purified bottled water). If, for any reason, the available water is of doubtful quality, add a water purifier, such as "Potable Aqua" brand (get it at a camping goods store before departure) or a few drops per quart of water of *blanqueador* (household chlorine bleach) or *yodo* (tincture of iodine) from the pharmacy.

Bottled water, soft drinks, beer, and fresh fruit juices are so widely available it is easy to avoid tap water, especially in restaurants. Ice and *paletas* (iced juice-on-a-stick) may be risky, especially in non-tourist villages and small towns.

Washing hands with soap before eating is a time-honored Mexican ritual that visitors should religiously follow. The humblest Mexican eatery will generally provide a basin and soap to *lavar las manos* (wash the hands). If it doesn't, don't eat there.

Hot, cooked food is generally safe, as are peeled fruits and vegetables. These days milk and cheese in Mexico are generally processed under sanitary conditions and sold pasteurized (ask, "*¿Pasteurizado?*") and are virtually always safe. Mexican ice cream used to be both bad-tasting and of dubious safety, but national brands available in supermarkets are so much improved that it's no longer necessary to resist ice cream while in town.

In recent years, much cleaner public water and increased hygiene awareness have made salads—once shunned by Mexico travelers—generally safe to eat in tourist-frequented Ixtapa-Zihuatanejo region cafés and restaurants. Nevertheless, lettuce and cabbage, particularly in country villages, are more likely to be contaminated than tomatoes, carrots, cucumbers, onions, and green peppers. In any case, you can douse your salad in *vinagre* (vinegar) or plenty of sliced *limón* (lime) juice, the acidity of which kills most (but not all) bacteria.

Sunburn

For sunburn protection, use a good sunscreen with a sun protection factor (SPF) rated 15 or more, which will reduce burning rays to one-fifteenth or less of direct sunlight. Better still, take a shady siesta-break from the sun during the most hazardous midday hours. If you do get burned, applying your sunburn lotion (or one of the "caine" creams) after the fact usually decreases the pain and speeds healing.

Tattoos

All health hazards don't come from the wild. A number of Mexico travelers have complained of complications from black henna tattoos. When enhanced by the chemical dye PPD, an itchy rash results that can lead to scarring. It's best to play it safe: If you must have a vacation tattoo, get it at an established, professional shop.

First-Aid Kit

In the bug-friendly tropical outdoors, ordinary cuts and insect bites are more prone to infection and should receive immediate first aid. A first-aid kit with aspirin, rubbing alcohol, hydrogen peroxide, water-purifying tablets, household chlorine bleach or iodine for water purifying, swabs, bandages, gauze, adhesive tape, Ace bandage, chamomile *(manzanilla)* tea bags for upset stomachs, Pepto-Bismol, acidophilus tablets, antibiotic ointment, hydrocortisone cream, mosquito repellent, pocket knife, and good tweezers is a good precaution for any traveler and mandatory for campers.

HEALTH PROBLEMS
Traveler's Diarrhea

Traveler's diarrhea (known in Southeast Asia as "Bali Belly" and in Mexico as *turista* or "Montezuma's Revenge") sometimes persists, even among prudent vacationers. You can suffer *turista* for a week after simply traveling between California and Philadelphia or New York. Doctors say the familiar symptoms of runny bowels, nausea, and sour stomach result from normal local bacterial strains to which newcomers' systems need time to adjust. Unfortunately, the dehydration and fatigue from heat and travel reduce your body's natural defenses and sometimes lead to a persistent cycle of sickness at a time when you least want it.

Time-tested protective measures can help your body either prevent or break this cycle. Many doctors and veteran travelers swear by Pepto-Bismol for temporary relief, for soothing sore stomachs and stopping diarrhea. Acidophilus, the bacteria found in yogurt, is widely available in the United States in tablets and aids digestion. Warm *manzanilla* (chamomile) tea, used widely in Mexico (and by Peter Rabbit's mother), provides liquid and calms upset stomachs. Temporarily avoid coffee and alcohol, drink plenty of *manzanilla* tea, and eat bananas and rice for a few meals until your tummy can take regular food.

MEDICAL TAGS AND AIR EVACUATION

Travelers with special medical problems should consider wearing a medical identification tag. For a reasonable fee, **Medic Alert** (2323 Colorado Ave., Turlock, CA 95382, tel. 209/668-3333, toll-free tel. 888/633-4298, www.medicalert.org) provides such tags, as well as an information hotline that will inform doctors of your vital medical background.

In life-threatening emergencies, highly recommended **Aeromedevac** (Gillespie Field Airport, 681 Kenney St., El Cajon, CA 92020, toll-free tel. 800/462-0911, from Mexico 24-hr toll-free tel. 001-800/832-5087, www.aeromedevac.com) provides high-tech jet ambulance service from any Mexican locale to a U.S. hospital for roughly $20,000.

Alternatively, you might consider the similar services of **Med-Jet Assist** (Birmingham, Alabama, Intl. Airport, 4900 69th St., Birmingham AL, 35206, toll-free U.S. tel. 800/527-7478, www.medjet assist.com; in emergencies, world-wide, call U.S. tel. 205/595-6626 collect).

Although powerful antibiotics and antidiarrhea medications such as Lomotil and Imodium are readily available over *farmacia* counters, they may involve serious side effects and should not be taken in the absence of medical advice. If in doubt, consult a doctor.

Chagas' Disease and Dengue Fever

Chagas' disease, spread by the "kissing" (or, more appropriately, "assassin") bug, is a potential hazard in the Mexican tropics. Known locally as a *vinchuca,* the triangular-headed three-quarter-inch (two-centimeter) brown insect, identifiable by its yellow-striped abdomen, often drops upon its sleeping victims from the thatched ceiling of a rural house at night. Its bite is followed by swelling, fever, and weakness and can lead to heart failure if left untreated. Application of drugs at an early stage can, however, clear the patient of the trypanosome parasites that infect victims' bloodstreams and vital organs. See a doctor immediately if you believe you're infected.

Most of the precautions against malaria-bearing mosquitoes also apply to dengue fever, which does occur (although uncommonly) in outlying tropical areas of Mexico. The culprit here is a virus carried by the mosquito species *Aedes aegypti.* Symptoms are acute fever, with chills, sweating, and muscle aches. A red, diffuse rash frequently results, which may later peel. Symptoms abate after about five days, but fatigue may persist. A particularly serious, but fortunately rare, form, called dengue hemorrhagic fever, afflicts children and can be fatal. See a doctor immediately. Although no vaccines or preventatives, other than deterring mosquitoes, exist, you should nevertheless see a doctor immediately.

For more good tropical preventative information, get a copy of the excellent pamphlet distributed by the International Association of Medical Advice to Travelers.

Scorpions and Snakes

While camping or staying in a *palapa* or other rustic accommodation, watch for scorpions, especially in your shoes, which you should shake out every morning. Scorpion stings are rarely fatal to an adult but are potentially very serious for a child. Snakebites are potentially very serious; get the victim to a doctor quickly.

WATER SAFETY

Viewed from the beach, the Pacific Ocean usually lives up to its name. Many protected inlets, safe for child's play, dot the coastline. Unsheltered shorelines, on the other hand, can be deceiving. Smooth water in the calm forenoon often changes to choppy in the afternoon; calm ripples that lap the shore in March can grow to hurricane-driven walls of water in November. Such storms can wash away sand, temporarily changing a wide, gently sloping beach into a steep one plagued by turbulent waves and treacherous currents.

Undertow, whirlpools, cross-currents, and occasional oversized waves can make ocean swimming a fast-lane adventure. Getting unexpectedly swept out to sea or hammered onto the beach bottom by a surprise breaker are potential hazards.

Never attempt serious swimming when tipsy or full of food; never swim alone where someone can't see you. Always swim beyond big breakers (which come in sets of several, climaxed by a huge one, which breaks highest and farthest from the beach). If you happen to get caught in the path of such a wave, avoid it by *diving directly toward and under it,* letting it roll harmlessly over you. If you are unavoidably swept up in a whirling, crashing breaker, try to roll and tumble with it, as football players tumble, to avoid injury.

Look out for other irritations and hazards. Now and then swimmers get a nettlelike (but usually harmless) jellyfish sting. Be careful around coral reefs and beds of sea urchins; corals can sting (like jellyfish) and you can additionally get infections from coral cuts and sea-urchin spines. *Shuffle* your feet along sandy bottoms to scare away stingrays rather than stepping on one. If you're unlucky, its venomous tail spines may inflict a painful wound.

While snorkeling or surfing, you may suffer a coral scratch or jellyfish sting. Experts advise you to wash the afflicted area with ocean water and pour alcohol (rubbing alcohol or tequila) over the wound, then apply hydrocortisone cream available from the *farmacia*.

Injuries from sea-urchin spines and sting-ray barbs are painful and can be serious. Physicians recommend similar first aid for both: Remove the spines or barbs by hand or with tweezers, then soak the injury in as-hot-as-possible fresh water to weaken the toxins and provide relief. Another method is to rinse the area with an antibacterial solution—rubbing alcohol, vinegar, wine, or ammonia diluted with water. If none are available, the same effect may be achieved with urine, either your own or someone else's in your party. Get medical help immediately.

MEDICAL CARE

For medical advice and treatment, let your hotel (or if you're camping, the closest *farmacia*) refer you to a good doctor, clinic, or hospital. Mexican doctors, especially in medium-sized and small towns, practice like private doctors in the United States and Canada once did before health insurance, liability, and group practice. They will usually come to you if you request it; they often keep their doors open even after regular hours and charge reasonable fees.

You will receive generally good treatment at the many local hospitals in Ixtapa-Zihuatanejo regional tourist centers and larger towns. If you must have an English-speaking, American-trained doctor, the **International Association for Medical Assistance to Travelers (IAMAT)** publishes an updated booklet of qualified member physicians, some of whom practice in Ixtapa-Zihuatanejo and Acapulco. IAMAT (1623 Military Road, #279, Niagara Falls, NY 14304, tel. 716/754-4883; or 2163 Gordon St., Guelph, Ontario N1K 1B5, tel. 519/836-0102, or 1287 St. Clair Ave. W, Toronto, Ontario M6E 1B8, tel. 416/652-0137, info@iamat.org or www.iamat.org) also distributes a very detailed *How to Protect Yourself Against Malaria* guide, together with worldwide malaria risk and communicable disease charts.

For more useful information on health and safety in Mexico, consult Drs. Robert H. Paige and Curtis P. Page's *Mexico: Health and Safety Travel Guide* (Tempe, AZ: Med to Go Books, 2004) and Dirk Schroeder's *Staying Healthy in Asia, Africa, and Latin America* (Berkeley, CA: Avalon Travel Publishing, 2000).

SAFE CONDUCT

Mexico is an old-fashioned country where people value traditional ideals of honesty, fidelity, and piety. Crime rates are low; visitors are often safer in Mexico than in their home cities.

This applies even more strongly in the Ixtapa-Zihuatanejo region. Don't be scared away by headlines about kidnappings and drug-related murders in border cities such as Tijuana and Ciuduad Juárez, or car hijackings in bad Mexico City neighborhoods. Violent crime, while not unknown in the Ixtapa-Zihuatanejo region, is nearly always associated with drug turf wars.

In Acapulco, around the *zócalo,* women are often seen walking home alone at night. Nevertheless, some Acapulco neighborhoods are friendlier than others. If you find yourself walking in a locality at night that doesn't feel too welcoming, do not hesitate to hail a taxi.

Although the Ixtapa-Zihuatanejo region is very safe with respect to violent crime, you should still take normal precautions against petty theft. Stow your valuables in your hotel safe, don't wear showy jewelry and display wads of money, and especially at a crowded market, keep your camera and valuables protected in a waist belt, secure purse, or zipped pockets. If you're parking your car for the night, do it in a secure garage or a guarded hotel parking lot.

Even though four generations have elapsed since Pancho Villa raided the U.S. border, the image of a Mexico everywhere bristling with *bandidos* persists. And similarly for Mexicans: Despite the century and a half since the *yanquis* invaded Mexico City and took half their country, the communal Mexican psyche still views gringos (and, by association, all white foreigners) with revulsion, jealousy, and wonder.

Fortunately, the Mexican love-hate affair with Americans does not usually apply to individual visitors. Your friendly *"buenos dias"* ("good morning") or *"por favor"* ("please"), when appropriate, is always appreciated, whether in the market, the gas station, or the hotel. The shy

MACHISMO

I once met an Acapulco man who wore five gold wristwatches and became angry when I quietly refused his repeated invitations to get drunk with him. Another time, on the beach near San Blas, two drunk campesinos nearly attacked me because I was helping my girlfriend cook a picnic dinner. Outside Taxco I once spent an endless hour in the seat behind a bus driver who insisted on speeding down the middle of the two-lane highway, honking aside oncoming automobiles.

Despite their ethnic and socioeconomic differences, all four men shared the common affliction of machismo, an affliction that seems to possess many Mexican men. Machismo is a sometimes-reckless obsession to prove one's masculinity, to show how macho you are. Men of many nationalities share the instinct to prove themselves. Japan's *bushido* samurai code is one example.

When confronted by a Mexican braggart, male visitors should remain careful and controlled. If your opponent is yelling, stay cool, speak softly, and withdraw as soon as possible. On the highway, be courteous and unprovoking – don't use your car to spar with a macho driver. Drinking often leads to problems. It's best to stay out of bars or cantinas unless you're prepared to deal with the macho conse-

quences. Polite refusal of a drink may be taken as a challenge. If you visit a bar with Mexican friends or acquaintances, you may be heading for a no-win choice between a drunken all-night *borrachera* (binge) or an insult to the honor of your friends by refusing.

For women, machismo requires even more cautious behavior. In Mexico, women's liberation is long in coming. Although a handful of Mexican women have risen to positions of political or corporate power, they constitute a small minority.

Female visitors should keep a low profile and wear bathing suits and brief shorts only at the beach. They can follow the example of their Mexican sisters by making a habit of going out in the company of friends or acquaintances, especially at night. Many Mexican men believe an unaccompanied woman wants to be picked up. Ignore their offers; any response, even refusal, might be taken as an encouraging sign. If, on the other hand, there is a Mexican man whom you'd genuinely like to meet, the traditional way is an arranged introduction through family or friends.

Mexican families, as a source of protection and friendship, should not be overlooked – especially on the beach or in the park, where, among the gaggle of kids, grandparents, aunts, and cousins, there's room for one more.

smile you will most likely receive in return will be your small, but not insignificant, reward.

Women

Your own behavior, despite low crime statistics, largely determines your safety in Mexico. For women traveling solo, it is important to realize that the double standard is alive and well in Mexico. Dress and behave modestly and you will most likely avoid embarrassment. Whenever possible, stay in the company of friends or acquaintances; find companions for beach, sightseeing, and shopping excursions. Ignore strange men's solicitations and overtures. A Mexican man on the prowl will invent the sappiest romantic overtures to snare a gringa.

He will often interpret anything but a firm "no" as a "maybe," and a "maybe" as a "yes."

Men

For male visitors, alcohol often leads to trouble. Avoid bars and cantinas; and if, given Mexico's excellent beers, you can't abstain completely, at least maintain soft-spoken self-control in the face of challenges from macho drunks.

The Law and Police

While Mexican authorities are tolerant of alcohol, they are decidedly intolerant of other substances such as marijuana, psychedelics, cocaine, and heroin. Getting caught with such drugs in Mexico usually leads to swift and severe results.

Equally swift is the punishment for nude sunbathing, which is both illegal in public and offensive to Mexicans. Confine your nudist colony to very private locations.

Although with decreasing frequency lately, traffic police in Ixtapa-Zihuatanejo and Acapulco sometimes seem to watch foreign cars with eagle eyes. Officers seem to inhabit busy intersections and one-way streets, waiting for confused tourists to make a wrong move. If they whistle you over, stop immediately or you will really get into hot water. If guilty, say *"Lo siento"* ("I'm sorry") and be cooperative. Although the officer probably won't mention it, he or she is usually hoping that you'll cough up a $20 *mordida* (bribe) for the privilege of driving away. Don't do it. Although he may hint at confiscating your car, calmly ask for an official *boleto* (written traffic ticket, if you're guilty) in exchange for your driver's license (have a copy), which the officer will probably keep if he writes a ticket. If after a few minutes no money appears, the officer will most likely give you back your driver's license rather than go to the trouble of writing the ticket. If not, the worst that will usually happen is you will have to go to the *presidencia municipal* (city hall) the next morning and pay the $20 to a clerk in exchange for the return of your driver's license.

Political Protest

The Ixtapa-Zihuatanejo region's customary tranquility has occasionally undergone episodes of public unrest. Recent protests have been the result of the longstanding backlog of unsettled grievances that run from local land disputes and strikes by underpaid teachers and government workers, all the way up to unsolved kidnappings and occasional drug-related killings and shootouts.

In recent years, the aggrieved, usually local community delegations, have both petitioned state and city authorities for redress and set up camp in plain view for visitors to see, in the Acapulco and Chilpancingo central plazas. There is no reason for visitors to be concerned by such peaceful demonstrations. During recent years, political protests have been generally tolerated by local authorities and could be considered a positive sign of a maturing Mexican democracy.

Pedestrian and Driving Hazards

Although the Ixtapa-Zihuatanejo region's potholed pavements and "holey" sidewalks won't land you in jail, one of them might send you to the hospital if you don't watch your step, especially at night. "Pedestrian beware" is especially good advice on Mexican streets, where it is rumored that some drivers speed up rather than slow down when they spot a tourist stepping off the curb. Falling coconuts, especially frequent on windy days, constitute an additional hazard to unwary campers and beachgoers.

Driving Mexican country roads, where slow trucks and carts block lanes, campesinos stroll the shoulders, and horses, burros, and cattle wander at will, is hazardous—doubly so at night.

Information and Services

MONEY
The Peso: Down and Up

At this writing, the Mexican peso (that is prefixed with the dollar sign, just like the American dollar), trades between 12 and 13 per U.S. dollar. Since the peso value sometimes changes rapidly, U.S. dollars have become a much more stable indicator of Mexican prices; for this reason they are used in this book for prices. You should, nevertheless, always use pesos to pay for everything in Mexico.

Since the introduction of the new peso, the centavo (one-hundredth of a new peso) has reappeared, in coins of 10, 20, and 50 centavos. Incidentally, the dollar sign, "$," also marks Mexican pesos. Peso coins *(monedas)* in denominations of 1, 2, 5, 10 and 20 pesos, and bills, in denominations of 20, 50, 100, 200 and

500 pesos, are common. Since banks like to exchange your travelers checks for a few crisp large bills rather than the often-tattered smaller denominations, ask for some of your change in 50- and 100-peso notes. A 500-peso note, while common at the bank, may look awfully big to a small shopkeeper, who might be hard-pressed to change it.

Banks, ATMs, Traveler's Checks, and Money-Exchange Offices

Mexican banks, like their North American counterparts, have lengthened their business hours. Hong Kong Shanghai Banking Corporation (HSBC) maintains the longest hours: as long as Monday–Friday 9 A.M.–6 P.M., Saturday 9 A.M.–2 P.M. Banamex (Banco Nacional de Mexico), generally the most popular with local people, usually posts the best in-town dollar exchange rate in its lobby, for example: *Tipo de cambio: venta $11.799, compra $11.933*, which means it will sell pesos to you at the rate of 11.799 per dollar and buy them back for 11.933 per dollar.

Since ATMs (automated teller machines), or *cajeros automáticos* (kah-HAY-rohs ahoo-toh-MAH-tee-kohs), have become the money sources of choice in Mexico, traveler's checks have become less useful. A growing number of banks, hotels, and restaurants no longer accept them. However, virtually every bank has a 24-hour ATM, accessible (with your usual PIN number) by a swarm of U.S., Canadian and European credit and ATM cards. *Note:* Some Mexican bank ATMs will "eat" your ATM card if you don't retrieve it within about 15 seconds of completing your transaction. Retrieve your card *immediately* after getting your cash.

To avoid too many one-time bank ATM charges, typically about $3, regardless of the transaction amount, best get the maximum cash possible (customarily $300–500 dollars) per ATM visit.

Even without an ATM card, you don't have to go to the trouble of waiting in long bank service lines. Opt for a less-crowded bank, such as Bancomer, Banco Norte, HSBC, or a private money-exchange office *(casa de cambio)*. Often most convenient, such offices often offer long hours and faster service than the banks for a fee (as little as $0.50 or as much as $3 per $100).

Keeping Your Money Safe

Travelers checks, the traditional prescription for safe money abroad, are accepted, but not as widely as before. Nevertheless, even if you plan to use your ATM card, you could buy some U.S. dollar travelers checks (a well-known brand such as American Express or Visa) for an emergency reserve. Canadian travelers checks and currency are not as widely accepted as U.S. travelers checks, and European and Asian travelers checks even less so. Unless you like signing your name or paying lots of per-check commissions, buy denominations of $50 or more.

In the Ixtapa-Zihuatanejo region as everywhere, thieves circulate among the tourists. Keep valuables in your hotel *caja de seguridad* (security box). If you don't particularly trust the desk clerk, carry what you cannot afford to lose in a money belt. Pickpockets and purse-snatchers love crowded markets, buses, and airport terminals where they can slip a wallet out of a back pocket or dangling purse or a camera from its case in a blink. Guard against this by carrying your wallet in your front pocket, your camera in your purse or backpack, and your purse, waist pouch, and daypack (which clever crooks can sometimes slit open) on your front side.

Don't attract thieves by displaying wads of money or flashy jewelry. Don't get sloppy drunk; if so, you may become a pushover for a determined thief.

Don't leave valuables unattended on the beach; share security duties with trustworthy-looking neighbors, or leave a bag with a shopkeeper nearby.

Tipping

Without their droves of visitors, Mexican people would be even poorer. Deflation of the peso, while it makes prices low for outsiders, makes it rough for Mexican families to get by. The help at your hotel typically get paid only a few dollars a day. They depend on tips to make the difference between dire and bearable poverty. Give the *camarista* (chambermaid) and floor attendant 20 pesos every day or two. And whenever uncertain of what to tip, it will probably mean a lot to someone—maybe a whole family—if you err on the generous side.

In restaurants and bars, Mexican tipping customs are similar to those in the United States: Tip waiters, waitresses, and bartenders about 15 percent for satisfactory service.

Credit Cards

Credit cards, such as Visa, MasterCard, and, to a lesser extent, American Express and Discover, are honored in the hotels, restaurants, craft shops, and boutiques that cater to foreign tourists. You will generally get better bargains, however, in hotels and shops that depend on local trade and do not so readily accept credit cards. Such businesses sometimes offer discounts for cash sales.

PACKING CHECKLIST

Use this list as a last-minute check to make sure that you've packed all of the items essential to your Mexico trip:

NECESSARY ITEMS
__ camera, film, extra memory card (expensive in Mexico)
__ comb, brush
__ guidebook, reading books
__ inexpensive watch, clock
__ keys, tickets
__ lightweight clothes, hat for sun
__ money, ATM card, and/or travelers checks
__ mosquito repellent
__ prescription eyeglasses, contact lenses
__ prescription medicines and drugs
__ purse, waist-belt carrying pouch
__ sunglasses, sunscreen
__ swimsuit
__ toothbrush, toothpaste
__ passport
__ windbreaker

USEFUL ITEMS
__ address book
__ birth control
__ checkbook, credit cards
__ dental floss
__ earplugs
__ first-aid kit
__ flashlight, batteries
__ immersion heater
__ lightweight binoculars
__ portable radio/cassette player
__ razor

__ travel booklight
__ vaccination certificate

NECESSARY ITEMS FOR CAMPERS
__ collapsible gallon plastic bottle
__ dish soap
__ first-aid kit
__ hammock (buy in Mexico)
__ insect repellent
__ lightweight hiking shoes
__ lightweight tent
__ matches in waterproof case
__ nylon cord
__ plastic bottle, quart
__ pot scrubber/sponge
__ sheet or light blanket
__ Sierra Club cup, fork, and spoon
__ single-burner stove with fuel
__ Swiss army knife
__ tarp
__ toilet paper
__ towel, soap
__ two nesting cooking pots
__ water-purifying tablets or iodine

USEFUL ITEMS FOR CAMPERS
__ compass
__ dishcloths
__ hot pad
__ instant coffee, tea, sugar, powdered milk
__ moleskin (Dr. Scholl's)
__ plastic plate
__ poncho
__ short (votive) candles
__ whistle

Whatever the circumstance, your travel money will usually go much further in the Ixtapa-Zihuatanejo region than back home. Despite the national 17 percent sales tax (IVA), local lodging, food, and transportation prices will often seem like bargains compared to the U.S. or Canada. Outside of the pricey high-rise beachfront strips, pleasant, palm-shaded hotel rooms often rent for $50 or less.

COMMUNICATIONS
Using Mexican Telephones
Although Mexican phone service continues to improve, it's still sometimes hit-or-miss. If a number doesn't get through, you may have to redial it more than once. When someone answers (usually *"Bueno"*), be especially courteous. If your Spanish is rusty, say, *"¿Por favor, habla inglés?"* (¿POR fah-VOR, AH-blah een-GLAYS?, "Please, do you speak English?"). If you want to speak to a particular person (such as María), ask, *"¿María se encuentra?"* (¿mah-REE-ah SAY ayn-koo-AYN-trah?).

Since November, 2001, when telephone numbers were standardized, Mexican phones operate pretty much the same as in the United States and Canada. In Ixtapa-Zihuatanejo, for example, a complete telephone number is generally written like this: 755/556-4709. As in the United States, the "755" denotes the telephone area code, or *lada* (LAH-dah), and the 556-4709 is the number (except in the case of calling a cell phone) that you dial locally. If you want to dial this number long distance (*larga distancia*) in Mexico, first dial "01" (like "1" in the United States), then 755/556-4709. All Mexican telephone numbers, with only three exceptions, begin with a three-digit *lada*, followed by a seven-digit local number. (The exceptions are Monterrey, Guadalajara, and Mexico City, which have two-digit *ladas* and eight-digit local numbers. The Mexico City *lada* is 55; Guadalajara's is 33; Monterrey's is 81. For example, a complete Guadalajara phone number would read 33/6897-2253.)

Although **Mexican cellular telephones** are as universally used (but more expensive than) those in the United States and Canada, at this writing, they operate a bit differently. Generally, in order to call a cellular number locally from within its local Mexican *lada* (area code), you must prefix it with "044." For example, in Ixtapa-Zihuatanejo, call Ixtapa-Zihuatanejo cell phone number 755/105-2345, by dialing 044-755/105-2345. The same is true for other locales; for example, in Acapulco, with area code 744, call the cellular number 744/119-3822 locally by dialing 044-744/119-3822.

However, if you're calling a cell phone long distance (from outside the cell phone's local area), you must first dial "045" instead of "044." For example, in Taxco, with area code 762, you must call the above-cited Zihuatanejo cell phone by dialing 045-755/105-2345. The same is true of the above-cited Acapulco cell phone by dialing 045-744/119-3822. This procedure is necessary for all long-distance calls to cell phones throughout Mexico.

In Ixtapa-Zihuatanejo region towns and cities, direct long-distance dialing is the rule—from hotels, public phone booths, and private telephone offices (*larga distancias*). The cheapest, often most convenient, way to call is by buying a **Ladatel phone card** (*tarjeta telefónica*), usable in public (often on the street) telephones. Buy them in 30-, 50-, and 100-peso denominations at the many outlets—minimarkets, pharmacies, liquor stores—that display the blue-and-yellow Ladatel sign.

Calling Mexico and Calling Home
To call a Mexico (non-cellular) phone direct from the United States, first dial 011 (for international access), then 52 (Mexico country code), followed by the Mexican area code and local number. For example, to call an Ixtapa-Zihuatanejo local number, such as 755/556-4709, from the U.S., dial 011-52-755/556-4709. Again, you must **dial cellular phone numbers a bit differently,** by entering a "1" before the area code. Thus, for the Ixtapa-Zihuatanejo cellular number 755/105-2345, from the U.S. you must dial 011-52-1-755/105-2345.

For station-to-station **calls to the United States and Canada from Mexico,** dial 001, followed by the U.S. or Canadian area code and the local number. For example to call San Diego (area code 619) local number 388-5390, from Mexico, simply dial 001-619/388-5390. For calls to other countries, ask your hotel desk clerk or see the easy-to-follow directions in the local Mexican telephone directory *(directorio telefónico)*.

By far the cheapest way to call home (about $0.50 per minute) is via one of the many public telephones with your Ladatel phone card.

Beware of certain private "To Call Long Distance to the U.S.A. Collect" (or "by Credit Card") telephones installed prominently in airports, tourist hotels, and shops. Tariffs on these phones often run as high as $10 per minute (with a three-minute minimum), for a total of $30, whether you talk three minutes or not. Always ask the operator for the rate *(tipo)*, and if it's too high, buy a 30-peso ($3) Ladatel phone card for a (six-minute) call home.

In smaller towns, with no public street telephones, you must often do your local or long-distance phoning in the *larga distancia* (local phone office). Typically staffed by a young woman and often connected to a café, the *larga distancia* becomes an informal community social center as people pass the time waiting for their phone connections.

Post, Telegraph, and Internet Access

Mexican *correos* (post offices) operate similarly, but less efficiently and less securely, than most of their counterparts all over the world. Mail services usually include *lista de correo* (general delivery, address letters *"a/c lista de correo,"*), *servicios filatelicas* (philatelic services), *por avión* (airmail), *giros* (postal money orders), and Mexpost secure and fast delivery service, sometimes from separate Mexpost offices.

Mexican ordinary (non-Mexpost) mail is sadly unreliable and pathetically slow (three weeks for letters and postcards to the U.S.). If, for mailings within Mexico, you must have security, use the efficient, reformed government Mexpost (like U.S. Express Mail) service. For international mailings, check the local Yellow Pages for widely available DHL, Federal Express, and UPS courier service.

Telégrafos (old-fashioned telegraph offices), usually near the post office, send and receive *telegramas* (telegrams) and *giros* (money orders). *Telecomunicaciones* (Telecom), the new high-tech telegraph offices, add computerized telephone, public fax, and sometimes Internet connection to the available services.

Internet service, including personal email access, has arrived in Ixtapa-Zihuatanejo region cities and towns. Internet "cafés" are becoming increasingly common, especially in Ixtapa-Zihuatanejo, Acapulco, Taxco, Iguala, and Chilpancingo. Access rates run an economical $1–2 per hour.

ELECTRICITY AND TIME

Mexican electric power is supplied at U.S.-standard 110 volts, 60 cycles. Plugs and sockets are generally two-pronged, nonpolar (like the pre-1970s U.S. ones). Bring adapters if you're going to use appliances with polar two-pronged or three-pronged plugs. A two-pronged polar plug has different-sized prongs, one of which is too large to plug into an old-fashioned non-polar socket.

The entire Ixtapa-Zihuatanejo region, all surrounding states, and Mexico City operate on U.S. Central Time, the same as central U.S. states such as Nebraska, Illinois, Tennessee, and Louisiana.

RESOURCES

Glossary

Many of the following words have a social-historical meaning; others you will not find in the usual English–Spanish dictionary.

abarrotes groceries, grocery store

aguardiente Mexican "white lightning": cheap distilled liquor made from sugarcane

aguas watch out!

alcalde mayor or municipal judge

alebrije fanciful wooden animal, mostly made in Arrazola and Tilcajete villages in Oaxaca

alfarería pottery

andador walkway, or strolling path

antojitos native Mexican snacks, such as tamales, chiles rellenos, tacos, and enchiladas

artesanías handicrafts

artesano, artesana craftsman, craftswoman

asunción the assumption of the Virgin Mary into heaven (as distinguished from the *ascención* of Jesus into heaven)

atole a popular nonalcoholic drink made from corn juice

audiencia one of the royal executive-judicial panels sent to rule Mexico during the mid-16th century

autopista automobile expressway

ayuntamiento either the town council or the building where it meets

barrio a town or village district or neighborhood, usually centered around its own local plaza and church

bienes raíces literally "good (or strong) roots," but commonly, real estate

bola small crowd of people

boleto ticket, boarding pass

brujo, bruja male or female witch doctor or shaman

caballero literally "horseman," but popularly, gentleman

cabaña ecoturísticas bungalow lodging for tourists

cabercera head town of a municipal district, or headquarters in general

cabrón literally, a cuckold, but more commonly, bastard, rat, or S.O.B.; often used affectionately

cacique local chief or boss

calenda procession, usually religious, as during a festival

camionera bus station

campesino country person; farm worker

canasta basket with handle, traditionally made of woven reeds

cantera volcanic stone, widely used for colonial-era monuments

Carnaval celebration directly preceding Ash Wednesday, the beginning of the fasting period called Lent. Carnaval is called Mardi Gras in the United States.

casa de huéspedes guesthouse, often operated in a family home

cascada waterfall

caudillo dictator or political chief

centro de salud local health center/clinic

charro gentleman cowboy

chingar literally, to "rape," but also the universal Spanish "f" word, the equivalent of "screw" in English

Churrigueresque Spanish baroque architectural style incorporated into many Mexican colonial churches, named after José Churriguera (1665-1725)

científicos literally, scientists, but applied to President Porfirio Díaz's technocratic advisers

coa (estaca) digging stick, used for planting corn

cofradia Catholic fraternal service association, either male or female, mainly in charge of financing and organizing religious festivals

colectivo a shared public taxi or minibus that picks up and deposits passengers along a designated route

colegio preparatory school or junior college

colonia suburban subdivision/satellite of a larger city

comal a flat pottery griddle, for cooking/heating tortillas

comida casera home-cooked food

comida corrida economical afternoon set meal, usually with four courses – soup, rice, entrée, and dessert

compadrazgo the semi-formal web of village and barrio *compadre* and *padrino* relationships that determine a person's lifetime obligations and loyalties

compadre a semi-formalized "best friend" relationship that usually lasts for life

comunal refers to the traditional indigenous system of joint decision-making and land ownership and use

Conasupo government store that sells basic foods at subsidized prices

correo mail, post, or post office

criollo person of all-European, usually Spanish, descent born in the New World

Cuaresma Lent, the 40 days of pre-Easter fasting, beginning on Ash Wednesday (Miercoles de Ceniza), and ending during the week before Easter Sunday.

cuota toll, as in *cuota autopista*, toll expressway

curandero, curandera indigenous medicine man or woman

damas ladies, as in "ladies room"

Domingo de Ramos Palm Sunday, one week before Easter Sunday

ejido a constitutional, government-sponsored form of community, with shared land ownership and cooperative decision-making

encomienda colonial award of tribute from a designated indigenous district

farmacia pharmacy, or drugstore

finca a farm

finca cafetelera coffee farm

fonda food stall or small restaurant, often in a traditional market complex

fraccionamiento city sector or subdivision, abbreviated "Fracc."

fuero the former right of Mexican clergy and military to be tried in separate ecclesiastical and military courts

gachupín "one who wears spurs"; a derogatory term for a Spanish-born colonial

gasolinera gasoline station

gente de razón "people of reason"; whites and mestizos in colonial Mexico

gringo once-derogatory but now commonly, even affectionately used term for North American whites

grito impassioned cry, as in Hidalgo's Grito de Dolores

guero a blond person

hacienda large-landed estate; also a government treasury

hamaca hammock

hechicero a "wizard" who often leads native propitiatory ceremonies

hidalgo nobleman or noblewoman; called honorifically by "Don" or "Doña"

hojalata tinware, a popular Mexican craft

indígena indigenous or aboriginal inhabitant of all-native descent who speaks his or her native tongue; commonly, but incorrectly, an **indio** (Indian)

jacal native label for thatched, straw, and/or stick-and-mud country house

jaripeo bull roping and riding

jejenes "no-see-um" biting gnats, most common around coastal wetlands

judiciales the federal "judicial," or investigative police, best known to motorists for their highway checkpoint inspections

jugería stall or small restaurant providing an array of squeezed vegetable and fruit *jugos* (juices)

juzgado the "hoosegow," or jail

lancha launch (a small motorboat)

larga distancia long-distance telephone service, or the *caseta* (booth or office) where it's provided

licencado academic degree (abbrev. Lic.) approximately equivalent to a bachelor's degree in the United States

licuado a blended drink of ice and usually fruit, whipped with a bit of milk and sugar; like a smoothie in the United States

lonchería small lunch counter, usually serving juices, sandwiches, and *antojitos*

machismo; macho exaggerated sense of maleness; person who holds such a sense of himself

malecón oceanfront walkway, typically used for strolling

mañanita early-morning mass

mano a hand, or the stone roller used to grind corn on the flat stone metate

mayordomo community leader responsible for staging a local Catholic religious festival

mescal alcoholic beverage distilled from the fermented hearts of maguey (century plant)

mestizo person of mixed native and European descent

metate a slightly concave, horizontal stone basin for grinding corn for tortillas

milagro literally a miracle, but also a small religious wish medal, often pinned to an altar saint by someone requesting divine intervention

milpa a small, family-owned field, traditionally planted in corn, beans, and squash

mirador viewpoint, overlook

molcajete a stone mortar and pestle, used for hand-grinding, especially chilies and seeds

mordida slang for bribe; "little bite"

olla a pottery jug or pot, used for stewing – vegetables, meats, beans, coffee

padrino, padrina godfather or godmother, often the respective *compadres* of the given child's parents

palapa an open, thatched-roof structure, often shading a restaurant

panela rough brown cane sugar, sold in lumps in the market

panga outboard motor-launch *(lancha)*

papier-mâché the craft of glued, multilayered paper sculpture, centered in Tonalá, Jalisco, where creations can resemble fine pottery or lacquerware

Pemex acronym for Petróleos Mexicanos, the national oil corporation

peninsulares the Spanish-born ruling colonial elite

peón a poor wage-earner, usually a country native

periférico peripheral boulevard that bypasses a town center

petate all-purpose mat, woven from palm fronds

piciete native tobacco, widely cultivated in northern Guerrero and Oaxaca states

piñata papier-mâché decoration, usually in animal or human form, filled with treats and broken open during a fiesta

plan political manifesto, usually by a leader or group consolidating or seeking power

Porfiriato the 34-year (1876-1910) ruling period of president-dictator Porfirio Díaz

Las Posadas Christmas, especially on Christmas Eve, procession, in which participants, led by costumed Holy Mary and Joseph, knock on neighborhood doors and implore, unsuccessfully, for a room for the night

pozahuanco horizontally striped hand-woven wraparound skirt, commonly worn in the Costa Chica coastal Mixtec district

pozole stew of hominy in broth, usually topped by shredded meat, cabbage, and diced onion

presidencia municipal the headquarters, like a U.S. city or county hall, of a Mexican *municipio*, county-like local governmental unit

preventiva local, state, or federal police, especially charged with catching crooks

principal, anciano a respected elder, often a member of a council of elders, whom the community consults for advice and support

pronunciamiento declaration of rebellion by an insurgent leader

pueblo town or people

puente literally a "bridge," but commonly a

long holiday weekend, when resort hotel reservations are highly recommended

pulque the fermented juice of the maguey plant, approximately equivalent in alcoholic content to wine or strong beer

puta whore, bitch, or slut

quinta a villa or upscale country house

quinto the colonial royal "fifth" tax on treasure and precious metals

ramada a temporary shade roof, of branches or palm fronds

regidor a community official, often a town council member, responsible for specific government functions, such as public works and treasury

retablo altarpiece, often of ornately carved and gilded wood

retorno cul-de-sac

ropa típica traditional dress, derived from the Spanish colonial tradition (in contrast to *traje*, traditional indigenous dress)

rurales former federal country police force created to fight *bandidos* (bandits) and suppress political dissent

Sabi the Mixtec god of rain

sabino "Mexican" or "Montezuma" bald cypress tree, *Taxodium mucronatum*

Semana Santa Holy Week, the week preceding Easter Sunday

servicios the indigenous ladder of increasingly responsible public tasks that, if successfully performed, leads to community approval, prestige, and leadership for a given individual by middle age

tapete wool rug, made in certain east-side Valley of Oaxaca villages

taxi especial privately hired taxi, as distinguished from *taxi colectivo*, or public collective taxi

telégrafo telegraph office, lately converting to high-tech *telecomunicaciones (telecom)*, that also offers computerized telephone and public fax services

temazcal traditional indigenous sweat room, enclosed and heated by a wood fire, usually used for healing, especially by women after childbirth

tenate basket of woven palm leaf, with tumpline instead of a fixed handle

tepache a wine, fermented from *panela* (sugarcane juice)

tequio an obligatory communal task, such as local road work, street sweeping, or child care, expected of all adult villagers from time to time

tianguis literally "awning," but now has come to mean the awning-decorated native town market

tono a usually benign animal guardian spirit

topil lowest municipal job, usually messenger, filled by youngest teenage boys

vaquero cowboy

vecinidad neighborhood

yanqui Yankee

zócalo the popular label originally for the Mexico City central plaza; now the name for central plazas all over Mexico, including Oaxaca

ABBREVIATIONS

Av. *avenida* (avenue)
Blv. *bulevar* (boulevard)
Calz. *calzada* (thoroughfare, main road)
Fco. Francisco (proper name, as in "Fco. Villa")
Fracc. *Fraccionamiento* (subdivision)
Nte. *norte* (north)
Ote. *oriente* (east)
Pte. *poniente* (west)
s/n *sin número* (no street number)

Spanish Phrasebook

Your Mexico adventure will be more fun if you use a little Spanish. Mexican folks, although they may smile at your funny accent, will appreciate your halting efforts to break the ice and transform yourself from a foreigner to a potential friend.

Spanish commonly uses 30 letters – the familiar English 26, plus four straightforward additions: ch, ll, ñ, and rr, which are explained in "Consonants," below.

PRONUNCIATION

Once you learn them, Spanish pronunciation rules – in contrast to English – don't change. Spanish vowels generally sound softer than in English. (*Note:* The capitalized syllables below receive stronger accents.)

Vowels

a like ah, as in "hah": *agua* AH-gooah (water), *pan* PAHN (bread), and *casa* CAH-sah (house)

e like ay, as in "may:" *mesa* MAY-sah (table), *tela* TAY-lah (cloth), and *de* DAY (of, from)

i like ee, as in "need": *diez* dee-AYZ (ten), *comida* ko-MEE-dah (meal), and *fin* FEEN (end)

o like oh, as in "go": *peso* PAY-soh (weight), *ocho* OH-choh (eight), and *poco* POH-koh (a bit)

u like oo, as in "cool": *uno* OO-noh (one), *cuarto* KOOAHR-toh (room), and *usted* oos-TAYD (you); when it follows a "q" the **u** is silent; when it follows an "h" or has an umlaut, it's pronounced like "w"

Consonants

b, d, f, k, l, m, n, p, q, s, t, v, w, x, y, z, and ch
pronounced almost as in English; **h** occurs, but is silent – not pronounced at all.

c like k as in "keep": *cuarto* KOOAR-toh (room), Tepic tay-PEEK (capital of Nayarit state); when it precedes "e" or "i," pronounce **c** like s, as in "sit": *cerveza* sayr-VAY-sah (beer), *encima* ayn-SEE-mah (atop).

g like g as in "gift" when it precedes "a," "o," "u," or a consonant: *gato* GAH-toh (cat), *hago* AH-goh (I do, make); otherwise, pronounce **g** like h as in "hat": *giro* HEE-roh (money order), *gente* HAYN-tay (people)

j like h, as in "has:" *Jueves* HOOAY-vays (Thursday), *mejor* may-HOR (better)

ll like y, as in "yes": *toalla* toh-AH-yah (towel), *ellos* AY-yohs (they, them)

ñ like ny, as in "canyon": *año* AH-nyo (year), *señor* SAY-nyor (Mr., sir)

r is lightly trilled, with tongue at the roof of your mouth like a very light English d, as in "ready": *pero* PAY-doh (but), *tres* TDAYS (three), *cuatro* KOOAH-tdoh (four).

rr like a Spanish r, but with much more emphasis and trill. Let your tongue flap. Practice with *burro* (donkey), *carretera* (highway), and Carrillo (proper name), then really let go with *ferrocarril* (railroad).

Note: The single small but common exception to all of the above is the pronunciation of Spanish **y** when it's being used as the Spanish word for "and," as in "Ron y Kathy." In such case, pronounce it like the English ee, as in "keep": Ron "ee" Kathy (Ron and Kathy).

Accent

The rule for accent, the relative stress given to syllables within a given word, is straightforward. If a word ends in a vowel, an n, or an s, accent the next-to-last syllable; if not, accent the last syllable.

Pronounce *gracias* GRAH-seeahs (thank you), *orden* OHR-dayn (order), and *carretera* kah-ray-TAY-rah (highway) with stress on the next-to-last syllable.

Otherwise, accent the last syllable: *venir* vay-NEER (to come), *ferrocarril* fay-roh-cah-REEL (railroad), and *edad* ay-DAHD (age).

Exceptions to the accent rule are always marked with an accent sign: (á, é, í, ó, or ú), such as *teléfono* tay-LAY-foh-noh (telephone), *jabón* hah-BON (soap), and *rápido* RAH-pee-doh (rapid).

BASIC AND COURTEOUS EXPRESSIONS

Most Spanish-speaking people consider formalities important. Whenever approaching anyone for information or some other reason, do not forget the appropriate salutation – good morning, good evening, etc. Standing alone, the greeting *hola* (hello) can sound brusque.

Hello. *Hola.*
Good morning. *Buenos días.*
Good afternoon. *Buenas tardes.*
Good evening. *Buenas noches.*
How are you? *¿Cómo está usted?*
Very well, thank you. *Muy bien, gracias.*
Okay; good. *Bien.*
Not okay; bad. *Mal or feo.*
So-so. *Más o menos.*
And you? *¿Y usted?*
Thank you. *Gracias.*
Thank you very much. *Muchas gracias.*
You're very kind. *Muy amable.*
You're welcome. *De nada.*
Goodbye. *Adios.*
See you later. *Hasta luego.*
please *por favor*
yes *sí*
no *no*
I don't know. *No sé.*
Just a moment, please. *Momentito, por favor.*
Excuse me, please (when you're trying to get attention). *Disculpe or Con permiso.*
Excuse me (when you've made a boo-boo). *Lo siento.*
Pleased to meet you. *Mucho gusto.*
How do you say...in Spanish? *¿Cómo se dice...en español?*
What is your name? *¿Cómo se llama usted?*
Do you speak English? *¿Habla usted inglés?*
Is English spoken here? (Does anyone here speak English?) *¿Se habla inglés?*
I don't speak Spanish well. *No hablo bien el español.*
I don't understand. *No entiendo.*
How do you say...in Spanish? *¿Cómo se dice...en español?*
My name is . . . *Me llamo . . .*
Would you like . . . *¿Quisiera usted . . .*
Let's go to . . . *Vamos a . . .*

TERMS OF ADDRESS

When in doubt, use the formal *usted* (you) as a form of address.

I *yo*
you (formal) *usted*
you (familiar) *tu*
he/him *él*
she/her *ella*
we/us *nosotros*
you (plural) *ustedes*
they/them *ellos* (all males or mixed gender); *ellas* (all females)
Mr., sir *señor*
Mrs., madam *señora*
miss, young lady *señorita*
wife *esposa*
husband *esposo*
friend *amigo* (male); *amiga* (female)
sweetheart *novio* (male); *novia* (female)
son; daughter *hijo; hija*
brother; sister *hermano; hermana*
father; mother *padre; madre*
grandfather; grandmother *abuelo; abuela*

TRANSPORTATION

Where is . . . ? *¿Dónde está . . . ?*
How far is it to . . . ? *¿A cuánto está . . . ?*
from...to . . . *de...a . . .*
How many blocks? *¿Cuántas cuadras?*
Where (Which) is the way to . . . ? *¿Dónde está el camino a . . . ?*
the bus station *la terminal de autobuses*
the bus stop *la parada de autobuses*
Where is this bus going? *¿Adónde va este autobús?*
the taxi stand *la parada de taxis*
the train station *la estación de ferrocarril*
the boat *el barco*
the launch *lancha; tiburonera*
the dock *el muelle*
the airport *el aeropuerto*
I'd like a ticket to . . . *Quisiera un boleto a . . .*
first (second) class *primera (segunda) clase*
roundtrip *ida y vuelta*

reservation reservación
baggage equipaje
Stop here, please. Pare aquí, por favor.
the entrance la entrada
the exit la salida
the ticket office la oficina de boletos
(very) near; far (muy) cerca; lejos
to; toward a
by; through por
from de
the right la derecha
the left la izquierda
straight ahead derecho; directo
in front en frente
beside al lado
behind atrás
the corner la esquina
the stoplight la semáforo
a turn una vuelta
right here aquí
somewhere around here por acá
right there allí
somewhere around there por allá
road el camino
street; boulevard calle; bulevar
block la cuadra
highway carretera
kilometer kilómetro
bridge; toll puente; cuota
address dirección
north; south norte; sur
east; west oriente (este); poniente (oeste)

ACCOMMODATIONS

hotel hotel
Is there a room? ¿Hay cuarto?
May I (may we) see it? ¿Puedo (podemos) verlo?
What is the rate? ¿Cuál es el precio?
Is that your best rate? ¿Es su mejor precio?
Is there something cheaper? ¿Hay algo más económico?
a single room un cuarto sencillo
a double room un cuarto doble
double bed cama matrimonial
twin beds camas gemelas
with private bath con baño
hot water agua caliente

shower ducha
towels toallas
soap jabón
toilet paper papel higiénico
blanket frazada; manta
sheets sábanas
air-conditioned aire acondicionado
fan abanico; ventilador
key llave
manager gerente

FOOD

I'm hungry Tengo hambre.
I'm thirsty. Tengo sed.
menu carta; menú
order orden
glass vaso
fork tenedor
knife cuchillo
spoon cuchara
napkin servilleta
soft drink refresco
coffee café
tea té
drinking water agua pura; agua potable
bottled carbonated water agua mineral
bottled uncarbonated water agua sin gas
beer cerveza
wine vino
milk leche
juice jugo
cream crema
sugar azúcar
cheese queso
snack antojo; botana
breakfast desayuno
lunch almuerzo
daily lunch special comida corrida (or el menú del día depending on region)
dinner comida (often eaten in late afternoon); cena (a late-night snack)
the check la cuenta
eggs huevos
bread pan
salad ensalada
fruit fruta
mango mango
watermelon sandía

papaya *papaya*
banana *plátano*
apple *manzana*
orange *naranja*
lime *limón*
fish *pescado*
shellfish *mariscos*
shrimp *camarones*
meat (without) *(sin) carne*
chicken *pollo*
pork *puerco*
beef; steak *res; bistec*
bacon; ham *tocino; jamón*
fried *frito*
roasted *asada*
barbecue; barbecued *barbacoa; al carbón*

SHOPPING

money *dinero*
money-exchange bureau *casa de cambio*
I would like to exchange traveler's checks. *Quisiera cambiar cheques de viajero.*
What is the exchange rate? *¿Cuál es el tipo de cambio?*
How much is the commission? *¿Cuánto cuesta la comisión?*
Do you accept credit cards? *¿Aceptan tarjetas de crédito?*
money order *giro*
How much does it cost? *¿Cuánto cuesta?*
What is your final price? *¿Cuál es su último precio?*
expensive *caro*
cheap *barato; económico*
more *más*
less *menos*
a little *un poco*
too much *demasiado*

HEALTH

Help me please. *Ayúdeme por favor.*
I am ill. *Estoy enfermo.*
Call a doctor. *Llame un doctor.*
Take me to . . . *Lléveme a . . .*
hospital *hospital; sanatorio*
drugstore *farmacia*

pain *dolor*
fever *fiebre*
headache *dolor de cabeza*
stomach ache *dolor de estómago*
burn *quemadura*
cramp *calambre*
nausea *náusea*
vomiting *vomitar*
medicine *medicina*
antibiotic *antibiótico*
pill; tablet *pastilla*
aspirin *aspirina*
ointment; cream *pomada; crema*
bandage *venda*
cotton *algodón*
sanitary napkins *use brand name, e.g., Kotex*
birth control pills *pastillas anticonceptivas*
contraceptive foam *espuma anticonceptiva*
condoms *preservativos; condones*
toothbrush *cepilla dental*
dental floss *hilo dental*
toothpaste *crema dental*
dentist *dentista*
toothache *dolor de muelas*

POST OFFICE AND COMMUNICATIONS

long-distance telephone *teléfono larga distancia*
I would like to call . . . *Quisiera llamar a . . .*
collect *por cobrar*
station to station *a quien contesta*
person to person *persona a persona*
credit card *tarjeta de crédito*
post office *correo*
general delivery *lista de correo*
letter *carta*
stamp *estampilla, timbre*
postcard *tarjeta*
aerogram *aerograma*
air mail *correo aereo*
registered *registrado*
money order *giro*
package; box *paquete; caja*
string; tape *cuerda; cinta*

AT THE BORDER

border *frontera*
customs *aduana*
immigration *migración*
tourist card *tarjeta de turista*
inspection *inspección; revisión*
passport *pasaporte*
profession *profesión*
marital status *estado civil*
single *soltero*
married; divorced *casado; divorciado*
widowed *viudado*
insurance *seguros*
title *título*
driver's license *licencia de manejar*

AT THE GAS STATION

gas station *gasolinera*
gasoline *gasolina*
unleaded *sin plomo*
full, please *lleno, por favor*
tire *llanta*
tire repair shop *vulcanizadora*
air *aire*
water *agua*
oil (change) *aceite (cambio)*
grease *grasa*
My...doesn't work. *Mi...no sirve.*
battery *batería*
radiator *radiador*
alternator *alternador*
generator *generador*
tow truck *grúa*
repair shop *taller mecánico*
tune-up *afinación*
auto parts store *refaccionería*

VERBS

Verbs are the key to getting along in Spanish. They employ mostly predictable forms and come in three classes, which end in *ar*, *er*, and *ir*, respectively:

to buy *comprar*
I buy, you (he, she, it) buys *compro, compra*
we buy, you (they) buy *compramos, compran*

to eat *comer*
I eat, you (he, she, it) eats *como, come*
we eat, you (they) eat *comemos, comen*

to climb *subir*
I climb, you (he, she, it) climbs *subo, sube*
we climb, you (they) climb *subimos, suben*

Here are more (with irregularities indicated):

to do or make *hacer* (regular except for *hago*, I do or make)
to go *ir* (very irregular: *voy, va, vamos, van*)
to go (walk) *andar*
to love *amar*
to work *trabajar*
to want *desear, querer*
to need *necesitar*
to read *leer*
to write *escribir*
to repair *reparar*
to stop *parar*
to get off (the bus) *bajar*
to arrive *llegar*
to stay (remain) *quedar*
to stay (lodge) *hospedar*
to leave *salir* (regular except for *salgo*, I leave)
to look at *mirar*
to look for *buscar*
to give *dar* (regular except for *doy*, I give)
to carry *llevar*
to have *tener* (irregular but important: *tengo, tiene, tenemos, tienen*)
to come *venir* (similarly irregular: *vengo, viene, venimos, vienen*)

Spanish has two forms of "to be":

to be *estar* (regular except for *estoy*, I am)
to be *ser* (very irregular: *soy, es, somos, son*)

Use *estar* when speaking of location or a temporary state of being: "I am at home." "*Estoy en casa.*" "I'm sick." "*Estoy enfermo.*" Use *ser* for a permanent state of being: "I am a doctor." "*Soy doctora.*"

NUMBERS

zero *cero*
one *uno*
two *dos*
three *tres*
four *cuatro*
five *cinco*
six *seis*
seven *siete*
eight *ocho*
nine *nueve*
10 *diez*
11 *once*
12 *doce*
13 *trece*
14 *catorce*
15 *quince*
16 *dieciseis*
17 *diecisiete*
18 *dieciocho*
19 *diecinueve*
20 *veinte*
21 *veinte y uno* or *veintiuno*
30 *treinta*
40 *cuarenta*
50 *cincuenta*
60 *sesenta*
70 *setenta*
80 *ochenta*
90 *noventa*
100 *ciento*
101 *ciento y uno* or *cientiuno*
200 *doscientos*
500 *quinientos*
1,000 *mil*
10,000 *diez mil*
100,000 *cien mil*
1,000,000 *millón*
one half *medio*
one third *un tercio*
one fourth *un cuarto*

TIME

What time is it? *¿Qué hora es?*
It's one o'clock. *Es la una.*
It's three in the afternoon. *Son las tres de la tarde.*
It's 4 A.M. *Son las cuatro de la mañana.*
six-thirty *seis y media*
a quarter till eleven *un cuarto para las once*
a quarter past five *las cinco y cuarto*
an hour *una hora*

DAYS AND MONTHS

Monday *lunes*
Tuesday *martes*
Wednesday *miércoles*
Thursday *jueves*
Friday *viernes*
Saturday *sábado*
Sunday *domingo*
today *hoy*
tomorrow *mañana*
yesterday *ayer*
January *enero*
February *febrero*
March *marzo*
April *abril*
May *mayo*
June *junio*
July *julio*
August *agosto*
September *septiembre*
October *octubre*
November *noviembre*
December *diciembre*
a week *una semana*
a month *un mes*
after *después*
before *antes*

Suggested Reading

Some of these books are informative, others are entertaining, and all of them will increase your understanding of Mexico. Some are easier to find in Mexico than at home, and vice versa. Many of them are out of print, but www.amazon.com, www.barnesandnoble.com, or libraries often have used copies. Take some along on your trip. If you find others that are especially noteworthy, let us know.

HISTORY

Brunk, Samuel. *Emiliano Zapata: Revolution and Betrayal in Mexico.* Albuquerque, NM: University of New Mexico Press, 1995. A detailed narrative of the renowned revolutionary's turbulent life, from his humble birth in Anenecuilco village in Morelos, through his de facto control of Mexico City in 1914–1915, to his final betrayal and assassination in 1919. The author authoritatively demonstrates that Zapata, neither complete hero nor complete villain, was simply an incredibly determined native leader who paid the ultimate price in his selfless struggle for land and liberty for the campesinos of southern Mexico.

Calderón de la Barca, Frances. *Life in Mexico, with New Material from the Author's Journals.* Charleston, SC: Bibliobazaar, 2006. A new copyright and printing of the humorous original 1843 book, by the brilliant, celebrated Scottish wife of the Spanish ambassador to Mexico.

Casasola, Gustavo. *Seis Siglos de Historia Gráfica de Mexico (Six Centuries of Mexican Graphic History).* Mexico City: Editorial Gustavo Casasola, 1978, republished in 1989. Fourteen fascinating volumes, in Spanish, of Mexican history in pictures, from 1325 to the present. Amazon.com advertises copies of individual volumes; large city and university libraries may have copies also.

Collis, Maurice. *Cortés and Montezuma.* New York, NY: New Directions Publishing Corp., 1999. A reprint of a 1954 classic piece of well-researched storytelling, Collis traces Cortés's conquest of Mexico through the defeat of his chief opponent, Aztec Emperor Montezuma. He uses contemporary eyewitnesses—notably Bernal Díaz del Castillo—to revivify one of history's greatest dramas.

Cortés, Hernán. *Letters from Mexico.* Translated by Anthony Pagden. New Haven, CT: Yale University Press, 1986. Cortés's five long letters to his king, in which he describes contemporary Mexico in fascinating detail, including, notably, the remarkably sophisticated life of the Aztecs at the time of the conquest.

De las Casas, Bartolome. *A Short Account of the Destruction of the Indies.* New York, NY: Penguin Books, 1992. The gritty but beloved Dominican bishop, renowned as Mexico's "Apostle of the Indians," writes passionately of his own attempt to moderate and humanize the Spanish conquest of Mexico. Undoubtedly, de las Casas's sad tale made a great impression on Spain's King Charles V, who, in 1542, the same year the book was written, promulgated the liberal New Laws of the Indies, that outlawed buying and selling human beings in Mexico 320 years before Abraham Lincoln's Emancipation Proclamation.

Díaz del Castillo, Bernal. *The Discovery and Conquest of Mexico.* New York, NY: da Capo (Perseus Books Group), 2003. A fascinating, still-fresh soldier's tale of the Conquest from the Spanish viewpoint.

Fernández, Miguel Ángel. *The China Galleon.* Translated by Debra Nagao. Photographs by Michel Zabé. Monterrey, Mexico: Vitro

Corporativo, S.A. de C.V., 2000. This authoritatively researched, masterfully translated, and gorgeously illustrated coffee-table volume traces the colorful history of the Manila galleon, and consequently Acapulco, from the fall of Constantinople in A.D. 1453 to the present day. The author shows how the allure of Asia's aromatic spices, glistening lacquerware, smooth silks, glittering gold and gems, and radiant porcelains propelled the Spanish to realize Columbus's old dream and transform the Pacific into the Spanish lake that it remained for 300 years.

Garfias, Luis. *The Mexican Revolution*. Mexico City: Panorama Editorial, 1985. A concise Mexican version of the 1910–1917 Mexican revolution, the crucible of present-day Mexico.

Gugliotta, Bobette. *Women of Mexico, the Consecrated and the Common* Encino, CA: originally published by Floricanto Press, 1989. Lively legends, tales, and biographies of remarkable Mexican women. Libraries, Amazon.com, and others have used copies.

León-Portilla, Miguel. *The Broken Spears: The Aztec Account of the Conquest of Mexico*. New York, NY: Beacon Press, 1962. Provides an intriguing contrast to Díaz del Castillo's account.

Meyer, Michael, and William Sherman. *The Course of Mexican History*. New York, NY: Oxford University Press, 2003. An insightful 700-plus-page college textbook in paperback. A bargain, especially if you can get it used.

Novas, Himlice. *Everything You Need to Know About Latino History*. New York, NY: Penguin Group, 2007. Chicanos, Latin rhythm, La Raza, the Treaty of Guadalupe Hidalgo, and much more, interpreted from an authoritative Latino point of view.

Reed, John. *Insurgent Mexico*. New York, NY: International Publisher's Co., 1994. Republication of 1914 original. Fast-moving, but not unbiased, description of the 1910 Mexican revolution by the journalist famed for his reporting of the subsequent 1917 Russian revolution. Reed, memorialized by the Soviets, was resurrected in the 1981 film biography *Reds,* starring Warren Beatty and Diane Keaton.

Ridley, Jasper. *Maximilian and Juárez*. London: Orion Pub. Group, 2001. This authoritative historical biography breathes new life into one of Mexico's great ironic tragedies, a drama that pitted the native Zapotec "Lincoln of Mexico" against the dreamy, idealistic Archduke Maximilian of Austria-Hungary. Despite their common liberal ideals, they were drawn into a bloody no-quarter struggle that set the Old World against the New, ending in Maximilian's execution, the insanity of his wife, and the emergence of the United States as a power to be reckoned with in world affairs.

Ruíz, Ramon Eduardo. *Triumphs and Tragedy: A History of the Mexican People*. New York, NY: W. W. Norton, Inc., 1992. A pithy, anecdote-filled history of Mexico from an authoritative Mexican-American perspective.

Shorris, Earl. *Life and Times of Mexico*. New York, NY: W. W. Norton, 2006. A grand 750-page narrative of the divided soul of Mexico, driven by 3,000 years of history, as told by Mexicans, from the ancient Olmecs, Benito Juárez, and Emiliano Zapata, to *maquiladora laborers,* prostitutes, and a movie director.

Simpson, Lesley Bird. *Many Mexicos*. Berkeley, CA: University of California Press, 1962. A much-reprinted, fascinating, broad-brush version of Mexican history.

GOVERNMENT, POLITICS, AND ECONOMY

Dillon, Samuel, and Julia Preston. *Opening Mexico: The Making of a Democracy.* New York, NY: Farrar, Straus and Giroux, 2005. Former Mexico City *New York Times* bureau chiefs use their rich personal insights and investigative skill to tell the story of the latter-day evolution of Mexico's uniquely imperfect democracy. Their story begins during the 1980s, tracing the decay of the 71-year-rule of the PRI, to its collapse, with the election of opposition candidate Vicente Fox in 2000. The actors are vivid and manifold, from rebellious anti-government campesinos to high federal officials conspiring with drug lords, to teachers striking for fair pay and an end to political assassination of their colleagues.

UNIQUE GUIDE AND TIP BOOKS

American Automobile Association. *Mexico TravelBook.* Heathrow, FL: 2003. Published by the American Automobile Association (1000 AAA Drive, Heathrow, FL 32746-5063, www.aaa.com, 800/922-8228). Short but sweet summaries of major Mexican tourist destinations and sights. Also includes information on fiestas, accommodations, restaurants, and a wealth of information relevant to car travel in Mexico. Available in bookstores, or free to AAA members at affiliate offices.

Church, Mike, and Terry Church. *Traveler's Guide to Mexican Camping.* Kirkland, WA: Rolling Homes Press (order by telephone P.O. Box 2099, Kirkland, WA 98083-2099, tel. 425/825-7846, www.rollinghomes.com). An unusually thorough guide to trailer parks all over Mexico, with much coverage of the Pacific Coast, including Ixtapa-Zihuatanejo and Acapulco. Detailed maps guide you accurately to each trailer park cited and clear descriptions tell you what to expect. The book also provides very helpful information on car travel in Mexico, including details of insur-

ance, border crossing, highway safety, car repairs, and much more.

Forgey, Dr. William. *Traveler's Medical Alert Series: Mexico, A Guide to Health and Safety.* Merrillville, IN: ICS Books, 1991. Useful information on health and safety in Mexico. Out of print, but available through Amazon.com.

Franz, Carl. *The People's Guide to Mexico.* Berkeley, CA: Avalon Travel, 13th edition, 2006. An entertaining and insightful A-to-Z general guide to the joys and pitfalls of independent economy travel in Mexico.

Graham, Scott. *Handle With Care: Guide to Socially Responsible Travel in Developing Countries.* Chicago, IL: The Noble Press, 1991. Should you accept a meal from a family who lives in a grass house? This insightful guide answers this and hundreds of other tough questions for people who want to travel responsibly in the third world. Out of print, but available through Amazon.com.

Guilford, Judith. *The Packing Book.* Berkeley, CA: Ten Speed Press, 4th edition, 2006. The secrets of the carry-on traveler, or how to make everything you carry do double and triple duty, all for the sake of convenience, mobility, economy, and comfort.

Jeffrey, Nan. *Adventuring With Children.* Ashland, MA: Avalon House Publishing, 1995. This unusually detailed book starts where most travel-with-children books end. It contains, besides a wealth of information and practical strategies for general travel with children, specific chapters on how you can adventure—trek, kayak, river-raft, camp, bicycle, and much more—successfully with the kids in tow.

Werner, David. *Where There Is No Doctor.* Berkeley, CA: Hesperian Foundation, 1992 (1919 Addison St., Berkeley, CA 94704, tel.

888/729-1796, www.hesperian.org). How to keep well in the tropical backcountry.

Whipperman, Bruce. *Moon Oaxaca*. Berkeley, CA: Avalon Travel, 6th edition, 2011. The most comprehensive guidebook of Oaxaca City and state, the Ixtapa-Zihuatanejo region's neighboring state. It's chock full of useful details of not only Oaxaca's renowned capital city and central valley, but also Oaxaca's little-known untouristed treasures, from the mountains to the sea.

LITERATURE

Bowen, David, ed. *Pyramids of Glass*. San Antonio, TX: Corona Publishing Co., 1994. Two dozen-odd stories that lead the reader on a month-long journey through the bedrooms, barracks, cafés, and streets of present-day Mexico.

Boyle, T. C. *The Tortilla Curtain*. New York, NY: Penguin-Putnam 1996; paperback edition, Raincoast Books, 1996. A chance intersection of the lives of two couples, one affluent and liberal Southern Californians, the other poor homeless illegal immigrants, forces all to come to grips with the real price of the American Dream.

Cisneros, Sandra. *Caramelo*. New York, NY: Alfred A. Knopf, 2002. A celebrated author weaves a passionate yet funny multigenerational tale of a Mexican-American family and of their migrations, which, beginning in Mexico City, propelled them north, all the way to Chicago and back.

De la Cruz, Sor Juana Inez. *Poems, Protest, and a Dream*. New York, NY: Penguin, 1997. Masterful translation of a collection of love and religious poems by the celebrated pioneer Mexican feminist-nun (1651–1695).

De Zapata, Celia C., ed. *Short Stories by Latin American Women: The Magic and the Real*. New York, NY: Random House Modern Library, 2003. An eclectic mix of more than 30 stories by noted Latin American women. The stories, which a number of critics classify as "magical realism," were researched by editor Celia de Zapata, who got them freshly translated into English by a cadre of renowned translators; includes a foreword by celebrated author Isabel Allende.

Doerr, Harriet. *Consider This, Señor*. New York, NY: Harcourt Brace, 1993. Four expatriates tough it out in a Mexican small town, adapting to the excesses—blazing sun, driving rain, vast untrammeled landscapes—while interacting with the local folks and while the local folks observe them, with a mixture of fascination and tolerance.

Finn, María, ed. *Mexico in Mind*. New York, NY: Vintage Books, 2006. The wisdom and impressions of two centuries of renowned writers, from D. H. Lawrence and John Steinbeck to John Reed and Richard Rodríguez, who were drawn to the timelessness and romance of Mexico.

Fuentes, Carlos. *Where the Air Is Clear*. New York, NY: Farrar, Straus and Giroux, 1971. The seminal work of Mexico's celebrated novelist.

Fuentes, Carlos. *The Years with Laura Díaz*. Translated by Alfred MacAdam. New York, NY: Farrar, Straus and Giroux, 2000. A panorama of Mexico from independence to the 21st century through the eyes of one woman, Laura Díaz, and her great-grandson, the author. One reviewer said that she, "as a Mexican woman, would like to celebrate Carlos Fuentes; it is worthy of applause that a man who has seen, observed, analyzed and criticized the great occurrences of the century now has a woman, Laura Díaz, speak for him."

Jennings, Gary. *Aztec*. New York, NY: Atheneum, 1980. Beautifully researched and written monumental tale of lust, compassion, love, and death in preconquest Mexico.

Nickles, Sara, ed. *Escape to Mexico*. San Francisco, CA: Chronicle Books, 2002. A carefully selected anthology of 20-odd stories of Mexico by renowned authors, from Steven Crane and W. Somerset Maugham to Anaïs Nin and David Lida, who all found inspiration, refuge, adventure, and much more in Mexico.

Perez-Riverte, Arturo. *Queen of the South*. New York, NY: Plume Books, 2005. In a gripping good read, the author tackles the dangerous world of Mexican drug trafficking. The story immediately races along with protagonist Teresa Mendoza, fleeing for her life from Mexico to Morocco. There, learning from her every step, threading her way through a snake nest of dangerous men, she finally triumphs as the ringleader of a big drug trafficking ring.

Peters, Daniel. *The Luck of Huemac*. New York, NY: Random House, 1981. An Aztec noble family's tale of war, famine, sorcery, heroism, treachery, love, and, finally, disaster and death in the Valley of Mexico.

Traven, B. *The Treasure of the Sierra Madre*. New York, NY: Hill and Wang, 1967. Campesinos, *federales,* gringos, and *indígenas* all figure in this modern morality tale set in Mexico's rugged outback. The most famous of the mysterious author's many novels of oppression and justice in Mexico's jungles.

Villaseñor, Victor. *Rain of Gold*. New York, NY: Delta Books (Bantam, Doubleday, and Dell), 1991. The moving, best-selling epic of the gritty travails of the author's family. From humble rural beginnings in the Copper Canyon, they flee revolution and certain death, struggling through parched northern deserts to sprawling border refugee camps. From there they migrate to relative safety and an eventual modicum of happiness in Southern California.

PEOPLE AND CULTURE

Castillo, Ana, ed. *Goddess of the Americas*. New York, NY: Riverhead Books, 1996. Here a noted author has selected from the works of seven interpreters of Mesoamerican female deities to provide readers with visions of goddesses that range as far and wide as Sex Goddess, the Broken-Hearted, the Subversive, and the Warrior Queen.

Casumano, Camille. *Mexico, a Love Story: Women Write About the Mexican Experience*. Berkeley, CA: Seal Press (Perseus Book Group), 2006. A dozen-odd writers share stories, some poignant, some entertaining, and all endearing, that express their love for Mexico and its people.

Cordrey, Donald, and Dorothy Cordrey. *Mexican Indian Costumes*. Austin, TX: University of Texas Press, 1968. A lovingly photographed, written, and illustrated classic on Mexican native peoples.

Finerty, Catherine Palmer, *In a Village Far From Home*. Tucson, AZ: University of Arizona Press, 2000. After a successful Madison Avenue career, the author packed up and eventually found herself the volunteer nurse in an isolated western Mexico village. From her eight-year diary, she shares the joys and sorrows of a cast of village characters, from a valiant Catholic padre and his frowning bishop, to Chuy, her indigenous housekeeper, and Chila, her landlord.

Lewis, Oscar. *Children of Sanchez*. New York, NY: Random House, 1961. Poverty and strength in the Mexican underclass, sympathetically described and interpreted by renowned sociologist Lewis.

Medina, Sylvia López. *Cantora*. New York, NY: Ballantine Books, 1992. Fascinated by the stories of her grandmother, aunt, and mother, the author seeks her own center by discovering a past that she thought she wanted to forget.

Palmer, Colin A. *Slaves of the White God: Blacks in Mexico.* Cambridge, MA: Harvard University Press, 1976. A scholarly study of why and how Spanish authorities imported African slaves into the Americas and how they were used afterward. Replete with poignant details taken from Spanish and Mexican archives describing how the Africans struggled from bondage to eventual freedom.

Toor, Frances. *A Treasury of Mexican Folkways.* New York, NY: Bonanza Books, 1947, reprinted 1985. An illustrated encyclopedia of vanishing Mexicana—costumes, religion, fiestas, burial practices, customs, legends—compiled during the celebrated author's 35 years of residence in Mexico in the early 20th century.

Wauchope, Robert, ed. *Handbook of Middle American Indians.* Vols. 7 and 8. Austin, TX: University of Texas Press, 1969. Authoritative but aging surveys of important native-speaking groups in northern, central (vol. 8), and southern (vol. 7) Mexico.

ARTS, ARCHITECTURE, AND CRAFTS

Morrill, Penny C., and Carol A. Berk. *Mexican Silver.* Atglen, PA: Shiffer Publishing Co., 2001 (4880 Lower Valley Road, Atglen, PA 19310). Lovingly written and photographed exposition of the Mexican silvercraft of Taxco, Guerrero, that was revitalized through the initiative of Frederick Davis and William Spratling in the 1920s and 1930s. Color photos of many beautiful museum-quality pieces supplement the text, which describes the history and work of a score of silversmithing families who developed the Taxco craft under Spratling's leadership. Greatly adds to the traveler's appreciation of the beautiful Taxco silvercrafts.

Mullen, Robert James. *Architecture and Its Sculpture in Viceregal Mexico.* Austin, TX:

University of Texas Press, 1997. The essential work of Mexican colonial-era cathedrals and churches. In this lovingly written and illustrated life work, Mullen breathes new vitality into New Spain's preciously glorious colonial architectural legacy.

Sayer, Chloë. *Arts and Crafts of Mexico.* San Francisco, CA: Chronicle Books, 1990. All you ever wanted to know about your favorite Mexican crafts, from papier-mâché and pottery to toys and Taxco silver. Beautifully illustrated by traditional etchings and David Lavender's crisp black-and-white and color photographs.

FLORA AND FAUNA

Beletzky, Les. *Tropical Mexico: The Ecotraveler's Wildlife Guide* San Diego, CA: Academic Press, 1999. Although not complete by any means, this is the best popular guide to Mexican Wildlife, with 500 pages, chocked with details covering a host of habitats southeast Mexico, including Yucatan, Chiapas, and Oaxaca (adjacent to the Ixtapa-Zihuatanejo region). Although half of the coverage is devoted to birds, many other species, from frogs and crocodiles to armadillos and ocelots are also included.

Goodson, Gar. *Fishes of the Pacific Coast.* Stanford, CA: Stanford University Press, 1988. More than 500 beautifully detailed color drawings highlight this pocket version of all you ever wanted to know about the ocean's fishes (including common Spanish names) from Alaska to Peru.

Howell, Steve N. G. *Bird-Finding Guide to Mexico.* Ithaca, NY: Cornell University Press, 1999. A unique portable guide for folks who really want to see birds in Mexico. Unlike other bird books, the author presents a unique and authoritative site guide, with dozens of clear maps and lists of birds seen at sites all over Mexico.

Howell, Steve N. G., and Sophie Webb. *A Guide to the Birds of Mexico and Northern Central America*. Oxford: Oxford University Press, 1995. All the serious bird-watcher needs to know about Mexico's rich species treasury. Includes authoritative habitat maps and 70 excellent color plates that detail the male and females of about 1,500 species.

Mason Jr., Charles T., and Patricia B. Mason. *Handbook of Mexican Roadside Flora*. Tucson, AZ: University of Arizona Press, 1987. Authoritative identification guide, with line illustrations, of all the plants you're likely to see in your travels in Mexico.

Morris, Percy A. *A Field Guide to Pacific Coast Shells*. Boston, MA: Houghton Mifflin, 1974. The complete beachcomber's Pacific shell guide.

Pesman, M. Walter. *Meet Flora Mexicana*. Globe, AZ: D. S. King, 1962. Delightful anecdotes and illustrations of hundreds of common Mexican plants. Out of print.

Wright, N. Pelham. *A Guide to Mexican Mammals and Reptiles*. Mexico City: Minutiae Mexicana, 1989. Pocket-edition lore, history, descriptions, and pictures of commonly seen Mexican animals.

Internet Resources

A number of websites may be helpful in preparing for your Ixtapa-Zihuatanejo adventure.

GENERAL TRAVEL
U.S. Department of State
www.state.gov/travel
The U.S. State Department's very complete information website. Lots of subheadings and links to a swarm of topics, including U.S. consular offices in Mexico, travel advisories, and links to other government information, such as importation of food, plants, and animals, U.S. customs and returning home; health abroad; airlines; and exchange rates.

Internet Travel Sites
www.travelocity.com, www.expedia.com, www.tripadvisor.com
Major sites for airline and hotel bookings.

TRAVEL INSURANCE
Travel Insurance Services
www.travelinsure.com
World Travel Center
www.worldtravelcenter.com
Both good for general travel insurance and other services.

MEXICO CAR INSURANCE
Sanborns Insurance
www.sanbornsinsurance.com
Site of Sanborn's Insurance, the longtime, very reliable Mexico auto insurance agency, with one of the few north-of-the-border adjustment procedures. Get your quote online, order their many useful publications, and find out about other insurance you many have forgotten.

SPECIALTY TRAVEL
Mobility International
www.miusa.org
Site of Mobility International, expertly organized and complete, with a flock of services for travelers with disabilities, including many people-to-people connections in Mexico.

Purple Roofs
www.purpleroofs.com
One of the best general gay travel websites is maintained by San Francisco–based travel agency Purple Roofs. It offers, for example, details about several gay-friendly Oaxaca hotels, in addition to a wealth of gay-friendly travel-oriented links worldwide.

Road Scholar
www.roadscholar.org
Site of Boston-based Road Scholar, Inc. (formerly Elderhostel, Inc.), with a huge catalog of ongoing senior-friendly study tours.

MEXICO IN GENERAL
MexConnect
www.mexconnect.com
A large Mexico site, with dozens upon dozens of subheadings, links, and forums, most helpful for folks thinking of traveling, working, living, or retiring in Mexico. For example, I entered "Zihuatanejo" into their very useful search box and got two dozen hits, on topics ranging from Guerrero recipes and snorkeling, to building construction and cooking schools.

Mexico Desconocido
www.mexicodesconocido.com.mx
The site of the excellent magazine *Mexico Desconocido* (Undiscovered Mexico) that often features unusual, untouristed destinations. It links to a large library of past articles, in a style not unlike a Mexican version of *National Geographic Traveler*. Solid, hard-to-find information, in good English translation, if you can get it. (The site is so voluminous that the Google automatic translator tends to bog down at the effort.)

Mexico Online
www.mexonline.com
An excellent, very extensive, well-organized commercial site with many subheadings and links. They cover Ixtapa-Zihuatanejo, Troncones, Acapulco, and Taxco, including dozens of accommodations, from luxury hotels to modest guesthouses.

Mexico Tourism Board
www.visitmexico.com
The official website of the public-private Mexico Tourism Board; a good general site for destination information. It has lots of summarily informative subheadings, not unlike an abbreviated guidebook. If you can't find what you want here, call the toll-free information number 800/446-3942 or email contact@ visitmexico.com, or contact your local Mexico Tourism Board office. If you can read Spanish, the Spanish-language version of www.visit mexico.com, www.cptm.org.mx, is much more specific and detailed.

On the Road in Mexico
www.ontheroadin.com
Helpful information and photos of dozens of Mexico RV and camping parks. Includes accurate and very usable for-sale maps and driving directions to out-of-the-way, hard-to-find locations, including three around Acapulco and another three around Ixtapa-Zihuatanejo. Information, however, tends to be two or three years old.

Planeta.com
www.planeta.com
Life project of Latin America's dean of ecotourism, Ron Mader, who furnishes a comprehensive clearinghouse of everything ecologically correct, from rescuing turtle eggs in Jalisco to preserving cloud forests in Peru. Contains dozens of subheadings competently linked for maximum speed. For example, check out the Mexico travel directory for ecojourneys, maps, information networks, parks, regional guides, and a mountain more.

Vacation Rentals By Owner
www.vrbo.com
A very useful site, ideal for picking a vacation rental house, condo, or villa, with photos, information, and reservations links to many individual owners. Prices vary from moderate to luxurious. Coverage extends over much of the Mexican Pacific coast, with dozens of rentals in Troncones, Ixtapa-Zihuatanejo, and Acapulco.

DESTINATIONS

Ixtapa and Zihuatanejo Convention and Visitor's Bureau
www.visit-ixtapa-zihuatanejo.org

The official site of Ixtapa and Zihuatanejo Convention and Visitor's Bureau, with listings of many hotels, restaurants, tours, sports, and more. At this writing, it's still a work in progress; a number of links lead to dead ends. Although it was not possible to book all hotel reservations directly, hotel email and web links to many hotel websites, especially the upscale ones, were available.

zihua.net
www.zihua.net

Similar to, but less extensive than, www.zihuatanejo.net, this site (along with its twin, www.ixtapa.net) nevertheless has lots of useful, mostly commercial, travel-oriented information and links.

Zihuatanejo.net
www.zihuatanejo.net

A top-notch, very complete, well-maintained commercial site listing nearly everywhere to stay (with reservation and email links) and dine, everything to do, and much more in Zihuatanejo, Ixtapa, Troncones, and Barra de Potosí. In English or Spanish.

Barra de Potosí
www.barra-potosi.com

A good site, with several links to Barra de Potosí bed-and-breakfasts, hotels, activities, and services.

Troncones
www.troncones.com.mx

Good site, especially for hotels, with many links to Troncones's small beachfront hotels and bed-and-breakfasts. Also links to a number of restaurants, services, real estate, and much more.

Troncones.net
www.troncones.net

A good alternative to www.troncones.com.mx, also with several hotel, bed-and-breakfast, restaurant, and activities links.

Index

A

Acapulco: 104-137; maps 106-107, 111
Acapulco Trailer Park: 15, 102, 125
accommodations: 290-294
air evacuation: 303
air travel: 267-270
alcohol: 297-298
Amusgo people: 213
Anson, George: 26
arts and crafts: 262-266
ATMs: 308
Atracadero: 15, 75-76

B

Bahía de Puerto Marqués: 117
Balneario Santa Fe: 17, 158
banks: 308
Bar Berta: 18, 189
Bar Estación: 18, 189
bargaining: 262
Barra de Coyuca: 100-101
Barra de Potosí: 15, 68-70
Barra de Tecoanapa: 210
beaches: general discussion 14-15, 285-286;
    Acapulco 114-118; Costa Chica 207, 209, 210,
    218-219; Costa Grande 89, 90-91, 97, 98, 99;
    Ixtapa and Zihuatanejo 27, 29-32, 66, 68,
    74, 75-76
Biblioteca Del Estado: 147
Biblioteca Taxco-Canoga Park: 184
biking: 56-57, 118
birds/bird-watching: general discussion
    234; Costa Grande 99, 100; Ixtapa and
    Zihuatanejo 68
Bistro de Roberto: 15, 72-73
boating: Acapulco 131; Costa Grande 97; Ixtapa
    and Zihuatanejo 55-56
Bonita: 17, 132
border crossings: 276, 284-285
botanical garden: 113-114
bribes (*mordidas*): 275-276
bullfighting: 289
bungee jumping: 17, 129
business visas: 284
bus transportation: 270-271, 273, 280-281

C

Cacahuatepec: 222
Café Dora: 18, 187

Calderón, Felipe: 248-250
Calle de Muerte: 183
Calle la Garita: 184
Camalote: 97-98
Campamento Playa Piedra de Tlalcoyunque:
    94
camping: general discussion 292-294;
    Acapulco 125; Costa Chica 207-208, 219;
    Costa Grande 96, 97, 98, 102-103; Guerrero
    Upcountry 158; Ixtapa and Zihuatanejo
    47-48, 70, 73, 74
canoeing: *see* kayaking/canoeing
Capilla de la Paz: 114
Carnaval (Taxco): 189
car rentals: 281
car travel: 273-277, 281, 284, 307; map
    278-279
Casa Borda: 183
Casa de Dolores Olmedo: 113
Casa de la Máscara: 17, 20, 113
Casa del Encanto: 16, 69
Casa de Piedra: 207
Casa Elvira: 13, 49
Casa Frida: 16, 69
Casa Humboldt: 20, 183-184
Casa Ki: 14, 71-72
caves/caverns: 159-160, 195
cell phones: 310
Centro Joyero de Iguala: 17-18, 172, 176
Cerro de las Peñas: 85
Cerro Madera: 29
Chilapa: 17, 160-164; map 161
Chilapa Sunday handicrafts market: 17, 161-162
children, traveling with: 284, 300-301
Chilpancingo: 17, 20, 142-153; maps 144-145,
    146
Chilpancingo Zoo: 17, 147
Christine: 14, 51-52
churches/temples: Acapulco 112; Costa Chica
    211, 224; Costa Grande 85; Guerrero
    Upcountry 162, 182-183, 184, 200
CICI Parque Aquatico: 176
ciclopista (Acapulco bike path): 118
ciclopista (Ixtapa bike path): 13, 57
climate: 228
Coconuts: 13, 50, 52
Colotlipa: 159-160
Concha: 18, 189
Coronel, Don Chico: 165
Cortés, Hernán: 237-239

Costa Chica: 202-225; map 204-205
Costa Grande and Acapulco: 80-137;
    map 82-83
Costera: 116-117
credit cards: 309-310
Cristo del Monte: 184-185
cruise travel: 277
Cuajinicuilapa: 20, 217-218
Cuauhtémoc: 198-199
Cuauhtémoc Mural: 184
Cuna (Cradle) de Vicente Guerrero: 154
currency exchange: 308
customs declarations, U.S.: 285

D

Dampier, William: 26
Day of the Dead: 176, 261
Del Ángeles: 18, 188
demographics: 254-258
diarrhea: 303-304
Díaz, Porfirio: 243-244
disabilities, travelers with: 299-300
Doña Marina: 238
Drake, Francis: 239
driving distances: 278-279
driving restrictions, Mexico City: 277
duendes (spirits): 258

E

economy: 250-252
ecotourism: 263
Eden Beach Hacienda: 14, 72
El Aguacate: 224
El Borbollón: 158
El Carrizal: 14, 98-99
electricity: 311
El Faro: 30
El Refugio de Potosí: 68
Estero Valentin: 55
Ex-Convento San Bernardino: 184

F

fauna: 233-236
Feria de San Mateo, la Navidad,
    y el Año Nuevo: 151
Festival of Santa Prisca: 189
festivals and events: 258-261
Fiesta de la Natividad de María: 152
Fiesta de la Virgen de la Asunción: 163
Fiesta de los Jumiles: 189-190
Fiesta del Señor de las Misericordias: 159
Fiesta del Señor del Perdón: 214-215
Fiesta de Pascua: 167

Fiesta de San Francisco (Iguala): 176
Fiesta de San Francisco de Asis (Olinalá): 167
Fiesta de San Juan: 163
Fiesta de Santa Ana: 158
Fiesta of Santiago: 158
Fiesta of the Virgin of Guadalupe: 190
fish/fishing: general discussion 19, 235-236,
    287-289; Acapulco 130-131; Costa Chica 207,
    210; Costa Grande 91, 97, 99; Ixtapa and
    Zihuatanejo 54-55, 68
flora: 229-233
food/restaurants: 294-299
Fox, Vicente: 247-249
Fuerte de San Diego: 17, 20, 112-113

G

gay and lesbian travelers: 301
geography: 226-228
golf: general discussion 289; Acapulco 132;
    Guerrero Upcountry 190; Ixtapa and
    Zihuatanejo 56
government: 252-253
gratuities: 308-309
Green Angels: 273
Grutas de Cacahuamilpa: 18, 195
Grutas de Juxtlahuaca: 17, 159-160
Guerrero Upcountry: 138-201; map 140-141
Guerrero, Vicente: 154-155

HI

health and safety: 302-307
hiking/walking: Acapulco 115, 132; Guerrero
    Upcountry 184; Ixtapa and Zihuatanejo 57
Hilltop Memorial Flag: 18, 172-173
home ownership: 42
Hotel del Parque: 17, 148
Hotel Los Flamingos: 15, 17, 115-116, 120-121
Hotel María Isabel: 17, 174
Hotel Resort Villas San Luis: 94-95
Huaxpáltepec Nazarene (pre-Easter) fair:
    223-224
Iglesia de Chavarrieta: 184
Iglesia de Santa María de la Asunción: 200
Iguala: 168-178; maps 168-169, 170
Iguala gold market: 17-18, 172, 176
immunizations: 11, 302
indígenas: 255-257
Inn at Manzanillo Bay: 14, 72, 73
International Association for Medical
    Assistance to Travelers (IAMAT): 305
internet access: 311
ISA (Instructional Surf Adventures) Mexico:
    16, 73

Isla Grande: 13, 32, 57
Isla Montosa: 100
Isla Roqueta: 17, 114-115, 132; map 115
Ixcateopan: 20, 200-201
Ixtapa and Zihuatanejo: 21-79; maps 23, 28, 34, 45, 67
Ixtapa Trailer Park: 15, 47

JKL

jai alai: 130
Jamiltepec: 20, 224-225
Jardín Botánico de Acapulco: 17, 113-114
José María Morales statue: 20, 147
Juárez, Benito: 242-243
Juxtlahuaca: 17, 159-160
kayaking/canoeing: general discussion 286; Costa Grande 97; Ixtapa and Zihuatanejo 55, 68
King of Chole monolith: 19, 85
Kookaburra: 17, 128
Laguna Chautengo: 207
Laguna Coyuca: 99
Laguna de Ixtapa: 31
Laguna de Potosí: 55, 68
land: 226-228
La Organera Xochipala Archaeological Zone: 17, 20, 155-157; map 156
La Quebrada: 17, 113
La Saladita: 15, 16, 75
Las Salinas: 87
Lázaro Cárdenas: 76-79; map 77
legends of Acapulco: 109
lesbian and gay travelers: 301
lighthouses: 115, 218
Linda de Taxco: 17, 132
Los Arcos: 181
Los Manantiales: 158
Los Patios: 13, 60
Los Tlacololeros: 151

M

machismo: 306
Majahua: 74-75
Mama Norma and Deborah: 13, 51
Manzanillo Bay: 14, 16, 73
Mario's: 18, 187, 189
markets (*tianguis*): 20, 211, 216, 217, 219-220, 224
Marquelia: 209
medical care: 305
medical tags: 303
Mercado de Oro: 16, 85

Mercado de Parrazal: 17, 132
Mexican names: 255
Mexico Tourism Board: 282-283
Mixtec people: 223
Mochitlán: 157-158
Moctezuma: 237-238
money: 307-309
Monte Taxco: 18, 184, 185
Monumento a los Héroes de la Independencia: 173
Monument to Vicente Guerrero: 153
Morelos, José María: 148-149, 241-242
Museo Arqueología de la Costa Grande: 13, 18, 27
Museo Comunitario: 217
Museo de las Culturas Afromestizos: 20, 218
Museo Ferrocarríl: 172
Museo Guillermo Spratling: 18, 20, 183
Museo La Avispa: 17, 147
Museo Regional de Chilpancingo: 20, 147
Museo y Santuario a la Bandera: 18, 20, 171-172

NO

names, Mexican: 255
national park: 195
National Silver Fair: 190
Ocozuchil: 158
Old Acapulco: 110
Olinalá: 164, 166-167; map 164
Ometepec: 20, 211-216; map 212
Ometepec Sunday Market: 211
100 Percent Natural: 17, 127
Our Lady of Solitude cathedral: 20, 112

P

packing tips: 12, 309
Padre Jesús: 86
Palma Sola Archaeological Site: 17, 20, 113, 132
Papanoa: 89-90
parks and gardens: 154, 171, 172, 175-176, 184
Parque Infantil del D.I.F.: 176
Parroquia de Padre Jesús: 19, 85
Parroquia de Santiago: 211
Paseo Costera: 29
Paseo del Pescador: 13, 24, 57
passports: 11, 282-284
Petatlán: 85-86
Petatlán gold market: 16, 85
petroglyphs: 20, 113
pets, traveling with: 284
phones: 310-311
Piedra Tlalcoyunque: 15, 16, 91, 94

Pinotepa Don Luis: 20, 220
Pinotepa Nacional: 20, 219-222
Pinotepa Nacional Market: 219-220
pirates of Zihuatanejo: 26
planning tips: 8-12
plants: 229-233
Playa Arroyo Seco: 88-89
Playa Blanca: 66, 68
Playa Caleta: 14, 17, 114
Playa Caletilla: 114
Playa Carey: 15, 32
Playa Cayacal: 88-89
Playa Cayaquitos: 89
Playa Coral: 14, 32
Playa Cuachalatate: 14, 32
Playa de Los Hornos: 114
Playa del Palmar: 30, 57
Playa El Almacén: 27
Playa El Calvario: 15, 16, 88-89
Playa Escolleros: 14, 16, 53
Playa Escondida: 14, 16, 90-91
Playa Hamacas: 114
Playa Hermosa: 30
Playa Hornitos: 116
Playa Icacos: 116
Playa La Barrita: 88
Playa Larga: 118
Playa La Ropa: 14, 15, 29
Playa Las Gatas: 13, 14, 16, 18, 29-30, 54
Playa Las Palmitas: 15, 17, 115
Playa las Peñitas: 14, 209-210
Playa Las Pozas: 14, 66
Playa Linda: 13, 31-32
Playa Luces Trailer Park: 15, 102-103, 125
Playa Madera: 27, 29
Playa Morro: 116
Playa Ojo de Agua: 15, 16, 90
Playa Paraíso: 96-97
Playa Pie de la Cuesta: 14, 99-104; map 100-101
Playa Quieta: 31
Playa Revolcadero: 14, 16, 117-118, 130
Playa Roqueta: 14, 115
Playa Varadero: 32
Playa Ventura: 15, 16, 207-209
Playa Villas Acapulco: 116
Plaza de Trigarantías: 171
Plaza y Monumento a la Bandera: 171, 172
poinsettias: 175, 231
politics: 252-253
population: 254-255
power sports: 286-287
pozahuancos: 220

Pozolería Tía Calla: 18, 187
Puerto Maldonado: 14, 218-219
Punta Maldonado: 16, 218-219

QR

Quechultenango: 158
rafting: 158
religion: 257-258
rental cars: 281
Restaurant Bandidos: 14, 52
Restaurant Bratwurst: 17, 126
Restaurant El Olvido: 17, 127, 128
Restaurant El Portal: 17, 151
Restaurant El Zorrito: 17, 126
Restaurant Il Mare: 13, 50
Restaurant La Perla: 13, 53
Restaurant Mi Pueblito: 16, 86
Restaurant Palao: 17, 115
Río Azul: 17, 157-158
Río Balsas dam: 15, 76
road safety: 274
Rumba Caliente: 14, 52

S

sailboarding: 55, 286
sailing: 55, 286
Sala de las Banderas: 171-172
Sala Plan de Iguala: 172
San Andres Huaxpáltepec: 223-224
San Jerónimo: 96
San José de la Barra: 207
San Luis de la Loma: 95
San Marcos: 206-207
San Pedro Amusgos: 20, 213, 222
Santa Anna, Antonio López de: 242
Santa Prisca: 20, 182-183
Santiago Jamiltepec: 20, 224-225
Santuario a la Bandera: 172
scuba diving/snorkeling: general discussion
     286; Acapulco 115, 130; Costa Grande 91;
     Ixtapa and Zihuatanejo 53-54
Semana Santa (Iguala): 176
Semana Santa (Ometepec): 214
senior travelers: 301
Señor Frog's: 14, 51
Sirena Gorda: 13, 48
Soledad de Maciel archaeological zone: 16, 19,
     84-85
spirits: 258
Splash: 14, 52
statue of José María Morelos: 20, 147
student visas: 284

surfing: general discussion 16, 286; Acapulco 116, 117, 130; Costa Chica 219; Costa Grande 89; Ixtapa and Zihuatanejo 30, 53, 73

T

Tamales y Atoles "Any": 13, 49
Tastee Freeze-La Vaca Negra: 17, 175
Taxco: 18, 179–195; map 180
Taxco Hieroglyph: 184
Taxco town market: 18, 183, 190–191
taxis: 281
Tecpán: 95–96; map 95
telephones: 310–311
Templo de San Francisco: 164
Templo de Santa María de la Asunción: 20, 147
Templo de Santiago Apóstol: 224
tennis: general discussion 289; Acapulco 132; Ixtapa and Zihuatanejo 56
tianguis (native markets): 20, 211, 216, 217, 219–220, 224
time: 311
time-sharing: 43
tipping: 308–309
Tixtla de Guerrero: 153–155
Tlacoachistlahuaca: 217
tlatchtli: 190
Torneo de Pez Vela: 55
tourist cards: 11, 283–284
tours: 277, 281
traveler's checks: 308
Troncones: 14, 70–74; map 71

trusts: 42–43
turtles: 92–93
Tuxpan: 178–179

UVW

U.S. customs: 285
vaccinations: 11, 302
vegetation zones: 229–233; map 230
Villa, Francisco (Pancho): 244
Virgin of Guadalupe fiesta: 103
visas: 11, 284
water, drinking: 302
water parks: 114, 130
weather: 228
wildlife refuge: 68
wildlife/wildlife-watching: 233–236
women travelers: 306

XYZ

Xochicalco: 18, 20, 195–199; map 196–197
Xochistlahuaca: 20, 216–217
Zapata, Emiliano: 244
Zihuatanejo: 21-66; maps 28, 34
Zihuatanejo Bay: 57
Zihuatanejo, name origin of: 32
zócalo (Acapulco): 17, 110–112; map 111
zócalo (Chilpancingo): 143, 147
zócalo (Iguala): 171
Zoe Kayak Tours: 16, 55, 68
zoos and aquariums: Acapulco 114; Guerrero Upcountry 147

List of Maps

Front color map
The Ixtapa-Zihuatanejo Region: 2-3

Ixtapa and Zihuatanejo
Ixtapa and Zihuatanejo: 23
Zihuatanejo: 28
Downtown Zihuatanejo: 34
Ixtapa: 45
Around Ixtapa and Zihuatanejo: 67
Troncones: 71
Lázaro Cárdenas: 77

The Costa Grande and Acapulco
The Costa Grande: 82-83
Tecpán: 95
Pie de la Cuesta: 100-101
Acapulco: 106-107
Around the Zócalo: 111
Isla Roqueta: 115
The Costera: 116-117

Guerrero Upcountry
Guerrero Upcountry: 140-141
Chilpancingo: 144-145

Downtown Chilpancingo: 146
La Organera Xochipala Archaeological Zone: 156
Chilapa: 161
Olinalá: 164
Iguala: 168-169
Downtown Iguala: 170
Taxco: 180
Xochicalco: 196-197

The Costa Chica
The Costa Chica: 204-205
Ometepec: 212

Background
Vegetation Zones: 230
Native Peoples of the Ixtapa-Zihuatanejo Region: 256

Essentials
Driving Distances to the Ixtapa-Zihuatanejo Region: 272
Driving Distances within the Ixtapa-Zihuatanejo Region: 278-279

www.moon.com

DESTINATIONS | ACTIVITIES | BLOGS | MAPS | BOOKS

MOON.COM is ready to help plan your next trip! Filled with fresh trip ideas and strategies, author interviews, informative travel blogs, a detailed map library, and descriptions of all the Moon guidebooks, Moon.com is all you need to get out and explore the world—or even places in your own backyard. While at Moon.com, sign up for our monthly e-newsletter for updates on new releases, travel tips, and expert advice from our on-the-go Moon authors. As always, when you travel with Moon, expect an experience that is uncommon and truly unique.

**KEEP UP WITH MOON ON FACEBOOK AND TWITTER
JOIN THE MOON PHOTO GROUP ON FLICKR**

MAP SYMBOLS

▰▰▰	Expressway	🄲	Highlight	✗	Airfield	⚓	Golf Course
▰▰▰	Primary Road	○	City/Town	✈	Airport	🅿	Parking Area
▰▰▰	Secondary Road	◉	State Capital	▲	Mountain	▱	Archaeological Site
▪▪▪	Unpaved Road	⊛	National Capital	✚	Unique Natural Feature	⚑	Church
------	Trail	★	Point of Interest			⛽	Gas Station
··········	Ferry	•	Accommodation	⚑	Waterfall	◌	Glacier
▰▰▰	Railroad	▼	Restaurant/Bar	⚑	Park		Mangrove
▰▰▰	Pedestrian Walkway	▪	Other Location	⬛	Trailhead		Reef
▥▥▥	Stairs	Λ	Campground	⛷	Skiing Area		Swamp

CONVERSION TABLES

$°C = (°F - 32) / 1.8$
$°F = (°C \times 1.8) + 32$
1 inch = 2.54 centimeters (cm)
1 foot = 0.304 meters (m)
1 yard = 0.914 meters
1 mile = 1.6093 kilometers (km)
1 km = 0.6214 miles
1 fathom = 1.8288 m
1 chain = 20.1168 m
1 furlong = 201.168 m
1 acre = 0.4047 hectares
1 sq km = 100 hectares
1 sq mile = 2.59 square km
1 ounce = 28.35 grams
1 pound = 0.4536 kilograms
1 short ton = 0.90718 metric ton
1 short ton = 2,000 pounds
1 long ton = 1.016 metric tons
1 long ton = 2,240 pounds
1 metric ton = 1,000 kilograms
1 quart = 0.94635 liters
1 US gallon = 3.7854 liters
1 Imperial gallon = 4.5459 liters
1 nautical mile = 1.852 km

°FAHRENHEIT °CELSIUS

WATER BOILS (100°C / 210°F)

WATER FREEZES (0°C / 30-40°F)

INCH 0 1 2 3 4

CM 0 1 2 3 4 5 6 7 8 9 10

MOON IXTAPA & ZIHUATANEJO

Avalon Travel
a member of the Perseus Books Group
1700 Fourth Street
Berkeley, CA 94710, USA
www.moon.com

Editor: Kevin McLain
Series Manager: Kathryn Ettinger
Copy Editor: Naomi Adler Dancis
Graphics and Production Coordinator: Elizabeth Jang
Cover Designer: Elizabeth Jang
Map Editor: Mike Morgenfeld
Cartographer: Chris Henrick
Indexer: Greg Jewett

ISBN: 978-1-61238-143-5
ISSN: 2165-3712

Printing History
1st Edition — June 2012
5 4 3 2 1

Front cover photo: looking out to Zihuatanejo Bay © Mauricio Tonetto / http://www.mauriciotonetto .com.br

Title page photo: Day of the Dead figures in Taxco © Bruce Whipperman
Interior photos: pp. 4 – 24 all © Bruce Whipperman, except p. 9 (top) © csp/123rf.com

Printed in Canada by Friesens

KEEPING CURRENT

If you have a favorite gem you'd like to see included in the next edition, or see anything that needs updating, clarification, or correction, please drop us a line. Send your comments via email to feedback@moon.com, or use the address above.